Science Technology Engineering Maths

STEM STARTERS FOR KIDS

GEOLOGY
ACTIVITY
Book

Written by Jenny Jacoby

Designed and illustrated by
Vicky Barker

www.bsmall.co.uk

Published by
b small publishing ltd.
www.bsmall.co.uk

· 4 5 ·

Production by Madeleine Ehm.
Printed in China by WKT Co. Ltd.

British Library
Cataloguing-in-
Publication Data.

A catalogue record for this
book is available from the
British Library.

ISBN
978-1-911509-90-5

WHAT IS GEOLOGY?

Geology is the study of what makes up our planet, Earth, our natural landscape and what is deep below us. That includes the rocks, how they came to be there, why they are the way they are, and the ways they change over time.

WHAT IS STEM?

STEM stands for 'science, technology, engineering and mathematics'. These four areas are closely linked, and each of them is used in geology. By studying the Earth, scientists and engineers can use technology to make our lives better, by the way we work with the natural landscape. That could be finding the best place to build a bridge, or working out how to protect ourselves against earthquakes.

Science   Technology   Engineering   Maths

GEOLOGICAL TIME

Planet Earth is older than it's possible to imagine – **4.543 billion years old.**
In that time rocks have been forming and re-forming over and over. But all this
happens very slowly – in our own lifetime the Earth hardly seems to change at all.

It is rocks that tell us the story of Earth's history. Because rocks change so
slowly they can tell us how Earth used to look over long periods of 'rock time'
(known as 'geological time') long before humans were around. And one of the
stories the rocks tell is that Earth has looked very different in the past.

Once, 335 million years ago, all of the
land on Earth was in one huge piece, a
supercontinent called Pangaea. Then,
175 million years ago, Pangaea slowly
began to break up into pieces.
Those pieces formed the continents
we know today.

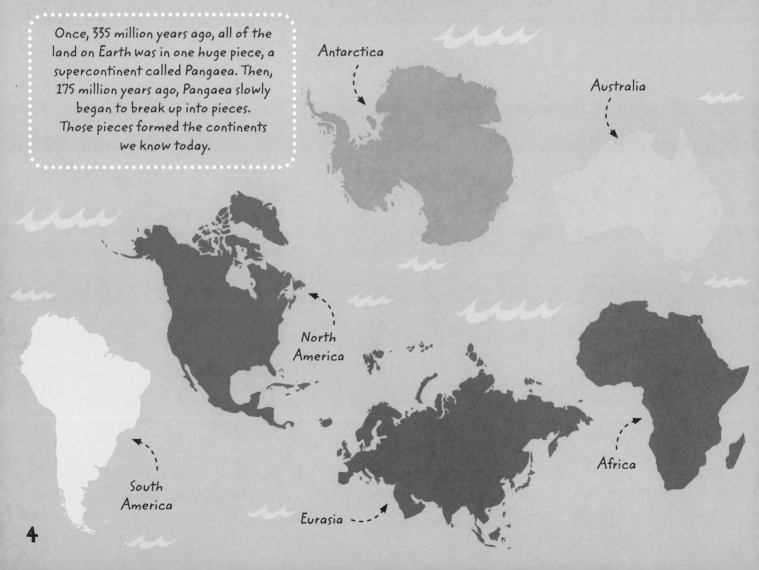

Antarctica

Australia

North
America

Africa

South
America

Eurasia

Can you spot today's continents within Pangaea? Colour them in the matching colours. Some are tricky!

Pangaea is not the only supercontinent that has been on Earth but it is the most recent one. Other supercontinents that came and went before Pangaea include Nuna, Rodinia and Gondwanaland. What name would you give a supercontinent?

_____

_____

Answers on page 30.

VOLCANOES

Most of our planet is extremely hot like a ball of fire. It's so hot that rocks melt. It is just the top layer, the crust, that makes up the things we recognise: the land and sea.

In some places the molten rock from the mantle rises up and bursts through the crust. This is a volcano. Some parts of the world, such as Indonesia and Iceland, have a lot of volcanoes.

CRUST

MANTLE

OUTER CORE

INNER CORE

Did you know?
Volcanoes don't keep erupting forever.
Eventually they die out and become perfectly
safe mountains.

MANTLE

ROCK FACTORY

Planet Earth is one giant rock factory. Rocks are made very slowly but every minute of every day they are being made, broken and re-made.

There are three types of rock and they're all made differently.

Igneous rocks
are rocks that were once melted – such as volcano lava – and then cooled down. Different rocks are made depending on how quickly the lava cools down and turns to rock.

Sedimentary rocks
are made very slowly by layers and layers of earth forming on top of each other. Over time, pressure from the layers above turns them to rock.

Metamorphic rocks
have been through changes — they may have started out as igneous or sedimentary but change type by getting very hot or buried under a lot of pressure.

MAGMA

Can you find these rocky words in this wordsearch?

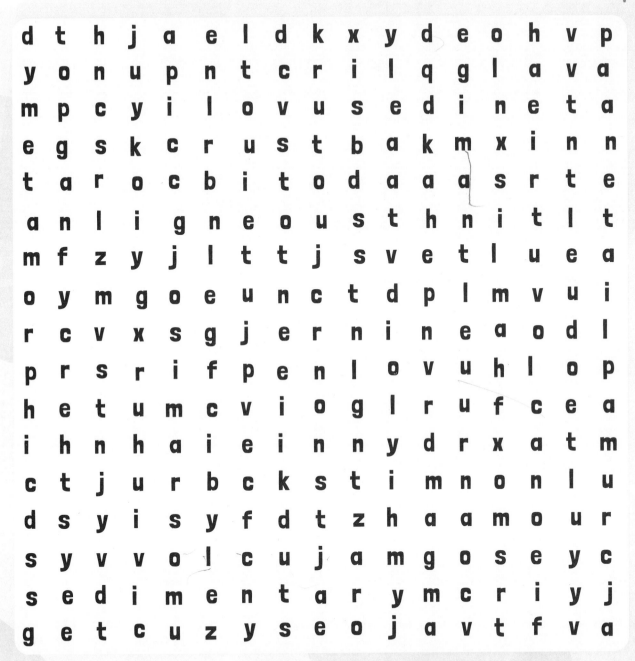

d t h j a e l d k x y d e o h v p
y o n u p n t c r i l q g l a v a
m p c y i l o v u s e d i n e t a
e g s k c r u s t b a k m x i n n
t a r o c b i t o d a a a s r t e
a n l i g n e o u s t h n i t l t
m f z y j l t t j s v e t l u e a
o y m g o e u n c t d p l m v u i
r c v x s g j e r n i n e a o d l
p r s r i f p e n l o v u h l o p
h e t u m c v i o g l r u f c e a
i h n h a i e i n n y d r x a t m
c t j u r b c k s t i m n o n l u
d s y i s y f d t z h a a m o u r
s y v v o l c u j a m g o s e y c
s e d i m e n t a r y m c r i y j
g e t c u z y s e o j a v t f v a

igneous   **volcano**   **river**

metamorphic **magma**   **lava**

sedimentary **mantle**

rock   **crust**   Answers on page 30.

9

EARTHQUAKES

The land and sea of the Earth's crust are all sitting on huge rocky 'plates'. Where the plates meet can be fragile and the plates are pushed apart in some places and crash together in others. Usually the plates rub together so gently you don't notice it, but sometimes the rubbing causes earthquakes that we do notice.

The central point of the earthquake, where the quake is usually strongest, is called the **epicentre**.

RICHTER SCALE

SCORE	EFFECT
1	Too weak to be noticed by people
2	Some people might notice wobbles but no damage done to buildings
3	Can be noticed by people, lamps and pictures may swing - but no damage
4	Most people will notice objects rattling or falling off shelves - but no damage
5	Everyone would notice the shaking and some buildings might be damaged
6	Violent shaking in the epicentre can be felt for hundreds of miles
7	Most buildings will be damaged and some completely destroyed
8	Even earthquake-resistant buildings will be damaged
9	Nearly total destruction and the ground permanently changed

HAITI

ENGLAND

ITALY

Can you grade these earthquakes using the Richter scale?

Draw scenes of what these earthquakes might look like...

CHILE

SOUTH ISLAND OF NEW ZEALAND

JAPAN

3 People sitting in their homes noticed the pictures on their walls started swinging.

6 The cathedral half collapsed, and a big bend appeared in the railway line.

8 All the buildings were destroyed, and a huge wave called a tsunami swept onto the shore from the sea.

WHAT'S THE USE OF A ROCK?

Some rocks are hard, some are soft. Some let water through and some do not. Some rocks are smooth, some are very strong, some can be polished to be shiny, and some leave marks. That's why rocks are so useful in so many different ways!

Did you know?
Rocks that let water through are called **permeable**.
Rocks that don't let water through are called **impermeable**.

ROCKS

Chalk:
wears away easily and leaves marks

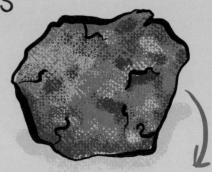

Granite:
hard and impermeable, doesn't wear away

Marble:
can be polished and looks attractive

Slate:
hard and impermeable and splits into thin sheets

JOBS

Tiling a roof

Drawing on a blackboard

Making a statue

Building a castle

FOSSIL SURPRISES

If an animal died and was very quickly buried in mud, sand or ash, its skeleton could turn into a fossil. But how? Over millions of years, more earth, rocks and mud ('sediment') would layer on top and press down and eventually turn to rock.

Meanwhile, water passing through the rock slowly dissolves the skeleton bones, but minerals in the water replace the dissolved bone and turn the skeleton into a new kind of rock – a fossil!

Over even more millions of years, the rock around the fossil might wear away so that a bit of the fossil pokes out of the ground. One day somebody might notice it – and that fossil hunter could be you!

Can you help this fossil hunter to find 15 fossils? First you'll need to help her find the fossil-hunting tools she needs.

Fossil-hunting tools

- Safety glasses
- Geological hammer
- Notebook and pen
- Plastic bag — to put fossil finds in
- Old newspaper — to wrap up delicate finds

ROCKY WEATHER

Even though they're big and strong, rocks don't last forever! Rocks that are exposed to the wind and rain slowly get worn away. This is called **weathering** and **erosion**. Water can seep into the rock and soften it so bits fall off more easily, or if the water freezes it can cause a crack to form in the rock. Where there are cracks, plants can start to grow, and their roots can make those cracks even bigger. Wind can carry sand and dust, so when it blows on the rock the blasting slowly wears it away.

When rocks wear away, the landscape can change. These two pictures show a scene before and after the landscape has changed due to weathering and erosion. Can you spot six differences?

SHAPING THE LANDSCAPE

In geological time, weathering causes all sorts of strange and beautiful changes to the landscape. Some of the Earth's most exciting scenery was created over a period of thousands of years.

Weathering

Grand Canyon, USA

Here are some amazing landscapes on Earth today, and a map of where they are found. Can you match them with the pictures of how they looked thousands of years ago when the climate was shaping the landscape? And can you find an explanation for each phenomenon?

Fjords, Norway

Fairy Chimneys, Cappadocia

The Siq, Jordan

Hard basalt rock wears down more slowly than the softer volcanic rock underneath it, leaving mushroom-shaped caps to chimney-like columns.

Glaciers are ice rivers that move slowly down the landscape, carving out valleys as they go.

Rivers erode the landscape, carrying away broken pieces of rock and leaving layers of rock exposed in their path.

The earth pulled apart, leaving a rift in the landscape that was worn smooth by wind and water over thousands of years.

OIL

Oil is very important to our lives: we use it to make medicine, cosmetics, paint, plastics and fuel. But what has it got to do with rocks? Oil is found deep underground, amongst the rocks, so to get to it we need to drill big holes in the ground.

How does oil get there?

Millions of years ago, when fish, plants and tiny sea creatures died, they fell to the bottom of the ocean floor. Their bodies were covered by sediment (sand and mud) and over time, as the layers burying them grew bigger and heavier, they turned to oil: a dark, sticky liquid.

How do we find oil?

Scientists use sound waves to find oil reservoirs. Because sound travels at different speeds through different types of rock, we can send sound waves through the ground and measure how fast they travel - to find the type of rock that holds oil. Then when a likely spot has been found, engineers drill down to see if there is oil where they think it should be.

Help this oil engineer find the best place to drill using the following information. Draw an oil rig on the land in the right place and draw a line from the rig to the oil.

- Oil sits on top of porous rock.
- Oil sits underneath impermeable rock.
- Sound waves travel through rock containing oil in this pattern:

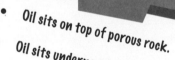

- Your oil rig could look like this:

20

POROUS ROCK

IMPEARMEABLE ROCK

GAS

POROUS ROCK

SUPER SOIL

Sitting in layers on top of rock, soil is made from tiny particles of rock mixed with air, water and bits of dead plants and animals. Soil has different characteristics depending on what kind of rock particles are in it. Soil is what plants grow in – so it is very important to look after it! It develops slowly – but not as slowly as rock.

True or false?

Can you tell which of these soil facts are true? Check your answers on page 32.

Soil can clean water

Soil can be turned into plates and mugs

Soil is home to lots of animals

Soil can be burned as a fuel

Clay soils can be turned into useful things! A lump of clay can be moulded and shaped into cups, plates and bowls – and when baked in a special oven they keep their shape and are less likely to break.

Decorate these pottery cups and bowls!

SEE-THROUGH SAND

Some soil contains a lot of sand, which is in fine grains like you see at the beach or in a sand pit. These small parts mean water passes easily through the soil. Sandy soil has a lot of uses:

An ingredient in cement and concrete

Silica in sand is used to make glass

An ingredient in bricks

Growing vegetables

How do you turn soil see-through? By taking the silica from the soil and heating it up with other ingredients you can make glass! If certain other chemicals are added, the glass can be 'stained' into colours. You can sometimes see beautiful stained-glass windows in places of worship, like churches and mosques.

Decorate your own stained-glass window here — there's one to colour in and one to design yourself. Fill each shape with one colour. Will you draw a pattern or a picture?

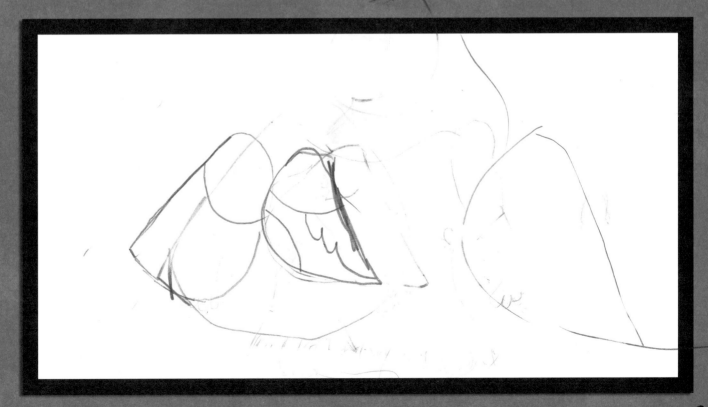

ROCKS FOR DINNER

Rocks are even important in our kitchens. We need minerals in our diet to keep us healthy – and these minerals are also found in rocks! Even our salt comes from rocks in the earth.

ROCK MENU

IRON:

eggs, lentils, fish, nuts

CALCIUM:

milk, kale, yoghurt, sardines, cheese

PHOSPHORUS:

cheese, cola, burgers

ZINC:

oysters, spinach, beef, lamb, nuts, dark chocolate

POTASSIUM:

avocado, dried apricot, sweet potato, banana

MAGNESIUM:

peanuts, wholegrain bread, black beans

Use the rock menu to choose a healthy meal that includes at least one of each mineral. Draw your chosen meal on the plates.

27

THE STONE AGE

Humans who lived around 3.4 million years ago were the first to use rocks and stones as tools. They knew that different stones had different characteristics, making particular rocks better for particular jobs. Here are two stones that we know were very important to Stone Age people:

Flint

A lump of flint can be turned into a sharp tool because – if it is hit carefully with a 'hammer' stone – parts of it flake off, leaving sharp, strong edges. It is so strong and sharp that one flake could be made into an arrow that could kill an animal.

Ochre

This rock is red-coloured due to the iron in it. When it is ground down into a powder it can be used as paint. One thing people in the Stone Age used this paint for is cave paintings, which have been found all around the world.

These flint axes were found deep in a dark cave. Can you find the matching shadow for each of these six axes among the shadows opposite?

Look at the way people and animals are drawn in the cave painting. Using similar colours, draw your own cave painting here.

ANSWERS

page 4-5

page 6-7

page 8-9

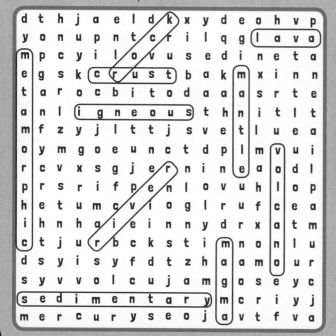

page 10-11

30

page 12-13
page 14-15

Tiling a roof

- SLATE

Drawing on a blackboard

- CHALK

Making a statue

- MARBLE

Building a castle

- GRANITE

page 16-17

page 18-19

Rivers erode the landscape, carrying away broken pieces of rock and leaving layers of rock exposed in their path.

Glaciers are ice rivers that move slowly down the landscape, carving out valleys as they go.

The earth pulled apart, leaving a rift in the landscape that was worn smooth by wind and water over thousands of years.

Hard basalt rock wears down more slowly than the softer volcanic rock underneath it, leaving mushroom-shaped caps to chimney-like columns.

page 28-29

page 22

Page 20-21

OIL AREA

Trick question! - They are all **TRUE!**

HISTORY &
BIBLIOGRAPHY
OF
BOXING BOOKS
collectors guide
to the history
of pugilism

DEDICATION

This book is dedicated to the collectors of boxing material,

and to all boxers and ex-boxers;

especially to those who never quite made it.

HISTORY & BIBLIOGRAPHY OF BOXING BOOKS
collectors guide to the history of pugilism

Incorporating a Bibliography
containing some 2100 titles on all aspects
of Pugilism published in the English language

BY

R. A. Hartley

With a Preface by
O. F. SNELLING

NIMROD PRESS LTD
15 The Maltings
Turk Street
Alton, Hants, GU34 1DL

ISBN 1-85259-074-2

Printed by Ptarmigan Printers

Publisher:
NIMROD PRESS LTD
15 The Maltings
Turk Street
Alton, Hants, GU34 1DL

CONTENTS

MENDOZA.

J. Gillray ad viv del et fecit.   Pub.d April 24.th by H. Lewis & sold by J. Aitken, Castle Street, Leicester Field.

From a Coloured Print by J. GILLRAY   *Ernest Betjemann, Esq.*

ACKNOWLEDGEMENTS

Firstly, I would like to acknowledge the enormous assistance I have derived in compiling this work, obtained from the manuscript of the late Mr G. Neville Weston. If I had not had the good fortune to acquire this collection of manuscript volumes in the course of my work as a second-hand bookseller, then the present volume would not have seen the light of day.

Mr Weston ceased his work in 1952; I have been fortunate in that I have been able to find the time to edit, condense, and supplement the results of his researches into more manageable form than he was able to attempt.

Secondly, thanks are also due to my wife, Vera, for her acceptance of long brooding silences on my part while I have been deep in thought, searching for ideas and words necessary to complete the book. I also owe Vera many thanks for the hours she has spent typing, revising, and finalising the manuscript.

I acknowledge with a deep sense of gratitude the assistance given by my friend, O.F. Snelling; for his Preface, for his advice on the layout of the book, his reading of the typescript, and his suggestions for improvement of the content and arrangement of the material. Mr Snelling has my thanks for undertaking the colossal task of cross-indexing the whole of the bibliographical section.

I feel sure that I am correct in stating that Fred Snelling offered all this assistance to me born out of his lifelong enthusiasm for everything connected with boxing and boxers, and his dedication to the literature of the game.

Thanks are also due to the Museo delle Terme for supplying and granting permission to reproduce the picture of the statue of the Sitting Boxer.

I am also grateful to a number of boxing collectors and enthusiasts, some of whom have allowed me access to their collections of books, and others who have passed on to me information on some inaccessible works. All of these have contributed towards the completion of what has been for me a labour of love, the result of which I now submit for, I hope, the approbation of all boxing enthusiasts.

PREFACE
by
O.F. Snelling

This is a book with which I am proud to be associated, albeit in a minor capacity. No work of the nature and scope of the present volume has ever before been published, or even quite attempted. It is unique.

Bibliographies, check-lists, and reference books of almost every activity and endeavour known to man are to be found in our libraries and institutions. They range from angling, ballistics, and cookery, to xenophobia, yachting, and zymotics. ABCs and XYZs, indeed. The world is fortunate in that certain indefatigable individuals have, for the benefit of scholars, collectors, and the merely curious, spent many years in listing, annotating, and searching out the details of all works on specific subjects, and thus adding to the sum total of human knowledge.

To the general reader, a book such as this one, attempting to list all books in our tongue dealing with the questionably salubrious subject of boxing, might at first glance appear to be a dubious endeavour. I would not agree.

Firstly, the art and science of pugilism, in all its many aspects, has captured the imaginations of writers and artists from the dawn of time. Cavemen etched crude drawings of fighters on their walls, unknown sculptors chipped and modelled gladiators, and the early classics of literature abound with the descriptions of boxing bouts. The thrill and fascination of physical combat is inherent in man. From Homer and Virgil, among the ancients, down through the years with Hazlitt, Borrow, Thackeray, Conan Doyle, and Bernard Shaw, in the 19th Century, to Hemingway, Mailer, and Schulberg, of those more modern, a stand-up fight between two men, using only their clenched fists and the reflexes of their brains has been celebrated by the written word. These writers were not mere depraved brutes.

Secondly, the aforementioned Shaw — a perceptive individual — once remarked to the effect that there are two certain ways of capturing the attention of the reader. One is to tell of the death or murder of a child — *vide* Charles Dickens — and the other is to describe a fight. Infanticide, as it happens, has no particular attraction for me, but short of actually watching a boxing match I like to read about one.

So do many thousands of other people, to the extent that all over the world there are avid connoisseurs and enthusiasts who spend a great deal of their time in accumulating everything they can find which deals with the subject close to their hearts. They will find this book a god-send, and as absorbing as any of the descriptive and historical pugilistic volumes already on their shelves.

It was a strange combination of circumstance and coincidence which led me to be now writing this preface. As a young man, a humble hoarder of boxing material myself, I was fortunate in meeting a certain solicitor from the Midlands; an inexaustible collector of fighting literature and mementoes named G. Neville Weston who spent every hour of his leisure — *and* a great deal of his time when perhaps he should have been more gainfully-employed — in searching out the details of all known works dealing with the subject of his interest. This was purely for his own satisfaction: the thrill of the chase. He had no particular desire to publish his researches, and no intention of doing so.

Among the books which came his way was a slim little effort by an American scholar, one Paul Magriel, who had earlier set out to compile a check-list of ring literature up to the year 1900. By the self-imposed limitations of this endeavour, it dealt almost exclusively with that era known as the London Prize Ring, or, more colloquially, "bare-knuckle fighting". But Weston had already traced almost 100 books not known to Magriel, and a considerable correspondence between the pair followed. Weston's own bibliography, a truly massive and detailed typescript, covered more than 50 ensuing years, embracing a host of published books dealing with the Queensberry Ring, or "glove-fighting". At the time I yearned for his researches to be available to us all.

It was in the early 1950s that G. Neville Weston, at the suggestion of his doctor, ceased his delving into and his collecting of boxing literature, and confined himself to his other love: cricket in general and W.G. Grace in particular. He requested me, in my capacity in the antiquarian book-auction world, to sell his enormous collection of pugilistica in London, and retained only his beloved bibliography.

Some 30 years passed. During this time I kept in touch with Weston, through frequent letters and occasional personal meetings, during which we discussed books and boxing. But he was now in poor health, elderly, and was drawing towards the end of his life. He was in no condition, or with much inclination, to pursue his studies.

It was a purely chance contact with an antiquarian bookseller I had heard of, named Robert Hartley, and who specialised in boxing material, which led me to inquire if he had in stock a long out-of-print book of my own, a copy of which a friend of mine was seeking. (I think it worth mentioning that this gentleman happens to be Stephen Massey, of the world-famous bookselling dynasty. How ubiquitous are boxing and books!) But no, Robert Hartley told me, he did not have my own volume at present, but during an interesting conversation I learned that he had not only acquired Weston's invaluable and enormous life-work, but had increased it considerably. He had traced works not mentioned in either Weston *or* Magriel, and had added details of volumes since published over another 30 years and more!

And so here, at long last, is Hartley's guide to the books published about the sport of boxing in the English language over almost the past two centuries and a half.

Exhaustive as it is, it cannot be quite complete and definitive: no bibliography or check-list ever was or ever could be. "Of making many books there is no end", Ecclesiastes informs us, and any and every work of this nature *must* be a never-finished task. The pedant and the literary nit-picker will, no doubt, find errors and omissions of various kinds. He will hasten to draw attention to his own superior scholarship — after all, there would be little justification to his petty existence if he didn't. There are such know-all people in every walk of life — but you will notice that these individuals, while ever-ready to draw attention to the minor lapses of others, rarely, if ever, attempt to undertake such a valuable chore themselves.

The book's plan and scheme is simple. All items in the bibliographical section are listed alphabetically under the names of the authors, editors, or compilers. In the instances where these are not given on the title-pages, and are not known, the names of the publishers or those responsible for producing the item are appended instead, with due explanation and acknowledgement. The title of the work follows, together with place of publication, publisher or printer, the date of appearance, plus pagination, etc., and minor bibliographical details when available. Notes of certain of the contents and relevant information frequently follow. As a handy cross-reference, for the benefit of a reader attempting to trace an item, the title of which might be known but nothing more, an abbreviated title-index has been compiled.

I feel sure that this book will be found to be a great boon to the collector of boxing literature, and also to many others. It is the only thing of its kind in the annals of sport.

NEW SCHOOL.

RICHARD HUMPHREYS

From the Mezzotint by J. YOUNG
After the Oil Painting by J. HOPPNER

Picture of the Statue of the Sitting Boxer, exhibited in the Museo Delle Terme in Rome (Bib. Ref. 722)

A SHORT HISTORY
OF THE
LITERATURE OF BOXING

A

FISTIANA;

OR,

THE ORACLE OF THE RING.

RESULTS OF

PRIZE BATTLES

FROM 1700 TO DEC. 1865, ALPHABETICALLY ARRANGED;

NEW RULES OF THE RING;

FORM OF ARTICLES, DUTIES OF SECONDS, BOTTLE-HOLDERS,
AND UMPIRES AND REFEREES;

Hints on Sparring and Boxing;

HEALTH IN GENERAL, AND THE CAUSES OF DEBILITY;

WITH USEFUL PRACTICAL HINTS.

BY THE

EDITOR OF "BELL'S LIFE IN LONDON."

TWENTY-SIXTH EDITION.

LONDON:
PUBLISHED BY WILLIAM CLEMENT, JUN.,
OFFICE OF BELL'S LIFE, 170, STRAND ; AND SOLD BY ALL BOOKSELLERS.
PRICE HALF-A-CROWN.

1866.

Title-Page 1866 Edition of F.L. Dowling's *Fistiana* (Bib. Ref. 539)

CHAPTER I
HOMER, VIRGIL, and OTHERS

BOXERS WITH THE CÆSTUS.

THOMAS CRIBB (Champion of England),

From the Painting by DE WILD, 1811.

A SHORT HISTORY OF THE LITERATURE OF BOXING

CHAPTER 1

HOMER, VIRGIL, and OTHERS

The above chapter heading is not intended to imply that the reader is familiar with the classics, or that perusal of the chapter will make him feel that he should pay a hurried visit to his local library or second-hand bookshop in order to obtain copies of Greek or Roman works, in an attempt to fill any gaps in his learning. Although strictly speaking they are not part of the lore of boxing, with which the present volume purports to deal, nevertheless sufficient written material has been handed down to us from hundreds of years before the dawn of Christianity which provides evidence that boxing was practised as a gladiatorial and combat sport two thousand years or more before the names of Figg, Cribb, Sayers, Fitzsimmons *et al*, and venues such as Thistleton Gap, Farnborough Common, the National Sporting Club, and Blackfriars "Ring", became of common usage in the vocabularies of ringside devotees of our beautiful game, in pubs, clubs, and places where they meet.

There are many references to boxing in the works of the early Greek and Roman poets and scribes. In the twenty-third book of *The Iliad* of Homer, we are told that during the games at the funeral of Petrocles the caestus fight was placed second in order only to the chariot race; the wrestling and the foot races were placed third and fourth respectively. The boxing contestants at the games were Epeus and Euralyus, the reward for the victor was "a stately mule", and for the loser "a goblet massive, large and round". This and similar contests were not fought with the bare knuckles, as became the custom centuries later, in England and America. In issuing his challenge, the poem tells us that Epeus proclaims:

> . . . Then let my foe
> Draw near, but first his certain future know,
> Secure, this hand shall his whole frame confound,
> Mash all his bones, and all his body pound;
> So let his friends be nigh, a needful train,
> To heave the battered carcase off the plain.

Later on we shall give consideration to the weapons to be used to back up the threat inherent in the above stanza. For the moment we may take note of the lines which follow, describing the acceptance of the challenge by Euralyus, urged on by his friend Tydides.

> Him great Tydides urges to contend,
> Warm with the hopes of conquest for his friend,
> Officious with the cincture girds him round;
> And to his wrists the gloves of death are bound

The final victory is gained by Euralyus, the condition of his opponent being described thus:

> . . . reeling through the throng,
> And dragging his disabled legs along,
> Nodding, his head hangs down his shoulders o'er;
> His mouth and nostrils pour the glotted gore;

This section of Homer's epic poem is recognised as being the first report of a prize-fight; the date was 1184 BC.

Another report of a caestus fight is given in the fifth book of *The Aenid* of Virgil, wherein is described the contest between Dares, referred to as a Trojan Pugilist, and Entellus. The rewards were, for the winner, "a bull with gilded horns, with fillets tied", and for the loser, "a sword and helm". Upon the announcement of the contest the poet describes the appearance of Dares as follows:

> Then haughty Dares in the lists appears;
> Stalking he strides, his head erected bears;
> His nervous arms the weighty gauntlets wield,
> And loud applauses echo through the field.

In the absence of an acceptance of his challenge Dares claims the bull as his prize. Despite his pleas of "staleness" and "want of condition", Entellus is persuaded to take up the challenge:

> Then just Aeneas equal arms supplied,
> Which round their shoulders to their wrists they tied,
> Both on the tiptoe stand, at full extent,
> Their arms aloft, their bodies inly bent;
> Their heads from aiming blows they bear afar,
> With clashing gauntlets then provoke the war.

The fight continues, with Entellus taking an early fall. He then inflicts much punishment on Dares and finally emerges as the victor. Virgil describes the end of the contest thus:

> But now the prince, who saw the wild increase
> Of wounds, commands the combatants to cease,
> And bounds Entellus' wrath, and bids the peace,
> First to the Trojan, spent with toil, he came,
> And soothed the sorrow for the suffered shame,
> The gauntlet fight thus ended, from the shore
> His faithful friends the unhappy Dares bore:
> His mouth and nostrils poured a purple flood,
> And pounded teeth came rushing with his blood,
> Faintly he staggered through the hissing throng,
> And hung his head and trailed his legs along,
> The sword and casque are carried by his train,
> But with his foe the palm and ox remain.

This must be the first reported case of an official stopping a contest to save one of the participants from taking too much punishment.

So far have been reported but two instances of the recording and reporting of fist fights; further reference to the classics, including the work of Plato, Aristotle, and Theocrites, show that we who dedicate our interest to the fight game are the inheritors of a tradition involving a method of combat similar to the one practised some 3000 years ago.

Before leaving this brief reference to the ancient foundations of our great sport, consisting of two men facing each other in an arena, we must look at the hand coverings which were used in Greek and Roman times, whether for protection of the knuckles, or as an aid in administering the maximum amount of punishment on the opponent, while at the same time providing some kind of defence against the retaliatory blows of the other man.

The two examples of Greek and Roman poetry relating to prize-fighting already quoted in this chapter, refer to cases where the contestants used the caestus as a covering for the hands, and from the information given in the extracts on the condition of the loser on each occasion, it is evident that the form of caestus used was indeed a fearsome weapon. There are illustrations showing the different types of caestus in some of the older books relating to pugilism, notably in Volume 1 of *Pugilistica* by Henry Downes Miles, published in 1880 and reissued in 1906. The most formidable of those so illustrated show a gauntlet made of strips of hide in several thickness to form a solid ring. This ring was supported on the hand by thongs bound round the wrist; there were holes in the solid offensive part of the caestus to allow the fingers and the thumb to grip the weapon. There were other designs, some more dangerous to the recipient of the blows than others. In several cases the leather thongs, which seemed to form the basis of all the different designs, were loaded with pieces of metal, described variously as being composed of brass, iron or lead.

It is likely that the most deadly forms of the caestus were used in gladiatorial combats in Roman times, both in Italy and in England after the Roman conquest, when slaves were forced into contention to provide entertainment for their masters, often resulting in the death of the loser of the contest. With the decline of the Roman Empire it is apparent that such pugilistic encounters ceased, as there have been no records handed down which relate to fistic encounters from that time until the 17th Century and the establishment of the Prize Ring era in England during the 18th Century.

Before leaving this chapter on the earlier written references to boxing it will be necessary to refer again to the period of Ancient Greece, particularly with regard to boxing as one of the sports which made up the programmes of the Olympic Games. These were held every four years. A feature of the Games was to encourage the development of the mental abilities of the Greek menfolk whose efforts were in the main directed to the soldierly and warrior-like abilities, as proof of individual strength, courage, and endurance. In these circumstances, where the Games were organised more as a sporting occasion than was the case in the gory contests of the Romans, the hand-coverings were made up from much softer leather.

Boxing was first introduced as an Olympic sport for the 23rd Olympiad held in 688 B.C. A kindred sport, known as the Pancratium, was included in the 33rd Olympiad in 648 B.C. This latter sport was a mixture of boxing and wrestling in which almost any form of offensive ploy was allowed; in fact from all accounts it seems to have been an early version of our present day All-in Wrestling. The death of an opponent in the pancratium meant that the contestant who remained alive was disqualified; however we are told that the boxing contests were subjected to stricter rules, but there were no weight divisions as we know them today; size and strength were the main qualifications and means of achieving victory.

With regard to the practice of boxing as a sport and an exercise, it should be recorded that for sparring and training purposes the ancient practitioners wore a protective headguard or helmet. This was made from thick hide and metal, fastened with straps under the chin or round the back of the head. This protector was known as the Amphotides; it protected the vulnerable parts of the head and ears, similar in many respects to the headgear worn by our present-day boxers in sparring sessions.

It may be of interest to today's boxers and retired professors of the Noble Art, who carry evidence of the occasions when they forgot to duck, in the form of a cauliflower ear, that this mark of the profession was also exhibited by many of the ancient boxers and pancreatic practitioners. Proof of this is apparent on examination of statues of old fighters and the figures of boxers decorating ancient examples of pottery, vases, and plaques, which have been recovered from city ruins, together with other evidences of the way of life of the people of ancient civilisations.

In looking at illustrations of these relics, one notices that the fighting stance adopted by the contestants bears in some respects a striking resemblance to the left foot forward and the left arm extended position adopted by modern boxers, excepting of course the cases of those who adopted the "southpaw" stance, with the positions of the feet and arms reversed. In looking at the stance adopted by the ancient progenitors of our sport, I have little doubt that present-day purists are not impressed by the position shown for the right hand; this is usually held high and wide on a level with the right ear, and in some cases it is extended to a position almost level with the left hand. In neither of these positions is the right hand of much use in launching an attack with that member, or for the same hand's use for defensive purposes.

From illustrations and descriptions of the ancient contests, it is evident that, although the poems describe the avoidance of blows by the sway of the head by the boxer on the defensive, together with the counter punch returned at the attacker who is caught off balance, there is some doubt as to whether they had discovered the effectiveness of straight punching. This doubt is borne out by the acceptance of the fighter concerned of the cauliflower ear as a kind of industrial hazard. One could make the point that the weight of the caestus on the hands would inhibit the launch of a straight left or right hand lead as is the accepted practice in modern boxing. Added to this is the fact that a round-arm swing, including the weight of the caestus, would land with terrific force on the person of the hard-pressed opponent. Indeed, the poems of Homer and Virgil speak of downward blows wielded by the attacker on to the receiver's head; in these instances the caestus-laden hand would be used like a club.

In winding up this chapter on the contribution of the Ancient Classics to the written word concerning boxing, and the means adopted to hand out punishment, let us just look at a quotation in translation from the *Epigrams* of Lucilius; this illustrates that the facial decorations which have been borne, not without some pride, by many pugilists since the birth of the modern school of fistic practitioners, were also displayed, perhaps with the same degree of pride, at gatherings of fighters and their retired colleagues in those far-off days. Here is one quotation:

This Olympus, who is now as you see him
Augustus, once had a nose, a chin, a forehead, ears and eyelids.
Then becoming a professional boxer he lost all,
Not even getting his share of his father's inheritance;
For his brother presented a likeness of his
He had and he was pronounced to be a stranger,
As he bore no resemblance to it.

The Grecian era was superseded by that of the expanding Roman Empire, with the circuses and gladiatorial combats, organised mainly for the entertainment of the nobility and soldiers of the conquering armies. The entertainments included cruel combat sports, involving the use of weapons, between individual opponents. The contests involved prisoners of war and also members of other subservient groups who had become victims of the conquest, the weapons on some occasions being fists encased in the caestus. It is recorded that the Roman Emperors Augustus and Marcus Aurelius were very fond of boxing bouts; and that the Emperor Caligula imported boxers from other countries, notably from Africa, in order to improve the quality of the encounters.

It is probable that the near 400-year period of the Roman occupation of Britain saw the disappearance of boxing as a sport as it had been practised in Greece, and consequently there was a long break in the literary output concerning the sport. We have to wait until the 17th Century before a study of the lexicography, literature, and some periodicals of that century, show any references to boxing, to be followed by an increasing number of books, periodicals, broadsides and instruction manuals relating to the beginning and the flowering of the Prize Ring era in Britain, and later in America.

F I G G .

CHAPTER II
SCHOLARS, SCRIBES & PIONEER PUGILISTS

BROUGHTON,

BUCKHORSE (John Smith), 1732-1746,
After an Etching by WILLIAM HOGARTH.

Picture of John Buckhorse, page 40 of *Pugilistica* (Bib. Ref. 266 and 1365)

CHAPTER 2

SCHOLARS, SCRIBES AND PIONEER PUGILISTS

The word *box* in relation to the use of the hands to administer punishment was frequently used by early English writers such as Chaucer, Shakespeare and Jonathan Swift, in the 14th, 16th and 17th Centuries respectively. In each case the word was used as a noun, and referred to a blow on the head; there are quotations from Shakespeare which illustrate the point, among which are the following:

If he took you a box o' the ear,
You might have an action for slander too.
(*Measure for Measure*. Act II, scene I)

He borrowed a box o' the ear of the Englishman
And swore he would pay him again when he was able.
(*The Merchant of Venice*. Act I, scene II)

I have sworn to take him a box o' the ear.
(*Henry V*. Act IV, scene VII)

The first report of a boxing match in an English newspaper appeared in the *Protestant Mercury* during January, 1681, reading as follows:

Yesterday a match of boxing was performed before His Grace the Duke of Albemarle between the Duke's footman and a butcher. The latter won the prize, as he hath done many times before, being accounted, though a little man, the best at the exercise in England.

Perhaps the unknown butcher could not read of the honour that was accorded him in this newspaper report. Certainly we can rest assured that if he had known of the position to which he was elevated in the world of 17th Century fist-icuffs, he could never have imagined in his wildest dreams the acclaim, the honour, and the kudos which would have been his, had he been born some two or three hundred years later!

The earliest dictionary definition of the word box is given in the first *Dictionary of the English Language*, the work of the celebrated Dr. Johnson, which was issued in 1755. The Doctor conjugates the word as follows:

Box n.s. A blow on the head given by the hand
To Box v.s. (From the noun). To fight with the fist
To Box v.s. To strike with the fist
Boxer n.s. (From Box). A man who fights with the fist

The inclusion of the word box and its derivatives in Dr. Johnson's *Dictionary* served to confirm the use of the word in relation to the sport and those who participated in it. The simple "box o' the ear" of Shakespeare had expanded to describe two men exchanging blows on the ear and other parts of each other's anatomy, and to describe a sport destined to become known and loved all over the world by generations of sportsmen as yet unborn.

Among other references to boxing given in the early 18th Century was a letter contributed to *The Spectator*, a journal edited by Joseph Addison; this was in the year 1714, and it reported on a gentleman, evidently a great patriot:

He hath had six duels and four and twenty boxing
matches in defence of His Majesty's title.

Sir Richard Steele, in *The Tatler* dated July 7th, 1709, includes a letter telling of a quarrel between two gentlemen, one a Major in the Train Bands; following the exchange of words, such as Rogue, Villain, etc., it is stated that "Satisfaction was demanded and accepted". The antagonists then repaired to a spacious room in the Sheriff's house; here they resolved not to shed each other's blood by engaging in a duel. They then "stripped, and in a decent manner fought full fairly with their wrathful hands", the engagement lasting a quarter of an hour. The Major appeared to be getting the better of the exchanges and expressed himself as satisfied, where-upon the combat ceased and the two are friends thereafter.

These reports appeared some years before James Figg became our first recognised champion boxer, and they reveal that boxing was practiced in England before the end of the 17th Century. The two gentlemen who boxed with each other instead of fighting a duel, and the footman and the butcher were only two pairs of fistic antagonists who helped to popularise the sport, which later became more systemised with the establishment of Figg's Academy and the framing of Broughton's Rules, of which more later.

Before commencing to annotate the first printed and bound books on the subject of boxing, it must be pointed out that most of these were instructional; James Figg was recognised as the first Champion of England in 1719; according to the list of champions given in Miles' *Pugilistica* there were only five other boxers to achieve that status until the year 1760, when Bill Stevens was added to the list. During the following eleven years, to 1771, six further champions were listed, and the momentum continued thus, with an emerging pattern of better organisation of championship bouts and more aspirants taking up the sport during following decades, thus providing the material for the ring historians such as Pierce Egan, John Badcock and other skilled reporters whose works are avidly assimilated by readers up to the present day.

When referring to the bibliographical section of the present work, readers will note that many of the early instructional books are not solely devoted to boxing; they included instruction in wrestling, sword-play, single-stick and quarter-staff. It is fair to assume that in the saloons and gymnasiums where this mixture of sports was on the curriculum, boxing gradually took over as the favourite exercise and the other combat sports were gradually eliminated in favour of the Noble Art.

The first Champion of England opened his Figg's Amphitheatre in 1719; it was situated in Tottenham Court Road, London, and later removed to Oxford Street (then known as Oxford Road). Figg issued a handbill to advertise his academy, the illustration on the bill showed a boxing ring with two figures inside, one holding a quarter-staff and the other a sword, with a crowd of spectators round the ringside. The announcement on the handbill read as follows:

James Figg, Master of the Noble Science of Defence on the right hand
in Oxford Road near Adam and Eve Court, teaches Gentlemen the use
of the small, backsword and Quarterstaff, at home and abroad.

We can now proceed to look at some of these early manuals, giving instruction on the mixture of sports.

The first bound book with specific boxing content was Sir Thomas Parkyn's *The Inn Play; or Cornish Hugg Wrestler*, originally published in 1713. As indicated in the title, the main subject of the book was wrestling, and there was also a section on fencing. There is some doubt as to whether the first edition included the subject of boxing, but the third edition, corrected with large additions and issued in 1727, contained from page 59 a section on boxing.

In the year 1744 was issued a book which did not follow the pattern of the early instructional works; this was entitled *The Gymnasiad, or Boxing Match*, an Epic Poem by Paul Whitehead. Although 1744 is generally accepted as being the date of the first publication of this work, there are differences of opinion regarding this; some authorities give the date as early as 1737, and others state the publication date to be later than that. The poem was included in collections of the works of Paul Whitehead entitled *Satires*, and in other later books of poems. It is possible that reference to the dates of issue of these collections resulted in confusion as to the correct date of the first issue. The poem describes the fight between John Broughton and George Stevenson, a coachman hailing from Yorkshire. The bout is reputed to have taken place in one of the fairground booths in Tottenham Court Road in 1741; if this date is correct, then the poem describing the affair could not have been written in 1737.

The fight lasted forty minutes, with Broughton returned as the winner, due to his opponent's inability to continue the battle. The poem consists of three parts, designated as follows:

Book I. The Invocation — The Night Before the Battle
Book II. Stevenson Enters the Lists — Broughton Advances
Book III. Description of the Battle

A short extract from *The Gymnasiad* is given herewith:

Incessant now their hollow sides they pound,
Loud on each Breast the bounding Bangs Resound:
Their flying Fists around the Temples glow,
And the Jaws crackle with the massy Blow,
And raging Combat every Eye appals,
Strokes following Strokes, and Falls succeeding Falls.
Now droop'd the Youth, yet urging all his Might,
With feeble Arm still vindicates the Fight,
Till on the Part where heaved the panting Breath,
A fatal Blow impress'd the Seal of Death.
Down dropp'd the Hero, welt'ring in his Gore,
And his stretch'd Limbs lay quiv'ring on the Floor.

A comparison of this extract with those given earlier from the Greek and Roman epics will illustrate the similarity in style, with which is combined the more satirical approach of Paul Whitehead to the subject.

The year 1747 was a significant one in the history of boxing books, as it saw the appearance of the most important of the early works on the subject of pugilism. The author was Captain Godfrey, and the title of his book *A Treatise upon the Useful Science of Defence*, connecting the small and back sword, and showing the affinity between them ... with some observations on boxing, and the characters of the most able boxers within the author's time. Printed for the author by T. Gardner, 1747.

Captain Godfrey's *Treatise* included nine pages of instruction on boxing and twelve pages on The Characters of the Boxers. The book was dedicated to His Royal Highness the Duke (of Cumberland), and as it was published only 28 years after the recognition of James Figg as the first Champion of the Prize Ring, the section on The Characters of the Boxers, while of necessity a short one, marked an important milestone in the history of books on boxing in that it was the first attempt to record historical and biographical material on the sport. The *Treatise* was widely quoted in sporting journals and in later works on boxing, among these being the *Annals of Sporting and Fancy Gazette*, the first volume of *Boxiana*, and Dowling's *Fistiana*. In these extracts and references to Godfrey it is made clear that he not only bent his energy to writing about boxing and related combat sports, but that he was also a competent performer in these exercises. Reference to his work appears in the first edition of *Fistiana, or The Oracle of the Ring*, (1842), as follows:

Captain Godfrey was the Captain Barclay of his day, and was distinguished by his proficiency in all the athletic sports of his time, testing the merits of the practitioners by personal trials in which Figg himself found him an awkward customer.

likewise, had improved under his tuition, and might be said a 'Chicken of his own rearing'. Belcher could not be persuaded of the difficulties he would have to encounter from the loss of an eye — but how did he fight? How he did fight will long be remembered by those who witnessed the grievous but honourable combat; a combat in which more unaffected courage was never seen —"

Pearce won the fight in 18 rounds, spread over 35 minutes, and did not contest the title any more; he died in 1809.

John Gully succeeded to the championship, mainly because of his game display in the bruising match with Pearce in 1805; during the two years after taking the title Gully took part in two punishing battles with Bob Gregson, both of which he won, and both of which are graphically described by Pierce Egan. The champion then quit the boxing scene and went into business, before throwing his hat into a more salubrious arena, when he entered Parliament as Member for Pontefract in 1832.

Following his substantial treatment of the Bristol School and their opponents, Egan passes to the Distinguished Heroes of the Second, or Intermediate Schools; the favourites of this group, according to the space given to them in *Boxiana*, were George Maddox, Tom (Paddington) Jones, and Daniel Mendoza. Of the first-named, Egan observed that he was comparable to the Austrian General Clairfayt, in being uncommonly brave but seldom victorious, "like a drum, never heard of but when he was beaten — Maddox was a good pugilist, but after any memorable achievement he again sank into his former obscurity". Despite his apparent lack of the qualities of which champions are made, Maddox is stated by Egan to have nobly contested his battles during a period of upwards of 35 years. When engaged in a desperate contest in Tothill Fields in 1776, George Maddox was seconded by his sister Grace, and on this occasion he came out the winner, as was the case when he disposed of Bill Richmond, the Negro pugilist, in 1804. Following this he contested every inch of ground before losing to Tom Cribb in a bout of two hours and ten minutes duration. After his retirement from the ring a benefit was arranged for Maddox in the Fives Court, which was graced with the presence of his old opponents Cribb, Richmond, and others. Soon after this Maddox met his death due to an accident, and Egan recorded that "he lived respected and died pitied, although following the humble occupation of costermonger".

Tom (Paddington) Jones, born 1769, weight 10st. 6lbs., was the first opponent of Jem Belcher in the metropolis; he is recorded as having beaten Sailor (One Eye) in three battles in 1786 and also to have been victorious over a character named the Chaffcutter. The hero of Paddington is stated in *Boxiana* to have fought more battles than any other pugilist then in existence, excepting Caleb Baldwin, and for seven years victory crowned all his attempts. The Ring in Hyde Park was the principle venue for his fistic forays, and he engaged in contests in this arena no less than nineteen times. Jones's first contest was fought in 1785, a half-crown being his reward on this occasion, when he was the loser, but within a few months he reversed this decision against an opponent by the name of Ned Holmes. Following an indecisive match against Nichols (of the Bristol School) at Norwood, Jones, on his way home, had a turn-up with a man named Carter, and is reported to have "set-to with pluck, and so soon convinced Carter that he was in the wrong, that he sheered off accordingly".

C

Pierce Egan reports on the fight between Jones and Belcher as follows:

Belcher was seconded by Bill Warr and Bill Gibbons acted as his bottle-holder; and Jones had for his attendants Joe Ward and Dick Hall. Belcher was at this period only nineteen years of age. The odds were, on setting-to, six to four on Jem. The spectators were much interested upon the commencement of the battle, from the very high character which had been promulgated by Bill Warr, upon the astonishing abilities that his pupil possessed, and the feats which he had achieved at Bristol. The first round considerable science was displayed on both sides — the experience and skill of Jones were well portrayed; and the dexterity and new mode of fighting, so exclusively Belcher's own, were soon exhibited; but on the termination of the round Belcher was knocked down. The advantages in the second and third rounds were perfectly reciprocal; but in the fourth and fifth Jones was levelled. In the sixth and seventh rounds Jones showed off in most excellent style — and the amateurs experienced some of the finest displays of the art; he saw, what always should appear prominent in trials of skill, manliness and fortitude, no shifting, nothing shy, Hugging out of the question, and hauling not resorted to; it was a clean fight throughout, stopping and hitting were the order of the day, and it might be deemed a model for pugilists in general to follow. Belcher, with all the gaiety and confidence of youth, portrayed a new feature as a boxer, and the spectators seemed not to be aware of its consequences. The odds had changed five to four on Jones. The eighth and ninth were spiritedly contested; but in the tenth round, Belcher put in some tremendous hits, with the rapidity of lightning. This immediately altered the appearance of things, Jem was looked upon as the favourite, and the odds were laid on him accordingly. Yet Jones nobly contested for victory for the space of thirty three minutes, before he gave in. Jem weighed in twelve stone six pounds and Tom Jones but ten stone five pounds in weight. It should not escape the memory, that Jones stood up to Belcher (before that distinguished pugilist lost his eye) a considerably longer time than any man ever did!

Modern-day enthusiasts (and the members of the Board of Control) will be aghast at the contest being allowed to proceed with two stone difference between the men; they will also note the comment that Jem Belcher not only had the weight advantage, but also that of being in possession of both eyes.

Paddington Jones died in his native borough in 1833, aged 64 years; this could be considered a good age for an ex-pugilist, as many former members of the profession passed on while still in their thirties and forties. The death of Jones is reported in Dowling's *Fistiana* as follows:

"Jones fought a vast number of minor battles, and was long the Master of Ceremonies at the Fives and Tennis Court."

Around the time when Paddington Jones was active in the ring, there was also a boxer named Jack Doyle, some one hundred and thirty years before the emergence of the more celebrated wielder of a devastating right hand, who bore the same name. The earlier Jack joined issue in a few contests in the London area, and while giving creditable displays, was mostly on the losing end; in the opinion of Egan "he conducted himself with great spirit, and in no instance have we learned that he ever disgraced the character of a good pugilist".

The name and triumphs of Daniel Mendoza are given long and honourable mention in the pages of *Boxiana*. He is described as "one of the most elegant and scientific pugilists in the whole race of boxers, and might be termed a complete artist". Although beaten by John Jackson early in his fighting career, Mendoza won the majority of his contests and met Richard Humphries on no less than four occasions. The final score being two wins each. Two of the fights were each of seventy minutes duration. Together with John Jackson, Daniel Mendoza was a noted teacher of pugilism. On retirement from boxing he became landlord of the "Lord Nelson" public house in Whitechapel, to which he retired with a wife and six children; however, Mendoza made a comeback in 1806, fifteen years after his final clash with Humphries. The return to action was the result of a difference of opinion with one Harry Lee over money matters. The bout resulted in a win for Mendoza in fifty-three rounds, lasting seventy minutes.

Up to the present, this chapter has attempted to convey an idea of the skill of Pierce Egan as a reporter, the scope of his work, and glimpses of some of the characters among whom he worked and of whom he wrote. It is impossible in a general work such as this on the literature of boxing to include more than a fraction of the content and quality of the five volumes of *Boxiana*, or to give even a glimpse of the careers of such as Elisha Crabbe, the Jew, a professor of some notoriety in the gymnastic art, Isaac Perrins, of Manchester, Tom Tring, of whom it is said "no boxer it appears, possessed such an attraction to publicity – his qualities were of a most tremendous nature"; a native of Leighton Buzzard, whose prize-fights were few, but his skirmishes numerous indeed.

There is insufficient space to recount fully the fistic talents of Caleb Baldwin (the veteran Champion of Westminster) but whom I feel merits the repetition of a passage from *Boxiana*, as an example of his abilities under the most trying circumstances, and of Pierce Egan's flippant but nevertheless engaging style of reporting:

In the vicinity of St. George's Fields, a man of the name of Jones, a Limner, and a neighbour of Dutch Sam's, who valued himself upon his milling qualities, publicly declared that he was Champion of that quarter, and had frequently importuned Sam to have a set-to, but who regaling himself at a public house near the Limner's dwelling, till glass succeeding glass of Deady's brilliant fluid, had nearly obliterated all the things of this world from Sam's pericranium, when Jones, learning the circumstances, soon entered the premises and attempted to provoke him, in his debilitated state, to a combat, but in vain, upon which Jones immediately struck him. This was too much, and Sam, reeling to and fro, returned it, and, scarcely intelligible, inquired 'whether he was right or wrong to defend himself', and who immediately went into the street to decide it. Sam, notwithstanding his intoxicated state, appeared to have the advantage, when Jones seized him by the hair of his head, threw him down, and beat him violently upon the stones. This act of cruelty operated contrary in its effect to what was expected by the perpetrator, by awakening Sam to a better recollection of what he was about, who started up, exclaiming 'Take care, take care, for now I'm coming!' and put in such a stomacher as nearly deprived Jones of his breath, and following it up by a tremendous hit over his eye, levelled this brute with the mud.

Volume I of Pierce Egan's classic ends with the championship of Cribb. This future champion's birthplace is given as in the parish of Bitton, on the borders of Gloucestershire and Somerset, within five miles of Bristol. Regarding Cribb's opponents in the ring, as Egan puts it: "The names of his brave competitiors render any further comment upon that head unnecessary; George Maddox, Tom Blake, Ikey Pig, Richmond, Jem Belcher (twice), Horton, Bob Gregson, Molyneux (twice) and Nichols."

There is an interesting footnote to the naming of Nichols as an opponent, which reads thus:

In every circumstance in which the public are interested, any thing like deception ought to be avoided, and the friends of the Champion acted injudiciously in with-holding the name of Nichols, who defeated Cribb, from the list of names which are placed under his whole-length likeness − it is calculated to mislead, and give importance to a circumstances, by endeavouring to obscure the fact, which it otherwise would not deserve. It was during the novitiate of Cribb, and by no means reflected discredit upon his conduct.

This note may be of comfort to modern record-compiling enthusiasts in the knowledge that the publication of inaccurate records is not a new phenomenon.

There are mentioned many times in *Boxiana* stories of the occasions when old-time fighters, either by accident or design, were drawn into skirmishes or street fights, but apparently Tom Cribb was more immune than most from this kind of activity.

Pierce Egan comments: "From the placid demeanour of the Champion, it appears he has never engaged in many Skirmishes; and the contests in which he has proved so conspicuous, have taken place on the principles of professed boxing".

As Cribb gained in experience he came to the attention of Captain Barclay, who took him into training for a match with Jem Belcher, with odds of six to four on the latter; Cribb proved the stronger man and was successful in forty-one rounds lasting thirty-five minutes. Egan commented on Tom's triumph thus:

From the above victory, Cribb rose rapidly into fame − his real qualities were hitherto unknown, and he had been viewed principally as a glutton of the first class, with a bottom unimpeached; but now his pretensions unfolded themselves, and the amateurs were completely surprised at his display and improvement in the science − his distances were well judged, and he stopped with great dexterity and neatness; and had he proved a quicker hitter, the contest might have soon been decided.

Cribb repeated his victory over Belcher at a later date, and the story of his two wins over Molyneux at Copthall Common and Thistleton Gap set the seal on his position as a Champion. Regarding the second win over Molyneux, Egan reported thus on some of the financial aspects: "It was reported that Cribb gained £400 by this set-to, and his patron, Captain Barclay, £10,000; and that a baker in the Borough sported all his blunt, personal property, together with the lease of his house, &c, amounting to £1700, upon the Champion".

Regarding the Cribb v. Molyneux fight at Thistleton Gap, I would like to add a small personal anecdote from my early days when starting my somewhat un-distinguised career as a boxer in the 1930s, while living in a Lincolnshire village. In those days I was friendly with an old gentleman, then in his seventies, who remembered his grandfather talking of having been present at the great fight on 28th September, 1811. At the time when my elderly friend told me of this memory from his own early days I did not give a second thought to the fact that here I had a direct personal link with one of the most historic occasions in the annals of pugilism. In later years I have often wished that I had probed more deeply into the memories of my septuagenarian friend on his grandfather's account of events on that historic field, which reverted thereafter to its windblown loneliness on the borders of three counties.

Picture of Pierce Egan, from a drawing

CHAPTER IV
TELLS MORE OF EGAN—
AND TWO CONTEMPORARIES

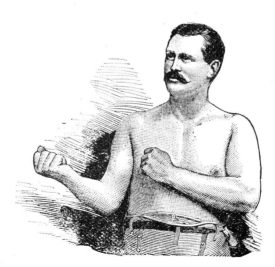

PADDY RYAN.

2.

Price Threepence.

BOXIANA;

OR,

Sketches of Ancient and Modern Pugilism,

FROM

THE DAYS OF FIGG AND BROUGHTON

TO THE PRESENT TIME.

WITH BIOGRAPHICAL MEMOIRS OF THE BOXERS.

BY ·PIERCE EGAN.

THE ART OF TRAINING, BY CAPTAIN BARCLAY.

LONDON:

PUBLISHED FOR THE PROPRIETORS,

BY W. M. CLARK, WARWICK LANE;

AND SOLD BY

Brittain, Paternoster Row; Strange, Paternoster Row; Pat tie, Brydges
Street, Covent Garden; Berger, Holywell Street; Purkiss, Coi mpton Street;
Clements, Pulteney Street; Hetherington, Strand; Clea e, Shoe
Lane; Watson, City Road; and all Booksellers.

Johnston, Printer, Lovell's Court, St. Paul's

Cover of Part 2 of *Boxiana*, as issued in parts. (Bib. Ref. 587)

CHAPTER 4

TELLS MORE OF EGAN –
AND TWO CONTEMPORARIES

Early in Volume II of *Boxiana*, one of the fighters to come under the scrutiny of Pierce Egan is Harry Harmer, who hailed from Bristol. Although he did not achieve championship status in the ring, Harmer is stated by Egan to have displayed superior style, and to have been an inoffensive, well-behaved man. One of the prime reasons for bringing Harmer to notice here is that he was a cousin of the Belcher brothers, Jem, Tom and Ned. The Belchers were in turn grandsons of Jack Slack, of earlier pugilistic fame, himself Champion of England, and by his relationship with the Belchers, grandfather of another champion in the person of Jem of that ilk.

In speaking of a pugilist by the name of Nosworthy, who was born in Devonshire, Pierce Egan coined one of those succinct and at the same time fully-descriptive phrases at which he was so expert when describing the qualities of a fighter, reading as follows:

In disposition he was cheerful, good natured and inoffensive; but in the ring Nosworthy was a glutton of the first mould; and he must be no common character that could attempt to satisfy his inordinate appetite.

One of Nosworthy's early encounters is described in the following passage:

It was with the mate of a vessel at Exeter, that the milling qualities of Nosworthy conspicuously burst forth, when he had scarcely attained his sixteenth year. Some difference of opinion occurring between them, a regular set-to was the consequence. The Mate flattered himself that he would soon be able to chastise the lad for his presumption in thus daring to contend with a man, and at once poured in a broadside to induce the enemy to cry for quarter. The action was kept up with great spirit on both sides for some considerable time, and notwithstanding the brisk and heavy firing of the man-of-war to enforce obedience, the superior skill and tactics of the frigate prevailed, and ultimately compelled the Mate to strike, by lowering his flag. It was a dearly purchased victory for Nosworthy, who had one of his arms broken.

At this stage it may be of interest to the reader to look at the dignified form in which challenges were made and accepted, as a preliminary to some of the ring battles. Here as an example is a challenge issued by Ned Painter to Tom Oliver, the Gardener, for a return fight, together with Oliver's reply:

Castle Tavern, Holborn, March 21, 1817.
Mr. E. Painter's compliments to T. Oliver, and challenges him to fight on Thursday, the 22nd day of May next, in a 24-feet ring, half-minute time between each round, a fair stand-up fight, for one hundred guineas a-side.

The place to be appointed by and stakes to be deposited with, Mr Jackson, who, Mr Painter understands, is willing to contribute a purse of twenty-five guineas to make up the one hundred. An early answer is required.

Mr. Oliver replied, with this acceptance:

Tom Oliver, with compliments to Mr Painter, informs him, he has received his most welcome challenge to fight him. Oliver certainly cannot refuse to fight him on the day appointed, but requests it to be understood, he will not fight for a lesser stake than £100 a-side, independent of the purse which may be thought proper to be given by the Club.

Oliver also begs leave to inform Mr Painter, he agrees to his own proposal, that is to make it a stand-up fight, in a 24-feet ring, at half-minute time between each round; and also the place to be appointed by Mr Jackson; and if it meets his pleasure, (which it does mine most exceptionally), to deposit the whole stakes in his hands. Your early answer to the above terms is requested, in order that I may apprise my friends to come and make a deposit. They will either meet you at my house, or I will meet you and them at Mr Thomas Belcher's in Holborn at his.
Peter Street, Westminster, 22nd March, 1817.

Unfortunately these courteous preliminaries were for the time being wasted, a complaint was laid with the police and Oliver was taken from his training quarters to Moorfields Police Station, he was bound over to keep the peace for twelve months under sureties of £400. Because of this interruption to their plans, the contestants and their supporters talked of transferring the promotion to France. Pierce Egan took the opportunity to ventilate his patriotism and to remind his readers of who was victorious at the Battle of Waterloo, with the following passage:

Oliver and Painter were both anxious for it, and the *Mounseers* would then have the opportunity of witnessing one of those national sports which have placed OLD ENGLAND at the top of the tree in the scale of nations, a trait that has routed out effeminacy from the composition of Britons — tempered their courage with generosity — and given them that true notion of bottom, never to flinch from their opponents while a chance of victory remains. This trait was nobly experienced at Waterloo — it was felt and acknowledged by all Europe — when the greatest Prize-fighter in the world was not only floored, but had the fight completely taken out of him. Of its national utility to Englishmen, the above facts speak more than a volume.

The idea of staging the contest in France did not materialise; Painter and Oliver did meet again in the ring in 1820 and the score between them came out at one victory each.

In his section on Ned Turner, who was born in Southwark of Welsh parentage, Pierce Egan describes at some length the contest between Turner and Jack Curtis;

this took place at Moulsey Hurst in October 22nd, 1816. The duration of the contest was 85 minutes, consisting of 85 rounds; the pathetic result of the fight is reported as follows:

> Notwithstanding the greatest exertion and humane care were taken in speedily removing Curtis from the ring after the battle terminated, to the nearest house of accommodation; in fact, but a few minutes had scarcely elapsed before he was put to bed at the *Red Lion* Inn, Hampton, and medical assistance procured, — yet the brave but unfortunate Curtis in the course of a few hours breathed his last. The subject of his death having very properly come under the cognisance of the Laws of the Country, an Inquisition was taken on the body at the above Inn on Friday October 25th, 1816, before Thomas Sterling Esq., Coroner for Middlesex.

The verdict of the inquest jury was one of manslaughter, and Turner was arrested. Evidence given at the inquest, and at the trial of Turner, indicated that he had not always followed up his advantage when Curtis was in a distressed condition during the fight, but he was found guilty and sentenced to two months' imprisonment; during his time in Newgate, Turner is reported as having conducted himself with much propriety and decorum.

Jack Curtis was 28 years of age at the time of the fatal contest. Ned Turner added to his fame by becoming one of the few boxers to defeat the great Jack Scroggins; in fact he achieved this considerable feat on two occasions, the contests lasting one hour and twelve minutes and one hour and thirty-one and a half minutes respectively. A sad postscript to the story of Ned Turner is that he did not long outlive the ill-fated Curtis; Ned died on April 17th, 1826, aged 36 years.

Two famous characters of the Prize Ring during the early years of the 19th Century, to whom Pierce Egan devoted considerable space in *Boxiana* were Jack Scroggins and Jack Randall. Scroggins was born in 1787 and Randall in 1794; their weights were given as 10st 12lbs and 10st 6lbs respectively. Despite these common features as to age and weight, and the fact that they were contemporaries in ring activity, there is no record of them having opposed each other within the roped square. The main reason for this may have been that Scroggins (real name John Palmer), was for a number of years at sea serving in the Navy.

Egan opens his introduction of Scroggins as follows:

> In point of attraction, what Kean has been to the boards of Drury Lane Theatre, Scroggins has proved to the Prize-Ring. Without the advantages of a patron — destitute of common introduction and merely relying on his natural strength and courage, he, *sans ceremonie*, entered himself as a competitor among the formidable list of London scientific boxers, and this too at a period, singular to remark, after he had been discharged from His Majesty's Services as an INVALID! Upwards of nine years Scroggins buffeted the ocean, five of which had been occupied in different merchantmen, and the remainder actively employed in fighting the enemies of his country on board the *Argo*, a 44-gun ship. During the above mentioned time, his constitution, it seems, while thus contending

with the rude elements, had acquired so fine a stamina, and a disposition so insensible to fear, that nothing could appal his feelings, or affect his dreadnought frame to acknowledge superiority in any man.

Jack is reported to have taken part in so many skirmishes while in the Navy, he is described as "full of pluck — fond of a lark and always ready for a turn-up, milling it appears formed the principal part of Scroggins' amusement when off duty".

During his schooldays in the New Cross district of London, Jack became cock of the walk, and when he left school he moved into service with a farmer in Kilburn; it was at this time that he took part in a number of turn-ups with the navigators (or "navvies") who were engaged on digging out the Grand Union Canal.

Scroggins had his first organised contest at the age of sixteen years; this followed a bull-baiting session at nearby Willesden Green. In fact, young Jack became very well known in the district now encompassed in the borough of Brent. In addition to his turn-ups at Kilburn and the first fight at Willesden Green, Jack also showed his prowess as a fighter in contests at the Swan at Sudbury and the Fox and Goose at Alperton, on the border of Wembley and Ealing. In the latter encounter Jack's opponent was a brickmaker weighing 14 stones, who was seen off in quick time. The diminutive Scroggins pursued his fistic career in the Wembley and Harrow district for some time, mostly at the expense of the canal diggers.

The circumstances under which Jack joined the Navy are recounted as follows by Pierce Egan:

It was owing to the following circumstances that our HERO was compelled to leave milling on the land, to fight the battles of his country at sea, by entering the Navy. In a row, with one Ellis, a constable at Sandford Green, the above representative of the Law, it appears, felt rather heavily the indignation of Scroggins. In consequence of which turn-up, an application was made to the Magistrate, Dr Glass, when our hero was depicted in such terrible colours, that a press-gang of seventeen was considered necessary to carry him safely out of the neighbourhood.

After his discharge from the Navy, Scroggins soon showed that his invalidity was not of a degree to inhibit his ring activities, for which purpose he returned to his old stamping ground at Willesden Green where he engaged in successful combat with one Jack Boots. Jack's spirited conduct in this contest so pleased the amateurs that the sum of four pounds was collected without any trouble and given to the victor as a reward.

As his fighting career met with continued success, Scroggins was enabled to take over as landlord of a public house, and for this purpose he returned south of the Thames to become landlord of the Waterman's Arms in Lambeth. After four months in the role of landlord, Jack resumed his ring career by engaging in a bout with a novice Yorkshireman named Whitaker. Either because of the soft living enjoyed as master of the Waterman's Arms, or because he did not train properly for the contest, Scroggins experienced difficulty in beating the Yorkshireman, as the battle extended to a period of seventy-six minutes, during which they fought forty-nine rounds. After one more successful bout the star of Scroggins appeared to be on the wane; it was then he became involved in fistic exchanges with the afore-mentioned Ned Turner, with whom he fought one drawn battle and by whom he was twice beaten. From then on "Scroggy", as he was fondly dubbed by Pierce Egan, lost the majority of his fights.

Jack Randall, otherwise "The Prime Irish Lad", also known as "The Nonpareil", was born in London of Irish parents and was active in the roped square from 1809 to 1821. The notable feature of Randall's career was his almost unparalleled success; he was unbeaten throughout the 12 years during which he was active in the ring. Among his successes were wins over Aby Belasco, West Country Dick, and Ned Turner (conqueror of Scroggins), in a match for £100 a-side.

Regarding Pierce Egan's reportage of a fight, a good eample of this may be given by taking a part of his account of the contest between Tom Spring and one Stringer, the latter being described as "A Yorkshireman from a place called Rawcliffe, thirty years old, and a mere novice". As a preliminary to his report of this bout Egan re-marks that very few big men had entered the Prize Ring for upwards of six years, since the reign of Cribb as Champion. Tom Spring (real name Winter),was a native of Herefordshire, and it was stated that not only had he disposed of all the rough commoners opposed to him with considerable ease, but he had likewise defeated the best men of that county in the best style. His debut in London area took place at Moulsey Hurst on Sept. 9th, 1817, against the Yorkshireman, who being described as a novice, put up a brave fight. Here are descriptions of some of the rounds:

Third — This round was most courageous fought. It was curious to observe the left hand of Stringer, pushing, as it were, against his opponent, with his right close upon it. *Yorky* did not appear wholly without judgement, though many of his blows were made at random. Both were down. The odds had now risen rapidly on Spring.

Sixth — This was a desperate round. The men stood up to each other, and hammered away like a couple of blacksmiths, as if both their frames were insens-ible of feeling; but Spring had the best of it. The latter nobly disdained taking an advantage when Stringer was on the ropes, and let him go down without extra punishment. Great applause from all parts of the ring.

Ninth — On setting-to *Yorky* received a facer, which nearly turned him round, but he recovered himself and planted a good hit. In closing Stringer got his arms round his opponent's body, but he nevertheless could not prevent Spring from administering some heavy punishment. The Yorkshireman, however, obtained the throw, and fell with all his weight upon Spring.

Twelfth — Both the combatants exhibited the severe marks of each other's handywork. The Claret was flowing copiously. Both down, a quarter of an hour had elapsed.

Sixteenth — This was as terrible a round as any in the fight. One minute occurred in hard milling, without intermission, till Spring got the best of it, when Stringer went down and fell upon his hands.

Twentieth — The men, upon setting-to, went as eagerly to work as if the fight had just commenced. Hit for hit and facer for facer were reciprocally given, till, in closing, both had enough of it, and went down.

Twenty-fifth — A more determined round was never fought, and the battle altogether was so terrible that many of the amateurs turned away from viewing it. In a rally, both men were hit to a stand-still; they at length got away from each other, when Stringer rushed in and got his arms round his opponent's body, but ultimately he was so severely fibbed, that he went down quite exhausted.

Twenty-ninth, and last — This round was, in point of finishing execution, the severest ever seen. Stringer received in his middle piece so tremendous a hit, from the right hand of his opponent, that he was only prevented from falling on his face by a quick repetition of it, which caught *Yorky*'s nob, and instantly floored him on his back. He was carried out of the ring by his seconds, in a state of stupor. It lasted thirty nine minutes.

Tom Spring's career is covered in later volumes of *Boxiana*; he went on to win the championship during a fighting life covering ten years of ring activity. During this time he defeated Ned Painter, and Spring also suffered one of his rare defeats at the hands of the same practitioner. Probably the highlights of Tom's achievements were his two wins over Jack Langan; the first in 77 rounds lasting 140 minutes, for £300 a-side, and the second in the same number of rounds, lasting 108 minutes, for £500 a-side.

Regarding the venues for the fights which were reported by Pierce Egan, the scene of the match between Jack Carter, the Lancashire Hero, and Tom Oliver, moved to Scotland. It was staged on the estate of Sir James Maxwell, a short distance from the famous blacksmith's shop at Gretna Green, which even in those days was known as the place where runaway lovers regularised their relationship by marrying over the anvil. The bout took place in October, 1816, for stakes of £100-a-side. Egan reported that there were 30,000 spectators to view the battle, and that during the day of the set-to the streets and houses of Carlisle and its vicinity were totally drained of the male population. The result of the bout was a win for Carter in 46 minutes, during which 34 rounds were contested, and Oliver was subjected to terrific punishment. Referring to the final round, Egan states: "The swelled appearance of his head beggared all description". Jack Carter was apparently an accomplished performer in other forms of exercise; he was supported by his backers in walking and running races, and he was credited with being a good dancer. Carter is stated to have "performed the clog-hornpipe with considerable talent, and after the manner of an expert clown, he stands upon his head and drinks off several gallons of ale in that position".

In the descriptions of fights culled from *Boxiana* and given in this volume, readers will note that the duration of the battle, divided by the number of rounds contested, indicates that the length of the round was on average quite short; in fact they were in many cases much shorter than the three-minute round, which is the standard for important contests at the present time. There was however a departure from this pattern in the case of a contest between a pugilist by the name of Fuller and Tom Molineux; the fight took place on May 31st, 1814, at Auchineaux, twelve miles from Glasgow, for an agreed 100 guineas a-side, in a forty-foot ring. The meeting had been arranged for four days earlier but it had to be postponed because of the intervention of the Sheriff of Renfrewshire, after the original set-to had been in progress for only eight minutes.

When the proceedings were resumed on the re-arranged date the contest lasted only two rounds, but the length of time taken to decide the issue was sixty-eight minutes! The first round was of twenty-eight minutes duration, and the second round lasted forty minutes, with Molineux the ultimate victor. In his description of the first round Egan states: "They sparred a considerable time with good skill, before any punishment was exhibited, when Fuller, by a tremendous hit, drew the cork of his antagonist". A typical example of Egan's elegant description of a common occurrence in the boxing ring: how one fighter hit his opponent on the nose and made it bleed.

Regarding these two prolonged rounds, one wonders whether the use of a forty-foot ring served to keep the antagonists at greater distance than usual from each other, thus reducing the amount of punishment meted out. According to Pierce Egan's description of the bout, this was not the case, and the fight was full of interest; in the second round for instance ". . . the whole *minutiae* of the milling art was resorted to, from the beginning to the end". In fact the conduct of Fuller in the fight so impressed the amateurs that a purse of 50 guineas was presented to him.

An amusing anecdote regarding the extra-curricular activities of Abraham Belasco, a Jewish fighter who was active from 1817 to 1824, is given in the following paragraph from Volume II of *Boxiana*:

Our hero, it seems was down at Moulsey-Hurst on Thursday April 3, 1817, to witness the fight between Randall and West Country Dick, and, in order not to lose sight of the "main chance", but to turn the penny to advantage, he filled up his time on the ground in disposing of oranges. Thus uniting pleasure with profit, when he was called upon unexpectedly to enter the ring with Jack the Butcher, for a subscription purse. Belasco, without hesitation, put down his basket of fruit, peeled *sans ceremonie*, and instantly prepared for action, with the utmost confidence.

This involuntary encounter was won by Belasco, the sixteen rounds lasting seventeen minutes.

Volume II of *Boxiana* concludes with a chapter on Sparring Exhibitions for the Benefit of the Various Pugilists. These were staged at the Fives Court, the Minerva Rooms, and other places of sport. The reports in this section deal with some of the contests, mostly boxed with the participants wearing mufflers, which rewarded a number of heroes who had decorated the fistic scene during the years prior to 1816. Pierce Egan introduced the Fives Court to his readers with the following passage:

The above national and manly place of amusement, which now holds its ranks among the numerous public exhibitions of the present liberal and enlightened era in the first Metropolis of the World, for the promulgation of the Art of Self Defence, is an object of great attraction among the amateurs of Scientific Pugilism. The Fives Court is well adapted for an exhibition of the Gymnastic Sports, and is calculated to contain conveniently 1000 persons; it has also to boast of the most respectable audiences. The combatants exhibit on a temporary stage, about four feet from the ground and which was first introduced by Tom Cribb. The doors are opened at two o'clock, and, previous to the time, it is nothing uncommon to witness crowds of amateurs assembled round them, anxious to gain admission, which is by tickets, sold at three shillings each. The proceedings are conducted with the utmost propriety and respect; but no pugilist whatsoever can obtain the Fives Court for his benefit without the acquiesence of Mr Jackson.

The beneficiaries of the proceedings at the Fives Court during the two years 1816 and 1817 included Harry Harmer, Isaac Bittoon, Tom Cribb, Ned Painter, Bill Richmond, Jem Belcher, Bob Gregson, Jack Scroggins, Jack Randall, and many other professors of the Science, who had in former years regaled their audiences with spirited displays of skill, and probably the more conspicuous quality, bottom.

The three later volumes of *Boxiana*, including the two volumes of the New Series, are to a great extent repetitive, with references to pugilists already mentioned in earlier volumes; however there are also new characters brought into the history as they appeared on the scene, concurrently with the publication years of the later volumes. Among the dozens of greater and lesser lights of the Prize Ring who came upon the scene, and are faithfully recorded by Egan, are such as Josh Hudson (The John Bull Fighter), Jack Cooper (The Gipsy), Tom Hickman (The Gas Light Man), Jack Martin, John Langan, Jem Ward, Barney Aaron (The Star of the East), and Young Dutch Sam.

Regarding Egan's fourth and fifth volumes of *Boxiana*, it has already been explained in this present work how these came to be prefixed *New Series*; in his opening to the first of these the author refers as follows to the court case in which it was ruled that the title of the additional volumes should be slightly amended:

Lincoln's Inn
PIERCE EGAN'S NOB IN CHANCERY!!!
Thursday July 24, 1823
BOXIANA
Sherwood and others v. Pierce Egan

Pierce then proceeds to give a verbatim account of the case, which resulted in the ruling on the extended title to be given to the two volumes, as already described.

In concluding this study of *Boxiana* and of Pierce Egan, with his references to The Fancy, The Flash Side, his Clodpoles or Johnny Raws, his Knights of the Cleaver and his Masters of the Rolls, together with other quaintly-dubbed pugilistic operators, it should not be overlooked that there were two contemporaries of Egan who also made substantial contributions to the lore of Fistiana. These two gentlemen were named William Oxberry and John Badcock, the latter being better known under his pen-name of Jon Bee. We shall now take a look at what is known of these two versatile characters.

William Oxberry was born in Moorfields in 1784, and he died in 1824; he crowded a wealth of experience into his comparatively short life. Oxberry had the benefit of a good education and started his working life by taking up artistic studies under Stubbs; he then transferred to bookselling before taking an apprenticeship with a printer in Tottenham Court Road. About this time he became friendly with an amateur actor named Searle, and took up acting. He made his first appearance on the stage in 1802, before cancelling his indentures as a printer and embarking on the career of an actor. This led to appearances in the plays of Shakespeare and the establishment of a reputation as a low comedian, with engagements in the provinces and in London with the Kembles at the Lyceum and Covent Garden Theatres in 1807. Oxberry became the manager of the Olympic Theatre, and later took over the Craven Head Chophouse in Drury Lane.

Before considering Oxberry's contribution to the literature of pugilism, and in order to give proper regard to his versatility, which, had he lived longer, could possibly have borne comparison with that of Pierce Egan, it would be appropriate to list some of the works for which he was responsible.

He was for a time editor of *The Monthly Mirror*, and the following works are attribtued to his pen:

The Banquet, or Actor's Budget, 1809. (2 volumes)
Pancratia, or A History of Pugilism, 1812.
The Encyclopedia of Anecdote, 1812.
The History of Pugilism, and Memories of Persons who have distinguished themselves in that Science, 1814.
Anecdotes of the Stage, 1827.

Editor, *The New English Drama*, 22 volumes, 1826.
Oxberry's Dramatic Biography, 5 volumes, 1826. (Published by Oxberry's widow after his death)

In addition, Oxberry wrote a play entitled *An Actress of All Work*, together with other pieces for the theatre, including editions of some of the plays of Shakespeare.

Regarding *Pancratia*, the book is divided into two parts, as follows:

Part I   (Boxing of the Classic Ages)
  1.   Amusements Arising from the contests of Animals.
  2.   Amusements Depending upon Bodily Exercises and Personal Contests.

D

Part II   (History of Pugilism in This Country)
From Figg and Broughton to Cribb's second fight with Molineux.

Early in my first two chapters dealing with *Boxiana* and Pierce Egan, the name of Oxberry was mentioned in connection with Egan's classic of the Prize Ring. This is better explained by reproduction of the following extract from *Sportsman's Slang* by Jon Bee, 1825, under Addenda to *Far-Fetched Words and Phrases*.

Pancratium — A place of boxing at Rome. But they knew nothing of the *Ars Pugnandi* as now practised; their wrists circled with iron, their knuckles defended by bullocks' hide, they larruped away incontinently, and two or three score proud Romans were thus murdered annually. Hence derived we have 'Pancratia' which is the title of a 'History of Pugilism', partly done by Bill Oxberry in 1811, the first fifty pages by another hand. Out of this volume, Smeeton, a printer, dished up 'Sketches of Pugilism', being a copy essentially, but a vulgarised one, of the comedian's book: for which piece of disservice the latter vowed vengeance . . .

The reference to Smeeton in this passage accuses the publisher of copying Oxberry's work.

The relationship between Pierce Egan, William Oxberry, and Jon Bee is further confused by the entry referring to *Pancratia* in the bibliography shown in the magazine *Famous Fights*, edited by Harold Furniss, (Vol.V, No.63), reading as follows:

Pancratia: A History of Pugilism. I Vol. 8vo. 1811, by J.B., London, Geo. Smeeton, St.Martin's Lane.

It will have been noted that Jon Bee, in his *Sportsman's Slang*, did not attribute full authorship of *Pancratia* to Oxberry, the first fifty pages being credited to 'another hand'. On the title-page of the work it is stated as being 'Published and Sold by W. Oxberry'; there is no claim here for any participation by Geo. Smeeton, so it is difficult to judge from whence Harold Furniss obtained his information, which led to him crediting Smeeton with publication. It is of course possible that Smeeton did indeed publish a later edition of *Pancratia*.

We do know however that Smeeton published a work similar to that of Oxberry, shortly after the latter's book was issued; this was of course the first volume of *Boxiana*, dated 1812. From the dates of publication of the two works, and taking account of the 1818 publication date of Egan's first volume of *Boxiana*, it is possible that Smeeton copied some of his first volume from Oxberry, and that Egan copied from Smeeton. Nevertheless the fact remains that Egan's 1818 volume, the first of his series of five, was allowed to remain thereafter with his name on the title-page as author.

One further curious fact emerges from the interplay between authors, titles, and dates of this series of books: Sherwood, Neely, and Jones, of Paternoster Row, were involved in the publication and selling of both works, i.e. *Boxiana*, 1812 and 1818 (two volumes), and *Pancratia*, 1811. The Sherwood company also issued a fourth volume of *Boxiana* in 1824, this being the work of Jon Bee.

The details of the birth and death of Jon Bee are not very clear, neither is much known on when he changed to the pen-name used instead of his proper name of Jonathan Badcock. He was active as a writer from 1816 to 1830, and as in the cases of Pierce Egan and William Oxberry, he was both versatile and prolific with his pen, especially on pugilism and on matters pertaining to horses and the Turf. Before dealing with Jon Bee's contribution to dissertations on prize-fighting, we must pay to him the same respect accorded to his two illustrious contemporaries, by listing some of the other works for which he was responsible:

Slang. A Dictionary of the turf, and ring, the chase, bon-ton and varieties of Life, forming the most complete and most authentic lexicon, balatronicum of the sporting world. 1823.

Sportsman's Slang. A new dictionary of terms used in the affairs of the turf, ca. 1825.

A Living Picture of London for 1828, and stranger's guide, showing the frauds and wiles of all description of rogues. (1828)

The Works of Samuel Foote, with remarks of each play, and an essay on the life of the author.

Editor of *The Fancy Gazette* section of the magazine *The Annals of Sporting and Fancy Gazette*; originally issued in monthly parts. 1822–1828.

There were also thirteen half-yearly volumes of this publication. The section edited by Jon Bee was almost entirely devoted to pugilism. There were also references to the Prize Ring in the main body of the magazine.

Bee was also credited with editing a new edition of *Treatise on the Horse and Rules for Bad Horsemen*. 1830.

There were at least two editions of Jon Bee's fourth volume of *Boxiana*. The title-page states that this volume contains "All the Transactions of Note, Connected with the Prize-Ring During the Years 1821, 1822, 1823". The volume was dedicated to Captain Barclay.

There is an advertisement in the preliminaries, reading as follows:

On the publication of a new volume of *Boxiana*, the Proprietors take the occasion to allude to the change which it has been necessary to make in the Editorship since the publication of the preceding Volumes. In making this change, they have been induced to avail themselves of the assistance of a gentleman of good practical knowledge and judgement of all the points on the subject, whereby they may have been able to introduce much improvement, both in the plan and execution of the work. With regard to such preceding parts of it as required reprinting, they have not to correct (by the same hand) the errors which had crept in; and this, with similar improvements in the style of elucidation, discernible in the present Volume, must contribute to render the whole work still more acceptable to the amateur taste of the present 'refined' times; these alterations will be mostly visible in the New Edition, just issued of Volume the Second.

Regarding the introduction of 'full length portraits' instead of 'Busts' they further expect the Purchasers approbation; for the alteration in this respect was only effected at considerable expense.

This advertisement clearly shows that the differences between the first and subsequent issues of Volume IV, were made while the work was still being published by Sherwood.

Jon Bee's volume includes a section on the "Art of Training", with elucidation of Captain Barclay's method. The text includes many of the stories of fights and fighters already covered in Pierce Egan's volumes issued in the 1820's. Bee also used appropriate nick-names for some of the pugilists, in some cases using the same soubriquets as adopted by Egan. For instance, we read again of Jack Martin being named "The Master of the Rolls", other appendages used by Bee included: Jack Cabbage, "The Iron Armed Bristolian"; Aby Belasco, "The Leary Israelite"; Pat Halton, "The Tight Irish Lad"; Alec Read, "The Chelsea Snob"; and others in similar vein.

In perusing the two chapters on Pierce Egan and his contemporaries in the fields of writing and publishing, during the period which saw the Prize Ring achieve the zenith of its popularity, the reader may feel some sympathy for the writer in the difficulties imposed by the constraints of the limited space available in which to do justice in honouring these early boxing historians.

If the brief glimpse afforded in these chapters gives impetus to the reader to pursue further research into the works of Egan, Oxberry, and Bee, then the efforts of the present writer will have been well worth while.

CHAPTER V
EARLY MEMOIRS, RECORDS, AND
JOURNALISTIC JOTTINGS

THE MUCH-ENQUIRED-FOR-WORK
AT LAST.
"BETTER LATE THAN NEVER."

THE

MEMOIRS

OF

JOHN SCROGGINS,

The Pugilistic Hero,

OTHERWISE

JOHN PALMER.

In which are given a correct Narrative of his

BIRTH, PARENTAGE, EDIFICATION, ORTHOGRAPHY,
(though loose) AND ODD EXPLOITS BOTH
AT SEA AND ON SHORE.

Including his many and determined OFF-HAND Fights in the

PRIZE RING.

With all the remarkable Circumstances attending those strange Proofs
of his

BRAVE AND HARDY MANHOOD.

Together with his peculiar ECCENTRICITIES through LIFE up
to the present Day.

TO WHICH WILL BE ADDED

SPORTING MISCELLANIES,
ANECDOTES,

And Original Rum Chaunts for the Fancy.

With, by way of a WIND-UP, or STALL-OFF,

An Appendix,

Containing Authentic

ANNALS OF PUGILISM,

From the early Days of FIGG, 1719, to those of SPRING and
LANGAN, 1824.

An eventful lapse of Time, big with Important Events, and truly *Illustrative*
of the *Origin, Rise, Progress, Illustrious Patronage,* and present improved and
refined state of the *Manly* and *Scientific*

ART OF BOXING,

During a lengthened Period of 105 Years.

By RICHARD HUMPHREYS.

London:

Printed by W. BARNES, Southwark, for, and Published by, J. SCROGGINS, Bond-street,
Borough road.

1827.

Title-Page *Memoirs of John Scroggins* (Humphreys) (Bib. Ref. 1033)

Chapter 5

EARLY MEMOIRS, RECORDS, AND
JOURNALISTIC JOTTINGS

A chapter which follows a review of the work of Pierce Egan and his contemporaries must of necessity be something of an anti-climax; however, a new generation of authors, journalists and pugilistic pundits made their appearance, to report and reminisce on fistic occasions and the state of the fight game. From the year 1818, which saw the publication of the first and second volumes of Pierce Egan's *Boxiana*, and the issue of the remainder of the series a few years later, up to the year 1880, and the publication of Henry Downes Miles' *Pugilistica* in three volumes, there were approximately one hundred books on boxing issued in Britain and America. These were in addition to the various periodicals dealing with the sport. Of the books which appeared during the sixty-two year period about one third were instructional items; some of these included lists showing results of contests from the earliest days of pugilism, and were thus the progenitors of the record books which were to become a regular feature among published material concerning boxing.

Among the books to include early records were titles such as *The Art of Boxing, or Science of Manual Defence*, by Thomas Belcher, (ca. 1820); *The Memoirs of John Scroggins*, by Richard Humphreys, (1827); and *The Handbook of Boxing*, by Owen Swift, (1840). The first venture into the publication of fighters' records was of course the well-known *Fistiana, or The Oracle of the Ring*, which was prepared by the editor of *Bell's Life in London*, otherwise Vincent George Dowling. This work appeared annually from 1841 to 1868; each annual issue was revised, or carried a supplement, showing results up to the date of issue.

In his preliminary address to the first issue of *Fistiana*, Mr. Dowling advises that the necessity for such a work was suggested by the innumerable questions which had been repeated to him, either for the gratification of curiosity or for the settlement of disputes or bets arising from bygone transactions of the Prize Ring. He pointed out that the circulation of previous works from which the information could be derived, such as Bee's *Chronology* and Egan's *Boxiana*, was limited, partly because of cost, and the publications were outside the reach of ordinary consultation. The editor also pointed out that there was no chronicle, beyond the columns of *Bell's Life in London*, of the matches made and decided between 1825 and 1841 and it being necessary to apply to the editor of that journal for information, the present work provided an instant channel, and avoided the loss of time heretofore experienced.

Mr. Dowling's reference to his work being used in order to settle disputes has of course applied in the use of record books by enthusiasts down to the present day. Friendly arguments still persist over the accuracy or otherwise of many boxers' records, and these records are constantly being researched, revised and supplemented by ardent and devoted statisticians who spend their time delving into magazine and newspaper files and any other sources judged as likely to yield up that odd elusive result of a battle contested long ago, which had hitherto lain unheeded in dusty archives, or which in recent years had achieved the dignity of being stored on micro-film.

There are those among us whose regard and enthusiasm for historical accuracy is not of sufficient magnitude to stir us from our fireside chair to delve into the roped-square activities of bygone fistic heroes, and we have cause to be grateful to the hard-working record-compilers. The achievements of many long-forgotten ring mechanics would have remained hidden in obscurity if it were not for the indefatig-able efforts of our boxing historians, and I pay my tribute to these gentlemen.

A title which will no doubt be familiar to all collectors of fistic material is *The Memoirs of Daniel Mendoza*, albeit that the mention of this title will in most cases ignite a mental spark in the mind of the collector, something like this: "Ah, issued by Batsford in 1951, author Paul Magriel". However, the Batsford edition is a re-issue of the original *Mendoza Memoirs*, first published in 1816. Both editions of the work contain Mendoza's account of events relating to his pugilistic career, but they tend to gloss over the first of his four encounters with Richard Humphries, while other histories of the sport, including *Boxiana*, do not agree regarding the result. The bout in question was not officially organised as to time and place; it was in fact a *turn-up*, or spur of the moment affair, which took place at the Cock Inn at Epping. Words were exchanged between the two pugilists, resulting in a fight being hastily arranged in the adjacent inn-yard. In his *Memoirs*, Mendoza claims that he succeeded in closing one of Humphries eyes, and bruising the other one, at which point the fracas was interrupted by a party of peace officers. Mendoza claimed that the keepers of the peace were brought in by friends of Humphries to save the latter from being beaten. Another account, given by H.D. Miles in his *Pugilistica* (1880), states that Humphries was rumoured to be having the best of the exchanges when the fight was interrupted. To add to the confusion, the *turn-up* at the Cock Inn is shown in the 1841 edition of Dowling's *Fistiana* as a win for Humphries, while the same fistic encounter is recorded in Owen Swift's *Handbook of Boxing* without a result being given. The results of the other three Mendoza v. Humphries encounters were two to one in favour of Mendoza.

It will not have escaped the notice of the reader that the author of the book *The Memoirs of John Scroggins*, mentioned earlier in this chapter, bore the name of Richard Humphreys. This was the same gentleman who did battle with Daniel Mendoza on four occasions. It would be interesting indeed if one were able to discover the circumstances under which Humphries abandoned pugilism to take up the more peaceful weapon of the pen, and at the same time pursue the business of coal merchant, upon which he embarked on his retirement from the ring.

Regarding the difference in the spelling of the name of the pugilistic provider of coal and reading matter to the citizens of London, the variations in the spelling of Richard's name persist in the various 19th Century works on pugilism. For instance, both *Boxiana* and *Fistiana* give the Humphries version, while the books on Scroggins and Mendoza give the name ending "eys".

Richard Humphreys' book *The Memoirs of John Scroggins* is dedicated to the Fancy, and the Sporting World in toto. The Editor's Preface commences as follows:

The many disadvantages which the Editor of the following Sheets has laboured under, (arising from very substantial reasons), they having all been written under Hatches, is the sole and real Apology for the Inaccuracies which will be found in them. He has, all along, had to contend (as well as the subject of them) with every Difficulty and Privation, solely emanating from stern and imperative necessity, during the time that has been occupied in their production: for like the Poet Savage, he has been compelled to get at them by bits and scraps, whenever the opportunity could be stolen, from the hollow, watchful Eyes, of lank and meagre Poverty. This, the Reader, it is hoped, will have the goodness to bear in mind, as a cause that could not be avoided, and which has been an Evil attendant on better Men than themselves, before now, and will no doubt happen to those who are to come.

The inimitable "Scroggy" was born in Deptford on 29th September, 1786, and was one of a family of fifteen children, fourteen boys and one girl; some of his exploits have already been recounted in an earlier chapter. In the *Memoirs*, Humphreys emerges as a great admirer of his subject, as witness the following passage:

As will be seen in the course of these his memoirs; for as long as the art of boxing exists in this country, when the professors of it act with an honest and upright principle, which he has ever done, there can be no doubt of its existence till time is no more, as his name will stand enrolled in the records of "milling fame" amongst the first pugilists the English nation has ever produced; for as a little man, who has ever done more? — always fighting under every disadvantage, as regards science, height and weight, being only 5 feet 3 inches, and his never fighting more than 10 stone 5 lb. &c. in all his battles: but his lion-like spirit knew no bounds nor fear, and bore down all his opposition, whatever might be the odds against him in every point of view, for a series of years, for whenever it was roused, he was far famed for "deeds in arms" as they were of the most decisive nature; but men as well as nations have their days of renown and greatness, when the full tide of unexampled prosperity flows on irresistibly, accompanied by their rising and setting suns.

Although fault may be found with the punctuation of this verbatim passage from the Memoirs, there is shining through the excerpt something of the great regard that was felt for Scroggins, expressed through the somewhat ragged prose of his biographer.

In addition to providing the reader with a look at the various phases of life as experienced by the diminutive Scroggins, covering his life on the Kilburn farm, in the Prize Ring, and in the Navy, the book by Humphreys is notable for the particularly elaborate title-page, a reproduction of which is included in the illustrations to the present work, showing the variety of printing types used in its preparation.

Pierce Egan also made his contribution to the instructional books on boxing which were issued during the mid-nineteenth Century; his *Every Gentleman's Manual — A Lecture on the Art of Self-Defence* was published in 1845. Owen Swift, who was active in the ring from 1829 to 1839, showed his literary as well as his pugilistic skill to good effect by his authorship of three titles of which details are given as follows: – *The Handbook to Boxing*, (1840); *Boxing Without a Master*, which ran to four editions in America in the 1840s; and *The Modern English Boxer*, (ca. 1840).

The period between the culmination of Pierce Egan's career, which came to its peak on completion of his five volumes of *Boxiana*, and the publication of H.D. Miles' *Pugilistica* in 1880, saw the first appearance on the literary scene of American books on the subject. One of the earliest titles, probably the first to be issued in U.S.A., was *The Complete Art of Boxing*, published by William Sharples in Philadelphia in 1829. This book was based on two British publications, *A Treatise on Boxing* (1802), and Sir Thomas Parkyn's *The Inn Play* (1727). An early biography was issued in America in 1854, also published in Philadelphia, under the imprint of A. Winch, the title of this was *The Life and Battles of Yankee Sullivan*.

From the year 1860 there appeared a large number of books and pamphlets on what was probably the most important prize-fight up to that date, and one of the premier occasions in the whole history of boxing. The bout in question was that between Tom Sayers and J.C. Heenan, which took place at Farnborough on April 7th, 1860. This contest was more widely reported and discussed through the medium of the printed page than any set-to in the history of the sport up to that time. The availability of the printed word to a wider public, and the ability of that public to read the reports and publications, contributed in great measure to arousing the interest of the man in the street, to this Great International Contest in particular, and to the activities of the Prize Ring heroes in general. This interest was fostered and kept alive by the public appearances of Sayers and Heenan in exhibitions of boxing at fairs and circuses in all parts of the country.

Even up to the present time the Sayers v. Heenan contest has not lost its fascination for followers and students of matters pugilistic; a book on the fight, and events surrounding it, was published as recently as 1977, the author being Alan Lloyd and his title *The Great Fight*. In addition to the many books and articles giving accounts of this great occasion, there was a poem entitled *The Combat of Sayerius and Heenanus. A Lay of Ancient London*, which is attributed in some learned quarters as being from the pen of Henry Makepeace Thackeray.

There were a number of books featuring the two heroes of Farnborough; these appeared from 1860, the year of the historic contest, when the public interest in the participants was at its height. The books included *the History of the Great International Contest Between Heenan and Sayers at Farnborough on 17th April 1860*; this was published by George Newbold in 1860. Adding to the output of books on Sayers was one by Henry Downes Miles, writing on this occasion under the pseudonym of "Philopugilis"; the title was *Tom Sayers, Champion of England: A Fistic Biography*, published by S.O. Beeton in 1864. In 1866 appeared another title with Sayers as the subject, with H.D. Miles this time appearing on the title-page as The Editor of *Pugilistica*, with the date 1866. The title of this work was *Tom Sayers, Sometime Champion of England, His Life and Pugilistic Career*. I have not been able to compare these two books by Miles, but I believe the 1866 edition to be a reissue of the 1864 work, but with a slightly different title.

Mention of Henry Downes Miles in the previous paragraph serves as a convenient point at which to introduce some mention of his best-known book on the subject of boxing. His *Pugilistica* was the first major work on the history of British boxing since the publication of the series of volumes of *Boxiana*. The physical details of the three volumes are given in the bibliographical section of th presnt work; however a few words on the prolific and versatile author would be appropriate. The following memoir of H.D. Miles is taken from *Modern English Biography;*

> **Miles, Henry Downes. b.1806; sub-editor of** *The Constitution,* **1833, which was started in opposition to** *The Times;* **subsequently on** *The Crown;* **ring reporter to the London daily press and** *Bell's Life in London* **many years, retired 1871; edited** *The Sporting Magazine;* **translated M.J. E. Sue's** *The Mysteries of Paris,* **1846 and** *The Wandering Jew,* **1846; edited** *The Licensed Victuallers' Year Book,* **1873 and** *The Sportsman's Companion,* **1863-4, twelve parts only; author of** *The Life of J. Grimaldi,* **1838;** *Dick Turpin,* **4 editions 1845;** *Claude du Val,* **1850;** *The Anglo-Indian Word Book,* **1858;** *The Book of Field Sports and Library of Veterinary Knowledge,* **1860-63;** *Miles' Modern Practical Farrier,* **1863-64;** *English Country Life,* **1868-69;** *Pugilistica, Being One Hundred Forty Four Years of British Boxing,* **3 Vols. 1880. Died Wood Green, Middlesex Feb. 1889.**

When one looks at the above entry, showing the range and quantity of the work attributed to Mr. Miles, it is not too surprising to learn that although his first volume of *Pugilistica* was published in 1866, he did not find the time to complete the three-volume set until 1880. In the meantime the whole work had been issued in twenty monthly parts, each presented in grey paper wrappers. The 1866 bound volume, marked Volume I, is believed to be very scarce, in fact some collectors of boxing material have thrown doubts on whether such a volume was issued. The scarcity of the earlier single volume suggests that the print run for this was quite small, but following the success of the enlarged version, in the monthly parts, it was probably decided to produce a uniform three-volume set, rather than to print two further volumes to add to the one already in circulation.

One further point of interest is that the period covered by the three volumes of *Pugilistica* ends in 1863, three years before publication of the single first volume; this suggests that the author had already decided at that time the full scope of the complete work, which appeared some fourteen years later.

Regarding the contents of the three-volume *Pugilistica*, it is stated on the front cover of each volume, in both the 1880 and 1906 editions, that the work contains one hundred portraits and illustrations; this is not correct; the 1880 edition has sixty-one plates, and there are two extra in the 1906 edition, issued by Grant of Edinburgh. The list of champions of England, which is shown in the preliminaries of the first volume of both editions, extends from James Figg, in 1719, to the year 1863, when Tom King is shown as champion, he having beaten J.C. Heenan on December 10th of that year. There are two curious features regarding the championship fight of 1863; the penultimate entry on the championship list states that Tom King beat Jem Mace, claimed the belt, and then retired, upon which Mace claimed the trophy, but later in the year we have Tom King named as champion of England, by virtue of his victory over Heenan, an American.

Heenan had returned to America following his 1860 bout with Sayers and the subsequent exhibiton tour of this country; however he expressed his intention of returning to challenge Sam Hurst, who was holder of the title at the time. When Heenan got back to England, Hurst had in the meantime lost the title to Jem Mace, who had in turn been beaten by King. When Heenan finally came to grips with Tom King, he did not show the same form as exhibited in his battle with Tom Sayers; although the Benecia Boy succeeded in bringing a majority of the 24 rounds to a close, only one of these rounds was terminated by a blow from Heenan. In the other rounds in which he succeeded in flooring Tom King, this was always achieved by a cross-buttock or a similar throw, instead of by a clean hit.

It is not the intention here to conduct a detailed comparison between *Boxiana* and *Pugilistica*; although they were for a time contemporaries, the two distinguished editors wrote at some thirty to forty years difference in time from each other. The later volumes are certainly better arranged chronologically than those of Pierce Egan and are thus easier to use as sources of reference.

Boxiana and *Pugilistica* cover the history of boxing since its inception, and the narrative of both runs parallel from the days of Figg and Broughton until the 1820s and the issue of Egan's volumes. Duplication occurs almost solely in dealing with the careers and contests of the earlier pugilists.

For some reason, not clearly elucidated in *Pugilistica*, Henry Downes Miles appeared to dislike Pierce Egan, and he was no admirer of Egan's work. On page after page of the first volume of *Pugilistica*, Miles draws attention to faults and errors in *Boxiana*, and he takes every opportunity to disparage Egan over errors in dates, style of writing, phraseology, and the use of so-called slang. In Miles' first volume there are mentions of Pierce Egan, or *Boxiana*, on more than one hundred pages; few of these references are complimentary, and on very few occasions does Miles directly acknowledge any assistance from *Boxiana*, which work must have been of great assistance to him in compiling his own history.

Another work of reference used in the compilation of *Pugilistica* was William Oxberry's *Pancratia*, but when quoting from this work Miles is never uncomplimentary regarding the composition or veracity of Oxberry's work. It is quite understandable that Mr. Miles should be pro-British, particularly as he lived and wrote in a period which saw the British Empire at the pinnacle of its ascendancy, and some resulting euphoria spilled over into the work of some contemporary writers. Instances of this occur in H. D. Miles' volumes, in his criticisms of the Hebrew race and particularly in his comments of those of Irish descent, including Pierce Egan. An example of Miles' predisposition is shown in the opening paragraph of his Appendix to Period Three, in Volume I of *Pugilistica*, this reads:

Andrew Gamble, another of Pierce Egan's Irish "champions" appears to have been a powerful, game, hard-hitting, clumsy, knock-kneed Hibernian, of six feet stature, and a strong fighting instinct. His euolgium may be read in *Boxiana*, volume I, pp.239 *et.seq.*

Regarding a bout between Andrew Gamble and Noah James, Miles states that this was Gamble's best fight, and continues:

. . . His warm-hearted friends, now overrating his capabilities, determined to match him with the best English pugilist of the day, the young Bristol champion, Jem Belcher. December 22nd, 1800 was fixed, and the friends of Gamble, having won the choice of place, named the old hollow, by Abbershaw's Gibbett, on Wimbledon Common, as the spot. How triumphantly he was thrashed may be read in the memoir of Jem Belcher; what disgraceful abuse, and worse, he received at the hands of his enraged "backers", may be read in *Boxiana*, p.242. We have extracted it as a specimen of "history", omitting the capitals, italics, and emphasised slang.

"Gamble's being so soon deprived of his laurels, created the most dreadful murmurings among his countrymen, many of whom were nearly ruined from Gamble being defeated. St Giles was in a complete uproar on this occasion, and the Paddies had not been so neatly cleaned out since the days of the renowned hero Peter Corcoran! It proved a most woeful day for the Irish indeed; dealers in wild ducks had not a feather left to fly with; the rabbit merchants were so reduced as to be even without poles, and not a copper to go next morning to market; never were men so completely dished and done up. Andrew's name had hitherto been a tower of strength, he was the tight Irish boy, and the darling of his country – but alas! the scene was changed, he was now called a cur, an overgrown thing, a mere apology, and was in danger of being tossed in a blanket by his enraged and disappointed backers. Gamble, from his defeat, lost the warm hearts of the Paddies ever afterwards. Gamble appeared truly contempt-ible in this fight, in comparison with even the worst of his former displays – and it was the opinion of the amateurs, that the evident superiority of Belcher completely frightened all Gamble's courage and science out of him."

Sic transit gloria, etc.; Andrew Gamble appears to have returned to Ireland, probably to his laborious calling.

Miles also engaged in detraction of Egan's reporting on the abilities and on the ring encounters of other Irish pugilists, such as Peter Corcoran, to whom Pierce Egan was said to have devoted several pages of fabrication in honour of "ould Ireland", and Jack Power, a Londoner of Irish descent.

For all his criticisms of Egan, regarding style, accuracy, use of slang, etc., Miles was not averse to using the earlier writer's reports of battles from the days when Egan was an active reporter. As an example, we can compare the reporting of the fight between Jack Randall and West Country Dick, on April 3rd, 1817, the wording of the Boxiana and Pugilistica reports reading as follows:

(Boxiana)

Round 1. On *setting-to* much caution was observed on both sides to obtain the first advantage, when Randall, with dexterity, put in a sharp *facer*. In returning Dick hit short – some few blows were exchanged in favour of Randall, who fought his way into a close, and commenced *fibbing* his adversary till they both went down. – 3 to 1 on Randall, who had drawn *Dick's cork*.

Round 2. *Paddy*, full of fire, immediately took the lead and *nobbed* Dick so successfully, that he turned round from his opponent. In closing, as before, he held Dick up, and *faced* him until he went down. Loud applause.

(Pugilistica)

Round 1. On setting-to much caution was observed on both sides to obtain the first advantage. Randall, with great dexterity, put in a sharp facer. In returning, Dick hit short. Some few blows were exchanged in favour of Randall, who fought his way to a close, and *fibbed* his adversary till both went down. (Three to one on Randall, who had drawn Dick's cork.)

Round 2. Randall, full of fire, immediately took the lead, and nobbed Dick so successfully, that he turned round from his opponent. In closing, as before, he held Dick up and faced him till he went down. (Loud applause.)

Many other examples could be quoted where the almost exact wording of the two reports, from the separate publications, show that Miles used material from *Boxiana* in his own three volumes.

There is no intention here to belittle the work of H.D. Miles, but rather to express the opinion that he had no reason to pursue his detraction of Pierce Egan to the extent shown in his book. The works of both editors contributed more to the lore of fistiana than those of any other chroniclers of the Noble Art.

Miles' *Pugilistica* supplemented and brought up to date the work of Pierce Egan, and one can afford to disregard the sometimes vitriolic criticisms he levelled at *Boxiana* and its editor. We certainly owe a debt of gratitude to H.D. Miles for his accounts of the lives and battles of pugilists with whom he was contemporaneous, and whose fights he could report on at first hand; in fact there were occasions when the services of Miles, in his role as a sporting journalist, were used in the office of choosing the ground to be used for a contest, a task which had sometimes been entrusted to Pierce Egan in previous decades.

An important factor regarding more speedy access to scenes of pugilistic encounters, which were still illegal when Miles was a boxing reporter to the press, was the coming of the railways. This innovation solved the problem of transport for the members of the Fancy, who had previously had to make their way by whatever means available to the scene of the action. These journeys often required the use of a coach, followed by a long tramp across country to the chosen venue. Many of the spectators were forced to make the whole of the journey by foot, and the old books include accounts of crowds of sportsmen leaving London in the small hours, hopefully trudging along the main exit roads, anxious to be in time for the action, and praying that the chosen stamping-ground would not have to be changed at the last minute, due to the intervention of local magistrates, or other officers of the law.

An early example of the use of the railway as a means of transport to the fight was for the bout between William Perry, otherwise known as the Tipton Slasher, and Charles Freeman. This encounter took place on December 6th, 1842, the Articles of Agreement stipulated that the fight should take place half way between Tipton and London; on the day before the event it was announced that there would be a a trip by the Eastern Counties Railway to the borders of Hertfordshire and Essex.

It was also intimated that a simultaneous departure by the nine o'clock train to Sawbridgeworth would suit all purposes. Consequently the London terminus of the chosen railway was besieged by intending spectators, among whom was the Tipton Slasher. Unfortunately the publicity given to the arrangements had become too wide-spread; on arrival in the vicinity of the chosen spot the fight fans found a magistrate and a police superintendent already in attendance. These guardians of the peace forbade the practice of organised mayhem taking place in Hertfordshire or Essex, whereupon the bloodthirsty convoy of supporters decided to proceed to Broxbourne. The representatives of the law having in the meantime withdrawn, it was decided to pitch the ring near to the originally chosen rendezvous, half a mile from Sawbridgeworth station, and close to a spot that had been the scene of famous fights in previous years.

Because of the time taken to find a suitable milling area, uncontaminated by the presence of legal busybodies, the fight did not commence until four o'clock, therefore the proceedings were overtaken by darkness, to which was added the complication of fog. After the bout had been in progress for one hour and twenty minutes, during which seventy rounds were contested, and despite the protestations of the principals, the contest was stopped. It is recorded in *Pugilistica* that many of the spectators had difficulty in finding their way back to Sawbridgeworth station in the darkness; some caught the six o'clock train, while the latecomers returned to London some hours afterwards.

Arrangements were made for a resumption of the Perry v. Freeman battle on Thursday of the following week at Thriplow Heath, about three miles from Royston but again their plans were thwarted by a magistrate, and the parties made a short move over the county boundary into Essex. The principals and their supporters had again used the railway as a means of conveyance to the battle ground, and scouts were left at Thriplow Heath to acquaint late arrivals of the inadvertent change of location.

The Tipton Slasher was among the latecomers at the original rendezvous; during the waiting at the new location, until the Slasher found his way to the ground, such was the enthusiasm of the spectators who had already arrived, that they were laying bets with each other on whether or not there would be a fight. However, the Tipton contingent finally arrived, only to be again frustrated by the appearance of a superintendent of police, who put an end to the prospects of a fight taking place that day.

The Perry v. Freeman match was finally decided on Tuesday, December 20th, 1842; this time the rivals and their supporters were conveyed down river by boat, from London to Cliff Marshes, below Gravesend. The final result was a win for Freeman on a foul. The Pride of Tipton was adjudged the loser, as he went down without a hit, after seven rounds had been fought, in thirty-nine minutes.

A note on the winner, Charles Freeman, might be of interest to the reader. This gentleman was brought to England from America by Ben Caunt; as Freeman was seven feet tall he quickly became known as the American Giant, and he seems to have been launched over here as a showpiece, rather than as a serious contender for fistic honours. However, by training under the supervision of Ben Caunt, the Giant was able to reduce his weight from twenty-three stones, and doubt was expressed on whether he would scale more than eighteen stones on the day of the clash with Bill Perry.

Although he was at first apparently regarded as something of a freak, Charles Freeman must also have had *some* boxing ability — after all he *did* extend the highly-regarded Tipton Slasher on two occasions, one of these resulting in a victory for him. Freeman has only the two bouts with the Slasher recorded against his name in *Fistiana*, where he is also reported to have died of consumption in Winchester hospital on October 18th, 1845; he was 28 years of age.

Before closing this chapter on the post-Egan period in boxing literature, which came to its culmination with the appearance of the three volumes by H.D. Miles, a period which saw the decline in the reputation of the Prize Ring as a reflection of the sporting proclivities of the nation, followed by the renaissance and revival of interest brought about by the appearance in the arena of fighters of the calibre of Tom Sayers and Tom King, may we refer to one other book on the Prize Ring. This was first published in 1855 and reissued in 1858 and 1860; the relevant title is *Fights for the Championship and Other Clebrated Prize Battles*. The author of this work was given on the title-page as the Editor of *Bell's Life in London*, and it was shown as having been compiled from *Boxiana, Bell's Life in London*, and other original sources. The editor concerned was of course Francis L. Dowling. His accounts of the earlier battles are taken from *Boxiana*, while the later reports are his own, taken from *Bell's Life*; these are in some cases repeated in *Pugilistica*. In the case of collectors who do not possess, or have no access to, copies of *Boxiana*, or *Pugilistica*, Mr Dowling's book is obviously a useful item to have on the bookshelf.

CHAPTER VI
ALL KINDS OF AUTHORS

THOMAS MOLINEAUX,

From a Drawing by GEORGE SHARPLES.

E

LIFE AND REMINISCENCES

OF A

NINETEENTH CENTURY GLADIATOR

BY

JOHN L. SULLIVAN

CHAMPION OF THE WORLD

WITH REPORTS OF PHYSICAL EXAMINATIONS AND MEASUREMENTS,
ILLUSTRATED BY FULL-PAGE HALF-TONE PLATES,
AND BY ANTHROPOMETRICAL CHART

BY

DR. DUDLEY A. SARGENT

" Why don't you speak for yourself, John?"—LONGFELLOW, *Miles Standish.*

COPYRIGHT

LONDON:
GEORGE ROUTLEDGE AND SONS, LIMITED
BROADWAY, LUDGATE HILL
MANCHESTER AND NEW YORK
1892

Title-Page of *Life and Reminiscences of a Nineteenth Century Gladiator* (Sullivan)
(Bib. Ref. 1802)

CHAPTER 6

ALL KINDS OF AUTHORS

The revival of interest in pugilism deriving from the 1860 Sayers and Heenan contest continued into the ensuing years, leading up to the turn of the century. During this period the tempo of the output of books on boxing gained momentum, this being a particular feature of the American literary scene. The leading American authors at the time were William E. Harding and Ed. James, with Richard K. Fox filling two roles, those of author and publisher; Fox was the editor of the *Police Gazette*, and reference to the bibliographical pages of this book will show the many titles that were issued under his imprint.

Many of the publications from this group were little more than pamphlets, with illustrated paper covers; they included a series entitled *Lives and Battles*, included among which were the following fighters: Joe Collins (Tug Wilson), John C. Heenan, John Morrissey, and James J. Corbett. In addition there were more general titles, such as *The Black Champions of the Prize Ring*, and *Prize Ring Champions of England*. There were also the usual instruction books from the pens of various operators, seeking to pass on the benefit of their experience to those with aspirations to hold their own in the battle of life generally, or to perfect their boxing skills to a stage whereby they would be able to adopt the Noble Art as a profession. Those who gave their names to such instruction manuals in the late 19th Century included Charlie Mitchell, George Dixon, Jem Mace and a highly respected amateur boxer from Birmingham named Anthony Diamond. There was also a gentleman who was probably the first to adopt the title of "Professor" in the context of the teaching of the Art of Self Defence; this was our own Ned Donnelly; his *Self Defence, or The Art of Boxing* was first issued in 1879, and it ran to several editions on both sides of the Atlantic.

A more substantial boxing autobiography was published in America and England in the year 1892; the subject was John L. Sullivan, and the title *Life and Reminiscences of a Nineteenth Century Gladiator*. There is a publisher's note to this volume which reads as follows:

> As several fragmentary sketches have been issued purporting to give the record of John L. Sullivan, but proving to be incorrect and unfair, it is proper to inform the public that this work, prepared by himself, is the only complete and authentic account of his life.

This was of course the original Sullivan autobiography; there have been other books on John L. since 1892, even up to the 1970s, when a book was issued with the title *I Can Lick Any Sonofabitch In The House*. There have been claims that this is the authentic autobiography of Sullivan. This claim is incorrect, as the later work was a reprint of the original *Reminiscences*, under a different title.

In 1894 the Pugilistic Publishing Company, Philadelphia and London, published a folio volume entitled *The Portrait Gallery of Pugilists of England, America, Australia*, by Billy Edwards, ex-Champion Lightweight; this book contains 96 sepia plates in one edition and 64 plates in another. The Introduction to the work reads as follows:

> The author believes that in presenting this volume to the public, he is fulfilling a long-felt want, particularly in the great sporting world. Of recent years the interest taken in the noble art of self-defence has been almost universal. The cultivation in our colleges and other institutions of learning of athletic exercises, and the interest taken by all classes of people in physical culture, would seem to indicate that this is the golden age of muscular development, and the establishment of perfect manhood and womanhood.

> THE PUGILISTIC PORTRAIT GALLERY has been prepared in the most careful manner, under my personal supervision. Every fact has been verified by exhaustive research and careful compilation of official data. Every important event in the fistic arena, from the first ring encounter to the present day, both in this country and abroad, is given a place. The biographical matter is historically correct, and the accompanying illustrations are taken from authentic photographs or sketches made from life.

Billy Edwards' work is an important item in the sphere of boxing literature. On the reverse of each picture is a short biography of the subject of the illustration. Many of the better-known fighters are also of course dealt with in other publications, but in the Edwards book some of the practitioners are not so internationally-famous. Information on these more remote figures from the world of fistiana is like Manna from Heaven to the more dedicated boxing historian. The portraits include boxers from all over the world, with the relevant short biography; they include such names as James Daly, Heavyweight Champion of Pennsylvania; Tommy Kelly, The Harlem Spider; Patsy Kerrigan (John L. Sullivan's protégé); Jimmy Carroll, of Lambeth; and Tom Tracy, of Australia.

Before the final decade of the 19th Century, the knuckle contests in the Prize Ring had been mainly wars of attrition, with victory going to the more durable of the two contestants; with the dawning of the glove era, these often bloody battles were supplanted by the better-organised glove contests, fought over an agreed number of rounds, each of equal duration, with a uniform period of rest between each round. However, there had been in preparation for a number of years one further contemporary account of happenings in the Prize-Ring; this was entitled *Fights of the Championship, the Men and Their Times*, by Fred Henning. The work was in two volumes, published by *The Licensed Victuallers' Gazette*, a newspaper in which his articles appeared under the nom de plume of "Tourist", his two volumes were made up of reprints from the *Gazette*.

As it was published some years later than the ring histories of Pierce Egan, H.D. Miles, and other Victorian writers, Henning's work extended the coverage of bare-knuckle fighting to include the final phases of the sport that had been initiated by James Figg and his contemporaries more than a century and a half earlier. The last bare-knuckle contest reported in *Fights For the Championship* was that between John L. Sullivan and Jake Kilrain, fought in 1889 for the *Police Gazette* Championship Belt and a prize of 20,000 dollars, the winner to be recognised as Champion of the World. Sullivan was the winner of a bruising battle over seventy-five rounds, lasting a total of two hours and sixteen minutes.

In his author's preface, Mr Henning states that his material was culled from many sources, and the fabric is a patchwork, neither more nor less. He claims that his two volumes treat more exhaustively of the fistic champions than any of the books published heretofore. He had borrowed from many sources matters of historical interest connected with the times of the men whose careers he had endeavoured to trace, which he hoped would lend a little colour to the grim picture which had been painted, perhaps with not too careful a brush.

Fred Henning says in his introduction that the articles from which his book was established had appeared under the title of *Fights for the Championship* in the *Licensed Victuallers' Gazette* over a period of 22 years. The research had been entrusted to less than half a dozen gentlemen, and but for these gentlemen, facts and incidents connected with prize-fighting would have been buried in the past. Three other persons beside himself had written the articles; his own contribution had been to chronicle the most up-to-date records. When the series of articles in the *Licensed Victuallers' Gazette* terminated there had been hundreds of letters from old readers of the paper, expressing regret, and suggesting that the series should be reissued from the beginning. The articles in the paper had been estimated to run to eight or nine million words; instead of attempting to repeat all of these, it was intended to deal only with championship fights in his two volumes.

As was the case with Pierce Egan and H.D. Miles, with their *Boxiana* and *Pugilistica* respectively, Henning gained much of his information on the earlier fights from Captain Godfey's *Treatise on the Useful Science of Defence*. As the Henning volumes dealt only with championship contests, the later author had more space in which to provide coverage of those select occasions. He was able to provide fuller details on the boxers, their backgrounds, their backers, and further anecdotal material. The reports of the contests are not given in the form of round by round summaries; the pertinent details are given in narrative style, interconnected with informative material on the principals. Some of the prose is identifiable as emanating from the same sources as that in *Pugilistica*, as parts of the text are identical with that presented by H. D. Miles. Generally speaking Fred Henning's accounts of the action are condensed, and the reports are more concise than those of the original historians of prize-fighting.

In the course of his continuing story of the bare-knuckle boxing champions, covering the final quarter century of that era, the second volume of *Fights for the Championship* deals with the careers of Jem Mace and his contemporaries. On reading of this period one becomes aware that boxing as a sport was now becoming more international; a number of British exponents, including Jem Mace, crossed the Atlantic to exchange punches with their American counterparts. Among those making the journey to the New World were Joe Wormald, Ned O'Baldwin, Tom Allen, and an accomplished Birmingham boxer named Charlie Mitchell. The latter could usually weigh in at around the 11 stone mark, and was thus called upon to give away weight to most of his opponents, who came from the heavyweight division; one of these was John L. Sullivan, who was held to a draw by Mitchell, in a contest lasting 3 hours and 11 minutes, over 39 rounds. This affair took place on Baron Rothschild's estate at Chantilly in France, for stakes of £500-a-side. These two protagonists also met in a four-round glove contest in America.

As the art of bare-knuckle fighting, as an organised sport, originated in England, it was appropriate that English pugilists should be deeply involved in the closing chapter of the historical period covering Prize Ring championship fights. One of the English participants concerned was Jem Smith, who, like others of his time, took part in the contests in their original form, with bare fists, and also in the trans-formation to the more civilised method of handing out punishment, with the hands encased in gloves. Jem was a skilled and successful ring mechanic, who in his time faced such opposition as Alf Greenfield, Jake Kilrain, and Frank Slavin, with the knuckles, and Peter Jackson, Ted Pritchard, and George Crisp (or Chrisp), with the gloves. Jem Smith's fight with Jake Kilrain took place on an island in the river Seine, and the match was abandoned as a draw, due to the coming of darkness, after the fighters had contested no fewer than 106 rounds. The date of the Smith v. Kilrain bout was December 19th, 1887, and Smith's last fight under Prize Ring rules took place on December 23rd, 1889, when he fought a 14-round draw with Frank Slavin. Jem Smith's pugilistic career lasted until the year 1897 when he was defeated by George Crisp in a glove-contest at Newcastle.

With the passing of the Prize Ring giving way to the use of boxing gloves, the sport became legalised, and therefore considered more respectable. The years from the 1890s, to the coming of the Second World War in 1939 embraced what many fight-followers regard as the Golden Age of British boxing. For the first three decades of this period the sport at championship level was governed by the National Sporting Club, the headquarters being situated in King Street, Covent Garden. One of the first books to record the founding and the early days of the Club was entitled *The National Sporting Club Past and Present*, edited by A. F. Bettinson and W. Outram Tristram, published in 1902. As well as giving details of the Club and the headquarters, the book gives a chapter by chapter account of the contests held within the building during the first ten seasons, 1891 to 1901. The first tournament, on March 5th, 1891, featured the very best amateur and professional talent in exhibition spars, the climax being the appearance together of Charlie Mitchell and Frank Slavin. The book is well illustrated; in addition to pictures of the founding fathers of the N.S.C., the sixty-three illustrations include some legend-ary ring artisans; such as Peter Jackson, Billy Plimmer, Dick Burge, Ben Jordan, Dido Plumb and Pedlar Palmer are among those who grace the pages. Many others who performed at the Club are mentioned in the text.

While on the subject of the National Sporting Club, mention should be made of another book which brought the history of that august institution up to the early 1920s. Mr A.F. Bettinson was also involved in *The Home of Boxing*; his co-author on this occasion was Ben Bennison, a famous sporting journalist. The sixty-two illustrations in this later work include more boxers than was the case with the earlier volume. The later masters of the Noble Art who are portrayed include such as Sam Langford, Joe Bowker,Kid Lewis, Dick Smith, Johnny Summers, and the great Welsh Trio, Jim Driscoll, Tom Thomas and Freddie Welsh, together with many others of similar calibre, names that are household words among the cognoscenti of the science of hit, stop, and get away.

March 4th, 1901 saw the appearance on the newstands of a weekly magazine entitled *Famous Fights Past and Present, (Police Budget* Edition), edited by Harold Furniss, each issue comprising sixteen pages. The magazine was published for three years, a full run being made up of one hundred and fifty-six copies. This item is included in the present bibliography, as more than eighty years after it ceased publication it is probably better known in the form of bound volumes than as a magazine. During the years of publication *Famous Fights* was issued in quarterly volumes, thirteen to a set, and also in annual bound volumes. The standard edition, as issued in magazine form, was printed on thin pink paper; a de-luxe edition in bound form was printed on better quality art paper. The cost of the quarterly volumes was one shilling each, the standard annual volumes three shillings and sixpence, and the de-luxe edition, bound in crimson cloth and gold, was ten shillings and sixpence. The original unbound magazines come to light occasionally but the flimsy paper is usually the worse for wear, mostly very worn at the edges and the spine.

The accounts of the boxing bouts given in *Famous Fights* do not appear in chronoligical order; for instance, the first issue includes the first of a series of seven articles on the Sayers v. Heenan contest, together with a report on Pedlar Palmer v. Dan Sullivan; there is then a reversion in time by way of an article on the Broughton v. Slack encounter. Through the whole of the series of this magazine there is a profusion of topical stories and anecdotes on the fight game; each issue carries a portrait with the title "Our Portrait Gallery of Pugilists", the subject of this in the first issue being Harry Ware.

There was a reissue of the *Famous Fights* magazine in 1907–08; this was subtitled "Shurey's Edition", with a run of only 53 copies. A striking feature of the magazine is the illustrations, which appear on almost every page; the pictures of the earlier contests and contestants are from drawings or reproductions of old prints, those of contemporary boxers, and the instructional illustrations are from photographs. The issue numbered 63, volume V, page 72, lists a bibliography of boxing books; the introduction to this reads as follows:

We have received many letters from subscribers, asking for information respecting works dealing with the old Prize-Ring. Our little paper FAMOUS FIGHTS seems to have revived a taste for knowledge anent the old-time fighters, and, a multitude of our readers are anxious to dive into the history of bye-gone fights and fighters. For the information of our correspondents we may say, that it is an extremely difficult matter to obtain any good works on the old Prize-Ring. We can boast of possessing the finest pugilistic library in the United Kingdom, but it represents a collection of three lifetimes. The writer himself has, during a period of over fifty years, by constant search on secondhand bookstalls, watching advertisements in sporting papers, and other means, succeeded in purchasing exactly five books on the subject. The others have been handed down to him by his relations, and have been in the family for very many years.

We have prepared a list of the principal works on the subject, which we subjoin. Should any of our readers come across any of them, they will no doubt be asked a fancy price, but if they can be had at anything like a reasonable figure, we would say by all means buy them. We have in our library all the books mentioned below, as well as several works which treat of matters other than and in addition to pugilism, and which we have not, on that account, included in our list. Of *Fistiana*, or The Oracle of the Ring, we have no less than nine copies. There were several editions published to keep pace with the times. This is why it is necessary to have so many copies. We may say that every edition teems with errors.

The writer of this introduction, and the owner of the books that were listed, is believed to have been Mr Frank Bradley, a well-known boxing writer and referee. There have been stories in circulation that Mr Bradley's collection of books was destroyed after his death.

In this writer's experience of some years' contact with collectors of boxing books, it is evident that these enthusiasts fall generally into categories regarding section, period or branch of the sport in which they are specially interested. In some cases the divide occurs between those whose chief interest lies in the bare-knuckle period, while others specialise in the modern, or glove, era. I feel that any serious collector of boxing material, and student of the history of boxing, should devote time to acquainting himself with the origins of boxing, and the development of the modern boxing match from the set-to and turn-up of our fistic ancestors. Essential reading for the acquisition of knowledge on the bare-knuckle period would be any two or three of the major works mentioned in the foregoing chapters. These are Pierce Egan's *Boxiana*, H.D. Miles' *Pugilistica*, F. Henning's *Fights for the Championship* and the Harold Furniss *Famous Fights Past and Present*.

Since the early days of the present century, no similar authoritative or comprehensive work has been published, to rank with the four mentioned above. This does not mean that we have been bereft of historical and biographical information since they were issued; on the contrary, when the reader refers to the bibliographical section of this book, it will become evident to him that we have been well-served by talented and knowledgeable writers during the period of eighty or more years. A glance at the names of authors and editors responsible for the prodigious output of books on boxing reveals that these writers make up a group consisting of journalists, boxing referees, boxers, (sometimes through 'ghost' writers), managers and trainers, theatrical impressarios, promoters, and famous writers of fiction, with a regard for the game which led them to take up the pen and add to the canon of fistic lore.

A quantity of instructional material came off the presses, when boxers such as Gunner Moir, Bombardier Billy Wells, Jim Driscoll, Georges Carpentier, Tommy Burns, Bob Fitzsimmons, and Len Harvey were among those who sought to convey through the printed page and by illustrations the fruits of their experience to the novice, eager to achieve success at boxing. In addition to his books on boxing and physical fitness, Bombardier Wells issued a course on boxing; this was illustrated on a series of cards; when the cards were flicked through the pack, by placing the thumb at the edge, this produced a cinematograph effect, showing the moves and the blows. This instruction course was issued in 1924. Famous boxing trainers and managers also went into print with instructional books; among this category of authors appear the names of Nat Seller, Wally Dakin, Joe Bloom, and Jack Goodwin.

The works of fiction with a boxing theme include offerings from the pens of Arthur Conan Doyle, Paul Herring, who wrote a novel based on the life of Bendigo, Jack London, Jeffrey Farnol, and George Bernard Shaw. Mr. Shaw's novel was entitled *Cashel Byron's Profession*; this did not meet with much success initially, but as the author rose to fame in later years, the Cashel Byron novel gained in popularity and several reprints were required. Shaw's book was dramatised for the theatre, and James J. Corbett played on stage in a pirated version in the United States. The copyrighted stage version of the book was entitled *The Admirable Bashville*, a play in three acts, first produced in London in 1903, with Ben Webster playing the part of Cashel Byron.

One very much sought-after work of boxing fiction is the book by A. G. Hales which is based on the life of Peter Jackson, the famous coloured heavyweight. The title of this is *Black Prince Peter*, also issued earlier under the title *The Romantic Career of Peter Jackson*. Mr Hales wrote other novels with a boxing background; one of the most interesting was entitled *Nut Brown Maid and Nut Brown Mare*. The opening scenes of this novel are laid in Reno, at the scene of Jack Johnson v. James J. Jeffries fight.

In consulting the bibliographical section of the present work, readers will note that it contains many titles which at first glance would not appear to be related to boxing, although they include boxing material. In some instances a glance at the author's name may give a clue; that is in cases where the reader has some knowledge of the names of people, who, while not professionally associated with boxing, have other links with the sport, which are not easily discernible. One author and his titles who may be given as an example is Harry Preston; Mr Preston was responsible for two books, the first entitled *Memories* and the second *Leaves from My Unwritten Diary*. The author, later to be awarded a knighthood, was a Brighton hotelier, who numbered Jack Dempsey and many other famous boxers among his friends. He combined his love for boxing with his charitable inclinations and organised boxing shows in aid of worthy causes. His two books, particularly his *Memories*, include many anecdotes and stories of boxers and their famous occasions.

In the case of a book with the title of *The Roosevelt that I Know*, the boxing enthusiast would not feel inclined to give this a second glance, unless he looked more closely and noted that the author's name under the title was Mike Donovan, Ex-Champion Middleweight of America, and Boxing Master to the New York Athletic Club. The glance at the name of the author would probably lead to the collector looking at the title-page, when all would be revealed; the sub-title reads — *Ten Years with the President, and Other Memories of Famous Fighting Men*, the President being of course Theodore Roosevelt. The book was published in New York in 1909.

As another example one could quote a book entitled *Rambles Around Luton*, by P. G. Bond, published in 1937. The boxing collector's heart would not miss a beat when he saw this title on the shelf, but on closer inspection he would find that the book includes information on the Bull Inn at Wheathamstead, a hostelry with prize-fighting associations. If some research was done on books associated with boxing, but which carry non-boxing titles, there would probably be enough material for another book, with *Obscure Boxing Titles* on the title-page!

In discussing writers of fiction who were able to weave the atmosphere of the training camp and the boxing arena into their writings, we should not overlook the contributions of American authors to this genre. Names such as Ernest Hemingway, author of *The Sun Also Rises*, (issued in U.K. under the title of *Fiesta*), W. C. Heinz, for *The Professional*, Budd Schulberg, who wrote *The Harder They Fall* and Jim Tully, for *The Bruiser* and *Emmett Lawler*, come to mind as providers of significant literary offerings from over the Atlantic.

Reverting to the broad categories of boxing authors given earlier in this chapter, it is possible that the section to provide more writers on the subject than any other group would be the journalists, among whom would be numbered Pierce Egan, H.D. Miles, and Fred Henning. Regarding the more recent Gentlemen of the Press who have subscribed to the reader's enjoyment of his favourite sport, we find such names as Trevor C. Wignall, Ben Bennison, Bohun Lynch, Charlie Rose (who could also be included in the category of boxing managers), Fred Dartnell A.G. Hales, H.E. Cleveland, and Denzil Batchelor. More recent candidates for membership of this group are Frank Butler, Peter Wilson, and Gilbert Odd; while broadcasters Harry Carpenter and Reg Gutteridge have exhibited their literary as well as their vocal skills by presenting us with a number of readable and informative volumes, such as *Masters of Boxing*, and *The Big Punchers*.

It will probably have been noticed that one journalist, in the person of the late Nat Fleischer, is not included in the names grouped together to represent the reporting profession in our list of journalists who also blossomed as authors; this is because Mr Fleischer surely deserves separate and honourable mention. I am confident that readers of boxing memorabilia and Nat Fleischer's fellow-journalists would not quarrel with this proposition. Mr Fleischer was the most prolific of all, the veritable Emperor of boxing scribes.

Nat Fleischer edited the *Ring* magazine from its founding in 1922 until his death in the 1970s; at the same time he arranged and supervised the publication of the *Ring Record Book* annually from 1942 onwards, and he was also able to write and publish his colossal output of books on all aspects of the fight game concurrently with his journalistic activities. The books included those on boxing instruction and physical culture, such as *How to Box, How to Second and Manage a Boxer*, and *Simple Exercises for Height Increase*. There were biographies of almost every American boxer of note, from John L. Sullivan and James J. Corbett onwards. Included in Fleischer's output was a biography of Adah Isaacs Menken, who was for a time married to John C. Heenan, the five volumes under a series-heading of *Black Dynamite*, the Story of the Negro in the Prize-Ring, and some books on wrestling, including a sought-after volume entitled *From Milo to Londos*, the Story of Wrestling through the Ages. Reference to the bibliographical section will confirm to the reader the extent of Nat Fleischer's contribution to the literature of boxing, as an author and as a journalist.

In contrast to the output of Nat Fleischer, the one title turned out by another American journalist may seem to be insignificant, but J. R. Fair's *Give Him to the*

Angels, the Story of Harry Greb, is one of the most prized and sought-after items in the whole range of boxing books. The Greb story has become something of a legend in the annals of fistiana, although one wonders whether some of the antics ascribed to Harry, both in and out of the ring, were quite so bizarre as stated in the book; nevertheless they make good reading.

Of the British muster of newspapermen who contributed through the medium of the printed page for the delectation of the bibliophile, Trevor C. Wignall must rank among the most notable. The books published with his name on the title-page include *The Story of Boxing* (1923), *The Sweet Science* (1926), and *Ringside* (1928). These volumes are crammed with information of value to the connoisseur, presented in the author's elegant style. In addition to some books of sporting reminiscences, including items of boxing interest, such as *Never a Dull Moment*, and *I Knew Them All*, Trevor Wignall was responsible for some works of fiction, written in the context of the boxing ring; these included *Jimmy Lambert* (1921), *The Ring* (1928), and *Sea Green* (1937). T. C. Wignall's daily sporting column in the newspapers from the 1920s onwards will no doubt be remembered by older readers.

One of the most fascinating books to come from the pen of a journalist was H. E. Cleveland's *Fisticuffs and Personalities of the Prize-Ring*, in which the author tells of old-time fighters with names bearing soubriquets denoting their trade or profession. The titles *Bellicose Boatmen, Combative Costers*, and *Milling Miners*, are reminiscent of Pierce Egan and his use of the soubriquet, together with an appropriate adjective.

Of boxing referees to take time off from totting up their score-cards and taking up the pen, probably the best-known was Eugene Corri. His *Thirty Years a Boxing Referee* (1915), *Gloves and the Man* (1930), and *Fifty Years in the Ring* (1933), deal with an exciting period in ring history, during which there were probably more very capable active boxers than at any time before or since. All these books are well illustrated; Mr Corri's *Refereeing 1000 fights* was issued in 1919; it is another version of his *Thirty Years a Boxing Referee*, produced in smaller format and with fewer illustrations.

Mr B. J. Angle was a famous boxing referee at the old National Sporting Club and other venues; he was the author of a book of autobiography with the title *My Sporting Memories*, published in 1925. Although this book includes reminiscences of other sports at which Mr Angle was adept, such as rugby football and rowing, the main emphasis is on boxing. The author officiated as referee in the great Peter Jackson v. Frank Slavin contest at the N.S.C. in 1892, and also in the Charlie Mitchell v. John L. Sullivan fracas with the bare-knuckles at Chantilly in 1888. Mr Angle is of course able to give first-hand accounts of these contests.

A referee named Joe Palmer is probably best-remembered for the controversy surrounding the disputed verdict which he gave in favour of Johnny Sullivan of Covent Garden against Len Harvey, at the Blackfriars 'Ring' on March 1st, 1926. Mr Palmer also has a book to his credit; this is entitled *Recollections of a Boxing Referee*, published in 1927, after he had been deprived of his referee's licence following the Sullivan-Harvey decision. The recollections bring in many names from the heyday of the glove era, including the author's relative, Pedlar Palmer. Despite the fact that Joe Palmer never refereed another contest following the loss of his licence, it is best to remember him for the positive side of his contribution to the boxing game. His book simply teems with the names of boxers who will be remembered for as long as history of the roped square survives. Among those to grace his pages are Phil Scott, George Cook, Charles Ledoux, Ted 'Kid' Lewis (whose contest with Georges Carpentier was refereed by Joe Palmer), Tommy Milligan, Johnny Basham, Eddie McGoorty, and others of similar exalted status in the roped square.

In more recent years referees such as Eugene Henderson, Moss Deyong, and Ruby Goldstein have recorded their memoirs for posterity; Mr Goldstein's book is appropriately entitled *Third Man in the Ring*.

Of the 20th Century boxers who took up the pen after taking off the gloves for the last time, one of the most distinguished, and certainly the most capable writer, was Gene Tunney. Gene is one of the few ex-fighters to produce his memoirs without the aid of a 'ghost' writer. There were two books from the pen of the retired heavyweight champion; the first was entitled *A Man Must Fight* (1933), and the second *Arms for Living* (1941). Both of these books are autobiographical, some of the material from the first book is repeated in the second. *Arms for Living* recounts Tunney's experiences up to the time of the Second World War, telling of how he again joined the U.S. Armed Forces, first as Athletic Director at various naval air stations, and later as Director of the Physical Training Programme for the U.S. Navy. The author uses his reappearance in uniform to turn back the clock, and revive his memories of service in his country's Marines in the First World War, when he won the Championship of the American Expeditionary Force, while serving in France. His *Arms for Living* is a scarce book, not so readily available as the Ex-Champion's first essay into print; however, either of the titles make an acceptable addition to the boxing collector's bookshelf.

Another boxer with more than average ability in the ring, and as a writer, was Eddie Eagan, boxer and scholar, who conquered the world as an amateur with his fists, but could not be persuaded to turn professional. Mr Eagan's book *Fighting for Fun* was published in 1932, with the sub-title "The Scrap Book of Eddie Eagan, Amateur Heavyweight Champion of the World". The author was of course a contemporary of Gene Tunney; he also won a boxing title at Middleweight in the 1918 post-war Allied Services Championships in France. On returning from the war Eddie won the American Heavyweight championship, still wearing the amateur vest, and went on to win the light-heavyweight title in the 1920 Olympic Games; he also won the British A.B.A. heavyweight championship in 1923. In between these successes in the ring, Eddie gained a Rhodes Scholarship to Oxford University, where he studied Law. His experiences, as narrated in his book, are unique, as although remaining an amateur boxer, he frequently crossed gloves with fighters of championship calibre, including Jack Dempsey and Gene Tunney, to whom he acted as a sparring partner. As Colonel Eddie Eagan, the ex-Olympic champion later became Chairman of the New York State Athletic Commission.

There were many other boxers turned writers whose work will be familiar to collectors; these include Jack Dempsey, Jack Johnson, Joe Louis, Mickey Walker, and on our own side of the Atlantic, such as Jimmy Wilde, Terry Downes, Alan Minter, Jim Watt and many others. There are also many ring artists who we would have liked to have had regale us with their reminiscences, but who, alas, never appeared in print, except perhaps with an instructional book, or with a series of newspaper articles. So far as I can ascertain, there was never issued a contemporary biography of Jim Driscoll; how pleasing it would have been if we could have had something in print to match Jim's elegant style of boxing. No doubt the reader can think of others of whom he would have liked to have read at first hand: such as Phil Scott— (what was the truth behind his abortive attempt to gain world heavy-weight recognition in his fight with Jack Sharkey?) Bombardier Wells, Nel Tarleton, Johnny Cuthbert, and a host of others. So one could go on, thinking of biographies that might have been, should have been, but never were, written.

One of the possibly lesser-known autobiographies is that of Jack Hare, known as "The Globetrotter"; his small closely printed book entitled *Gladiators of the Prize Ring and My World Travels* was published in 1925. Jack announces himself as Bantam-Weight Champion of South Africa, 1899. On reading his book, one wonders how he found the time to win the championship, as he did not appear to stay in one place long enough to take part in contests on shore. Jack's travels aboard ship, as boxing instructor and in other roles, took him across the seven seas, and made his name known world-wide, particularly in boxing circles. The book is very well illustrated from photographs, and the chapter "Ring Idols of Yesterday" brings to memory heroes of many hitherto long-forgotten battles.

The best known theatrical impressario to become involved with boxing was C. B. Cochran, better known perhaps by devotees of the theatre for his shows featuring his "Young Ladies". Mr Cochran wrote four autobiographical books; these were *Secrets of a Showman* (1925), *I Had Almost Forgotten* (1932), *Cock-A-Doodle-Doo* (1941), and *Showman Looks On* (1945). All these books include stories and anecdotes concerning his experiences as a boxing promoter, which started in 1913. Mr Cochran's chief venues for his boxing shows were the Holborn Stadium, the Albert Hall, and Olympia. Even after he ceased to promote shows he maintained an interest in boxing, as witness the mention in his writings of such boxers as Jack Petersen, Jack Doyle, Joe Louis, and Billy Conn; all of whom came to the fore some time after C. B. Cochran's time as a promoter. In addition to the books mentioned above, there was a biography of Mr Cochran written by Charles Graves; this was entitled *The Cochran Story*, published in 1951, and including stories of "C.B.'s" essay into the world of fisticuffs.

Some boxing promoters, managers, and trainers also felt the urge to leave the story of their boxing experiences to posterity via the printed word. These included Jack Solomons, as promoter, trainer Jack Goodwin, and with a managerial contribution from the pen of Ted Broadribb. The relevant books were entitled respectively *Jack Solomons Tells All, Myself and My Boxers*, and *Fighting Is My Life*. The Jack Goodwin book takes the reader back nostalgically to the days when trainers took their charges to a hostelry in rural surroundings for a period of preparation before an important fight. These establishments were usually situated on the outskirts of large cities; as for instance in the case of Jack Goodwin, who sometimes took his boxers to The Norfolk Arms, a public house in a road beside the railway in North Wembley. Jack handled such useful fighters as Alf Mansfield, Tommy Noble, Joe Fox, George Cook, Augie Ratner, and Sid Burns, all of whom are mentioned in

Myself and My Boxers.

In an earlier chapter brief reference occurred to boxing record books, and their place in the range of boxing literature; this category is well-documented in the bibliographical section of the present work. The most famous continuous series of record books is of course *Nat Fleischer's Ring Record Book*, which started life as the *All-Time Ring Record Book*; this series continues to make its annual appearance. In Britain we had the *Boxing News Annual and Record Book*, published annually since 1945, and more recently the well-researched and produced *British Boxing Yearbook*, edited by Barry Hugman. This manual was first issued in 1985, and it promises to give fingertip information to the boxing statistician for many years to come. For those wishing to delve further back into the recorded history of boxing bouts, and the records of the exponents, there were a number of record books produced, but of course the older ones of these are now difficult to come by. Our forebears in the writing and publishing professions did not anticipate the demand which would arise in future years from the army of eager readers who would wish to study, and often to supplement, the career details of bygone fighters.

For the aficionado of the early years of pugilism, the very first boxing record book was V. G. Dowling's *Fistiana, or The Oracle of the Ring*, first issued in 1841. In subsequent years, before the turn of the century, attempts were made to establish the issue of a record book on a regular basis in America. The New York *Clipper Annual* included other sports in its pages, in addition to boxing. Among other record books to succeed these early efforts in the United States were those of T. S. Andrews, the *Everlast Record Book*, and that issued by the U.S. *Boxing News*. All of these have long since ceased publication. The issue of record books on the British side was rather limited during the first forty years of the present century; the *Sporting Life* issued one covering each of the years 1909 and 1923, and the *Boxing* magazine (forerunner of *Boxing News*) was responsible for record books produced in 1914, 1921, and 1939. The 1914 issue covered records up to June 30th of that year, while the other two carried statistics to the end of the year prior to that of publication.

In each of the record books mentioned above, there are cases of entries concerning busy fighters who took part in 20 to 30 bouts during a year; a few instances of these are given herewith.

An American middleweight named Jack Dillon took on 29 opponents in 1912, and faced 23 in 1913. Frank Moran boxed 42 times in 1919 and 29 times in the following year. Of our own native fighters, Frank Moody had 23 bouts during 1919, whilst 1938 was a busy year for George Marsden (Nottingham), and Len Wickwar (Leicester), who boxed 33 and 28 times respectively during that period. In those fistically busy times the pay was small, compared with the present day, and competition was fierce. Almost every town held its coterie of fighters, and many places all over the country boasted a hall where the local favourites could show their skills, before moving on to larger venues, and hopefully to eventual stardom in the boxing game.

In drawing to a close this brief look at the literature of boxing, which serves as an introduction to the bibliographical section of the book, there is another category of written work which I feel deserves to be mentioned; these are the boxing anthologies. My own favourite in this category is *The Boxing Companion*, by Denzil Batchelor, while running this one a close second must be *The Fireside Book of Boxing*, by W. C. Heinz. These were published in 1964 and 1961 respectively.

Although the basic idea behind these two books is to present to the reader a comprehensive and interesting sample of pieces from the range of works with boxing content, very little of the material is duplicated. Denzil Batchelor's volume covers extracts from the works of authors ranging alphabetically from James Agate to Trevor Wignall, and within these alphabetical extremes the reader is treated to gems of fact and fiction which make this book essential reading for anyone seeking guidance to further study of the literature of The Beautiful Game.

W.C. Heinz, in his *Fireside Book of Boxing*, ventures across the ocean to Britain for some of his material; for instance, he uses excerpts from Arnold Bennett and P. G. Wodehouse. Fortunately for the reader he draws on literature from his own country for the bulk of his anthology. The pieces provided for the delectation of the reader come from the pen of such masters of phraseology as Damon Runyon, Nelson Algren, Bob Considine, and O. Henry. Of the two anthologies discussed above, that by W. C. Heinz is much the better illustrated, including photographs and cartoons; the endpapers carry coloured reproductions, showing Stillman's Gym and the well-known aquatint by C. Turner, *The Interior of the Fives Court*.

There is one more book of milling miscellany which should be brought to the attention of those pugilistic pundits who have not had the good fortune to acquire a copy; this is the work by O.F. Snelling, entitled *A Bedside Book of Boxing*, published in 1972. The book is dedicated to A. J. Liebling. If that brilliant writer was still with us to express his thoughts, he would no doubt be proud to have been chosen as the dedicatee. Mr Snelling poses questions and gives his opinion on such topics as "Did Jack Johnson Quit?", referring of course to Johnson's losing fight with Jess Willard; the author also discusses such diverse subjects as "Fight Films", "Pet Punches", and "Old-Timers versus Moderns". His chapters entitled "Ring Oddities", and "The Ring and The Book" alone entitle this volume to occupy a prominent place on the bookshelf of the boxing bibliomaniac.

This look at the history and the progress of boxing literature, which serves as an introduction to the Boxing Bibliography in this volume, has of necessity had to be condensed. To some enthusiasts, who are more experienced and more deeply-versed in the pleasure emanating from the collecting of boxing books and study of the history of the sport, the information presented may appear to be elementary. Nevertheless it is hoped that this short survey of some of the pages from the works of our boxing historians may serve to enlighten the reader, and that a perusal of the pages may encourage him to embark on further research, in order to broaden his knowledge of the written history of the sport which is closest to our hearts: the Noble and Manly Art of Self-Defence.

BOXIANA;

OR

SKETCHES

OF

ANCIENT AND MODERN

Pugilism;

FROM THE DAYS OF THE RENOWNED

BROUGHTON AND SLACK,

TO

The HEROES OF THE PRESENT *MILLING ÆRA!*

DEDICATED TO THAT DISTINGUISHED PATRON OF THE

Old English Sports,

CAPTAIN BARCLAY.

BY ONE OF THE FANCY.

LONDON:
PRINTED BY AND FOR G. SMEETON, 139, ST. MARTIN'S LANE;
AND SOLD BY
SHERWOOD, NEELY and JONES, Paternoster Row, and all other Booksellers

M.DCCC.XII.

Title-Page 1st Vol. *Boxiana* 1812 (Egan) (Bib. Ref. 587)

BIBLIOGRAPHY

F

FISTIANA;

OR,

THE ORACLE OF THE RING.

COMPRISING A

DEFENCE OF BRITISH BOXING;

A BRIEF HISTORY OF PUGILISM,

FROM THE EARLIEST AGES TO THE PRESENT PERIOD;

PRACTICAL INSTRUCTIONS FOR TRAINING;

TOGETHER WITH

CHRONOLOGICAL TABLES

OF

PRIZE BATTLES,

FROM 1780 TO 1840 INCLUSIVE, ALPHABETICALLY ARRANGED
WITH THE ISSUE OF EACH EVENT.

SCIENTIFIC HINTS ON SPARRING,

&c. &c. &c.

[BY THE EDITOR OF BELL'S LIFE IN LONDON.]

LONDON:

PUBLISHED BY WM. CLEMENT, JUN.
AT THE OFFICE OF BELL'S LIFE IN LONDON, 170, STRAND,
AND TO BE HAD OF ALL BOOKSELLERS AND NEWSPAPER
AGENTS THROUGHOUT THE KINGDOM.

1841.

Title-Page *Fistiana* 1841 (Bib. Ref. 539)

1. **ABINGER, Edward**
Forty Years at the Bar. Being the Memories of Edward Abinger, Barrister of the Inner Temple. London, Hutchinson and Company (Publishers) Limited. 1930.
286pp illus.
Chapter XIII contains references to boxing mentioning in particular Bat Mullins and Charlie Mitchell

2. **ABRAHAMS, H.M., B.A., LLB, and BRUCE-KERR, J., B.A.** (Compilers and Arrangers).
Oxford versus Cambridge
London, Faber and Faber Limited. 1931.
Includes an Analysis of Results 1827–1930, with results of the boxing contests.

3. **ADAMS, Caswell.** (Editor).
Great American Sports Stories
Philadelphia (U.S.A.), Davis McKay Company. 1947.
(Copyright 1947 by King Features Syndicate Inc).
304pp. Illus. Bound in light blue cloth, yellow lettering on cover and spine.
This is a collection of colourful news-stories written by some of the great news-men, with a selection of notable sports photos.
Includes many boxing items, by authors such as Dan Parker, Damon Runyon, George E. Phair, Bob Considine, etc. Covering bouts involving Joe Louis, Max Schmeling, Dempsey, Tunney, Carnera v. Schaef, Max Baer and others; with 21 boxing photos.

4. **ADAMS, Joe.** (American Connection)
From Gags to Riches
Published in New York. 1947.
Includes a chapter "From Punches to Punch Lines" which is largely about Tony Canzoneri.

5. **ADAMS, W.T.**
Fighting Joe. A Boxing Novel.
Boston (U.S.A.). 1876 or earlier.

6. **AFLALO, F.C., F.R.G.S., F.Z.S.**
The Sport of the World
London, Cassell and Company Ltd.
416pp illus.
Includes an illustrated article "Boxing in the British Army and Navy" by R.P. Watson.

7. **AFLALO, F.G., F.R.G.S., F.Z.S.** (Editor)
The Sportsman's Book for India
London, Horace Marshall. 1904.
567pp illus.
Part IV includes "Some Minor Sports and Games" (Boxing).

8. **AGATE, James**
Alarums and Excursions
London, Grant Richards Ltd. 1922.
263pp.
Includes an Essay entitled "Big Pugs and Little", which deals principally with Bombardier Wells and Joe Beckett, but also refers to other notable boxers.
This essay appeared in other books by the same author, in some cases with alterations & additions.

9. **AGATE, James**
Ego One. (Autobiography)
London, George G. Harrap and Co. Ltd. January, 1935. Second and third impression issued in February, 1935.
388pp.
Contains brief reference to boxing, and a picture of Jimmy Wilde. The work is split into two sections, Book 1 and Book 2.

10. **AGATE, James**
Ego 3. Being still more of the Autobiography of James Agate.
London, George Harrap and Co. Ltd. 1938.
360pp.
Includes a number of references to boxing, boxers and devotees of the sport, covering boxing bouts and personalities in the years 1936, 1937 and 1938.
Note. The author's Ego 4 published in 1940 did not include any boxing.

11. **AGATE, James**
Speak For England
An Anthology of Prose and Poetry for the Forces. Chosen by James Agate.
London, Hutchinson and Co. (1939).
251pp.
Chapter IV, "Sport", includes an essay by James Agate entitled "The Fight"; this describes the bout between Teddy Baldock and Archie Bell at the Albert Hall, May 5th, 1927.

12. **AGATE, James**
Ego 5. Again more of the Autobiography of James Agate.
London, George G. Harrap and Co. Ltd. 1942.
283pp.
Contains only slight reference to boxing.

13. **AGATE, James**
Ego 6. Once more the Autobiography of James Agate.
London, George G. Harrap and Co. Ltd. 1944.
307pp.
Contains only slight reference to boxing.
Note. The author's Ego 7 published in 1945 contained little or no reference to boxing.

14. AGATE, James
Ego 8. Continuing the Autobiography of
James Agate.
London, George G. Harrap and Co. Ltd.
1946.
269pp.
Includes some small boxing references.

15. AGATE, James
Ego 9. Concluding the Autobiography of
James Agate.
London, George G. Harrap and Co. Ltd.
1948.
351pp.
Includes some boxing references, bringing the
author's reminiscences up to the time of Bruce
Woodcock v. Tami Mauriello, Ike Williams v.
Ronnie James and Joe Louis v. Billy Conn.
Note. James Agate passed away 6 days after he
completed this work.

16. AGATE, James
Essays of Today and Yesterday
London, George G. Harrap and Co. Ltd.
1926.
Issued in paper covers with a label on the front
cover.
Includes a section "Big Pugs and Little" from
Alarums and Excursions, mainly dealing with
Joe Beckett v. Bombardier Wells. There is also
mention of Jimmy Wilde, Johnny Basham, Kid
Lewis and others of that period.

17. AGATE, James
Here's Richness. An Anthology Of and By
James Agate.
Foreword by Osbert Sitwell.
London, George G. Harrap and Co. Ltd.
1942.
271pp.
Includes at page 77 – Diversions: "Boxing",
which had previously appeared in *Alarums and
Excursions*.

18. AGATE, James
Kingdoms for Horses
With Decorations by Rex Whistler.
London, Victor Gollancz Ltd. 1936.
150pp.
Chapter IV is devoted to boxing and pugilism.
There is one boxing illustration.

19. AGATE, James
Responsibility. A Novel.
London, Grant Richards Ltd. 1919.
(Later reissued by Hutchinson and Co.
[Publishers] Ltd)
329pp.
Chapter V contains considerable reference to
boxing, dealing with a small East End Booth.

20. AGATE, James
White Horse and Red Lion. Essays in
Gusto.
London, Collins, 28 Pall Mall. 1924.
273pp.
Bound in blue cloth with label on the spine.
Commencing at page 139 this book includes
"Exit Kid Lewis" dealing with Lewis's loss of the
British Middleweight title to Roland Todd.

21. AINSWORTH, William Harrison
Jack Sheppard. A Romance.
London, Richard Bentley. 1839. (3 vols)
There were many subsequent editions, in
single volumes and in weekly parts and
penny numbers.
This romantic novel first appeared in *Bentley's
Miscellany*, with 27 illustrations by George
Cruikshank. The first edition in book form was
published concurrently with the serialisation. This
edition included the Cruikshank illustrations.
The book contains a number of references to Figg.

22. ALGREN, Nelson
Never Come Morning
London, Neville Spearman. 1958.
284pp.
This vivid novel is the story of "Lefty" Bicek, a
third-rate pug from the Chicago slums. The author
famous for his *The Man with the Golden Arm*, was
said by the press to show every promise of "taking
up Steinbeck's cudgel, of continuing the Hemingway tradition".

23. ALGREN, Nelson
Stanley Ketchel. A Biography.
This item is referred to in *The Knockout* magazine,
Volume 15, No.11 (March 15th, 1941) as follows:
"Wants Ketchel Dope. Nelson Algren, Chicago
writer, wants to contact anyone who knew or saw
the great Stanley Ketchel fight. Nelson is writing a
biography and is in search of a few Ketchel anecdotes."

24. ALI, Muhammad,
(with DURHAM, Richard)
The Greatest. My Own Story.
New York, Random House Inc. 1975.
St. Albans (Herts), Hart-Davis McGibbon
Ltd. 1976.
415pp, (U.K. edition 413pp).

25. ALI, Muhammad
My Own Story
London, Hart-Davis. 1976.
413pp. Illus.

26. ALKEN, Henry
The National Sports of Great Britain.
Fifty Engravings, with Descriptions in
English and French.
London, Thomas McLean, Printed by W.
Lewis, 1820 and 1821.
London, Printed for Thomas McLean at the
Colombia Press. 1823.
London, Reissued for Thomas McLean,
1825.
There was also an edition published in 1825
with the letterpress in English only.
Further reprints of the 1823 edition were
issued in 1903 (Folio) and 1903 and 1904
(Octavo).
There is one plate dedicated to pugilism; it is
entitled "Prize Fight".

27. ALKEN, Henry
Symptoms of Being Amused
London, Thomas McLean, Repository of Wit
and Humour, 26 Haymarket. 1822 (Vol 1).
Although this item is marked Volume 1, the
second volume was not completed and
published.
There are 42 coloured plates in this volume, each
containing several designs.
Plate 37 contains (*inter alia*) "Of a Few Neat Ones
Going to a Mill".

28. ALKEN, Henry
Moments of Fancy and Whim
London, Thomas McLean (Repository of
Wit and Humour) 26, Haymarket. 1823.
This is a series of plates, all marked 'moments of
Fancy", all marked "Henry Alken Delt" and all
bearing McLean's imprint, London.
Issued in 2 parts, in printed wrappers.

29. ALLANSON-WINN, R.G.
Boxing. (The All-England Series)
Prefatory Note by Bat Mullins.
London, George Bell and Co. 1890.
A later edition was issued in 1892 and a
new edition in 1920.
There are two American issues of this book:
New York, Stokes. 1890.
New York, Stokes, Manuals of Sport, 1894.
The author was winner of the Middleweights at
Cambridge University in 1876- 1877 and the
Heavyweights in 1877- 1878.
The 1920 edition of this book included extra
portraits of notable boxers such as Carpentier,
Wells, Basham, Driscoll and others.

30. ALLANSON-WINN, R.G., B.A.,   Cantab.
Boxing.
Edited by B. Fletcher Robinson.
London, A.D. Innes and Co. 1895.
(The Isthmian Library No.5).
284pp. Bound in green cloth, gilt titles and decor-
ations. Illus.
Although this book is mainly an isntructional item
it includes many references to the old prize-
fighters, with reports of their battles.

**31. ALLANSON-WINN, R.G., and WALKER,
Charles Edward.**
Self Defence.
Being a Guide to Boxing, Quarter-Staff and
Bayonet Practice, The Walking-Stick Cudgel,
Fencing, etc.
London, Laurence and Bullen Ltd. 1903.
206pp. Bound in red cloth, gilt lettering on spine,
design in black on front cover.
Chapters I to XI dealing with boxing, with instruc-
tions on Positions, Hitting and Guarding, Slipping,
Ducking, etc., with a Summary of Hints for Boxing
in Competitions and Contests.
There are 50 outline illustrations and diagrams.

32. ALLEN, (Publishers)
A Most Extraordinary Man. (John Gully).
The Life and Extraordinary Career of John
Gully, Butcher Boy, Prize-Fighter, Great
Betting Man, Publican, and Member of Parli-
ament for Pontefract.
London, Printed by McCallum and Co., 13
Rolls Buildings, Fetter Lane.
Sold by various booksellers. (1863). Priced
One Penny.

33. ALLEN, Neil
Olympic Diary – Rome 1960
London, Nicholas Kaye, 1960.
111pp. Illus.
There are many mentions of the Olympic boxing in
Rome, including the final of the light-heavyweight
class, won by Cassius Clay, pp.80–81.

34. ALLEN, Neil
Ringside Seat
London, Newman Neame, Take Home
Books. 1963.
115pp Illus.

35. ALLEN, Neil
Olympic Diary – Tokyo 1964
London, Nicholas Kaye. 1965.

continued

115pp. Illus.
There are mentions in this book of Muhammad Ali (Cassius Clay), pp.2–3, the Olympic boxing final, including a report of "Billy Joe Frazier", who won it, pp. 96–97, and the future of British amateur boxing, pp.101–102.
During this period, 1956–1976, the author was athletics and boxing correspondent of the London *Times*, during which he reported six summer Olympics. He later became the featured writer on these sports for the London *Standard*.

36. ALLEN, Roland
All in a Day's Sport
London, W.H. Allen, Ltd. 1946.
186pp.
A book of sporting reminiscences, including ten chapters on boxing.

37. ALLEN, Thomas
The History and Antiquities of the Parish of Lambeth, and the Archiepiscopal Palace, in the County of Surrey.
Including sketches of the Most Eminent and Remarkable Persons who have been Born, or have Resided There, from the Earliest Record.
Illustrated by Numerous Engravings.
Kennington (London), J. Allen, 1826.
458pp. Illus.
Chapter X – "District of St. Mary", includes references to the death of John Broughton at the "Ship' public house, Walcot Place, on January 6th,1789.

38. ALLIED NEWSPAPERS LTD. (Publishers)
Famous Fighters. (The New Wonder Books— No. 8)
Presented with the *Boy's Magazine*.
Manchester. 1932.
A booklet in coloured paper covers, with boxing illustrations on front and back covers with 25 pages of text.
Contains articles on the history of boxing and on past and present champions; includes a number of illustrations, with woodcuts at the heads of various articles.

39. ALLISON, Dean and HENDERSON, Bruce
Empire of Deceit
Bromley, Kent, Columbus Books. 1986.
380pp.
This book tells the story of one Harold Smith, a 'con' man, who defrauded many influential financial and boxing celebrities during the Muhammad Ali era.

40. ALLISON, William
My Kingdom for a Horse

Yorkshire, Rugby, Balliol, The Bar, Bloodstock and Journalistic Recollections.
London, Grant Richards Ltd. 1919.
352pp.
This book includes the following references to boxing:
Chapter XIV, (*inter alia*), Boxing with Tom Evans. (He was a noted pugilist in his day and a first-rate instructor at any time, especially as regards footwork).
Chapter XVI, (*inter alia*), Boxing at Blake's; Boxing Incidents.

40A ALL TIME RING RECORD BOOK. See NAT FLEISCHER'S ALL TIME RING RECORD BOOK
Although this famous publication is generally known as the *All Time Ring Record Book*,or the *Ring Record Book*, its correct title is prefaced by its editor's name. Strangely, Fleischer never included a title-page in any of these annual publications, and bibliographical information as regards exact titles and dates have necessarily been taken from the covers and spines of the various editions.

41 ALPHA POWER. (Publishers)
Boxing
The Art Fully, Simply and Concisely Explained.
Sydney, N.S.W. (Australia), 1946.

42. AMALGAMATED PRESS LTD (Publishers)
Encyclopedia of Sports, Games and Pastimes (The History, Principles and Practice of All Outdoor and Indoor Sports and Pastimes, with Rules and Regulations and their up-to-date Records Alphabetically Arranged for Ready Reference).
London, 1935.
Complete in one volume with 64 Art Plates and about 1250 illustrations.
Includes sections on various aspects of boxing, eg. Amateur Boxing, Broughton's Rules, the N.S.C., etc.

43. AMATEUR, An
Sword and Hand; A History of Noted Fencers and Fighters with Results and Descriptions of Fencing Matches and Prize Battles from 1700 to 1800.
Published in 1801.

44. AMATEUR, An
The Battle! An Impartial and Scientific Account of the Battle between Cribb and
continued

Molyneux, which was fought at Copthall Common on Thursday, December 18th, 1810. Illustrated with striking portraits of the combatants.

London, John Fairbairn. 1810.

24pp. 8vo.

Coloured folding plate of Cribb and Molyneux by George Cruikshank.

This work is exceedingly rare.

45. AMATEUR, An

Recollections of Pugilism and Sketches of the Ring.

London. 1811.

8vo

46. AMATEUR An (Pierce Egan?)

Real Life in London

London, Printed for Jones and Co. 1821-22. This work was originally published in 56 parts, and on completion was issued in boards. A few Large Paper Copies were printed on Royal paper, with proof impressions of the plates.

Although authorship of this book is usually attributed to Pierce Egan, it has also been attributed to Jon Bee (John Badcock). There are variations in the contents of different issued of *Real Life in London*; in some cases the volumes appear to have been made up from different issues of the parts.

There were further editions issued in 2 volumes as follows: 1822-23, 1829-30, and an undated edition published by T. Johnson and Co.

Messrs. Methuen and Co. Ltd. included these two volumes in their series "The Illustrated Pocket Library of Plain and Coloured Books" in May 1905. (Reprinted 1911.) This edition was founded on that printed for Jones and Co. in 1821.

The text contains references to the Prize-Ring as follows:

Volume 1.

Chapter VII (*inter alia*) A man of science (An Account of a visit to the Fives Court).

Chapter XVII (*inter alia*) The joys of milling. This includes four verses entitled "The Joys of a Mill, or a Toddle to a Fight".

Chapter XXV contains an account of the fight between Jack Randall and Jack Martin at Crawley Downs, Sept. 11, 1821, won by Randall in one round.

There are other pugilistic references spread throughout the two volumes. Information is given on the plates as follows: (all coloured):

Volume I - Frontispiece. This is a composite picture and includes figures of pugilists; all stripped and wearing mufflers.

Engraved Title-page. In the word "Life" there is a figure of a pugilist on the letter "F".

Sparring at the Fives Court. Shows two pugilists, sparring on a raised stage.

Road to a Fight. Plates 1 and 2, each consisting of 3 strip pictures.

A Private Turn-up. Shows two pugilists sparring, with patrons sitting or standing round in a drawing-room.

Volume II. In this volume the frontispiece is a composite, including boxing gloves or mufflers.

This item is described by R.V. Tooley in his work *Some English Books with Coloured Plates* as follows:

"Real Life in London; or Rambles and Adventures of Bob Tallyho, Esq. and his cousin, the Hon. Tom Dashall &/c through the Metropolis; exhibiting a Living Picture of Fashionable Characters, Manners and Amusements in High and Low Life, by an Amateur, Embellished and Illustrated with a Series of Coloured Prints, designed and engraved by Messrs. Alken, Dighton, Brooke, Rowlandson & Co. London: Printed for Jones and Co. Oxford Passage, Warwick Lane."

47. AMATEUR ATHLETIC UNION OF THE UNITED STATES (Publishers)

Official Boxing Rules and Guide

New York. 1943-1944, and subsequently.

Paper Covers.

Includes names of officers of the Amateur Athletic Union, with details of National Championship winners for years since the introduction of the various weight classes. There are also winners of Olympic titles and guidance to referees and judges, and other similar information.

48. AMATEUR OF EMINENCE, An

The Complete Art of Boxing, according to the modern method. To which are added the general history of boxing, containing an account of the most eminent professors of that noble art, who have flourished from its commencement to the present time.

London, Printed for M. Follingsby and M. Smith. 1788.

91pp. With a folding frontis. showing Humphries and Mendoza in action.

New editions were issued as follows:

1788, with frontis. as before.

1789, to which is added "Capt. Godfrey's Treatise on the same subject".

49. AMATEUR SAILOR, AN (Norman Lee)

My Personal Log of Stars (mostly glamorous) People (famous and infamous), and Places (of the world).

The Autobiography of an Amateur Sailor who finds the Land more exciting than the

continued

Sea.
London, Quality Press Ltd. 1947.

127pp.
This work includes boxing items as follows:
Part II – Star Spangled Country – Knee deep in Glamour. This tells of spending an hour at Jack Dempsey's long bar, drinking beer and watching the cabaret.
Part III – Land of Illusions – the Stars Come Out Again. The story of how Victor McLaglen began his film career.

50. AMATEUR SPORTSMAN, An

Sporting Anecdotes: Original and Select.
London, Printed by James Cundee and Thomas Hurst, J. Harris and J. Wheble. 1804
542pp.
A Second Edition was issued in 1807 – Printed for J. Cundee and J. Harris.

579pp.
Both editions contain the same pugilistic references as follows:
Broughton the Bruiser
Pugilistic Lingo
The first edition is slightly larger in format but has fewer pages than the later edition.

51. AMERICAN SPORTS PUBLISHING CO. (Publishers)

Boxing. A perfect treatise on the science of Self-Defence, London Prize-Ring Rules, Marquess of Queensberry Rules, Amateur Athletic Union Rules.
New York 1890.

42pp. Illus.
(Spalding's Athletic Library)

52. AMERICAN SPORTS PUBLISHING CO. (Publishers)

Boxing. A Manual of the Art of Self-Defence, London Prize-Ring Rules, Marquess of Queensberry Rules, and Rules of the Amateur Athletic Union.
New York. 1893.

Spalding's Athletic Library. Vol. II. No. 4

53. AMERICAN SPORTS PUBLISHING CO. (Publishers)

Boxing. A Guide to the Manly Art of Self-Defence, giving accurate instructions for becoming proficient in the science of Boxing.
New York. (Copyright 1902).
Spalding's Athletic Library Group XIV – No. 162.
Blue paper covers, lettered in white with picture of a boxer on front cover.
In addition to the usual Hints on Training, Rules

for Boxing, etc., there are 64 instructional plates illustrating the text.
This, with the two preceding items, would appear to be much the same, apart from the slight differences in wording on the title-pages, and numbers in the series.
The book ran through many editions; one of these issued after 1910 included a picture of the Johnson v. Jeffries fight.

54. AMERICAN SPORTS PUBLISHING CO. (Publishers)

Amateur Athletic Union of the United States, Official Boxing Rules.
New York, 1932–1942.
The book was published annually.

55. ANDREWS, Alexander

The Eighteenth Century, or Illustrations of the Manners and Customs of Our Grandfathers.
London, Chapman and Hall. 1856.

334pp.
Chapter V, "Public Entertainments, Sports and Amusements" includes "Boxing – Female Prize-fighters"

56. ANDREWS, Eamonn (Compiler and Editor)

Amateur Boxing Spotlight.
Dublin, The Parkhouse Press. 1946.

Illus.
Deals with Irish amateur boxing.

57. ANDREWS, Eamonn, and MACKAY, Angus

Sports Report
London, William Heinemann Ltd. 1954.

200pp. Illus.
A book based on the famous B.B.C. radio programme. It includes contributions on boxing from Peter Wilson, Freddie Mills, Bill McGowran, Jack Solomons and Raymond Glendenning.

58. ANDREWS, Eamonn, and MACKAY, Angus

Sports Report No. 2
London, William Heinemann Ltd. 1954.

192pp. Illus.
A second book based on the famous radio programme. It includes Jack Solomons and Peter Wilson on boxing.

59. ANDREWS, Eamonn

This is My Life. The Autobiography of Eamonn Andrews.
London, McDonald and Co. Ltd. 1963.

251pp. Illus.
There are items of boxing interest in this book,

continued

relating how the author took up the sport as a young amateur, and went on to win an All-Ireland juvenile championship. He later became a boxing commentator on radio. One of his broadcasts was from the Rocky Marciano v. Don Cockell World Heavyweight title fight.

Freddie Mills and Floyd Patterson are featured in the illustrations.

60. ANDREWS, Tom. (Gin and Beer)

Foxhunting Memories of "Gin and Beer".

See entry under PHILLIPS AND PROBERT. (Publishers)

61. ANDREWS, T.S. (Compiler and Publisher)

Ring Battles of the Centuries.

Only and Most Complete Record of the Roped Arena from Figg, 1719, to the Present Day.

Wisconsin, (U.S.A.). 1914.

253pp. Illus.
The contents include:
Tribute to the Man who Helped Greatly to Advance the Boxing Game. (To Captain Barclay by Pierce Egan in 1812).
Short History of British Boxing, from the Time of Figg, in 1719, down to the Advent of Tom Sayers.
Marquess of Queensberry Rules, drafted in 1865.
The text then proceeds to tell the stories of English and American boxers.
There are 164pp. of boxers' records, also many illustrations.

62. ANDREWS, T.S. (Author and Compiler)

Ring Battles of the Centuries, (Revised Edition), and Sporting Almanac. (The Blue Book and Almanac of all Sports, including the most complete history of boxing from the days of history to the modern roped arena.)

Associate Editor: C.R. Diegie.

Milwaukee (Wisconsin), T.S. Andrews Publishing Co. 1924.

262pp. Illus.
The chapters include:
Boxing from the Dawn of History — John L. Sullivan Biography —
Lord Lonsdale —
Fighters of Today and Yesterday —
Early American Biographies —
History of Titles from the First Holders —
Boxing Records (Weights for boxers, complete records of all celebrities of the ring in all nations, from the time of James Figg, 1719, to the present day).

63. ANDREWS, T.S.

World's Sporting Annual Record Book.
Published 1903 to 1938.
Published at Milwaukee, Wisconsin, until

1937. The 1938 edition was issued by Associated Publishers' Corporation, Chicago. There were variations in the title of the Annual, as follows:

1903–1928 – T.S. Andrews' World's Sporting Annual Record Book.

1929–1934 – T.S. Andrews' World's Sporting Annual.

1935–1937 – T.S. Andrews' World's Boxing Annual.

1938 – T.S. Andrews' Authentic and Complete Boxing Record.

The Annual, from first publication in 1903, consisted largely of boxers' records, with illustrations, showing portraits of boxers and others connected with the sport; many of the issues carried a picture of a boxer on the front cover.

The Annual was bound in paper covers, the contents of each issue followed the same pattern, consisting of Ring Notes, lists of past and present Champions and Pugilistic Records brought up to the end of the year prior to that of issue.

64. ANGELO, Henry

Angelo's Picnic; or Table Talk.

Including recollections of Public Characters who have figured in some part or another of the Stage of Life for the last fifty years; forming an endless Variety of Talent, Interest and Amusement. With a Prefatory note on the Angelo Family by C. Swynnerton.

With 26 fine plates (15 in colour) from contemporary drawings and prints in the collection of Joseph Greco.

400pp.

Edition-de-Luxe, printed on handsome paper, (with two extra coloured plates) limited to 50 numbered copies. 4to.

The Plates include 'Mr. John Jackson', from a picture in the possession of Sir Henry Smyth, Bart; painted by B. Marshall, engraved by Charles Turner.

The original edition, published by John Ebers of 27 Old Bond Street, London in 1834 was limited to 500 copies; it was bound in red cloth and contained no reference to pugilists or prize-fighters.

Henry Angelo, (1760–1839) was a Fencing Master and at one time was a partner of John Jackson, the pugilist.

65. ANGELO, Henry

Reminiscences of Henry Angelo, with memories of his late Father and Friends, including numerous Original Anecdotes and curious traits of the Most Celebrated Characters that have flourished during the last Eighty Years.

London, Henry Colbourn and Richard Bentley. 1828 and 1830.

(Two volumes)

These volumes contain many references to the old prize-fighters, including Jack Broughton, Jack Slack, John Gully, Tom Hooper, Isaac Perrins, Daniel Mendoza, and others.
There was a re-issue of the two volumes in 1904, as follows:
The Reminiscences of Henry Angelo, with an Introduction by Lord Howard De Walden and Notes and a Memoir by H. Lavers Smith, B.A.

London, Kegan Paul, Trench Trubner and Co. Ltd. 1904.

Limited to 100 copies, bound in red cloth.

The plates in this edition included two on prize-fighting as follows:
Volume II No.13 'A Country Fight' by T. Rowlandson.
No.15 'Mendoza and Humphries' by Isaac Cruikshank.

66. ANGLE, Bernard John (The famous Boxing Referee)

My Sporting Memories
London, Robert Holden and Co. Ltd. 1925.
Dedicated 'To My Old Friend, John H. Douglas'.
Bound in red cloth, gilt titles on spine.
23 full page illustrations.
252pp.

The author was an experienced amateur boxer and a famous referee in both bare-knuckle and glove contests. He participated in other sports, such as rugby football, walking and rowing, but the majority of his autobiography is devoted to boxing.
The reminiscences extend from Famous Boxers of the Sixties, The Pelican Club and the Hey-Day of the National Sporting Club and the early days of the Amateur Boxing Association.
B.J. Angle is probably best remembered as the referee of the famous Peter Jackson v. Frank Slavin contest at the National Sporting Club in 1892.

67. ANKRAH, Roy

My Life Story
Accra, West African Graphic Co. 1952.
30pp.

68. ANNUAL REGISTER

or a Review of the History and Politics of the Year
Published in America in 1860.

This work included reference to John C. Heenan.

69. ANSTEY, Christopher

The Patriot
A Pindaric Address to Lord Buckhorse.
(Buckhorse the Prizefighter).
Cambridge, Printed by Fletcher & Hodson and sold by various London Booksellers.
1767. 44pp.
2nd Edition with Appendix, 1768 67pp.
A New Edition, printed for J. Dodsley in Pall Mall, 1779.

70. ARKELL, Reginald

Meet these People
Caricatures by Bert Thomas.
London, Herbert Jenkins. 1928.
(There were 2 more printings in 1928 and a new and enlarged edition in 1930).
151pp.
This is a book of verse, including:
'A Sporting Lord' (Lord Lonsdale)
'The Passing of a Pugilist' (Phil Scott).
The caricatures include Lord Lonsdale and G.B. Shaw.

71. ARMSTRONG Anthony ("A.A")

Yesterdailies
Being some extracts from the Press of the Past, Discovered and Collected.
London. Methuen and Co. Ltd. 1931.
Re-issued in 1931 and 1932.
106pp.
This book includes 'Extracts from the *Esquiline Herald*, Rome, 59 A.D.' in which is a Sporting Page, including the following announcement:
"Tonight's Great Fight — Contestants interviewed — Eugenides Expresses Himself Confident — Mirmillo's 'I Shall Win' — Both Gladiators' full statement — By Our Special Representative."
There is an illustration of the contestants.

72. ARMSTRONG, Henry

Gloves, Glory and God
An Autobiography.
London, Peter Davies. 1957.
224pp Illus.
The story of a boxing phenomenon, holder of World Titles at feather, light, and welterweight at the same time, who later turned to preaching the Gospel.
This book was later issued in a Sportsmans Book Club edition.

73. ARMY BOXING ASSOCIATION
Army Boxing Association Official Handbook
Aldershot and London, Gale and Polden.
1921.

74. ARMY SPORTS CONTROL BOARD (The)
Games and Sports in the Army
London, First Issue believed to be 1931.
The 1941 edition included a section entitled
'Boxing', with the following sub-sections:
Part I, The Imperial Services Boxing Association.
Part II, The Army Boxing Association.
Training for Boxing.
The Noble Art of Self Defence.

75. ARNOLD, Peter
History of Boxing
London, Deans International Publishers.
1985.
188pp. 4to. Illus.

76. ASCHE, Oscar
Oscar Asche, His Life, By Himself
London, Hurst and Blackett Ltd. 1929.
256pp. Illus.
This famous actor's autobiography includes a few
references to boxers, including Peter Jackson,
Frank Slavin and others.

77. ASHTON, John
Dawn of the XIXth Century in England. A
Social sketch of the times.
First Edition (Two Volumes) 1886.
116 Illustrations.
A one-volume edition appeared in 1890 and
a fifth edition was published in London by
T. Fisher Unwin in 1906, with 114
illustrations.
Chapter XXV includes a section on prize-fighting,
including George IV as a patron of the Ring, and
attempts to put down prize-fighting.

78. ASHTON, John
Gossip in the First Decade of Victoria's
Reign.
London, Hurst and Blackett Ltd. 1903.
315pp. Illus.
Chapter IV contains a section entitled "Lords and
Pugilists", referring to Young Dutch Sam.

79. ASHTON, John
Social England Under the Regency
(A New Edition with 90 illustrations)
Ward and Downes, 1890.
Chatto and Windus, 1899.

Chapter XXXIII includes "Prize-Fighting".
There is one boxing illustration, "Boxiana, or the
Fancy", a caricature.

80. ASSOCIATED NEWSPAPERS LTD
(Publishers)
Tom Webster's Sporting Cartoons
London. From 1920.
This famous cartoonist worked for Associated
Newspapers from 1919, and his drawings appeared
in the *Daily Mail, Evening News* and *Weekly
Despatch.*
Webster's cartoons, from all three papers, were
published in volume form for a number of years,
each volume including a number of boxers among
the subjects.
The 1920 issue was entitled *Tom Webster of the
Daily Mail Among the Sportsmen*; then the title was
changed to *Tom Webster's Annual.*
Each edition included good boxing coverage for
the year under review, with such well-remembered
contests as Joe Beckett v. Bombardier Wells, and
Dempsey v. Carpentier. Through this medium the
public became acquainted with the 'Horizontal
Heavyweight', and also God's gift to the cartoonist
the arrival and exit of Jack Doyle.
(See also WEBSTER, Tom, item No.1932).

81. ASTLEY, Sir John Dugdale, Bart.
Fifty Years of My Life, in the World of
Sport at Home and Abroad
(Edited by Richard Thorold).
London, Hurst and Blackett Ltd. 1894.
(2 volumes).
A one-volume edition was issued by the
same publishers in 1895.
This book contains a number of references to
boxing and the prize-ring, particularly in Chapter
XIX. The author tells of his presence at the
Sayers v. Heenan contest and also talks of the
National Sporting Club and Slavin v. Jackson.

82. ASTOR, Gerald
And a Credit to His Race
The Hard Life and Times of Joseph Louis
Barrow, also known as Joe Louis.
New York, *Saturday Review* Press. 1974.
275pp.

83. ASTOR, Gerald
Gloves Off. The Joe Louis Story
London, Pelham Books Ltd. 1974.
275pp. Illus.

84. ATHLETIC PUBLICATIONS LTD.
(Publishers)
Boxing's Book of Records
London, Issued by the Publishers of *Boxing.*

continued

1914.

231pp.
Includes records of all boxers who have achieved international fame, up to June 30th, 1914.
A further issue was published 1921, giving records up to May of that year.
173pp.

85. ATHLETIC PUBLISHING COMPANY (Publishers)
The Modern Gladiator
Being an Account of the Exploits and Experiences of The World's Greatest Fighter, John Lawrence Sullivan.
First Accurate History of the Life and Record of the Samson of the Prize Ring.
His Battles are Described by an Eye Witness of High Expert Authority.
How Professor Muldoon Trained Him.
Muldoon's System of Physical Development Fully Described.
St. Louis. 1889.

384pp.
The book is profusely illustrated, with pictures of Sullivan's opponents and contemporaries, including Paddy Ryan, Alf Greenfield, Tug Wilson, The Maori, Charley Mitchell, Jem Smith and others.

86. ATLAS PUBLISHING and DISTRIBUTING CO. LTD. (Publishers)
True, The Man's Magazine, Boxing Yearbook 1964.
Edited by William A. Wise.
64pp.
Also issued in 1965 and 1966 under the editorship of William A. Wise and Lee Greene respectively.
The British edition was issued by arrangement with Fawcett Publications Inc., Greenwich, Conn., U.S.A.

A magazine-type publication, with features on contemporary boxers.

87. ATYEO, Don, and DENNIS, Felix
The Holy Warrior, Muhammad Ali
An illustrated biography.
London, H. Bunch Associates Ltd. 1975.
111pp. Stiff paper covers. Illus. 4to.

88. ATYEO, Don
Violence in Sport
New York and London, Paddington Press. 1979
277pp Illus.
Section 3, entitled 'Blood and Canvas — Combat

Sports', includes boxing and wrestling. It traces the history of these sports since Roman times, and the renaissance of pugilism with the advent of the gloves. There are quotations from writers and professors of the art from early times to the reign of Muhammad Ali and other modern greats.
As indicated by the title of the book, the author tends to dwell on the more punishing and brutal side of boxing.

89. AUSTIN, Sam C.
Boxing and How to Train
New York City, Richard K. Fox, (Fox's Athletic Series). 1904 and 1913.

90. AUTHOR UNKNOWN
The American Boxer
Little is known about this book. However, it is mentioned in an article entitled "How American Books First Broke Into Print", by Fairfax Donney which appeared in a U.S. periodical, *The Sportsman*. The article mentions an exhibition of sporting books at the Grolier Club in New York, stating that "The Prize-Ring was represented by *The American Boxer* and *The American Fistiana*".

91. AVIATION TRAINING DIVISION (Publishers)
Boxing
Annapolis, (U.S.A.). 1943.
286pp. Illus. 8vo

92. AVIS, F. C.
Boxing Reference Dictionary
London, published by the author. No date.
127pp.
This small book contains the A to Y of boxing. (There is no entry under the letter 'Z').

93. AXON, William E. A. (Editor)
The Annals of Manchester.
A Chronological Record of the Earliest Times to the end of 1885.
Manchester and London, John Heywood. 1886.
456pp.
Contains some references to pugilists, including Isaac Perrins.

94. AYE, John
Humour in Sports
Introduction by Trevor Wignall. Preface by Ian Hay.
London, Universal Publications Ltd.
Includes at pp.63 to 88 a section entitled 'Boxing'

95. BAERLEIN, Henry
The Squire of Piccadilly
Memories of William Stone, in Conversation with Henry Baerlein.
London, Jarrolds (Publishers) Ltd. 1951.

Mention occurs in the text of John Jackson and his School for pugilism in the Albany Building, Piccadilly.

96. BAGNATO, Vince
Half-a-Buck Nobody, and Me
Erin, (Ontario), Boston Mills Press. 1984.
152pp. Illus.

97. BAILEY, J.
The Improved Art of Self Defence, or Scientific Boxing Displayed in an Easy Manner.
London, No Date.

This work was issued in at least 3 editions.

98. BAILEY, John Wendell.
(Class of 1915)
The Mississippi Book of Athletics — Mississippi State College.
Richmond, Virginia, U.S.A.
Published by the Author, 1947.
2 volumes.

This work covers all sports in which 'varsity teams participated in Mississippi State College; it has been referred to as the most complete work on the subject of intercollegiate athletics ever published. The book covers thoroughly the history, development and records of 'varsity teams in all sports at State College from 1880 to 1947.
Volume I = 1880–1930
Volume II = 1930–1947
The topics include boxing, and a directory of 'M' Men.

99. BAILLIE, Albert Victor, K.C.V.O., D.D.
(Formerly Dean of Windsor)
My First Eighty Years
London, John Murray. 1951.

259pp. Illus.
Part IV. Windsor. Chapter XV, The Deanery (Section 1) includes the Dean's friendship with professional boxers Paddy Peters and Joseph Rottenburger (of Mulhous in France).
The chapter also refers to Len Harvey (whom the Dean knew only slightly), and to Jackson, "the great boxer of the Regency".

100. BAILY, J. (Printer and Publisher)
Book of Sports; or Man of Spirits Companion
London, 1819.

This book deals with a number of sports, i.e. Fencing, Single-Stick, Riding, etc, as well as boxing.
The work consists of twelve pamphlets, published separately by J. Baily, including:
1) The Art and Practice of British Boxing. 28pp; folding plate by I.R. Cruikshank.
2) The Inn-Play; or Cornish Hugg Wrestler, (Sir Thomas Parkyns); folding plate (The Art of Wrestling).

101. BAILY, Tom
The Man With The Malacca Cane

This book mentions the fight between Joe Gans and Battling Nelson at Goldfield, Nevada, Sept. 3rd, 1906.

101A. BAKER, Carlos
Ernest Hemingway. A Life Story.
London, Collins. 1969.

702pp. Illus.
The subject of this biography was a lifelong enthusiast of boxing, both as an observer and a participant. There are frequent mentions of his activity with the gloves as well as reference to his writings, which include the famous short story "Fifty Grand", loosely based on the Jack Britton v. Benny Leonard contest, which appeared in *Men Without Women* (q.v.)

102. BARCLAY, Captain Robert. (Allardyce of Ury)
Training for Pedestrianism and Boxing. 1816

This item is included in the Bibliography of Boxing that appeared in the Harold Furniss *Famous Fights Past and Present*, Volume V No.63 as follows:

"*Training for Pedestrianism and Boxing*, 8vo, by Captain Robert Barclay (Allardyce of Ury). This pamphlet contains an account of the Captain's training of Cribb for his fight with Molyneaux".

There is also a section in Volume IV of *Boxiana* 1824 (Jon Bee), with wording in the title similar to that given above for the Barclay item.

103. BARDSLEY, Geoffrey W. (Compiler and Editor)
British Boxing Records
Published under the direct authority of the National Boxing Association. 1939.

136pp. Paper covers.
Contains 150 boxers' records up to December, 1938 and includes a portrait of the editor and an article by Harry A. Flower, Hon. General Secretary of the N.B.A.

104. BARING, Mrs. Henry (Editor)
Diary of the Rt. Hon. William Windham.
1784 to 1819
London, Longmans Green and Co. Ltd.
1866. (One Volume)

continued

This work contained a number of pugilistic items, including an account of the fight between Jackson and Fewtrell; there were also references to Big Ben Brain, Richard Humphries, Sam Martin and others. The diary also mentions various prize-fights not mentioned in the pages of *Fistiana*.

105. BARNARD, E.A.B., F.R.S., F.R.Hist.S.

The Prattinton Collections of Worcestershire History
Evesham, The Journal Press. 1931.

This work had been in the possession of the Society of Antiquaries since 1841.
Vol.XX. Biography, I–R–, includes four letters from John Jackson, "The Pugilistic Champion of England, 1795 to 1803".

106. BARNETT, Charles A.

Barnett's Boxing Book for 1913
"A Reliable and Invaluable Guide for followers of Ye Noble Art of Self Defence, —Rules and Records, together with an interesting History of the Ring".
Cardiff, *Evening Express*. 1913.

In the Introduction the author expresses his thanks to Mr Bettinson and the Directors of the N.S.C. for their kind permission to use their copyright Rules on Boxing; he also thanks Mr Tom Andrews the famous American Sporting Writer, for supplying the records.

107. BARRINGTON, George

The New London Spy; or the Frauds of London detected
Containing also a Sketch of Night Scenes and Notorious Characters in a Ramble round the Metropolis, to which is prefixed a Treatise on Boxing by J. Belcher.
London, Printed for Tegg and Co. 1802.
Four more editions were issued up to 1807, the fifth edition being considerably enlarged.

A coloured cut of a prize-fight appeared on the title page of the first edition; one of the boxers being Jem Belcher.
An American edition was published in Boston in 1832.

108. BARRY, The Rev.Edward, A.M. and M.D. Chaplain to the Lord Bishop of Kildare

A Letter on the Art and Practice of Boxing Addressed to the King, Lords and Commons.

London, Printed for the author by A. Grant and sold by J. Bew. 1789.

A Dedication to Sir Watkin Lewes, Kt. and M.P. for the City of London refers to "The Brutal Practice of Boxing".
This work was re-issued in 1791, included in a work entitled *Theological and Moral Essays*, pages 273 to 300.

109. BARRY, Duke

The Blue Book of Boxing. (A Directory of Who's Who in Boxing).
Davenport, Indiana, U.S.A., 1929 (Compiled by Duke Barry. (International Boxing Authority)

110. BASS, A.L., and others (Editors)

Medical Aspects of Boxing
Proceedings of a conference held at Goldsmith's College, London, November, 1965.

Oxford, Pergamon Press. 1965.
124pp.

111. BASS, Howard

The Sense in Sport
(With a Foreword by C.B. Fry)
London, Arthur H. Stockwell. 1945.

96pp.
Includes the following items of boxing interest:
Chapter III – A World's Sports Association, (*inter alia*) Boxing Board of Control.
Chapter IV – An Annual World Games, (*inter alia*) Broadcasting.
Chapter V – The Professional with the Amateur (*inter alia*) Joe Louis, Henry Armstrong, Jackie Paterson.
Chapter XI – Seven Modern Wonders (*inter alia*) Joe Louis.
Chapter XII – Sport in Wartime (*inter alia*) Joe Louis.

112. BASSEY, Hogan, M.B.E. (Former Featherweight Champion of the World)

Bassey on Boxing
With Foreword by Dr. Nnambi Azikewe, Governor-General of the Federation of Nigeria.
London, Thomas Nelson and Sons Ltd. 1963.

119pp including Hogan Bassey's fighting record. Illus.

113. BATCHELOR, Denzil

British Boxing. (Britain in Pictures Series)
London, Collins. 1948.
48pp
8 illustrations in colour and 27 in black and white; also includes a short bibliography of boxing.

114. BATCHELOR, Denzil

Gods With Gloves On
London, Claud Morris Books Ltd. 1946.
123pp. Stiff paper covers.
Chapter headings include: "Come Out Fighting" (Sayers v. Heenan), "A White Man" (Peter Jackson) "The Game Bantam" (Joe Bowker), "Ex-Sergeant Barrow" (Joe Louis) etc.

115. BATCHELOR, Denzil
Days Without Sunset
London, Eyre and Spottiswoode Ltd. 1949.
283pp.
Contains a section on boxing, including references to Lesnevich v. Mills (first fight), and Carpentier v. Ted 'Kid' Lewis.

116. BATCHELOR, Denzil
They Laugh That Win. A Boxing Novel.
London, Robert Hale Ltd. 1951.
224pp.
Bound in black cloth, lettered in green on the spine

Tom Barlow, the hero, is typical of those young men who slog their way to championships in the ring.

117. BATCHELOR, Denzil
The Turf of Old
London, H.F. and G. Witherby Ltd. 1951.
208pp.
This book includes references to pugilism as follows:
Chapter IX – Glorious John. (John Gully)
The following prize-fighters or pugilists are also mentioned: John Broughton, Deaf Burke, Tom Cribb, Dutch Sam, Bob Gregson, J.C. Heenan, Hooper (The Tinman), John Jackson, Tom Molyneux, Tom Oliver, Tom Sayers, Tom Spring. Also Captain Barclay and Will Warr (Trainers).

118. BATCHELOR, Denzil. (Editor)
Best Boxing Stories
London, Faber and Faber Ltd., 1953.
288pp.
Contains a wide selection from the literature of Boxing. The authors include Damon Runyon, D.B. Chidsey, Bernard Darwin, Trevor C.Wignall, George Borrow, Gene Tunney, Etc.

119. BATCHELOR, Denzil
Big Fight
The Story of World Championship Boxing.

London, Phoenix House Ltd. 1954.
235pp. With Appendices showing Champions under Prize-Ring Rules and modern World Champions at the various weights.
Illus.
This book was later issued in the Sportsmans Book Club series.

120. BATCHELOR, Denzil
Jack Johnson and His Times
London, Phoenix Sports Books. 1956.
185pp Illus.
This book was later issued in the Sportsmans Book Club series.

121. BATCHELOR, Denzil
Babbled of Green Fields

London, Hutchinson and Co. 1961.
224pp.
This autobiography includes a chapter on boxing.

122. BATCHELOR, Denzil (Editor)
The Boxing Companion
London, Eyre and Spottiswoode. 1964.
451pp, plus Index to Authors. Illus.
This anthology includes extracts from works dealing with boxing in all its aspects.
The text is divided into five parts, with the following headings:
Part I   The Fascination of Boxing
Part II   History and Know-how
Part III   Bare Fists and the Prize-Ring
Part IV   The Glove Fighters
Part V   Fights in Fantasy

123. BATEMAN, H.M.
H.M. Bateman, by Himself
London, Collins. 1937.
133pp, plus Appendix
An autobiography, embellished with examples of the author's drawings. Includes a short account of the youthful Bateman's brief experience of boxing, with a suitable drawing.

124. BATES, H.E.
The Black Boxer. (A book of short stories)
Only the first story, under the same title as the book, refers to boxing.
The picture on the dustcover shows a coloured boxer taking a count.
The central character of the story, Zeke Pinto, is based on the famous coloured boxer, Sam Minto who was active in Britain for many years.

125. BATES, William, B.A., M.R.C.S.E., etc. (Professor of Classics in Queens College, Birmingham)
George Cruikshank, The Artist, The Humourist and The Man. With some account of his Brother Robert.
A Critico-Biographical Essay. With numerous illustrations by Cruikshank, including several from original drawings in possession of the author.
London, Houlston and Sons. 1878.
Birmingham, Houghton and Hammond.1878
Second edition, revised and augmented by a copiously annotated Biographical Appendix and Additional Plates, on India Paper. 1879.
This item includes a number of references to Pugilism, the joint work of the Cruikshank brothers, and the illustrations of Pierce Egan's works.

126. BATT, Peter, and GILLER, Norman
Barry McGuigan: Fighting Folk Hero

continued

London, Stanley Paul and Co. Ltd. 1985.
112pp. Illus.

127. BAUM, Vicki
Grand Hotel. A Novel.
London, Geoffrey Bles. 1930.
314pp.
Reprinted later in the same year and in many
further editions.
The novel contains an account of a boxing match,

128. BAVIN, Bill
The Strange Death of Freddie Mills
London, Howard Baker Press Ltd. 1975.
153pp. Illus.

129. BAYNE-POWELL, Rosamund
Eighteenth Century London Life
London, John Murray. 1937.
A section entitled 'Amusements' includes refer-
ences' to a number of famous pugilists, such as
James Figg, John Broughton, Richard Humphries
Daniel Mendoza, and others.

130. BEACH, Rex.
The Spoilers. A Novel.
New York, A.L. Burt and Co. April, 1906.
Bound in light brown cloth, lettered in
black on front cover and spine. Coloured
picture on front cover.
314pp. 22 chapters, 4 illus.
This item is described as an Alaskan epic; one of
the characters, 'Broncho Kid', is based on Tex
Rickard, who later became a world-famous
promoter of boxing.

131. BEANLAND, V.A.S.
Great Games and Great Players
Some thoughts and recollections of a sports
journalist.
London, W.H. Allen and Co. Ltd. 1945.
147pp.
Reference to boxing occurs in Chapter 27, which
mentions in particular Jake Kilrain (who fought
J.L. Sullivan), Charlie Mitchell, Jimmy Wilde, and
Boxing venues such as the Free Trade Hall,
Manchester.

132. BEAUDIN, M.
Willie de Witt. The Lord of the Ring.
Scarborough (Ontario), Avon Books. 1985.
223pp. Illus.

133. BEBBINGTON, William. (for 22 years Senior Jockey Club detective)
Rogues Go Racing
London, Good and Betts. 1947.
191pp.

Chapter XVII: "Colombo's Death — and Some
Frauds", mentions (inter alia) the Goudie Case
(The Liverpool Bank Fraud), which involved Dick
Burge, the former Lightweight Champion and
founder of the Blackfriars 'Ring'.

134. BELCHER, Mr. Jem
A Treatise on the Art of Boxing
See BARRINGTON, George. *The New
London Spy, or the Frauds of London
Detected*, 1802—1807.

135. BELCHER, Thomas
The Art of Boxing, or Science of Manual
Defence, Clearly Displayed on Rational
Principles. Whereby Every Person may make
themselves masters of that Manly Acquire-
ment so as to ensure Success both in Attack
and Defence. To which is added Memoirs
and Delineations of the Most Celebrated
Pugilists and an account of their Principal
Battles.
London, W. Mason. ca. 1820.
34pp. Frontis. (Crib and Molineaux)

136. BELL, Ernest, M.A. (Trinity College Cambridge) (Editor)
Handbook of Athletic Sports. (Volume III)
London, George Bell and Sons. 1890.
This volume deals with Boxing, Wrestling,
Fencing, Broadsword and Single-stick; with
91 pages and 31 illustrations on boxing.
The boxing section is instructional and is con-
tributed by R.G. Allanson-Wynn, Inns of Court
School of Arms, winner of Cambridge University
Middle and Heavyweight Championships 1876
and 1877 respectively.
The Prefatory Note is by Bat Mullins, late
Lightweight Champion of the World.

137. BELL, John
A Catalogue of Books, Newspapers etc.,
Printed by John Bell, born 1745, died 1831,
of *The British Library, The Morning Post,
Bell's Weekly Messenger* etc. and by John
Browne Bell, born 1799, died 1855, son of
the above. Founder of *Bell's Weekly
Messenger, The News of the World*, etc.
Exhibited at the First Edition Club, 17
Bedford Square, London, 15th April—5th
May, 1931.
The Catalogue contains details of and notes on the
papers mentioned above; also of other papers
published by the two Bells and of papers bearing
the name of Bell who were not connected with
the two Bells in the title of the Catalogue.
These other papers include *Bell's Life in London*
continued

and *The Sporting Chronicle*, with mention of Pierce Egan.
Before compiling *Life in London* Egan was a sporting writer for *Bell's Weekly Despatch.*

138. BELL, Leslie
Focus on the Fight Game, No.3
(A Background Sports-Photo Book)
"Focus on Freddie Mills"
Art Editor Bobby Naidoo.
London, Background Books Ltd. 1949.

24pp. Action picture of Freddie Mills on front cover. 3 pages of text, followed by 21 pages of various fights and poses, involving Freddie Mills.

139. BELL, Leslie
The Fight Racket. (Fiction)
London, Background Books Ltd. 1949.

11 chapters, illustrated paper covers. Price 1s.
This story brings in the author's ideas on the future of the boxing game.

140. BELL, Leslie
These Fists for Hire. (Fiction)

This book was mentioned on the title-page of *The Fight Racket* by the same author and published by Background Books Ltd. 1949. However, there is some doubt as to whether *These Fists for Hire* was ever published.

141. BELL, Leslie
Focus on the Fight Game No. 4.
"Focus on Bruce Woodcock"
Art Editor Bobby Naidoo.
London, Background Books Ltd. 1949.

24pp. Paper covers with action picture of Bruce Woodcock on front cover. 3 pages of text and 21 pages of pictures.

142. BELL, Leslie
Boxing Spotlight
London, Findon Publications Ltd. 1949.

64pp. Illus. Paper covers.
Although largely written by Leslie Bell, this booklet also contains contributions by Joe Bromley, Tim Riley, Nat Seller, Ron Franks, Maurice Woolf, and Bobby Naidoo.

143. BELL, Leslie
Men Behind the Gloves
London, C. and J. Temple Ltd. 1950.

191pp. Illus. Bound in yellow cloth, picture of Carpentier v. Wells, at the National Sporting Club on the front of dustwrapper.
Includes chapters on Patsy Hagate, (The Voice of them All). Freddie Mills, Terry Allen, Laurie Buxton, The Gutteridge Family, Bruce Woodcock, etc.

144. BELL, Leslie
Inside the Fight Game
London, Rockliff Publishing Corporation Ltd. 1952.

190pp. Bound in red cloth. 22 Illus. Price 16s
Consists of 14 chapters on various aspects of boxing, including the roles of the Board of Control and The Professional Boxers' Association.

145. BELL, Leslie
Bella of Blackfriars
London, Odhams Press Ltd. 1961. 237pp.

The story of Bella Burge, who took over management of the Blackfriars 'Ring' following the death of her husband, Dick Burge, the former lightweight champion.

146. BELL, Neil
Child of My Sorrow. A Novel.
London, Collins of Pall Mall. 1944.

Contains a number of references to the old-time prize-fighters.

147. BELL, Norman
The Fighting Life of a Fighter. (Joe Louis, World Heavyweight Champion)
London, The War Facts Press. 1945.

68pp. Stiff paper covers, with a boxing picture on the front cover.
Traces the career of Louis from his early days on the farm to his career as World Champion and his time in the Army; together with his record and his ring earnings.

148. BENEDICT, G.H.
Handbook to Manly Sports
Chicago, A.G. Spalding and Brothers, 1883.
118pp. Illus.
The text gives full instructions on the arts of boxing, fencing and wrestling.

149. BENEDICT, G.H.
Philadelphia Reach
New York, A.G. Spalding and Brothers. (copyright), 1883.
New York, A.G. Spalding and Brothers. 1886.

This item is described as — "Manual of boxing, club swinging and manly sports, giving full instructions in the arts of boxing, fencing, wrestling, etc."

150. BENNETT, John
Tom Fox, or the Revelations of a Detective.
London, Published by the author. 1860.
A Second Edition, with two illustrations, was published by George Vickers in 1860.

continued
G

The illustrations include two cuts in the text entitled "A Sparring Match" and "A Pugilist"

151. BENNISON, Ben
Giants on Parade
Some Sporting Reminiscences.
London, Rich and Cowan Ltd., 1936.
290pp.
These memoirs written by a famous sporting journalist, include 118 pages on boxing; there are also further boxing items in the final chapter entitled "Random Recollections"

152. BENNISON, Ben
Fighting. Famous Fights and Fighters Remembered and Recorded.
Kingswood (Surrey), The World's Work (1913) Ltd. 1938.
159pp. Illus. by woodcuts in the text.
Chapters include: Pages from My American Diary; Farr Still in America; The Rise and Fall of Harry Mizler; Notable Invaders of London, (Loughran, Palmer, Lazer); The Re-birth of the National Sporting Club. etc.

153. BENTLEY, Nicholas. (Editor)
Fred Bason's Diary
London, Allan Wingate (Publishers) Ltd. 1950.
Frontis. 175pp.
The diary runs from 1921 to 1950, with many references to boxing.

154. BENTLEY, Richard and Son (Publishers)
A New Book of Sports. (Reprinted from the *Saturday Review*)
London, 1885.
This book includes the following articles:
Boxing and Sparring,
Savate, Boxe and Canne,
Wrestling

155. BENTON, B.H. (Rob Roy). (Compiler and Editor)
Little Fistiana
Boston (Mass.), Lanpher and Co. 1895 and 1898.
Illus.
This work, issued in the years shown above, gave official records of the prize-ring and of boxing.

156. BERGER-WHEELER, Captain F.E.A. (Compiler)
The International Bulldog Year Book. (including "Bulldog Pedigrees")
Published 1934.
Includes an article entitled "Old Time Celebrated Bulldog Men", (Tom Cribb, Champion of England) by Captain F.A.E. Wheeler. Illustrated by a repro-

duction of Tom Cribb, from an old print.

157. BERKELEY, The Hon. Grantley F.
My Life and Recollections
London, Hurst and Blackett. 1865 and 1866 (4 volumes).
This work contains many references to pugilism and the old prize-ring, including the following:
Volume I, Chapter III -
Mentions Colonel Hanger conducting the Prince Regent to a prize-fight, and tells of Lord Barrymore's retention of a boxer in his service as a footman. There is also a story of an encounter between His Highness and the Brighton Butcher, Jackson, the pugilist.

Chapter V -
Tells of the experiences of the author and his family in pugilism; including mention of Pierce Egan.

Chapter XIV -
Relates a remark of Mr. Cobden, that if Mr Bright had not been a Quaker, he would have been a prize-fighter.

Volume II, Chapter IV -
Combat between a monkey and a dog, the latter a small white bull-terrier belonging to Tom Cribb.

Chapter V -
A Prize-Fighter employed to punish Lord Waterford.

Chapter XIII -
At Home and Abroad. My introduction to Heenan and my opinion of him.

Volume III, Chapter II -
Jack Musters as a boxer.

Chapter IV -
Lord Byron and Jackson, my master in "Self Defence".

Volume IV, Chapter I -
Includes a verse on John Gully, prize-fighter and Member of Parliament.

Chapter VII -
Tells of the vociferous multitude, mainly consisting of prize-fighters, impeding the progress of a Royal carriage at the Coronation. Among those recognised being Peter Crawley, Josh Hudson, and Richmond, the Black.

158. BERNARD, George Charles
The Morality of Prizefighting. A dissertation etc.
(Studies of the Catholic University of America in Sacred Theology, Series 2, No.71)
Washington, Catholic University of America Press, 1957.
190pp.

159. BERREY, R. Power
The Romance of a Great Newspaper
London, the *News of the World*, 1930.
The History of the start and progress of the weekly paper.
57pp. small 4to. Illus.
The section "A Master of Crafts", which deals largely with John Bell, who founded a paper called *The World* in 1787, this was an earlier version of the *News of the World* and is stated to have gained further prestige and circulation when the famous prize-fighters Humphries and Mendoza challenged each other through its columns.

160. BERRY, Lester V., and VAN DEN BARK, Melvin
The American Thesaurus of Slang. A Complete Reference Book of Colloquial Speech.
New York, Thomas T. Crowell Co.
London, Constable and Co.
Part II, Special Slang, All Sports and Games, pp 695-706 refers to terms used in boxing.

161. BERRY, Ron
So Long, Hector Bebb. A Novel.
London, Macmillan and Co. Ltd. 1970
224pp.
Set in Wales, this novel gives a vivid and loving picture of the world of boxing.

162. BESANT, Sir Walter
London in the Eighteenth Century
London, A. and C. Black. December 1902.
This work is divided into sections and these are divided into chapters. Chapter 9 in the Section "Society and Amusements" is headed "The Art of Self Defence" it includes one illustration showing Humphries and Mendoza, from a print.

163. BETHEL, W.
Book on Physical and Moral Defence
Manchester, Messrs. Hulton. 1907.
32pp.

164. BETTINSON, A.F., and BENNISON, B.
The Home of Boxing
London, Odhams Press Ltd. 1923.
Dedicated to Lord Lonsdale. "A Great Sportsman"
253pp. Illus.
This is the story of the National Sporting Club. Chapter I is entitled "A Glance Over the Last Twenty Years"; those following trace the history of the Club in more detail.
There are 63 full-page illustrations of boxers and personalities associated with the Club.

165. BETTINSON, A.F., and BENNISON, B.
Famous Fights and Fighters, from Jem Mace to Tommy Farr.
Ringside Recollections of A.F. Bettinson and B. Bennison.
Kingswood (Surrey), The World's Work (1913) Ltd. 1937.
128pp. Paper Covers.
The foreword states: "Ben Bennison is the senior critic of Boxing in this country. He has known and watched all the champions during the past forty years. For many of the early chapters Mr. Bennison acknowledges the collaboration of the late A.F. Bettinson, for so many years the live figure at the National Sporting Club; Mr. Bettinson's word was law and his decision was never doubted"

166. BETTINSON, A.F., and OUTRAM, W. Tristram
The National Sporting Club Past and Present
London, Sands and Co. 1901.
(Large Paper Edition, white covers with gilt decoration and title on fromt cover)
The same publisher reissued the book in 1902, in smaller size, bound in blue cloth, with same design and gilt lettering in front cover.
205pp. Illus.
The contents of the two issues are the same.
The text is divided into 3 parts:
Part 1 - The Past. Being the History of the Club House from 1664 to 1856. (14 pages)
Part 2. The Present. Being the Club Record from March 5th 1891 to March 15th 1901. (113pp).
Part 3. Connects the National Sporting Club with such agreeably diversified places of Entertainment as Somerset House etc. There is also a short talk by A.F. Bettinson on the Decline of English Champions. With a Recipe for Their Revival.
This book is profusely illustrated, with 64 full-page pictures, including some of the interior of the Club and of boxers and other personalities associated with its activities over the years.

167. BINSTEAD, Arthur M. (Pitcher)
Pitcher in Paradise.
Some Random Reminiscences, Sporting and Otherwise
London, Sands and Co. 1903.
292pp.
This book includes some mention of the old boxers

168. BINSTEAD, Arthur M. (Pitcher), and WELLS, Ernest, (Swears).
A Pink 'Un and a Pelican.

continued

Some Random Reminiscences, Sporting and Otherwise.
London, Sands and Co. March 1898.
Reprinted April 1898 and March 1900.
282 pp.
This book contains many references to boxing, at the Pelican Club and elsewhere; particularly in Chapters IV and V.

169. BINSTEAD, Arthur, and FITZGIBBON, Gerald (Editors)
The Sporting Annual (Illustrated). 1903.
London, Anthony Treherne and Co. Ltd.
The Contents Include:
Boxing in 1902
The Queensberry Rules
Contests for Endurance
The Amateur Boxing Association Rules
The National Sporting Club Rules, and other similar information.

170. BIRD, T.H.
Admiral Rous and the English Turf. 1795—1879.
London, Putnam. 1939.
331pp. Illus.
Includes a number of references to John Gully, particularly in Chapter XI.

171. BIRKENHEAD, The First Earl of. (F.E. Smith)
Fifty Famous Fights in Fact and Fiction
Selected and introduced by the author.
London, Cassell and Co. Ltd. 1932.
Boxing items include extracts from *Boxiana*, "The Fight" from Hazlitt's *Essays*, Extracts from George Borrow's *Lavengro*, Thomas Hughes' *Tom Brown's Schooldays*, and other literary works.

172. BIRKENHEAD, The Earl of
Frederick Edwin, Earl of Birkenhead, The Last Phase. By his Son.
London, Thornton Butterworth Ltd. 1935.
The illustrations include one of the Earl of Birkenhead sparring with Carpentier.

173. BIRRELL, Augustine
Res Judicatae. Essays and Papers
London, Elliot Stock. 1892.
280pp.
This book consists of the following essays:
IV. George Borrow.
This mentions Borrow's passion for the ring and gives an extract from the 26th chapter of *Lavengro* on the bruisers of England.

VII. William Hazlitt,
quoted as "always writing about really interesting things – including prize-fights".

174. BIRRELL, Augustine
William Hazlitt. (English Men of Letters Series).
London, Macmillan and Co. Ltd. 1902.
Issued in a New Pocket Edition, 1902.
230pp.
Among the boxing items in this work are a number of references to the essay "The Fight".

175. BIRTLEY, Jack
The Tragedy of Randolph Turpin
London, New English Library. 1975.
160pp. Illus.

176. BIRTLEY, Jack
Freddie Mills, His Life and Death
London, New English Library. 1977.
201pp. plus Mills' boxing record. Illus.

177. BISHOP, John George
Brighton in the Olden Time, with Glances at the Present
Brighton, J.G. Bishop, of the *Brighton Herald* office. 1880.
390pp.
This book contains a number of references to pugilism, including "Fatal Prize Fight in 1800" and "Sparring at the Union Inn".
A plate entitled "The celebration of a Royal Birthday of Brighthelmston" includes two pugilists in action.

178. BLACK, Ladbroke
Seconds Out of the Ring. A Boxing Novel.
London, Odhams Press Ltd. 1920.
187pp.
Red cloth, lettered in black on cover and spine.
12 chapters.

179. BLACKIE and SON Ltd. (Publishers)
Blackie's Boys Annual. 1922.
London and Glasgow.
Includes an article "Boxing for Youths", by Fred G. Shaw.

180. BLACKMANTLE, Bernard. (Charles Molloy Westmacott)
Fitzalleyne of Berkeley
A Romance of the Present Time
London, Sherwood and Co. 1825. Two Volumes.
This story is founded on the affair between Peagreen Hayne, a well-known patron of the ring and Maria Foote, the actress. The novel contains many pugilistic references, as follows:
Volume I – Chapters III, VII and IX
Volume II – Chapter XXIII

continued

At the end of Volume II is a 16pp catalogue of Sporting Books published by Sherwood Jones and Co. including books on pugilism.

181. BLAINE, Delabere P.

An Encyclopedia of Rural Sports, or a Complete Account, Historical, Practical and Descriptive of Hunting, Shooting, Fishing, Racing and Other Field Sports and Athletic Amusements of the Present Day. Illustrated by Six Hundred Engravings on Wood by R. Branston, from Drawings by Alken, T. Landseer, Dickes, etc.

London, Longman, Orme, Brown, Green and Longman. 1840. 1240pp.

A further edition was issued in 1852, 8vo, by "Ephemera" (Edward Fitzgibbon) and others; with over 600 engravings on wood.

Further editions were published in 1858, 1870 and 1880 with engravings from illustrations by various artists.

The First Edition was set out in parts and 4082 sections. Sections 4010–4082 in Part X were entitled "Boxing", edited by Vincent George Dowling.

182. BLAND, ERNEST A. (Editor)

Fifty Years of Sport
Records of Sporting Events from 1896, Compiled by Experts.
London, Published by *The Dail Mail*, 1946.
756pp. plus adverts.
Paper covers.
Includes a section on boxing by C.E. Nash, Boxing Correspondent, *London Evening News*.

183. BLAND, Ernest A. (Editor)

Fifty Two Years of Sport
Records of Sporting Events 1896 to 1949.
London, Published by *The Daily Mail*, 1949.
640pp.
Includes 58 pages of text and 16 pages of pictures on the Olympic Games (including Boxing) in addition to many other boxing references.

184. BLAND, Ernest A. (Editor)

Olympic Story
The Definitive Story of The Olympic Games from their revival in 1896. Illustrated with an Appendix of Results and Records. Foreword by J. Sigrid Edstrom, President, International Olympic Committee.
London, Rockliff Publishing. 1948.
Bound in light red cloth, gilt lettering on spine.
252pp.
The items of boxing interest are as follows:
In the Editor's Preface there is acknowledgement of the authoritative articles on the 17 sports of the XIVth Olympiad contributed by experts. These included Ben Bennison, Fred Dartnell and G. Wagstaffe Simmons on Boxing.
Chapter XX – Boxing
Chapter III – The Ancient Games
Appendix– Record of Olympic Champions, 1896 to 1936, including boxing.

185. BLEACKLEY, Horace, M.A., F.S.A.

Jack Sheppard
With an Epilogue on Jack Sheppard in Literature and Drama. A Bibliography, a Note on Jonathan Wilde and a Memoir of Horace Bleackley by S.W. Ellis.
Edinburgh and London, William Hodge and Co. Ltd. 1933.
(Notable British Trials Series)
260pp.
Chapter XVI, "The March to Tyburn" tells of Sheppard, on his way to execution, being allowed to call upon James Figg at the sign of the "City of Oxford" in the Oxford Road, Marylebone, for a farewell drink.

186. BLONSTEIN, Dr. J.L.

Boxing Doctor
London, Stanley Paul and Co. Ltd. 1965.
125pp. Illus.
The author was Chief Medical Officer to the Amateur Boxing Association.

187. BLOOM, Joe. (Well-known Physical Culturist, Trainer and Manager of Champions)

Boxing
Edited by James Saunders
London, Bear Hudson Ltd. (The "How To" of Sport No.1). 1948.
62pp. Eight half-tone illustrations and fourteen line drawings.
Stiff paper covers. Price 2s-6d.

188. BLUMENFELD, Ralph D.

R.D.B.'s Procession

London, Ivor Nicholson and Watson Ltd. 1935.

329pp.

In the section entitled "Twenty Three Kings of the Ring", mention occurs of a number of prominent boxers, including Peter Jackson, John L. Sullivan, Joe Beckett, Frank P. Slavin, Gunboat Smith, Primo Carnera, and others.

189. BLUNDEN, Edward

Cricket Country

London, Collins. 1944.

224pp.

Includes in Chapter XI a comparison between the literature of cricket and that of other sports, including boxing.

190. BOARDMAN, W.H. (Billy)

Vaudeville Days

Edited by David Whitaker

London, Jarrolds, Publishers. 1935.

288pp. Illus.

This book of reminiscences contains a number of references to boxing and prominent boxers, including the following:

Chapter 2 – Boxing at Newcastle.

Chapter 5 – Sir Harry Preston, Jack Callaghan and Charlie Mitchell

Chapter 8 – Jim Corbett, John L. Sullivan, Bob Fitzsimmons, Jimmy Wilde and Bombardier Billy Wells

Chapter 9 – Sir Harry Preston and boxing tournaments at Brighton

Chapter 11 – John L. Sullivan, Jim Corbett and Bob Fitzsimmons as Music Hall Artists.

191. BOASE, Frederick

Modern English Biography

Containing Many Thousand Concise Memoirs of Persons who have Died Since the Year 1850. With an Index of the Most Interesting Matter.

Truro, Published for the author by Netherton and Worth.

This work was issued in 6 volumes, those numbered 1, 2 and 3 in 1892, 1897 and 1901 respectively; these were limited to 250 copies of each. Supplementary volumes 4, 5 and 6 came out in 1908, 1912 and 1921, and were limited to 125 copies of each.

The volumes contain many memoirs of pugilists and patrons of the prize-ring. Information is given on these as follows:

Volume 1–24 boxing memoirs, from Allardice (Captain Robert Bridges Barclay), known as Captain Barclay, to Dowling, Frank Lewis, (publisher of *Fistiana*).

Volume 2–33 boxing memoirs, from Jackson,

George (Tom Sayers was his pupil), to Queensberry, 7th Marquess of.

Volume 3–14 boxing memoirs, from Reardon, Patrick to Wormald, Joseph.

Volume 4–(Supplement to Volume 1) 6 boxing memoirs, from Aaron Barnett (Jewish pugilist, known as Barney Aaron), The Star of the East, to Couper, John Robertson, (South African Champion).

Volume 5–(Supplement to Volume 2),–9 boxing memoirs, from Davis, Charles to Knifton, John. (A pugilist known as Napper's 81-tonner).

Volume 6–(Supplement to Volume 3)–3 boxing memoirs, from Morris, Peter (lightweight pugilist), to Wilson, Tug (Joe Collins), who claimed to be Champion of England and fought J.L. Sullivan in America.

192. BOGEY, Colonel, The Late

Sport in a Nutshell

Edited by C. E. Hughes and his unrivalled staff of assistants, namely Fred Buchanan (who illustrated the book).

London, Jarrolds Publishers (London) Ltd.

This book includes a section entitled "Boxing" which contains a sub-section entitled "Boxing Results in the good old days and nowadays".

193. BOKRIS, Victor, and WYLIE, Andrew

Ali, the Greatest Champ

New York, Zebra Books. 1976.

Illus. Paperback

194. BOLT, Ben

The Pride of the Ring

(A Novel of the Prize-Ring, with Tom Cribb as the Hero).

London, Ward Lock and Co. Ltd. June 1921

Also published by G. Heath Robinson & J. Birch Ltd., London.

255 pp.

195. BOND, P.G.

Rambles Around Luton

With a Foreword by Sir Williams Beach Thomas, K.B.E.

Luton, Gibbs, Bamforth and Co. (The Leagrave Press). 1937.

(First Edition in book form). Cheap edition, 1941.

In Chapter VIII "Exploring Hertfordshire Lanes", reference is made to the "Bull Inn" at Wheathamstead and its association with bare-knuckle fighters.

196. BOON, Eric

How to Box

London, Scion Press. 1953.

80pp. Illus.

197. BOOTH, J.B.
Old Pink 'Un Days
London, Grant Richards Ltd. 1924.
413pp. Illus.
Contains a quantity of boxing material, referring to Jim Jeffries, The National Sporting Club, Bob Fitzsimmons, Carpentier and Beckett, Pedlar Palmer, Abington Baird (The Squire), Charley Mitchell, Peter Jackson, and many other personalities associated with the ring.

198. BOOTH, J.B.
Pink Parade
London, Thornton Butterworth Ltd., 1933.
312pp. Illus.
Contains two chapters on boxing and boxers.

199. BOOTH, J.B.
Bits of Character, a Life of Henry Hall Dixon ("The Druid")
London, Hutchinson and Co. (Publishers) Ltd. 1936.
287pp. Illus.
Contains references to Tom Sayers, John Gully and other pugilists.

200. BOOTH, J.B.
A Pink 'Un Remembers
With a Foreword by C.B. Cochran.
London, T. Werner Laurie Ltd. 1937.
286pp. Illus.
Chapter XI of this book deals with "The Squire" (Abington Baird), and his interest in prize-fighters, particularly Charlie Mitchell.

201. BORROW, George
The Zingali. (The Gypsies of Spain)
London, John Murray. 1841.
Two Volumes.
The introduction contains a section "The English Gypsies" – with mention of a prize-fight and the Gypsies' interest therein.

202. BORROW, George
Lavengro. The Scholar – The Gypsy – The Priest
London, John Murray, 1851. Three Volumes
There were further editions in 1851 (2nd), 1872 (3rd), 1888 (4th) and 1896 (5th)
A 6th (definitive) edition appeared in March 1900, edited by Prof. W.I. Knapp, containing the original text and some previously suppressed episodes. This edition has been reprinted many times.
The book includes many pugilistic references, including Ben Brain, The Flaming Tinman, The Game Chicken, John Gully, Ned Painter; also sections entitled "Days of Pugilism" and "Bruisers of England".
The notes of Professor Knapp in the 6th edition give further details on some fistic items.

203. BORROW, George
The Romany Rye. (A Sequel to *Lavengro*)
London, John Murray, 1857. Two Volumes.
Further editions were issued in 1858 (2nd), 1872 (3rd), 1888 (4th), and 1896 (5th).
A 6th (definitive) edition appeared in 1900, edited by Professor W.I. Knapp; this includes a Bibliography of the Editor's sources. This edition was reprinted many times.
The book includes references to pugilism including Broughton's Guard, A Defence of Pugilism, (which refers particularly to Tom Cribb), Tom Spring, and the Game Chicken.
The Bibliography of the Editor's sources refers to Pierce Egan's *Boxiana*.

204. BORROW, George
Romano-Lavo-Lil. Word Book of the Romany or English Gypsey Language.
London, John Murray. 1874.
Reprinted; 1905, 1907, 1908, 1909, 1914, and 1919.
The section "Metropolitan Gypseyries" includes an account of George Borrow's visit to the wife of Gypsey (Jack) Cooper, the well-known pugilist who fought Jack Scroggins, Bishop Sharpe, Alec Reid, Young Dutch Sam, and others.

205. BORROW, George
The Works of George Borrow, (Norwich Edition)
London, Constable and Co. Ltd.
Contains in Vol. XVI (Vol. II of the *Miscellanies*), a story "The Young Boxer", from the Persian.

206. BORTSTEIN, Larry
Ali
New York, Tower Publications. 1971.
173pp. Paperback.
This author produced another book with the same title in 1976. (q.v.)

207. BORTSTEIN, Larry
Ali
New York, Scholastic Books. 1976.
92pp. Paper covers.
This author produced a similar book under the same title in 1971 (q.v.)

208. BOULTON, William B.
Amusements of Old London. Being a Survey of the Sports and Pastimes, Teagardens and Parks, Playhouses and the Diversions of the People of London from the 17th to the beginning of the 19th Century.
London, John C. Nimmo. 1901. Two Vols.
Includes 12 hand-coloured illustrations from contemporary sources. (1 on boxing).
Volume II, chapter IX, deals with pugilism.

209. BOVET, P.
Fighting Instinct. (Fighting psychology)
New York, Dodd, Mead and Co. 1923.

210. BOWEN-ROWLANDS, Ernest
In Court and Out of Court. Some personal Recollections.
London, Hutchinson and Co. 1925.
Chapter X, entitled "Clubmen" includes reference to the Pelican Club, and the Great Fight between Frank Slavin and Peter Jackson.
The illustrations include a portrait of Peter Jackson

211. *BOXING* **MAGAZINE (Publishers)**
Johnson v. Jeffries Souvenir
The Story of the Great Fight for the Championship of the World, 4th July, 1910. Pictures of every round, with enthralling graphic description, including a special coloured supplement of Jack Johnson.
London, 1910.
The 36 illustrations show the contestants and the preliminaries before the bout, the Reno arena during the preliminaries, and pictures of the fight.

212. *BOXING* **MAGAZINE (Publishers)**
The Life and Fights of Bombardier Billy Wells, Heavyweight Champion of Great Britain
London, 1912.
Contains Graphic Descriptions of the Bombardier's Sensational Contests and the Whole Story of his Boxing Career.
6 Illus.

213. *BOXING,* **The Editor of,**
Boxing Handbook. (Up-to-date information)
London, Sports Journals Ltd., 1936.
(Further editions of this item were issued from 1937)
40pp.
The contents include the Rules of Boxing, for Amateur Professional and Imperial Services tournaments; also details of champions, amateur and professional, at all weights.

214. *BOXING NEWS,* **The Editor of, and KENRICK, Jim**
How to Box. All the Modern Methods.
London, War Facts Press. N/D. (ca.1950).
94pp. Stiff paper covers. Line Illus.

215. *BOXING WORLD AND ATHLETIC CHRONICLE* **(Publishers)**
The Big Fight. (Jack Johnson v. Jim Jeffries). A full and detailed account of the great championship battle, specially cabled from the ringside.
London, 1910.
An illustrated booklet. Price 1d.

216. BOYD, Frank M.
A Pelican's Tale.
Fifty Years of London and Elswhere.
London, Herbert Jenkins. 1919.
315pp. Illus.
This book contains references in Chapters III, IV and IX to John L. Sullivan and Charlie Mitchell.

217. BRADLEY, Frank. (Editor of the *Mirror of Life***)**
History and Art of Boxing
On the basis of a sight of the advance proofs, this work was reviewed by Gerard Austin in the *Mirror of Life* dated November 8th, 1905, and was stated to be plentifully embellished with photos of fistic celebrities.
The work was also mentioned by Mr. Bradley in his Introduction to Norman Clark's book entitled *How to Box*, published in 1922 (q.v.). Mr. Bradley stated there that it traced the whole history and development of the science of boxing from Roman times to the date of writing, but that its bulk had frightened away all publishers from the start.
As Mr. Bradley's library of boxing books is believed to have been destroyed after his death in 1924, it is very doubtful whether his *History of Art of Boxing* was ever published.

218. BRADLEY, Frank
Boxing. (The Science of Self Defence. How to Acquire the Noble Art).
London, *Mirror of Life* Handbook. 1909.
Illus.
Also published under the title *Art of Boxing.*

219. BRADLEY, J. Frank
Jim Driscoll, His Life, Fights and Experiences
London, *Mirror of Life* Handbook, 1909.

220. BRADLEY, J. Frank
Johnny Summers, His Life, Fights and Ex-
continued

periences.
London, *Mirror of Life* Handbook. 1909.

221. BRADLEY, J. Frank
Freddie Welsh, His Life, Fights and Experiences
London, Published by the *Mirror of Life*.
1909. Price 2d.

222. BRADLEY, J. Frank
The Boxing Referee
An exhaustive treatise on the duties of a referee and an explanation of the Queensberry Rules relating to Boxing Contests and Competitions.
London, The Queenhithe Printing and Publishing Co. Ltd. 1910.
92pp.
Bound in green cloth with gilt titles. Frontis. A second edition was published in 1914 with red paper covers; this later edition lacks the frontispiece but contains eight additional pages. The extra pages give an explanation of the National Sporting Club Rules.

223. BRADLEY, J. Frank
Life and Fights of Owen Moran
London, *Mirror of Life* Handbook. 1910.
Price 2d.

224. BRADSHAW, Percy V.
Seen in Perspective 1895–1945. A
Panorama of Fifty Years
London, Chapman and Hall. 1946.
219pp. Illus.
Chapter IX "Double, Double Toil and Trouble" includes mention of boxers and boxing, including Jimmy Wilde, Jack Dempsey, Joe Beckett and others.

225. BRADY, F.A. (Publisher)
Career of the Champions
New York. ca. 1860
105pp. Illus.
A history of Tom Sayers and John C. Heenan and their achievements in the ring. Collated from various sources and reliable authorities, with a full report of their great fight for the Championship.

226 BRADY, James
Strange Encounters. Tales of Famous Fights and Fighters.
London, Hutchinson and Co. (Publishers) Ltd. (Hutchinson's Library of Sports and Pastimes). 1947.
Bound in red or blue cloth. 16 Illustrations. 12 Chapters and an Appendix.

216pp. Illus.
This book was advertised for publication as follows: A vivid account of prize-fighting in the 18th and first half of the 19th centuries by an author who knows his subject thoroughly . . . With skill and knowledge the author describes such notable boxers as "Gentleman" Jackson, Jem Belcher, Pearce, Gully, Cribb, Tom Spring, Tom Sayers, and others, and describes most vividly their famous fights.
The Appendix contains the various sets of Rules, including 'contests for endurance'.
There is also a Bibliography consisting of a list of books and journals, ancient and modern — which the author searched through and read in order to acquire and check the information contained in his book.

227. BRADY, William A.
The Fighting Man
Indianapolis (U.S.A.), The Bobbs-Merril Co., 1916.
Bound in red/brown cloth. Gilt titles on cover and spine.
227pp. 35 Illus.
The story of the author's varied life, as a sports reporter, actor, theatrical and boxing manager. He claims that he was given the name of "The Fighting Man" because of his toughness in theatrical deals.
William A. Brady managed James J. Corbett and Jim Jeffries in their fighting careers and he also arranged tours during which these boxers appeared on the stage, J.J. Corbett in *Gentleman Jack*, and Jim Jeffries in *The Man From The West*.
The illustrations in the book include Jim Corbett and Gus Rhulin, Jake Kilrain, Charley Mitchell, Jess Willard, Jem Mace, Frank Moran and others.

228. BRADY, William A.
Showman: My Life Story
New York City, E.P. Dutton and Co. 1937.
227pp. Illus.
Contains mention of many famous boxers, including John L. Sullivan.

229. BRAMSTON, Dr. John Byrom (Man of Taste)
Dodsley's Collections. 1777.
This item includes various poetic pieces by the author and others, including "Sketches of Pugilism" and allusions to the "Fashionable Art of Boxing, or Self Defence".

230. BRANDT, Francis Frederick. (Of the Inner Temple, Barrister at Law)
Habet
A Short Treatise on the Law Of The Land As It Affects Pugilism.
London, Robert Hardwicke. 1857.

continued

Bound in red cloth with gilt lettering and design on the front cover showing two infants fighting.

92pp.

The 10 chapters discuss the legality of pugilism, Riot and Tumult, Breaches of the Peace, Unlawful Assembly, The Regulation of Prize-fighting, Rules of the Ring, etc.

Note on the title: The word "Habet" was the cry with which the Roman gladiator was saluted when he had received a more than usually effective stroke, delivered with the sword or the caestus.

231. BRASHER, Chris

Sportsmen of Our Time

London, Victor Gollancz Ltd. 1962.

144pp. Illus.

The chapter on boxing is entitled "There is not enough honour in Boxing", this refers mainly to Ingemar Johannson.

232. BREAKWINDOW, Mr. (Editor)

Jack Randall's Diary of Proceedings of the House of Call for Genius; to which are added several of Mr. B's minor pieces.

London, Printed for W. Simpkin and R. Marshall, 1820.

A note in *The Slang Dictionary* by John Camden Hotton, comments on this book as follows:—

Randall's (Jack) 'The Pugilist', formerly of the "Hole in the Wall" Chancery Lane, Diary of Proceedings at the House of Call for Genius, edited by Mr. Breakwindow, to which are added several of Mr. B's minor pieces.

12mo. 1820.

(Believed to have been written by Thomas Moore.) The verses are mostly parodies of popular authors, and abound with the slang of pugilism, and the phraseology of the fast life of the period.

Extracts from this book are to be found in the pages of Pierce Egan's *Boxiana* and in the *Annals of Sporting and Fancy Gazette*.

The title is included in a list dated Nov. 1824, published by Sherwood, Jones and Co., London. This suggests that there was a later edition of the work.

233. BREAKWINDOW, Mr. (Editor)

Jack Randall, A Few Selections from His Scrap-Book

Published: 1822.

John Camden Hotten, in his *Slang Dictionary*, lists this book as follows:—

Randall, Jack, a Few Selections from his Scrap Book, to which are added Poems of the late Fight for the Championship. 12mo. 1822.

Extracts from this item are also to be found in the pages of *Boxiana* and the *Annals of Sporting and Fancy Gazette*.

The book is also listed in an 1823 issue of Volume I of *Boxiana* dated 1824, as being lately published by Sherwood Jones and Co., Paternoster Row.

234. BRENNER, Teddy
(As told to Barney Nagler)

Only the Ring was Square

New Jersey, Prentice Hall Inc. 1981.

164pp.

Tells of the author's experiences as matchmaker at Madison Square Garden.

235. BREWER, The Rev. E. Cobham, LLD.

A Dictionary of Phrase and Fable

First published in 1868, with a new and enlarged edition in 1894. A revised and up-dated edition was later issued by Cassell and Co. Ltd., London.

This work contains descriptions of many pugilistic terms and the derivation of certain expressions taken from the names of famous pugilists.

236. BRIDGES, J.A.

A Sportsman of Limited Income

Recollections of Fifty Years.

London, Andrew Melrose, 1912.

309pp. Illus.

Includes, Chapter XXII "Changes in Sports, the P.R.", in which mention occurs of The National Sporting Club, George Borrow, Sayers and Heenan, and Joe Goss.

237. BRIER, Warren J.

The Frightful Punishment

Con Orem and Montana's Great Glove Fights of the 1860's.

Missoula, Montana, University of Montana Press. 1969.

113pp. plus Appendix, which includes details of Orem's pugilistic career, with a bibliography of newspaper and other sources.

238. BRITISH BOXING BOARD OF CONTROL, No.3 (South Western) Area.

Ringside Annual 1948.

The sport in No.3 (South Western) Area of the B.B.B.C.

This item is described as:—

64 pages of interesting Facts and Figures covering the counties of Cornwall, Devon and Somerset.

239. BRITISH BOXING BOARD OF CONTROL (1929). (Publishers)

Referees' Guide

Boxing Rules and Explanatory Notes.

London, ca. 1963.

23pp.

continued

Stiff paper covers. With sheets showing amendments to 1962 and 1963.

240. BRITISH BROADCASTING CORPORATION. (Publishers)

The B.B.C. Handbook

The Handbook under this title was published in 1928, 1929 and 1939.

The 1929 edition included a section entitled "Other Sporting Events" with a sub-section entitled 'Boxing'; this gave an account of the first broadcast description of a boxing match in England. This was relayed from the Albert Hall on October 6th, 1927; the bout was between Teddy Baldock of Poplar and Willie Smith of South Africa. There is also a picture taken during the fight.

The 1939 Edition of the B.B.C. Handbook includes a section entitled "Television in 1938", which mentions the Emitron cameras peering through the tobacco smoke at Harringay to see Ben Foord v. Eddie Phillips and Jock McAvoy v. Len Harvey; this being among the highlights of the year in outside broadcasting.

241. BRITISH BROADCASTING CORPORATION. (Publishers)

The B.B.C. Yearbook. 1930 and 1948.

(Issued in other years as the B.B.C. Handbook)

In the 1939 edition is a section entitled "The Range of Broadcasting", a list selected from the programmes broadcast by the old B.B.C., Nov. 15th, 1922–Dec. 31st, 1926, which includes a reference to the first Outside Broadcast of boxing, in March 1926, sounds of the fight between Phil Scott and Ted Sandwina on Jan. 31st, 1929, and another equally successful commentary on the Lightweight Championship of Great Britain on May 2nd, 1929 between Fred Webster and Sam Steward.

The 1948 yearbook contains an article by Stewart McPherson entitled "On the Spot in Front of the Mike", which includes considerable mention of boxing, including Jackie Paterson v. Peter Kane on 9th June, 1943.

242. BRITISH SPORTS AND SPORTSMEN LTD. (Publishers)

Athletic Sports — Tennis — Rackets, and Other Ball Games

London, ca. 1928.

Folio. Full crimson morocco, gilt edges. Illus.

The boxing references in this volume include "The Olympic Games Past and Present" and mention of amateur boxing. There is also an article "Records of Boxing", with fifteen boxing illustrations.

243. BROADBENT, R.J.

Annals of the Liverpool Stage, from the Earliest Period to the Present Time.

Together with some account of the Theatres and Music Halls in Bootle and Birkenhead.

Liverpool, Edward Howell. 1908.

393pp. Illus.

In the section "The Variety Stage — The Free and Easies and the Concert Rooms" reference is made to Jem Ward. Another chapter also includes a reference to Jem Mace.

244. BROADRIBB, Ted

Fighting is My Life

London, Frederick Muller Ltd. 1951.

149pp. 21 Illus.

This autobiography covers the author's career in the boxing game from his early days as a boxer to his successes as a manager of such as Tommy Farr, Freddie Mills and many others.

245. BROEG, Bill, and BURRILL, Bob

Don't Bring That Up. Skeletons in the Sports Closet.

New York, A.S. Barnes and Co. 1946.

272pp (including Index). Illus. by Vic Donahue.

Contains many memorable sports stories, showing the 'Greats' at their worst, a wonderful collection of tales you will enjoy.

Consists of seventeen stories, some devoted to boxing, including "Walk into my Parlour" (Battling Siki, Mike McTigue etc), "Indelible Infamy" (Harry Thomas), "Fate's Tragic Touch" (Death in Sport), and "Pardon My Gloves" (Wholly devoted to Boxing).

246. BROGAN, D.W.

The English People (Impressions and Observations)

London, Hamish Hamilton. 1943.

260pp.

Chapter III "England as a Democracy" includes a reference to English boxing, and Chapter VI "India" contains an anecdote of James J. Corbett.

247. BROMBERG, Lester

World Champs

New York, Retail Distributors Inc. 1958

253pp. Paperback

248. BROMBERG, Lester

Boxing's Unforgettable Fights

Foreword by Jack Dempsey

New York, The Ronald Press Co. 1962.

343pp. Illus.

The fights are covered in three sections of the book, entitled 'Old Timers', 'The Golden Age', and 'Moderns'. The period covered extends from John Sullivan v. Paddy Ryan to Floyd Patterson's return bout with Ingemar Johansson, with a wealth of fisticuffs in between.

249. BROOME, J. E. and ROSS, John Adrian
History Repeats Itself (A Humorous Book)
London, Hutchinson and Co. (Publishers) Ltd. 1938.
The text is by J.A. Ross and the illustrations by J. E. Broome.
120pp.
Includes a section entitled "Seconds Out" which contains 3 humorous boxing stories and 4 illustrations.

250. "BROUGHTON" (Gilbert E. Odd) (Editor)
Boxing News Amateur Boxing Annual 1948.
London, War Facts Press and Pallas Publishing Co. Ltd.
Coloured paper covers, with picture of a boxing match on the front cover.
This was the first of three annuals covering the amateur side of the sport; the contents included the following:
A Notable Season, a Survey of Events in 1947–48, by Gilbert E. Odd.
The Great Johnny Ryan, by An Admirer
Eight New Titleholders.
Complete A.B.A. Results.
Complete Olympic Results.
Complete Amateur Records.
List of Champions – A.B.A., British Empire, Olympic, European, etc.
The Annual included a number of illustrations of well-known boxers and their contests.

The other two Annuals in this series were issued as follows:
Boxing News Amateur Boxing Annual, 1950 (Issued in 1949)
Boxing News Amateur Boxing Annual, 1951 (Issued in 1950)
Both of these were edited by "Broughton" (Gilbert E. Odd).
The contents of both following editions were similar to those of the first issue, with the records brought up to date.

251. BROUN, Heywood Hale (Compiler)
Collected Edition of Heywood Broun
New York, Harcourt, Brace and Co., 1941.
561pp. with a bibliography of Broun's work. These collected pieces of journalism, ranging from 1908 to 1939, embrace "Sport for Art's Sake", (Dempsey–Carpentier), p.97; "The Orthodox Champion", (Leonard–Rocky Kansas), p.113; and "The Champion", (Joe Louis), p.528.

251A. BROWN Gene (Editor)
The Complete Book of Boxing
A New York *Times* Scrapbook History.
New York, Bobbs-Merrill Co. Inc. 1980.
204pp.
New York *Times* reports of fights from Corbett v. Sullivan to Holmes v. Norton.

252. BROWN, Ned. (Editor)
Pardon My Glove. (Official Dope Sheet and Programme of Boxing and Wrestling)
New York, Published by the Editor. 1933.
Price 5 cents.

253. BROWN, Thomas, The Younger (Editor)
The Fudge Family in Paris
London, Printed for Longman, Hurst, Rees, Orme and Brown. 1818.
168pp.
The author of this book was Thomas Moore, the poet. The first 150 pages comprise the text of the title-piece; page 151 states "The following occasional papers have already appeared in my friend Mr. Perry's paper, and are here by desire of several persons of distinction, reprinted. T.B."
Pages 165 to 168 include: Epistle from Tom Cribb to Big Ben, concerning some Foul Play In a Late Transaction. (Written soon after Bonaparte's transportation to St.Helena.)
(Lines on a political matter with pugilistic terms and cant of that age.)
This book ran to at least three editions.

254. BROWN, Warren, (Of the *Chicago Herald American*)
Win, Lose or Draw
New York City, G.P. Putnam's Sons. 1947.
The author was a sports writer on the *Chicago Herald-American* who had seen all the big sporting events and knew all the sporting characters of his time; he was friendly with Jack Dempsey, and Gene Tunney. Others mentioned in the book include Tex Rickard and Jack Kearns.

255. BROWN, Wesley
Self Defence
New York, A.S. Barnes and Co. 1951.
(Part of the "Barnes Sports Library").
91pp.

256. BRUNO, Frank
Know What I Mean? His Own K.O. Story, with Norman Giller.
London, Stanley Paul & Co. Ltd. 1986.
160pp. Illus.

257. BRYANT, Arthur
The Years of Endurance. 1793–1802.
London, Collins and Co. 1942.
370pp.
Chapter I is entitled "Freedom's Own Island" and

continued

includes mention of boxing.

The passage opens "Boxing was the favourite pastime of the nation" and it proceeds with reference to pugilists who were active in the last days of the 18th Century; such as John Gully, Bob Gregson, Tom Cribb, and Gentleman Jackson.

258. BRYANT, Arthur
English Saga. (1840–1944)
London, Collins, with Eyre and Spottiswoode. 1940.

340pp.

Includes a short reference to the Sayers v. Heenan fight.

259. BRYDEN, Bill
Benny Lynch. Scenes from a short life. A Play.
Edinburgh, Southside (Publishers) Ltd. 1975.
97pp. Stiff paper covers.

260. BUCHAN, John
Great Hours in Sport
London, Thomas Nelson and Sons Ltd. 1921.
288pp.
In the section entitled "Boxing" is included a contribution by Bohun Lynch: "A Great Fight", (Oxford v. Cambridge, 1906).

261. BUCHANAN-TAYLOR, W.
Shake the Bottle
London, Heath Cranton Ltd. 1942. Reissued 1942, 1943, 1944 and 1946.
221pp. Illus.
Chapter XXII, entitled 'Champs', is of boxing interest. There are accompanying illustrations of Billy Wells, Joe Beckett and Joe Louis.
Chapter XXVII includes mention of Frank Moran.

262. BUCHANAN-TAYLOR, W.
Shake It Again
London, Heath Cranton Ltd. 1943.
2nd, 3rd and 4th editions were issued in 1943 and 1944.
136pp. Illus.
This author is known principally for his books of theatrical reminiscences. Some of these include boxing references; this title includes the following:
Chapter III, Blackpool; includes material on Jimmy Wilde and an account of his visits to a boxing show in Blackpool.
Chapter XXV, Handy Pandy; refers to the state of boxers' hands and the advantages of pickling these, as recommended by Jem Carney.
One illustration shows Jimmy Wilde.

263. BUCHANAN-TAYLOR, W. (In collaboration with James Butler)
What Do You Know About Boxing?

London, Heath Cranton Ltd. 1947.
Bound in blue cloth, with gilt lettering on spine.
236pp.
In the preliminaries the publishers acknowledge with gratitude the following sources of information:
Boxiana, Pugilistica, Fistiana, The Prize Ring (Bohun Lynch), *The Boxing Referee* (Frank Bradley), Hazlitt's *Essays, Lavengro* (George Borrow).
There are also thanks for permission to reproduce excerpts from *Rodney Stone* (Conan Doyle), *The World I Knew* (Louis Golding), *Masterson* (Gilbert Frankau), and *Burning Daylight* (Jack London).

264. BUCKAMAGA, C.V.
The American Indian Boxers of Minnesota
Ponsford (Minnesota), Pine Point Publications. 1980.
192pp.

265. BUCKHORSE, Blunden, M.A.
The Devil to Pay at W—r, or St. J—s In An Uproar
London, printed for J. Raymond, ca. 1750.
Contains a number of references to pugilism, including Broughton's Amphitheatre.

266. BUCKHORSE (John Smith)
Memoirs of the Noted Buckhorse. In which, Besides a Minute Account of his past Memorable Exploits, That Celebrated Hero is carried into the higher Life.
Containing some very Extraordinary Events, Interspersed with Remarkable Anecdotes of some Bloods of Fortune and Eminence, Companions of Mr. Buckhorse.
London, Printed for S. Crowder and H. Woodgate, at the Golden Ball, in Paternoster Row. 1756. (2 volumes.)
Vol 1: 246pp; Vol 2: 272pp.
Buckhorse was probably more noted for his exploits outside of the ring, where he was famous for his participation in "Battles Royal", involving a number of fighters.

267. BUCKINGHAM, James Silk
Autobiography of James Silk Buckingham
London, Longman, Rees, Orme, Browne and Green. 2 Volumes. 1855.
The pugilistic references here deal with the career of John Gully. Extracts from this book appear in *Racing in The Olden Days* by William Fawcett, 1933 (q.v.)

268. BUCKMASTER, Herbert
Buck's Book

continued

London, Grayson and Grayson. 1933.

29 pp. Illus.
Includes a number of references to boxers and boxing.

269. BUILDER PRINTING WORKS
(Publishers)
Souvenir of the Burns-Squires Boxing Contest for the World Championship
Sydney (Australia) ca.1908.

64pp. 16 Illus.
As well as dealing with the contest this item contains articles, records and portraits of famous boxers.
(Burns knocked out Squires in 13 rounds in Sydney, August 24th 1908)

270. BURCHARD, Marshall
Muhammad Ali
New York, Putnam 1975.
(Sporting Hero Biographies)
96pp.

271. BURCHARD, S.H.
Sports Star, Sugar Ray Leonard.
San Diego, Harcourt Brace Jovanovich. 1983.
53pp. Illus.

272. BURDON, Randall
New Zealand Notables
This includes a reference to Bob Fitzsimmons.
New Zealand Notables, Series Two
New Zealand, The Caxton Press, 1945.

190pp.
The second series also contains reference to Bob Fitzsimmons in the form of a chapter which contains scarce information on his early life in New Zealand.

273. BURKE, Thomas
The Real East End
The Lithographs by Pearl Binder.
London, Constable and Co. Ltd. 1932.
163pp. Illus.

The section "Its People" contains an account of the Premierland boxing arena.

274. BURKE, Thomas
Murder at Elstree, or Mr. Thurtell and his Gig.
London, Longmans Green and Co. 1936.
177pp.
This book contains a number of references to pugilists and the prize-ring, among them the following:

Chapter I Mr. Thurtell Stages a 'Cross' (The Story of a fight). Mentioning Tom Cribb, Belcher, Randall, Tom Spring, George Borrow and Pierce Egan.

Chapter XI Mr. Thurtell faces the Music. (The story of Thurtell's Execution and last hours). This tells of an interview with Pierce Egan in jail, when the condemned man asks for news of the result of the Spring v. Langan contest.

275. BURKE, Thomas
English Nightlife
(From Norman Curfew to Present Black-Out)
Illustrated from Prints, Paintings, Drawings and Photographs.
London, B.T. Batsford Ltd. 1941.

150pp. Illus.
A Chapter "We Won't Be Home Till Morning" contains references to old pugilists, including Cribb, Thomas Belcher, John Jackson and others; there are also references to later boxing at the N.S.C. and other venues.
There are two boxing illustrations, after Thomas Rowlandson and R. Cruikshank.

276. BURKE, Thomas
Travel in England,
From Pilgrim to Pack Horse to Light Car and Plane.
London, B.T. Batsford Ltd. 1942.
154pp. Illus.
Chapter IV – "Down the Road to Glory" includes reference to the prize-ring, with two extracts from works by Pierce Egan.
There is an uncoloured reproduction from the plate "The Road to the Fight" from *Real Life in London*.

277. BURNETT, W.R.
Iron Man. A Boxing Novel
London, William Heinemann Ltd.
312pp.
Bound in red cloth with gilt lettering on the spine.

278. BURNS, Tommy
Scientific Boxing and Self Defence
London, *Health and Strength* Ltd. 1909.
172pp. (1914).
There were two issues of this book in 1909; the standard edition was bound in green cloth with black titles on front cover and spine. A Souvenir Edition was issued in blue binding, with gilt lettering and an inscription on the title-page, reading "Special Autograph Edition, as a souvenir of the Author's visit to England, 1907–1908".
The text and illustrations are the same in both issues.
2nd and 3rd editions of this book were
continued

published in 1934 by Athletic Publications Ltd. London.

There are 11 chapters and 40 illustrations, most of these including Tommy Burns. Some of the illustrations were omitted from the 2nd and 3rd editions.

279. BURRAGE, A. Harcourt
Carry on Rippleton. A School Story.
London, Sampson Low. Marston and Co. 1947.

248pp. 8 Illus.
The story includes a considerable amount about boxing. The principle character is called "The Champ".

280. BURRILL, Bob
Who's Who in Boxing
Foreword by Jack Dempsey
New Rochelle, New York, Arlington House, 1974.

208pp.
Arranged from A to Z, including a potted biography of each entry, with career highlights and overall records.

281. BURROWS, John
Benny
The Life and Times of a Fighting Legend.
Edinburgh, Mainstream Publishing Ltd. 1982.
219pp. plus Epilogue and Postscript, and Benny Lynch's record.
This biography includes background material on Benny's early years, before he achieved undying fame in the ring.

282. BURTON, Edmund
Fists of Fortune. A Novel.
The Story of an Obscure Boxer's Rise to Fame.
London, U.T.B. Ltd. 1945.
32pp. Coloured paper covers, with boxing picture on front cover.

283. BUTLER, Frank
(*News of the World* Boxing Correspondent)
Randolph Turpin — Sugar Ray Robinson.
Their Story in Pictures.
London, *News of the World*, 1951.
32pp. Paper covers

284. BUTLER, Frank
Success at Boxing
London, Phoenix Press, 1956.
128pp. Illus.
Incorporating hints from famous contemporary boxers, including Ron Barton, Don Cockell and Dai Dower.

285. BUTLER, Frank
A History of Boxing in Britain
London, Arthur Barker and Co. 1972.
207pp. Illus.

286. BUTLER, Frank.
Muhammad Ali
London, Hamish Hamilton's Children's Books, (Profile Series), 1981.
64pp. Card covers. Illus.

287. BUTLER, James
Kings of the Ring
With a Foreword by the Rt. Hon. Earl of Lonsdale, K. G.
London, Stanley Paul and Co. Ltd. 1936.
Includes a dedication "To My Son, Frank Butler".
256pp. Illus.
The famous boxing journalist looks back on a lifetime's experience as a boxing writer; the book includes references to all the great glove artists from before the turn of the century to Kid Lewis, Young Stribling, Tommy Milligan and many others.
The dedicatee, Frank Butler, became as famous as his father as a boxing writer.

288. BUTLER, James, and BUTLER, Frank
The Fight Game
Kingswood, Surrey. The World's Work (1913) Ltd. 1951.
223pp. Illus.
The journalist-authors, father and son, reminisce on fighters with whom they became acquainted over a period of fifty years.
This book was also issued in a Sportsmans Book Club Edition.

289. BUXTON, Laurie
The Changing Years
A Book of Philosophic Verse
London, Printed by Robins and Co., Islington, 1951.
The author was a successful professional boxer, being a member of the famous boxing family from Watford; he was Chairman of the Professional Boxers' Association.
All proceeds from the sale of "The Changing Years" were devoted to the funds of the Professional Boxers' Association.

290. BYRNE, Donn
Destiny Bay
London, Sampson, Low, Marston and Co. Ltd. 1928.
Boston (U.S.A.), Little, Brown and Co. 1928

continued

432pp.
Includes in Chapter III "Tales of James Carabine" (A Story of the Ring).
See also, William D. Cox: *Boxing in Art and Literature*, 1935.

291. BYROM, John, M.A. F.R.S.

Miscellaneous Poems

Manchester, Printed for J. Harrop, 1773 (2 volumes)

Leeds, Printed for James Nichols. 1814 (2 volumes)

The first volume of each issue contains "Extempore Verses on a Trial of Skill between the Two Great Masters of the Noble Science of Self-Defence, Messrs. Figg and Sutton".

292. BYRON, George Gordon, (Sixth Baron)

The famous poet took a keen interest in the prize-ring, and was friendly with John Jackson (Conqueror of Mendoza), who had sparring rooms in Bond Street, London.

There are references to the prize-ring and pugilism in some of Byron's works, including the following:
1. *Don Juan* first edition (Canto XI, Stanza XXI)
2. *Detached Thoughts* (15th Oct. 1821)
3. *Hints from Horace*

There are also pugilistic references in a number of works about Lord Byron, including the following:
1. Moore, Thomas, The Life, *Letters and Journals of Lord Byron*, Volumes I and II, 1830.
2. Jeaffreson, John Cody, *The Real Lord Byron*. (New Views of the Poet's Life) 2 volumes, 1883.
3. Armstrong, J.L., *Life of Lord Byron*, 1846.

Some of the items mentioned above are included in *Boxing in Art and Literature* by Wm. D. Cox, 1936 (q.v.)
Lord Byron's enthusiasm for boxing is well described in *The Prize Ring* by Bohun Lynch (q.v.)
Chapter VI of this book is entitled "Lord Byron's Screen" and describes the screen as being decorated between 1812 and 1816, at the time of Byron's friendship with John Jackson.
Among the plates in the Bohun Lynch book is one showing Lord Byron sparring with John Jackson, and also a number of pictures of the panels which make up the screen.
All of these show pugilists.

293. CAFFYN, W. (Printer & Publisher)
Caffyn's Scrap Sheet No.1
London, 1844.
Four large pages of woodcuts, including Young Dutch Sam, Deaf Burke, Fred Mason, and the Parlour of the Champion of England (Ben Caunt)

294. CALDER-MARSHALL, Arthur
Dead Centre
London, Jonathan Cape. 1935.
287pp.
A story of life in a Public School, with a short passage on schoolboy boxing.

295. CALDER-MARSHALL, Arthur
Glory Dead
London, Michael Joseph Ltd. 1939.
286pp. Illus.
This book is about Trinidad and Part 2 gives an account of the author's experiences while in that country, including "Fight! Fight! Black is White!", an amazing account of some amateur boxing boys.

296. CALIFORNIA ATHLETIC COMMISSION (Publishers)
Rules and Regulations and the Laws Regulating Boxing and Wrestling Matches
Sacramento, 1926. (Fourth Edition)

297. CALIFORNIA STATE ATHLETIC COMMISSION (Publishers)
Rules, Regulations and Laws regulating Boxing Matches and Wrestling Exhibitions in California
Sacramento, 1964.
116pp.

298. CALLOW, Edward
Old London Taverns. Historical, Descriptive and Reminiscent. With Some Account of the Coffee Houses, Clubs, etc.
London, Downey and Co. 1899.
354 pp.
This book contains some references to old prize-fighters in Part II "Westward Ho!" which discusses the pugilistic associations of taverns in the Strand and Leicester Square areas.

299. CAMPBELL, Colonel Ronald, and DRISCOLL, Jim
Boxing and Bayonet Fighting
An Army Service Manual, published during the 1914-1918 War.

300. CAMPBELL, Ronald (Col. Ronald Bruce Campbell, C.B.E., D.S.O., One Time Inspector of Army Physical Training)
A Ten-Round Contest
London, Cassell and Co. 1926.
242pp.
This book consists of 10 boxing stories, told by 'Professor Ben Barlow' in intervals between lessons at his boxing academy.
The book was published again in 1951 under the title *The Spirit of the Fist* (q.v.)

301. CAMPBELL, Ronald (Col. Ronald Campbell, C.B.E., D.S.O., One Time Inspector of Army Physical Training)
The Spirit of the Fist
Edinburgh and London, Oliver and Boyd. 1951.
237pp.
A note on the verso of the title-page says "All but one of these stories were published by Messrs Cassell and Co. Ltd. in 1926 under the title *A Ten Round Contest*.
The additional story is entitled "The Morphia Punch"; this is included instead of "The Treble Cross" one of the stories in the original book *A Ten Round Contest*. (q.v.)

302. CAMPBELL, Capt. R.B.
Private Spud Tamson
Edinburgh and London, Wm. Blackwood and Sons. 1915.
There were at least eight impressions of this novel.
The book includes one chapter on Boxing.
Chapter VI: "The Garrison Lightweight"

303. CANNON, Jimmy
(Of the *New York Post***).**
Nobody Asked Me
New York, The Dial Press. 1951.
Bound in green cloth with black spine, lettered in gold.
This book includes: "The Fighter", with sections entitled – Club Fighter – Night at Sugar Ray's – Fight Man Soliloquy, I and II – Louis and Conn, Second Fight – Baer Had Everything – Petrolle – Joe Louis, Stay Retired – Tony Zale, Working Man – The Heavyweights and Damon Runyon, and other references to Boxing.

304. CANTWELL, Robert
The Real McCoy
The Life and Times of Norman Selby
Princeton, Auerbach Publishers Inc. 1971.
184pp. including Notes, Index and Bibliography. illus.
The story of the fighter who was the original of the phrase "The Real McCoy".

305. CARLETON, Patrick

continued
H

The Hawk and the Tree. A Novel.
London, Philip Allen. 1933.
357pp.
This item includes boxing in the story.

306. CARLETON, William
City Ballads
New York, Harper and Brothers, 1886
London, Sampson Low and Co. 1886
London, (Rose Library), 1887.
Further editions were issued in New York in 1898 and in London in 1907. In the section entitled "Vice" is included a poem "The Slugging Match".

307. CARNEGIE, Dale
Dale Carnegie's Biographical Round Up
Kingswood (Surrey), The World's Work, 1946.
Includes material on Jack Dempsey.

308. CARNEGIE, Dale
How to Stop Worrying and Start Living
Kingswood (Surrey), The World's Work Ltd. 1948.
Includes items of boxing interest:
Pages 273–274 – "I Go to the Gym to Punch the Bag, or Take a Hike Outdoors", by Colonel Eddie Eagan, (Chairman, New York State Athletic Commission, Former Olympic Light-Heavyweight Champion).
Pages 287–289 – "The Toughest Opponent I Ever Fought Was Worry", by Jack Dempsey.

309. CARPENTER, Harry
Masters of Boxing
London, William Heinemann Ltd. 1964.
241pp. Illus.
The author reviews the careers and gives the fight records of 19 great boxers at all weights, from Benny Lynch to Jack Dempsey and Joe Louis.

310. CARPENTER, Harry
Boxing, A Pictorial History
With a Foreword by Muhammad Ali.
London, William Collins, Sons and Co. Ltd. 1975.
189pp. 4to.

311. CARPENTER, Harry
Boxing
Glasgow, Collins, 1975.
London, Collins, 1982. (Revised edition)
192pp (both editions). Illus.

312. CARPENTER, Harry
The Hardest Game
London, British Broadcasting Corporation.
1981.
121pp. Illus.
Harry Carpenter discusses professional boxing and some of its practitioners.

313. CARPENTER, Tom
(World's Champion Ball Puncher)
Ball Punching
London, Athletic Publications Ltd. 1923.
69pp. Illus.

314. CARPENTIER, Georges
(Champion of Europe)
My Methods or Boxing as a Fine Art
Translated into English by F. Hurdman-Lucas
London, Published at the offices of Boxing, by Ewart, Seymour and Co. Ltd., 1914.
Re-issued in 1920.
Dedicated "To My Friends the Public and to All Those Interested in Boxing"
95pp. Card covers. Portrait of Carpentier on front cover.
The chapters are all instructional; with photographic illustrations of boxing poses, the author, the translator and Carpentier's manager, Francois Descamps.

315. CARPENTIER, Georges
(Champion Heavyweight Boxer of Europe)
My Fighting Life
London, Cassell and Co. Ltd. 1920.
The Dedication reads as follows:
To All British Sportsmen I dedicate this, The Story of My Life. Were I of their own great country, I feel I could have no warmer more lasting place in their friendship.
253pp. Illus. Bound in green cloth, 17 chapters, 7 illustrations
The chapter headings include: I Become Descamps' Pupil – My Professional Career Begins – My Fights with Wells – and a Sequel – Arranging the Beckett Fight – Men I Have Fought, etc.

316. CARPENTIER, Georges
Brothers of the Brown Owl.
A Story of the Boxing Ring.
London, Cassell and Co. 1921.
276pp.
Bound in pictorial cloth with 4 coloured illustrations and a number in black and white.

317. CARPENTIER, Georges
The Art of Boxing
London, G. Harrap and Co. Ltd. 1926
New York, George H. Doran Co. 1926

continued

English Edition 167pp; U.S.Edition 172pp. Illus.

318. CARPENTIER, Georges
Carpentier by Himself
London, Hutchinson and Co. (Publishers) Ltd. 1955.
204pp. Illus.

319. CARROLL, Ted
Picture Story of Joe Louis and Jack Dempsey. Their Complete Ring Careers.
New York, 1947.
400 Drawings by Ted Carroll.
Foreword by Dan Parker, Sports Editor of New York *Daily Mirror*.
Stiff paper covers, with action pictures of Joe Louis and Dempsey on front cover.
Contains 208 pictures of Dempsey and 240 of Louis, with text on both of their careers.

320. CARTER, Rubin (Hurricane)
The Sixteenth Round
From No.1 Contender to No.45472.
New York, The Viking Press. 1974.
337pp. plus Carter's Prize-Fighting Record. Illus. The story of the boxer whose identity became hidden behind a State Prison number, in place of the label of top contender for the World Middleweight boxing crown.

321. CASEY, George (Editor)
Sunday Pictorial Sports Parade
London, *Sunday Pictorial* Newspapers Ltd. 1949.
Stiff paper covers, printed on semi-art paper. illustrated.
This book includes boxing articles by Peter Wilson and Nel Tarleton, plus other items on Bruce Woodcock, Freddie Mills, Rinty Monaghan, Tommy Farr, Eddie Thomas and other boxers.

322. CASPER, KREUGER, DORY CO. (Publishers)
Complete Guide to Boxing
Milwaukee, Wisconsin, U.S.A. 1929.

323. CASSELL AND COMPANY (Publishers)
Wonders of Bodily Strength and Skill. In All Ages and All Countries. Translated and Enlarged from the French of Gulliame Depping. With Numerous Illustrations.
London, No Date.
Bound in blue cloth, red decorations on front cover and spine.
Divided into three books, the first of which is entitled "Bodily Strength", including two sections with boxing content:
III — Pugilism among the Ancients
V — Boxing in England
Most of the illustrations are in the text, some of these show pugilistic scenes.

324. CASSELL AND COMPANY LTD (Publishers)
Cassell's Complete Book of Sports and Pasttimes
London, 1896.
The section entitled "Manly Games and Exercises" includes a section of boxing, illustrated by four figures.
Also published in Paris and New York as *Cassell's Book of Sports and Pastimes*

325. CATTARUZZI, Humbert (Al. Williams, pseud)
How to Out-Think Your Opponent, or T.N. tactics for close-in fighting.
San-Francisco, J.J. Newbiggin. 1918
86pp.

326. CATTO, Max
The Flanagan Boy. A Boxing Novel.
London, George G. Harrap & Co. Ltd., 1949.
225pp. The description on the dust-wrapper states, (*inter alia*):
The boxing sequences are described in a manner which vividly reproduces the atmosphere of the boxing booth, with its flares, its eagerness and zest, and the primaeval emotions which govern its occupants.

327. CAULFIELD, James
Portraits, Memoirs and Characters of Remarkable Persons Collected from the most Authentic Accounts Extant
(Four Volumes)
Volume I and II, London, H.R. Young, 1819
Volumes III and IV, London, T.H. Whitely, 1820.
Volumes II and IV include short biographies of James Figg and George Taylor respectively, with a portrait of each.

328. CAVANAGH, Timothy (Ex-Chief Inspector of Police)
Scotland Yard — Past and Present. Experiences of thirty-seven years.
London, Chatto and Windus. 1893.
229pp.
There is reference in this book to Kangaroo, a negro pugilist known as Nat Langham's Black.

329. CAVANAGH, William J.

continued

Instructions on Boxing, both individual and mass for beginners and those who are advanced in the manly art of self-defence; mass boxing as it should be taught to classes of boys or men.

Cornwall, New York. The Cornwall Press Inc 1928.

125pp. Illus.

330. CAXTON PRESS, THE
(Outhwaite Brothers, Printers)

Bronte Society Publications. Vol VI, Part XXXV.

Shipley (Yorks), 1925.

This section includes an article on Patrick Bronte in which an extract is given from a letter sent by him to a friend. This includes a pen and ink sketch of Benjamin Caunt in a fight with Bendigo. There is also a short biographical sketch of each of the contestants.

331. CELEBRATED PUGILIST, A.

The Art and Practice of English Boxing; or Scientific Mode of Defence, Displayed in an Easy Manner, whereby Every Person may comprehend this most Useful Art, without the aid of a Master. To which is added, Descriptions of Pugilistic Attitudes, The Art of Attack and Self Defence, as practised by the Most Celebrated Boxers of the Present Day. Got Up under the Superintendence of a Celebrated Pugilist.

London, Printed and Sold by J. Bailey. ca. 1819.

The frontis. consists of a folding plate showing nine boxing attitudes, drawn by I.R. Cruikshank.

This item was issued in at least four editions during 1819; these varied in that there were slight differences in the layout and the title-pages.

In 1819 J. Bailey published a work entitled *Book of Sports or Man of Spirit's Companion*; this item was made up of twelve pamphlets, including *The Art and Practice of English Boxing*. The text of this is similar to the third edition of the separate work; it includes the folding plate, but has no separate title-page. It is fair to assume that this pamphlet was treated as a fourth edition.

Jon Bee, in an article in the *Annals of Sporting*, Vol. III, No.17 (May 1823), in the section entitled "The Fancy Gazette", suspects that the author of *The Art and Practice of English Boxing etc.* to be Henry Lemoine.

See also *Book of Sports and Man of Spirit's Companion*, 1819; *Art and Practice of Self Defence etc.*, Published by E.T. Fordyce, Newcastle.

332. CELEBRATED PUGILIST, A.

Treatise on the Art and Practice of Self Defence; or Instructions how to obtain a scientific mode of boxing, with the rules to be observed.

London, 1826.

Coloured frontispiece and illustrations.

333. CELEBRATED PUGILIST, A.

Art and Practise of Self Defence; or Scientific Mode of Boxing. Displayed in an Easy Manner, whereby every person may comprehend this most useful Art, without the aid of a Master. To which are added Descriptions of Pugilistic Attitudes. Also the Art of Attack, as practised by Crib, Spring, Deaf Burke, Bendigo, Molyneux, Renwick and other famous Boxers of the Present Day, by a Celebrated Pugilist.

Printed and Sold by W and T Fordyce, 15 Grey Street, Newcastle. ca.1830.

24pp.

The text of this item is very similar to the item published by J. Bailey, but it has no frontispiece.

334. CHAMPION, A.

The Noble Art of Boxing

London, R. March and Co. 1874. price 1d.

Bound in yellow covers.

30pp.

Contents include the Queensberry Rules and the Rules of The Prize-Ring, in addition to instructions on boxing such as Attitude, Leading Off, Counter Hitting, Defence of the Head and other similar chapters.

335. CHANCELLOR, E. Beresford

Life in Regency and Early Victorian Times. An Account of the Days of Brummell and D'Orsay, 1800 to 1850.

London, E. T. Batsford and Co. 1926.

130pp. Illus. including colour frontis.

There are a number of references to pugilism in the text, including the following:—

Chapter VI — Fun and Frolic, some pages dealing with the prize-ring, and including a cut of a prize-fight.

3 of the illustrations are of boxing interest, including Cribb v. Molyneux and The Interior of the Fives Court.

336. CHANCELLOR, E. Beresford

London's Old Latin Quarter. Being an Account of Tottenham Court Road and its Surroundings.

London, Jonathan Cape. 1930.

293pp. Illus.

continued

This book includes mention of some of the very early pugilists such as Figg, Broughton and George Taylor. It identifies the location of hostelries and houses in the area which were kept and frequented by the aforementioned pugilists, and also by Randall, Slack, Stevenson and others, including the poet, Thomas Moore.

337. CHANDLEY, H.G.H.
The Amateur Boxer's Textbook
London, The Amateur Boxing Association, 1945.
51pp. Paper covers. Illus.
Contains instructional chapters and the Rules of Boxing.

338. CHANDLEY, H.G.H. and HEDGER, H.A.
Referee's and Judge's Manual
London, Referee and Judge's Association of the A.B.A., 1962.

339. CHANDLEY, H.G.H.
The Instructor's Guide and Amateur Boxer's Textbook etc.
London, The Amateur Boxing Association, 1965 (Fifth Edition)
63pp. Illus.

340. CHAPMAN and HALL LTD.
(Publishers)
Sport and Athletics in 1908
An Annual Register including the results for the year 1908 (to November) of all the important events in Athletics, Games, and every form of Sport in the United Kingdom etc.
London, 1908.
Includes a section entitled "Boxing", which is divided into sub-sections, each giving results of different competitions or championships, including A.B.A., University, Public Schools, Army and Navy and principal contests at the National Sporting Club. There is also a section entitled "Olympic Games 1908 (Fourth Series) Held in England"; this includes details of the boxing competitions.

341. CHAPPELL, Connery
Two Pleasures For Your Choosing
The World of William Crockford.
London, The Falcon Press, 1951.
226pp.
Part novel, part biography; includes many references to the prize-ring in the days of the Game Chicken, Tom Johnson, Jack Slack, and others, together with stories of gaming on the turf and the dice-table.

342. CHAPPELL and Sons
(Publishers)
The Literary Humbug, or Weekly Take In
London, 1823. (Six weekly issues only).
There was only one volume of this work, with a title change half way through its lifetime, when it became *The Literary Expose*, published by John Miller; the publication ran to six issues under each title. The first issue, under the original name, appeared on May 14th, 1823 and continued until issue No.6 dated June 18th, 1823; Issue No.7 (as *The Literary Expose*) came out on 30th July, 1823 and the final issue (No.12) was dated September 3rd, 1823.
Items on boxing interest appeared in each issue in a section entitled "Sporting Intelligence", giving reports of current prize-fights and other items concerning pugilistic personalities of the period.
Among the battles mentioned were Peter Crawley v. Dick Acton at Blindley Heath, Topsham Joe and Henry the Ostler at Exeter, Israel Belasco's benefit at Birmingham, the great Fight for the Championship between Spring and Neat at Hinckley Down, Randall's Benefit at the Fives Court, and many others.
With the change of name, the first issue of *The Literary Expose* carried the following announcement:
"Our Sporting Intelligence, (which has hitherto given decided satisfaction), will be derived principally from the same sources as before; for when we inform our readers that the majority of our 'milling information' is gleaned from a periodical paper, the sporting department of which is under the care and superintendence of the renowned Pierce Egan, we are convinced on that report they will faithfully place implicit reliance and sporting belief.

343. CHARLES, Wyndham
Champion of the World (Floyd Patterson)
Illus. by Hookway Cowles
Exeter, (Devon), Haldon Books, 1967.
38pp. Illus.

344. CHARTERIS, The Hon. Evan
William Augustus, Duke of Cumberland —
His Early Life and Times, 1721—1748
London, Edward Arnold. 1913.
Chapter XXI "Suppression of the Jacobites" includes a reference to John Broughton, to whom the Duke of Cumberland was known as "Duke William".

345. CHESTER, Joseph Lemuel, F.R.H.S., etc. (Editor and Annotator)
Westminster Abbey Registers
The Marriage, Baptismal and Burial Registers of the Collegiate Church or Abbey of St.

continued

Peter, Westminster.
London, Mitchell and Hughes, Printers,
Wardour Street, 1876.
(Private Edition)

These Registers carry records of the burials of Mrs.
Elizabeth Broughton (wife of John Broughton) on
7th December, 1784, aged 59 years; also the burial
of John Broughton, Yeoman of the Guard, January
21st, 1789, aged 86 years.

346. CHIDSEY, Donald Barr
John the Great
The Life and Times of a Remarkable
American, John L. Sullivan.
Garden City, New York, Doubleday Doran &
Co., 1942.
London, Chapman and Hall, 1947.

335pp.
With an introduction by John P. Marquand.
Bound in green cloth with gilt titles on the spine.
27 Chapters, plus an Appendix and 7 page bibliography and 7 illustrations.

347. CHILD, Harold
(With R. Vaughan Williams)
Hugh the Drover, or Love in the Stocks
A Romantic Ballad Opera in two acts.
London, J. Curwen and Sons Ltd, 1924.
Germanstown (Philadelphia), Curwen Incorp.

This Opera is of pugilistic interest, as a realistic
prize-fight is presented in the finale of Act 1.

348. CHINNERY, H. J.
Sporting Recollections of H.J. Chinnery
From the *Sporting Life* 1909.
Bicester, T. W. Pankhurst, Printer.

52pp.
Includes a section entitled "Boxing"

349. CHOLMONDLEY-PENNEL, H.
Puck on Pegasus.
Illustrated by Leech, Tenniel, Doyle,
Millais and others.
London, Chatto and Windus, 1874.

This book contains two pugilistic poems, "The
Fight for the Championship" (Sayers v. Heenan)
and "The Fight".

350. CHRISTIE, O.F., M.A.
A History of Clifton College, 1860–1934
(Written for the Old Cliftonian Society)
Bristol, W. J. Arrowsmith, 1935.

Includes on pages 315 to 317 – Gymnastics and
Boxing.

351. CLARK, Dudley
Bateman and I in Filmland

Illustrated by H. M. Bateman
London, T. Fisher Unwin, 1926.

91pp. Illus.
The section 'Sport' includes a description of a filmland boxing match and the life of a filmland
boxer.

352. CLARK, Norman
A Technical Comparison of two of the
greatest boxers of recent Times
(Jim Driscoll and Jimmy Wilde)
Foreword by Frank J. Bradley.
London, Published at the offices of the
Mirror of Life and Boxing World, 1918.
This comparison first appeard in the *Mirror
of Life*.

353. CLARK, Norman
Boxing
London, C. Arthur Pearson, 1921.
Foreword by Eugene Corri.

123pp.
Illustrated by twenty figures in the text;

354. CLARK, Norman
How to Box. With an introduction by Frank
Bradley. With Action Photographs of Jim
Driscoll and the Author.

205pp.
London, Methuen and Co., 1922.
12 instructional chapters, with 60 illustrations.

355. CLARK, Norman
(Secretary, British Boxing Board of Control)
The Boxing Referee
London, Methuen and Co. Ltd., 1926.
170pp.
Contains six chapters on the various sets of boxing
rules.

356. CLARK, Norman
All in the Game.
Memoirs of the Ring and other Sporting Ex-
periences.
London, Methuen and Co. Ltd., 1935.
324pp.
Contains several chapters on boxing, including
"The Brummagem Bruisers", "The Golden Age of
Heavyweights", "The Old National Sporting Club"
etc.
Includes a number of boxing illustrations.

356A. CLARK, Tom

continued

The World of Damon Runyon.
With illustrations by the author
New York, Harper and Row Publishers, 1978
291pp. plus a bibliography. Illus.
Damon Runyon, apart from being a syndicated newspaper sports columnist and world-famous writer of short stories, was also a dedicated fight fan, and this publication mentions many of the boxers who were contemporary with him and who inhabited his 'world'. These include Jack Dempsey, Mickey Walker, Harry Greb, Max Baer, James J. Braddock and others.

357. CLARK, W.M. (Publisher)
The "Great" Fight
A Full and Authentic Report of the 'Great' Fight between Charles Freeman, The American Giant, and William Perry, The Tipton Slasher, for £100 a side, on Tuesday, December 6th, 1842; with memoirs of the men.
Published in London, 1842. Price 1d.

358. CLARK, W.M. (Publisher)
British Pluck
London, ca. 1860.
An eight-page pamphlet with the title-page on the front cover.
The title-page shows this item as "Short Sketches of Tom Sayers, the Champion of England and of John C. Heenan the Renowned Benecia Boy", With full-length portraits.

359. CLARKE, Richard S.
Boxing for Boys
A handbook containing valuable information in connection with the Art of Boxing in Clubs and Schools.
Introduction by H.W. Rodgers, Hon. Sec. and Treasurer N.C. A.B.A.
London, Thorsons Publishers Ltd., 1946.
64pp. Illus by the author. Stiff paper covers. Price - 2s 6d.

360. CLARKE, Richard E.
Amateur Boxing. A Handbook for the Amateur Boxer.
London, Thorsons Publishers Ltd. 1948.
104pp. Bound in light brown cloth. Also issued in Paper covers

361. CLARKE, William
(Author of *The Cigar*)
Every Night Book, or Life After Dark
London, T. Richardson and Sherwood and Co., 1827.
192pp.
The Preface states (*inter alia*): we have given

Cribb's and Belcher's as specimens of the sporting houses; Harry Harmer's, Holt's, Randall's, Burn's, Cy Davis's, Hudson's &c &c we deemed it unnecessary to notice.
Space is given in the text to Belcher's Castle Tavern in Holborn and to Cribb's Crib in the Haymarket.

362. CLEAVER, Hylton
Boxing for Schools
(How to Learn It and How to Teach It)
London, Methuen and Co. Ltd., 1934.
133pp.
Illustrated with seventeen figures in the text by Stanley White.

363. CLEAVER, Hylton
Sports Problems – Can we solve them
(150 Intricate Sports Questions and Authentic Rulings)
London, Frederick Warne and Co. Ltd, 1937
64pp.
Includes a number of boxing problems and answers

364. CLEAVER, Hylton
Knight of the Knuckles
(A Boy's story dealing with Boxing)
London, Frederick Warne and Co. 1940.
Coloured Frontis.
256pp.

365. CLEAVER, Hylton
Sporting Rhapsody
London, Hutchinson and Co. (Publishers) Ltd 1951.
(Hutchinson's Library of Sports & Pastimes)
223pp. Illus.
This book contains a number of references to boxing (principally amateur). These include:
Chapter III – From Self Defence to Snobbery
Chapter XIV – These Were the Men (Includes Harry Mallin)
There are 2 boxing illustrations.

366. CLEAVER, Hylton
Danger at the Ringside (Fiction).
London, Hutchinson and Co. 1952
216pp.
The stirring tale of an Oxonian who takes up professional boxing.

367. CLERKE and COCKERAN –
Publishers Ltd. (Publishers)
Every Boy's Book of Sport
London, 1948–1951.
Four editions of this book were published up to 1951; each was designated *Every*

continued

Boy's Book of Sport for the year following the one in which it was published.
Further information is given on the boxing content of each issue:—
Every Boy's Book of Sport for 1949. 190pp.
Meet the Champs
Champions Old and New (with portraits)
Boxing for Beginners
The Champions Show You How (with pictures of Bouts)
They Do Come Out Fighting
The Masked Marvel (fiction)
Man to Man Throughout the Ages (includes Bare-Fist Fighting)

Every Boy's Book of Sport for 1950. 192pp.
The Best in Boxing (with pictures of contemporary boxers)
Training for the Ring
The Fighting Canadian (fiction)
The Story of Freddie Mills
No Gloves — No Limits (includes 'Fighting Farr')

Every Boy's Book of Sport for 1951. 160pp.
The Men Who Decide (Referees and Judges)
Ringcraft (How to Win at Boxing) (illustrated)

Every Boy's Book of Sport for 1952. 140pp.
Stars of the Ring
Fenton Proves His Point (fiction)
Sporting Scrapbook (includes Anecdotes of Jem Mace)

368. CLEVELAND, Harry
Fisticuffs and Personalities of the Prize-Ring
Dedicated to "Harry Preston, A Great Sportsman, This Book is Dedicated by His Friend, The Author"
London, Sampson Low, Marston and Co. Ltd. (1924)
208pp.
Frontis. showing a five-part composite picture of John Broughton.
Harry Cleveland was a well-known Birmingham sporting journalist, who sometimes wrote under the pseudonym of 'Pal'; he contributed a weekly column to *Boxing* magazine for a number of years. Mr. Cleveland's book consists of three parts, each referring to a group of pugilists by identifying them with a trade or profession, or with their own personal characteristics. Examples of these are given as follows:
Battling Basket-Makers, - - Bellicose Boatmen, - - Combative Costers, - - Scrapping Shoemakers, - - Colossean Battlers, - - Pugilists who were Un-defeated, - - Titanic Punchers, etc.
On the title-page of his book, Harry Cleveland is stated to be the author of the following works:

"A Short History of English and American Champions"
"Old Time Mills"
"Glove Contests Re-Told"
"Gossip About Famous Pugilists"

"Noted Black Country Fighters"
It is unlikely that these were published as separate items; it is more likely that they were published in newspapers, as a series of articles under each title.

369. CLIFFORD, Arthur
Smoky Arena. A Novel of Prize-Fighting
London, Hodder and Stroughton Ltd., 1952
192pp.
Bound in red cloth, black titles on spine.
15 chapters.

370. CLOUGH, James
Charles Blake Cochran. (Lord Bountiful)
London, Pallas Publishing Co. Ltd. 1938.
(How They Did It Series)
Chapter III "War and Post War" contains reference to Mr. Cochran's boxing activities, including prom-otions at Holborn Stadium and Olympia.

371. COBB, Irvin S.
A Laugh a Day Keeps the Doctor Away
His Favourite Stories, as told by the Author
Garden City, New York, Garden City
Publishing Co. Inc., 1923.
246pp.
Includes the following pugilistic items:
Section 41 –
One Detail was missing (Jack Johnson and James J. Jeffries)
Section 139 –
Not Listed among the Leading Ones Anyway
(The Willard v. Dempsey Fight)
Section 253 –
Hail and Farewell.(Boxing in a Small Town in Ohio)
Section 272 –
There was No Hurry about it. (Negro prize-Fighter)
Section 338 –
The Proper Rate of Exchange. (Anecdote by Charles E. Van Loon about boxing at a little town just over the International boundary be-tween Mexico and California.)

372. COBBETT, Martin
The Man on the March
London, Bliss, Sands and Co. 1895.
370pp.
This book contains many references to pugilism and boxing, particularly in Chapter IV "On Boxing".

373. COBBETT, Martin
("Geraint" of *The Referee*)
Sporting Notions, of Present Days and Past.
Edited by Alice Cobbett (daughter of the Author)
Edinburgh and London, Sands and Co.
366pp.
This includes:
Chapter II – Boxing

continued

Chapter III – Boxers

374. COCHRAN, Charles B.
Secrets of a Showman
London, William Heinemann Ltd., 1925.
486pp. Illus.
Bound in white cloth, lettered in red and black on front cover and spine.
The Foreword is by James Agate and this gives some examples of C.B. Cochran's ventures into boxing promotion, with the financial results.
Two chapters of the book are devoted entirely to boxing, as follows:
Chapter 26 –
Tells of C.B. Cochran's early promotions at Holborn Stadium, commencing with Beckett v. Wells in 1919.
Chapter 27 –
Gives details of Cochran's bid to promote the Dempsey v. Carpentier bout, and why he finally gave up boxing promotion.
The illustrations include cartoons and pictures of boxing personalities, including Joe Beckett, B.J. Angle and Georges Carpentier.

375. COCHRAN, Charles B.
I Had Almost Forgotten
With a Preface by A.P. Herbert.
London, Hutchinson and Co. (Publishers) Ltd., 1932.
304pp.
Illustrated.
Includes a number of boxing references telling of Cochran's experiences as a boxing promoter, mentioning Young Griffo, Joe Walcott, the Milligan v. Walker match, etc.
The boxing illustrations include J.L. Sullivan, Jim Corbett, Mickey Walker and Tommy Milligan.

376. COCHRAN, Charles B.
Cock-A-Doodle-Doo
London, J.M. Dent and Sons Ltd., 1941.
386pp. Illus.
Includes references to boxing, notably in chapters II, III, XI, XIII and XV.

377. COCHRAN, C.B.
Showman Looks On
London, J.M. Dent and Sons Ltd., 1945.
Reprinted in 1946.
323pp. Illus.
Bound in blue cloth.
Contains items of boxing interest, principally as follows:
Chapter II – Brighton Front. (The Marquess of Queensberry)
Chapter V – Early Days in America. (Pugilism, Friendship with Jim Corbett, etc.)
Chapter VI – America on Business and on Holiday. (My First World Championship – Freddie Welsh and Willie Ritchie, – Tex Rickard, etc.)
Chapter VIII – Beauty in Woman. (Marquess of Ailesbury and Abington Baird)

Chapter XVI – Celebrities of the Ring. (The lucky Carpentier – Jack Dempsey – The Wily Doc Kearns)
Chapter XVII – Farewell to Boxing Promotion. (Outstanding Personalities, etc.)
Chapter XVIII – A Wrestling Interlude. (Hackenschmidt and Ahmed Madrali)
Chapter XIX – Last Faces (Lord Lonsdale – Black versus White).

378. COE, Charles Francis
Knockout. A Boxing Novel.
London, Hutchinson and Co. Ltd., 1938.
254pp.
Dedicated "To a lad whose courage carried him beyond the Styx, my friend Ernie Schaaf, I dedicate this book".
Ernie Schaaf died after being beaten by Primo Carnera, and was booed as he was carried from the ring in a coma. A fictionalised account of this incident appears in Budd Schulberg's novel *The Harder They Fall*. (q.v.).

379. COEBURN, Joe
Elliott's Guide to the Art of Boxing
London, 1864.
The author was possibly Joe Coburn, born in Middleton, County Armagh (Ireland), who fought Jem Mace.

380. COHANE, Tim
Bypaths of Glory
A Sportswriter Looks Back.
New York, Harper and Row Publishers, 1963.
Includes three chapters on boxing; reminiscing on Rocky Marciano, Dempsey, Tunney, Archie Moore, and others.

381. COHEN, O.R.
Kid Tinsel. A Boxing Novel.
New York City, Appleton-Century Co.,1941.
281pp.

381A. COHN, Albert M., B.A. (Oxon)
A Bibliographical Catalogue of the Printed Works Illustrated by George Cruikshank
London, Longmans Green and Co., 1914.
226pp.
This volume contains brief details of boxing items illustrated by George Cruikshank, among which are the following:
Annals of Sporting and Fancy Gazette, Bell's Life in London, The Sporting Mirror
The works of Harrison Ainsworth and Pierce Egan.

382. COHN, Albert M., B.A. (Oxon)
George Cruikshank. A Catalogue Raisonne of the work executed during the years 1806-1877, with Collations, Notes, Approximate Values, Facsimiles and Illustrations.
London, Published from the Office of *The Bookman's Journal*, 1924.
(Limited to 500 numbered copies)

continued

375pp. Illus.
This work contains details of a number of boxing items.
Part III, entitled "Caricatures and Separate Prints", includes a number of subjects of pugilistic interest.

383. COKE, The Hon. Henry J.
Tracks of a Rolling Stone
London, Smith Elder and Co., 1905 (2nd Edition). (Enlarged).
368pp.
Bound in red cloth, lettered in gold on front cover and spine. 48 untitled chapters.
Chapter XLII describes the fight between Tom Sayers and J.C. Heenan, at which the author was present.

384. COKES, C. and KAYSER, H.
The Complete Book of Boxing for Fighters and Fight Fans
Palm Springs (California), ETC Publications, 1980.
144pp.

385. COLE, William (Editor)
The Best of A.J. Liebling
London, Methuen, 1965.
First published in New York by Simon and Schuster under the title *The Most of A.J. Liebling.*
358pp.
Liebling, possibly the most famous of all American contributors to *The New Yorker*, was an ardent boxing enthusiast and wrote much about the ring. Herein are two of his finest pieces, "Fun-Lover", about Sonny Liston, and "Ahab and Nemesis", dealing with the contest between Rocky Marciano and Archie Moore.

386. COLLINS, Mike E. (Editor)
Ring Battles of the Ages
Minneapolis (Minnesota), Boxing Book Publishing Co., 1932.
Illustrated paper covers, 20 illus., plus some cuts in the text. 48pp. including covers.
The book opens with an introduction "Meet Mike Collins, Editor and Ring Authority"; it then proceeds, chapter by chapter to relate a history of boxing from the use of the cestus through the period to 1932.

387. COLMAN, C.S. and WINDSOR, A.H. (Editors)
The Sportsman's Year Book
(With Contributions from Various Hands)
London, Laurence and Bullen, 1899.
This includes a section: Boxing (Amateur).

388. COMBAT ANNUAL (Publishers)

Combat Annual
London, 1947 and 1948.
This annual was made up of bound issues of the *Combat* magazine. The first annual, issued in 1948 included numbers 1 to 12, to February 1948, and the second issue consisted of numbers 13 to 21, March to November 1948.
Each issue of the magazine contained 20 pages, devoted mainly to boxing and wrestling.

389. COMPTON and RITCHIE (Printers)
The Young Sportsman's Miscellany
London, 1826.
This little book comprises three parts, each entitled "The Young Sportsman's Magazine" and dated respectively:
  September 1 – 1823
  October 1 – 1823
  November 1 – 1823
It will be noted that the three parts are dated 1823, while the complete work is dated 1826. It is possible that it started life as a periodical in 1823 as *The Young Sportsman's Pocket Magazine* and ran only to three numbers, leaving the printer with a number of unsold copies on his hands; these being later provided with a title-page for each set of three issues and marketed as a book under the title of *The Young Sportsman's Miscellany.*
Each of the monthly sections has a sub-section entitled "Pugilism" which gives results of some ring battles fought during the month; some of these include a short report on the fight.

390. CONNORS, Chuck (Mayor of Chinatown)
Bowery Life
New York, Richard K. Fox Publishing Co., 1904.
Red Paper Covers. Price 50 cents.
Illustrated by photographic pictures.
The text includes "One way to train".

391. CONNORS, Professor James
Illustrated History of the Great Corbett-Sullivan ring battle at New Orleans, Sept. 7th, 1892, for the Heavyweight Championship of the World and a purse and stake of $ 45.000.
Every legitimate hit scored by the contestants.
Buffalo, (U.S.A.), Press of the Courier Co., cop. 1892.

392. CONPRESS PRINTING LTD.

continued

(Printers and Publishers)
Vic Patrick. The Champ.
(*Daily Telegraph* Sports Book No.3)
Sydney (N.S.W.), (1946)

Stiff paper covers. Pictures of Vic Patrick and
Ronnie James on front and back covers respectively. Illus.

393. CONSIDINE, Robert Bernard

It's All News To Me. A Reporter's Depos-
ition.
New York, Meredith Press, 1967.
150pp.

394. CONSOLIDATED PRESS LIMITED
(Publishers)

The Daily Telegraph Sports Year Book. 1948.
Sydney, (N.S.W.)

256pp. Stiff paper covers with many sports illus-
trations on front cover, including boxing.
This item has a boxing section which includes
World Champions, Australian Champions (includ-
ing amateur and professional) together with
Empire Games Champions.
Similar *Sports Year Books* were issued by the same
publisher in 1949 and 1950.

395. CONSTABLE, Thomas

Archibald Constable and His Literary Corres-
pondents. A Memorial by his son.
Edinburgh, Edmonston and Douglas, 1873.
Three volumes.

Volume 1 contains an account of the fight between
Jem Belcher and Tom Cribb, as given by Alex
Gibson Hunter, Forfarshire laird and Edinburgh
bookseller, who was present at the fight.

396. CONSTABLE and COMPANY LIMITED
(Publishers)

The Victoria History of the Counties of
England
First published in volumes in London in
1902; first issued in parts in 1920.
Constable and Company were the original
publishers, but from 1923 the work was
published by St. Catherine Press (W.H.
Smith and Son Ltd) and in 1938 the pub-
lication passed to the Oxford University
Press.

A number of the *Victoria County Histories* contained a "Sport" section, and when the *History*
was issued in parts in 1920 this section formed a
separate part.
The "Sport" section of the following counties
contained a sub-section dealing with, or referring
to, pugilism:
A History of Berkshire
    Edited by F.H. Ditchfield, M.A., F.S.A., and
    William Page. (First issued in volume form

in 1906).
    Page 16 "Pugilism" by the Rev. P.H. Ditchfield.

A History of the County of Hereford
    Edited by William Page, F.S.A. (first issued in
    volume form in 1920).
    Part 16 Sport, "Pugilism", by Charles T. Part,
    M.A., D.L., J.P., Bob Grimston (including his
    portrait).

A History of the County of Lancaster
    Edited by William Farrer, D.Litt., and J.Brown-
    hill, M.A. (first published in volume form in
    1908).
    Part 16 Sport, Edited by The Rev. E.E.Dowling
    M.A., F.S.A. "Wrestling" by Major Arthur
    Willoughby-Osbourne (contains references to
    some old Lancashire pugilists).

A History of the County of Middlesex
    Edited by William Page, F.S.A. (first published
    in volume form in 1911, 2 volumes).
    Volume II includes "Sport Ancient and
    Modern" containing a section on Boxing by
    C.J.B. Marriott, M.A.; this refers to pugilists
    from James Figg to Jem Smith, the Pelican
    Club etc. There is also mention of Canon J.J.
    McCormick, D.D., the Cambridge Double
    Blue, who in his University days could hold his
    own with the scientific Langham and other
    leading Professionals.

A History of the County of Nottingham
    (First published in 1910) (2 Volumes)
    The section "Old Time Sports", is in volume 2
    of this book and it includes mention of Sir
    Thomas Parkyn's "Inn Play or Cornish Hugg
    Wrestler".

397. CONTEH, John

I Conteh. An Autobiography.
London, Hatchards, 1982.
152pp. Illus.

398. CONTEST PUBLICATIONS
(Publishers)

Tense Moments
Hanley, (Stoke-on-Trent), June 1952.

48pp. Illus. paper covers. Price 2s. Vol.1, No.1.
The proceeds from the sale of this item were used
in aid of the Professional Boxers' Association.
Foreword by W. Barrington Dalby. The contents
consisted of a number of articles by well-known
boxers and people connected with the sport; ex-
amples of these are given as follows:
Introduction by Laurie Buxton
Gloves Against Granite, by Len Harvey
He Fouled But Failed, by Kid Berg
A Date at Madison Square Garden, by Dave
    Crowley
The Fight That Thrilled the World, by Nat
    Fleischer
Delayed Delivery, by Jackie Rankin, etc.

**399. COOK, Theodore Andrea, and
NICKOLLS, Guy**
Thomas Doggett, Deceased
A Famous Comedian.
London, Archibald Constable and Co., 1908.
156pp. Illus.
This item is divided into two parts:
Part I – "The Man", by T.A. Cook, and
Part II – "The Race", by Guy Nickolls
Part II, Chapter XII, includes a section on John
Broughton, winner of the Doggett's Coat and
Badge in 1730; with a portrait of Broughton.
There are also references to Lyons, Champion
Pugilist in 1769, B.J. Angle, the famous referee,
and to Tom King, the pugilist.

400. COOK, Theodore Andrea
International Sport
A Short History of the Olympic Movement
from 1896 to the Present Day.
Containing an Account of a Visit to Athens
in 1906 and of the Olympic Games in 1908
in London, Together with the Code of Rules
for Twenty Different Forms of Sport and
Numerous Illustrations.
London, Constable and Co. Ltd., 1910.
Includes a number of references to boxing, among
them the following:
Chapter XIV – The Amateur Definition (Page
180, Boxing)
Chapter XVI – The Royal Oakleaves, Prizewinners
in the Olympics of 1908 (Page 203, Boxing)
Chapter XVII – First Rate Performances (Page 228,
Boxing)
Appendix IV – The Rules of Sport (Page 33,
Boxing)
The illustrations include a picture of A.L. Oldman
(City Police), Gold Medal Heavyweight Boxing,
1908.

401. COOPER, Henry
Henry Cooper, An Autobiography
London, Cassell and Co., 1972.
184pp. including Cooper's record. Illus.

402. COOPER, Henry
The Great Heavyweights
London, Hamlyn Publishing Group Ltd.,
1978.
176pp. Illus. 4to.

403. COOPER, Henry
Henry Cooper's Book of Boxing
London, Arthur Barker Ltd., 1982.
168pp. Illus.
This book is part instructional, with additional
chapters on various aspects of the fight game.
There are two chapters on those judged by Henry
to have been the Greatest Characters of His Time.

404. COOPER, Henry
H for 'enry
More than just an Autobiography.
London, Willow Books, 1984.
135pp. Illus.

405. COOPER, Henry
Henry Cooper's Most Memorable Fights
London, Stanley Paul and Co. Ltd., 1985.
192pp. Illus.

**406. COOPER, R. and PAGE, R.
(Engravers)**
Fifty Wonderful Portraits
A Gallery of Eccentrics, with eight pages of
text, giving   a short description of each
person.
London, 1824. 4to.
This work portrays fifty rather unusual characters,
including John Broughton (Pugilist), and Henry
Lemoine (Eccentric Bookseller and Author),
author of *Modern Manhood, or the Art and
Practice of English Boxing.* (q.v.)

407. CORBET, Henry
Tales and Traits of Sporting Life
London, Rogerson and Tuxford, 1864.
202pp.
Coloured frontispiece and title page.
The foreword states:
"These papers have been collected from the
columns of *Bell's Life in London* and *All the Year
Round*, in which works they originally appeared."
The book includes a section on John Gully.

408. CORBETT, J.J.
New Ideas of Boxing
New York, Springer and Welty Co., 1894.
47pp. Illus.

409. CORBETT, James J.
Scientific Boxing
Together with Hints and Training and the
Official Rules.
(Fox's Authletic Library No.9)
Photographic poses by Jimmy Britt, Frankie
Neil and Kid Murphy, George McFadden and
Danny Duane.
New York, Richard K. Fox, 1905.
128pp. Illus.
Red stiff paper covers, lettered in black and white;
action portraits of Jim Corbett on front cover.
This book contains an Introduction and 25 instruc-
tional sections, a section on fouls, Rules for
Boxing and many illustrations.
Another edition was issued by the Padell Book
and Magazine Co., New York City, in 1944.

410. CORBETT, James J.
My Life and Fights
(Edited by Frederic A. Felton)
London, John Ousely, 1910.
125pp. Illus.

411. CORBETT, James J.
The Roar of the Crowd
The True Tale of the Rise and Fall of a
Champion.
London and New York, G.P. Putnam's Sons,
The Knickerbocker Press, 1925. (Copyright
1925 by James J. Corbett, 1st Printing
February 1925, 2nd Printing April 1925.)
329pp. Illus.
Bound in green cloth, gilt titles on cover and spine.

Another edition was issued in 1926 by
Garden City Publishing Co., New York. This
was bound in red cloth, with black lettering
on cover and spine.
The book is made up of 21 chapters, with
17 illustrations.
This book was re-issued in a Sportsmans
Book Club edition in 1953.

412. CORBETT, Young
(W.H. Rothwell)
How to Punch the Bag
New York, The American Sports Publishing
Co., 1906.
London, The British Sports Publishing Co.,
1906.
A revised and enlarged edition was issued in
1927.

413. CORDELL, Alexander
Peerless Jim
London, Hodder and Stoughton, 1984.
368pp.
A fictional account of the life and times of the
great Welsh-born boxer, Jim Driscoll, written somewhat in the style of A.G. Hales in his much earlier
Black Prince Peter: an approach to biography
which later came to be known as "faction".

414. CORINTHIAN
(Of the *Daily Chronicle* and *Lloyd's Weekly*
***News*)**
Our Famous Boxers, Their Virtues and Their
Faults.
London, Simpkin Marshall, Hamilton Kent
and Co., 1916.
101pp.
Bound in paper covers. Illustrated with 16 plates.
This book consists of a series of articles in which

the merits and demerits of many contemporary
boxers are discussed, including the following:
Billy Wells, Johnny Basham, Freddie Welsh,
Jimmy Wilde, Kid Lewis, Pat O'Keefe, Willie
Farrell, Digger Stanley, Llew Edwards, Dick Smith,
Jim Sullivan, Joe Bowker, Owen Moran, Harry
Curzon, D.C.M., Young Fox, Johnny Summers,
Bill Beynon, Curly Walker, Seaman Hayes, Percy
Jones, Jim Driscoll and others.
The illustrations include some action photos of
these boxers.

415. CORRI, Eugene
Boxing
London, Heath Robinson and J. Burch Ltd.
(Hearth and Home Library No.9)
A thirty-page booklet.

416. CORRI, Eugene
Thirty Years a Boxing Referee
With Foreword by the Earl of Lonsdale.
London, Edward Arnold, 1915.
266pp. Illus.
13 chapters, 16 illus.
This book deals with many boxers who were
active during the author's thirty years of
refereeing; these include:
Johnny Summers
Carpentier v. Gunboat Smith
Bombardier Wells
Slavin v. Jackson
Willie Ritchie and Freddie Welsh
Tommy Burns
Matt Wells
Jimmy Wilde
and others
The second edition of this book was issued under
the title *Refereeing 1000 Fights*, 1919 (q.v.)

417. CORRI, Eugene
Refereeing 1000 Fights. Reminiscences of
Boxing.
London, C. Arthur Pearson, 1919.
190pp. Illus.
A note on the verso of the title page says: "The
First Edition of this book was published in 1915
under the title 'THIRTY YEARS A BOXING
REFEREE'. Second Edition 1919".
These memoirs deal with many famous boxers
who were active in the early part of the 20th
century, including Johnny Summers, Carpentier,
Gunboat Smith, Bombardier Wells, Bob
Fitzsimmons, Willie Ritchie and Freddie Welsh,
Matt Wells, Johnny Basham, and others.
There are 4 illustrations.

418. CORRI, Eugene
Gloves and the Man. The Romance of the
Ring.
London, Hutchinson and Co. (Publishers)

continued

Ltd., 1928.

288pp. 16 Illus. Bound in black cloth. Gilt titles. This book gives wide coverage of the boxing scene, boxers and boxing personalities, from the 1890's to the date of publication.

The subjects include: Slavin v. Jackson, Carpentier, Bombardier Wells, Joe Beckett, Charlie Smith, Milligan and Moore, Phil Lolosky, Tommy Noble, Elky Clarke, Alf Mancini, Johnny Summers, Johnny Sullivan, the two Lens, (Harvey and Johnson), Teddy Baldock, Billy Bird, Harry Corbett, Johnny Curley, Jim Driscoll, Kid Socks, Ernie Rice, and many others.

419. CORRI, Eugene
Fifty Years in the Ring
London, Hutchinson and Co. (Publishers) Ltd., 1933.

256pp. Illus.
Contains the author's reminiscences as a boxing referee and devotee of the sport, covering the period from the meeting of Slavin and Jackson ("The Greatest Heavyweight Fight I Ever Saw") to the days of Dempsey and Tunney.

420. CORRIS, P.R.
Lords of the Ring
Australia, Cassell and Co., 1980.
200pp. Illus.

420A. CORRY, Eoghan
(Of the *Sunday Tribune*)
McGuigan. The Unauthorised Biography.
Dublin, Magill Publishers Ltd., 1985.
191pp. Illus. Stiff paper covers.

421. COSELL, Howard
Cosell
Written with the editorial assistance of Mickey Herskowitz.
Chicago (Illinois), The Playboy Press, 1973.
390pp. Illus.
The author is reputed to be the best sports commentator of this or any other time. This is his autobiography.
Among the boxing content is a chapter on Muhammad Ali.

422. COSELL, Howard
Like It Is
Chicago (Illinois), The Playboy Press, 1974.
305pp.
These further memoirs of the famous sports commentator include some boxing.

423. COTGREAVE, A.
(F.R. Hist. Soc., Chief Lib. West Ham Public Libraries)
A Contents-Subject Index

London, Elliott Stock and West Ham Public Libraries.

Entries on Boxing and Pugilism include dates of relevant articles and essays on the sport in various magazines and periodicals.

424. COTTRELL, John
Man of Destiny
The Story of Muhammad Ali/Cassius Clay
London, Frederick Muller Ltd., 1967.
354pp. Illus.

425. COUNTRY and SPORTING PUBLICATIONS LTD. (Publishers)
Sporting Record Sports Annual, 1949–1950
London, 1949.

Bound in grey cloth; printed on art paper.
Introduction by W.T. Mann (Managing Editor of *Sporting Record*).
The annual is divided into sections, each dealing with a different sport; each section has a short introduction, but otherwise consists chiefly of illustrations.
The introduction to the boxing section is by Len Harvey and is entitled "Many Titles Change Hands"; this includes 18 boxing illustrations.
A similar annual, from the same publishers, was issued in 1950 under the title *Sporting Record Sports Annual 1950–51*.
This issue was bound loose-leaf style in red boards.
The foreword to the boxing section is by Harry Carpenter and includes 13 illustrations.

426. COUNTRY and SPORTING PUBLICATIONS LTD. (Publishers)
Sporting Record Junior Annual — Sports Thrills
London, 1950.

Bound in coloured boards. Illus. front cover.
Includes an article by Trevor Wignall: "According to the Queensberry Rules", with 5 boxing illustrations.

427. COUPER, John Robertson
Mixed Humanity. A Story of Camp Life in South Africa.
London, W.H. Allen (Publishers to the India Office), 1892. Price 6s.
A cheaper edition was issued in 1893, price 2s.
400pp.
Bound in red cloth, lettered in gold on front cover and spine.
This book is a novel of 47 chapters with a frontis. and 7 plates; it contains a quantity of boxing material.
The author was born in Edinburgh about 1853 and had a varied career before settling in South Africa where he taught boxing and fought for the championship of the country. He fought and won
continued

against Wolf Bendoff for a purse of £4000 and side bets. Couper lost the money in speculations and committed suicide in 1897.

428. COWDEN-CLARKE, Charles and Mary
Recollections of Writers
London, Sampson Low, Marston, Searle and Rivington, 1878.
A second edition was published in the same year.

347 pp.
This book includes a section devoted to John Keats in which the poet describes to John Cowden-Clarke a prize-fight between "the two most skillful lightweights of the day", Randall and Turner, which took place on December 5th, 1818 at Crawley Down.
Randall defeated Turner in 34 rounds, extending to 2 hours 19 min.

429. COX, William D. (Editor)
Boxing in Art and Literature
New York, Reynal and Hitchcook, 1936.

227pp. Illus.
Bound in green cloth, 4to. 45 illus.
This anthology of boxing contains extracts from 37 literary works, including those of Homer, Plato, Artistotle and modern authors such as J.B. Priestley and Ernest Hemingway.
The illustrations show ancient marble and bronze statues of boxers and also reproductions of old prints.

438. CRAWFORD, Morris De Camp
Come-Back. A Boxing Novel.
New York, Milton Balch and Co., 1925.
309pp.

439. CRITCHLEY, Macdonald
Punch Drunk Syndromes: The Chronic Traumatic Encephalopathy of Boxers
Paris, Maloine, Editeur, rue de l'Ecole de Medecine, 1949.
London, Printed by Solicitors' Law Stationery Society.
14pp. Paper covers

440. CROOKES, C.
A Monody on the Death of Dan Donnelly, Late Champion of Ireland
Dublin, 1820.
22pp.

441. CROOME, A.C.M. (Editor)
Fifty Years of Sport at Oxford and Cambridge and the Great Public Schools.
Arranged by the Right Hon. Lord Desborough of Taplow, K.C.V.O.
London, Walter Southwood and Co. Ltd., 1913. (Two volumes)

4to. Bound in full crimson morocco, gilt titles and decorations.
Volume II includes "Boxing and Fencing" and "Biographies of Blues, Half-Blues and Others", including many University Boxers.
Illustrations in Volume II include W.G. Gubian (Cambridge), G.D. Dewar (Oxford) and G.W.V. Hopley (Cambridge).

442. CROSS, Thomas
(Stage Coach Proprietor)
Autobiography of a Stage Coachman
London, Hurst and Blackett, 1861. (Three Volumes)

Volume III gives references to pugilism and the death of Brighton Bill following his fight with Owen Swift in 1838.
A two-volume edition was issued in 1904 by Kegan Paul, Trench, Trubner and Co. Ltd., with forty-two plates (none of pugilistic subjects). This edition was limited to 500 copies and included the chapter with boxing interest from the first edition.

443. CROUSE, Russell
Mr Currier and Mr Ives
A Note on Their Lives and Times
New York Garden City Publishing Co. Inc., 1936, with 32 illus. in colour and in black and white.

138pp.
Dedicated to Nathaniel Currer and James Merritt Ives.
The prints from which the pictures appearing in this book were made are from the famous Currer and Ives collection owned by Mr. Harry T. Peters.
Includes in Chapter XI "My Hat and Fisticuffs" a short life history of John Morrissey, The American Champion, who defeated John C. Heenan.
The plates include one each of Tom Sayers and John Morrissey.

444. CRUIKSHANK, Robert
(Assisted by his Brother)
Emblematical Synopsis of Life in London
London, W.I. Moncrieff, July 1826.

An etching with a background representing different sports: Hunting, Bull-baiting, Boxing, Running, etc., with taverns on either side and with Tom and Jerry with the Prize Cup in the foreground.

445. CRUIKSHANK, R.J.
The Roaring Century, 1846–1946
London, Hamish Hamilton, 1946.

Includes reference to boxing as follows:
Chapter XIII The Rise of Sport
Chapter III The Corinthian Fancy

446. CUMING, E.D.

Squire Osbaldeston: His Autobiography
Edited (with Commentary) by E.D.Cuming.
Introduction by Sir Theodore Cook.
London, John Lane The Bodley Head Ltd.,
March 1926.
New York, Charles Scribner's Sons, 1926.
Reprinted, March 1926, April 1926, July
1926.
All the above editions were size 11 x 9ins.
A further edition in smaller format was
issued in 1927.
All the larger editions contain 16 illus-
trations in colour and 75 illustrations in
black and white, with a map.
The 1927 edition includes only 6 black and
white illustrations.
248pp.
This book contains many references to pugilists
and prize-fighting, among which are the following:
Chapter XII – (*inter alia*) Accidents at the Spring-
Langan fight
Chapter XIV – (*inter alia*) Reed v. Paddy Gill,
Johnny Broome v. Bungaree, Harry Broome v.
The Slasher, Harry Broome v. Orme, Mackeye
v. Byrne
The following references occur in the Commentary
by E.D. Cuming:
Chapter II – (*inter alia*) A Side Show at the Hunt
Ball, Belcher and Richmond give an exhibition
of the pugilistic science at the Green Dragon,
Lincoln
Chapter V – Scenes at the Spring v. Langan fight
Chapter VI – The Squire's debut as a referee in
the Prize-Ring, Cannon v. Hudson, Mackaye v.
Byrne, Fatal Results of the Fight, Ben Caunt
v. Bendigo, Thieves at Prize-Fights.
The illustrations include many pictures and
portraits of the Squire and one plate of pugilistic
interest: "The Fight between Spring and Langan
on Worcestershire Racecourse, January 7th,
1824, for the Championship of England".

447. CURTIS, James

The Gilt Kid. A Novel.
London, Jonathan Cape, 1936.
293pp.

448. CURTIS, James

There Ain't No Justice. A Novel.
London, Jonathan Cape, 1937.
283pp.
The "Author's Note" says:—
It should be understood that the Boxers' Union
and the British Boxing Board of Control have
remedied, if not eradicated, many of the abuses
which spoil a noble sport and which are touched
on in this novel.
If, however, the author succeeds in gaining for the
small-time preliminary boy any ventilation of his
grievances he will be more than happy.

449. CUTLER, Charles

A Miracle of Grace. The Life Story of
Charles Cutler, The Converted Boxer.
London, Published by the author, 1928.
85pp.
So far as can be ascertained from the book, Charles
Cutler did not box in organised contests in rec-
ognised arenas. He states that he was a public
house and booth fighter; the conversion mentioned
in the sub-title took place when he gave up drink-
ing and fighting and took up religion.
Although most of the text consists of repentance
for his previous conduct, mention is made of Jem
Smith, Jake Kilrain, Alf Greenfield and Peter
Jackson.

450. CUTTER, Bob

The Rocky Marciano Story
New York, Twayne Publishers Inc., 1954.
79pp.

451. DAGLEY, R.

Death's Doings. Consisting of numerous Original Compositions in Prose and Verse, The Friendly Contributions of various Writers, Principally Intended as Illustrations of Twenty Four Plates, Designed and Etched by R. Dagley.

London, 1826.

Second edition, with considerable additions, London, J. Andrews and W. Cole, 1827. (2 volumes)

Boston, (U.S.A.), Charles Ewer, 1828. (From the 2nd edition)

The work includes 2 items of prize-ring interest:
1 – "Death in the Ring", by S. Maunder, illustrated by a plate
2 – "The Fancy", by A. Querist

452. *DAILY MAIL*, The (Publishers)

Daily Mail – News In Our Time – Golden Jubilee Book of the *Daily Mail*, 1896–1946.

Includes boxing items:, Carpentier knocked out Beckett, 1923; a page of sporting cartoons by Tom Webster, including boxing.

453. DAISY BANK PRINTING AND PUBLISHING CO. (Publishers)

Boxing or the Art of Self Defence
Manchester, 1905. (Daisy Bank Publication No.28)

32pp. Boxing picture on front cover.
Contains four photographic illustrations of contemporary boxers.

454. DAKIN, Wally

(Eastern Counties Middleweight Champion, 1927–1931)

The Beginning of Instruction for an Aspiring Boxer. (Boxing Essential for Self Defence) Recommended and with a Foreword by Jimmy Wilde.

White paper covers. Illus. price 2s.

455. DALBY, W. Barrington

(Star Referee and Boxing Expert)

Famous Last Rounds
Foreword by Raymond Glendenning
London, Hood Pearson Publications Ltd., 1947.

63pp. Illus. paper covers, 12 illus.
20 chapters, including: The Boon-Danahar Epic, Jack Petersen Breaks Through, A Memorable Evening at the White City, The Mizler Classic, etc.

456. DALBY, W. Barrington

Come in Barry
With a Preface by W. Onslow Fane, President British Boxing Board of Control.
London, Cassell and Co. Ltd., 1961.

168pp. Illus.
Reminiscences of fifty years in the boxing game, as referee and broadcaster.

457. DANE, Elliott

Crime Takes the Count
(A Background Sports-Crime Novel)
London, Background Books Ltd., 1949.

123pp. Paper covers.

458. DANIEL, Daniel M.

(Associate Editor of *The Ring*)

The Mike Jacobs Story
New York City, *The Ring* Bookshop, 1950.

128pp. Illus. Bound in black cloth. Also issued in soft covers.
Introduction entitled "Curtain Raiser", by Nat Fleischer.
Previously published in serial form in *The Ring* magazine.
8 chapters and numerous illustrations, spanning the career of Mike Jacobs, ex-colleague of Tex Rickard, and later head of the Twentieth Century Sporting Club and world's leading boxing promoter.

459. DANZIG, Allison, and BRANDWEIN, Peter (Editors)

Sport's Golden Age
a Close-Up of the Fabulous Twenties
New York, Harper and Brothers, 1948.

296pp. Illus.
The boxing items include:
"The Golden Panorama", by Grantland Rice,
"Boxing", by James P. Dawson
There are 3 boxing illustrations, showing Dempsey v. Tunney, and Dempsey v. Firpo.

460. DANZIG, Allison, and BRANDWEIN, Peter

The Greatest Sports Stories form the *New York Times*. Sports Classics of a Century.
New York, A.S. Barnes and Co., 1951.

This work, including the introduction, contains a number of boxing items; these are divided into three periods:

The First Fifty Years (1851–1900)
The In-Between Period (1901–1919)
The Golden Age of Sport (1920–1930)
In Sport's Golden Age (1931–1951)
the stories being of boxers and bouts during those periods.
There are 5 boxing illustrations.

461. DARTNELL, Fred (Long Melford)

continued

I

"Seconds Out!" Chats about Boxers, Their Trainers and Patrons. With a Preface by Georges Carpentier.
London, T. Werner Laurie Ltd., 1924.
276pp. Illus.
The chapter headings include: Trainers and Methods, Sparring Partners, Manager and Boxers, Coloured Fighters, etc.
An American edition of this book was published in Chicago in 1925. The title was also included (abridged and unillustrated) in the Mellifont Sports Series, No. 15. (q.v.)

462. DARWIN, Bernard (Editor)
The Game's Afoot! An Anthology of Sports, Games and the Open Air.
London, Sidgwick and Jackson, 1926.
331pp.
This book includes a section entitled "The Ring" which gives selections from the works of George Borrow, Pierce Egan and William Hazlitt.

463. DARWIN, Bernard
John Gully and His Times
London, Cassell and Co., 1935.
230pp. 12 chapters, 4 illus.
The story of the 19th Century prize-fighter who became a prosperous colliery and racehorse owner and Member of Parliament for Pontefract.

464. DARWIN, Bernard
Life is Sweet Brother
Reminiscences by Bernard Darwin
London, Collins Publishers, 1940.
285pp.
Chapter 15 is of boxing interest, including mention of several prize-fighters and the scenes of their battles, such as Royston Heath, Six Mile Bottom and Thistleton Gap.

465. DARWIN, Bernard
British Sports and Games
London, Longmans Green and Co. (For the British Council), 1940.
44pp. Illus.
This is the sixth of a series of ten booklets entitled *British Life and Sport*. In 1941 the booklets were published in one volume under the same title.
Includes a section "At the Elder Shrine" which includes a mention of boxing.

466. DARWIN, Bernard
Every Idle Dream. A Book of Essays.
Illus. by Eleanor Darwin
London, Collins, 1948.
254pp.
Includes "A Look Around the Room", dealing chiefly with portraits of pugilists.

467. DATAS (The Memory Man)

Datas, The Memory Man. By Himself.
London, Wright and Brown, 1932.
208pp. Illus.
Includes boxing reminiscences in chapters II to VI, including mentions of Jem Mace, Tom Sayers, Frank Slavin and others. With illustrations of Jem Mace and Tom Sayers.

468. DAVIES, Charles (Publisher)
Gawthrop's Journal of Literature, Science and Art, and of Institution Reports
Liverpool, Printed by Hugh Gawthrop, 1842.
Numbers 16 and 17 (February 19th and March 5th 1842) contain an essay entitled "On the Demoralising Tendency of the Practice of Prize Fighting", by J.B. Jackson.

469. DAVIES, The Rev. C. Maurice, D.D.
Unorthodox London; or Places of Religious Life in the Metropolis
London, Tinsley Brothers, 1874—75 (4 volumes)
448pp.
Volume II contains mention of Bendigo (William Thompson) the famous pugilist.
The 3rd edition (1875) includes mention of The Surrey Chapel, (later the Blackfriars "Ring").

470. DAVIS, F.J.
Handbook of Refereeing and Judging Boxing under Imperial Services Boxing Association Rules.
Aldershot, William May and Co., 1935.
40pp. Illus.

471. DAVIS, John, Gent
The Ring. In Two Parts. A Poem.
London, Andrews and Co. Ltd., 1847.
Second Edition, in Three Parts, 1848.
This item refers almost exclusively to horse racing and betting; there is however some slight reference to the prize-ring.

472. DAVIS, Lenwood G.
Joe Louis. A Bibliography of articles, books, pamphlets, records and archival material.
Compiled by Lenwood G. Davis, with the assistance of Marsha L. Moore.
Westport (Conn.), Greenwood Press, 1983.
232pp.

473. DAVIS, Percy, and YATES, Frederick
Barefists and Courage. The Adventures of a Welsh Prizefighter during the reign of Queen Victoria.
Risca, Newport, (Gwent), The Starling Press
continued

Ltd., 1978.

138pp. Stiff paper covers.
A novel describing adventures which could have happened to a Welsh family living in the Rhondda Valley. The hero is a young unemployed miner, who earns his living with his bare fists.

474. DAVIS, Robert H.

"Ruby Robert" Alias Bob Fitzsimmons
With an Introduction by W. O. McGeehan – Sports Editor, The New York *Herald Tribune*.
New York, George H. Doran Co., 1926.

134pp. Illus.
Bound in red cloth, lettered in black, white dust-wrapper with portraits of Fitzsimmons on the front.
The text is divided into Parts 1 to 10 and includes such headings as "Fitzsimmons Reveals the Genesis of His Art", "The Solar Plexus Blow is Born", "Fitzsimmons Wins", "Remarkable Performances at the Close of His Career", and "Bob's Home Life and Rare Sense of Humour".
There are 9 illustrations in the book.

475. DAWSON, Daniel L.

With The Gloves
London, Ward, Lock, Bowden and Co.

This article was issued in a book entitled *Four Complete Novels by Famous Authors*, from *Lippincott's Monthly Magazine*.
The article is illustrated by 7 cuts in the text showing various boxing positions and blows and comprises 8 pages.

476. DAWSON, Captain Lionel, R.N.

Lonsdale, The Authorised Life of Hugh Lowther, Fifth Earl of Lonsdale, K.G., G.C.V.O.
London, Odhams Press Ltd., 1946.

Bound in light blue cloth, gilt lettering on spine.
286pp Illus.
A note on the dust-wrapper points out that the book had been printed shortly before Lord Lonsdale's death (in 1944), but owing to conditions prevailing at the time the issue was delayed and that due to Lord Lonsdale's death certain references were out of date; but the publishers were confident that such circumstances would not diminish the pleasure the reader would obtain from the book.
The text deals with the Earl's experiences in the numerous sports to which he was devoted; these of course included boxing.
Chapter VII is entitled "Boxing – The Belts" and there is also reference to the Pelican Club (Boxing Committee) in the Appendix.

477. DAWSON, Peter

Fifty Years of Song
London, Hutchinson and Co. (Publishers) Ltd 1951.

239pp. Illus.
Includes some references to boxing:
Chapter VII – Jimmy Clabby, Les Darcy, Tommy Uren, George Cook and Albert Lloyd
Chapter XVI – Les Darcy v. Eddie McGoorty; Les Darcy v. Fred Dyer; Carpentier v. Siki.
The author was a famous Australian singer, and in the text he comments "My interest in boxing is well known in Australia".

478. DAY, J. Wentworth

(Editor *The Illustrated Sporting and Dramatic News***)**
Falcon on St. Paul's
Being a Book about the Birds, Beasts, Sports and Games of London. Introduction by The Viscount Castlerosse.
London, Hutchinson and Co. (Publishers) Ltd., 1930.

254pp. Illus.
Includes some short references to pugilism and pugilists, including Chapter IX, "On Duelling – The Old Battling Days" etc.

479. DAY J. Wentworth

Gamblers' Gallery
(The story of great gamblers past and present)
London, Background Books Ltd, 1948.

127pp.
Includes items on boxing interest in chapters II, IV, VII, XII and XIII; including (*inter alia*) stories of John Gully, and Abington Baird (The Squire), a well known supporter of prize-fighting.

480. DAY and MASON (Publishers)

The Story of the Prize Ring
Windsor (Berks), 1949.

24pp.
Illustrated paper covers, with reproduction of the picture "The Fives Court" on the front cover.
The text consists of 7 sections, these being articles by Trevor Wignall, Harry F. Maxted and others; these refer to old-time fighters such as Tom Sayers, Tom Cribb, Dan Donnelly, etc.
There are a number of illustrations of pugilists and associated items.

481. DAY, MASON and FORD (Publishers)

Day and Mason Boxing Annual, 1950

32pp. Paper covers with picture of Dave Sands on the front.
Fully illus. with action and other pictures and cartoons.
A similar annual was published in 1951, with a picture of Randolph Turpin v. Ray Robinson on the front cover.

482. DAY, William

William Day's Reminiscences of the Turf.
With Anecdotes and Recollections of Celeb-
continued

rities.
London, Richard Bentley and Son, 1886.
466pp.
Chapters IV, V and XI include pugilistic material; particularly referring to John Gully, for whom the author's father trained racehorses at Danebury.

483. DEAKIN, A. (Publisher)
Hints to Pugilists on Training, or Golden Rules for the Guidance of Boxers, Wrestlers Runners, Walkers, Rowers etc.
London, 1865.
16pp.

484. DEAN, T. St.John
Olympic Referee, etc.
What Our Boxers Struck
(South African Olympic Boxing Team, 1924)
Johannesburg, Published by the Author, 1925.
32pp. Stiff paper covers. Frontis. showing the South African Team and Officials.
The story of the visit to England and France for the Games, with information on the bouts and the results.

485. DEAN, T. St.John
Olympic Referee, Member of the S.A.N.A. B.A. Examining Board etc.
The Third Man in the Ring Speaks
Practical Tips on Scoring in Boxing Contests
Johannesburg, N/d.
16pp. inc..covers.

486. DEARDEN, Rev. Albert E.
Billy McLeod, Ex-Champion Lightweight Prize-Fighter
London, James Clarke and Co. and the Kingsgate Press. N/Date.
144pp.
Bound in light green cloth, with gilt lettering on front cover and on spine, with an action picture of McLeod on the front cover, which also carries an inscription "The Life Story of a Converted Prize Fighter".
The author's preface says (*inter alia*) – "The Life of Billy McLeod has been written during an enforced leisure of six months of sanatorium life. I know the ex-champion well, and have fought by his side many times in warfare against sin".

487. DEARDEN, Seton
The Gypsy Gentleman. A Study of George Borrow.
London, Arthur Barker Ltd, April, 1939.
London, John Murray, November, 1939.
327pp.

Chapter II deals with Borrow's interest in the prize-ring.
The illustrations include one of Borrow and one of "A Prize-Fight in 1825" (The Fives Court).

488. de COY, Robert H.
The Big Black Fire. An uncensored biography of the first black heavyweight champion, Jack Johnson.
Los Angeles (California), Holloway House Publishing Co., 1969.
311pp. Paper covers.

489. DE CRESPIGNY, Sir Claude Champion, Bart.
Forty Years of a Sportsman's Life
London, Mills and Boon Ltd., 1910.
There was a new and revised edition issued in 1925 by the same publisher; this edition contained two additional chapters covering the years 1910 to 1924. There was also a cheaper popular edition issued in 1912.
318pp. Illus.
The author was a well-known Corinthian and a member of the National Spprting Club.
There are a number of references to boxing in the book, as follows:
Chapter II "Sport and Sportsmen" (Sayers v. Heenan)
Chapter III "Foxhunting and Other Delights" mentions the Marquess of Queensberry and the formation of the Rules of Boxing, and also the author's entry for the Amateur Lightweight Championship.

490. DE CRISTOFARO, S.
Boxing's Greatest Middleweights
Introduction by Billy Conn
Rochester (New York), Published by the author, 1982.
168pp. Illus.

491. DE FOREST, Jimmy
The Golden Age of Boxing
New York City, 1924.
56pp.

492. DEGHY, Guy
Noble and Manly
The History of the National Sporting Club.
Incorporating the Posthumous Papers of the Pelican Club.
London, Hutchinson and Co. (Publishers) Ltd., 1956.
223pp. Illus. Cold Frontis.

493. DE GROUCHEY, William J. (Compiler)
continued

How Champions Play
(Baseball – Boxing – Bowling – Softball – Wrestling)
Helpful Hints by Top Experts, Told Entirely in Pictures.
New York, Street and Smith Publications Inc. 1948.

494. DELGADO, Alan
Winner on Points
London, Max Parrish and Co. Ltd., 1964.
140pp.
A fast-moving story with a background of boxing.

495. DEMPSEY, Jack
Round by Round. An Autobiography. Written in Collaboration with Myron M. Stearns.
New York and London, Published by Whittlesey House, A Division of the McGraw-Hill Book Co. Inc., 1940.
The book was also published by Chapman and Hall Ltd., London, 1941.
The American edition was issued in dark red cloth with gold titles on the spine.
The English edition was issued in bright red cloth with black titles on the spine.
The text and illustrations are the same in both editions, with some variation in the format and the illustrations.
283pp. Illus.
There are 31 chapters, these are presented in 5 parts, entitled as follows:–
Part 1 – Growing Up in the West
Part 2 – Early Fights
Part 3 – Breaking Through
Part 4 – On Top of the World
Part 5 – Advice to Future Champions
There are 32 pages of illustrations.

496. DEMPSEY, Jack
How to Fight Tough
Published in U.S.A. 1942.
127pp.
An announcement regarding this item appeared in *Knockout* magazine dated November 21st, 1942, stating:– "Dempsey writes: Jack Dempsey has written a short book entitled *How to Fight Tough*, which is required reading for Service Men".

497. DEMPSEY, Jack
Championship Fighting, Explosive Punching and Aggressive Defence
Edited by Jack Cuddy.
Illustrated by Ed. Igoe.
New York, Prentice-Hall Inc., 1950.
London, Nicholas Kaye Ltd., 1950. Reprinted 1951.

264pp. Many instructional illustrations.
The English edition contains only 205pp. as many of the illustrations are included in the text instead of on separate pages.

498. DEMPSEY, Jack
Dempsey, By the Man Himself. As Told to Bob Considine and Bill Slocum.
New York, Simon and Schuster, 1959.
398pp.
This book was issued in U.K. by William Heinemann Ltd. under the title of *Massacre in the Sun* (q.v.)

499. DEMPSEY, Jack
(With Bill Considine & Bill Slocum)
Massacre In The Sun
An Autobiography
London, William Heinemann Ltd., 1960.
(First English Edition)
242pp. Illus.

The U.S. edition of this book appeared in 1959.

500. DEMPSEY, Jack
(with Barbara Piatelli Dempsey)
Dempsey
Introduction by Joseph Dureo
New York, Harper and Row Publishers Inc., 1977.
288pp. Illus.

South Yarmouth, Ma., John Curley and Associates Inc., 1978. (Large print edition, 2 volumes).
316pp.
Announced as the biography of a living legend – Jack Dempsey's own story of his fabulous career.

501. DENKER, Henry
I'll Be Right Home Ma (Fiction)
New York, Thomas B. Crowell Co.
Copyright by the author, 1949.
Second printing March, 1949.
278pp.
Bound in yellow cloth.
A hard-driving story of a prize-fighter.

502. DENT, Regimental Sergeant-Major E.B.
Boxing
Aldershot and London, Gale and Polden Ltd., 1917.
56pp. 36 Illus. Price 2s.
Further editions were issued in 1918 and 1920.
The 1918 edition carried two extra plates and
continued

also two that differed from those in the original issue; however the text was the same.

503. DENT, Regimental Sergeant-Major E.B.
Boxing for Boys
Foreword by Col. R.B. Campbell, C.B.
Aldershot & London, Gale and Polden, 1920.

504. DESMOND, Shaw
London Nights of Long Ago
London, Duckworth, 1927.
252pp. Illus.
Chapter XVI "A Night With the Gods at Olympia" deals with boxing — Bill Lang v. Sam Langford, etc.
The boxing illustrations include — The Coffee Cooler (Frank Craig) and Lang v. Langford at Olympia.

505. DESMOND, Shaw
Life and Foster Freeman. A Novel.
London, Hutchinson and Co. (Publishers) Ltd., 1940.
Another edition was issued in 1941.
518pp.
This novel contains some references to boxing, particularly in Chapter XIX ("The Noble Art").

506. DESMOND, Shaw
The Edwardian Story
London, Rockliff Publishing Coporation Ltd., 1949.
356pp. Illus.
Contains some slight reference to boxing, including the author's contributions when he was a boxing editor in Fleet Street.

507. DESMOND, Shaw
Personality and Power
London, Rockliff Publishing Co., 1950.
340pp. Illus.
Includes mention of boxing in two chapters.

508. DE WITT, R.M. (Publisher)
The Lives and Battles of Tom Sayers and J. C. Heenan. With Full Accounts of their various contests in the Ring, as revised by the Pugilistic Benevolent Association of England.
New York, 1860.
Illus.

509. DEYONG, Moss
"Everybody Boo — "
Foreword by Sir Noel Curtis-Bennett
London, Stanley Paul and Co., 1951.

180pp. 15 Illus.
In his dedication to his book of Memoirs, the author records his sincere appreciation of Mr. Leslie Bell's great literary assistance.

510. DIAMOND, Anthony
(10 stone Champion of the World, Amateur Lightweight Champion, 1883, 1884, 1885, Amateur Heavyweight Champion, 1886)
Modern Boxing — Up To Date. An Exposition of the Art and Science of Self Defence.
Birmingham, Hurt Brothers, Publishers, 1892.
Bound in yellow paper covers, with picture of the author on the front cover.
The book contains illustrations of the various positions in boxing, with a sketch of the career of Anthony Diamond and a résumé of the Ring and kindred subjects.
The textual descriptions of the various blows and positions are matched by a cut of the particular move on the opposite page.

511. DIAMOND, Wilfrid
How Great Was Joe Louis?
New York, The Paebar Co., Publishers, 1949.
A British Edition was Published by The World's Work Ltd., in 1955.
(Wilfrid Diamond was Sports Editor of *Muscle Power* and *Your Physique*).
128pp. Illus.
This book portrays the big scenes in over 30 of Joe Louis' important battles with 30 photographs of dramatic moments in the fights. These are shown in the original edition; the British edition contains fewer illustrations.

512. DIAMOND, Wilfrid
Blood, Sweat, and Jack Dempsey
Kingswood (Surrey), The World's Work (1913) Ltd., 1953.
107pp. plus an Appendix showing a list of World's Heavyweight Champions, together with their principal fights. Frontis.

513. DIAMOND, Wilfrid
Kings of the Ring
Kingswood (Surrey), The World's Work (1913) Ltd., 1954.
127pp.

514. DIAMOND, Wilfrid
This Guy Marciano
Kingswood (Surrey), The World's Work (1913) Ltd., 1955.
157pp. Illus.

515. DIBBLE, R.F.
John L. Sullivan. An Intimate Narrative.
Boston, U.S.A., Little, Brown & Co., 1925.
209pp. Illus.
Bound in green cloth with black lettering on front cover and spine.
8 chapters. 10 illustrations.
The book was dedicated to H. L. Mencken.
The Author's Preface states – "Certain pages from this book appeared in the July 1924 issue of the *American Mercury*. Since most of the data has been compiled from a variety of newspapers, there may be a question as to the authenticity of some episodes. I have taken great pains however to exclude whatever seemed irrelevant, and nothing that seemed relevant, to the generally recognised facts of Sullivan's life".

516. DICK, William B.
Manual of Boxing for Amateurs and Professionals
New York, Dick and Fitzgerald, 1894.

517. DIGBY, Reginald
Triumphs of Sport and Speed
Illustrated by J. E. Connell
London, The Thames Publishing Co., 1946.
125pp.
This boy's book of fictional stories includes a boxing story entitled "The Fighting Featherweight".
This is illustrated by 11 pictures in the text and a coloured plate.

518. DIPPLE, Edwin (Publisher)
The Guide to British Boxing, or Pugilistic Pocket Book, 1852.
This item was published in 4 parts, each in green wrappers and priced 3d. The 4th part contains the title-page, preface and contents-page.
The title on the cover shows John Hannan as part-author, while the title-page attributes this to James Shaw.

The contents include: Illustrated Rules for Boxing by John Hannan (or James Shaw) – Biographical Sketches of Modern Pugilists – An Essay on Pugilism – The Conduct of a Prize-Fight – Rules of the Ring – Ring Directory – Anecdotes, etc. by Francis Benjamin Thompson, Editor of *The Sporting Life*, the *Sporting Times* etc. – A Practical Guide for Training Pugilists, by Robert Fuller, Pedestrian and Trainer. Illustrated by Full-length Portraits of the Most Eminent Boxers.
There is also a sub-section on Pugilistic Literature, giving a list of authors of works on the subject.

519. DIPROSE AND BATEMAN (Publishers)
The Authentic History of the Prize-Ring
London, 1860.
Verbatim Accounts from the *Times* and *Bell's*

Life newspapers, an authentic history of the Prize Ring and Championships of England; together with a faithful record of the Great International Pugilistic Encounter between Sayers and Heenan. Likewise a most interesting and well-written letter by Mr. Wilkes, on behalf of Heenan and the Yankees, the Hug, etc. Price 1 penny.

520. DISHER, M. Willson
The Greatest Show on Earth. As Performed for over a Century at Astley's (afterwards Sanger's) Royal Amphitheatre of Arts, Westminster Bridge Road.
Recorded with illustrations by M. Willson Disher, with an Introduction by D. L. Murray.
London, G. Bell and Sons Ltd., 1937.
306pp.
Includes Chapter V, "Equestrian Drama", 3. "The Female Mazeppa". This section refers to the life of Adah Isaacs Menken, with mention of her husband, John C. Heenan, and also of Tom Sayers.

521. DISNEY, John
(Of the Inner Temple, Barrister-At-Law)
The Laws of Gaming, Wagers, Horse Racing and Gaming Houses
London, Printed for J. Butterworth, Law-Bookseller, and for J. Cooke, Ormond Way, Dublin, 1806.
Chapter IV, "Of Games", section I – Of Games which are legal and those which are not, quotes cases discussing the legality of Prize-Fighting.

522. DIXON, George
A Lesson in Boxing by George Dixon
Published in America, 1893.

523. DOBSON, Austin, Hon., Ll. D.
(Edinburgh)
William Hogarth
London, William Heinemann, 1891.
Re-issued 1898, 1902, and 1907.
The following information is taken from the 1907 edition:
Part II – Bibliography and Catalogue – a Catalogue of Paintings by or Attributed to Hogarth – includes a section "Paintings of Uncertain Date" contains items of pugilistic interest as follows:
1 – John Broughton, the Prize Fighter
2 – James Figg, the Prize Fighter.
Part II also includes "A Catalogue of the Principal Prints by, or after Hogarth":
1 – Ticket for James Figg
2 – James Broughton, Prize-Fighter
3 – Broughton v. Slack.
The frontispiece is a portrait of Hogarth, from the Original Painting in the National Gallery, and the

continued

following illustrations include:
  1 – The Rake's Progress No.11, from the original painting
  2 – Southwark Fair, from Hogarth's engraving
The plate "The March to Finchley" (Part) shows two pugilists in action.

524. DOHERTY, W. J.
("The Fighting Quarryman"), One-Time Middleweight Champion of South Africa and Heavyweight Champion of Australia)
In the Days of the Giants. Memories of a Champion of the Prize-Ring. Introduction by Viscount Knebworth.
London, George G. Harrap and Co. Ltd., 1931.
American Edition, New York, 1931.
272pp. Illus.
The English edition was issued in variable bindings, one in a dark blue and the other in light blue cloth. There are 12 illustrations (some coloured) and the 19 chapters include the following: My First Fight – Jem Mace – Peter Jackson – Joe Goddard – Griffo – The Middleweight Title – Mick Dooley – Nine Rounds with Kid McCoy, etc.

525. DONALDSON, Charles
From Figg to Tunney
Glasgow, Kirkwood and Co., Printers.
84pp. Paper covers.
In his preface the author states that he had many requests from readers to put his articles from *The Evening Chronicle* into book form. This book is an abridged version.
This small book has four chapters, the first three containing boxing material. The fourth chapter is entitled "A Chat About the Coffin"; this was a licensed restaurant in Whitevale Street, Glasgow, E1, owned by the author. Mr. Donaldson gives information on many sportsmen, including boxers, who visited his establishment.

526. DONNELLY, Edward
Art of Boxing. (Manual of Sparring and Self-Defence)
New York, 1881.
New York, Excelsior Publishing House, ca. 1910.
New York, Fitzgerald Publishing Corporation, ca. 1910.
This item was published in England under the title of *Self-Defence; or The Art of Boxing*, by Ned Donnelly (q.v.)

527. DONNELLY, Ned
Professor of Boxing to the London Athletic Club
Self-Defence; or The Art of Boxing
London, Weldon and Co., 1879.

There were at least five editions of this book published in London up to 1897, in which year Wyman and Sons re-issued the work.
127pp. including adverts. Illus.
The first edition was bound in green boards, with gilt titles and action picture of Prof. Donnelly on the front cover.
There were also four editions published in America from 1881 to 1910 under the title *Art of Boxing*, (q.v.)

528. DONOGHUE, Steve
Donoghue Up
The Autobiography of Steve Donoghue
London, Collins Publishers, 1938.
294pp. Illus. (None of boxing interest)
The author refers to his friendship with Jimmy Wilde, to whom he was introduced by Jim Driscoll.

529. DONOVAN, Dick
(Joyce E. P. Muddock)
Thurtell's crime – The Story of a Strange Tragedy
London, T. Werner Laurie, 1906.
Re-issued in *Daily Mail* Sixpenny Novels, 1907.
This is a fictionalised account of a true story, the murder near Elstree of Mr. William Weare, a London gentleman. The murderer was one John Thurtell, a native of Norwich, with a reputation as a gambler and backer of prizefighters.
The story is told against a background of gambling, duelling and prize-fighting, with some romantic interest.
Thurtell was hanged for the crime, after his accomplice, Joseph Hunt, turned King's Evidence.
See also Watson, Eric R. – *Trial of Thurtell and Hunt*, (Notable British Trials), 1920.
Burke, Thomas – *Murder at Elstree*, 1936.
Egan, Pierce – *Account of the Trial of Thurtell and Hunt*, 1824.

530. DONOVAN, Joseph G.
Galento the Great. The authentic and authorised story of the life and ring battles of Tony (Two Ton) Galento, World's Heavyweight Contender.
New York City, Published by George Winn, 1938.
Foreword by Tony Galento and Abe J. Greene, Boxing Commissioner, State of New Jersey.
119pp.
The 16 chapters progress the story from Galento's first amateur fight in 1926 to the one with Joe Louis in 1938.
12 illustrations.

531. DONOVAN, Professor Mike

continued

(Ex-Middleweight Champion of America and Instructor of Boxing, New York Athletic Club)

The Science of Boxing

New York, Dick and Fitzgerald, 1893.

78pp. Illus.

Bound in grey cloth, black titles with brown design on front cover, including a pair of boxing gloves. Gilt titles and design on the spine.

There was also an edition with yellow paper covers, lettered in black, with a full length action picture of Donovan on the front cover.

The preliminaries include a section entitled "Expert Opinions" in which a number of experts, having read the advance sheets, give their opinion of the book; among these experts are the following:—

Bob Fitzsimmons, Peter Jackson, Jos. B. Choynski, Parson Doyle, George Siler, etc.

The text is divided into sections, each giving instruction on the movements, positions, guards and blows of boxing, with appropriate illustrations.

Also included are the Rules of the Ring and the author's record.

532. DONOVAN, Mike

(Ex-Champion Middleweight of America and Boxing Master of the New York Athletic Club)

The Roosevelt that I Know

Ten Years of Boxing with the President — and other Memories of Famous Fighting Men

Edited by F.H.N.

New York, B.W. Dodge and Co., 1909. There was also an Authorised Special Limited Edition.

234pp. Illus.

The standard edition is bound in green cloth with pictorial cover and white lettering.

The Authorised Special Edition is bound in red cloth, gilt titles on cover and spine, six pairs of boxing gloves in relief on the front cover.

The narrative covers not only the author's meetings with the Governor (Roosevelt), who is described as "no ordinary amateur", but with other great fighters of the period, including J. L. Sullivan, J. J. Corbett, Jake Kilrain, and his own fight with Jack Dempsey (The Nonpareil).

There are 6 illustrations and 15 cartoons by Robert Edgren.

533. DORAN, B.J.

Science of Self Defence. A Manual for Beginners.

Cincinatti (Ohio), Press of Schiffer Printing Co., 1889.

This item was also issued in Toronto (Canada) in 1893.

108pp.

534. DOUBLESPUR, Dr.

The Great Fight at Gateshead, between Cumberland Hodge and Brimstone Harry

Printed and sold by W. T. Fordyce, Newcastle on Tyne, ca. 1830.

A 24-page pamphlet in verse.

This is actually a religious tract and the text contains nothing of boxing interest except for a woodcut on the title-page and the descriptive title.

535. DOUGLAS, Lord Alfred

The Autobiography of Lord Alfred Douglas

London, Martin Secker, March, 1929.

Reprinted April, 1929.

New Edition 1931.

340pp. Illus.

The boxing references mostly concern the author's father, the Eighth Marquess of Queensberry, who established the Queensberry Rules of Boxing.

536. DOUGLAS, Captain R.J.H. (Compiler)

The Works of George Cruikshank

Classified and arranged with Reid's Catalogue, and their approximate values.

London, Printed by J. Davy and Sons, at the Dryden Press, 1903.

This item contains many boxing references already dealt with in this bibliography under the various works on George Cruikshank.

537. DOWLING, Francis L.

(Editor of *Bell's Life in London*)

Fights for the Championship, and Celebrated Prize Battles

London, Published at the Office of *Bell's Life*.

There were 4 issues of this book in England, as follows:—

    1855 — 410pp.

    1858 — 410pp. plus Appendix

    1859 — as the 1858 edition except for the date

    1860 — with Appendix, plus "The Championship of England", 80pp.

The American Edition of the work was published in New York by Robert M. de Witt in 1859 with paper covers.

The title-page of the book reads as follows:— "Fights for the Championship and Celebrated Prize-Battles; or Accounts for all the Prize Ring Battles for the Championship from the Days of Figg and Broughton to the Present Time; And Also of Many Other Game and Extraordinary Battles Between First-Rate Pugilists of Ancient and Modern Times. Compiled from *Bell's Life in London, Boxiana* and Original Sources".

Chapter I of the book deals with the early Champions from Figg to Mendoza; succeeding chapters from II to X inclusive are devoted to Gully, Tom

continued

Cribb (2 chapters), Tom Spring, Jem Ward (2 chapters). Following chapters refer to later champions and their meetings in the ring.

The Appendix to the later editions continues the History of the Championship to the date of publication.

The supplementary information entitled "The Championship of England" in the 1860 edition brings the story up to the time of Sayers v. Heenan in 1860; it also deals retrospectively with a number of Sayers' bouts and also the one between Morrissey and Heenan.

538. DOWLING, Francis L.

(Editor of *Bell's Life in London***)**

The Championship of England

Being a continuation of *Fights for the Championship*, to which is added a brief History of Tom Sayers and the Benicia Boy and an account of their Chief Prize Battles.

London, *Bell's Life* Office, 1860.

For further details of this item see *Fights for the Championship and Celebrated Prize Battles*, 1855, 1858 and 1860.

539. DOWLING, Vincent George
(Editor, *Bell's Life in London***)**

Fistiana, or The Oracle of the Ring

London, William Clement, Junior. First Issued 1841.

There were at least 26 editions of this work, all except the final one being published by William Clement, Junior.

Up to the year 1852 all editions of *Fistiana* were edited by V. G. Dowling; after Mr. Dowling's death in that year the editorship was taken over by his son, Frank Louis Dowling, until he too passed away in October, 1867.

F.L. Dowling was preparing a further edition at the time of his death; this came out in 1868, and was not numbered.

There are conflicting opinions regarding the date of the final issue of *Fistiana*; for instance, Henry Downes Miles, in the Bibliography included in Volume I of his *Pugilistica* gives the year as 1864, while Paul Magriel, in his *Bibliogrpahy of Boxing* dated 1948, states that the series was published until 1870. Illustrations in the present volume show the title pages of the 1841 and 1866 editions.

The first edition of 1841 consisted of 306pp. with a frontispiece entitled "The Ring" and four pages of line drawings showing various blows and holds. This volume can claim to be the first devoted to the provision of boxers' records, as in addition to the contents shown on the title-page, the Chron-

ology of the Ring, alphabetically arranged from 1785 to 1840, occupies 143 pages. The remaining chapters provide such pieces of information as Training as Regards Pugilists, Time and Quantity of Eating, Training for Pedestrians, Training Jockeys, etc., Ages of Living Pugilists, Taverns and Public Houses kept by Ex-Pugilists in London and its Vicinity, Duties of Seconds and Bottle-Holders, Duties of Umpires and Referees, etc.

The second edition of Mr. Dowling's work was issued in two parts, dated 1843 (Part First) and 1842 (Part Second). It will be noted that Part Second of this second issue was dated a year earlier than what appears to have been the first issue of the second edition. Although this signifies the issue of books under the title *Fistiana* during the years 1841, 1842 and 1843, there does not appear to have been a third edition dated as such.

The 1844 edition — designated "Fourth Edition", states in the Address (*inter alia*) — "The rapid sale of the three previous editions of *Fistiana*, which are now out of print, has induced the Editor to send forth a Fourth Edition, with such additions and corrections as the events of the past year render desirable.

This indicates that the three former editions, now out of print, were in fact the 1841 issue plus the two parts of the second edition, issued in 1842 and 1843.

The contents of the later editions were broadly the same as those of earlier issues, each being updated to include the results of bouts contested in the preceding year. These were not so large regarding the number of pages, as was the case with the first edition; the later ones contained around 150 to 160 pages per issue. They were mostly bound in soft linen covers.

All the editions up to 1867 were numbered; the 1868 edition remained un-numbered. The list of Sporting Houses extended to cover 3 pages, listing establishments in London, Birmingham, Sheffield, Derby, Manchester, The Potteries and Liverpool.

The 1868 edition was published at the Office of *Bell's Life in London*, with 152pp.

540. DOWNES, Terry

My Bleeding Business

London, Stanley Paul Ltd, 1964.

194pp. Illus.

Memoirs of a colourful champion, told in his own inimitable style.

541. DOYLE, A. Conan

Songs of the Road

London, Smith Elder and Co., 1911.

Bound in blue cloth, gilt titles on spine and design on front cover.

The contents include "Bendy's Sermon" a poem which first appeared in the *Strand Magazine* for April, 1909; this is described as "A Story in Verse" and consists of 19 verses.

The poem is illustrated from facsimiles, old prints and drawings by A. J. Gough as follows:

Bendigo in the Ring
Bendigo as a Preacher

continued

It Was a Lovely Sight to See Him Floor His Men

Listenin' to the Words of Grace From Mr. Bendigo

"Bendy's Sermon" was also included in The Collected Edition of *The Poems of Arthur Conan Doyle* – published by John Murray in 1922.

542. DOYLE, A. Conan

The Last Galley

Impressions and Tales by Arthur Conan Doyle

London, Smith Elder and Co., 1911.

298pp.

Includes in Part II, No.IV "The Lord of Falconbridge" – A Legend of the Ring. (A Story about Tom Spring and Tom Cribb.)

This story first appeared in the *Strand Magazine* for August, 1909. (Vol.XXXVIII No.224).

543. DOYLE, A. Conan

Tales of the Ring and the Camp

London, John Murray, 1922.

The section "Tales of the Ring" includes 4 boxing stories, as follows:

The Croxley Master (q.v.)

The Lord of Falconbridge (q.v.)

The Fall of Lord Barrymore (q.v.)

The Bully of Brocas Court

The final item above first appeared in the *Strand Magazine* in 1921.

It is about Tom Hickman, the Gas Man, who was killed with Mr. Rowe, returning from the fight between Josh Hudson and Tom Shelton on Dec. 10th, 1822.

544. DOYLE, A. Conan

"Danger" And Other Stories

London, John Murray, 1918.

Story No.IV, "The Fall of Lord Barrymore" contains mention of Hooper the Tinman (1789–1797)

The story first appeared in the *Strand Magazine* for December, 1912, when it was illustrated in colour by H.M. Brock, R.I.

545. DOYLE, Arthur Conan

Rodney Stone

London, Smith Elder and Co., 1896.

The book was also published in the same year in the Bell's Indian and Colonial Library series.

366pp.

The story first appeared serially in the *Strand Magazine*, Volume XI, January to June 1896, and Volume XII, June to December of the same year. The serial included a large number of illustrations by Sidney Paget. Eight of these were included in the first edition in book form.

The work consists of 22 chapters, and it is claimed by some authorities to be the finest novel ever written about the prize-ring.

In the Preface the author expresses his indebtedness to a number of works for material in his book,

these include Egan's *Boxiana*, Miles' *Pugilistica* and Robinson's *Last Earls of Barrymore*.

546. DOYLE, A. Conan

The Croxley Master

This boxing story first appeared as a three-part serial in the *Strand Magazine*, October, November and December, 1899, with illustrations by Sidney Paget.

The story was included in a number of anthologies, among which are the following, all published in London:

The Green Flag and other Stories of War and Sport 1900, Smith Elder and Co.

Tales of the Ring and the Camp, 1922, John Murray

Best Sporting Stories, Edited by J. Wentworth Day, 1922, published by Messrs. Faber.

"The Croxley Master" was published as a separate item in New York and Toronto respectively; details as follows:

New York, McClure Phillips and Co, 1907

Toronto, The Musson Book Co., 1907.

547. DOYLE, A. Conan

The Green Flag, and Other Stories of War and Sport

London, Smith Elder and Co., 1900.

348pp.

This book includes the boxing story "The Croxley Master".

548. DOYLE, A. Conan

Through the Magic Door

London, George Bell and Sons, 1907.

274pp.

Chapter V refers to George Borrow and his interest in the prize-ring.

549. DOYLE, A. Conan

The House of Temperley. A Play.

Harold Locke, in his *Biographical Catalogue of the Writings of Conan Doyle*, 1928, states that this play is a dramatised version of the book *Rodney Stone*, although there are variations between the plots of the play and the book.

The play was first produced at the Adelphi Theatre in London on December 27th, 1909.

The magazine *The Play Pictorial* for January 1910 includes a souvenir of the play and an article entitled "Romance of the Prize-Ring" by B.W. Findon (Editor). There are a number of illustrations of scenes from the play which are of boxing interest.

550. DOYLE, A. Conan

continued

Memories and Adventures
London, Hodder and Stoughton Ltd, 1924,
2nd edition, January, 1930.

408pp
Chapter XXIV "Some Recollection of Sport" includes (*inter alia*) Boxing, Past and Present — Carpentier and France — The Reno Fight (A letter is reproduced from Irving Jefferson Lewis, Editor of the New York *Morning Telegraph*, inviting Conan Doyle to referee the Jeffries v. Johnson fight in Reno).
This Autobiography first appeared in the *Strand Magazine*.

551. DRACKETT, Phil
Fighting Days
Incidents in the Life of Bill Lee, as told to Phil Drackett.
Foreword by Matt Wells.
London and Montreal, Anglo-American Publications, 1944.

26pp. Stiff paper covers.
Chapters include: The Bermondsey School of Arms; Jack Goodwin. Jem Smith and Others, etc.
There is an illustration showing Bill Lee in his "Fighting Days".

552. DRAGO, Harry Sinclair
The Champ
Novelized by Harry Sinclair Drago
A Metro-Goldwyn-Mayer Production starring Wallace Beery and Jackie Cooper.
London, Readers Library Publishing Co. Ltd., ca.1932.

226pp.
The Readers Library was an early venture at producing some of the world's literary classics at sixpence a time in hard covers, and sold in department stores like Woolworth's. It proved to be uneconomical, and the publishers were obliged to novelise popular movies and to issue them as "the book of the film". This was one of the first.

553. DRAWBELL, James Wedgewood
Night and Day
London, Hatch and Co. (Publishers) Ltd, 1945.
272pp.
This book includes an article "Deaf Burke Couldn't Take It", which consists largely of an extract from *Recollections, Political, Literary, Dramatic and Miscellaneous of the Last Half Century* by the Rev. J. Richardson, LL.B., 1856.

554. DREISER, Theodore
A Book About Myself
New York, 1922.
Re-published in 1931 as *Newspaper Days*.
London, Constable and Co. Ltd., 1929.
502pp.

The English edition gives an account of the author, as a young reporter, meeting John L. Sullivan after the latter's fight with James J. Corbett, with a glimpse of Sullivan's personality.

555. DRISCOLL Jim
(Retired Undefeated Feather-weight Champion of the World)
The Straight Left and How to Cultivate It.
London, Ewart Seymour and Co. Ltd.,1914.
74pp.
Card covers; picture of a Straight Left on the front cover.
The book has 8 chapters, with 8 instructional photographs, showing boxing positions; these are posed by Jim Driscoll, Packy McFarland, Jimmy Wilde, Fred Dyer, and Bombardier Wells.
There have been at least 6 editions of this book, some of the later ones issued by Athletic Publications Ltd. The 6th edition was completely revised by Gilbert Odd and issued in 1945; this contained an additional chapter on the life story of Jim Driscoll, with his principal fights and his record.

556 DRISCOLL, Jim
(Ex-Featherweight Champion of the World)
Ringcraft
London, Ewart Seymour and Co. Ltd., 1914.
(A *Boxing* Handbook)
This book ran through at least 5 editions.
94pp.
3 Instructional chapters, 21 Illustrations.

557. DRISCOLL, Jim
(Retired Featherweight Champion Boxer of the World)
Text Book of Boxing
London, Ewart Seymour and Co. Ltd.,1915.
94pp. Illus.
Bound in red, black and white boards, with action portrait of Jim Driscoll on the front cover.
This was later re-issued by Athletic Publications Ltd, London; this issue was revised and brought up to date by Jim Kenrick. The same publisher was responsible for a 3rd edition in 1944.
The 2 later editions included a section entitled "Peerless Jim" by Jim Kenrick.
The text of each issue was almost exactly the same.
There were 34 illustrations showing punches and strategy, in addition to the instructional text.

558. DRISCOLL, Jim
(Retired Undefeated Feather-weight Champion of the World)
Out-Fighting and Long Range Boxing
London, Ewart Seymour and Co. Ltd.
(*Boxing* Handbook No.13). Re-issued
continued

1921.

Illus.

The Preface gives a short history of Driscoll's career; there are 5 instructional chapters, the illustrations showing some famous boxers in action.

559. DRUID, THE (Henry Hall Dixon)

Silk and Scarlet

London, Rogerson and Tuxford, 1859.

398pp.

Includes memories of Dick Christian, the famous Huntsman, in which he tells of how he witnessed the Cribb v. Molineux fight at Thistleton Gap, 28th September, 1811. Dick Christian also refers to Captain Barclay, The Game Chicken, Mr. Asheton Smith, and other prize-ring personalities.

560. DRUID, THE (Henry Hall Dixon)

Saddle and Sirloin, or English Farm and Sporting Worthies (Part North)

London, Rogerson and Tuxford, 1870.

London, Frederick Warne and Co., 1871 and 1878 (New Edition).

486pp.

Chapter XI includes reference to John Gully.

561. DUBLIN EVENING HERALD

(Publishers)

The Prize Fighters of Princes Street

This extract from the Dublin Newspaper was printed as a pamphlet in 1893.

562. DUDLEY, Ernest

Meet Doctor Morelle Again. A Further Collection of Chapters from His Case Book.

London, John Long Ltd., 1944.

208pp.

This item includes "The Case of the Man in the Squared Circle". A story of the Ring.

563. DUKE CIGARETTE COMPANY,

America (Publishers)

The Life of Jake Kilrain

This is a tiny book issued by the above company, printed on very thin paper with a coloured portrait of Kilrain on the front cover.

The book was one of a series of 50 *Histories of Poor Boys and Other Famous People*, issued in 1908.

564. DUNCOMBE, J. (Publisher)

Sinks of London Laid Open

A Pocket Companion for the Uninitiated, To Which is Added A Modern Flash Dictionary, Containing All the Cant Words, Slang Terms and Flash Phrases Now in Vogue, With a List of Prime Coves, The Whole

Forming a True Picture of London Life etc. Embellished with Humorous Illustrations by George Cruikshank.

London, 1848.

The "Modern Flash Dictionary" contains many terms used in connection with the prize-ring.

565. DUNDEE, Angelo

I Only Talk Winning

His Own story, as told to Mike Winters

London, Arthur Barker Ltd., 1983.

263pp. Illus.

The memoirs of the famous American boxing trainer/manager.

566. DURANT, John, and RICE, Edward

Come Out Fighting

New York, Duell, Stern and Pierce Inc., 1946.

246pp. Illus.

A note on the dust-cover of this book claims it to be the only pictorial history of the ring ever published. It is illustrated with over 200 prints and photographs, supplemented by about 30,000 words.

A further cheap edition of this book was published in 1948 by Zebra Picture Books of Cincinatti, Ohio, with illustrated paper covers and 96 pages of picture and text. This edition deals only with heavy-weights and concluded with a picture of Ezzard Charles defeating Joe Baksi.

567. DURANT, John

The Heavyweight Champions

Foreword by Col. Edward P. Eagan

London, Arco Publications, 1961.

152pp. Illus.

In addition to discussion on the fights for the championship, the book includes an appendix giving additional information on British and American Champions, with various facts about the Champions.

THE

BLACK

CHAMPIONS

OF

THE · PRIZE · RING

FROM MOLINEAUX TO JACKSON.

ILLUSTRATED.

NEW YORK :
RICHARD K. FOX, Publisher,
FRANKLIN SQUARE.

1890.

Title-Page *Lives & Battles of Famous Black Pugilists* (Fox Pub.) (Bib. Ref. 741)

568. EAGAN, Eddie
Fighting for Fun
The Scrapbook of Eddie Eagan
(Amateur Heavyweight Champion of the
World)
New York, Macmillan and Co., 1932
London, Lovat Dixon and Co., 1932.
278pp. Illus.
The author won the Olympic Heavyweight Title in
1920; he studied at Oxford University as a Rhodes
Scholar and won the British A.B.A. Heavyweight
Championship in 1923. Eddie Eagan trained with
Mike McTigue when the latter was preparing for his
fight with Battline Siki, and he also sparred with
Jack Dempsey and Gene Tunney. Eagan was
approached on several occasions with proposals
that he should box as a professional. He later be-
came Chairman of the New York State Athletic
Commission .

569. EARL, J.C.
Boxing, with the Queensberry Rules etc. for
the Gloves
London, Dean, 1893.

570. EARL, J.C., and ELLIOTT, W.J.
Boxing, Attack and Defence
London, Dean, 1898.
8vo. Price 1s.

571. EARL, J.C.
Earl's Handbook of Boxing
London, Dean's Champion Handbooks,
1904.
32pp.

571A "E.B.T." – One of Jackson's Pupils
Fencing and Fighting
Being the Lives and Histories of the Champ-
ions of Defence, from James Figg to John
Jackson.
Published in London, 1815.

572. EDDOWES, J. (Printer)
An Exhortation in Christian Love
Shrewsbury, 1769.
The title-page states as follows: An Exhortation in
Christian Love, to all who frequent Horse Racing,
Cock Fighting, Throwing at Cocks, Gaming, Plays,
Dancing and other Vain Diversions.
34pp.
This work consists mainly of quotations from the
Scriptures. Whilst it does not actually mention
pugilism or boxing it is obviously aimed at such
pursuits as well as those mentioned in the preface.

573. EDGAR, George
The Blue Bird's Eye
(A Tale of the Old Prize Ring)
London, Mills and Boon Ltd., 1912, price 6s

Cheap edition, 1913 – price 1s.
London, George Newnes, Ltd., 1916.
311pp.

573A. EDGAR, George
The Pride of the Fancy
A Novel of the Prize Ring
London, Mills and Boon Ltd., 1914. Price 6s
386pp.
Further editions were issued by the same
publishers in 1917 and 1920 price 2s and 6d
each.

574. EDGAR, George
Kent the Fighting Man
A Story of the ring
London, Mills and Boon, 1916.
311pp.

575. EDGEWORTH-JOHNSTONE, Capt. W.
Royal Irish Rifles, Assistant Inspector of
Gymnasia, Amateur Heavyweight Champion
of England 1895 and 1896.
Boxing, The Modern Style of Glove Fight-
ing.
London and Aldershot, Gale and Polden Ltd
1895.
Reissued 1901 and 1906.
168pp. Illus.
Mainly instructional but includes reference to con-
temporary boxers, such as George (Kid) Lavigne,
Pedlar Palmer, Frank Craig, Bob Fitzsimmons, etc.

576. EDITOR OF *BOXIANA*
(Pierce Egan)
Impartial Enquiry Into the Existing Doubts
and Various Reports Relative to the Late
Pugilistic Contest between the Renowned
Dutch Sam and Nosworthy at Moulsey
Hurst, December 8th, 1814.
London, Printed by and for G. Smeeton,
(1815).
The title-page announces that – The En-
quiry is Tending to Remove all undue
Prejudices and unfounded assertion, from
beginning to end. Supported by Documents
and Facts – Dedicated to the Sporting
World, with Great Respect and Deference,
by the Editor of *Boxiana* .
This item includes articles on the two fighters, and
accounts of the fight, with comments.
There is also an advert, regarding the New Series
of *Boxiana* – to be published in February, 1815,
price 6d each number, to be embellished with a
Portrait of a Distinguished Pugilist. The series to

continued

be a continuation from May, 1813 (When the First Volume Closed), to the Present Day.

577. EDITORIAL FEATURES INC.
(Publishers)
Champs
(Heavyweight Battles in Pictures — Big Fights Since Sullivan)
Rochester, (N.Y.), 1938.
Contains pictures, cartoons and articles featuring famous bouts from Sullivan to Braddock and Louis.

578. EDMONDS, Anthony O.
Joe Louis
Grand Rapids, (Michigan), William B. Eardman's Publishing Co., 1973.
112pp.

579. EDMUNDSON, Joseph
Great Moments in Boxing
London, Carousel Paperback, 1974.
126pp. Illus.

580. EDUARDO-GONZALES, C.F.
Boxing Fan's Glossary
Minneapolis, Published by the author, 1980.
47pp.

581. EDWARD, Paul (Editor)
Best Sport Stories
London, Faber and Faber, 1966.
222pp.
Includes one boxing story, "Blood Wedding in Chicago", by Robert Lowry. This is sub-titled "For the Middleweight Championship; Ray Robinson and Jake LaMotta".

582. EDWARDS, Audrey
The Picture Life of Muhammad Ali
New York and London, F. Watts, 1976.
47pp. (Mainly illustrations).

583. EDWARDS, Billy
The Portrait Gallery of Pugilists of England, America, Australia
London and Philadelphia, Pugilistic Publishing Co., 1894.
This work was originally published in parts.
The complete volume is bound in green or purple cloth, with gold lettering on the front cover. One bound version contains 96 plates; it is also found with only 64 plates. Each measures 14ins. x 11ins. and they portray pugilists of England, Australia and America. Most of the plates show the subject in boxing pose, with a biographical description on the reverse side.

Among the plates are 8 of Young Griffo and Young Campbell, entitled "A Boxing Lesson", showing various punches and guards.

584. EDWARDS, H.J.W.
The Good Patch. The Story of the Rhondda.
Introduction by Arthur Bryant
London, Jonathan Cape, 1938.
246pp.
Chapter X, "Sport in the Rhondda", includes mention of boxing in the valley, referring to people Tommy Farr, Llew Edwards, Jimmy Wilde, Tom Evans, Job Churchill, Mr Emlyn Michael (London Boxing Critic) and to boxing venues at Judges Hall, Trealaw, and Llwynpia Baths.

585. EDWARDS, William
(Ex-Champion Lightweight of America)
Art of Boxing and Science of Self Defence, together with a Manual of Training
New York, Excelsior Publishing House, 1888.
New York, Platt and Nourse Co., (Cop. 1888).
111pp. Illus. (posed by Billy Edwards and Arthur Chambers)
A further edition was issued in wrappers by M. Ottenheimer, Baltimore, Maryland, U.S.A. in 1948.

586. EDWARDS, William
Gladiators of the Prize Ring, or Pugilists of America and their contemporaries from James J. Corbett to Tom Hyer, with authentic records of their victories and defeats, embracing all the men of note of all nations connected with the pugilistic arena.
Chicago, The Athletic Publishing Co., 1895.
196pp. Portraits.

587. EGAN, Pierce
Boxiana, or Sketches of Ancient and Modern Pugilism
This Classic of the Prize-Ring was issued in parts and in volumes between 1812 and 1829, as well as being issued in single volumes and in sets of later days. It passed through several phases as to authors and publishers.
A brief history of publication is given as follows:
A single volume, with the author given as "One of the Fancy", originally appeared in parts and was published as a single volume by George Smeeton in 1812.

continued

Pierce Egan produced three volumes, published by Sherwood, Neely and Jones, the first two in 1818 and the third in 1821.

Jon Bee was the author of a single volume for Sherwood, Neely, and Jones in 1824; this was designated volume four.

Pierce Egan wrote fourth and fifth volumes in his own series in 1828 and 1829; these were published by George Virtue.

Finally, there was a volume of plates from *Boxiana*; this was issued ca.1840 and contained all the plates from the volumes. There were 62 plates, these being made up by 57 plates from the volumes, plus three single figures of boxers who were originally shown in combat with another pugilist on a folding plate.

There are also three plates in this volume which were not included in the original issue of *Boxiana*.

The first volume, dated 1812, and published by George Smeeton, had previously been issued in 21 parts. Smeeton was not responsible for the publication of any further volumes of the work, although another volume was advertised to appear under his name; this was due for publication on 1st February, 1815. The proposed issue was advertised in "An Impartial Enquiry into the Existing Doubts and Various Reports Relative to the Late Pugilistic Contest between the Renowned Dutch Sam and Noseworthy at Moulsey Hurst, (Dec. 8th, 1814) etc.", by the editor of *Boxiana*, printed by and for G. Smeeton, 17. St. Martin's Lane, London, 1815.

It was proposed to issue this new series in parts, but for some reason neither the parts nor any further volumes were issued by Smeeton.

Four volumes were published by Sherwood, Neely and Jones, (afterwards Sherwood, Jones and Co.), as follows:

1. First Volume, published in 1818, under the authorship of Pierce Egan. This material was largely taken from Smeeton's single volume, issued in 1812; the plates were identical and the imprints unaltered. The dedication from Smeeton's volume, much disfigured by Egan, was incorporated into the 1818 issue, as was the Smeeton title-page.

Pierce Egan was at one time a compositor in Smeeton's office, and the publisher apparently did not object to the public-ation of his original volume in Egan's name, so it would appear that he did not disagree with Egan taking over the work.

2. Sherwood and Co. published a second volume under the name of Egan in 1818.

3. Sherwood and Co. published a third volume by Egan in 1821.

4. The Sherwood Company published a fourth volume in 1824; the compiler of this was Jon Bee (John Badcock), who was the editor of the Pugilistic Section of *The Annals of Sporting*.

This fourth volume was the last original issue published by Sherwood; this company sought an injunction against Pierce Egan selling his own fourth volume to another publisher (George Virtue), as a result of this the Lord Chancellor ordered Egan to prefix the words "New Series" to his book. This finalised the matter.

The first of Pierce Egan's "New Series" of *Boxiana* appeared in 1828, and the second volume under this designation in 1829. They were published by George Virtue. This publisher reissued all Egan's five volumes in parts at 6d each; he also issued them as a five volume set in 1830.

Some volumes of *Boxiana* were reissued by a publisher named W.M. Clark, of Warwick Lane, Paternoster Row, London; but this publisher was not involved in the issue of any of the original volumes.

W.M. Clark advertised the publication as follows:

"The work will be published in weekly numbers and monthly parts; every alternative number will contain a Portrait of a Celebrated Boxer, and from sixteen to twenty-four pages of letter press. The work may be had in five volumes, at ten shillings each"

The plates bore no imprint and the five volumes comprised those by Egan, as issued by Virtue; the price of the parts was 1s each.

As previously stated, Egan's first three volumes, together with the two designated "New Series", were issued by George Virtue in a five volume set. Some may be found with the names of the following publishers in the front cover:

continued
J.

145

(a) Strange, 21 Paternoster Row, London
(b) B. Steill, 20 Paternoster Row, London
(c) Berger, Holywell Street, London
These volumes carry an advertisement on the back cover for other works published by Strange. In these instances the name of Virtue is still shown on the title-page as the publisher.

There does not appear to have been an American edition of *Boxiana* though an advertisement appeared in the *New Sporting Magazine* for December, 1835, as follows:

"The Publisher, having disposed of the whole of the Copper and Stereotype of *Boxiana* to an American bookseller, for re-publication in that country, he begs to inform the public that a very few copies of the work remain on hand, and will in the course of a few months be entirely out of print, and will not then be purchased for double its price of publication. The work was originally published in five volumes at Four Pounds, and is now offered to the public at half price"

(The publisher was then George Virtue)
Regarding the plates in *Boxiana*, these were distributed among the volumes as follows:
Pierce Egan's five volumes
Vol. 1 - 21 plates, plus illustrated title-page
Vol. 2 — 6 plates
Vol. 3 — 7 plates
Vol. 4 — 8 plates
Vol. 5 — 7 plates

588. EGAN, Pierce

The Art of Boxing, So Clearly Elucidated that on Perusal the Greatest Novice May Easily Make Himself the Master of that Noble and National Sport.
A New Edition, by the Author of *Boxiana*.
London, George Smeeton, ca.1816.
24pp. Frontis.

589. EGAN, Pierce

Key to the Picture of The Fancy —
Going to a Fight at Moulsey Hurst
London, R. Jones, 1819.
This item is advertised in a list of books "recently published by Sherwood Jones and Co. at Paternoster Row, London", dated "London November 1824", which appears at the end of Volume I of *Boxiana*, published by Sherwood Jones in 1823.
The *Boxiana* advert reads as follows:

"The Road to the Fight. A Picture of the Fancy Going to a Fight at Moulsey Hurst (Measuring in length 14 feet). Containing numerous Original Characters, Many of them 'Portraits' in which all the Fun, Frolic, Lark, Gig, Life, Gammon and trying-it-on are depicted incident to the pursuit of a PRIZE MILL: dedicated, by permission, to Mr Jackson, and the Noblemen and Gentlemen comprising the Pugilistic Club".
The book *Key to the Picture of the Fancy*, etc. shows a cut of two pugilists in action on the title-page and is signed 'Pierce Egan' and dated 1819; it is shown as being designed and etched by I.R. Cruikshank.
This work is also reviewed in *The Sporting Magazine* Volume 7 (Dec. 1819), the review being headed "Curiosities of Literature".

590. EGAN, Pierce

Sporting Anecdotes, Original and Selected
London, Sherwood, Neely and Jones, 1820.
The frontispiece comprises eight small vignettes, one of them a prize-fight.
The book contains a number of items of pugilistic interest, including the following:
Captain Barclay (Mentioning his interest in the prize-ring) — Pugilism in Italy — On the Advantages resulting from a Sound Knowledge of Training Possessed by that Class of Society Termed "The Sporting World" — Epistle from Tom Crib to Big Ben Concerning Some Foul Play in a Late Transaction (Five Verses) — Russian Pugilsim — On the Usefulness of Pugilism — Tom Crib's Memorial to Congress — Sketch of Some of the Professors of the Old School of Boxers — Song Made on the Prize Ring in 1819, by the Author of *Boxiana* — Sketch of Mr. John Jackson, etc.
A New Edition, Considerable Enlarged and Improved was issued by the same publishers in 1825; information is given as follows:
Bound in boards with a woodcut of greyhounds and a hare on upper cover, wild duck and a funeral urn on the spine; advertisement for *Annals of Sporting* on the back cover with a woodcut of a deer. This edition contains additional material on pugilism, not included in the first issue:—
Description of Cruikshank's visit to the Fives Court — The seasons; A Pugilistic Fragment — Tom Crib. A Biography — Canons of Pugilism. The Dictae of an Amateur. (Some of these taken from the *Annals of Sporting*.)
The frontis is similar to that in the 1820 edition but there are 2 plates of pugilistic interest, as follows:
A visit to the Fives Court. Designed and etched by J.F. Cruikshank. Tom Cribb. Engraved by Percy Roberts from a painting by Sharples.

591. EGAN, Pierce

Life in London. Or The Day and Night Scenes of Jerry Hawthorn Esq. and his Elegant Corinthian Tom, Accompanied by Bob Logic, the Oxonian, in Their Rambles and Sprees through the Metropolis of
continued

146

London, Printed for Sherwood, Neely and Jones, 1821.

A second edition was dated 1822 and there were further editions in 1823 and 1830.

Reprints were issued by Hotten in 1869 and by Methuen's in 1904.

Some copies of the first edition were issued on large paper and some copies of this version have 23 extra plates by Heath. There was an American edition, in two volumes, issued by M. Kean of New Orleans in 1837 and by James Rice of Louisville in the same year. This edition was not illustrated.

The text of the work contains many references to pugilism, particularly in Book II, chapter III. The coloured plates include 2 of pugilistic interest, both drawn and engraved by I.R. and G. Cruikshank as follows:
1. Art of Self Defence, Tom and Jerry receiving instruction from Mr. Jackson at his rooms.
2. Cribb's Parlour, Tom introducing Jerry and Logic to the Champion of England.

592. EGAN, Pierce

The Fancy Togs Man versus Young Sadboy, The Milling Quaker

London, Published by the Author, 71 Chancery Lane, 1823.

33pp.

Ludicrous report by the author of *Life in London* of a suit at law, between a tailor against a young Quaker, a minor; for the amount of bill for clothes. The defendant's pleas were "minority" and that such dress did not come under the heading "Necessary". The promising young spark used to attend prize-fights.

Counsel's speech for the Defendant includes "His Sketch of the illustrious Belcher's Parlour" – "A glimpse of Dick Curtis' White Surtout and Pearl Buttons", etc.

593. EGAN, Pierce (Editor)

Grose's Classical Dictionary of the Vulgar Tongue. Revised and Corrected.

London, Printed for the Editor, 1823.

282pp.

Includes a considerable number of entries of pugilistic interest, with interpretations of the meaning of words in current use with reference to the prize-ring.

594. EGAN, Pierce

Pierce Egan's Account of the Trial of John Thurtell and Joseph Hunt. With an Appendix, Disclosing Some Extraordinary Facts Exclusively in the Possession of the Editor.

With Portraits and Many Other Illustrative

Engravings.

London, Knight and Lacy, 1824.

The appendix has a separate title-page and comprises 44 pages which contain many references to Thurtell's interest in the prize-ring, in particular to his part in organising the bout between Painter and Oliver at North Walsham near Norwich.

A note on John Thurtell in *The Concise History of National Biography* describes him as a murderer, son of the Mayor of Norwich, who took to prize-fighting and gambling; lost money to William Weare, whom he murdered on the St. Alban's Road, 1823. In spite of a powerful speech in his own defence, he was hanged.

595. EGAN, Pierce

Pierce Egan's Anecdotes (Original and Selected) of the Turf, the Chase, the Ring and the Stage; the whole forming a Complete Panorama of the Sporting World. Writing with it a Book of Reference and Entertaining Companion to the Lovers of British Sports.

Embellished with Thirteen coloured plates, designed from Nature and etched by Theodore Lane.

Dedicated to Sir Bellingham Graham, Bart.

London, Printed for Knight and Lacy, and Pierce Egan, 1827.

Issued in pictorial boards.

One of the coloured plates is of boxing interest. The text includes Anecdotes, Obituaries, Verses and Stories of pugilistic interest.

596. EGAN, Pierce

Pierce Egan's Book of Sports and Mirror of Life. Embracing the Turf, The Chase, The Ring and the Stage. Interspersed with Original Memoirs of Sporting Men, etc.

Dedicated to George Osbaldeston Esq.

London, Printed for T.T. and J. Tegg and R.Goffon and Co.,

Glasgow, 1832.

Illus. by R. Seymour

This work was originally issued in 25 weekly parts, with a woodcut on the first page of each part; it was afterwards issued complete in boards and also in six parts with four copies in each part, with one copy unaccounted for.

There were further editions in 1836 and 1844.

The work contained many pugilistic items and articles, including a series "Doings and Sayings in the Prize Ring".

597. EGAN, Pierce

Every Gentleman's Manual
London, Sherwood and Bowyer, 1845.
London, Flintoff, 153 Fleet Street, 1851.
A Lecture on the Art of Self Defence — by the Author of *Boxiana* etc. With Animated Sketches of the Most Celebrated Pugilists During the Last Century. Also a Visit to the Irish Champion's Tomb. Embellished with several Attitudes of the Most Accomplished Boxers in the Prize-Ring.
Dedicated to Lord Panmure.
Likewise A Spirited Etching of John Jackson Esq., illustrating the advantages of a Knowledge of the Art of Self Defence to the late Lord Byron.
199pp.
The First Edition is found with various bindings and with a different number of plates.
The two editions are similar, except that the frontis in the later edition is in some cases coloured, while some issues have no frontis.

598. EGAN, Pierce

Bill Neat v. Tom Hickman
London, Printed and Published by John Fairburn, Broadway, Ludgate Hill.
This item is advertised in *The Devil Among the Fancy*, 1822, as follows:
The Bristol Victor!! and the Gas Light Hero!!!; This Day is published, price Sixpence, An Account of the Great Fight for the Championship of All England, between Neat of Bristol, and Hickman. The Gas Light Hero, On Hungerford Downs, Tuesday December 11th 1821, for Two Hundred Guineas A-Side. By Pierce Egan, Author of *Sporting Anecdotes, Life in London* &c. &c., To which are Added Lines on the Defeat of Hickman, and a Song "Neat Valiant Neat, That Extinguished the Gas".

599. EGAN, Pierce

Boxiana. Sketches of Ancient and Modern Pugilism. Introduction and Additions by Dennis Prestidge.
Leicester, Vance Harvey Publishing, 1971.
482pp. Illus., including the original title-page and plates.
A Facsimile Edition of Pierce Egan's first volume.

600. EGAN, Pierce

Boxiana, or, Sketches of Ancient and Modern Pugilism. A Selection, edited and introduced by John Ford.
London, The Folio Society, 1976.
208pp. Bound in Caxton Kingsway cloth. Issued in a slip-case.

This edition contains 8 coloured illustrations from engravings by Thomas Rowlandson, Robt. Cruikshank, and others. The coloured endpapers show a reproduction of the panoramic engraving by Robt. Cruikshank, "The Fancy On The Road To Moulsey Hurst".

601 EICKLER, Alfred

Gentle Giant
A Boxing Romance.
London, G. Swann Limited, 1943.

603. ELKIN, Robert

Queen's Hall 1893—1941
London, Rider and Co., 1941.
Foreword by Sir Malcolm Sargent.
160pp. Illus.
Information on boxing matches held in the Queens Hall is given in Chapter XIII, entitled "Diverse Occasions".

604. "ELLANGOWAN"
(James Glass Bertram)

Sporting Anecdotes
London, Hamilton, Adams and Co., 1889
Glasgow, Thomas D. Morison, 1889.
352pp.
Bound in blue cloth with gold lettering on the spine.
This item contains the following pugilistic anecdotes:
The Fruits of Boxing Fame — Johnny Broome the "Pug of Fame" — How Jem Burn the Pugilist took an Insult from a Customer — First Appearance of the Champion of England (Jem Ward) — Gregson, the Poet of the Pugilists — Glove Fights — Gentleman Jackson — Billy's Epitaph (Cribb's Song) — How Sir Tatton Sykes punished a Pugilist — Jem Ward and the Editor's Lady — The Bold Bendigo and Jem Burn — Prize Fighting on the Derby Day — How the Pugilist of the Period is Trained — L.S.D. of a Great Pugilistic Event (Sullivan v. Kilrain) — Pugilists after the Fight.

605. ELLIOTT, Ernest C.

Fifty Leaders of British Sport
A Series of Portraits with Biographical Notes and a Preface by F.G. Aflalo.
London, John Lane, The Bodley Head, 1904
Includes entries on Captain Walter Edgeworth-Johnstone and The Earl of Lonsdale, with portraits.

606. ELLIOTT, W.J.

The Art of Attack and Defence in use at the Present Time. Fencing . . . and Boxing.
London, Dean and Son, 1886.
40pp. 12mo.

607. ELMER, Professor William
Boxing
New York, American Sports Publishing Co., 1902.
(Sportsman's Athletic Library, Vol.14 No. 162)
209pp. Illus.

608. ELMER, Professor William
Spalding's Boxing Guide, an accurate instructor of the Science of Self Defence, Rules of Boxing
Sydney, Australian Sports Publishing Co., ca. 1905.
(Spalding's Athletic Library)
140pp. Illus.

609. EMINENT PUGILIST, An
The Art and Practise of English Boxing, containing Explanatory Illustrations of Pugilistic Attitudes in the Art of Attack and Self Defence, as practised by the most celebrated Boxers of the present day; with Broughton's Rules as observed at his Amphitheatre in Tottenham Court Road.
Written under the direction of an Eminent Pugilist.
London, W. Glinden, Printer and R. Walker, 1807.
Price 6d.
36pp. with a folding coloured plate showing nine boxing Attitudes.
A second edition was issued in 1809, to which was added an authentic account of the battles between Broughton and Slack, April 11th, 1750, Humphries and Mendoza, January, 1788, and Cribb and Jem Belcher, Feb. 1st, 1809.
36pp with coloured plate similar to that in the first edition.

610. ENCINOSA, Enrique G.,
and KAPLAN, Hank
Boxing – This is It!
Palm Springs (California), ETC Publications. ca.1984.
245pp. Illus.

611. ENCYCLOPEDIA BRITANNICA
COMPANY LTD. (Publishers)
The Encyclopedia Britannica
London and New York, First issued in 1768. Fourteenth Edition, 1929, A New Study of Universal Knowledge.
Volume 3, (Baltimore to Braila), includes a section on Boxing, written in part by E.B. Osborn, Literary Editor of *The Morning Post* (London), and by Gene Tunney (Ex-World Heavyweight Champion

U.S.A.). The section includes a short bibliography of boxing books, together with instructional and other illustrations.
Volume 18 (Plants to Raymond of Tripoli) has a section on Pugilism, including "Boxing in Classical Days" and "Pugilism in England".
In the Annual Supplement to the Eleventh Edition, issued in 1913, and entitled *The Britannica Yearbook*, short mention occurs of boxing in Section VIII, "Sports and Games".

612. ENTERKIN, Hamilton
Dames Out Of The Ring
A collection of short stories told by a trainer, an old hand at the boxing game.
U.S.A., Published by Kaner, 1948.
64pp. Cold. paper covers.

613. ETHERINGTON, Harry,
and PALMER, A. and Son (Publishers)
The Sporting Mirror
London, 1881 to 1886 (10 volumes)
The first 9 volumes were published by H. Etherington and the final volume by A. Palmer and Son.
This publication was issued in monthly parts and also in bound volumes, each made up of six monthly issues.
The magazine was illustrated by full page plates of prominent sportsmen; it included a number of articles and plates of boxing interest.
Articles, many of them illustrated, appeared on such as R. Frost-Smith and G.H. Vize (Famous Amateur Boxers), Ned Donnelly, John Gully, Jem Mace, Tom Sayers, Jem Ward and others.

614. EVANS, B.J.
How to Become A Sporting Journalist
Foreword by C.B. Fry
London, W.H. Allen and Co. Ltd., 1946.
98pp.
Bound in pink cloth, gilt lettering on front cover.
21 chapters, 3 of these are devoted to boxing, as follows:

Chapter 4 – Reporting a Big Fight
Chapter 5 – The Old N.S.C.
Chapter 6 – I Refereed a Fight
Chapter 21 – Famous Sporting Journalists, includes writers on boxing.

615. EVANS, Godfrey
Behind the Stumps
London, Hodder and Stoughton, 1951.
207pp.
This autobiography includes information on the author's short career as a professional boxer, during which he had at least three fights.

616. *EVENING NEWS*
(Allied Newspapers Ltd) (Publishers)
Hitler Passed This Way. (170 pictures from the London *Evening News*) with an Introduction "Four Years of Bombs" by Crawford Snowden.
Published in London.

This item was printed on art paper and deals with London buildings damaged by wartime bombs; these are shown before and after the damage.
Two articles and sets of pictures refer to the destruction of the Blackfriars "Ring" and the Holborn Stadium (also known as The Stadium Club). Both of these buildings were well-known boxing venues.

617. EVERLAST BOXING RECORD BOOK 1922
"Boxing Blue Book"
New York, Everlast Sporting Goods Manufacturing Co., 1922.

352pp.
The chief articles of the 1922 edition were as follows:
Biographies of the Officers of the N.Y.State Athletic Commission (William Muldoon and Henry P. Burchell)
Biography of Tex Rickard
Boxing's Greatest Year, 1921.
"Battle of the Century", (Dempsey v. Carpentier)
Benny Leonard v. Ritchie Mitchell contest
Brief Histories of Jack Dempsey, Geo.Carpentier, Johnny Wilson, Jack Britton, Benny Leonard, Johnny Dundee, Johnny Kilbane, Johnny Buff, Jimmy Wilde, Pete Herman.

618. EVERLAST BOXING RECORD
This annual publication ran from 1922 to 1938. During that time it was issued variously by the Everlast Sporting Goods Manufacturing Co. the Everlast Sports Publishing Co. the *Boxing News*, and independent individuals. The annuals contained not only boxers' records but also articles by famous boxing authorities, and were fully illustrated with pictures and cartoons.
The standard contents of each issue consisted of the following:
Authentic ring records of important present-day boxers
Complete records of all champions and descriptive matter pertaining to them
Boxing Laws, Rules and Regulations of the New York State Ahtletic Commission
Boxers' and Managers' Directory

The details of each issue are listed in the adjacent 17 entries.

619. EVERLAST BOXING RECORD BOOK 1923
"Boxing's Baedeker"

New York, Everlast Sports Goods Manufacturing Co., 1923.

416pp.
The principal special articles in this issue were as follows:
Biographies of Senator James Walker, Tex Rickard and Joe Humphries
History of Self Defence
Boxing Enjoyed a Bumper Year
Second Battle of the Century, (Leonard v. Tendler)
When Greb Wrested Title from Tunney
Mickey Walker Wins Title from Jack Britton
Siki v. Carpentier Battle; Round by Round Description
Filipino Ascends American Flyweight Throne
Brief Histories of Boxers: Battling Siki, Harry Greb Mickey Walker, Joe Lynch, Pancho Villa, together with others repeated from the 1922 edition.

620. EVERLAST BOXING RECORD, 1924
New York, Everlast Sports Goods Manufacturing Co., 1924.
Editor-in-Chief: Robert Ripley
The Introduction to this edition says (*inter alia*): "In presenting this, the third issue of the *Everlast Boxing Record*, we again bring to your attention the most complete and carefully compiled record of boxing statistics and news of fistiana for 1923".
398pp.

The contents include:

By Way of Greeting, by Robert L. Ripley
Dempsey Says a Few Words to Ripley
Luis Angel Firpo, by W.G. McGeehan
A Truly Remarkable Man (Johnny Dundee)
Tricky Old-Timers in Action, by Robert Edgren
Dempsey v. Firpo Bout (Round by Round Description)
McTigue Wins Light Heavyweight Championship of World
Tunney Regains Title from Greb
Dempsey-Gibbons Bout. (Round by Round Description)
Benny Leonard Conquers His Greatest Rival
Brief Histories of Boxers, as in previous issues.

621. EVERLAST BOXING RECORD, 1925
New York, Everlast Sports Publishing Co. Inc 1925.
Editor: Robert Ripley
416pp.

This edition includes the following articles:

Man to Man, by Grantland Rice
Boxing in Europe, by T.C. Wignall
Wills-Firpo Bout. (Round by Round Description)
Carpentier-Tunney Bout. (Round by Round Description)
Goldstein-Lynch Bout. (Round by Round Description)

continued

Brief Histories of boxers, Mike McTigue and others, as in previous issues.

622. EVERLAST BOXING RECORD, 1926

New York, Everlast Sports Publishing Co.Inc 1926.

352pp.

This issue contains the following articles:

Pancho Villa, by Will Gould
Gene Tunney, by Ned Brown
Paul Berlanbach, byEd. Sullivan
Boxing Needs New Blood, by Jimmy De Forest
Rocky Kansas, by Ed. Van Every
Bouts that Drew $120.000 or over
The Year 1925 in Review, by Francis Albertanti

623. EVERLAST BOXING RECORD, 1927

New York, Everlast Sports Publishing Co.Inc 1927.

448pp.

The main features of this issue are given as follows

Topsy Turvy Year, by George Underwood
Walker Wins Second Title in Record Time
The Nebraska Wild Cat, by Will Gould
Harry Greb's Career, byEd. Van Every
Dempsey-Tunney Battle Realised Rickard's dream, by Martin J. Berg
Tunney-Dempsey, Round by Round
Articles on boxers: Jack Delaney, Jack Sharkey, Jim Maloney, Sammy Mandell, Pete Latzo, Johnny Green, Charles "Phil" Rosenberg.

624. EVERLAST BOXING RECORD, 1928

New York, Everlast Sports Publishing Co.Inc 1928.

Edited by S.Jay Levin. Cartoons by Will Gould.

454pp.

This issue contains the following articles:
Tex Rickard's 1928 Forecast
Blindness, the Fighter's Menace, by Joe Williams
Books and Boxing, by Al. Gould
Loud Demand for George Godfrey, by Murray Lewis
England Cannot Boast a Single Boxing Champ. by Fairplay
Articles on boxers: Gene Tunney, Leo Lomski, Tom Heeney, Tommy Loughran, Roberto Roberti, Tiger Flowers.

625. EVERLAST BOXING RECORD, 1929

New York, Everlast Sports Publishing Co.Inc 1929.

Edited by John J. Romano
Cartoons by Will Gould
392pp.

Among the articles in this issue were the following:

Arguments of Old Timers versus Present Day Boxers, by Hype Igoe

'Color' Leaves the Game, by Paul Gallico
The Bayonets and Boxing
A Period in Prize-Fighting History, by Joe Villa
William Muldoon's Philosophy of Health, by Ed. Van Every
Where, Oh Where Is the Puncher, by Sparrow McGann
Ancient Boxers Still Going Strong, by Wilbur Wood
The Chicago Stadium, by John J. Romano
Some Famous Series in the Ring, by Wilbur Wood
Dempsey's Come Back, by Joe Williams
Boston's Place in Boxing, by Eddie Mack
Evil-Eye Sharkey and that Superiority Complex, by Will Gould
Broadcasts Boost Boxing, by Jimmy Bronson
The March of Kearns' Musketeers, by Gene Fowler

626. EVERLAST BOXING RECORD, 1930

New York, Everlast Sports Publishing Co.Inc 1930.

Edited by John J. Romano

352pp.

In addition to the usual features this edition contained the following:

A Testimonial to William Muldoon, by Ed. Van Every
Jack Sharkey, the Warrior, by Paul Gallico
Dempsey in a New Role, by Robert F. Keeley
Jimmy McLarnin, by Hype Igoe
Johnny Dundee's Birthday, by Ed. Sullivan
Reducing the Hazards of Boxing, by Dr. H.G. Goldman
Boston in Fistdom, by Eddie Mack
Kid Chocolate, Picture Fighter, by Wilbur Wood

This issue and those following it contained articles on the boxing scene in many of the States of the USA.

627. EVERLAST BOXING RECORD, 1931

New York, Everlast Sports Publishing Co.Inc 1931.

Edited by John J. Romano

352pp.

Among the articles in this edition were the following:

Canzoneri, Now One of the King's Immortals, by Hype Igoe,
Battling Battalino, by Damon Runyon
A Talk with Jim Corbett, by Joe Williams
The Last Bell, by Lou Jaffa
Gans Could Match Brains, by Ed. Van Every
There were also articles on Gene Tunney, Max Schmeling, Frank Wiener, Jack Sharkey, and Pete Sanstol.

628. EVERLAST BOXING RECORD FOR 1932

New York, Everlast Sports Publishing Co.Inc 1932.

continued

Edited by John J. Romano

The principal articles in this issue included:

James J. Johnston, by Sparrow McGann
Those Were theDays, by Hype Igoe
Michigan's Big Three, by E.W. Dickerson
K.O.'s Few in Amateur Ring, by Will Wedge
Max Schmeling's Rise to Fame, by Joe Williams
Everlast National Boxing Poll for 1931.

629. EVERLAST BOXING RECORD FOR 1933

New York, Everlast Sports Publishing Co.Inc 1933.

Edited by John J. Romano

192pp.

Included the following articles:

Charley Retzlaff, by John J. Romano
With the American Team in Los Angeles
Boxing in Argentina, by Ricardo Carjabal

630. EVERLAST BOXING RECORD FOR 1934

New York, Everlast Sports Publishing Co.Inc 1934.

Edited by "J.J.G."

180pp.

This issue included the following articles:

Boxing the Compass, by Eddie Eagan
The Old Man Reminisces, by Paul Gallico
Lightweight Title Goes Back 200 Years, by
  Edward J. Geiger
What has Become of All the Irish Lightweights?
  by Joe Williams
Will Brown's Tonic to Revive the Fistic Game,
  by Damon Runyon
Tony Canzoneri, by Sam Taub
Paolino Uzcudun, by Walton L. Robinson
The Art of Fistiana, by Will Gould
Dai Dollings (Trainer Extraordinary)

631. EVERLAST BOXING RECORD FOR 1935

New York, Everlast Sports Publishing Co.Inc 1935.

Edited by Billy Stevens

Cartoons by Lank Leonard and Will Gould

160pp.

The articles in this edition included the following:

Record Boxing Gate Receipts for All Time
Setups and Upsets for 1934, by Don Granger
One Man's Opinion, by Edward G. Foster.
Corbett, a Good Bet, by Pat Frayne
Barney Ross, by Joe Foley
Champions of All Classes, by Frank G. Menke

There were a number of full-page portraits of boxers by Lank Leonard.

This was the final issue of this record book actually produced by the Everlast Sports Publishing Co. For the final three years of publication is was issued by *Boxing News*, Eddie Borden, and Maurice Waxman.

632. EVERLAST BOXING RECORD FOR 1936

New York, *The Boxing News*, 1936.

Edited by George Winn

Cartoons by D. D. Golomb

128pp.

The principal articles included the following:

As I See Them, by George Winn
Louis, Iceberg in the Ring or Out, by Wilbur Wood
Barney Ross is a Busy Champion, by Hype Igoe
Manager with a Million Friends – Pete Reilly
When Opportunity Knocked, Joe Gould Answered
  by Tex Sullivan
Britisher Destined for Great Heights (Jock
  McAvoy), by Duke Ballard
Freddie Miller, Recognised Almost Universally as
  the World Featherweight Champion, Maurice
  Waxman
It Takes a Thoroughbred to Come Back, by D.D.
  Colomb.

633. EVERLAST BOXING RECORD, 1937

New York, Eddie Borden, 1937.

Edited by Eddie Borden

192pp.

A preliminary announcement to this edition states:

"This year's record book removes all superfluous reading matter. Those stories can always be read in the daily newspaper".

Additional contents are as follows:

Manager with a Million Friends (Pete Reilly) by
  Maurice Waxman
Bringing Back Boxing, by Sam Taub
Boxing Writers and Sporting Editors

634. EVERLAST BOXING RECORD, 1938

New York, Maurice Waxman, 1938.

Editors: Maurice Waxman and Charles Vackner

196pp.

This, the last issue of this publication, included articles and material as follows:

Game and Mighty Handy, is Tom of Tonypandy
  (Tommy Farr)
Boxing is on the Upgrade in New Jersey, by
  Solar Plexus
Gould and Braddock are Modern Damon and
  Pythias, by Wilbur Wood
Always Johnny on the Spot, That's Johnny
  McAvoy, By Charles Vackner
King Mike the First is the Promotorial Ace, by
  Lester Scott
Two Prospective Champions (Pete Scalzo and
  Schmeling)
Sixto, The Brain, by Julio Garson
Greek Hercules of the Lightweights (George
  Zengaras)

This issue included cartoons of Max Schmeling,
continued

Tommy Farr, Ted Burman, Vittorio (Vic) Venturi, Mike Belloise, Allie Stolz, Sixto Escobar, and Tiger Jack Fox.

635. EWART SEYMOUR AND CO. LTD.
(Publishers)
Boxing Rules and Guide to Refereeing, Judging, etc. (Royal Army and Navy Boxing Association)
London, 1918.
47pp.

636. EWART SEYMOUR AND CO. LTD.
(Publishers)
How to Become a Boxer
London, ca. 1920.
46pp. Bound in Boards. Illus.

637. EWART SEYMOUR AND CO. LTD.
(Publishers)
Boxing for Amateurs

(*Boxing* Handbook No.6)
Illus.

638. EXPERT, An
Boxing; With Hints on the Art of Attack and Defence, and How to Train for the Prize Ring
New York, Richard K. Fox, 1889.
49pp. Illus.
Includes chapters on the Origin of Boxing, Important Points of Boxing, Prize Ring Rules and Instructional Chapters.
The illustrations are mostly instructional, with additional pictures of Jake Kilrain, Jack McAuliffe, Peter Jackson, John L. Sullivan and others.

639. EXPERT BOXER AND ATHLETE, An
Art of Boxing, Swimming, and Gymnastics Made Easy etc.
New York, 1883.
99pp. Bound in wrappers.
This is assumed to be the work of Ned Donovan. A work with the same title was attributed to Henry Llewellyn Williams (q.v.)

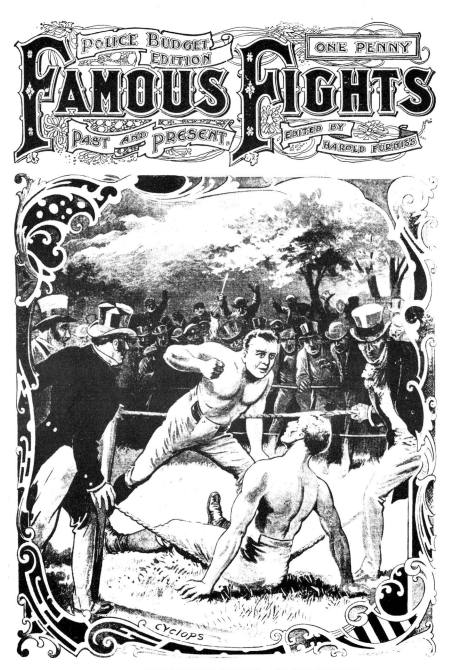

Front cover No.56 Vol.V *Famous Fights* Magazine (Bib. Ref. 759)

640. FAIR, James R.
Give Him to the Angels.
The Story of Harry Greb.
New York, Smith and Durell, 1946.

184pp. Bound in yellow cloth, with full-length action portrait of Harry Greb as frontis.
This is the biography of one of the legendary characters of boxing.

641. FAIRBAIRN, W.E.
Defendu. Scientific Self-Defence
Shanghai, 1926.

171pp. Illus.
See *Scientific Self-Defence* (1931) and
All-in Fighting (1942).

642. FAIRBAIRN, W.E.
Scientific Self-Defence
New York and London, D.A.Appleton and Co., 1931.

Preface by Douglas Fairbanks.

179pp.
This book is based on an earlier work by the same author issued in Shanghai in 1926 under the title - *Defendu.* (q.v.)

643. FAIRBAIRN, Captain W.E.
(Late Assistant Commissioner Shanghai City Municipal Police)
All-in Fighting
London, Faber and Faber, 1942.

132pp.
Deals principally with individual fighting in war-time, but contains some references to boxing. The Introduction states: "This book is based on earlier works under the titles of *Defendu*, which was written for the police forces of the Far East, and *Scientific Self Defence*, published by D. Appleton of New York.

644. FAIRBAIRN, Capt. W.E.
Get Tough!
How to Win in Hand to Hand Fighting. As taught to the British Commandos and the U.S. Armed Forces.
Boulder (Colorado), The Paldin Press, 1942.

110pp. Illus. by line drawings.
Although not a boxing item, this book may be deemed to be collectable by students of the Art of Self Defence.

645. FAIRBURN, John
(Printer and Publisher)
The Devil Among the Fancy: or The Pugilistic Courts in an Uproar.
London, 1822.

Illustrated with a tinted plate of Sporting Life in High Life and in Low Life. Drawn and engraved by Mr. Cruikshank.
This item includes an account of a trial in the Court of Common Pleas on May 8th, 1822, the action being brought by Samuel William Hunt, the proprietor of the Tennis Court in Windmill Street, Haymarket, against Robert Bell, the Editor and Proprietor of the *Sunday Dispatch*, to recover damages for an alleged libel published in that newspaper in a letter signed by Thos. Cribb, Thomas Belcher, John Randall, John Martin, Edward Turner, Joshua Hudson, Jack Scroggins and others.
Pages 3 to 10 comprise introduction to the case and pages 10 to 18 an account of the trial. The jury gave a verdict for the Defendant.
Among the witnesses called was Daniel Mendoza.

646. FAIRFAX, John and Sons Ltd.
(Publishers)
A Century of Journalism — The Sydney *Morning Herald* and its Record of Australian Life
Sydney (N.S.W.), 1931.

Includes reports of prize-fighting in 1832, when the *Herald* was apparently not opposed to the sport. But the paper later changed its attitude, as articles appeared in 1847 attacking pugilism.

647. FALK, Bernard
The Naked Lady, or Storm over Adah
A Biography of Adah Isaacs Menken
London, Hutchinson and Co. (Publishers) Ltd., 1934.
(There were at least 3 impressions of this book)

306pp. Illus. of which 3 include J.C.Heenan.
This book contains many references to famous pugilists, particularly to J.C. Heenan, the second husband of Adah Isaacs Menken, a well-known actress. Although most of the boxing passages refer to Heenan (including the marriage and divorce). mention is also made of Tom King and Jem Mace.

648. FALK, Bernard
Five Years Dead
A Postscript to *He Laughed in Fleet Street*
London, Hutchinson and Co. (Publishers) Ltd., 1937.

377pp. Illus.
Includes a number of slight references to boxing:
Chapter XVI — Tells how the Berry brothers (newspaper proprietors) founded the magazine *Boxing* following the success of a publishing venture; and of one of the brothers' interest in the sport.
Chapter XX — tells of the author's friendship with Lord Lonsdale and how the latter was persuaded to write his memoirs for *The People*.

649. FARMER, John, and

\continued

HENLEY, W.E.
A Dictionary of Slang and Colloquial English Abridged from the seven volume work entitled *Slang and its Analogues* 1894–1904.
London, George Routledge and Sons Ltd., 1905.
New York, E.P. Dutton and Co., 1905.
533pp.
Contains many items of pugilistic interest. An example being "The Auctioneer", the nickname given to Tom Sayers' right hand.

650. FARMER, John S. and
HENLEY, W.E.
Slang and its Analogues
London, George Routledge and Sons Ltd., 1894–1904.
(2 Volumes)
See *A Dictionary of Slang and Colloquial English.*

651. "FARMER'S SON, A"
A Fortnight's Ramble Through London; or, A Complete Display of All the Cheats and Frauds Practised in That Great Metropolis with the Best Methods of Eluding Them.
Being the true and pleasing narrative of the Adventures of a Farmer's son, Published at his request for the Benefit of his country.
London, Printed and sold by Dean and Munday, 1795.
Cold. frontis. by Isaac Cruikshank.
12 chapters. Chapter IX includes (*inter alia*) "The Battle between Ward and Mendoza – I love money".

652. FARNOL, Jeffery
The Amateur Gentleman
A Romance.
London, Sampson Low, Marston and Co. Ltd., 1913.
Boston, (U.S.A.), Little Brown and Co., 1913.
A de-luxe edition was issued by the same London publishers; this included 21 coloured illustrations by C.E. Brock.
599pp.
One of the chief characters in this novel is Jack Bart, an ex-pugilist.

653. FARNOL, Jeffery
Epics of the Fancy
A Vision of Old Fighters.
London, Sampson, Low, Marston and Co. Ltd., 1928.

Boston, (U.S.A.), Little Brown and Co., 1928.
(The American edition was issued under the title of *Famous Prize-Fights; or Epics of the Fancy*)
310pp. 21 chapters, with 19 of these referring to specific fights or fighters, and each chapter including a short biography of the boxers mentioned. 27 Illus.

654. FARR, Finis
Black Champion
The Life and Times of Jack Johnson
London, Macmillan and Co. Ltd., 1964.
237pp. Illus.

655. FARRAR, Arthur Hobart
How to Fight
A Fighters Manual, a thorough-going Comprehensive Self-Instructor of Fighting, in and out of the Ring.
New York City, Padell Book Co., 1943.
Bound in wrappers.
Black and white illustrations by "Seaman" in the text.

656. FARRELL, James T.
Fellow Countrymen
Collected Stories of James T. Farrell.
London, Constable and Co., 1937.
Another edition was issued in 1941.
439pp.
This book contains a boxing story entitled "Twenty-Five Bucks".

657. FARRELL, James T.
More Fellow Countrymen (Short Stories)
London, George Routledge and Sons Ltd., 1946.
223pp.
Includes story No. 8: "The Downfall of Machine Gun McGurk".

658. FAWCETT, William
(Hunting and Racing Editor of *The Field*)
Racing In The Olden Days
London, Hutchinson and Co. (Publishers) Ltd., 1933.
192pp.
This book contains a number of references to the old pugilists and others interested in the prize-ring; including John Gully, Colonel Mellish, Tom Cribb, Henry Pearce and others.

659. FAWCETT PUBLICATIONS INC.
continued

(Publishers)

Joe Louis, Champion of Champions

The Epic Story of a Farm Boy's Climb to the Heavyweight Championship of the World.

This is a 36-page comic, first issued in the U.S.A.

The English edition was published by L. Miller and Son, Hackney Road, London, in 1951.

There were 2 issues of the comic, both containing 36 pages, including covers.

660. FELLOWS, Bert, and
MARGOLIES, Hank
(Compilers)
Fight's

(South Africa's Premier Boxing Magazine), Boxing Annual of South Africa.

Johannesburg, Sporting Publications (Pty) Ltd., 1950.

208pp. Stiff paper covers. Picture of Vic Toweel on front cover.

661. FELSTEAD, S. Theodore

In Search of Sensation. Being Thirty Years of a London Journalist's Life.

304pp.

This book has some items of boxing interest, including the following:

Chapter II – From Sin, Sand and Sorrow to Grub Street, (Mentions Hugh D.McIntosh, Jack Johnson and Tommy Burns)

Chapter III – Test Cricket and Boxing. A Famous Referee. (Eugene Corri). Mentions C.B. Cochran and some famous contests promoted by him

Chapter IV – Great Days in Fleet Street. (Mentions a visit to Blackfriars 'Ring', with Hannen Swaffer)

Chapter XI – Gamble in Millions (Jimmy White). Mentions White's entry into boxing, including the proposed fight between Jack Johnson and Bombardier Billy Wells)

Chapter XV – Off Stage in the Film Studios. (Mentions Victor McLaglen)

662. FELSTEAD, S. Theodore

Stars Who Made the Halls

London, T. Werner Laurie Ltd,, 1946.

2nd Impression, 1947.

187pp. Illus.

This book contains a number of references to prominent boxers and others connected with the sport; these include Hugh D. McIntosh, Eugene Corri, Jem Mace, Victor McLaglen, Jim Corbett, Jack Johnson, etc.

663. FERRY, Francis J.

(Cousin of the late Champion)

The Story of Les Darcy, Late Middleweight Champion of the World.

N. Manley (N.S.W.) Published by the Author 1935, 10pp.

Second edition, 1936, 56pp.

The second edition was issued in pink pictorial paper covers, with an introduction by Dave Smith. A third edition was issued later in white paper covers, with a picture of Les Darcy on the front.

664. FEWTRELL, Thomas

Boxing Reviewed; or The Science of Manual Defence etc.

London, Printed for Scatchard and Whitaker and Champante and Whitrow, 1790.

Frontis. showing full-length portrait of Thos. Johnson (in action).

This is an interesting item in that it is possibly the first boxing book written by an active pugilist.

In one of his bouts Thomas Fewtrell was beaten by John Jackson at Croydon on June 9th, 1788.

665. FINN, Ralph L.

Everyday Cameos

London, Rich and Cowan, 1946.

128pp;

The author's note says (*inter alia*):– "Most of the Cameos which appear in these papers originally saw the light of day in *The People* – at the time of writing they are still being featured in each Sunday's issue of the paper".

One of the Cameos is entitled "Punch Drunk Old-Timer".

666. FINNEGAN, Chris
(With Walter Bartleman)

Finnegan, Self Portrait of a Fighting Man

An Autobiography

London, McDonald and Jones, 1976.

667. FISHER, Art, and Others

Garden of Innocents

New York, E.P.Dutton and Co. Inc., 1972.

186pp.

668. FISHER, Ham.
Author and Illustrator

Joe Palooka Comics, "Joe Tells How He Became World Champ".

Featuring America's most famous Comic Hero.

London, The McIntosh Publishing Co. Ltd., 1946.

20pp.

Coloured paper covers.

669. FISHER, Norman
Great Days in Sport
London, The Mitre Press, 1943.

95pp. Coloured paper covers.
Among the 28 "Great Days" given in the book there are 8 devoted to boxing as follows:

Jimmy Wide v. Pete Herman
Joe Louis Becomes World Champion
Jack Johnson, Batters Tommy Burns
Jack Dempsey wins the Heavyweight Title
Carpentier Loses to Siki
Tunney's Long Count Against Dempsey
Jim Jeffries' Greatest Mistake
Len Harvey Ends His Boxing Career.

670. FISHER, Tom
Boxing Was My Sport
The Story of Croydon Boxers from 1920 —
in Words and Pictures
West Wickham (Kent). Printed and Published by Belvedere Printing Co. Ltd., 1976.
(Limited Edition)
Edited by G.M. Allnutt.
Foreword by Paul Nihill, M.B.E.

56pp. plus Index. Stiff paper covers, with picture of Tom Fisher, with boxing prizes on front cover.
A Second and updated Edition was issued by the Croydon Ex-Boxers' Association in November, 1984.

671. FISTIC EXPERT, A. (Louis Shomer)
Scientific Boxing
(Easy Instructional Series)
New York City, Luellen Publishing Co. Inc., 1937.

64pp. Paper covers. Illustrated by Seaman.
Includes Practice and Diet, Correct Punching, Fight Training, Encyclopedia of Fisticuffs, Defensive Blocks, and Knockout Punches.
Featuring – Action Illustrations by the Slow Motion Movie Pictures.
A later edition of this book was issued by Padell Book and Magazine Co. Inc., 1941. (q.v.)

672. FISTIC EXPERT, A.
Scientific Boxing
New York, Padell Book and Magazine Co., 1941.

63pp. Paper covers. Illus.
Deals with Diet, Training, Scientific Boxing, K.O. Punching, Ring Rules, and History.
This is a later edition of a book with the same title issued by Louellen Publishing Co. in 1937. (q.v.)

673. FITZ-BARNARD, Captain L.
Fighting Sports
London, Odhams Press Ltd., 1928.
Dedicated "To My Old Friend Eugene Corri, the Best Sportsman in the World, I Dedicate

This Book".

292pp.
The book includes a large section entitled "Man Fighting", which contains biographies of a number of pugilists. There are also sets of rules, and references to 20th Century boxers, such as Jimmy Wilde, "The World's Greatest Fighter".

674. FITZGIBBON (publishers)
Fitzgibbon's Sporting Almanack For 1900.
An Epitome of All Sports With Full Records and Fixtures for 1899.
London, Published at the Offices, 4 and 5 Adam Street.

434pp.
This almanack is bound in orange cloth with titles and a contents list on the front cover and spine. It includes a number of sports, with 2 chapters on boxing, as follows:
Boxing, by George T. Dunning. This chapter gives a brief history of the sport, and a review of some of the great fights up to the date of publication; including Jackson v. Slavin, the two bouts between Charley Mitchell and John L. Sullivan and others.
Boxing versus Savate, by Arthur M. Binstead. This describes two bouts between practitioners of the two sports.
The Annual carries a number of picturesque adverts at the front and rear of the book.
At the end of the Preface is a paragraph which reads:
"Without further parley we present the first edition of FITZGIBBON'S ALMANACK to the public, content to think that, should it prove a trustworthy servant, it will have no difficulty in becoming a hardy annual."

675. FITZSIMMONS, Robert
Robert Fitzsimmons, His Life and Battles
Published in New York, 1895.
91pp.

676. FITZSIMMONS, Robert
(Middle and Heavyweight Champion of the World)
Physical Culture and Self Defence
With an introduction by A.J.Drexel Biddle
London, and Aldershot, Gale and Polden, 1902.
Second edition, 1907.
185pp.
Illustrations from poses by Robert Fitzsimmons and George Dawson.
Certain of the articles and illustrations have been published earlier by the New York *Journal*.

677. FLEETWAY HOUSE (Publishers)
continued

The Champion Annual for Boys, 1947.
London.
Includes articles on boxing, mentioning Nel Tarleton, Tom Thomas, Tom Cribb, etc.

678. FLEISCHER, Nat (Editor)

The Ring's Fight Pictures of the Century: Special Heavyweight Issue. Arranged by Frank Butler, in conjunction with Nat Fleischer.
Great Britain issue published by Hermitage Publications Ltd., London.
Coloured paper covers; picture of Jack Dempsey on front cover.
The contents include: Giants on Parade – Pictures that made Boxing History – The Tragedy of Ernie Schaaf – The Dempsey/Tunney Battles The Revenge of Joe Louis, etc.

679. FLEISCHER, Nat

How to Second and How to Manage a Boxer
Foreword by William A. Brady, Manager of J.J. Corbett and J.J. Jeffries
New York, Published at *The Ring* Bookshop.
(*The Ring* Athletic Library No.4)
There were several editions of this work.
72pp. Illus.
The Revised Edition contains 17 chapters on subjects such as:
    The Importance and Duties of Seconds
    Seconding is an Art
    What to do Between Rounds
    Handling a Badly Beaten Man, and How to
    Manage a Boxer

680. FLEISCHER, Nat

(Editor and Publisher of *The Ring*)
Training for Boxers
New York City, *The Ring* Athletic Library, Book No.2, 1927.
There were a number of later editions of this book, including 3rd and 9th (revised) editions, 1929 and 1938 respectively.
The 1929 edition consisted of 22 instructional chapters, including hints on proper and improper training methods and on seconding a boxer.
The illustrations include pictures of many famous boxers, including Jack Dempsey, J.J. Corbett, Gene Tunney, Jack Johnson, Battling Nelson, Tom Sharkey, Bob Fitzsimmons, Benny Leonard, and many others; some are shown in their favourite training exercises.

681. FLEISCHER, Nat

Young Griffo, The Will O' The Wisp of The Roped Square

New York, *The Ring* Incorporated, 1928.
96pp. 30 illus. plus 18 plates in Chapter XX entitled "A Boxing Lesson".
Bound in red paper covers.
The book traces the life of Griffo, the legendary "Will O' The Wisp", from his early days in Australia to his death in America in 1927 at the age of 56.

682. FLEISCHER, Nat

The Universal Home Boxing Course
New York City, Published at *The Ring* Bookshop, 1929.
A mail order course comprising nine lessons, each in booklet form.
Fully illustrated.
The author had the collaboration of Jack Dempsey Tony Canzonieri and Tommy Loughran in compiling this course.

683. FLEISCHER, Nat

Jack Dempsey, Idol of Fistiana. An Intimate Narrative.
(*The Ring* Athletic Library No.5)
New York, *The Ring* Publishing Co. 1929.
Dedicated to the Greatest Exponent of Clean Sport in America: William A. Muldoon the "Grand Old Man" of Boxing.
Foreword by Jack Dempsey.
309pp. 147 illus.

A revised edition was published in 1936 (*The Ring* Athletic Library No.12)
157pp. 20 Illus.

As indicated by the difference in the number of pages in each, there are differences in the two editions; the original edition consists of 66 chapters, while there are only 41 chapters in the revised edition. This variation is also reflected in the reduced number of illustrations in the 1936 issue.

685. FLEISCHER, Nat

How to Box
Foreword by Jim Corbett
New York, *The Ring* Bookshop, 1929.
(*The Ring* Athletic library No.3)
111pp.
38 chapters with many illustrations, which include the demonstration of punches and tactics by many famous American boxers. These include Jim Corbett, Jack Dempsey, Tommy Ryan, James J. Jeffries, Terry McGovern, Gene Tunney, Tom Gibbons, Phil Kaplan, Benny Leonard, and others.

686. FLEISCHER, Nat

(Editor and Publisher of *The Ring*)
Gene Tunney, The Enigma of the Ring
New York City, *The Ring* Inc. 1931.

continued

Bound in red cloth, black lettering on cover and spine, with portrait of Tunney on the front cover. 127pp. Illus.

This book covers the whole of Gene Tunney's career; including his ancestry and birth, school life, his work as a shipping clerk and stenographer, his early fights and service in the Great War and his return to civilian life, culminating in his wins over Jack Dempsey for the Heavyweight Championship of the World.

The three final chapters recount Gene Tunney's Farewell to the Ring, his Complete Record and chapter XVIII consists of An Appreciation by William Muldoon.

687. FLEISCHER, Nat.

How to Referee and How to Judge a Fight
New York, *The Ring* Bookshop, 1933.
(*The Ring* Athletic Library-Book No.9)

Contains 6 chapters including instructions on the duties of referees and judges, together with information on the various sets of Rules of Boxing.

688. FLEISCHER, Nat.

Simple Exercises for Height Increase
New York, *The Ring* Bookshop, 1934.
(*The Ring* Athletic Library No.10)
Illus.

689. FLEISCHER, Nat.

(In collaboration with Benny Leonard, Tony Canzoneri, Jack Dempsey, Tommy Loughran and Charley Massera)
Scientific Blocking and Hitting and Other Methods of Defence
(*The Ring* Athletic Library No.11)
New York, *The Ring* Bookshop, 1935.

48pp.
Bound in green stiff paper covers, lettered in black on front cover, with diagram.
Includes instructional chapters, 30 plates plus instructional cuts in the text.

690. FLEISCHER, Nat.

Black Dynamite
The Story of the Negro in the Prize-Ring from 1782 to 1938.
New York, Published in the series *The Ring* Athletic Library, 1938 to 1947.

All the volumes are bound in orange cloth with black lettering and boxing figures on the front covers.

All except volume I have the title on the spine; the spine on this volume was left plain.

All the volumes are copiously illustrated with copies of old prints and with line drawings.

Details are given of the volumes as follows:
Volume I
The Ring Athletic Library, Book No.14 – Black Dynamite. Preface by Daniel M. Daniel. Takes the story from the first Negro fighter in 1791 to those of the late 19th Century. 182pp. 1938.
Volume II
The Ring Athletic Library Book No.15 "Jolting Joe" and "Homicide Hank" The story of Joe Louis and Henry Armstrong. 165pp. 1938.
Volume III
The Ring Athletic Library, Book No.16 –The Three Coloured Aces. The story of George Dixon, Joe Gans and Joe Walcott, and several contemporaries. 314pp. 1938.
Volume IV
The Ring Athletic Library, Book No.18 "Fighting Furies" Story of the Golden Era of Jack Johnson, Sam Langford and their contemporaries, 282pp. 1939.
Volume V
The Ring Athletic Library. Issued 1947. "Sockers in Sepia" Continuation of the Drama of the Negro in Pugilistic Competition. 250pp.
The fifth volume was not given a number in *The Ring* Athletic Library Series.

692. FLEISCHER, Nat.

The Flaming Ben Hogan
Pugilist, Pirate, Gambler, Civil War Spy, Oil Magnate, Evangelist.
New York, *The Ring* Bookshop. 1941. (Limited to 900 copies)

32pp. 5 Illus.
Bound in green covers with a portrait of Hogan on the front cover.
The illustrations include Tom Allen, Bare Knuckle Champion of the World, who successfully defended his title against Ben Hogan in 1869.

693. FLEISCHER, Nat.

(Editor of *The Ring* Magazine)
The Boston Strong Boy
(The Story of John L. Sullivan, the Champion of Champions)
New York, *The Ring* Bookshop Inc. 1941.
64pp. Illus. Stiff paper covers.

694. FLEISCHER, Nat.

The Saga of John L. Sullivan
This was the pre-publication title of *The Boston Strong Boy*, 1941. (q.v.)

695. FLEISCHER, Nat.

continued

Reckless Lady —
The Life Story of Adah Isaacs Menken.
New York City, *The Ring* Bookshop, 1941.
Limited Edition of 900 copies.

36pp. 6 Illus.
Bound in stiff blue covers, with picture of Menken on front cover.
The text refers to John Camel Heenan and his marriage to Adah Isaacs Menken.
The illustrations include J.C. Heenan.

696. FLEISCHER, Nat.

Max Baer, The Glamour Boy of the Ring
New York, *The Ring* Bookshop, 1941.
Further editions were issued in later years.

42pp. 11 Illus.
Bound in red stiff paper covers, with picture of Baer on front cover.

697. FLEISCHER, Nat.

Commando Stuff
New York, *The Ring* Bookshop, 1942.

128pp. Brown paper covers.
Contains in the text some 40 tricks with numerous black and white illustrations demonstrating these. In this book Nat Fleischer drew on his experience as a writer on various sports, including boxing, wrestling and physical fitness. The work was highly recommended to instructors in the armed forces and to soldiers in combat units.

698. FLEISCHER, Nat.

"Gentleman Jim"
The Story of James J. Corbett
New York, *The Ring* Bookshop, 1943.
128pp. 24 Illus.
(Limited to 2000 copies)

699. FLEISCHER, Nat.

"Terrible Terry" — The Brooklyn Terror
The Fistic Career of Terry McGovern
New York City, *The Ring* Bookshop, 1943.
64pp. Illus.
Blue stiff paper covers; picture of McGovern on the front cover.

700. FLEISCHER, Nat.

Nat Fleischer's All Time *Ring* Record Book.
1941 Edition
New York, Published at the Offices of *The Ring*, 1942.
548pp. Bound in stiff grey paper covers.

The record books appearing under this title were published from 1942 up to and including the 1944 edition, and are probably the most comprehensive volumes of their kind ever to appear. The title was then changed to *Nat Fleischer's Ring Record Book*, and covered the careers, for the most part, of

active boxers.
The 1941 edition appeared in 1942, and the Foreword opens as follows:
"In this All-Time record of boxing achievements, I believe I have compiled the most extensive, the most accurate compendium of ring performances yet put together. If exhaustive research, if access to the greatest number of records yet placed at the disposal of any writer on boxing, if the most careful editing, can produce the ideal work, this book is exactly that.
In making this record book, I had at my command the most extensive library, set of old manuscripts and lists of performances available anywhere in the world. Including the only existing complete file of the *Police Gazette* as well as *Police News and Illustrated Record*, this vast accumulation of data comprises the reference Library of *The Ring* Magazine".
The records of the *currently active* boxers in this issue are up to December, 1941.
The remaining contents are summarised as follows:
Facts worth Knowing
Histories of the various weight categories, from Heavyweight to Flyweight
World Boxing Champions for 1941
Measurements of Heavyweight Champions and Giants of the Roped Square
Joe Louis's Ring Earnings
Statistics of Johnson–Jeffries Battle, July 4th, 1910
Ages at which Heavyweight Titles Were Won
Boxing's Big Gates
Odds in Heavyweight Championship Fights
Bareknuckle Heavyweight Champions from Figg, 1719 to John L. Sullivan, 1892.

In the preliminaries to the book the editor acknowledges his appreciation to his staff: Joan Phillips Fleischer, Alice Sloan, William Shulkin, Meyer Ackerman, Eddie Borden, George T. Pardy, and Daniel M. Daniel for their aid.

701. FLEISCHER, Nat.

Nat Fleischer's All Time *Ring* Record Book, 1943 Edition
New York, Published at the Offices of *The Ring*, 1943.
592pp. Bound in red cloth.
The opening statement, "About This Book", commences as follows:
"This is the second edition of the All Time record of boxing performance and achievement. It is a more complete work, a more thorough presentation, than the first edition, which came out a year ago, and excited the approval of fistic experts and sports writers all over the United States, Canada, Central and South America, and the British Dominion.
This second edition shows errors corrected, commissions taken care of, structural faults revised. It is the best job a thorough hardworking organisation, with vast statistical resources and an eagerness for perfection, could turn out..."
The Preface to the first edition is repeated in this volume.

continued

K

There is a Dedication to Boxers in Service.
Some of the features and articles from the First Edition are repeated in this volume; information on additional material is given as follows:

Famous Holiday Fights
Famous Firsts in Boxing
New York Boxing Laws
Membership List of the National Boxing Association
World Champions for 1943
John L. Sullivan's Earnings

There are 555pp. of boxer's records.

702. FLEISCHER, Nat.

Nat Fleischer's All Time *Ring* Record Book.
1944 Edition
New York, Published at the Offices of *The Ring*, 1944.

592pp. Bound in green cloth.
The introduction "About This Book" states as follows (*inter alia*):
"This is the third edition of *All Time Ring Record Book*. The 1942 (sic) and the 1943 issues, which were limited in number and had to create a field for themselves, already have taken their places among the rarities of boxing literature and are bringing far beyond their original costs. Those who are fortunate enough to possess the three editions have the most complete record of boxing, since the sport achieved recognition in England . . . that it is possible to compile".
The contents of this edition are very similar to those of the 1943 issue; additional features are noted as follows:
The records of 420 boxers not to be found in the earlier editions.
The records of all boxers who in 1943 participated in four or more contests, either as service men or civilians.
The War Service Roll of Boxing.
A directory of professional managers and promoters of boxing.
There are 555pp. of boxer's records, including the names of some boxers on whom additional data has been located.
With the additional information the 1944 All Time Record Book claims to bridge the gap completely between Tom Cribb and Jimmy Bivins.

703. FLEISCHER, Nat.

Nat Fleischer's *Ring* Record Book, 1945
Edition
New York, Published by *The Ring* Bookshop Inc., 1945.

370pp. Bound in green cloth.
The record books compiled by Nat Fleischer had been issued from 1942 to 1944 under the title of *All Time Ring Record Book*; from 1945 the title changed to that shown above, and concentrated on active boxers.
The records of current fighters in this issue are up to Dec.31, 1944.
Page 1,, "About This Book" states (*inter alia*):

This is the fourth edition of *All Time* (sic) *Ring Record Book*.
The 1942, 1943 and 1944 issues, all Limited, have become rarities in the literature on the sport of boxing. As a matter of fact, while this is the fourth book in the series of All Time Records compiled, edited and published by Nat Fleischer, this is not the fourth edition of the original volume.
The 1945 issue contains only the complete records of all active boxers who participated in two or more contests during the year 1944. The purchaser of this book is warned that the 1945 edition does not list the records of men who in 1944 were not active in the ring, except those of champions who were in service, and whose titles were frozen. For records of men who were not active in 1944 you will have to get the editions of 1942, 1943 and 1944.
The principal contests of this edition are as follows:

Histories of all the weight classes from heavy to flyweight
Joe Louis's Ring Earnings
World Champions for 1944
343pp. of boxers' records.

704. FLEISCHER, Nat.

Nat Fleischer's *Ring* Record Book, 1946
Edition
New York, Published by *The Ring* Bookshop Inc., 1946.

496pp. Bound in grey cloth.
The records of current fighters in this issue are up to Dec.31, 1945.
Page 1, "About This Book" states (*inter alia*):
"The first three volumes, published 1942, 1943 and 1944 contain the complete records since 1719. Then came the first yearly or supplement, the 1945 edition. In that, as in the latest volume, only the records of active fighters are to be found. The 1942, 1943 and 1944 issues, all limited, already have become rarities in the literature on the sport of boxing. The 1942 edition is out of print but the publisher still has a few copies of the 1943 and 1944 issues for sale. Also the 1945 edition.
The features and articles in this volume are very similar to those in the 1945 edition, they are given as follows:

Histories of all the weight divisions of boxing
Joe Louis's Ring Earnings
List of current world champions
Membership list of the National Boxing Assoc.
Boxing's Big Gates
Ages at which heavyweight titles were won
List of world's outstanding promoters
List of boxing managers (All these are American)
456pp. of boxers' records.

705. FLEISCHER, Nat.

Nat Fleischer's *Ring* Record Book, 1947
Edition.
New York, Published by *The Ring* Bookshop Inc., 1947.

continued

688pp. Bound in red cloth.
The records of the fighters in this issue are up to Dec. 31, 1946. Page 1, "Out Latest Record Book" says (*inter alia*):
"This is the third supplement to *The All Time Ring Record Books*. In our effort to supply the public with complete records of old-timers and present-day fighters, three *All Time Record Books* have appeared. These have been acclaimed as the greatest reference works yet published on boxing. The 1942 edition is out of print and sells for a premium — when a copy can be found. A few copies of the 1943 and 1944 issues are still available".
The contents of the 1947 issue comprise the following:

> Measurements of Heavyweight Champions. Compiled from Official Weight-in Records
> Title Bouts during 1946
> Joe Louis's Ring Earnings and Title Defences
> John L. Sullivan's Ring Earnings
> Jack Dempsey's Ring Earnings
> Fights below the Light-Heavyweight that grossed over $100.000
> Odds in Heavyweight Championship Fights
> Ring Deaths in 1946
> History of Junior Titles
> Membership of the National Boxing Assoc.
> Histories of the Various Weight Classes in boxing
> Directory of Fight Managers
> List of World's Outstanding Promoters
> 639pp. of boxers' records.

706. FLEISCHER, Nat.

Nat Fleischer's *Ring* Record Book, 1948 Edition.

New York, Published by *The Ring* Bookshop Inc., 1948.

699pp. Bound in black cloth.
The records of the fighters in this issue are up to Dec. 31, 1947.
The introduction to this volume says (*inter alia*):
"This is the fourth supplement to our *All Time Ring Record Books* which made their first appearance in 1942. In this issue will be found the complete records of all active fighters the world over. In addition to the records of the American boys, this issue contains the data on the outstanding fighters from England, Ireland, Scotland and Wales, France, Italy, Belgium and Holland, Australia, New Zealand, South Africa and Central and South America. It is the most complete record book on active fighters that has ever been compiled. *The Ring* Editor and his staff are proud of their accomplishment . . ."
In addition to the features and articles listed as included in the 1947 edition, the 1948 issue contains the following:

> Oddities of 1947
> Zale v. Graziano Bout Sets Records
> Winner of the Ring Magazine Annual Merit Award
> Number of Championship Bouts Fought by Heavyweight Kings
> Record Lows in Title Bouts in Light-Heavyweight Class
> Receipts in Garden Shows for 1947

Jack v. Ted Kid, Fight by Fight. (Britton v. Lewis)
647pp. of boxers' records.

707. FLEISCHER, Nat.

Nat Fleischer's *Ring* Record Book, 1949 Edition.

New York, Published by *The Ring* Bookshop Inc., 1949.

792pp. Bound in red cloth.
The records of current fighters in this issue are up to Dec. 31. 1948.
The introduction to the volume says (*inter alia*):
"This is the fifth supplement to our *All Time Ring Record Books* which made their first appearance in 1942, revised editions of which were published in 1943 and 1944. All these are now out of print . . . "
Many of the features and articles which appeared in previous issues are repeated in the present one. with the addition of the following:

> Winners of the Edward J. Neil Trophy, (for the person adjudged to have done the most for boxing in the previous year. Awarded by the Boxing Writers' Association of New York)
> Receipts for Outstanding Light-Heavyweight and Heavyweight Bouts
> Number of Championship Bouts Fought by Heavyweight Kings
> Retired Undefeated World Champions
> Most Championship Bouts Engaged In
> Here is a Record of Louis' Return Bouts
> Most Consecutive Fights Without a Loss (Lifetime)
> Record Exhibition Gate
> Knockouts, Most Scored
> Battles of the Long Count
> Boxing's Twenty Year Men
> Heavyweight Title Bout Referees
> Untarnished Records
> Super Champions
> Longest Title Held in Each Division
> One Round Knockouts in Title Bouts
> championship Fights with Record Knockdowns
> Famous Holiday Fights
> World's Outstanding Promoters and Match-makers
> 720pp. of boxers' records

The previous volumes included a few photographs of boxers, principally champions; the 1949 edition, and those for the following years, carried an increased number of illustrations.

708. FLEISCHER, Nat.

Nat Fleischer's *Ring* Record Book, 1950 Edition.

New York, Published by *The Ring* Bookshop Inc., 1950.

810pp. Bound in green cloth.
The records of current fighters in this issue are up to Dec. 31. 1949, or as close to that date as possible.
Included in the introduction is the statement:
"Additions to old time records and historic data

continued

appear in this issue; also corrections of errors found in previous issues"

Additional features to be found in this volume include the following:

Recipients of the James J. Walker Memorial Award (awarded annually since 1940 by the Boxing Writers' Association of New York to an individual for long and meritorious service to boxing)

Odds in Heavyweight Championship Fights

New York State Boxing Taxes

Brothers in Boxing

Famous Fights in Boxing

New York Boxing Laws

Statistics of Johnson–Jeffries Battle, July 4th, 1910

Last Rounds of Famous Heavyweight Fights 739pp. of boxers' records.

As in the 1949 issue, this edition carries a number of illustrations.

709. FLEISCHER, Nat.

Nat Fleischer's *Ring* Record Book, 1951 Edition.

New York, Published by *The Ring* Bookshop Inc., 1951.

813pp. Bound in light brown cloth.

The records of the current fighters in this issue are up to Dec. 31. 1950, or as close to that date as possible.

The introduction to the volume includes the following:

"This Tenth Anniversary Edition, more complete than ever, with the usual Ring Record Book authenticity and reliability, lists all the boxers, the world over, who competed in three or more bouts from January 1. 1950, to January 1951, and those with past records who engaged in any contests, plus the complete records of all world champions in every division from the start of pugilism in America to the present day . . ."

As well as the features which were included in previous issues, the 1951 edition contains the following:

Biographical Sketches of Champion and those who lost their title in 1950

Famous Postponements

First Pictures of a Fight

When Jack Kearns Fought

Title Bouts During 1950

Madison Square Garden Receipts 1925–1949

Tragic Endings of Famous Fighters

How a Fight is Scored

Birthplaces of Champions

Facts Worth Knowing

One Round Kayoes

720pp. of Boxers' Records.

In addition to a number of photographic illustrations, this volume includes a section entitled "Portfolio of Champions"; this is printed on blue-tinted paper and shows pictures of all the current world champions in action.

710. FLEISCHER, Nat.

Nat Fleischer's *Ring* Record Book,

1952 Edition.

New York, Published by *The Ring* Bookshop Inc., 1952.

813pp. Bound in light blue cloth.

The Introduction to this volume includes the following:

"Added features in *The Ring Record Book* are biographical, sketches of all title holders of 1950 and 1951, Fighting Names, Television Firsts and Famous Fighting Fists"

Except for the bringing up to date of the statistical section of the record book the contents and articles in this volume are very similar to those included in the editions for 1950 and 1951.

722pp. of boxers' records.

The separate section entitled "Portfolio of Champions" is printed on yellow-tinted paper. There are a number of other photographic illustrations, both full-page and in the text.

711. FLEISCHER, Nat. (Editor)

Nat Fleischer's *Ring* Record Book, 1953 to 1972.

The individual issues of this publication up to and including the year 1952 are dealt with in the Bibliographical Section of the present work. (q.v.) *The Record Book* continued to appear under Nat Fleischer's name until the Editor's death in 1972.

With the 1973 edition the name of Fleischer disappeared from the title; the book was issued thereafter as *The Ring Boxing Encyclopedia and Record Book*.

The 1973 edition included a tribute to Nat Fleischer, who had served for 50 years as Editor of *The Ring* magazine. The tribute included a statement saying that before he died, Mr. Fleischer enjoined Nat Loubert, his son-in-law and successor in *Ring* enterprises, not to let the *Record Book* miss even one edition; Loubert gave Nat Fleischer his firm promise on this.

The compilers of the 1973 edition were given as Nat Loubert, John Ort, George Girsch and Dan Daniel; this quartet continued as compilers until 1975, after which the name of George Girsch was not among those credited with the compilation.

Nat Loubert and John Ort continued their work on the record book for a number of years; later on Bert Randolph Sugar became associated with the publication.

712. FLEISCHER, Nat.
(Editor of *The Ring* Magazine)

Jack McAuliffe. The Napoleon of the Prize-Ring.

New York, *The Ring* Bookshop, 1944.

Bound in yellow stiff paper covers, with portrait of McAuliffe on the front cover.

10 chapters telling of the subject's career, commencing as an amateur. 17 Illus.

713. FLEISCHER, Nat.
(Editor of *The Ring* Magazine)

The Michigan Assassin. The Saga of Stanley

continued

Ketchel. World's Most Sensational Middleweight Champion.
New York, Published at the offices of *The
Ring*, 1946.
114pp. Illus.
Bound in blue cloth, lettered in black on front
cover.
Contains 13 chapters, from "Fighting His Way Up"
to "His Fighting Record"

714. FLEISCHER, Nat.
Leonard the Magnificent
The Life Story of the Man Who Made Himself "King of the Lightweights"
New York, *The Ring* Bookshop Inc., 1947.
121pp. Bound in grey cloth.
30 Illustrations.

715. FLEISCHER, Nat.
The Heavyweight Championship
An Informal History of Heavyweight Boxing
from 1719 to the Present Day
New York, G.P. Putnam's Sons, 1949.
London, Putnam and Co. Ltd., 1949.
292pp. Illus.

New York, G.P. Putnam's Sons, 1961.
New and Revised Edition.
307pp. Illus.
The later edition takes the heavyweight story up
to the championship of Floyd Patterson; it includes a supplement on Patterson v. Liston.
The earlier edition was also issued in the Sportsmans Book Club Series.

716. FLEISCHER, Nat.
John L. Sullivan, Champion of Champions
New York, G.P. Putnam's Sons, 1951.
Published concurrently in Canada by
Thomas Allen Ltd., Toronto.
213pp. Illus.
This biography of John L. Sullivan also carries an
Appendix; this includes summaries of the earnings
of Sullivan and of Joe Louis, also the History of
the Heavyweight Championship from the days of
the Last of the Bareknuckle Contests to date of
publication.
There was an English Edition of this book, pub-
lished in London by Robert Hale Ltd., in 1952.
This was bound in red cloth, the contents and
illustrations were the same as in the American
Edition.

717. FLEISCHER, Nat.
The Louis Legend
New York, *The Ring* Inc., 1956.
181pp. Illus.
Including the Joe Louis Ring Record.

718. FLEISCHER, Nat.

50 Years at Ringside
New York, Fleet Publishing Corporation,
1958.
296pp. Illus.
The memoirs of an internationally-renowned
boxing authority. In his final chapter, entitled
"Summing Up" Mr Fleischer gives his assessment
of the fighting abilities of a number of boxers,
and also his all time rankings.

**719. FLEISCHER, Nat., and
ANDRE, Sam**
A Pictorial History of Boxing
Secacous (New Jersey), Citadel Press, 1959.
Toronto (Canada), George G. McLeod, Ltd.,
1959.
London, Spring Books, 1960.
316pp. 4to. Illus.
Further editions were published in 1964, 1966 and
1975. (Revised and Enlarged)

720. FLEISCHER, Nat.
Jack Dempsey
New Rochelle, (New York), Arlington House
1972.
256pp. Illus.

721. FLEMING, Denis
The Manchester Fighters
Manchester, Neil Richardson, 1986.
64pp. Illus. Limp paper wrappers.
The author of this book is the son of Harry
Fleming, Manchester manager of boxers. He tells
the story of the famous fighters developed in his
vicinity, among them Joe Bowker, Boy McCormick
Len Johnson, and the famous trio guided by his
father, Jackie Brown, Johnny King, and Jock
McAvoy. Also appended is an extensive "Who's
Who" of Manchester and Salford boxers active in
the 1930s.

722. FLETCHER, J.S.
History of the St.Leger Stakes, 1776–1901
London, Hutchinson and Co., 1902.
503pp. Illus.
The boxing references occur in Chapters III and
V; these are respectively: Doncaster Races in the
Olden Days, Pugilism as an attraction.
Associations of the St.Leger, John Gully, a Man of
Many Parts, Greville's description of him in
1832.
There is a head and shoulders portrait of Gully as
an old man.

**723. FLOWER, Harry A.
(Hon.Gen.Secretary, National Union of
Boxers)**
Boxing from Behind the Scenes

continued

London, National Union of Boxers, 1938.
14pp. Stiff paper covers.

724. FLYNN, Brian
They Never Come Back.
A Detective Novel.
London, John Long Ltd., 1940.
256pp.
Announced as "A Legend of the Ring – that a boxer never comes back".

725. FOLEY, Tom J.
(Editor and Publisher)
The Old Timer – Sporting Record Compendium
San Francisco (California), ca.1930.
The contents include: Recollections of Old Days – Fighters' "Stage" Names – Refereeing – Boxing – How To Box – Pugilistic Records – Boxers' Records (to 1907).
The Illustrations include one of the author as Gymnastic Instructor on board S.S. "Malolo".
There are also many instructional photographs and pictures of famous boxers.

726. FORD, J.
Prizefighting. The Age of Regency Boximania.
Newton Abbot, David and Charles, 1971.
108pp. Illus.
Traces the Chronology of the Prize-Ring 1787-1824 includes a chapter entitled "Pugilism in Print" and a select book list.

727. FORD, J. Murray
(Thomas Le Breton)
Memoirs of a Poor Devil
London, A.M. Philpot Ltd., 1926.
215pp.
Contains in Part II (Sport),
Chapter II: "Boxing and Wrestling".

728. FORE PUBLICATIONS LTD
(Publishers)
Boxing Stars, Past, Present and Future, No. 1
London, 1949.
32pp. (Including covers)
This item comprises 32 pictures of boxers, with a short description of each beneath each picture.

729. FORESTER, C.S.
Two and Twenty
A Novel.
London, John Lane The Bodley Head, 1931.
(Cheap Edition 1933; Reprinted 1940)
312pp.
The dust wrapper has a picture of a boxer being counted out.
23 Chapters, the first two being entitled "The

Dressing Room" and "The Ring" respectively.

730. FOTHERGILL, G.A.
Hunting, Racing, Coaching and Boxing Ballads
London, Heath Cranton Ltd., 1926.
Includes a section entitled "Fistiana", pp.117–123.

731. FOWLER, Gene
Shoe the Wild Mare
A Novel
Copyrighted by the author in 1931.
Also issued by Avon Book Co., New York, 1944.
376pp.
Information is given on the 4th printing:
Bound in black cloth, lettered in red on front cover and spine.
One of the principal characters in this book is a boxer who wins a title; an injury resulting from this causes him to lose his sight and almost his sanity.
There is mention of a number of famous fighters in this story.

732. FOWLER, Gene
Good Night, Sweet Prince
The Life of John Barrymore
New York, The Viking Press, 1944.
413pp.
Contains a number of references to boxers, such as Corbett, Sullivan and Dempsey. There are no descriptions of fights. Barrymore's father Maurice was a friend of Jim Corbett, and as a boy John Barrymore often met Sullivan.
The boxing references are spread through the book; mention also occurs of Damon Runyon, William Muldoon and Kid McCoy.

733. FOWLER, Gene
Skyline
A Reporter's reminiscences of the 1920's.
New York, Viking Press, 1961.
314pp.
Randy Roberts gives this book as providing Prime Source material for his book *The Manassa Mauler* (q.v.)

734. FOWLER, J.K. ('Rusticus')
Recollections of Old Country Life – Social, Political, Sporting and Agricultural
London, Longmans, Green and Co., 1894.
235pp.
Boxing references are included in Chapter IV (*inter alia*): Prize-Fight between Tom Hatton and Mickey Gannon (Gannon beat Hatton for £50 a-side, in 39 rounds 1 hour 3 minutes, Home Circuit, 29th April 1862). The Archdeacon's Opinions. Jem Mace, Champion of England.

735. FOX, Charles (Publisher)
Famous Fights in the Prize Ring
Compiled by the Promoter of *The Sporting Life* and *Illustrated Sporting News*.
London, 1877.
This work was originally issued in thirty-six parts, each part containing a large folding plate; it was later issued in three bound volumes.
The cover of each issue showed portraits of pugilists or scenes from fights.
Each issue included reports of prize-ring battles; in many cases the narrative on one bout was carried over to the next issue of the magazine, thus in these cases each issue carried the story of one, two or three bouts and two part-stories, one being the first part of the story to be continued in the next issue.

736. FOX, Richard K. (Publisher)
John L. Sullivan, Ex-Champion Pugilist of the World, His Life and Battles In the Prize-Ring
New York City, 1883 and 1892.
(Revised and enlarged edition)
Printed on Pink paper.
The biography traces Sullivan's career from his debut in the ring to his loss of the title of Champion of the World.
The book is profusely illustrated.

737. FOX, Richard K. (Publisher)
Lives of Tom Hyer, John C. Heenan, Yankee Sullivan and John Morrisey
(Complete in one Volume)
New York, 1888.

738. FOX, Richard K. (Publisher)
The Life and Battles of Jack Dempsey
A Compete History of all the Battles fought by the "Nonpareil".
Fully Told and Handsomely Illustrated.
New York, 1889.
82pp. Paper covers. Illus.

738A. FOX, Richard K. (Publisher)
Prize Ring Heroes
Life and Battles of Tom Hyer, Yankee Sullivan, John Morrissey, John C. Heenan, Tom King
New York, 1889.
This is possibly a later version of *The Lives of Tom Hyer, John C. Heenan, Yankee Sullivan and John Morrissey* from the same publisher. (q.v.)

739. FOX, Richard K. (Publisher)
Tom Sayers, England's Great Pugilist.
His Life and Battles.
New York, 1889.
40pp. Illus.

740. FOX, R.K.
Prize-Ring Champions of England from 1719 to 1889.
New York, Published by the author, 1889.
65pp. Illus.

741. FOX, Richard K. (Publisher)
Lives and Battles of Famous Black Pugilists, or Black Champions of the Prize-Ring from Molineaux to Jackson
New York City, 1890.
The first of the above titles is given on the front cover and the alternative or sub-title is shown on the title-page.
57pp. Illus.
The book is bound in stiff paper covers with an action picture of Tom Molineaux on the front cover.
The text recounts the battles of famous coloured pugilists such as Molineaux, Bob Smith (The Liverpool Darkey), Bill Richmond, Bob Travers, Harry Woodson, George Godfrey, Peter Jackson, George Dixon and others.

742. FOX, Richard K.
Life and Battles of James J. Corbett, Champion Pugilist of the World
New York, Published by the Author, 1892.
48pp. Illus.

743. FOX, Richard K. (Publisher)
The Police Gazette Sporting Annual
New York, Published Annually from 1898 to 1918, and in 1930.
First published by Richard K. Fox and later by the Richard K. Fox Publishing Co. Inc., New York.
The earlier issues were compiled by Sam C. Austin, Sporting Editor of the *Police Gazette*.
The annuals are not solely devoted to boxing but also contain records and statistics of other sports.
Each issue is illustrated and includes portraits of boxers and boxing personalities.

744. FOX, Richard K. (Publisher)
The Life and Battles of Jack Johnson, Champion Pugilist of the World. Together with the Complete Records of Peter Jackson, Joe Jeanette, Sam Langford, Joe Walcott, Joe Gans, Jack Blackburn and George Dixon.
New York, 1909 (Fox's Athletic Library No.22)
continued

Sole Agents for Great Britain — Abel Haywood and Sons, Manchester.

71pp.
Red paper covers with action picture of Jack Johnson on the front cover.
14 other illustrations.

745. FRANK, Stanley
Sports Extra
New York, A.S. Barnes and Co., 1944, (3rd Printing 1945).

282pp.
These are Sports Page Classics, described as wonderfully entertaining pieces, by Damon Runyon, Ring Lardner, Heywood Broun, Grantland Rice, Irvin S. Cobb and others.
Bound in red cloth lettered in yellow on front and spine.
The boxing contributions include pieces by John P. Marquand, Arthur Brisbane, Jack London, Irvin S. Cobb, Paul Gallico, Gene Fowler, Dan Parker, etc.

746. FRANKAU, Gilbert
My Unsentimental Journey
London, Hutchinson and Co. (Publishers) Ltd., 1926.

285pp.
The chapters in this book are designated "Stages", the boxing references are included in Stages 9, 10, 11 and 17 in which the author tells of his meetings in America with boxing personalities and his visits to boxing arenas as a spectator.

747. FRANKAU, Gilbert
Masterson.
The Story of an English Gentleman
London, Hutchinson and Co. (Publishers) Ltd., 1926.

415pp.
This novel includes the following references to boxing:—

Chapter 12 — Section 2 and 3 — "Tonight's fight at the Albert Hall; Bob Brackley and Patsy Kynes"

Chapter 13 — The whole of this chapter is devoted to the Brackley v. Kynes fight.

748. FRANKS, Ron
(Editor and Compiler)
Focus on the Fight Game
(A Background Sports Photo Book)
London, Background Books Ltd., 1948.

25pp. Paper covers. Picture of Louis v. Walcott on front cover.
Includes a foreword and 22 pages of pictures of bouts and boxers from around the period of publication.

749. FREDERICK, Oswald

(O.F. Snelling)
Fight Quiz
London, Bertrand, Snelling (Publications) and Co., 1946.

20pp. Coloured illustrated covers, with 15 pictures or portraits to identify.
Consists of 5 sets of questions on boxing; ranging from those considered to be easy, through those considered to be very hard, to a set of catch questions.

750. FREDERICK, Oswald
(O.F. Snelling)
Battling Bruce — The Story of the Fighting Career and Rise to Fame of Bruce Woodcock.
London, Bertrand, Snelling (Publications) and Co., 1946.

44pp. Illus.
Stiff Paper Covers. Price 2s.

751. FREDERICK, Oswald
(O.F. Snelling)
White Hope.
The Story of the Jack Johnson Era
London, Pendulum Publications Ltd., 1947.
Price 2s-6d.
(Pendulum Popular Sports Series)

101pp. Illus.
Bound in boards. Coloured dust-wrapper with a picture of Johnson v. Jeffries on the front.
17 chapters. 8 illustrations.

752. FREDERICK, Oswald
(O.F. Snelling)
Boys' Book of Boxing
London, Bernard Henry, 1949. Price 1s-6d.
32pp. (Including covers). Illus.
Chapters include:
  Great Britain—Home of Boxing
  First Steps in Boxing, by Jock McAvoy etc.

753. FREEMAN, William, F.R.S.A.
Fellow of the Institute of Journalists
The Life of Lord Alfred Douglas.
Spoilt Child of Genius
London, Michael Joseph Ltd, 1948.

Chapter 1, "The Family Album" deals with the ancestors of Lord Alfred Douglas, including the 8th Marquess of Queensberry, who formulated the Queensberry Rules for the conduct of boxing.

754. FRUDD, Percy G.
Fighter Blake, Knight of Silver Street
London, Heath Cranton Ltd., 1938.
284pp.
A work of fiction, with a single boxing sequence.

755. FULLER, Peter

continued

The Champions.
The Secret Motives in Games and Sports
London, Allen Lane Penguin Books Ltd.,
1978.
First published in the United States by
Urizen Books, 1977.

386pp. (Revised English Edition)
Chapter 4 (pages 170–270) is entitled "Muhammad
Ali, the Piece of Fur and the People's Champ".

756. FULLERTON, Hugh

Two Fisted Jeff
Chicago, Consolidated Book Publishers Inc.,
1929.
This book was also issued in a Limited and
Numbered Autographed Edition.

319pp. Illus.
Bound in red cloth, with black lettering on front
cover and spine.
23 chapters, 11 illustrations.
Copyright by James J. Jeffries, 1929.
Dedicated "To the Memory of My Mother and My
Father To Whom I Owe All the Good That was In
Me and To Whom I Was never a World Champion,
but Just Their Boy Jim"
The preliminaries include the Ring Record of
James J. Jeffries, Jeffries' classification of the
Heavyweight Champions and the Near Heavy-
weight Champion, Tom Sharkey.
There are also tributes to Jeffries by Jack Dempsey,
Eddie Graney, (The west's Most Famous Third
Man in the Ring), from James J. Corbett, Tom
Sharkey, and a number of other boxing person-
alities.
The chapter headings include the following:
Chapter I – The Jeffries Clan
Chapter II – My Early Fights
Chapter IV – I Start to be a Fighter
Chapter VII – The Fight at Carson City
Chapter IX – I Meet the Sailor
Chapter XVI – I Beat My Teacher
Chapter XXI – Red Robert Falls Again
Chapter XXIII – I Settle the Corbett Question
Chapter XXVIII – I Return to the Ring
Chapter XXIX – The Johnson Affair

757. FURBER, Edward, C.B.E.

London Doctor
London, Geoffrey Bles. 1940.

222pp. Illus.
Includes references to boxers and boxing as
follows:

Chapter VII – Billy Wells and Fred Storbeck, at
  the National Sporting Club, 28/12/1911.
Chapter IX – Pat O'Keefe v. Bandsman Blake, at
  the National Sporting Club, 28/1/1918.
Chapter XIII – Major Michael Leahy, (One-legged
  boxer); also Joe Beckett v. Georges
  Carpentier, 4/12/1919.

758. FURNESS, Harry "Kid"

Historic Battles of the Prize Ring, 1719 to
1910, James Figg to Jem Mace.
Manchester, Miller and Fazackerly, 1927.

32pp. This is a pamphlet bound in blue wrappers,
with a picture of a fight on the front cover.
10 Illus.
Includes a Preface, text and a list of births and
deaths of champions entitled "In Memory of our
Fistic Heroes".

759. FURNISS, Harold (Editor)

Famous Fights – Past and Present. (*Police
Budget* Edition)
London, Numbers 1 to 20 published by
Frank Shaw.
London, Numbers 21 to 156, Printed and
Published by Harold Furniss 1901–1904
(156 copies).
Weekly publication of this journal com-
menced March 4th, 1901, the first 15 issues
were dated, but the remainder carried no
date. Following the appearance of the final
issue (No.156) the magazine was incorpor-
ated with *The Illustrated Police Budget*.
Famous Fights was reissued in 1907–1908
as Shurey's Edition, numbers 1 to 53 only;
a folding plate "The Fight between Tom
Sayers and J.C. Heenan" was presented with
No.1 of this series.

A useful and interesting Boxing Bibliography was
printed in No.63 of the magazine; this bibliography is reputed to be the work of Mr. Frank
Bradley, *Famous Fights* was issued in 12 quarterly
bound volumes of 13 issues per volume, and also
in 3 annual volumes, one for each year of issue.
The weekly parts were printed on rather thin
pink paper, but a "De Luxe" edition available
in the bound annual volumes, was printed on
thicker glossy paper.
The price of each quarterly volume was 1/- and
that of each annual volume 3/6d; the "De-Luxe"
edition was priced at 10/6d per annual volume.
Famous Fights magazine consisted of articles on
past and contemporary boxers and their contests,
and was profusely illustrated. The cover of each
issue carried a full-page picture of a boxer or a
scene from a fight. Most of the earlier numbers
included a picture and an article entitled "Our
Portrait Gallery of Present Day Pugilists", the
subjects including both British and American
Boxers.
Later issues included a series of illustrated instructional articles entitled "Tips for Tyros"

760. FURNISS, Harry

Our Joe, His Great Fight.
Original Cartoons by Harry Furniss
London, William Heinnemann, 1903.

continued

57 pp. 4to. Paper covers, with coloured cover showing the subject of the work.

The cartoons feature Joseph Chamberlain as being at the time of publication the most interesting figure in the political world. The cartoons show him as a boxer dealing as such with various political situations and opponents.

761. FURNISS, Harry

The By Ways and Queer Ways of Boxing.
Pictured and Described by Harry Furniss
London, Harrison and Sons, 1919.

227pp. Illus.
Large 8vo. Bound in green cloth, with pictorial cover.

The author, who was an artist and illustrator, states in a preliminary note that he has engaged more than one model to sit for him who has been a boxer in his day, and from these old boxers he heard much of the By Ways and Queer Ways of the "Great Game".

The author also notes that although he was the author of a story entitled "Gentleman Chick" he is no relation to the artist and journalist named Harold Furniss who edited the periodical *Famous Fights* which appeared for 3 years in the early part of the century.

The *By Ways and Queer Ways* are spread over 18 chapters, profusely illustrated by the author's drawings.

762. FUTURE PUBLICATIONS (Publishers)

Olympic Games-London, 1948.
Official Souvenir
London, 1948.
Printed in Photogravure throughout.

Illustrated paper covers. magazine style.
This publication includes all information on winners, including boxing; with short articles on the history of Boxing and on Olympic Boxing.

763. FYFE, James G.

Games, Sports and Pastimes.
The Gresham Library of Knowledge, No.8 of a series of 12.
London, The Gresham Publishing Co. Ltd., 1934.

305pp. Illus.
The Section "Self Defence" includes – "Boxing for Youths" by Fred G. Shaw, F.G.S., illustrated by 1 plate and 4 figures in the text.

JOSEPH F. HESS.

764. GABRIEL, John
The Last of the Corinthians (A Novel)
London, Odhams Press, 1920.
190pp. Bound in light brown cloth.

765. GAINS, Larry
The Impossible Dream
London, Leisure Publications, [1976]
141pp. Illus.
Autobiography of a heavyweight who fought at
championship level for many years.

766. GALE, Benjamin Thomas
(Editor and Publisher)
Gale's Almanack. For Sporting Men and
Licensed Victuallers.
London, Published by the Editor at the
Offices of the *Licensed Victuallers' Mirror*
and *Gale's Special*.
This publication appeared annually for a
number of years, commencing in 1889 and
was still being issued in 1900.
Each issue included an article entitled "The Year's
Boxing".

767. GALE, Frederick
The Life of The Hon. Robert Grimston
London, Longmans Green and Co., 1885.
Frontis. portrait of The Hon. Robert Grimston.
Chapter IV "Oxford" includes information on
Grimston's interest in boxing and the prize-ring.

768. GALE, Frederick,
(The Old Buffer)
Sports and Recreations in Town and Country
London, Swann Sonnenschein, Lowrey and
Co., 1888.
224pp.
Bound in green cloth, gilt titles on spine.
The 2 boxing articles in this book originally
appeared in a weekly paper called *Ashore and
Afloat*; these are entitled:

"Tom Spring's Back Parlour" and
"Boxing and Athletics".

769. GALE AND POLDEN LTD
(Publishers)
Boxing Rules and Guide to Refereeing,
Judging, etc.
Aldershot and London, 1921.
This item was produced for the Imperial Services
Boxing Associations.
94pp.

770. GALLICO, Paul
Farewell to Sport

New York, Alfred A. Knopf Inc., 1936.
A special edition of this book was published
for the Armed Forces overseas during the
Second World War.
Contains 26 chapters, several of these on boxing,
including Primo Carnera, Gene Tunney, Tex
Rickard, etc.

771. GALLICO, Paul
The Golden People
Garden City, New York, Doubleday and Co.
Inc., 1964.
315pp. Illus.
The memoirs of a famous ex-sportswriter; includes
chapters on Jack Dempsey, Gene Tunney, and Tex
Rickard.

772. GALLICO, Paul
Confessions of a Story-Teller
London, Michael Joseph, 1961.
Harmondsworth (Middx.), Penguin Books,
1966.
434pp.
This book is a remarkable collection of stories by
the former sports editor of the New York *Daily
News*, who, after fourteen years as a columnist
gave up his job and came to Europe in 1936 as a
full-time writer of fiction. Each of these tales is
prefaced by a note explaining how Gallico came
to write it. "The Roman Kid", anthologised as a
classic detective story, is based on the statue of the
Sitting Boxer in the Museo delle Terme, in Rome,
the original of which was proved by the author to
have been a southpaw from the evidence in the
sculpture. This book also contains "Oh, Them
Golden Mittens", a story about the Golden Gloves
tournament, which Paul Gallico originated and
promoted.

773. GARDNER, L.
Fat City
London, Rupert Hart-Davis Ltd., 1970.
London, Panther Books (Paperback), 1972.
127pp.

774. GARNETT, David
The Sailor's Return
London, Chatto and Windus. 1925. (Limited
Edition of 160 copies)
London, Chatto and Windus. (Phoenix
Library), 1928.
New York, Garden City Publishing Co.
(Sundial Library), 1928.
162pp.
In this book the Targett family appear as charac-
ters, and one member of the family is killed in a
fight with a boxer.
See also "Targett's Prize Fight", one of the
chapters in the book.

775. GAY, K., and BARNES, B.E.
Your Fight Has Just Begun!
The Sport of Boxing
New York, Julian Messner, 1980.
190pp.

776. GEER, Alpheus
(Marshall Stillman pseudonym)
Boxing and Self Defence Taught by the
Marshall Stillman Method
New York, Marshall Stillman Association,
1919.
94pp. Illus.

777. GEER, A.
(Marshall Stillman pseudonym)
Manual of the Fist and Self Defence
Three rounds of shadow boxing, eight bone-
breaking holds and releases, eight holds in
standing wrestling.
Nutley, Jew Jersey, Marshall Stillman Association, 1918.
28pp.

778. GEER, A.
Five Short Cuts to Good Boxing.   Mass
Boxing, Success through Boxing.
New York, 1920.

779. GEER, A.
(Marshall Stillman pseudonym)
Booklet on Boxing and Self Defence (In 6
parts)
New York, Marshall Stillman Association,
1922.
Each of the booklets has a black/grey cover, with
an illustration on the front.
The contents consist of the following:

Book 1 – 5 Short-cut Lessons to Good Boxing,
    64pp.
Book 2 – Scientific Blows and Guards, 46pp.
Book 3 – Great Fighters and Boxers, 95pp.
Book 4 – Shadow Boxing and How to Train. With
    36 instructional illustrations, 48pp.
Book 5 – Daily Exercises and Home Development,
    63pp.
Book 6 – Ju-Jitsu and other Defences against
    Violent Assault. Wrestling With 54 Instruction-
    al Illustrations, 46pp.
The No.3 booklet consists of short biographies of
boxers, lists of some of their principal fights and
descriptions of a few contests.   There are 82
boxers mentioned in this section with 65 portraits.

780. GERALD, Frank
A Millionaire in Memories

London, George Routledge and Sons Ltd.,
1936.
344pp.
This book contains a number of references to Jem
Mace, Peter Jackson, Frank Slavin, Bob Fitzsimmons and Larry Foley in chapter 7 entitled "The
Hub of Sport".

781. GEROULD, Katherine Fullerton
Ringside Seats
New York, Dodd, Mead and Co., 1937.
226pp.
This book includes an essay entitled "Ringside
Seats" (A woman's impression of the first fight
between Gene Tunney and Jack Dempsey on
September 23, 1926).

782. "G.G."
Sporting Stories and Sketches
London, Kegan Paul, Trench and Trubner
and Co. Ltd., 1895.
This book contains a story of the ring entitled
"A Little Scrap".

783. GIAMBRA, Joey and
VILLANI, Fred
The Uncrowned Champion
Las Vegas, Joey One Inc., 1979.
259pp. Illus.
The life story of Joey Giambra.

784. GIBBONS, M.J.
How to Box Scientifically
St.Paul (Minnesota), Gibbons Athletic Assoc-
iation, 1923.
Illus.

785. GIBBONS, M.J.
How to Train for Boxing
Complete Instruction for Preparing for
Boxing
St.Paul, (Minnesota), Gibbons Athletic Asso-
ciation, 1922.
48pp. illus.

786. GIBBS Harry
Box On. The Autobiography of Harry Gibbs
As told to John Morris.
London, Pelham Books Ltd., 1981.
155pp. Illus.
A Referee's story of his life.

787. GIFFORD, William
(Editor of *A Quarterly Review*)
Warreniana

continued

London, Printed for Langman, Hurst, Rees, Orme and Green, 1824.

This item includes:
"The Dream", A Psychological Curiosity" by S.T.C.
This poem is preceded by an "Advertisement to the Reader", which includes the following paragraph:
"The circumstances that led to its original composition are as follows: I had been considering in what way I might best introduce the subject, when suddenly falling asleep over a provincial newspaper which detailed the battle between Cribb and Molineux, the thoughts of my waking hours assumed the aspect of the present poetical reverie".
There is another poem entitled "The Battle of Brentford Green". A Poem in two cantos. By Sir W-- S--.
S.T.C. would be the poet Samuel Taylor Coleridge, 1762-1834. Sir W-- S- would probably be Sir Walter Scott.

788. GILLINGHAM, The Revd. George W. (Rector of Ombersley)

Ombersley — An Omnibus of History and Sport

Worcester and London, Ebenezer Baylis and Sons Ltd., Trinity Press, 1948.

105pp. Illus.
Chapter XXII — Sport — The Noble Art, refers to Boxing Academies "started under the patronage of the nobility and gentry", claiming that the sport was thus named "The Noble Art of Self Defence", deriving from a book published in 1795 by a certain noble pupil of the great Mendoza.

789. GILMORE, Al-Tony

Bad Nigger!
The National Impact of Jack Johnson
Port Washington, (New York), Kennikat Press 1975.
162pp.

790. GILMOUR, R.

The Champion Breed
A Book Length Novel of the Ring, and other stories
London, Gerald G. Swan Ltd., 1946.
This was No.1 in a series entitled *Boxing Yarns*. No.2 in the series was entitled *Boxing Shorts*, also issued in 1946.
Issued in paper covers, illustrated on front cover.

791. GINGRICH, Arnold (Editor)

Esquire's Second Sports Reader. (An Anthology of Short Stories)
New York, A.S. Barnes and Co., 1946.
427pp.

Includes eleven stories on boxing by Harry Sylvester, L.A.G. Strong, Paul Gallico and others.

792. GLANVILLE, Brian

People in Sport
London, Martin Secker and Warburg Ltd., 1967.
255pp.
This is a compendium of the writings of the author on sport over ten years.
There are a number of boxing references, including "Are Boxers People?", "Talking to Patterson", "Listening to Liston", "Terry Downes and Sugar Ray", etc.

793. GLENDENNING, Raymond

Raymond Glendenning's Book of Sport for Boys
London, Sportsguide Publication Ltd.
There were three editions of this book up to 1952 as follows:
1950 Edition –
160pp. This included the following items of boxing interest:
"Comeback" by Richard Gibson (Fiction)
"The Six Greatest Fights of All-Time" by Trevor Wignall
"Close-Up of a Champion" (Marcel Cerdan)
"Building of a Boxing Champion" by Nat Seller.
There were a number of boxing illustrations, including the Turpin brothers.

1951 Edition –
160pp. Boxing items included:
"Tales of the Great in Boxing" by Trevor Wignall
"Sports Brains Trust" (including Danny O'Sullivan)
"My Sunday Morning Nursery" by Jack Solomons,
plus numerous illustrations.

1952 Edition –
160pp. Boxing items included:
"Our Most Exciting Fights" by Raymond Glendenning and Barrington Dalby
"Close-Up of a Champion" (Sugar Ray Robinson)
"Where's Drake", a short boxing story by Kenneth Wheeler.
Plus numerous illustrations.

794. GLENDENNING, Raymond

Just a Word in Your Ear
Foreword by Gordon Richards
London, Stanley Paul and Co. Ltd., 1953.
188pp. Illus.
The author gave radio commentaries on many boxing matches during his career; his book includes reminiscences of his boxing broadcasts.

**795. GLENDENNING, Raymond and
BATEMAN, Robert**
Sportsman's Who's Who
London, Museum Press Ltd., 1957.
250pp.
The entries include 12 boxers, amateur and professional, who were active at the time of compilation.

796. GLOECKNER, Carolyn
Marvellous Marvin Hagler
Edited by Dr. Howard Schroeder
Mankato (Minnesota), Crestwood House,
1985.
48pp. Illus.

797. GLOECKNER, Carolyn
Sugar Ray Leonard
Edited by Dr. Howard Schroeder
Mankato (Minnesota), Crestwood House,
1985.
48pp. Illus.

798. GODBOLD, Ernest (Editor)
The Magazine of Sport
An Illustrated Record and Review
Coventry, Iliffe, 1888–1889.
This magazine included "History of the Birmingham Amateur Boxing Club" by E. Lawrence Levy, author of *Autobiography of an Athlete*.

799. GODFREY, Captain John
A Treatise Upon the Useful Science of Defence.
London, Printed for the Author by T. Gardner, at Cowley's Head, opposite St. Clements Church in the Strand, 1747.
This book contains sections on The Theory of the Sword and on Boxing with a chapter on the Character of Boxers. This chapter deals with the following pugilists:
John Broughton, Tom Pipers, George Cretting, Bob Whitaker, Venetian Gondolier (Tito di Carnari), Nathaniel Peartree, George Taylor, Prince Boswell, Tom Smallwood, George Stevenson and Jack James.
This is probably the oldest book on the history of the old prize-fighters, and it is probable that later works on the history of pugilism are based on the section "The Characters of the Boxers".
A Treatise Upon the Useful Science of Defence is menioned in other noted books on boxing, such as the following:
Annals of Sporting and Fancy Gazette, Vol.III, No. 17 (May 1st, 1823)
Boxiana by Pierce Egan, Vol.1, 1812.
The Complete Art of Boxing According to the Modern Method, by An Amateur of Eminence, 1788.
Famous Fights, Past and Present, by Harold Furniss

Vol.V. No.63.
Fistiana, or The Oracle of the Ring, edited by Vincent Dowling, 1st edition, 1841.

It is interesting to note that in the section "The Theory of the Sword", the chapter entitled "Characters of the Masters" deals with Tom Figg in his capacity of a swordsman, as follows:
"Figg was the Atlas of the Sword, and may he remain the gladiating statue! In him, Strength, Resolution and unparallelled judgement conspired to form a matchless Master. There was a majesty Shone in his Countenance, and blazes in all his actions, beyond all I ever saw".

800. GOGARTY, Oliver St.John
Mad Grandeur
A Novel
London, Constable and Co., 1943.
406pp.
Deaf Burke is one of the characters in this novel: Book 1. Chapter IV: "What Deaf Burke Heard", includes an account of a fight between Burke and Herbert (Bert) Wallins in Ireland.

801. GOLD, Kid
Brown Flash
A Boxing Novel
London, Carter Warren Ltd., 1951.
128pp. Paper covers, with coloured illustrations on front cover.

802. GOLD, Kid
Frisco Champ
A Boxing Novel
London, Curtis Warren Ltd., (1951)
128pp. Illus. paper covers.

803. GOLD, Kid
Kid Gloves
A Boxing Novel
London, Curtis Warren Ltd., 1951.
128pp.
Coloured paper covers with a boxing action picture on the front cover.

804. GOLD, Kid
Punch Money
A Boxing Novel
London, Curtis Warren Ltd., (1951)
128pp. Illus. paper covers.

805. GOLD, Kid
Right Cross
A Boxing Novel
London, Curtis Warren Ltd., 1951.
128pp. Coloured paper covers.

806. GOLDBERG, Samuel
Fighter In The Naptha Ring
New York, Carlton Press Inc., 1967.
255pp.
The author boxed in his younger days under the name of Young McGowan; he fought Benny Leonard, Ellis O'Keefe and other well-known lightweights. His autobiography tells of these fights and of his experiences as a union organiser in the dry-cleaning industry.

807. GOLDING, Claud
Cavalcade of History
London, Hutchinson and Co. (Publishers)Ltd
1937.
This book, divided into monthly sections, includes a few pugilistic items, referring to Daniel Mendoza, Sayers v. Heenan etc.

808. GOLDING, Claud
The Second Cavalcade of History
London, Hutchinson and Co. (Publishers)Ltd
1938.
830pp.
This book is divided into months, each containing short biographies of celebrities who were born or died in that month.
Among the pugilistic entries are the following: Tom Spring, Jack Langan, Ben Caunt, John Jackson, Josh Hudson, Harry Broome and others.
See also *Cavalcade of History*, 1937 by the same author.

809. GOLDING, Louis
Store of Ladies. A Novel
New York City, Alfred A. Knopf Inc., 1927.
London, Bear Hudson Ltd., 1948. (Bear Pocket Books)
308pp.
This is the story of Mrs Horsham, a wealthy widow from Belgravia, and her involvement with Jimmy Barton, a young boxer from Bermondsey, after meeting him at a party; following this she attended some of his fights.

810. GOLDING, Louis
Adventures in Living Dangerously
London, Morley and Michael Kennerly Junior, 1930.
52pp.
A book of reminiscences, with slight reference to boxing.

811. GOLDING, Louis
Magnolia Street
London, Hutchinson and Co., January,1932.
The first print of this book sold out very

quickly and it has since been reissued many times.
607pp.
One of the principal characters in the novel is Battling Kid Mick Shulman, World's Lightweight Champion.
Magnolia Street was produced as a play by C. B. Cochran at the Adelphi Theatre in London in 1934.

812. GOLDING, Louis
Black Frailty
London, The Centaur Press, 1934.
Issued in a Limited Edition of 75 signed copies.
49pp. Illus.
The hero of the story is Tom Molineux.

813. GOLDING, Louis
The World I Knew
London, Hutchinson and Co.(Publishers)Ltd, 1940.
328pp.
This book includes material of boxing interest as follows:

Chapter 11 – "Madison Square Garden". (Golden Gloves Inter-City Tourney between boxers of New York and Chicago)
Chapter 18 – "Boxing Fan", refers to the author's enthusiasm for boxing, finding the sport 'exciting and beautiful'.

814. GOLDING, Louis
Pale Blue Nightgown. A Book of Tales.
London, Hutchinson and Co., 1943.
This book contains two stories of the Prize-Ring, as follows:

15 – He Fought a Ghost. The story of Deaf Burke v. Samuel O'Rourke contest in New Orleans, May 30th, 1857.
16 – There were Men Once. The Story of Bendigo's third fight with Ben Caunt near Sutfield Green, Oxon, Sept. 9th, 1845.

815. GOLDING, Louis
Boxing Tales
A collection of Thrilling Stories of the Ring by the famous author of *MagnoliaStreet*, etc.
London, Findon Publications Ltd., Printed and Published by the Argus Press Ltd., 1947.
78pp. Paper covers carrying a picture of Freddie Mills being K.O'd by Lloyd Marshall.
This book is made up of 8 chapters of true-life and fictional boxing stories.

816. GOLDING, Louis
Bare Knuckle Lover and Other Stories

continued

London, Polybooks Ltd., 1947.

Paper covers. Illus.
Contains six stories, the first of which deals with pugilism. It is a fictional fight between George Stevenson and John Broughton in 1741.

817. GOLDING, Louis
My Sporting Days and Nights
With illustrations by "Joss" of the London *Star*.
Dedicated to "Sir Arthur Elvin, a Tribute in the Year of the Olympic Games at Wembley".
London, Findon Publications Ltd., 1948.
15 Chapters, Paper covers.
The Chapters on boxing include the following:

II – What's wrong with British Boxing?
III – The worst fight I ever saw (Petersen v. Doyle)
IV – Harvey was a real champion
V – The Blonde Tiger (Walter Neusel)
VI – Petersen v. Gains
VII – The fallen giant (Carnera)
VIII – English v. American boxing
X – Kid Lewis

818. GOLDING, Louis
The Bare Knuckle Breed
London, Hutchinson and Co. (Publishers)Ltd 1952.
232pp. Illus.
A book of bare-knuckled fights and fighters, with a few glove fights.

819. GOLDSTEIN, Alan
A Fistful of Sugar
New York, Coward, McCann, and Geoghegan, 1981.
296pp. plus Appendix. Illus.
A biography of Sugar Ray Leonard.

820. GOLDSTEIN, Ruby
Third Man In The Ring
As Told to Frank Graham
New York, Funk and Wagnalls, 1959.
213pp. Illus.
Memoirs of a fighter who later became a world-famous referee.

821. GOLESWORTHY, Maurice
The Encyclopedia of Boxing
London, Robert Hale and Co., 1960.
Further revised and updated editions were published in following years.
230pp. Illus.

822. GOODRICH, Thomas
Thomas Eakins. His Life and Work.

New York, The Macmillan Co., for the Whitney Museum of American Art, 1933.
72 Illustrations.
The subject of this book was an artist, and information is given on his interest in prize-fighting and his pictures thereof.

823. GOODWIN, Jack, and
EVANS, B.J.
Boxing
Foreword by the Rt. Hon. Earl of Lonsdale.
Bristol, W.J. Arrowsmith.
London, Simkin Marshall and Co., 1922.
144pp.
This item is mainly instructional, including chapters on Health Hints, The Duties of Seconds, American Training, etc., with contributions by Joe Fox and Albert Lloyd.
Illustrated from photographs.

824. GOODWIN, Jack
(The Famous Trainer)
Myself and My Boxers
Edited By B.J. Evans
London, Hutchinson and Co., 1924.
255pp. Illus.
The text of this book gives information on the author's fighting days, together with his other experiences, and also stories of the many famous boxers to whom he acted as trainer, such as Harry Mansfield, Charlie Hardcastle, Louis Ruddick, George Cook, Joe Fox, Bermondsey Billy Wells and others.

825. GOODWIN, John C.
Queer Fish
Dedicated to W.L. George
London, Hutchinson and Co., 1926.
127pp.
This book is based on the author's experiences during walks round London, mixing with all kinds of people, including prizefighters.
Chapver V is entitled "The Prizefighter".

826. GOODWIN, John C.
One of the Crowd
London, Hutchinson and Co. (Publishers) Ltd., 1936.
287pp.
The theme of this book is the London crowd, and Chapter VI entitled "Seeing Stars" deals with boxing crowds at different venues.

827. GORDON, Adam Lindsay
The Poems of Adam Lindsay Gordon. (Including Several Never Printed Before)
Arranged by Douglas Sladen.
London, Constable and Co., 1912.

continued

390pp.

The introduction mentions that Adam Lindsay Gordon took to spending his holidays in Jem Edwards, the prizefighter's, boxing saloon at the Roebuck Inn, Cheltenham.

Included in the poems, Part VII "Poems not included in the Collected Poems", edited by Marcus Clarke, is one about Jem Edwards.

828. GORDON, D.V.

Boxing for Schoolboys
London, The Mitre Press, 1946.

31pp. Stiff Paper Covers. Illus.
The author was Light-Heavyweight Belt holder of the 2nd Battn. The Middlesex Regt., and later a Physical Training Instructor at several schools.

829. GORDON, Lord Granville

Sporting Reminiscences
Edited by F.G. Aflalo
London, Grant Richards, 1902.
New York, E.P. Dutton and Co., 1902.

209pp. Illus.
Includes Chapter VII – "On Pig Sticking and Glove Fights".

830. GOUGH, Ex-Chief Inspector W.C.

From Kew Observatory to Scotland Yard. Being Experiences and Travels of 28 Years of Crime Investigation.
London, Hurst and Blackett Ltd., 1919.

284pp.
The boxing references include:
Chapter IX – The Liverpool Bank Frauds, involving Dick Burge, one-time Lightweight Champion of England.
Chapter XVI – A drama in Black and White, mentions Frank Craig "The Harlem Coffee Cooler".

831. GRAFFIS, Herb. (Editor)

Esquire's First Sports Reader
New York, A.S. Barnes and Co., 1945.
(Three Printings)

292pp.
Contains real-life stories of boxing by Abe Simon, J.R. Fair, Westbrook Pegler and others.

832. GRAHAM, Carroll

Only Human
A Boxing Novel
Toronto (Canada), F.E. Howard Publications Ltd., 1940.

Bound in stiff paper covers with coloured boxing picture on the front.
18 chapters.

833. GRAHAM, Stephen

Twice Round London Clock and More London Nights

London, Ernest Benn Ltd., 1933.

224pp.
The section "More London Nights" includes, "Premierland" (East London Boxing Arena).

834. GRAHAM, Winston

Angell, Pearl and Little God
London, Collins, 1970.

380pp.
A novel with boxing interest.

835. GRANT HUGHES LTD
(Publishers)

British Boxing Stars
London, 1948.

16 pp. (including covers). Pictures only (15). Each page shows a photographic picture of a current British boxer.
Acknowledgements to the various photographic agencies for permission to reproduce the pictures are given on the front page.

836. GRANT HUGHES LTD
(Publishers)

International Boxers
London, 1948.

Paper covers.
Is made up by illustrations only of 16 contemporary boxers. Portrait of Freddie Mills on the front cover.
(See also items under Hughes, Grant).

837. GRANT, James L.

The Great John L.
A Novelization of the Screen Play
Cleveland (USA) and New York City, The World Publishing Co., February 1945, second printing April 1945.

180pp. Illustrated by 4 full-page pictures taken from the film.
The subject of this film and book is John L. Sullivan.

838. GRANT, Keith

The Skeets Gallaher Story
A Biography
Dumbarton, Dumbarton District Libraries, 1983.

80pp. Stiff paper covers. Illus.
The Biography of the World's Best Amateur Flyweight Boxer, 1946. One of the British Amateur All-Time Greats.

839. GRANVILLE, Taylor

The Star Bout
A Romance of the Prize-Ring
Baltimore (U.S.A.), J and H Ottershaw, 1908
90pp. Illus.
Bound in wrappers.

L

840. GRAVES, Charles
Panorama
London, Ivor Nicholson and Watson, 1932.
392pp.
This book includes a chapter headed "The L.S.D. of Prize-Fighting".

841. GRAVES, Charles
The Price of Pleasure
London, Nicholson and Watson, 1935.
Reprinted, June 1935, Sept., 1935.
Cheap Edition Sept. 1936.
392pp.
One Chapter is entitled "The Price of a Blow".

842. GRAVES, Charles
Other People's Money
London, Ivor Nicholson and Watson Ltd., 1937.
304pp.
This book contains a number of references to boxers and boxing, including the sections "Boxers in Training" and "The Industry of Sport".

843. GRAVES, Charles
The Bad Old Days
London, Faber and Faber, 1951.
218pp.
Contains many references to boxers, boxing and others interested in the sport; including the National Sporting Club, Jack Bloomfield, Frank Goddard, Billy Wells, Joe Beckett, Phil Scott, etc.

844. GRAVES, Charles
The Cochran Story
London, W.H. Allen and Co. Ltd., 1951.
281pp. Illus.
This biography of the well-known showman, who also promoted boxing, includes many references to boxing in chapters VII, VIII, IX, XIV and XV.

845. GRAVES, George
Gaieties and Gravities.
The Autobiography of a Comedian.
Foreword by C.B. Cochran.
London, Hutchinson and Co. Ltd., 1931.
287pp.
Includes the following items of boxing interest:

Chapter XIX – The Beckett v. Carpentier Fight
Chapter XXII – Amateur Boxers, – The National Sporting Club Bouts, Latter-Day Corinthians.

846. GRAVES, Rev. Richard
The Heir Apparent, or the Life of Commodius, the Son and Successor of the good

Marcus Aurelius Antonius, Emperor of Rome, Translated from the Greek of Herodian. With a preface adapted for the present time.
London, 1789.
(3 volumes)
The translator appears to have taken Commodius as the ancient precursor of the modern "buck" and patron of pugilism – indeed he terms him the Imperial Prize-Fighter.
The preface attacks fashionable follies, introducing Humphries and Mendoza, the famous pugilists.

847. GRAYDON, John Allen
Sports Thrills. (Never to be Forgotten)
London, Findon Publications Ltd., 1945.
Paper covers, composite picture on front cover including boxing. The frontispiece – "Eight-Nine-Ten" shows Dempsey knocking out Firpo.
The boxing references are as follows:

Chapter I – Dempsey vs. Firpo
Chapter II – Baer vs. Carnera
Chapter XVII – Boon vs. Danahar
See also *More Sports Thrills*, 1946.

848. GRAYDON, John Allen
(London Sports Editor, Kemsley Newspapers)
More Sports Thrills
(More Never-To-Be-Forgotten Sports Thrills)
London, Findon Publications Ltd., 1946.
Price 1s.
Black and White paper covers. Illus.
The boxing references in this book are as follows:
Chapter 4 – When John L. Sullivan was really amazed
Chapter 18 – Tommy Farr gives Louis his Biggest Boxing Fright
The illustrations include one of John L. Sullivan chatting to convalescent soldiers.

849. GRAYDON, John Allen
(London Sportswriter, Kemsley Newspapers)
Still More Never-To-Be-Forgotten Sports Thrills.
London, Findon Publications Ltd., 1946.
The boxing entries in this publication are as follows:
Chapter 2 – Britain's Amateurs Surprise the Americans. (May 1946 at Wembley Pool)
Chapter 4 – When Freddie Mills Lost – But Won The Heart of "Boxidom". (versus Gus Lesnevitch at Harringay, May 14th 1946)
The one boxing illustration shows Lesnevitch battered and worn, turning away as the referee begins to count.

850. GRAZIANO, Rocky
Somebody Up There Likes Me
The Story of My Life So Far
Written with Rowland Barber.
London, Hammond, Hammond and Co.,1956
284pp.
The story of Rocky's fight with life and with the guys in the other corner of the ring.

851. GRAZIANO, Rocky
Rocky's Boxing Book
New York, Sayre Publications, 1978.

852. GRAZIANO, Rocky, and
CORSEL, Ralph
Somebody Down There Likes Me Too
This sequel to Graziano's *Somebody Up There Likes Me* was published in America, ca. 1985.

853. GREEN, Benny
Shaw's Champions
G.B.S. and Prizefighting, from Cashel Byron to Gene Tunney
London, Elm Tree Books, 1978.
Tells of Shaw's lifelong obsession with prizefighting, the transformation of his novel *Cashel Byron's Profession* into a stage play, and his friendship with boxers, including Gene Tunney.

854. GREEN, F.L.
On the Night of the Fire
London, Michael Joseph Ltd., 1939.
317pp.
One of the characters in this book is a champion boxer. In the film of the same title the boxer's part was played by Dave Crowley.

855. GREEN, Isidore (Editor)
The Weekly Sporting Review Annual
Wembley (Middx), Published by the Editor.
This annual number of *The Weekly Sporting Review* covered show business and a number of sports, including a large section devoted to boxing, which was well illustrated.
The annual issue ran for at least four years, 1948-1949 to 1951-1952; the size varied from large quarto to folio, with a coloured cover (illustrated).

856. GREENWOOD, James
The Wilds of London
With 12 Illustrations by Robert Concanen.
London, Chatto and Windus, 1874.
The text of this book contains very little on boxing, but 2 of the illustrations are of pugilistic interest, these are tinted full-page plates, as follows:

"Sunday Evening with 'The Fancy'" by A. Concanen. (A scene in a bar of a public house, showing pictures of pugilists on the walls.)
"An Evening with Forty Thieves". A scene in the bar of a public house, showing pictures of pugilists on the wall, also a bill of a benefit for Bos Tyler.

857. GREENWOOD, J.
Low Life Deeps; Strange fish to be found there.
A curious account of London life in the middle of the 19th century.
With a frontispiece and several other tinted lithographs.
Illustrated by A. Concanen.
London, Chatto and Windus, 1876.
Includes a portrait and reference to Bendigo (William Thompson) the champion pugilist.

858. GREY, Clifford
Boxing
London, Reynolds and Co. No Date.
Reynolds and Co. Sixpenny series of Recitations, No.3.
Any introductory note states "May be performed freely everywhere, excepting Theatres and Music Halls".

859. GREYVENSTEIN, Chris
This Brutal Glory
Capetown, Boren Publishing Pty., Ltd.,1969.
162pp. Illus.
Includes a short bibliography of boxing books.

860. GREYVENSTEIN, Chris
The Fighters
A Pictorial History of S.A.Boxing from 1881
Capetown, Don Nelson, 1981.
448pp. inlcuding Index and Bibliography.
4to Profusely Illus.

861. GRICE, Edward
Great Cases of Henry Curtis Bennett, K.C.
London, Hutchinson and Co. (Publishers) Ltd., 1937.
152pp.
This book contains a chapter entitled "The Banned Big Fight", which refers to the proposed bout between Bombardier Wells and Jack Johnson, to be promoted by James White at Earls Court on Oct. 2nd, 1911.
The illustrations include one of Jack Johnson with the Rev. F.B. Meyer who led the "Stop The Fight" campaign.

862. GRIERSON, Henry
The Ramblings of a Rabbit

continued

London, Chapman and Hall Ltd., 1924.

238pp. Illus

This work includes items of boxing interest as follows:

Chapter III — Jerry Driscoll coaching at boxing at St. Pauls

Chapter VI — Anecdote of Bombardier Billy Wells

Chapter VIII — Anecdote of Joe Beckett

Chapter XIII — Anecdote of Jack Bloomfield

863. GRIFFIN, Marcus

Wise Guy — James J. Johnston; A Rhapsody in Fistics

With a Foreword by Damon Runyon.
New York, The Vanguard Press, 1933.

315pp. Bound in brown or green cloth.
The story of the famous boxing promoter and manager, including many of the notable fighters, American and British, with whom he was involved.

864. GRIFFITH, J.L., and
CLARK, G.P.

Fundamentals of Boxing
Chicago, Wilson-Western Sporting Goods Co.
Issued between 1910 and 1928.

865. GRIMAULT, Dominique, and
MAHE, Patrick

Piaf and Cerdan. A Hymn to Love.
Translated from the French by Barbara Mitchell.
London, W.H. Allen and Co., P.L.C., 1984.

236pp. Illus.
The fictionalised love story of Edith Piaf and Marcel Cerdan, (World Middleweight Champion).

866. GRIME, Billy
(Triple Australian Champion)

The Art of Boxing
Melbourne (Austr.), The National Press Pty., 1946.

56pp. 29 Illus. Stiff Paper Covers.

867. GROMBACH, John V.

The Saga of Sock
New York, A.S. Barnes and Co., 1949.

374pp. Illus.
Bound in blue cloth with red titles on front cover and on spine.
The text is contained in 10 chapters and an appendix, described as follows:

Chapter I — Origins, Early History and the First Golden Age of Boxing

Chapter II — The Rebirth of Boxing and the Bare Fist Era

Chapter III — The Padded Glove Era

Chapter IV — Development of Weight Classifications, and Outstanding Performers in Each

Chapter V — Amateur and Inter-Collegiate Boxing

Chapter VI — Mirrors of Boxing. 'The First in Literature', 'Art', 'Theatre', 'Movies', and 'Radio'.

Chapter VII — Boxing and the World. Civilisation, Politics, New York State Athletic Commission, National Boxing Association, Suggestions for National Control, Oddities, War

Chapter VIII — Great Actors of Boxing, In and Out of the Ring

Chapter IX — Development of Boxing Technique, and Summary of Current Theory — Stance, Footwork, Offense and Defence

Chapter X — Homes, Finance, Results, Fatalities, and Future of Boxing.

The Appendix contains what is termed 'Boxing's Most Famous Poem "The Nonpareil's Grave"', and gives lists of Champions of different countries and the World; there are also various statistics such as record gates; etc.
The book is profusely illustrated, showing boxers of all periods. This book re-issued in 1977 under the title *The Saga of the Fist* (q.v.)

868. GROMBACH, John V.

The Saga of the Fist
The 9,000 Year Story of Boxing in Text and Pictures.
New York, A.S. Barnes and Co. Inc., 1977.
London, Thomas Yoseloff Ltd., 1977.

242pp. 4to. Illus.
This is a revised and updated version of *The Saga of Sock*, 1949, by John V. Grombach (q.v.), with new material.

869. GROOME, Francis Hindes

In Gipsy Tents
Edinburgh, William P. Nimmo and Co., 1880.
387pp.
Chapter I includes a Gipsy camp-fire discussion about Gipsy prize-fights, naming pugilists such as Cooper, Winter, Oliver, Jem Mace, and the family relationships of Mace.

870. GUTTERIDGE, Reg. (Editor)

Reg. Gutteridge World Boxing Year- Book, 1970 Edition
London, Atlas Publishing Co. Ltd.
A magazine-type publication, cold. paper covers, picture of Muhammad Ali on front cover.
Foreword by Ray Robinson.
Other Contributors include Eamonn Andrews, Joe Bugner, W. Barrington Dalby, Mark Rowe, and Alan Rudkin.

Re-issued by the same publisher in 1971 as *1971 Reg. Gutteridge World Boxing Year-book.*

continued

80pp. Foreword by Jack Dempsey.
Other contributors include Peter Wilson, Hugh McIlvanney, Richards Davies, and Bob Waters.

871. GUTTERIDGE, Reg.
Boxing, The Great Ones
London, Pelham Books, 1975.
152pp. Illus.

872. GUTTERIDGE, Reg.
The Big Punchers
Seconded by Henry Cooper
London, Stanley Paul and Co. Ltd., 1983.
223pp. Illus.
Includes the career records of a number of prominent fighters. The author's selection of big punchers ranges through all the weight divisions, from Jimmy Wilde to Ingemar Johannson and Henry Cooper.

FIG'S CARD,
Distributed to his Patrons and at his Booths at Southwark Fair and elsewhere.

ROMANTIC CAREER

OF

PETER JACKSON.

HIS FIGHTS RE-TOLD.

BY

A. G. HALES,

Author of "Outlawed," "McGlusky," "Angel Jim," "Little Blue Pigeon,"
"Driscoll, King of Scouts," "Camp Fire Sketches," &c.

———

PRICE ONE SHILLING.

———

The UMPIRE Publishing Co., Ltd., Manchester and London.

Title-Page *Romantic Career of Peter Jackson* (Hales) (Bib. Ref. 882)

873. HACKWOOD, Frederick

Old English Sports

London, T. Fisher Unwin, 1907

361pp. With 6 coloured plates and 32 half tone plates from old prints.

The text includes the following items of boxing interest:

Chapter XII – Quarter-Staff and Single Stick, etc.
Chapter XIII – Wrestling. (Including "Cornish Hug" and Cornish Rules)
Chapter XIV – Prizefighting – Pugilism.
The plates include – "A Private Turn-Up" drawn and sketched by H. Alken (coloured), and the following Half Tone plates:
"Single Stick. Somersetshire Gamesters"
"Cornish Wrestling"
"A Sparring Match in the Fives Court"

874. HADATH, Gunby

Pulling His Weight

A Public School Story

London, Hodder and Stoughton, 1924.

Dedication to "Troop A.S.M. Hutchinson, who knows why"

320pp.

This story contains several chapters about boxing, and a fine account of a boxing match in Chapters XXI, XXII and XXIII.

875. HAGEDORN, Hermann

The Life of Theodore Roosevelt

Illustrated with Photographs, Cartoons and Reproductions from Theodore Roosevelt's Own Diaries.

London, George G. Harrap and Co. Ltd., 1919.

Chapter XXII tells of Roosevelt's interest in boxing and wrestling and of him luring Mike Donovan, the ex-lightweight champion, to Albany to spar with him.

876. HAILS, Jack

Classic Moments in Boxing

London, Morland Publishers, 1983.

159pp. Illus.

877. HAISLET, Edwin L.

(Assistant Professor of Physical Education, Boxing Coach, University of Minnesota. Director of Northwest Golden Gloves)

Boxing

New York, A.S. Barnes and Co. Inc., 1940.

A "Barnes Sports Book", Barnes Dollar Sports Library.

118pp. Illustrated by 96 Instructional cuts in the text.

878. HALDANE, Robert A.

Giants of the Ring

The Story of the Heavyweights for Two Hundred Years.

There were two editions of this book, as follows:

A De Luxe Edition, in red cloth cover, with gilt titles on cover and spine.

A Cheap Edition, with stiff paper covers including a boxing picture on the front.

164pp. Illus.

The text is divided into two sections, "The Bruisers" and "The Queensberry Boxers".

879. HALDANE, R.A.

Champions and Challengers

100 Years of Queensberry Boxing

London, Stanley Paul and Co. Ltd., 1967.

244pp. Illus.

880. HALES, A.G.

Black Prince Peter

The Romantic Career of Peter Jackson

London, Wright and Brown (No Date)

The Dedication reads:

"This book 'Black Prince Peter' is dedicated – for old memories sake, to Harry Preston Esq."

352pp.

A Preliminary note states:

"The Author of this interesting Story, Mr. A.G. Hales, Author, War Correspondent, and World Rover, was intimately acquainted with Peter Jackson from his early years, and in close touch with him throughout his romantic career. Mr. Hales travelled all the way from Australia specially to witness and report the historic battle in the National Sporting Club, London, between the Black Prince and Frank Slavin, the greatest ring battle ever fought"

The story of Peter Jackson is told in the form of a novel.

The story was also published under the title *Romantic Career of Peter Jackson. His Fights Re-told*. (q.v.)

881. HALES, A.G.

Nut Brown Maid and Nut Brown Mare

A Novel

The Dedication reads: "Dedicated to the memory of Charley Mitchell, who, before he went west helped me to sketch out the chapters relating to the Making of a Real Champion"

253pp.

15 of the 21 chapters relate to boxing.

882. HALES, A.G.
Romantic Career of Peter Jackson
Manchester, The Umpire Publishing Co. Ltd.
ca. 1911.
Manchester, Empire News Ltd.
296pp.
Paper covers.
This is the life story of Peter Jackson, told in the form of a novel. The text is identical to that in A.G. Hales *Black Prince Peter*. (q.v.)

883. HALES, A.G.
My Life of Adventure
London, Hodder and Stoughton Ltd., 1918.
(Dedicated to the author's son, Trooper Walter F. Hales)
387pp.
This book contains many references to boxers and boxing:

Chapter VIII – I take seriously to Boxing, in which mention is made of such as Larry Foley, Peter Newton, Mick Nathan, Charlie Mitchell, John L. Sullivan, Joe Goddard, Jim Hall, Jem Mace, Young Griffo, Peter Jackson, Jim Corbett, Kid McCoy, Dick Burge and Georges Carpentier.

884. HALES, A.G.
Broken Trails
(The Record of a Wandering Life)
London, John Long Ltd., 1931.
320pp. Illus.
Chapter XXVI includes several pages devoted to boxing and boxers, particularly Australian boxers.

885. HALL, George
The Gipsy's Parson
London, Sampson, Low and Marsden, 1915.
307pp.
Chapter XIV   deals with Stephen, a Gipsy coal-dealer of Lynn, who travelled with Barney and Pooley Mace with a boxing-booth.

Chapter XVII   refers to Jem Mace, at the age of 18, with Nat Langan at Lincoln and Horncastle Fairs; Jem beat the local champion of Horncastle.

886. HAMILL, Pete
Flesh and Blood. A Novel.
London, Macmillan Ltd., 1971.
276pp.
The tough, lyrical story of a man who became the best heavyweight for years.

887. HAMMETT, Dashiell
(Author of *The Thin Man*)

Red Harvest. A Novel.
New York, Alfred Knopf, February 1929.
New York, Grossett and Dunlap, July, 1931.
This story also appeared in two Dashiell Hammett omnibus volumes published by Alfred Knopf in 1935 and 1942. There was also a Pocketbook edition in December 1943.
270pp.
The following chapters cover the boxing interest in this book:
Chapter 8 – A Tip on Kid Cooper
Chapter 9 – A Black Knife

888. HAMPDEN, John
An Eighteenth Century Journal. Being a Record of the Year 1774–1776.
London, MacMillan and Co. Ltd., 1940.
405pp.
Includes an account of two fistic battles in a field behind Montague House, London, taken from *The Morning Post* of 19th April, 1774.

889. HANCHANT, W.L.
The Newgate Garland, or Flowers of Hemp
London, Desmond Harmsworth, 1932.

A Collection of Broadsheet Ballads and Songs, with a Glossary of Slang and Cant.
This includes as ballad "The Leary Man" with a pugilistic theme, mentioning Ben Caunt and Bendigo.

890. HANGER, Colonel George
The Life, Adventures and Opinions of Colonel George Hanger. As Written by Himself.
London, Debrett, Piccadilly, 1801. (Two Volumes)
There is a slight reference to boxing in this work; in Volume I page 15 and Volume II, Chapter V.

891. HANKINSON, J.T., and FAULKNER, R.G.B.
Boxing for Schools
London, George Allen and Unwin, 1952.
72pp. 28 Illus. from photographs.

892. HARDING, W.E.
Life of John Morrisey, or John Morrisey, his Life Battles and Wrangles
New York City, Richard K. Fox, (*The Police Gazette*), 1880 and 1887. (Fistiana Heroes No.2)
49pp. Illus.
This work traces the life story of John Morrisey from his birth in Ireland until he died, a state senator.

893. HARDING, William E.
(**Sporting Editor**, *National Police Gazette*)
The Champions of the American Prize Ring
A Complete History of the Heavyweight Champions of America, with their Battles and Portraits, Executed Expressly for this book. Complete and Authentic. The only Book of its kind in the World.
New York, Richard K. Fox, 1881.
There were further issues of this book in1888 and 1893.
51pp. Illus.

894. HARDING, William E.
Jem Mace of Norfolk England, Champion Pugilist of the World. His Life and Battles. (Fistiana's Heroes, No.1)
New York City, Richard K. Fox, 1881.
Bound in wrappers, with portraits and illustrations.

895. HARDING, W.E.
History of the Prize Ring, With Lives of Paddy Ryan and John L. Sullivan
Giving Illustrations and Portraits of all the Champions and their Fights.
New York City, Richard K. Fox, 1881 and 1882.

896. HARDING, W.E.
Life and Battles of Joe Collins (Tug Wilson) Champion Pugilist of England
New York, Richard K. Fox, 1882.
47pp. 16 Illus.
Tug Wilson went to America from Britain and his backer in the U.S. was Richard K. Fox. Wilson's bouts in America included two with John L. Sullivan.

897. HARDING, W.E.
John L. Sullivan, the Champion Pugilist. His Life and Battles with a full History of his Great Battle with Paddy Ryan.
New York, R.K. Fox, 1883. Police Gazette Library, Vol.1 No.6.
24 Illustrations.

898. HARDING, W.E.
The Sporting Man's Companion
Containing Prize-Ring, Pedestrianism, etc.
New York City, Richard K. Fox, 1887.
This item was possibly the predecessor of the *Police Gazette Sporting Annual*, which first appeared in 1898.

899. HARDING, William Edgar
Jake Kilrain's Life and Battles
New York, Richard K. Fox, 1888.
Also a complete history of the great Prize Fight with Jem Smith.

900. HARDING, W.E.
Prize Ring Champions of England
New York, Richard K. Fox, 1889.
There was also an issue of this item in 1879.
65pp. Printed on pink paper. Illus.

901. HARDING, W.E.
John C. Heenan, His Life and Battles
(Fistic Heroes No.3)
New York City, Richard K. Fox, 1889.
64pp. Illus.
A Full Account of all his Great Battles, with portraits of all the men he fought with.

902. HARE, Jack (The Globe Trotter)
Gladiators of the Prize Ring,
and My World Travels
Nottingham, Printed and Published by Willson's of Mount Street, 1925.
304pp. Illustrated card covers with a picture of Jack Hare and Jack Dempsey on the front cover.
The author was Bantamweight Champion of South Africa in 1899.
The Introduction to the book consists of facsimile letters from Jack Dempsey, G.T.Dunning (*The Sportsman*) and A.J. Daniels (*The Sporting Life*).
The narrative recounts Jack Hare's experiences as a boxer, boxing instructor, trainer, referee and promoter, aboard ship and in places all over the world; with anecdotes concerning the boxing personalities he met during those travels.
There are many illustrations, both full-page and in the text.
Statistics are given in the final part of the book, including Ring Records and Fistic Facts with Jack Hare's listing of the World's Greatest Fighters, taken country by country.

903. HARE, Jack
The Knock-Out Blow and How to Avoid It.
Southampton, Published by the author, 1933.
This item ran into several editions. The following information is taken from the 4th edition.
Bound in green paper covers, with a picture of the author on the front cover. Profusely illustrated.
In this work there is only one chapter on the knock-out blow; the contents cover a much wider field including chapters on The Development of Boxing — The Sport, Past, Present and Future — My World Travels — The Last Knuckle Fight —

continued

Remarkable Fighters (How the Men of 20 or 30 years ago compare with the fighters of today).
Jack Hare served for many years at sea, and among other offices he held was that of Boxing Instructor aboard H.M.S. Prince George.

904. HARKINS, Philip
Southpaw From San Francisco
New York, William Morros, 1948. (Morros Junior Books)
247pp.

905. HARKINS, Phil.
Knockout
New York City, Holloway House, 1950.
242pp.

This book is described as "Fast moving fiction designed for the teen-age sports fan, telling what amateur boxing tournaments, like the Golden Gloves, can mean to the poor kid from the city streets".

906. HARMAN, Thomas T. (Compiler)
Showell's Dictionary of Birmingham
Oldbury, Walter Showell and Sons (Cross Wells Brewery), 1885.
(Originally issued in 24 parts, 1884-1885)
The section entitled 'Sporting Notes' contains a sub-section "Prize Fighting".

907. HARRIS, Frank
My Life and Loves
Volume III
Privately Printed.

While the author of this book was a brilliant editor, as well as being a novelist and short story writer, he will probably be remembered as one of the greatest literary charlatans, mountebanks, and outrageous liars of all time. His five volumes of "autobiography", while making fascinating reading, cannot be relied upon for the true facts, and are notorious for their salacious sexual content. One chapter in the third volume, entitled "Prize-Fighting", proves that he knew what he was talking about in this direction, but whether or not he was actually present at the Sullivan-Mitchell contest in France, which he claims, is a moot point. "My Life and Loves" was originally published by Harris himself, was banned, seized, and pirated, and in later years was issued in Britain legally by W.H. Allen and Corgi Books.

908. HARRIS, Richard, K.C. (Editor)
The Reminiscences of Sir Henry Hawkins (Lord Brampton)
London, Edward Arnold, 1904 (Two Volumes)
A one volume edition was issued in 1905 and was reissued a number of times afterwards.

There are a number of references to the prize ring and pugilists in the first edition, including the following:

Volume I,
Chap.VII   "Newmarket Heath", tells of Hawkins' visit to the fight between Caunt and Brassey at Six Mile Bottom. Oct. 27th 1840.

Volume I,
Chap. XXII "Farmer Ryde", mentioning a prize-fight on Frimley Common.

Volume II,
Chap.XLVIII
            "The Sporting Tailor", Appeal of Coney, the ex-prize fighter and reference to the fight between Brassey and Caunt.

The later editions include the first two items, namely:

Chap.VI   "An Incident on the Road to New-market"

Chap.XVIII
           "The Prize-Fight on Frimley Common".

909. HARRISON, John
(Member of the Royal College of Surgeons), late Resident Surgeon, Bath Hospital
Athletic Training and Health; an Essay on Physical Education
Oxford and London, James Parker and Co., 1869.

Contains a number of references to prominent pugilists; chiefly regarding their training and physical condition. Including Sayers, Heenan, Gentleman Jackson, "Old Joe Ward", etc.

910. "HARRY HIEOVER"
(Charles Bindley)
The World; How to Square It
London, T.C. Newby, 1854.

This book has no actual reference to boxing, but at pages 163 to 166 there is a description of dealings between buyers and sellers in terms of an imaginary boxing contest.

911. "HARRY HIEOVER"
(Charles Bindley)
The Sportsman's Friend in a Frost
London, T.C. Newby, 1857.

There are two sections holding boxing interest; as follows:
The Ring, (Pages 260–273
The Prize-Ring, (Pages 357–372

912. HART, James D.
The Oxford Companion to American Literature
New York, Oxford University Press Inc., Copyright 1941.
Published by the Oxford University Press, London, New York and Toronto. First print 1941. Second printing with corrections 1944.

This work contains many items of boxing or pugilistic interest, with short biographies of boxers such as J.J. Corbett, Jack Dempsey, J.C. Heenan, J.L. Sullivan and Gene Tunney.
Also included are short biographies of authors who were responsible for books or periodicals of boxing interest, such as Damon Runyon, Jim Tully, Ring W. Lardner, Jack London, Ernest Hemingway, and others, with short descriptions of some of their works.
Two further items of boxing interest is a short biography of Adah Isaacs Menken and a history of Madison Square Garden.

913. HARTE, James Lambert
The Amazing Story of James J. Braddock
Emmaus, Pa., U.S.A., Rodale Press, 1938.
183pp. Illus. (Two Portraits of Braddock)

914. HARVEY, Len.
System of Training and Self Defence
Illustrated by photographs by Spearman of Windsor.
London, The Queensway Press, 1934.
252pp.
Bound in green cloth, black lettering on the spine.
Introduction by Harry Preston.
23 chapters covering all aspects of boxing including training, gymansium work, road work, etc.
There are 42 instructional illustrations.

915. HARVEY, Len.
(Former Middle, Cruiser and Heavyweight Champion of Great Britain; Heavyweight Champion of the British Empire, and outright winner of the Lonsdale Belt at Middleweight)
Modern Boxing, (Blackie's Sports Series)
London and Glasgow, Blackie and Son Ltd., 1937.
Preface by Len Harvey. Foreword by Ben Bennison.
88pp.
The 6 chapters are instructional, with an Appendix showing the Rules of Boxing.
The illustrations consist of 9 poses and 4 sets of "moving pictures"; these latter are activated by flicking the pages in sequence.
The sparring partner shown with Len Harvey in the "moving picture" sequences is George James the Welsh heavyweight.

916. HARVEY, Sir Paul (Compiler and Editor)
The Oxford Companion to English Literature
Oxford, The Oxford University Press, at the Clarendon Press, 1932.
Reprinted December, 1932, and reprinted with corrections in January, 1933, March, 1933 and January, 1934.

Includes many items of boxing or pugilistic interest as follows:
Short biographies of The Benicia Boy (J.C. Heenan) and Tom Sayers.
Short biographies of authors or artists who were responsible for items of boxing interest, as follows:
W. Harrison Ainsworth, Henry Alken, William Hogarth, John Keats, George Borrow, Pierce Egan, John Masefield, George Bernard Shaw and others.
Also described are certain works of boxing interest, such as *Lavengro, The Romany Rye, The Connoisseur* (magazine) etc.
Of further interest are descriptions of articles with boxing connotation, such as The Belcher (A neckerchief), The Cestus, The Queensberry Rules etc).

917. HASKINS, James
Sugar Ray Leonard
New York, Lothrop, Lee and Shepard Books 1982.
157pp.

918. HATUGARI, Leopold M.
Langton "Schoolboy" Tinago.
Boxing's Dancing Master.
Gwelo (Zimbabwe), Mambo Press, 1979.
("Zimbabwe Profiles" Series).
44pp. Illus.

919. HAUSER, Thomas
The Black Lights,
Inside the World of Professional Boxing.
New York, McGraw Hill, 1986.
257pp.

920. HAY, Jack
A Pair of Jacks
California (U.S.A.), Hwong Publishing Co., 1983.
324pp. Soft covers.
The author claims to be the illegitimate son of Jack Dempsey, the Manassa Mauler, the other Jack mentioned in the title of the book.

921. HAY, William, Esquire
Deformity. An Essay.
London, Printed for R. and J. Dodsley, and sold by M. Cooper, 1754.
An interesting item in defence of deformity, by a hunchback only 5 feet high. Contains a two-page

continued

attack on prize-fighting, with reference to Broughton's Theatre.

922. HAYDON, Thomas
Sporting Reminiscences
London, Sands and Co., 1898.
281pp.
Chapter I – Athletics – deals principally with boxing in Australia and mentions Jem Mace, Larry Foley, Feter Newton, of Victoria, Ned Bitton, Joe Goddard, Peter Jackson and others.

923. HAYENS, Herbert
Play Up Tigers. A School Story.
London, William Collins Sons and Co. Ltd., 1937.
282pp.
This book contains several chapters on boxing, also a coloured frontis.

924. HAYES, Frank and Co. (Publishers)
Champions of the Ring from Tom Sayers (1860) to Jack Johnson (1910), containing Records, Lives and Battles of Great Fighters, and many rare photographs.
Melbourne (Australia), 1910.
120pp. 90 Rare Illus.
Contains chapters on the old prize-ring champions back to 1795, and also an excellent history of Australian boxing.

925. HAYES, Matthew Horace, F.R.C.V.S.
Among Men and Horses
London, T. Fisher Unwin, 1894.
Published in New York in the same year.
358pp.
Chapters II and XX include (*inter alia*) reference to pugilism; including Charlie Mitchell, Bat Mullins, Wolff Bendoff, etc.

926. HAZARD, T.G.
The Life of Dan Donnelly, Champion of Ireland, with a Full Account of his Battles and Actions.
Dublin, Published by the author, 1820.
32pp.

927. HAZLITT, William
The Fight. An Essay.
This is an account of Hazlitt's visit to the fight between Thomas Hickman (The Gas man) and William Neat. The essay first appeared in the *New Monthly Magazine* in 1822.
The first appearance of the piece in a book occurred in *Literary Remains of the Late William Hazlitt. With a Notice of His Life* by his son; and *Thoughts on his Genius and Writings* by E.L. Balfour M.P. and Mr. Serjeant Talfourd M.P.

This was published in 2 volumes by Saunders and Otley in 1836.
"The Fight" has been published separately on many occasions and has appeared in many anthologies.

928. HEALD, J.
Observations on the Art of Boxing
No Date. (ca.1800)
65 pages of closely-written manuscript. So far as can be ascertained this work has been seen only in manuscript form and was never published. It is of considerable historical interest as the author was apparently a pupil of John Broughton. The manuscript describes boxing as being divided into three parts; first Square Boxing, second Round or Circular and third, Half Round or Half Circular Boxing. It then proceeds to describe the methods. Also given are Terms of Boxing and Miscellaneous Observations, particularly those of Mr. Broughton.

929. HEALTH and STRENGTH LTD (Publishers)
Training for Athletics
A Comprehensive Manual Dealing With All Branches of Sport.
London, 1907.
Each sport is dealt with by a different author who is an expert in his particular field.
The boxing section is made up as follows:

Ball Punching, by Gunner Moir, Champion of Eng.
How to Train for Boxing, by Tommy Burns, Champion of the World
Methods of Joe Carroll, Middleweight Champion of the World
Methods of Peter Gotz, 10st-6lbs Champion of the World
There are 6 illustrations in this section.

930 HEALTH and STRENGTH LTD (Publishers)
The Fighting Life of Jimmy Britt. (Ex-Lightweight Champion of the World)
London, 1909.
Gives a full account of his brilliant battles, with many facts never before published.
The illustrations include Jimmy Britt, Young Corbett, Joe Gans and Johnny Summers.

931. HEALTH and STRENGTH LTD. (Publishers)
Full and Graphic Story of the Great Fight — Burns v. Johnson. (Secret History of the Fight, Incidents of the Training, Special Illustrations)
London, 1909.
Includes: What happened after the contest, interviews with the combatants, expert opinions, the history of the rivals and the arrangement of the
continued

contest.

932. HEALTH AND STRENGTH LTD
(Publishers)
The Life and Fights of Tommy Burns
Special Descriptions of his Chief Contests,
Training, Methods, Expert Opinions etc.
London, ca.1909.

A narrative of Burns' career from boyhood, with
accounts of his contests with Marvin Hart, Bill
Squires, Gunner Moir, Bill Lang and Jack Johnson.
Particulars of his training, opinions of experts,
interviews and photos.
Illus.

933. HEALTH AND STRENGTH LTD
(Publishers)
The Burns-Moir contest at the National
Sporting Club for the Championship of the
World; with remarks by Gunner Moir
London, ca.1909. Price 1d.

A similar publication was published by the *Sporting Life* at about the same time.

934. HEALTH AND STRENGTH LTD
(Publishers)
The Life and Battles of Jas. J. Corbett,
One of America's Most Famous Boxers
London, ca.1909.

A complete history of "Pompadour Jim's" career,
with graphic accounts of his many famous fights,
photographs of his principal opponents, together
with many interesting incidents of his life.

935. HEALTH AND STRENGTH LTD
(Publishers)
The Fighting Career of Owen Moran, The
Famous Birmingham Boxer. Vivid descriptions of his Fights, and his Full Record.
With notes on his Marvellous Career.
London, 1909. Price 1d.

Paper covers, printed on pink paper. 5 Illustrations
including action portrait of Own Moran on the
front cover.

936. HEALTH AND STRENGTH LTD
(Publishers)
The Ring Career of Jim Driscoll
London, 1909.
6 Illus.

937. HEALTH AND STRENGTH LTD
(Publishers)
The Life and Fights of Robert Fitzsimmons.
Graphically Described From the Stories of
Eye-Witnesses. Detailed Accounts of all the
Principal Contests of this Unique Boxer,

embodied in a complete narrative of his
career, with splendid photos of himself and
his great contemporaries.
London, 1909.
32pp. 4 Illus.

938. HEALTH AND STRENGTH LTD
(Publishers)
The Life and Fights of "Iron" Hague
A Narrative of the Career of England's
Heavyweight Champion; with accounts of
his Contests, Training Methods, Opinion of
Experts, Personal Sketch, and His Future.
London, 1909. Price 2d.

This paper covered booklet includes a Chronology of The Ring (Heavyweights 1709-1908),
and contains 6 illustrations, including one of
Iron Hague on the front cover.

939. HEALTH AND STRENGTH LTD
(Publishers)
The Life and Fights of Jack Johnson
Accounts of the many Victories gained by
the World Champion, with Character Sketch
Training Methods, Anecdotes etc.
A narrative of the career of Jack Johnson,
the first coloured boxer to win the World
Heavyweight Championship, with personal
and splendid photos.
London, 1909. Price 2d.
Illus.

The 6 illustrations include the Champion and his
formidable opponents, Sam McVea, Joe Jeanette,
Sam Langford and Tommy Burns.

940. HEALTH AND STRENGTH LTD
(Publishers)
The Life and Fights of James J. Jeffries
Graphically described from the Stories of
Eye-Witnesses, With the Opinions of Experts
and Special Photos.
The Life Story of the Emperor of the
Boxing Arena, who retired undefeated after
twice meeting Fitzsimmons, Corbett,
Sharkey and other celebrities, and who is
now to fight Jack Johnson.
London, 1909. Price 2d.
This item was issued in at least two editions.
5 Illustrations. (One of James J. Jeffries on front
cover)

941. HEALTH AND STRENGTH LTD
(Publishers)
The Life and Battles of Sam Langford
Whose victory over "Iron" Hague, coupled
with Jack Johnson's default constitutes him
continued

the World's Champion Boxer.
A narrative of the Career of the phenominal pugilist, with Accounts of his Chief Contests a World Picture, Expert Opinions and Numerous Illustrations.
London, 1909. Price 2d.
Paper covers, picture of Langford on front cover. 9 other Illus.

942. HEALTH AND STRENGTH LTD
(Publishers)
The Life and Fights of Jem Mace, England's Veteran Hero
(With numerous hitherto unpublished Incidents in his career)
London, 1909.
Specially Illustrated.

943. HEALTH AND STRENGTH LTD
(Publishers)
The Life and Battles of Charlie Mitchell. Heavyweight Champion of England and One of the Cleverest Boxers on Record.
London, 1909.
A Narrative of the Famous Boxer's Career, with Graphic Descriptions of the Contests with J.L. Sullivan, J.J. Corbett, Jake Kilrain, Frank Slavin, and Jack Burke.
4 Illus. (including one of Mitchell on the front cover)

944. HEALTH AND STRENGTH LTD
(Publishers)
The Life and Battles of Gunner James Moir Ex-Heavyweight Champion of England
London, 1909. Price 2d.
A Narrative of the Ex-Champion's Career, containing graphic descriptions of the contests with Ben Taylor, Bill Heveron, Jem Casey, Slouch Dixon, Jack Palmer, Tiger Smith, Tommy Burns, Iron Hague etc., together with splendid portraits of his chief opponents.
London, 1909. Price 2d.
There are 8 illustrations, including an action portrait of Gunner Moir on the front cover.

945. HEALTH AND STRENGTH LTD
(Publishers)
The Life and Fights of John L. Sullivan
London, 1909.
Full-length action portrait of Sullivan on the front cover.
This item describes Sullivan as "One of the Most Remarkable Figures in the History of Pugilism".
The booklet claims that the famous fighter's career has never been fully told in this country before; it contains a fully detailed account of his

many battles in the ring.

946. HEALTH AND STRENGTH LTD
(Publishers)
The Life and Fights of Johnny Summers
Early Battles in Australia and Later Fights in America, France and England.
London 1909. Price 1d.
Paper covers. Printed on pink paper. 7 Illus.

947. HEALTH AND STRENGTH LTD
(Publishers)
The Life and Battles of Freddie Welsh
The Most Skilful Light-Weight Boxer in the World.
Being an Account of the Sensational Career of an Unbeaten Briton at Home and Abroad. Showing how he fought Sixty-five Battles against the best men of two Continents, and preserved an unbeaten record.
London, 1909.
Fully illustrated. Two Parts (I and II). Price 1d. each.
The first part ends with Welsh's fight against Phil Brock on May 30th 1908 and the second part with Welsh's fight against Joe Fletcher on Sept. 6th 1909.
8 Illustrations in Part I and 6 in Part II.

948. HEALTH AND STRENGTH LTD
(Publishers)
The Life and Fights of Packy McFarland
London, 1910. Price 1d.
Pink paper booklet, with an action picture of Packy McFarland on the front cover.
5 Illus.

949. HEDGEHOG, Humphrey, Esq.
The Busy Body, or Men and Manners
London, J. Johnston. 1816-1817.
This monthly periodical was reissued in volume form every six months. Volume III (March to August 1817) included "Pugilism Extraordinary".

950. HEIMER, Mel
The Long Count
New York, Atheneum, 1969.
Published simultaneously in Canada by McLelland and Stewart Ltd.
262pp. Plus Bibliography, Illus.
Written around the legendary Battle of the World Championship, when Prize-fighting was a National Sport and Jack Dempsey and Gene Tunney were its heroes.

951. HEINZ, W.C.
The Professional. A Novel.

continued

New York, Harper and Row, Publishers, Inc.
1958.

338pp.

The professional is in this case the manager of a
boxer; the story follows the manager and his
fighter from the moment of leaving home for the
training camp until the moment of the title fight.

952. HEINZ, W.C. (Editor)

The Fireside Book of Boxing
New York, Simon and Schuster, 1961.

404pp. Illus.

The author delves into the fact and fiction of fight
ligerature to provide a feast of reading. The extracts range from "The Dioscuri" of Theocritus to
Damon Runyon on Dempsey v. Tunney and Rocky
Marciano on "How It Feels to Be Champ".

953. HEINZ, W.C.

Once They Heard The Cheers
Garden City, New York, Doubleday and Co.
Inc., 1979.

489pp.

The famous sporting journalist's story of a trip
across America in search of yesterday's sporting
heroes. There are a number of interviews with
members of the boxing fraternity, such as
Rocky Graziano, Willie Pep, Floyd Patterson, Jack
Hurley, Carmen Basilio, Sugar Ray Robinson, and
other well-remembered glove artists.

954. HEINZ, W.C.

American Mirror.
A Distinguished Writer on Courage.
With a Foreword by Red Smith.
Published in America, ca. 1985.

An anthology of articles by the famous American
sports writer. Seven of the thirteen chapters
refer to boxing. The boxers mentioned include
such as Tony Zale, Lou Ambers, and Rocky
Graziano; three chapters are devoted to the latter
boxer.

955. HELLER, Peter

In This Corner
Forty World Champions Tell Their Stories
Introduction by Muhammad Ali.
New York, Simon and Schuster, 1973.
London, Robson Books Ltd, 1975.

420pp. Illus.

The book is divided into sections, each covering a
period during which the various champions
reigned. The periods are designated 1912-1919;
The Twenties; The Thirties, and so on up to The
Sixties.
This item was also issued in paperback.

956. HELLIWELL, Arthur

The Private Lives of Famous Fighters

Windsor (Berks), Cedric Day, 1949.
(Agents, Day and Mason, London)

98pp. Illus.

Thirteen Chapters, Twelve of which each feature
a different boxer.

957. HEMINGWAY, Ernest

The Sun Also Rises
New York, Charles Scribner's Sons, 1926.
London, Jonathan Cape Ltd., 1927. (Pub-
lished in England under the title of *Fiesta*)

259pp.

The central character of this novel is one Robert
Cohn "once middleweight boxing champion of
Princeton", but the book deals much more with
the bull ring than the boxing ring. The Cohn
character was based on Harold Loeb, whose much
later book, *The Way It Was*, gives his own version
of the events described in Hemingway's novel.
Loeb was so incensed when *The Sun Also Rises*
first appeared that he was said to be looking for
Hemingway with a gun.
The black-skinned boxer who makes a brief appearance in the book was actually Larry Gains, later to
become British Empire heavyweight champion.
Hemingway had a managerial interest in him in
Paris in the early 1920s.

958. HEMINGWAY, Ernest

Men Without Women
A Book of Short Stories
New York, Charles Scribner and Sons, 1928.
London, Jonathan Cape Ltd, 1928.

Includes boxing stories entitled "The Killers" and
"Fifty Grand".
The second of these stories appears in Cox W.D.
Boxing in Art and Literature (q.v.)

959. HEMINGWAY, Ernest

Winner Take Nothing
New York, Charles Scribner's Sons, 1933.
London, Jonathan Cape Ltd, 1934.

244pp.

This collection of short stories includes "The Light
of the World"; this story includes reference to the
Stanley Ketchel v. Jack Johnson fight.

960. HENDERSON, Edwin Bancroft

The Negro in Sports
Washington D.C., The Associated Publishers
Inc., 1939.
(Revised Edition)

371pp. Illus.

Parts of this book deal with Negro boxers, as follows:

Chapter II   — Past Heroes of the Prize-Ring
Chapter III   — Louis, Armstrong, and Lewis
Chapter XVI — Promotion (Includes amateur box-
                       ing)

The Appendix contains records of famous Negro
continued

boxers, from Tom Molineux to John Henry Lewis. There are full-length action pictures of some of the boxers mentioned.

961. HENDERSON, Eugene
"Boxing" Teaches a Boy
Edinburgh, The Moray Press, 1952.
31pp. Illus.
Stiff paper covers. Picture of the author on the front cover.

962. HENDERSON, Eugene
Box On
London, Stanley Paul and Co. Ltd, 1957.
149pp. Illus.
Memoirs of a famous referee.
Also issued in a Sportsmans Club Edition.

963. HENDERSON, Robert W.
(Compiler)
Early American Sport — A Chronological Check-List of Books Published Prior to 1860 Based on an Exhibition held at the Grolier Club. With an Introduction by Harry T. Peters.
New York, The Grolier Club, 1937.
400 copies only.
This work contains details of many rare American items dealing wholly or partly with boxing or pugilism, including some of the works of Pierce Egan, George Barrington, Donald Walker, Owen Swift, etc.

964. HENDERSON, William
King of the Gorbals
London, New English Library, 1973.
173pp. Paper covers.
This story is based on the life of Benny Lynch.

965. HENDRYX, James B.
Without Gloves
London, Hutchinson and Co. (Publishers) Ltd., 1925.
This book appeared in various cheap editions following the first issue.

966. HENLEY, William Ernest
Essays. (Volume 2 of the Collected Works of W.E.Henley)
London, Macmillan and Co. Ltd., 1921.
A Prefatory Note says: The biographical sketches here entitled "Byron's World" served as notes to an edition of Byron's Letters, of which one volume was published by Mr. Heinnemann in 1897, the other essays included in this volume made their first appearance in the *Pall Mall* magazine.

The following essays include pugilistic matter: William Hazlitt on the fight between Neat and Hickman.
"Byron's World", on Gentleman Jackson and Bob Gregson. "Old England" deals largely with the prize-ring and after, referring to the works of George Borrow, containing a review of Thormanby's "Boxers and their Battles", and information on some works of pugilistic interest.

967. HENNING, Fred W.J.
Some Recollections of the Prize Ring With Original Illustrations by Robert Prowse and Matt Stretch.
London, Henning and Co., 1888.
192pp.
Bound in coloured paper covers, with a picture of the bare fist on the front.
17 chapters, 5 illustrations.
The chapters are headed by the names of the pugilists whose particular battle is described in the chapter, such as — Bendigo and Ben Caunt — Johnny Walker and Ned Adams — Joe Goss and Jack Rooke — Deaf Burke and Bob Castles — Pooley Mace and Louis Gray, etc.

968. HENNING, Fred (Tourist)
Fights for the Championship — The Men and Their Times
London, Published at the Offices of the *Licensed Victuallers' Gazette*. 1899. Two Volumes.
Volume I = 364pp. Volume II = 525pp.
The contents of this comprehensive work consist of articles re-printed from the *Licensed Victuallers' Gazette*. The volumes are profusely illustrated with portraits taken from old prints. It is not possible to summarise fully the contents of this item in a limited space, except to note that it covers the period from the time of James Figg and Ned Sutton, Jack Broughton and George Stevenson through the time of Sayers and Heenan to the days of Jem Mace, J.L. Sullivan and Charlie Mitchell, Jem Smith and his battles, Frank Slavin and Jake Kilrain.
Among the illustrations is one of the *Police Gazette* Heavyweight Prize Ring Belt of the World, offered for competition by Richard K. Fox in 1884 and contested for by J.L. Sullivan and Jake Kilrain in 1889. The Belt is described as being fifty inches long and eight inches wide and weighing about 200 ounces in silver and gold.

969. HENRY, Detective Inspector Jack
Detective Inspector Henry's Famous Cases.
London, Hutchinson and Co. (Publishers) Ltd., 1944.
Illus. 182pp.
This item contains a number of references, embracing the National Sporting Club, Police Boxers and various boxing personalities.
There is an illustration of the author as a boxer in the Police Force.

970. HENRY, Ex-Divisional Detective Inspector Jack (Late of Scotland Yard)
What Price Crime?
London, Hutchinson and Co. (Publishers) Ltd., 1945.
112pp. Illus.
A number of boxing references occur in this book, including Jack Johnson, Sydney Hulls (Promoter), Tommy Farr, Covent Garden and Hammerstein's Opera Houses (when these were used as boxing arenas); Frank Moran v. Billy Wells, Joe Beckett v. Boy McCormick, etc.

971. HENRY, O.
Options. (A Book of Short Stories)
New York, Doubleday, Doran and Co., 1909
254pp.
Includes a story "Higher Pragmatism" which refers to an amateur boxer.
This story is also included in Cox W.D. *Boxing in Art and Literature* (q.v.)

972. HERBERT, A.P.
The Man About Town
London, William Heinemann Ltd., 1923.
286pp.
This volume includes an essay entitled "La Boxe", which is the story of a visit to a boxing arena in South East London.

973. HERMAN, H.M.
(Boxing Master at Dulwich Preparatory School)
Boxing for Beginners
A Little Book of Boxing for boys and beginners.
Foreword by Sir Harry Preston.
London, Hutchinson and Co. (Publishers) Ltd., 1936.
Illus.

974. HERRING, Paul
Bold Bendigo, A Romance of the Open Road
London, Sampson Low, Marston and Co. Ltd., 1927.
313pp.
This novel is based on the career of Bendigo (William Thompson) the Champion Pugilist; the story first appeared in the *Nottinghamshire Weekly Guardian*.

975. HERRING, Paul
Sir Toby and the Regent. A Novel.
London, Sampson Low, Marston and Co.Ltd 1929.
There were at least 2 impressions of this book
312pp.
This novel contains a great deal about the prize-ring and pugilism, particularly about Tom Cribb. There are 41 chapters and an epilogue.

976. HESS, Joseph F.
The Autobiography of Joseph F. Hess, The Converted Prize-Fighter
A Book of Thrilling Experiences and Timely Warnings to Young Men.
Dedicated to the cause of Total Abstinence and Religion.
Rochester, N.Y., Published by the Author, 1888 (Second Edition).
The author does not refer to his first prize-fight until late in the second chapter; in the meantime he had indulged in all manner of dissipation. In fact the whole book is devoted to his telling of his roistering, interspersed with accounts of his few appearances in the boxing ring.

977. HEYN, Ernest V. (Editor)
(Editor of the magazine *Sport*)
Twelve Sport Immortals
New York, Macfadden Publications Inc.1949
Publishers of the magazine *Sport*.
The editor selected for this book the very best "Sport Specials" by three master writers, Jack Sher, Ed Fitzgerald and Tom Meany.
These include the following items of bxing interest:

| Chapter III | – Jack Dempsey, Fighter from Manassa. By Jack Sher. |
| Chapter IX | – Brown Bomber, The Saga of Joe Louis. By Jack Sher. |

There are 6 boxing illustrations.

978. HEYN, Ernest V. (Editor)
Twelve More Sport Immortals
New York, Bartholomew House Inc. Publishers, 1951.
This item includes the following boxing material:

| James J. Corbett | – "Gentleman Jim" by Jack Sher. |
| John L. Sullivan | – The Boston Strong Boy by Jack Sher. |

There are full-length action portraits of these two boxers.

979. H.G.H.C. (H.G.H. Chandley)
Amateur Boxing Association. Its History.
London, 1963.
58pp. Illus.

980. HICKEY, Kevin
"Boxing" The A.B.A. Coaching Manual
London, Kaye and Ward, 1980.
303pp.

M

980A. HICKS, Seymour

Seymour Hicks, Twenty Four Years of an Actor's Life. By Himself.
London, Alston Rivers Ltd., 1910.

321pp. Illus.
Chapter VI – U.S.A. refers to the author attending a performance of John L. Sullivan appearing in a play entitled *Honest Hearts and Willing Hands* at the time of the Jack Dempsey (The Nonpariel) v. Bob Fitzsimmons fight.

981. HICKS, Seymour

Night Lights. Two Men Talk of Life and Love and Ladies.
London, Cassell and Co. Ltd., 1938.

244pp. Illus.
Part III "Talk Idle Talk" includes a section entitled "The Noble Art"

982. HICKS, Seymour

Vintage Years; When King Edward the Seventh was Prince of Wales.
London, Cassell and Co. Ltd., 1943, January A second Edition was issued in February, 1943.

185pp.
Pages 135 to 141 deal with boxing.

983. HICKS, Stephen

Sparring for Luck
London, Tower Hamlets Art Project Ltd., 1962.

111pp. Paper covers. Illus.
The author of this autobiography was an East Londoner who boxed under the name of Johnny Hicks.

984. HICKS, W.J. (Editor)

News Chronicle Boys' Book of All Sports
London, *News Chronicle* Publications Dept., 1950.

This book contains a number of boxing items, as follows:

The Toughest Man I Ever Fought, by Bruce Woodcock
Freddie Mills, World Cruiserweight Champion (Portrait)
Sport as it Used to be Played, by Norman Wymer, (includes boxing and a picture, Cribb v. Molineaux)
The Young Idea (Page of Junior Boxing

A further issue of this item appeared in 1951, under the same title and with the same editor. The boxing items in this issue include:

The Fighting Turpins, by John Camkin; with a picture of Randolph Turpin and Ray Robinson.

No Room for the Bully Where Boxing is Taught, by C.F. Gosling.
No Easy Path To Fame, by Jack Gardner.

985. HIGHLAND OFFICER, A

Anti-Pugilism, or the Science of Self Defence exemplified in short and easy lessons for the practice of the Broadsword and Single Stick.
London, J. Aitken, 1790.
48pp. Illus. 8vo.
The text in this book appears to contain nothing relating to boxing, but there is a plate of a man using his fists against an adversary with a single stick.

986. HILDEBRAND L.

Sparring! Or the theory and practice of the art of self defence. A complete guide. Classified and explained in a most simple manner.
Philadelphia, Fisher and Brothers,
Baltimore, Fisher and Denison, 1864.
Further issues of this work were published Chicago and Philadelphia in 1865, 1892 and 1893.

987. HILTON, Jack

Champion. A Boxing Novel.
London, Jonathan Cape, 1938.
350pp.

988. HILTON, Trevor

British Boxers
First Series: Dai Dower, Joe Erskine, Peter Waterman, Dick Richardson. Action-crammed lives of the top fighters.
London, Beverley Books, 1956.
64pp. Stiff paper covers. Illus.
Includes a chapter on each of the four boxers named above, together with their records.

989. HINDLEY, Charles

The True History of Tom and Jerry; or The Day and Night Scenes of Life in London, from the Start to the Finish.
With a Key to the Persons and Places, Together with a Vocabulary and Glossary of the Flash and Slang Terms Occurring in the Course of the Work.
London, Charles Hindley, 41 Bookseller's Row, 1857.
This work is based on Pierce Egan's *Life in London* 1821, and *Finish to the Adventures of Tom and Jerry and Logic in their Pursuits through life in*
continued

and out of London, 1830.

The book contains many items of pugilistic interest both in the text and among the woodcuts with which it is illustrated.

990. HINDLEY, Charles

Curiosities of Street Literature. Comprising "Cocks" or "Catchpennies" A Large and Curious Assortment of Street-Drolleries, Squibs, Histories, Comic Tales in Prose and Verse, Broadsides on the Royal Family, Political Litanies, Dialogues, Catechisms, Acts of Parliament, Street Political Papers, a "Variety of Ballads on a Subject", Dying Speeches and Confessions.

London, Reeves and Turner, 1871. Only 456 copies printed.

236pp. Illus.

Division III "A Collection on a Subject", includes "Sayers and Heenan's Great Fight for the Championship".

991. HINDLEY, Charles

The Life and Times of James Catnach. (Late of Seven Dials), Ballad Monger.

London, Reeves and Turner, 1878. (Only 500 copies printed).

230 woodcuts.

Includes a number of references to pugilists and pugilism; including the works of Pierce Egan. There is also mention of Jack Randall, Simon Byrne and Deaf Burke.

992. HIPKISS, James

Self-Defence Made Simple.

The governing principles of the Japanese art of Ju-Jitsu, adopted and arranged in easy Practical Lessons for the Business Man and Woman.

Copyright by James Hipkiss.

(Drapkin and Morton, Printers, Fleet Street, Birmingham), March 1931.

Paper covers.

The Foreword is by Jack Hood (British welter-weight boxing Champion). This is entitled "An Appreciation of Ju-Jitsu".

993. HIS MAJESTY'S STATIONERY OFFICE (Publishers)

Recreation and Physical Fitness for Youth and Man

(Board of Education Physical Training Series No.15)

London, 1937.

This book includes;

Chapter 3, Section V. Boxing

The section includes 30 instructional pictures and 3 diagrams.

Appendix IV is entitled "A Boxing Meeting".

994. HOBY, Alan

One Crowded Hour

London, Museum Press Ltd., 1954.

156pp. Illus.

A Sportswriter's Memories. Two chapters on boxing.

995. HODDER, Thomas Knowles (Editor)

Daily Express Book of Popular Sports

The Sportsman's and Sportswoman's Book of Instruction and Reference to all Sports, and Pastimes.

Explained and Illustrated with Playing Rules, Records and Results.

London, *Daily Express* Publications Ltd, 1936.

Introduction by Trevor Wignall.

The boxing section includes a short Historical Summary, leading to a section on Boxing including references to both Amateur and Professional Boxing.

There are eight instructional illustrations and a reproduction of the famous engraving by C. Turner, "In the Fives Court".

996. HODE, Hal

This Hero Business (Fiction)

New York, Gold Label Books, 1944.

181pp.

997. HODGSON and Co. (Publishers)

The Sportsman's Magazine, or Chronicle of Games and Pastimes

This was published monthly from January 1823 to January 1825 (20 issues). It was afterwards issued in 3 volumes.

There was an engraved title-page, the same for each volume, depicting several branches of sport, including two pugilists fighting on a raised stage and a gloved boxer standing over his vanquished opponent.

The name of Hodgson and Co. is substituted by that of William Cole as Publisher of the 3rd volume.

The 14 issues making up the first 2 volumes are not numbered, the 6 issues making up Volume III are numbered XV to XX inclusive.

This work includes many pugilistic items and also plates of famous pugilists. The contents consist of reviews of fistic literature, results of contests, memoirs of famous fighters, correspondence relating to pugilism, etc.

998. HODGSON and Co. (Publishers)

continued

The Art of Boxing
London, 1830, Price sixpence.
viii, 64pp. Frontis.

999. HOFF, Syd
Gentleman Jim and the Great John L.
Tadworth, The World's Work, 1979.
48pp. Illus. (Cold)

1000. HOGG, James and Son (Publishers)
The Habits of Good Society. A Handbook of Etiquette for Ladies and Gentlemen.
London (1860)
Part I – "The Individual"; Chapter V: "Accomplishments", contains sections entitled 'Self Defence', 'Boxing' and 'The Sword and the Fist'.

1001. HOLE, Christina
English Sports and Pastimes
Illustrated from Paintings, Prints and Photographs.
London, B.T. Batsford Ltd., 1949.
182pp. Illus.
Part I – Games and Sports, Chapter II, "Games of Skill and Strength" includes Wrestling and Prize-Fighting, and Broughton's Rules.
The illustrations include "A Sparring Match in the Fives Court" from a print by T. Blake.

1002. HOLLAND, John
Sixty Years in Boxing
Bognor Regis (Sussex), New Horizon Ltd, 1982.
164pp.
The author was known as "Mr. Boxing" in Ayr, where he settled following travels with boxing booths. His book includes reminiscences of many boxing favourites from pre-war years, particularly of Scottish Boxers, such as Elky Clark, Tommy Milligan, and Benny Lynch.
Mr. Holland was very active in amateur boxing in Ayr, where he had a hand in the emergence of Evan Armstrong from the boxing section of the local Y.M.C.A. to achieve success and fame, both as an amateur and professional.

1003. HOLLAND, Fritz
Uppercuts. Stories of the Ringside.
Sydney, (Australia), New Century Press Ltd, 1929.
Also published in Wellington (New Zealand) by the same Co.
Yellow paper covers; The cover design, by Jack Gilmour, shows a boxing scene..
The Introduction gives a brief outline of the author's boxing career.
The author records his thanks to the proprietors of *The Sun* newspaper, Christchurch (N.Z.) for permission to republish the articles in book form.

1004. HOLLANDER, Zander (Editor)
Madison Square Garden
A Century of Sport and Spectacle on the World's Most Versatile Stage.
175pp. Illus.
The section on Boxing is by Barney Nagler.

1005. HOLLANDERSKY, Abe
The Life Story of Abe the Newsboy. Hero of a Thousand Fights.
Los Angeles, Published by the author, 1930.
There were at least 23 editions of this book.
500pp Profusely illustrated.
Bound in blue cloth, decorated on cover and spine.
The dustwrapper includes pictures of a battleship, President Theodore Roosevelt, and the Author.
The Dedication is "To My Dearest Friends the President, and the Officers and Men of the U.S. Navy".
Abe Hollandersky could not enlist in the Navy because of defective eyesight; however he served in the capacities of newsboy, boxer and boxing instructor.
The reverse of the dustwrapper features a cartoon in the "Believe it or Not" series, by Ripley. This claims that Abe the Newsboy fought 1043 battles.

1006. HOLLENDER, Bertie
Before I Forget
London, Grayson and Grayson, 1935.
260pp. Illus.
Includes mention of many boxers and persons interested in the sport, including Georges Carpentier, John Hopley, J.W.H.T. Douglas, Jem Smith, George Cook, Same McVea, etc.

1007. HOLLIMAN, Jennie, Ph.D.
American Sports (1785–1835)
Durham, N.C. U.S.A., The Seeman Press, 1931.
222pp.
Bound in green cloth. Gilt titles on the spine.
The introduction includes information on how British Sailors influenced the introduction of new sports into America, particularly boxing.
Chapter IX – "Gouging and Boxing", mentions the names of a number of boxers, and gives details of American teachers of the art from the late 18th century.
The book also gives a list of reference sources for boxing material.

1008. HOLT, Alfred Henry
Championship Sketches (With Portraits)
London, George Newbold, 1862.

1009. HONE, William
The Every-day Book or Everlasting Calendar of Popular Amusements, Sports, Pastimes, etc.

continued

London, Hunt and Clarke, Two Volumes in four parts.

Volume I – 1826, Volume II – 1827.

Volume II, June 8th, includes Figg the Prizefighter; referring to a challenge by Edward Sutton, and the answer by Figg.

1010. HOOPER, S. (Bookseller)

Hogarth Moralized. Being a Complete Edition of Hogarth's Works. Containing near Fourscore Copper Plates, most elegantly engraved. With an explanation, pointing out the many Beauties that may have Hitherto escaped Notice; and a Comment on their Moral Tendency, Calculated to Improve the Minds of Youth and Convey Instruction, under the Mask of Entertainment. Now First Published, with the Approbation of Jane Hogarth, Widow of the Late Mr. Hogarth.

With 78 Plates (Including Frontispiece and Title-page)

London, Sold by S. Hooper, 1768.

The Plates include – "Southwark Fair" – "The March to Finchley" – "The Rake's Progress" and others.

There are also references in the text to Figg and Broughton.

1011. HOOPER, Stanley
(Ex-Flyweight Champion of the Eastern Counties)

The A.B.C. of Boxing
London, Messrs. Drane, 1923.
Illus. Foreword by Eugene Corri.
142pp.

1012. HORLER, Sydney

The Breed of the Beverlys
A Story of the Modern Prize Ring
London, Odhams Press Ltd, 1921 Price 2s.
London, George Newnes Ltd, 1931 Price 6d.
(Cheap Edition), 1931.
London, Cherry Tree Books, 1938, Price 6d.
(Paperback)

1013. HORLER, Sydney

The Black Heart
London, Hodder and Stoughton, 1932.
Price 6d.
316pp.

1014. HORNIBROOK, F.A.

The Lure of the Ring

London, Pendulum Publications, 1946.

Stiff paper covers;
Picture of a black and white boxer on the front cover.
The author's introduction stated (inter alia): "Books on boxing are usually written by Sporting Correspondents – I have written this book entirely on a good memory. I have never been a boxer or a Sporting Writer, just an enthusiast. If therefore there are any slight errors, I crave the reader's indulgence".

1015. HOTTEN, John Camden

The Slang Dictionary; or The Vulgar Words, Street Phrases, and "Fast" Expressions of High and Low Society.

Many with Their Etymology, and a Few with their History Traced.

London, Compiled and Published by the Author, 1864.

(First published as The Dictionary of Modern Slang, Cant and Vulgar Words 1859, 2nd edition, 1860)

The 1864 edition was considerably enlarged.

This book includes many words associated with prize-fighting; ranging alphabetically from "Back Hander" to "Set To".

Also included is a Bibliography of Slang, Cant and Vulgar Language, or a List of Books which have been Consulted in Compiling this Work, Comprising Nearly Every Known Feature on the Subject.

1016. HOTTEN, John Camden
(Compiler and Publisher)

Dictionary of Colloquial English
In Two Volumes.
London, 1864.

The words and phrases in current use, commonly called "Slang" and "Vulgar", their origin and etymology traced and their use illustrated in examples.
Includes words and phrases associated with pugilism.

1017. HOTTEN, John Camden

The Book of Wonderful Characters
With Memoirs and Anecdotes of Remarkable and Eccentric Persons – Chiefly from the text of Henry Wilson and James Caulfield.
Illustrated with sixty-one full page engravings.
London, Published by the Author, 1869.

Contains references to pugilistic personalities, John Broughton, Henry Lemoine and John Smith (Buckhorse), with relevant portraits engraved by R. Cooper.
There was a later issue of this item by Reeves and Turner (London), slightly smaller in size than the original edition.

**1018. HOULSTON and WRIGHT
(Publishers)**
The Dictionary of Daily Wants
London, 1858–1860, Three Volumes.
Volume I includes a short section giving a descrip-
tion of boxing, The Art of Self Defence.

**1019. HOUSTON, Graham
(Editor of *Boxing News*)**
Superfight
The Story of the World Heavyweight Boxing
Champions.
From John L. Sullivan to Muhammad Ali.
New York, Bounty Books, 1975.
176pp. Illus. Stiff paper covers.

**1020. HOWARD, Major General Sir Francis,
K.C.B., K.C.M.G.**
Reminiscences 1848–1890.
London, John Murray, 1924.
This book includes the following references to
boxing:
Chapter III – Bridgemans. (Boxing and Fencing
– Masters and Boys – Sayers and
Heenan)
Chapter XII – Leave in London. (Boxing-
Sword Play-The Pelican Club)

1021. HUGHES, Grant (Publisher)
International Boxers
16pp. inc. covers, pictures only.
Picture of Freddie Mills on the front, and Ernie
Roderick on the back cover. The remaining pic-
tures show contemporary boxers at all weights.

1021A. HUGHES, Grant (Publisher)
British Boxing Stars
London, 1948.
16pp. inc. covers, pictures only.
Picture of Ernie Roderick on the front, and Nel
Tarleton on the back cover. The remaining pic-
tures show British boxers at all weights.
(see also items under Grant Hughes)

1022. HUGHES, Rupert
The Patent Leather Kid
London, The Readers Library Publishing Co.
Ltd., ca. 1927.
252pp.
The romantic story of a young New York Prize-
fighter, Curly Boyle, and an enchanting cabaret
dancer bearing the nick-name shown in the title.
This is another example of a book based on a film,
in this case a silent movie made by First National
and starring Richard Barthelmess as Curly Boyle.

1023. HUGHES, T.
The Art and Practice of English Boxing etc.
With Broughton's Rules. (Written under the

Direction of an Eminent Pugilist)
London, 1807.
Includes a folding frontis, showing nine attitudes of
fighting.
36pp.

1024. HUGHES, Thomas
Tom Brown's Schooldays
London, Macmillan and Co.
First published in 1857 over the signature
of "An Old Boy".
Part V, Chapter V is entitled "The Fight" (Tom
Brown v. Slogger Williams).
See also Cox, W.D., *Boxing in Art and Literature*,
1935.

1025. HUGMAN, Barry J. (Editor)
The 1982/3 George Wimpey Amateur Box-
ing Yearbook.
London, Wimpey Group Services P.L.C., and
Tony Williams Ltd., 1982.
336pp. Illus.
Contains full records of A.B.A. title-holders since
formation of the Association, and also records of
Amateur Clubs.

**1026. HUGMAN, Barry J.
(Editor and Compiler)**
British Boxing Yearbook 1985
In Association with the British Boxing Board
of Control.
Feltham, Middx., Newnes Books, 1984.
544pp. Illus.
This detailed and comprehensive publication is
without doubt the best of all British record books.
The compiler of the records is Vic Hardwicke, and
there are contributions by Ray Clarke, Alexander
H. Elliot, Harry Mullan, Ron Olver, Simon Block,
and Dr. Adrian Whiteson.
The 1986 edition, produced the following year,
brought things up to date and carried articles by
Ray Clarke, Harry Mullan, Ron Olver, O.F. Snelling, and Derek O'Dell.

1027. HUIE, J.L. (Publisher)
A Key to Tom and Jerry, or Life in London.
A Musical Extravaganza in Three Acts.
Founded on Pierce Egan's Popular Work of
Life in London. Performed at The Caledon-
ian Theatre Edinburgh. To which is Prefixed
a Vocabulary of Flash and Cant, Incidental
to the Piece. With an Etching of Mr.Stanley
and Bob Logic.
Edinburgh, 1823.
Sold by W. Hunter, 23 Hanover Street, and
J. Watt, Leith.
The Vocabulary of Flash and Cant includes many
pugilistic terms.

continued

There are also pugilistic items in the piece as follows:

Act II, Scene XX – Life in Fancy, a turn into Cribb's Parlour etc.

Act III, Scene XIV – Life in Bond Street. having a touch at Jackson's Rooms, etc.

1028. HULTON PRESS LTD
(Publishers)

The *Eagle* Book of Records and Champions

Part II of this book, by John Findlay, includes boxing and contains information on Past World Title Holders, Fistic Facts and six illustrations of boxers.

1029. HUME, David

Below the Belt

A Boxing and Mystery Novel.

London, W. Collins and Co. Ltd., 1934.

252pp.

1030. HUME, David

Stand Up and Fight

A Boxing and Mystery Novel.

London, Collins, 1941.

252pp.

1031. HUMPHRIS, E.M.

The Life of Fred Archer

Edited by Lord Arthur Grosvenor, with a Preface by Arthur F.S. Portman.

London, Hutchinson and Co. (Publishers) Ltd., 1923.

A second edition was issued in 1933.

320pp. Illus.

Contains a number of references to Tom Sayers and also to Jem Edwards of Cheltenham, the bare-fist Middleweight Champion.

1032. HUMPHRIS, Edith and SLADIN, Douglas

Adam Lindsay Gordon and his friends in England and Australia

With 16 sketches by Gordon, and numerous other illustrations.

London, Constable and Co., 1912.

464pp.

The book contains many references to Gordon's interest in the prize ring and pugilists, particularly in Jem Edwards and Tom Sayers, and contains the following chapters:

Part 1, Chapter X – "The Knock Out of Edwards by Lindsay Gordon"

Part 1, Chapter XI– Another boxing chapter, "Such as Jem Earywig Can Well impart".

(Both these chapters were written by Miss Edith Humphris).

Some photographic illustrations are of boxing interest.

1033. HUMPHREYS (sic) Richard

The Memoirs of John Scroggins, The Pugilistic Hero

London, Printed by J. Barnes and Published by J. Scroggins, 1827.

This item is described on the title-page as follows: "John Scroggins, The Pugilistic Hero, otherwise John Palmer. In which are given a correct narrative of his Birth. Parentage, Edification, Orthography (though loose) and Odd Exploits, Both at Sea and on Shore, Including his many and determined OFF HAND Fights in the Prize-Ring".

In addition to the life of Scroggins, the contents include a series of Miscellanies, giving news of other pugilistic celebrities, their deaths and funerals, also poems, chaunts and songs (two by Pierce Egan), paying tribute to the Fancy and celebrating some of their battles.

The Appendix contains authentic annals of pugilism from the early days of Figg in 1719 to those of Spring and Langan, 1824.

1034. HUMPHRIES, Richard

The Odiad, or Battle of Humphries and Mendoza; a heroic Poem. To which is added Prefaratory Discourse of Boxing.

London, Lowndes and Christie, 1788. Price 1s.6d.

"Humbly Dedicated to the Boxing Academies, Several Illustrious Personages, the Patrons and Amateurs of the Most Ancient Art".

1035. HUNT, Leigh

A Saunter Through the West End

London, Hurst and Blackett, 1861. (in one volume).

First published in 1847 (from Atlas).

251pp.

Chapter VII includes a section "Broughton's Boxing Academy".

1036. HUNTER, David

Reminiscences of Hunter. The Genial Yorkshire Stumper.

Scarborough (Yorkshire), W.H. Smith and Sons, 1909. Price 3d.

Includes a section entitled "David and the Other Gloves", with a picture of Hunter as a boxer "Contributed by the Anonymous Caricaturist".

1037. HURDMAN-LUCAS, F.

From Pit Boy to Champion Boxer. The Romance of Georges Carpentier.

continued

London, Ewart Seymour and Co., 1913.
72pp. Red paper covers, with inset portrait of Carpentier on the front cover and a frontis. picture of Carpentier.

1038. HURST, Norman
Thrilling Fights
London, Horace Marshall Limited, 1946.
Bound in stiff white paper covers with a cartoon by Tom Webster on the front cover.
136pp. 13 illus.
The opening chapter is entitled "Behind the Scenes in the Fight Game" and each succeeding chapter deals with a famous fight or fighter, examples are given as follows:

Jim Driscoll v. Spike Robson,
Art Delmont v. Owen Moran
Len Harvey v. Frank Moody
Larry Gains v. Don McCorkindale
Tommy Harrison v. Charles Ledoux
Joe Jeanette v. Sam McVea
Nel Tarleton v. Johnny Cuthbert
etc.

1039. HURST, Norman
Big Fight Thrills
London and Manchester, Withy Grove Press Ltd., 1948.
(A Cherry Tree Special)
128pp. Illus. Paper covers.

1040. HUSSEY, George (Compiler)
The Champions Chart (The Greatest Compilation on Figures on Past and Present Ring Champions)
Los Angeles, Boxing News Bureau, 1934.

16ins. x 24ins.
Gives the history of Champions, even to the number of rounds fought.

1041. HUTCHINSON, John
Herefordshire Biographies
Being a Record of Such of Natives of the County as have Attained to More than Local Celebrity
Hereford, Jakeman and Carver, 1890.
There is mention of Thomas Winter (Tom Spring) in the Preface, and he is also given a section in the Herefordshire Biographies (Natives).

1042. HUTCHISON, David Chapel
Boxing
New York, Outing Publishing Co., 1913.
(Outings Handbooks No.44)
Reissued in 1923 and 1932.
120pp. Illus.

1043. HYER, T.
Prize Ring Heroes
New York, 1885.
85pp

1044. HYMAN, Dick
Jinxes and Jonahs
New York, Elliott Publishing Co. Inc., 1943.
Paper covers, magazine size.
Contents include "A Superstitious Sports World", mentioning Joe Louis, Mike Jacobs, Billy Petrolle, Tami Mauriello, Jack Britton and other Boxers.

1045. IDELL, A.E.
Pug. A Boxing Novel.
New York, The Greystone Press, 1941.
245pp.

1046. ILLUSTRATED POLICE NEWS, The
(Publishers)
The Life, Death and Funeral of Tom Sayers
London, 1865, Price One Penny.

This item is described as follows:
− Being his complete life, and containing his various battles; account of the Fight for the Championship at Farnborough. Full particulars of his funeral etc., etc.
The front cover acts as the title-page and contains a head and shoulder portrait of Tom Sayers (stripped).

1047. INCH, Thomas
Ex-World's Champion Weight-Lifter,
Holder of many World and British Records
Manual of Physical Training
London, Thorsons Publishers Ltd., ca.1940.

In the Section "Physical Culture Systems" is included 'Shadow Boxing'. Illustrated by a plate.

1048. INCH, Thomas
Spalding's Book of Boxing and Physical Culture
Aldershot, Gale and Polden Ltd., 1945.

Bound in red cloth with black titles on front cover and spine.
There are 13 chapters, mostly instructional, but also including: The History of the Ring; Errors That Cost Championships; Famous Boxers-Champions Compared, and Giants of the Ring. The book is profusely illustrated, showing guards and blows in boxing and also instruction in other methods of self-defence.

1049. INCH, Thomas
Boxing
With Illustrations by Richard Clarke.
London, Sir Isaac Pitman and Sons Ltd., 1948.
(Pitman's Games and Recreations Series)
187pp. Bound in cloth.
Foreword by Ted Broadribb.

1050. INCH, Thomas
Boxing for Beginners − From Novice to Champion
Kingswood (Surrey), The World's Work (1913) Ltd., 1951.
176pp. Illus. Bound in red cloth.

1051. INCH, Thomas
Boxing − The Secret of the Knockout

"You are O.K. if you K.O."
Illustrated by Richard Clarke.
Kingswood (Surrey), The World's Work, (1913) Ltd., 1953.
158pp.

1052. INGLE, Jimmy
The Jimmy Ingle Story
With an Introduction by Patrick Myler.
Cooleen, Dingle, Co. Kerry; Dover N.H., Brandon, 1984.
93pp. Illus.

1053. INGLIS, Gordon
Sport and Pastimes in Australia
London, Methuen and Co. Ltd., 1912.

Chapter XIX, "A General View", contains a subsection entitled 'Boxing'. This deals wih both amateur and professional boxing.

1054. INGLIS, William O.
Champions Off Guard
New York, The Vanguard Press, 1932.
Dedicated to the Memory of Mike Donovan, Warrior and Sage.

311pp. Illus.
The chapters include:
    The Mighty Sullivan
    The Magic of Jim Corbett
    Mike Donovan and Theodore Roosevelt
    Bob Fitzsimmons, Master Hypnotist
    McCoy and His Winning Corkscrew

1055. INGRAM, Wallie
Wallie Ingram's World of Sport
Published in New Zealand, ca.1947.

The author was a sports-writer and broadcaster; his broadcast talks included tales of the immortals in boxing. Some of these stories are incorporated into this book.

1056. INNES, Nelse
Ring Records and Fistic Facts
Boston (U.S.A.), Published by the Author.
1895−1896 (2 volumes).

1057. INTERNATIONAL AMATEUR BOX-
ING ASSOCIATION (Publishers)
Articles of Association and Rules for International Competitions and Tournaments.
London, 1966.
55pp. Stiff paper covers.

1058. INTERNATIONAL BOOK AND RE-
VIEW PUBLISHERS LTD., The
(Publishers)

continued

Life Science Boxing Annual, 1949.
Published for Life Science (A Non-Profit
Society), 1949.
A note on the contents page says:
Articles are for the good of boxing and not for
personal prestige. Author's names, therefore, are
not quoted. Reproductions must contain ack-
nowledgements to Life Science.
Coloured paper covers, action portrait of Don
Cockell on the front cover. Contents include:

> Psychological Training Behind Don Cockell
> Britain's World Championship Hope
> The Boxer's Mind
> The Boxer's Scale of Personality
> Formula for Winning and the Purpose of
> Life Science.

1059. IRELAND, Samuel
Graphic Illustrations of Hogarth, from
Pictures, Drawings and Scarce Prints in the
Possession of Samuel Ireland, author of
this work.
London, R. Faulder, 1794–1799. (In 2
volumes)
Volume 1 of this work mentions an etching by
Simpson of Hogarth's drawing for Figg's business
card.
Volume II includes information on a picture of
Figg which was claimed in some quarters to be
the work of Hogarth; also in this volume there
is information on a sketch of Broughton and
Slack fighting, which was intended for use as an
admission card to a great contest of skill.

1060. IRISH AMATEUR BOXING ASSOCI-
ATION (Publishers)
Rules of the Irish Amateur Boxing Association. Dublin, 1948.
74pp. Paper covers.

Made up by three sections: Origin and Adminis-
tration – Rules of Amateur Boxing – Appendices.
There is an illustrated section showing Some
Common Forms of Foul Practices in Boxing.

1061. IRVING, Anchell
Never a Champion
New York, Vantage Press Inc., 1974.
172pp.
The author gives his recollections of tough battles
in the streets of Brownsville and East New York,
and of how he gave up his dream of becoming an
artist and became a pugilist.

1062. IRVING, Joseph
Annals of Our Time
1875.
This American Publication contains reference to
John C. Heenan.

1063. IRVING, Leigh Hadley
"Our Jim" – The World's Champion
New York and San Francisco. The Crown
Publishing Co. (copyright 1892).
93pp.
The title refers to James J. Corbett, who had just
beaten John L. Sullivan.

1064. IZENBERG, Jerry
The Rivals
New York, Holt Rinehart and Winston Inc.,
1968.
Publishedssimultaneously in Canada.
284pp.
The author wrote as a syndicated sports columnist.
Chapter II entitled "Second Time Around",
includes stories of boxers such as Joe Louis, Billy
Conn, Lou Nova and Max Schmeling.

1065. JACKSON, George F.
Soul Brother Superfighter
Published by the author in the U.S.A., 1985.
285pp. Illus.

1066. JACKSON, Mr. John
A Sketch of the Life of
Issued from St. Martin's Lane, March 17th,
1813.
Bernard John Angle in his book *My Sporting Memories*, 1925, (q.v.) says in Chapter XXIII:
"A Memento that I prize is a private presentation of a SKETCH OF THE LIFE OF Mr. JOHN JACKSON – My copy of the book in question is in a good state of preservation. It contains a fine steel engraving of Jackson from a picture which now hangs in the dining room of the National Sporting Club".

1067. JACKSON, Mason
The Pictorial Press
London, Hurst and Blackett, 1885.
Pugilistic material is included in this work, by a number of references to *Bell's Life in London*.

1068. JACKSON, Stanley
The Life and Cases of Mr. Justice Humphries
London, Odhams Press Ltd., 1952.
239pp. Illus.
Chapter 4 "For the Prosecution" includes an account of the case at Bow Street regarding the proposed fight between Jack Johnson and Bombardier Billy Wells.

1069. JACKSON, Stanley
The Great Barnato
London, William Heinemann Ltd., 1970.
267pp. plus a bibliography.
The biography of Barney Barnato, the youth from London's East End who became a South African diamond magnate. There are some boxing references including how Barnato took Woolf Bendoff, an East End boxer, to South Africa to fight J.R. Couper, the champion of that country. There is also mention of the N.S.C., of which Barney Barnato was a member.

1070. JACOB, Naomi
"Our Marie" (Marie Lloyd)
A Biography.
London, Hutchinson and Co. (Publishers) Ltd., 1936.
287pp. Illus.
This book includes a number of references to Dick Burge and his wife Mrs. Dick Burge (formerly Bella Orchard); Bella performed on the stage with Marie Lloyd's sister, Rosie, as "The Sisters Lloyd". Bella Burge later ran the Blackfriars "Ring" following the death of her husband.

1071. JACOMB, William J.
Boxing for Beginners. With chapters showing it in relationship to bayonet fighting.
Philadelphia, Lea and Febiger, 1918 and 1923

1072. JACOMB, WILLIAM J.
Practical Self-Defence
Philadelphia, Lee and Fabiger 1918 and 1923.

1073. JAMES, David
Better Boxing
London, Kaye and Ward, 1974.
95pp.
The author was formerly the A.B.A. National Coach.

1074. JAMES, Ed.
Manual of Sporting Rules
Comprising the Latest and Best Authenticated Revised Rules, Governing (*inter alia*) The Prize Ring, Amateur Sparring, Queensberry, Blackened Glove and Glove Contests.
(Illustrated with Original Engravings)
New York, Published by the author, 1877.
This item ran through at least 12 editions and dealt with all the Sets of Rules shown in the sub-title.
There was also a single-sheet supplement, headed by a cut of pugilists in action and entitled "Marquess of Queensberry Rules Governing Contests of Endurance" which gives 12 rules and also notes as to weights, etc.

1075. JAMES, Ed.
The Life and Battles of John Morrisey
With portraits from the life of John Morrisey, John C. Heenan, Yankee Sullivan and Bill Poole.
(From the New York Clipper, with the permission of Frank Queen Esq.)
New York, Published by the author.
No date (ca. 1871).
This is the first of Ed. James' "Copyright Pugilistic Series".

1076. JAMES, Ed.
The Complete Book of Boxing and Wrestling With Full and Simple Instructions on Acquiring those Useful, Invigorating and Health-Giving Arts
New York, Published by the author, in his "Standard Sporting Series", No.7, 1878.

continued

44p. Illus.

24th edition, 1878.

55pp. Illus.

1077. JAMES, Ed.

The Lives and Battles of the Champions of England, from the Year 1700 to the Present Time.

New York, Published by the Author, 1879.

Bound in green boards with the picture of pugilists on the front cover.

The contents include: The LIves and Battles, Authentic Records, Anecdotes, Personal Recollections, etc., with Portraits from Life.

The pugilists covered range in time from that of James Figg to the last championship match between Joe Goss and Henry Allen.

There are 26 illustrations.

1078. JAMES, Ed.

Life and Battles of Sir Dan Donnelly, Champion of Ireland.

New York, Compiled and published by Ed. James, 1879.

Ed.James' "Copyright Pugilistic Series", No. 4.

24pp. Illus.

1079. JAMES, Ed.

The Life and Battles of J.C. Heenan

(Ed. James' "Pugilistic Series" No.3)

(The Life and Battles of John C. Heenan, Hero of Farnborough)

New York City, Published by the Author, 1879.

24pp. Bound in wrappers.

1080. JAMES, Ed.

The Life and Battles of Tom Hyer

With portraits from the life of Hyer

New York, Published by the author, 1879.

(Ed. James' "Copyright Pugilistic Series" No. 2).

1081. JAMES, Ed.

Practical Training for Walking, Running, Boxing, Rowing, etc.

New York, Published by the Author, ca.1879.

1082. JAMES, Ed.

The Life and Battles of Jack Randall

New York, 1880.

40pp. Illus.

1083. JAMES, Ed.

The Life and Battles of Yankee Sullivan

New York, Published by the Author, 1880.

(Ed. James' "Copyright Pugilistic Series" No. 6).

1084. JAMES, Harry A.

A Professional Pugilist

Illustrated by Kenneth M. Skeaping

London, The Leadenall Press Ltd., 1894.

(Simkin, Hamilton, Kent and Co.)

86pp. plus 18 pages adverts.

Stiff paper covers.

1085. JAMES, Roy

Left Hooks and Right Crosses

(Stories of Vic Patrick and other famous boxers)

Sydney (Australia), Market Printing Pty. Ltd 1946.

Stiff paper covers, picture of fight on the front.

7 Illus.

1086. JAMES, Roy

Ring Review

Sydney (Australia), Jno. Evans and Son Printing Co., 1946.

Paper covers, with coloured picture of Vic Patrick on front cover.

The contents include information on main events fought at Sydney, Melbourne, Newcastle and Brisbane Stadiums during 1946 and also comments and items concerning Australian boxing personalities. There is also some wrestling material.

There are a number of boxing illustrations.

1087. JAMIESON, David A.

Powderhall and Pedestrianism, The History of a Famous Sports Enclosure (1870–1943)

Edinburgh and London, W. and A.K. Johnston Ltd., 1943.

320pp.

Reference is made in this book to the participation of Bombardier Wells in the 100 yards handicap in the year 1912.

The illustrations include one of a group of sports celebrities, among whom are Tancy Lee and Alex Ireland.

1088. J.C.

Recollections of an Octogenarian

London, 1805.

This work is one of those listed in the Bibliography of Boxing given on pages X and XI of H.D. Miles *"Pugilistica"*, Volume I.

The *Recollections* are further quoted on pages 29 and 30 of the same volume of the Miles work; here the "Octogenarian" gives reminiscences of John Broughton.

1089. JEAFFRESON, John Cordy

The Real Lord Byron
— New Views of The Poet's Life
London, Hurst and Blackett, 1883.

Chapter X — Cambridge, includes a section "The Noble Art of Self-Defence".

1090. JEFFRIES, C.A.

Famous Fights at the Stadium
Sydney (Australia), The Platypus Press, 1914

Includes stories of the battles of many Australian boxers, as well as those visiting that country from the U.K. and America; including Squires, Burns, Johnson, Fitzsimmons, Bill Lang, the McVea—Langford series of bouts and others.
Many photographs.

1091. JEFFRIES, James J.

My Life and Battles
Edited and Illustrated by Rogert Edgren
Published in New York, 1910.

Bound in paper wrappers, Illus.

1092. JENKINS, Edward

Lisa Lena. A Novel.
London, Sampson Low, Marston and Co. Ltd., 1880 (2 volumes)

One of the characters in this story is John C. Heenan.

1093. JENKINS, Herbert

The Life of George Borrow
London, John Murray, 1921 and 1924.

496pp. Illus.
Contains a number of references to the prize-ring, including the old prize-fighter's recipe for a quiet life: "Learn to box and keep a civil tongue in your head".

1094. JENKINS, Herbert

Malcolm Sage, Detective
London, Herbert Jenkins, 1921.

315pp.
This volume of detective stories includes:

Chapter XV — The Missing Heavyweight
Chapter XVI — The Great Fight at Olympia

Herbert Jenkins is a now somewhat mythical figure about whom little is known personally. Although he wrote a series of tales introducing a character known as "Bindle", he is best remembered for his foresight in publishing the unique series of books by P.G. Wodehouse, and the fact that this author remained under the Jenkins' imprint.

1095. JEPTHA, Andrew

A South African Boxer in Britain. Experiences of Andrew Jeptha. Written by the Boxer himself.

Cape Town (South Africa),Progress Printing Works, price 1s. (No date)

Green paper covers, lettered in black. Action picture of the author on front cover.
The text consists of 14 chapters; there are 2 pages at the front of the book containing instructional material and 2 pages at the back with a record of some of Jeptha's fights.

1096. JESSOP, Gilbert, and SALMOND, J.B.

The Book of School Sports
London, Thomas Nelson and Sons Ltd., 1920

Includes a section on boxing by J.B. Salmond, illustrated by eight cuts in the text and by a plate "The Value of the Feint".
(Carpentier v. Wells)

1097. "J.E.W."

The Great Fight, or America versus England
(Tom King v. John C. Heenan, December 10th, 1863)
This is a Song Sheet published by the Musical Bouquet Office and F. Pitman in London, 1864.

The front cover includes a picture of Tom King, seated and dressed in ordinary clothes. There is also an announcement stating "Sung at All the Music Halls and Concerts".
Pages 2 to 5 comprise the words and music of the song, and at the head of the music states "Written by J.E.W., Air-Yankee Doodle".
There are 6 verses to the song.

1098. JOHANNSON, Ingemar

Seconds out of the Ring
Translated from the Swedish by Ian Rodger and Jan Jonsjo
London, Stanley Paul and Co. Ltd., 1960.

176pp. plus Johannson's record.
Also issued in a Sportsmans Book Club Edition.

1099. JOHN O'LONDON (Editor)

London Stories
London, George Newnes Ltd., 1906.
(John O'London's Little Stories No.6)

This book includes shortened versions (unillustrated) of two of the stories that appeared in London Stories (1912), as follows:
A Prize-Fighter buried in Westminster Abbey
Doggett's Coat and Badge.

1100. John O'London (Editor)

London Stories
Being a Collection of the Lives and Adventures of Londoners of All Ages.
London and Edinburgh, T.C. and E.C. Jack, 1912 (2 volumes)

continued

The Preface discloses that many of the stories are by authors other than the editor; and that the illustrations are by George Morrow, W.W. Jacobs, Percy Billinghurst, D.Lewis Morris, Will Dyson, J.P.S. Percival, and Hedley Whitton.

The 1st volume includes the following stories:

A Prize-Fighter Buried in Westminster Abbey (John Broughton)

The Race for the Doggett's Coat and Badge, with also mentions Broughton

Tottenham Court and its Fair, mentioning Figg, Broughton, George Taylor, and other pugilists; including Broughton's defeat by Slack and Slack's defeat by Taylor.

Volume II contains:

Evan's Supper Room (These Rooms were later the site of the old original National Sporting Club)

Gentleman Jackson, the Pugilist

The later years and death of Pierce Egan.

There are a number of illustrations to these articles.

1101. JOHN O'LONDON (Wilfred Whitten)

More London Stories

(John O'London's Little Books No.13)

London, George newnes Ltd., March 1928.

This book contains an entry: "Gentleman Jackson, The Pugilist".

1102. JOHNSON, Alexander

Ten — And Out!

The Complete Story of the Prize-ring in America.

With a Foreword by Gene Tunney.

New York, Ives Washburn, Publisher, 1927. (Second printing January, 1928)

London, Chapman and Hall Ltd, 1928.

Further editions were published in 1936, 1943, 1945 and 1947.

347pp. (English edition 1928)
440pp. (New enlarged edition, 1943)
There are variations in the illustrations included in the various editions, these being changed to bring in contemporary boxers in the later issues. For instance, pictures of Joe Louis were shown from 1936.

1103. JOHNSON, Duff

Come Out Fighting. A Boxing Novel.

London, Hamilton and Co. (Stafford) Ltd.

127pp. Coloured illus. paper covers.

1104. JOHNSON, Duff

Sucker Punch. (Fiction)

London, Hamilton and Co. (Stafford) Ltd.,

127pp.

The book is described thus:

"From the Bowery He Came, Battlin' more than Leather-Slingers, a Dynamite-Packed Story by Fight Reporter Duff Johnson".

1105. JOHNSON, Jack
(Former World Heavyweight Champion)

Jack Johnson — In The Ring — And Out

With Special Drawings by Edward William Krauter, and other illustrations.

Chicago, National Sports Publishing Co., 1927.

London, Proteus, 1977. (Reprint edited by Gilbert Odd)

Dedicated by the author to his mother.

256pp. plus Appendix giving Johnson's record.
The U.S. edition has a Foreword by J.B.Lewis and Introductory Articles by "Tad", of the New York Evening Journal, and by Damon Runyon.
This book was also reprinted under the title *Jack Johnson Is A Dandy* with an introduction by Dick Schaap, 1969. (q.v.)

1106. JOHNSON, Jack

Jack Johnson is a Dandy. An Autobiography

Introductory Essays by Dick Schaap and The Lampman.

New York, Chelsea House Publishers, 1969.

262pp. 4to. Illus.
The chapter headings and text of this book are the same as in the original Jack Johnson autobiography entitled "In the Ring and Out" published in Chicago in 1927. (q.v.). The essays by Dick Schaap and the Lampman in this later issue replace the Foreword and Introductory Articles by J.B. Lewis, "Tad", and Damon Runyon, included in the 1927 edition.
The piece by Mrs. Irene Johnson given in the preliminaries of the earlier work is included as an Epilogue in the 1969 version.

1107. JOHNSON, John Weldon

Black Manhattan

New York, Alfred A. Knopf, 1930.

Chapter VII deals with activities in professional sports, including references to Tom Molyneux and Bill Richmond.

1108. JOHNSTONE, F.

Romance of a Boxer

London, Digby, Long and Co., September, 1891.

144pp.

1109. JOHNSTONE, John

Coaching for Boxing

Ann Arbor, Michigan U.S.A., Edwards Bros. 1932.

1110. JOKL, Ernst, M.D.,
Head of the Dept. of Physical Education,
Witwaterstrand Technical College,
Johannesburg, S/Africa
The Medical Aspects of Boxing
Pretoria, South Africa, J.L. Van Schaik Ltd.,
1941.

Cloth covers, lettered in black with a boxing
picture on front cover.
This book gives extensive coverage of medical
aspects and the effects of various blows on those
sustaining punishment while boxing. It also gives
case histories and the results of experiments.
There are 54 illustrations and 4 plates, together
with a useful bibliography of books on the subject
of boxing injuries and their effects.

1111. "JON BEE" (John Badcock)
Fancy Chronology: A Brief History of
Pugilism During the Reign of George III.
London, Printed for the author, 4 Long
Lane, Smithfield/T. Hughes, 36 Ludgate
Street; and to be had of All Booksellers.

The information on this item is obtained from the
same author's *Fancy Ana* (3rd Edition).
The work is described as "Giving compressed but
luminous accounts of every remarkable Turn-
Up, Spree, Boxing Match and Prize-Fight within
that long period, brought down to 1821 – closely
printed in Black and Red (Almanack Fashion),
2s-6d, or in a Handsome Black Carved Frame,
6s. – This Royal Sheet of Pugilism at One View
contains a clear and perspicuous sketch of over
600 Battles, with the date of its occurrence and
the place where fought, etc".
"Also a Key to accompany the same, price 1s;
or the whole (containing 800 Battles), done up,
Book Fashion, 3s-6d".

1112. "JON BEE" (John Badcock)
Lives of the Boxers
London, 1811.

8vo.
The title of this item is sometimes given as *Life
of the Boxers.*

1113. "JON BEE" (John Badcock)
Fancy Ana, or A History of Pugilism
First edition probably published ca. 1820.

The information given below refers to the
third edition:
London, Printed by W. Lewis, 21 Finch
Lane, Cornhill, for J. Waller, 44 Paternoster
Row, T. Hughes, 35 Ludgate Street, and the
Editor, at 4 Long Lane, Smithfield.
The Title-Page refers to Jon Bee, Esq. as the
Editor of the (Original) *Fancy, Fancy
Gazette, Sportsman's Slang*, etc.
Page 6 of the Third edition gives particulars
of the various issues of the work, in four

different sizes and/or bindings.
The book contains a Scale of Relative Merit, which
is referred to as follows:
"Among nearly One Hundred Boxers, Made up to
the period of the latest Battle of each Man".
There is also advice on the Practical Use of the
Table.

1114. "JON BEE" (John Badcock)
The Fancy List, or Brief History and Scale of
Pugilism

This item was advertised in *The Fancy*, Volume I,
No.IV (June 2 1821), Page 104, as follows:
N.B. The Fancy List, or Brief History and Scale
of Pugilism, occupying 16 pages, will appear this
day fortnight. This compressed and luminous
Review of all that has passed in the Ring and
around it, for nearly a century, with the most
prominent characteristics of every leading occurrence, will be found highly acceptable and entertaining to lovers of "The Fancy" of all degree; as
containing vivid sketches of every transaction,
practical, anecdotal and elucidatory. THE SCALE
formed upon the principle of a Carpenter's Rule,
will enable any man who has seen one of the men
therein named in a pitched battle, to estimate the
probabilities of the event of any pending fight
between either of the parties; being altogether a
novelty of the Fancy Age in which we live.

1115. "JON BEE" (John Badcock)
Sportsman's Slang
London, Printed for T. Hughes, 35 Ludgate
Street, 1823.
London, Printed for the Author by W. Lewis
21 Finch Lane, Cornhill, 1825 (2nd edition)
216pp. 1825 Edtn - 222pp.
The title-page of the 1st edition reads as follows:
A Dictionary of the Turf, The Ring, The Chase,
The Pit, Of Bon-Ton, and the Varieties of Life,
Forming the Completest and Most Authentic
Lexicon Salatronicum Hitherto Offered To The
Notice of The Sporting World. For Elucidating
Words and Phrases that are necessarily or pur-
posely cramp, mutative, and unintelligible out-
side their respective spheres. Interspersed With
Anecdotes And Whimsies, With Tart Quotations,
And Rum Ones; With Examples, Proofs, And
Monitory Precepts, Useful and Proper For Novices,
Flats and Yokels – By Jon Bee Esq., Editor of
*The Fancy, Fancy Gazette, Living Pictures of
London.* Printed for T. Hughes, 35 Ludgate
Street, 1823.
The book was bound in boards, with a label on
the spine.
Pages 1 to 197 give the Dictionary of Varieties,
and pages 198 to 216 consist of an Addendum of
Obsolete and Far-Fetched Words and Phrases.
The 2nd edition is similar in content to the earlier
one, but is slightly larger in format; it was bound in
boards, with a cloth spine which bears a label.

continued

The contents are made up of 197 pages entitled "Dictionary of Varieties", with a longer Addendum than that of the earlier edition. The 1st edition was not illustrated, the 1825 edition has a folding frontispiece entitled "Life In Its Varieties"; there are also some full-page woodcut illustrations in this issue.

1116. "JON BEE" (John Badcock)

Prize Ring Companion, 1824

This item was advertised in *Fancy Ana*, Jon Bee, 1824, as follows:

"Shortly will be published, of the same size and shape as *Fancy Ana*, *The Prize Ring Companion*, Price 1s-6d".

"Consisting of new, curious, and useful Intelligence on Pugilistic Transactions, arranged Alphabetically, and adapted to the meanest Capacity".

1117. "JON BEE" (John Badcock)

Boxiana, or Sketches of Modern Pugilism
Volume IV
London, Printed for   Sherwood, Jones & Co., 1824.

660pp. 8 plates.

This volume is described on the title-page as "Containing All the Transactions of Note, Connected with the Prize-Ring during the Years 1821, 1822, and 1823.

The volume was written when Pierce Egan went over to George Virtue, for the latter to publish the two "New Series" of *Boxiana*, and Jon Bee took over the writing for Sherwood, Jones and Co.

1118. "JON BEE" (John Badcock)

A Living Picture of London for 1828 — and stranger's guide through the streets of the Metropolis; showing the Frauds, the Arts, Snares and Wiles of all descriptions of Rogues that everywhere abound: to which is added "Hints for Improvement of the Police".

London, 1828.

There is very little mention of the prize-ring in the text; however the frontispiece is a coloured folding plate with a number of small cuts; one of these shows a ring with pugilists in action, with spectators.

1119. JONES and COMPANY
(Temple of Muses) (Publishers)

The Universal Songster; or Museum of Mirth.

Forming The Most Complete, Extensive and Valuable Collection of Ancient and Modern Songs in the English Language: with a Copious and Classified Index, which will, under its Various Heads, refer the Reader to the Following Description of Songs viz: (*inter alia*) Sporting.

Embellished with a humorous Characteristic Frontispiece and 29 Woodcuts designed by George and Robert Cruikshank, and engraved by J.R. Marshall.

London, 1832. (3 volumes)

Volume 1 includes:
"The True Bottom'd Boxer; or The Champion of Fame" (T. Jones)
Air – "Oh! nothing in Life can sadden us".
(Three verses referring to Tom Spring).

1120. JONES, Bernard E.

Freemasons' Guide and Compendium
London, George G. Harrap and Co., 1950.

Book III "The Grand Lodges (1717–1813)", chapter eleven "The First Grand Lodge (1717)". In describing the personages in the early lodges this chapter includes "The Pugilist James Figg, of the Lodge at the Castle Tavern, St. Giles". In 1725 he had an academy of boxing and swordsmanship; he fought a broadsword duel in the Haymarket Theatre to provide a spectacle for a visiting Freemason, the Duc de Loraine, and gave exhibitions of bear baiting and tiger fighting.

1121. JONES, Bob

Bob Jones's 1972 New Zealand Boxing Yearbook
A complete record of boxing in New Zealand over the past year.
Wellington, Robert Jones Holdings Ltd.

72pp. Illus.

With this issue was an announcement that it was proposed that this would be an annual publication.

1122. JONES, Jimmy

King of the Canebrakes
Macon (Georgia), Southern Press, 1969.

127pp. Illus.

The story of Young Stribling, the "Georgia Peach".

1123. JONES, Reginald B.

Full and Authentic Account of the Great Battle for the World's Championship, Black v. White – Jack Johnson and Jim Jeffries, fought July 1910.

Manchester, Daisy Bank Printing and Publishing Co. (Daisy Bank Publications No.29), 1910.

32pp. Yellow Paper covers, with boxing portrait on front cover.

1124. JOSE, Arthur Wilberforce, and
CARTER, James Herbert

The Australian Encyclopedia

continued

Sydney, Angus and Robertson, 1925 and 1926, (2 Volumes)

Volume II includes an article on pugilism by William Lawless, ("Solar Plexus" of *The Referee* Sydney).
Note:
The first recorded battle in Australia took place on Sydney Racecourse (now known as Hyde Park), on 7th January, 1814, when John Berringer defeated Charles Lifton.

1125. J.T.R.
Art of Self Defence
A Treatise on Fencing, Smallsword, and Boxing.
1780.

JOHN L. SULLIVAN IN COSTUME

1126. KALETSKY, Richard
Ali and Me. Through the Ropes.
Bethan (Conn.), Adrianne Publications,
1982.
88pp. Paperback. Illus.

1127. KANDEL, Aben
City for Conquest
London, Michael Joseph Ltd., 1936.
479pp.
There is a good description of a fight in this novel,
and the film version of the book featured James
Cagney as the boxer.

1128. KARNEY, Jack
There Goes Shorty Higgins. A Boxing Novel
New York City, William Morrow and Co.,
1945.
243pp.

1129. KEARNS, Jack ("Doc")
The Million Dollar Gate
As Told to Oscar Fraley, Veteran Sports-
writer.
New York, The Macmillan Co., 1966.
333pp. Illus.
Described as "The Lusty, gutsy adventures of the
greatest fight manager of them all".

1130. KEATH, Walter
Stack
London, William Collins Sons and Co. Ltd.,
1971.
320pp. (Fiction)
The story of an East End boy, ill-educated and
penniless, who takes to the boxing ring to escape
from the squalor of his environment.

1131. KEEPING, James
The Pulse of Life
A Novel dealing with a Young Boxing Idol.
London, John Long Ltd., 1940.
256pp.

1132. KELLEY, Robert F. (Editor)
The Sportsmans Anthology
New York, 1944.
396pp.

1133. KEMP, Boris
They Like 'Em Rough
London, Curtis Books, 1953.
160pp. Paperback (Fiction)

1134. KENNEDY, Bart
The Human Compass
London, Sampson, Low, Marston and Co.,
Ltd., 1911.
New and cheap editions were published in
1912 and 1916.
325pp.
The section enetitled "From Any Points" includes
at pages 280–286 "Pugilism".

1135. KENNEDY. C.E.
Boxing Simplified, prepared especially for
schools
Springs, Ohio, U.S.A., Antioch Press Corporation, 1929.
75pp. Illus.

1136. KENT, George
Annals of British Pugilism, and Portraits of
English Boxers.   From the Days of
Broughton and Figg to those of the present
era, their biography, ages, weights, etc., em-
bellished with engravings.
London, Printed by R. Gray, 1818
34pp. 8vo.

**1137. KENT, John — Private Trainer to the
Goodwood Stable**
Racing Life of Lord George Cavendish
Bentinck, M.P. Edited by the Hon. Francis
Lawley
Edinburgh and London, William Blackwood
and Sons, 1892.
482pp. Illus.
Includes in Chapter XVII some reference to John
Gully

1138. KENT, Thomas
The Entertainer
Containing Several Prize Battles, with re-
marks &c. Also some Glorious Chaunts
about the Double Refined Victorious
Pugilists, with Randall's Farewell to the Ring
and the Description of the Belt, the Road to
a Fight, with some Country Hits in Prose
and Verse, with Toasts and Songs inter-
spersed with Pieces on Various Subjects;
and the Whole Compiled to Gratify the
Sporting Reader,
London, September, 1825.
Contains fights between various pugilists, including
Neate, Hickman, Crawley, Acton, etc. Also the
"Fancy at Fault, or the No Fight".

1139. KENT, William   continued

The Lost Treasures of London
With an Introduction by Norman Brett-James
M.A., BB.Litt., F.S.A.
London, Phoenix House Ltd., 1947.

150pp. Illus.
Walk 4 includes Blackfriars Road and refers to the
Blackfriars 'Ring' (previously the Surrey Chapel)
on the East side.

1140. KENYON, James W.

On My Right –
(A Boy's Boxing Story)
London, Thomas Nelson and Sons Ltd.,
1940.
Reprinted 1945. (The Coronet Library
No.12)

221pp. Illus.
First issue bound in light blue cloth, gilt lettering
on front cover.

1141. KENYON, James W.

Peter Trant – Heavyweight Champion. A
Novel.
London, Methuen and Co., 1946.

192pp. Illus.
Dedication to "My Brother Teddy, Globe Trotter
and Boxing Enthusiast"

1142. KENYON, James W.

Lightweight Honours
(A Boy's Boxing Story)
Illustrated by J. Phillips Paterson
London, Thomas Nelson and Sons Ltd. 1947

221pp. 4 Illus.
Bound in red cloth with cream spine.
The chief character in this story is Jerry Webb,
lightweight champion of Great Britain, who was
featured in Mr. Kenyon's earlier story *On My
Right* (q.v.).

1143. KENYON, J.W.

Boxing History
London, Methuen and Co., 1961.
(Methuen's Outline Series)

80pp. Illus.

1144. KESSLER, Gene

Joe Louis, The Brown Bomber
Illustrated with photos from Wide World
Press Inc.
Racine, Wisconsin, Whitman Publishing Co.,
1936.
(The Big Little Book Series)

242pp. Illus.
The chapter headings range from "Up from the
Cotton Fields" to "On the Threshold of the
Championship".

1145. KERSH, Gerald

Selected Stories
Modern Reading Library No.2
London, Staples and Staples Ltd., 1943.

120pp. Stiff cardboard boards
This wartime project to promote reading con-
centrated on the shorter forms of writing. Gerald
Kersh was a prolific author of novels and stories
at that time, and in this collection there appears
the brilliant sketch "The Drunk and the Blind",
a tale loosely based on old-time second-raters of
Irish origin from the turn of the century, like
Peter Maher, Dominick McCaffrey, and Mike
Morrissey.

1146. KETTON-CREMER, Robert W.

The Early Life and Diaries of William
Windham
London, Faber and Faber Ltd., 1930.

317pp.
This book includes a number of references to
Windham's interest in the prize-ring and his love
of a prize-fight, together with his patronage of
Broughton's Amphitheatre. It is stated that in
later years William Windham "watched with critical
enthusiasm every prize-fight he could reach".
During his days at Eton he was known as
"Fighting Windham".

1147. KEVERNE, Richard

Tales of Old Inns
London, Collins, St James Place, May,1939.
2nd impression December, 1939.
Revised and edited by Hammond Innes,
May, 1947, 3rd edition April, 1949.
Published in association with Trust Houses
Limited.

The boxing references are as follows:
Chapter IV   – A Round of Hertfordshire Inns
               – This refers to the "Two Brewers"
               at Chipperfield, used by boxers as
               training quarters.
Chapter V   – South East into Kent and Sussex
               – Includes reference to Crawley
               Downs and Copthall Common,
               scenes of many historic prize-
               fights.

1148. KEYNES, Geoffrey

Bibliography of William Hazlitt
London, Printed for the Nonesuch Press,
1931.

135pp.
This edition consists of 750 copies, of which 185
are for the U.S.A. Includes the famous essay
"The Fight".

1149. KIERAN, John

Story of the Olympic Games
776B.C.–1936A.D.

continued

New York, Frederick A. Stokes and Co.,
1936.

319pp. Illus.
The section on boxing gives winners at all weights
for the years 1904, 1920, 1924, 1928, 1932, and
1936.

1150. KIERAN, John
The American Sporting Scene
New York, The Macmillan Co., 1941.
Reprinted in 1946.

212pp. Illus. by Joseph W. Golinken
49 pages are devoted to boxing, mostly referring to
the Joe Louis fights.
34 boxing illustrations.

1151. KING, Don
I Am King
A Photographic biography of Muhammad
Ali
Baltimore, Penguin Books Inc., 1975.
Harmondsworth (Middx), Penguin Books
Ltd., 1975.

128pp. Stiff paper covers. Illus.

1152. KINNEY, Joe and
CASO, Adolph
Young Rocky
A True Story of Attilio "Rocky" Castellani
Brookline Village, (Ma), Brandon Publish-
ing Co., 1985.

1153. KIRCHER, Rudolph
Fair Play — The Games of Merrie England
A German impression of what the author
calls the "Play Spirit" of the English people.
Translated by R.N. Bradley.
London, William Collins Sons and Co. Ltd.,
1928.

221pp. Illus.
The section "The Sports of Their Public" in the
sub-section "Premierland", deals with boxing in the
East End of London.
There are no boxing illustrations.

1154. KIRSCH PUBLISHING CO.
(Publishers)
The All-Time Heavyweight Tournament
Championship
Devised by Murray Woroner
Wyncote, Pa. 1967.

24pp. Paper covers. Illus.
This pamphlet contained all information for pro-
cessing through the computer to find the All-Time
Champion.

1155. KLAUS, Frank
(Ex-Middleweight Champion of the World)

The Art of In-Fighting — A Treatise on a too
neglected Science
London, Ewart Seymour and Co. Ltd., 1913.
There were two further editions of this
book, one in 1919.

74pp. Illus.
An edition, completely updated and revised by Jim
Kenrick was issued by Link House Publications Ltd
London. It comprised 62pp. and sixteen illus-
trations posed by Jim Kenrick and Jimmy Kelly.

1156. KNEBWORTH, Viscount
Boxing. A Guide to Modern Methods, with
a Contribution by W. Childs, Coach to Cam-
bridge University Boxing Club.
With over fifty illustrations.
Volume XI of the Lonsdale Library of
Sports, Games and Pastimes.
London, Seeley Service Co. Ltd., 1931.

279pp. Illus.
This item was issued in 3 different types of bind-
ing, Full leather, light brown buckram, and
quarter leather.
The series is dedicated to H.R.H. The Prince of
Wales and the Editor's Introduction is by the
Earl of Lonsdale.
The text consists of a History of the Prize-Ring and
the Queensberry Ring, chapters on the Amateur
Ring, Training, Seconding, Refereeing, together
with a number of instructional chapters.
The Appendix deals with the various sets of Rules
of Boxing, from Broughton's Rules to those of the
Amateur Boxing Association.
In addition to numerous instructional illustrations
there are plates showing many pugilists of note.

1157. KNIGHT, Dame Laura
Oil Paint and Grease Paint
(An Autobiography)
London, Ivor Nicholson and Watson, 1936.

397pp. Illus.
Book III, Chapter XVII includes reference to box-
ing and Joe Shear's training camp.
There are 2 boxing illustrations.

1158. KNIGHTS, Henry (Printer)
A Handbook of Sparring
Published in London, 1960.
Printed by Henry Knights at Ipswich.

This book is divided into 3 sections, each on a
series of hits.

1159. KNOLLYS, Major, F.R.G.S.,
93rd Sutherland Highlanders
Shaw, The Life Guardsman
An Exciting Narrative
(Deeds of Daring Library)
London, Dean and Son, 1876.

continued

Illus.

Bound in brown cloth, with design in black on front cover, black titles on cover and spine.

This book ran through a number of editions; the following information is taken from the 3rd edition.

The subject of this book is mentioned in *Fistiana* as follows:

"Shaw, Jack (Life Guardsman): beat Burrows 13 rounds, 17 minutes, Combe Warren, July 12, 1812. Beat Painter, 50 gns, 28 rounds, Hounslow April 18, 1815. (Killed at Waterloo)".

1160. KNOX, E.V. (Evoe)

Here's Misery! A Book of Burlesque.
London, Methuen and Co. Ltd., 1928.
Second and cheaper edition, 1931.

Includes III – "The Boxer Explains" (By A. Hayright)
Illustrations include: "Psycho-Analysis is the Principal Necessity in the Ring".

1161. KOFOED, Jack

Thrills in Sport
Memories of those supreme moments in sport that will live for ever. Baseball, boxing, football, fully reviewed.
New York, Holborn House, 1932.

The boxing references are as follows:

Chapter I   – Dempsey v. Firpo
Chapter VII   – The Double Knockout.
                   (Wolgast v. Rivers)
Chapter XV   – Fair Lady (Female Boxing in Berlin)

Chapter XIX   – Ma Stribling
Chapter XXII   – The Boilermaker (James J. Jeffries)
Chapter XXVI   – The Battler (Battling Nelson)

1162. KOFOED, Jack

Brandy for Heroes. (A Biography of The Honourable John Morrissey, Champion Heavyweight of America and State Senator)
New York, E.P. Dutton and Co. Inc., 1938.
282pp. 10 Illus.

1163. KRAY, Charles (with Jonathan Sykes)

Me and My Brothers
London, Everest, 1976.
256pp. Illus.
Includes references to the brothers' participation and interest in boxing.

1164. KROUT, J.A.

Annals of American Sport
(The Pageant of America, Vol. XV)
Published in New Haven, Connecticut, 1929
322pp. Illus.

1165. KUHLER, Hugh MacNair

The Big Pink
A Boxing Novel
New York, Farrar and Rhinehart Inc., 1931.
Reissued in 1932.

OLD SCHOOL.

1166. LAFOND, Eddie and
MENENDEZ, Julie
Better Boxing
An Illustrated Guide
New York, Ronald Press Co., 1959.
(Ronald Sports Series)
118pp. Illus.

1167. LA MOTTA, Jake
Raging Bull.
My Story.
Eaglewood Cliffs, N/Jersey, Prentice Hall
Inc., 1970.
218pp. Illus.

1168. LAMBERT, J.M., and Alec
Boxing
London, E.E. Owens, 1914, Price 6d.
Alec Lambert was a famous boxing trainer, with a
gymnasium in the Edgware Road area of London.

1169. LAMBERT, Margaret
When Victoria Began to Reign
A Coronation Year Scrap-Book
London, Faber and Faber Ltd.,1937.
319pp.
There are pugilistic references in the following
chapters:

    Chapter V – News and Views
    Chapter XIII – Topical Events of the Year

There are 2 illustrations connected with prize-
fighting.

1170. LAMBERT, Richard S.
The Cobbett of the West
(A Study of Thomas Latimer and the
Struggle between Pulpit and Press at
Exeter)
London, Nicholson and Watson Ltd., 1939.
254pp.
Includes in Chapter VIII a mention of Latimer's
visit to the Sayers v. Heenan contest and his
account of the fight.

1171. LAMBTON, Arthur
The Galanty Show
London, Hurst and Blackett Ltd., 1933.
288pp.
Part 1, "Sport and Drama" includes reference to
the following Fights:

    Sayers and Heenan – 1860
    Frank Slavin and Peter Jackson – 1892
    Corbett and Fitzsimmons (Film of the Fight)

1172. LANCHESTER, Elsa
Charles Laughton and I
A Biography
London, Faber and Faber Ltd., 1938.
271pp. Illus.
Mentions boxing and all-in wrestling in Hollywood

1173. LANDSEER, Thomas
The Gorilla Fight
London, Thomas Maclean, 1863.
This consists of 4 etchings on size 4to paper, the
pictorial wrapper containing a further drawing on
the front cover.
The drawings were intended to depict in satire the
fight between Sayers and Heenan in 1860, and are
sometimes attributed to W.M. Thackeray, whose
figure is shown among the spectators on one of
the drawings, as is that of Thomas Landseer. In
a later work Thackeray denied that he had been
present at the fight.

1174. LANDSEER, William
Monkey-Ana, or Men in Miniature
Designed and etched by Thomas Landseer.
London, Moon, Boys and Graves, 1828.
This item was made up of six parts, including
a total of 24 plates, issued from January to
December, 1928. Some of the plates were
dated 1827.
The plates show monkeys depicted in various
professions – Lawyers, Overseers, etc.
Plate 13 "Pugilists", is the boxing item.

1175. LANGDON, Claude
(Britain's Adventurous Showman)
Earls Court
Foreword by the Marquess of Milford Haven
O.B.E., D.S.C.
London, Stanley Paul and Co. Ltd., 1953.
Autobiography of Claude Langdon, pioneer of
speedway and of ice-shows. Includes a section on
boxing at the Empress Hall.

1176. LANGLEY, Tom
The Tipton Slasher
Edited and produced by Harold Parsons,
Editor of *The Blackcountryman*
Tipton (Staffs), The Black Country Society,
N/d (ca. 1970)
112pp. Stiff paper covers. Illus.
The author describes the early life and environ-
ment of William Perry, The Tipton Slasher; with
descriptions of some of his fights taken from
Pugilistica.

1177. LANGLEY, Tom

continued

The Life of Tom Sayers
Leicester, Vance Harvey Publishing, 1973.
78pp. Illus. by Rigby Graham.

1178. LANGLEY, Tom
The Life of John L. Sullivan,
The Boston Strong Boy
Leicester, Vance Harvey Publishing, 1973.
78pp. Illus. by Rigby Graham.

1179. LANGLEY, Tom
The Life of Peter Jackson
Leicester, Vance Harvey Publishing, 1974.
78pp. Illus. by Rigby Graham.

1180. LANPHER, F.K. and Co. (Publisher)
The Little Boxer
Boston (Mass.), 1894.
(Another issue appeared in 1895)
Green paper covers, lettered in red on front and back.
The following information is taken from the 1895 edition:
The Little Boxer 1895. Official Records of the Prize-Ring and of Boxing.
Records of the champions, Classification of the Fighters and All Principal Battles from 1719 to 1895 . . .
Also given are lists of champions from different areas The World – America – England and Australia.
Various boxing statistics are included such as:
The Longest Bare Knuckle Battle on record –
The Longest Glove Fight – The Largest Purses, etc.

1181. LARDNER, John
It Beats Working
Illustrated by Willard Mullen
253pp. Illus.
This book is made up of reprints from the author's contributions first published in the *Newsweek* magazine.
This author is described as one of the foremost sports humorists of the day.
The boxing content is included in Chapters 1, 2, 4, 6, 8, 10, 12 and 13, which refer to many boxing personalities from the period when John Lardner first joined *Newsweek* in 1939.
There are at least 21 cartoons of boxing interest.

1182. LARDNER, John
White Hopes and Other Tigers
Philadelphia and New York, J.R. Lippincott and Co. 1951.
190pp. Illus.
Bound in light blue cloth, darker blue lettering on front cover and spine.
The author's acknowledgement says:– "Much of the material in this book first appeared in *The New Yorker* and is used here with the permission of the

magazine's editors"
The book includes 2 chapters on Firpo, the "Wild Bull of the Pampas" and deals further with the various "White Hopes" who were brought forward with the object of dethroning Jack Johnson.

1183. LARDNER, John
Strong Cigars and Lovely Women
Drawings by Walt Kelly
New York, Published for *Newsweek* by Funk and Wagnalls Co., 1951.
127pp.
This is a selection of John Lardner's weekly columns which appeared in the Sports section of *Newsweek* during 1949, 1950 and 1951; these are typical examples of his unique style of humour and satire.
The headings of the boxing items are as follows:

When in Doubt, Hang the Judge (Walcott v. Charles)
Murder to Music (Tony Galento)
Minstrel Memories (Al Jolson)
Death of a Simian and a Scholar (Tunney and Gargantua)
Now Pitching for Bartletts (Joe Jacobs)
Morgan Rises Above It (Dumb Dan Morgan)
The Doctor Rides Again (Doc Kearns)
The Voice at Home and Abroad (Eddie Egan)
The Adios That Bounced (Joe Louis)

1184. LARDNER, Rex
The Legendary Champions
New York, American Heritage Press, 1972.
272pp. Illus.
Consultants in preparation: Turn of the Century Fights Inc., William Cayton and Jim Jacobs.
Pictorial Research and Commentary by Alan Bodian.

1185. LARDNER, Rex
Ali
New York, Tempo Books, 1974.
84pp. Illus.

1186. LARDNER, Ring W.
Round-Up. The Stories of Ring W. Lardner.
New York, Charles Scribner's Sons, 1929.
London, Williams and Norgate Ltd., 1935.
There was also a cheaper edition issued by Scribner's in 1933.
This book contains 2 stories of boxing interest:

Chapter IX – "Champion"
Chapter XXXII – "A Frame-Up"

1187. LARDNER, Ring
Some Champions. Sketches and Fiction.
New York, Charles Scribner's Sons, 1976.
In his book *The Manassa Mauler* (q.v.) Randy Robert includes this title as providing source material for his work.

1188. LARWOOD, Jacob, and HOTTEN, John Camden

A History of Signboards

From the Earliest Times to the Present Day, With One Hundred Illustrations in Facsimile by J. Larwood.

London, John Camden Hotten, 1866.

536pp.

This work ran to a number of editions; a new edition was issued in 1951 under the title *English Inn Signs*. (q.v.)

There are a number of boxing references in this book; these refer to signboards naming tea-gardens or public houses kept by a pugilist or ex-pugilist, or in other cases where the house has been used as a place of call by boxers or others connected with the sport such as writers. In some cases the particular house identified with the signboard had been built on the site of an earlier sporting venue.

A public house bearing the name "Tom Sayers" in the Pimlico district of Brighton was one of several houses in the area claiming to be the birthplace of the great pugilist.

1189. LARWOOD, Jacob and HOTTEN, John Camden

English Inn Signs

Being a revised and modernised version of *The History of Signboards* with a chapter on Modern Inn Signs by Gerald Miller.

London, Chatto and Windus, 1951.

(Chatto and Windus took over the publishing business of John Camden Hotten when the latter died in 1874)

336pp.

The pugilistic references in this edition are not generally so lengthy or comprehensive as those in the original edition, and at least two have been omitted altogether.

1190. LATHAM, Edward

A Dictionary of Names, Nicknames and Surnames of Persons, Places and Things.

London, George Routledge and Sons Ltd., 1904.

New York, E.P. Dutton and Co., 1904.

334pp.

Includes items of pugilistic interest, referring to participants in the sport who bore nicknames, i.e. The Benecia Boy, etc.

1191. LATTIMER, R.B., M.A., and MORGAN, R.B., M.A., M.Litt. (editors)

Adventures in British Sport

London, John Murray 1926. (Modern English Series)

177pp. Illus.

Nine of the chapters are devoted to different sports.

Chapter V "Boxing" consists of "The Smith's Last Battle", a chapter from *Rodney Stone* by A. Conan Doyle.

1192. LAUDER, Sir Harry

Roamin' in the Gloamin'

London, Hutchinson and Co. (Publishers) Ltd., 1928.

Re-issued in 1930 and 1933.

Philadelphia, J.B. Lippincott Co., 1928.

New York, Grosset and Dunlap, 1930.

287pp. Illus.

Sir Harry tells of his meetings with famous boxers during his travels, particularly in America. He describes meetings with John L. Sullivan, Gene Tunney, Jim Corbett, Jim Jeffries, Jack Dempsey and Bob Fitzsimmons. He also recounts his attendance at bouts involving Jim Driscoll and Pancho Villa.

1193. LAURENCE, John

Philosphical and Practical Treatise on Horses and on the Moral Duties of Men towards the Brute Creation. Two Volumes.

London, Printed for J. Longman, Vol.1, 1796, Volume II 1798.

Vol. II of the First Edition includes a reference to pugilism in Chapter 1, on the Philosophy of Sports.

The third edition of this work contains a great deal more on pugilism in both volumes.

1194. LAWLESS, Peter

Rugger's an Attacking Game

Foreword by Howard Marshall.

London, Sampson Low, Marston and Co., 1946.

116pp.

The author played Rugby Football for the Barbarians and Richmond. There is fleeting reference to boxing in Chapter II "Growing Pains" in which mention is made of the Belsize Club, Bombardier Wells, and Dick Smith.

1195. LAWLESS, Will (Solar Plexus)

Boxing Made Easy

A Complete Manual of Instruction.

Sydney (N.S.W.), New Century Press Ltd., 1919.

Stiff Paper covers, with portrait of the author on the front cover.

Contains instructional chapters, with historical material and pictures relating to Australian boxing.

1196. LAWLEY, The Hon. Francis

The Life and Times of The Druid (Henry Hall Dixon)

London, Vinton and Co. 1895.

continued

334pp. Illus.
Includes some slight reference to the prize-ring and pugilism.

1197. LAWLOR, Jim
Seconds Out-Time
Memoirs of an exciting life on land and sea.
A Private publication, a limited edition of 500 copies. April, 1975.
Edited by Norman Smithson (Leeds)

114pp. Paper covers. Picture of Jim Lawlor on front cover. Illus.
The author established a well-deserved reputation as a knock-out king in the busy days before the War. In January 1939 Jim was ranked No.8 in the list of world welterweights. On top of that list was Henry Armstrong!

1198. LAWSON, Joseph
Progress in Pudsey
A Letter to the Young, on Pudsey during the Last Sixty Years.
Stanningley (Yorks), J.W. Birdsall, 1887.

136pp.
Letter No. IX, Manners, Customs, Sports and Pastimes, includes references to Pugilists visiting local feasts, and to local Prize-fights.

1199. LEGGE, Harry
A Penny a Punch
Christchurch, Curtis Publications, 1981.

204pp. Illus. Stiff paper covers, 8vo.
Harry Legge was a famous lightweight during the war and immediate post-war years, and Western Area title-holder, as well as participant in hundreds of booth contests. He is remarkable in that he overcame the disability of a withered right leg, due to polio, during his career, and after retirement taught himself to write prose and eventually produced this autobiography and reminiscenes of the colourful life of the boxing booth.

1200. LEIGH-LYE, Terry
The Truth About Boxing
Illustrated with Cartoons by famous artists.
London, Claud Morris, 1945.

32pp. Illus. paper covers.
Dedicated to "John Murray, a life-long fighter in the cause of better boxing".
The 12 sections include the following:

Peerless Jim, the Idol of Wales
The Old General, Crowley of Clerkenwell
Fight to Fame – Braddock's Amazing Story
Ballyhoo – The Press and the Pugilist

1201. LEIGH-LYE, Terry
"In This Corner"
Introduced by Peter Wilson, of the
Sunday Express

London, Background Books, Ltd, 1946.

46pp. Illus. paper covers. Price 2s-6d.
Chapters include:
They Never Come Back
The Matinee Idol
The Dempsey Era
The Clown Prince
etc.

1202. LEIGH-LYE, Terry
The Count of Ten
London, Background Books Ltd, 1947.

48pp. Stiff paper covers
Foreword by George Harrison, sports columnist of *The News of the World*.

1203. LEIGH-LYE, Terry
— And for the Heavyweight Championship of the World. Focus on the Fight Game No. 2. (A Background Sports Photo Book)
London, Background Books Ltd., 1949.

24pp. Illus. Paper covers. Picture of Louis v. Conn on front cover.
Covers fights from Tommy Burns v. Jack Johnson to Joe Louis v. Lou Nova.

1204. LEIGH-LYE, Terry
Fight Reporter
London, Scion Press Ltd., 1951.

96pp. 12 illustrations. Bound in stiff paper covers with a picture of Randolph Turpin on the front cover.
In each chapter the text describes a famous boxing match, from Eric Boon v. Arthur Danahar to Randolph Turpin v. Ray Robinson.

1205. LEIGH-LYE, Terry
The Squared Circle
From Corbett to Ezzard Charles.
London, Scion Ltd. 1951.

95pp. Illus. Stiff paper covers, a picture of Ezzard Charles on front cover.
The 12 chapters each deal with a famous fight or fighter; these include Bob Fitzsimmons, Marvin Hart and Tommy Burns, Max Baer and Carnera, the fights of Joe Louis and others.

1206. LEIGH-LYE, Terry
Personalities of The Ring
Intimate Pictures of the Great Names in the Boxing World.
London, Scion Ltd., 1952.

96pp. Paper covers. Illus.
An odd feature of this book is that the title is shown on the cover as "Personalities of Boxing" and on the title-page as "Personalities of The Ring". The personalities mentioned include, Promoters, Trainers, Managers and Boxers.

1207. LEIGH-LYE, Terry
The Heavyweight Story
London, Transworld Publications, 1955
(Corgi Books)
187pp.

1208. LEIGH-LYE, Terry
From the Ringside
London, Transworld Publications, 1958.
160pp. Paper covers. Illus.

1209. LEIGH-LYE, Terry
In This Corner
The Story of the Heavyweight Crown.
London, Mayflower Books Ltd, 1963.
127pp. Paper covers. Illus.

1210. LEIGH-LYE, Terry
A Century of Great Boxing Drama
With an Introduction by Henry Cooper.
London, Mayflower Books, 1971 (paperback)
144pp. Illus.
This book is mostly about heavyweights. In his penultimate chapter "Who Was the Greatest?", the author names his own choice as Joe Louis, with Cassius Clay placed second.

1211. LEIGHTON, Isabel (Editor)
The Aspirin Age 1919-1941.
New York, Simon and Schuster, 1949.
London, The Bodley Head, 1950.
491pp.
Includes a section by Gene Tunney entitled "My Fights with Jack Dempsey".

1212. LE MARCHANT, Sir Denis
Memoir of John Charles, Viscount Althorp, Third Earl of Spencer
(Edited by Sir H.D. Le Marchant)
London, Richard Bentley, 1876.
Includes references to Viscount Althorp's interest in the Ring, and also the fights he attended; including Mendoza v. Humphries and John Gully and Hen Pearce (The Game Chicken).

1213. LEMOINE, Henry
Ars Pugnantis
Henry Lemoine, in the Preface to *Modern Manhood*, 1788, mentions a small tract entitled *Ars Pugnantis*, and other items from all which "the present sheets are partly compiled".

1214. LEMOINE, Henry
Modern Manhood: or the Art and Practice of

British Boxing
Including the History of the Science of Natural Defence, and Memoirs of the Most Celebrated Practitioners of that Manly Exercise.
London, Printed for the Editor and sold by J. Parsons, Paternoster Row, and other booksellers, 1788.
There is a folding frontis. depicting Humphries and Mendoza, with their seconds and bottleholders and a number of spectators; the title of the book is in the centre, with a four-line verse on each side, entitled "The Gymnastic Contest".
Mention also occurs of a number of rare boxing publications, including *Ars Pugnantis*, Sir Thomas Parkyn's *Inn-Play and Cornish Hug*, Captain Godfrey's *Science of Defence*, etc.

1215. LENNOX, Lord William
Merrie England
Its Sports and Pastimes
London, T.C. Newby, 1857.
361pp.
Contains a section entitled "English Sports" with a subsection entitled "The Ring", which includes: "If pugilistic encounters are to take place that they will be divested of the brutality and dishonesty that have too often characterised them".

1216. LENNOX, Lord William Pitt
Drafts on My Memory
London, Hurst and Blackett, 1866.
Two volumes.
These volumes contain some references to the prize-ring and pugilism.

1217. LENNOX, Lord William Pitt
My Recollections from 1806 to 1873
London, Hurst and Blackett, 1874.
2 Volumes.
This item contains a number of references to pugilists and prize fights as follows:

Volume I, Chapter IV (*inter alia*): Pugilistic Encounters — The Fighting Life-Guardsman — Byron's Fistic Career — A Pugilistic Guard of Honour — George IV a Patron of the Ring — Prize Fights.

Volume II, Chapter IV (*inter alia*): The Art of Boxing.

1218. LENNOX, Lord William Pitt
Celebrities I Have Known, with Episodes Political, Social, Sporting and Theatrical
London, Hurst and Blackett. Published in 4 volumes, the first 2 in 1876 and the second 2 in 1877.

continued

These volumes include some reference to boxing in Volume II (1st series), including Tom Cribb, Captain Barclay, etc.

1219. LENNOX, Lord William Pitt
Fashion Then and Now
London, Chapman and Hall, 1878.
(Two Volumes)
Volume II, Chapter XVI includes some remarks on pugilism.

1220. LEONARD, Benny
My Greatest Ring Battles
12 pages. Compliments of the Sable Hat Co. Philadelphia Pa.

This was a tiny booklet which was given away to customers on the purchase of certain articles. Its contents included very small detail facts about some of Leaonard's greatest fights, including those with Ritchie Mitchell, Freddy Welsh, Charlie White,etc.

1221. LEVY, E. Lawrence
Birmingham Ahtletic Club 1866-1916
Pen Pictures of a Popular Past. A Jubilee Issue.
72pp. Illus.
Includes mention of a number of famous Birmingham boxers of the period; with three boxing illustrations.

1222. LEVY, E. Lawrence
The Autobiography of an Athlete
Birmingham, J.G. Hammond and Co. Ltd., 1913.

Contains many references to boxing and boxers, dealing with amateur and other boxing in Birmingham at the end of the nineteenth and beginning of the twentieth centuries.

1223. LEWIS, Claude
Cassius Clay
New York, McFadden Books, 1965.
126pp. Illus. Paper covers.

1224. LEWIS, Clifford
The Life and Methods of Primo Carnera
With a Special Chapter by Leon See.
London, Athletic Publications Ltd., 1933.
56pp.
Eleven chapters, frontis. showing Carnera with his manager, Leon See.

1225. LEWIS, Franklin
Sportistics
U.S.A. Cleveland Press, 1945.

Bound in red paper covers.
Includes a section on boxing, giving such information as Record Boxing Gates and the History of the Heavyweight Boxing Championship.

1226. LEWIS, Ted (Kid)
The Last Gong
A book under this title was advertised for publication by Hutchinson and Co. in the 1930s, but was withdrawn.
The autobiography of Ted (Kid) Lewis did in fact appear, with the title shown above, in a series of newspaper articles.

1227. LIBBY, Bill
Rocky, The Story of a Champion
New York, Julian Messner, 1971.
192pp. Ilius.
This book deals with the career of Rocky Marciano

1228. LIBBY, Bill
Joe Louis, The Brown Bomber
New York, Lothrop, Lee and Shepard Books, 1980.
224pp. Illus.

1229. LIEBLING, A.J.
The Sweet Science
London, Victor Gollancz, 1956.
256pp.
The famous sportswriter expounds on boxing, in his immaculate English.

1230. LIEBLING, A.J.
Between Meals
An Appetite for Paris.
London, Longmans, 1963.
191pp.
While this *bon viveur*, in this book, largely expounds upon gastronomy, he digresses widely, and boxing was probably only of secondary interest to him than eating. He writes engagingly of many personalities of the Ring.

1231. LINDSAY, Vachel
Collected Poems
New York, The Macmillan Company (copyright), 1920 and 1948.
This collection includes a poem entitled "John L. Sullivan The Strong Boy of Boston", this celebrates the victory of Sullivan over Jake Kilrain in the last bare-knuckle championship fight, July 8th 1889.

1232. LIPSYTE, Robert
The Contender
New York, Harper and Row Publishers Inc. 1967.
London, Pan Books Ltd. 1969 (paperback)
A tough, gripping novel of sporting life.

1233. LISTER, Dudley
Play The Game, No.1 Boxing
New Sporting Record Sports Series.
London, The Raymond Press, for *Sporting Record*, 1948.
32pp. Stiff paper covers.
Foreword by J.M. Wyatt Esq, F.R.C.S., President of the A.B.A.

1234. LISTER, Dudley S.
How to Box
London, Eyre and Spottiswoode, 1952.
("How to Play" Series)
256pp. Illus.
The author was A.B.A. Heavyweight Champion in 1925, and later Sports Editor of *Everybody's Weekly*.

1235. LLEWELLYN, Richard
How Green Was My Valley. A Novel.
London, Michael Joseph Ltd., 1939.
651pp.
Two of the characters in this novel are Dai Bando and Cyfartha Lewis, "Prizefighters, rough but gentlemen".
There is considerable mention of boxing in the book; chapter XXXVII contains an account of a fight between Dai Bando and Big Shoni, in which Dai wins the fight but loses his sight.

1236. LLOYD, Alan
The Great Prize Fight
London, Cassell and Co. Ltd., 1977.
188pp. Illus.
A well-researched book on the Sayers v. Heenan championship contest, 1860.

1237. LOCKER-LAMPSON, Frederick
My Confidences.
An Autobiographical sketch addressed to my descendants.
Edited by Augustine Birrell
London, Smith Elder and Co., 1896.
London, Thomas Nelson and Sons (1908)
(Nelson's Shilling Library)
440pp.
In his book the author speaks of a visit to the grave of Tom Sayers, and of his thoughts being taken back to the fight between Sayers and Heenan at Farnborough in 1860. There is also an account of a meeting with Tom Sayers while walking on Hampstead Heath.

1238. LODER, Vernon
(J.G.H. Vakey)
Kill in the Ring. A Boxing Novel.
London, The Crime Club Ltd., 1938.
London, W. Collins Sons and Co. Ltd., 1939.
252pp.
Vernon Loder was one of the pseudonyms of George Haslette-Vakey.

1239. LONDON, Charmian
(Mrs Jack London)
Jack London
With 41 illustrations and a bibliography.
London, Mills and Boon Ltd., 1921. (2 vols.)
This book contains many references to Jack London's writing on boxing and his love of the sport.
London was engaged by newspapers to report for them on famous fights including the Burns v. Johnson and the Jeffries v. Johnson bouts.

1240. LONDON, Jack
The Game
With Illustrations and Decorations by Henry Hutt and T.C. Lawrence.
London, William Heinemann, 1905.
Copyright 1905 by The Macmillan Co. New York City.
182pp. Illustrated by six coloured plates and many decorations and cuts in the text.
Bound in blue cloth with gilt titles and with a boxing design on the front cover.

1241. LONDON, Jack
Burning Daylight. A Novel.
New York, The Macmillan Co., 1910.
London, William Heinemann, 1910
Some mention of boxing is made in this item.

1242. LONDON, Jack
When God Laughs (Collected Stories)
New York City, The Macmillan Co., Jan. 1911.
London, Mills and Boon Ltd.
312pp.
Among the stories appearing in this book is "A Piece of Steak" the story of a poverty-stricken and ill-nourished boxer.

1243. LONDON Jack
The Abysmal Brute. A Novel.
Toronto, The Century Co., 1913.
169pp. Frontis.
Also published in London by George Newnes.

1244. LONDON, Jack
The Human Drift. A Book of Short Stories.
New York, The Macmillan Cp., 1917.
London, Mills and Boon Ltd., 1917.
190pp.

continued

These articles were arranged by Jack London for publication shortly before his death, and were published posthumously.

The book includes a sketch entitled "The Birthmark", this was written by London for Bob Fitzsimmons and his wife, Rose Julian. The sketch has a boxing theme.

1245. LONDON, Jack
Love of Life and Other Stories
Introduction by George Orwell
London, Paul Elek, 1946.

265pp.
Red cloth covers, gilt lettering on spine.
This collection of Jack London's short stories includes "A Piece of Steak", telling the story of an old prize-fighter's last battle against a youthful opponent.

1246. LONGHURST, Henry
It Was Good While It Lasted
Illustrated by 60 photographs
London, J.M. Dent and Sons Ltd., 1941.

342pp. Illus.
In the chapter entitled "Failure of a Mission" (dealing with the author's visit to America), reference is made to the fight between Joe Louis and Al Ettore.

1247. LONGHURST, Percy
Boxing (Warnes Recreation Books)
London and New York, Frederick Warne and Co., 1928.

64pp.
This instructional item appeared in several more editions up to 1947.

1248. LONSDALE LIBRARY OF SPORTS AND PASTIMES, THE
The following volumes in this series contain items of boxing interest. (q.v.)
Volume XI   – Knebworth, Viscount, *Boxing*
Volume XII – Parker, Eric (Editor) *The Lonsdale Anthology of Sporting Verse*
Volume XV   – Vesey-Fitzgerald, Brian (and others) *The Lonsdale Library of Sporting Records.*

1249. LOUIS, Joe
Born to Fight. Joe Louis' Own Story.
Chicago, Gene Kessler, 1935.

16pp. Illus. Limp card covers.
This booklet, which appeared only about a year after Joe Louis had turned professional, and had boxed only one contest in New York, that versus Carnera, is probably the earliest so-called 'autobiography' of the great pugilist. It was almost certainly written by Gene Kessler, who also published it and offers a brief introduction under his own name.

1250 LOUIS, Joe
My Life Story
New York, Duell, Sloan and Pearce (An Eagle Book), 1947.

Bound in green cloth, lettered in white and green, with portrait of Joe Louis on the dust wrapper. 21 Chapters with an added Postscript, profusely illustrated by photographs.
London, Eldon Press Ltd., 1947.
189pp. Illus.
The English edition is bound in blue cloth and consists of 21 chapters; the illustrations are spaced throughout the book and not bound in all together at the end, as in the American edition.

1251. LOUIS, Joe
How to Box
Edited by Edward J. Mallory.
Philadelphia, David McKay Co., 1948
London, Findon Publications Ltd., 1948 (paper covers)

64pp.
The U.S. Edition is bound in green-brown cloth.
The book contains chapters on Mind Discipline, Training and Defence and Attack.
There are many illustrations, including some of Joe Louis in contests with opponents such as Schmeling, Galento, Abe Simon, Billy Conn, Jim Braddock and others.

1252. LOUIS, Joe
My Life Story
Written with the editorial aid of Chester L. Washington and Haskell Cohen.
New York, Grossett and Dunlap, 1953.
147pp. Illus.
First published in 1947 under the title *My Life Story*. (q.v.)

1253. LOUIS, Joe
(With Edna and Art Rust, Jr)
Joe Louis: My Life
Brighton (Sussex), Angus and Robertson Ltd 1978.
277pp. including the Louis record. Illus.

1254. LOW, A.M.
Wonderful Wembley
London, Stanley Paul and Co. Ltd., 1953.
186pp. Illus.
A chronicle of post-Exhibition activities at Wembley Stadium and Pool. Chapter X carries references to boxing.

1255. LOWRY, Robert James
The Violent Wedding

continued

The Story of a Fighter who fought to win, and of the Girl who loved him and lost.
London, Arthur Barker Ltd., 1954.
London, The Harborough Publishing Co. Ltd., (Ace Books Paperback)
158pp.

1256. LUBBOCK, Alfred
Memories of Eton and Etonions. Including My Life at Eton, 1854–1863
London, John Murray, 1899.
320pp. Illus.
Chapter XIV, "Fagging, Bullying, Betting, etc." includes Sayers' fight with Heenan and Sayers' Circus at Windsor.

1257. LUCAS, E.V. (Editor)
Good Company. A Rally of Men.
London, Methuen and Co., 1909.
361pp.
Includes in chapter XI:
The Old Swordsmen, Broughton and Whitaker, by Capt. John Godfrey.
Tom Cribb, John Jackson, Jack Randall, by H.D. Miles
Jack Randall, by J. Hamilton Reynolds, (The Fancy).

1258. LUCAS, E.V.
The Phantom Journal, and other Essays and Diversions
London, Methuen and Co. Ltd., 1919.
Second Edition, 1920.
207pp. Illus.
One essay includes a reminiscence of Frank Bradley, regarding talks on pugilism with George Borrow.

1259. LUCKMAN, George and PETERSON, John
John L.Sullivan v. James J. Corbett, New Orleans, 1892
Published in U.S.A. by the authors.
Edition limited to 500 copies.
33pp. Paper covers. Illus.
Includes a reprint of the original story of the fight from the *Chicago Tribune*.

1260. "LUD"
(Sports Editor *Hudson Dispatch* Union City, New Jersey)
Relief to Royalty — The Story of James J. Braddock — World Heavyweight Champion
Foreword by Damon Runyon
Copyright 1936 by Ludwig Shabazian. All rights of publication, translation, abridgement, dramatic rights, as well as all other rights, are reserved.

191pp. Illus.
The Dedication reads "Dedicated to Haddon Ives Who Gave Me My Chance To Draw and Write".
Bound in green cloth, gilt lettering on front cover and spine.
There are 23 chapters and a photographic portrait of Jim Braddock and 20 illustrations by the author

1261. LUFTSPRING, Sammy
(with Brian Swarbrick)
Call Me Sammy
Foreword by Gordon Sinclair
Scarborough (Ontario), Prentice Hall of Canada Ltd,, 1975.
195pp. Illus.
The autobiography of the Ex-Welterweight Champion of Canada, and his fight against adversity.

1262. LUMLEY, Arthur T.
(Editor and Proprietor of the *New York Illustrated News*)
Bob Fitzsimmons. The Life, Battles and Records of the World's Champion.
Sold in London by the *Mirror of Life* Co., 1898.
Includes "The only correct Diagram of the Blows, as taken by Billy Madden during the Corbett-Fitzsimmons Fight at Carson City, Nevada".
Illustrated with full-length Portraits of Bob Fitzsimmons, James J. Corbett, Peter Maher, Dan Creedon, and Tom Sharkey.
Double-page illustrations of scenes in the ring in the Fitzsimmons-Corbett fight and full details of the battle.

1263. LUNDIN, Hjalmar
On The Mat and Off
Memoirs of a Wrestler
New York, Albert Bonnier Publishing House, 1937.
166pp. Illus.
This book contains a number of references to famous boxers in the following sections:

Trying out the Gloves (Anecdote of Bob Fitzsimmons)
My First Meeting with Young Corbett
Samuelson and Sharkey (Tom Sharkey as a Wrestler)
Bill Brown (Commissioner on the New York Athletic Board).

1264. LYALL, J.G.
Round Goes the World
Stamford, Haynes and Son, 1937.
111pp.

continued

These memoirs of a racehorse trainer, include some references to boxing. Mr. Lyall tells of his early memory of going to a circus with his father where Tom Sayers was giving exhibitions of boxing, and of sitting on Sayers' knee.

He also tells of visiting a field at Thistleton Gap to buy some cattle when he noticed the odd shapes of some of the trees; he was told by local people that these trees had been cut away to enable spectators to have a better view of the Cribb v. Molyneux fight in 1811.

1265. LYBURN, Dr. E.F. St.John, B.Ch., M.B., B.A., etc.

The Fighting Irish Doctor
An Autobiography
Dublin, Morris and Co, 1947.

200pp.
The author's story refers to his early days in Dublin, continuing the study of medicine while fighting his way up to the championship class in the boxing ring, stories of Battling Siki and his fight with Mike McTigue, and the later experiences of boxing in London, Birkenhead and at Oxford University.

1266. LYNCH (Colonel) Arthur

My Life Story
London, John Long Ltd., 1924.

319pp.
This book contains a number of references to prominent boxers, including the following:

Chapter III — Brothers, Speaks of the author's meeting with John L. Sullivan
Chapter XXIX— Meeting with Roosevelt. Gives further reminiscenes of John L. Sullivan
Chapter XXX— Great Men. Mentions sayings connected with the prize-ring and includes anecdotes of John L. Sullivan and Tom Sayers.

1267. LYNCH, Bohun

The Complete Amateur Boxer
London, Methuen and Co. Ltd., 1913 and 1924.
New York, Messrs. Stokes, 1914.
(Published as *The Complete Boxer*)

235pp. Illus.
There are differences in the text and layout of the two English editions; the first comprising 238pages and the second having 178 pages. The headings of the first 15 chapters vary slightly between the two editions in that an additional chapter (No.4) appears in the 1924 issue, entitled "Boxing in Literature", while in the earlier edition there are additional chapters numbered XVI and XVII entitled respectively "Military Boxing, Its Origin and Growth" and "Regimental Boxing Clubs and Military Tournaments" by W.Knight Bruce.
Both editions carry an appendix, the first including 4 sections and the second 2 sections. Common to

both are those entitled "Rules of the Amateur Boxing Association" and "Rules of the National Sporting Club". The 1913 edition includes in addition the sections "Rules of the Royal Navy and Army Boxing Association" and "Conditions of Public School Boxing".
Both editions are profusely illustrated.

1268. LYNCH, J.G.B.
(Bohun Lynch) Formerly Captain of Oxford University Boxing Club)

Prominent Pugilists of Today
London, Max.Goschen Ltd., 1914.
160pp. Illus.

1269. LYNCH, Bohun

Knuckles and Gloves
With a Preface by Sir Theodore Cook
London, W. Collins, Sons and Co. Ltd., 1922
209pp. Illus.
Large 8vo. Bound in green cloth with black lettering.
This book is divided into two parts:

Part I	— "Knuckles", has 20 chapters, dealing with pugilists from John Broughton to Tom Sayers and J.C. Heenan.
Part II	— "Gloves" has 14 chapters, from Jackson v. Slavin to Georges Carpentier and George Cook.

1270. LYNCH, Bohun

The Prize Ring
Illustrated by Reproductions of Old Prints Several Oil Paintings, and of the famous Byron Screen
London, Country Life Ltd., 1925.
(The English edition was limited to 750 copies)

52pp of text, 80pp. containing 40 plates, with descriptions, plus Index.
4to, bound in marbled boards, calf spine.
In the Preface the author points out that he has not attempted to write a complete history of boxing, but to give a brief introduction to a series of pictures and prints which cover the most interesting periods of the Prize-Ring.
The illustrations in the book consist of reproductions of well-known prints such as "The Interior of the Fives Court", and engravings by artists such as the Cruikshanks; there are also scenes from boxing matches, including Jack Randall v. Martin, the Baker, Johnson and Perrins, etc. from the heyday of the Prize-Ring era.
Regarding Lord Byron's screen, the poet is stated to have made this up at the height of his friendship with John Jackson. It is possible that Jackson assisted in the selection and cutting out of some of the material with which the screen is decorated; this consists of clippings from

continued

Boxiana and from newspapers. The panels from the screen are reproduced in the book and described by the author.

1271. LYND, Robert
The Sporting Life and Other Trifles
London, Grant Richards Ltd., 1922.
251pp.
This includes: V. What a Night's Boxing is Like. (Georges Carpentier v. George Cook).

1272. LYND, Robert
The Goldfish
(A Book of Essays)
London, Methuen and Co., 1927.
Second Edition, The Gateway Library, 1929.
214pp.
Includes "On Brutality" (a discussion of boxing in general and of the fight between Mickey Walker and Tommy Milligan, June 30th, 1927, in particular).

1273. LYTTON, The Earl of
Antony (Viscount Knebworth), a Record of Youth
Foreword by J.M. Barrie
London, Peter Davies, December, 1935.

A Second Impression was published in the same month.
368pp. Illus.
The subject of this biography won lightweight, and later welterweight, boxing competitions while at Eton, also a Public Schools competition. After going up to Oxford Viscount Knebworth was selected to box for the University against Cambridge.
He was later commissioned to write a book on boxing for the *Lonsdale Library of Sport* series, (Volume XI), published by the Seeley Service Co., in 1931.
Viscount Knebworth was killed in a flying accident in 1933.
(See Entry under Knebworth, Viscount).

1274. LYTTON, Edward George Bulwer (Lord Lytton)
Kenelm Chillingley. His Adventures and Opinions.
Edinburgh, Blackwoods of Edinburgh, 1873.
(3 volumes).
A second edition was published in the same year.
There is what is reported by W.E.Henley as a "good turn-up" in this novel.

O

PUGILISTICA:

THE HISTORY

OF

BRITISH BOXING.

CONTAINING

LIVES OF THE MOST CELEBRATED PUGILISTS,
AND FULL REPORTS OF THEIR BATTLES FROM CONTEMPORARY NEWSPAPERS
AND PERIODICALS, WITH AUTHENTIC PORTRAITS FROM
ORIGINAL PRINTS, PAINTINGS, AND BUSTS, BIOGRAPHICAL DETAILS,
PERSONAL ANECDOTES, SKETCHES OF THE PRINCIPAL PATRONS OF THE P.R., ETC.,

BEING THE ONLY

COMPLETE AND CHRONOLOGICAL HISTORY OF THE PRIZE RING.

BY

HENRY DOWNES MILES,

MANY YEARS RING REPORTER TO THE LONDON DAILY PRESS AND BELL'S LIFE IN LONDON,
EDITOR OF THE SPORTSMAN'S MAGAZINE, AUTHOR OF "THE BOOK OF FIELD SPORTS," ETC., ETC.

VOL. I.

LONDON:

PUBLISHED FOR THE PROPRIETOR,
AT THE OFFICE OF THE "SPORTING LIFE," 148, FLEET STREET, E.C.

1866.

Title-Page 1866 Edition *Pugilistica* (Miles) (Bib. Ref. 1365)

1275. MACADAM, John

The Macadam Road

London, Jarrolds, 1955.

192pp. Illus.

Reminiscences of a sports journalist.

This book was also issued later in the *Sportsmans Book Club* series.

1276. MacCONNELL, Brian

The Evil Firm. The Rise and Fall of the Kray Brothers.

From an investigation by a *Daily Mirror* team.

London, Mayflower, 1969.

The story of the Kray borthers, who were well-known in boxing circles.

1277. MacDONALD, Philip

Gentleman Bill. A Boxing Novel.

London, Herbert Jenkins Ltd., 1922.

255pp.

The novel was reviewed as follows:

"Really a sort of picture of the present-day position of heavyweight boxing . . . other characters can be identified as Dempsey, Carpentier, Lord Lonsdale, Tex Rickard, Eugene Corri, etc."

1278. MacDONALD, Philip

Patrol. A Novel.

London, Wm. Collins and Co., 1927.

245pp.

Further editions 1929, 1930, 1932, 1933, 1934.

Penguin Books edition 1935.

U.S. edition, Harper and Bros., New York, 1928.

U.S. edition, A.L. Burt and Co., New York, 1930.

This book includes a section on boxing and a chapter entitled "Rough Stuff".

1279. MacDONALD, Philip

Death on My Left

(Murder of a Boxing Champion). A Novel.

London, Wm. Collins and Sons and Co., Ltd. ("Crime Club"), 1933.

Reissued by the same publisher in 1934, 1935, 1936, 1937, the latter being in the Collins' Sixpenny Novels Series.

Published in New York by Doubleday Doran & Co.,1933.

Published in New York by A.L. Burt Co., 1934.

255pp.

1280. MacDONALD, R. (Printer)

The Handbook of Boxing, 1863

33pp. Green paper covers. Price 2d.

Picture of Tom Sayers on front cover.

This is a book of instruction in sparring and training, including Rules of the Ring.

The title-page bears a picture of J.C. Heenan; the folding frontis shows the British Champion's Belt, a facsimile of which was presented to both Sayers and Heenan following their battle in 1860.

1281. MACE, Jem, Junior

Boxing

London, Phelp Bros. No.date.

Bound in blue boards. Gilt lettering.

1282. MACE, Jem

(Retired Champion of the World)

Boxing

Edited with an Appendix by Edmund Sampson

London, Printed and Published by Fred Henning, at the *Sporting Truth* Offices, 1889

47pp. Illus.

Bound in red boards. Gilt lettering.

1283. MACE, Jem

Fifty Years a Fighter

The Life Story of Jem Mace (Retired Champion of the World)

Told by Himself.

London, C. Arthur Pearson Ltd., 1908.

128pp. 22 chapters, paper covers with a portrait of the author on the front cover. 7 illus.

The chapter-headiings include "My Early Days" "Tom Sayers and Other Memories", and "I Fight Davies Twice and Leave America for Australia".

1284. MACHRAY, Robert

The Night Side of London

Illustrated by Tom Brown, R.I., R.B.A.

London, John Macqueen, 1902 (large 8vo)

London, T.Werner Laurie, 1906 (small 8vo)

300pp.

Both editions are similar to each other except for size.

The book contains many references to boxing, particularly in the following chapters:

Chapter XVII – The National Sporting Club

Chapter XVIII – School for Neophytes. Refers to Bob Habbijam's gymnasium

Chapter XIX – Wonderland.

There are illustrations of boxing interest.

1285. MACKAY, George (Journalist)

The History of Bendigo

(The History of the Australian Town)

Melbourne, Ferguson and Mitchell, 1891.

195pp.

Details the naming of the town after a shepherd (also a bruiser) called "Bold Bendigo", after the English pugilist.

.continued

1286. MACLEAN, Catherine McDonald
Born Under Saturn
A Biography of William Hazlitt.
London, Collins, 1943.
631pp. Illustrated with portraits of Hazlitt and others.
Includes references to Hazlitt's visit to the fight between Hickman, The Gas Man, and Bill Neate, the Bristol Bull, at Hungerford. It gives Hazlitt's account of the fight as it appeared in *The New Monthly Magazine*.

1287. MACQUEEN-POPE, W.
Twenty Shillings in the Pound
London, Hutchinson and Co (Publishers) Ltd., 1948.
414pp. Illus.
The boxing interest is in the following chapters:

Chapter II – Seen But Not Heard. This speaks of the cinema in embryo, called The Wheel of Life, and of the author viewing two boxers pummelling each other through this apparatus.

Chapter XVIII – When Britain Held the Championship. Discusses the National Sporting Club and the spread of interest in boxing to the Middle Classes.

1288. MACQUEEN-POPE, W.
Ghosts and Greasepaint
A Story of the days that were
London, Robert Hale Ltd., 1951.
334pp. Illus.
Mention of boxing is given in Chapter V, "A Prince and a Pugilist", referrring to Jem Carney. The illustrations include a full-length portrait of Jem Carney.

1289. MADDEN, Joe
(The Markee)
Set 'Em Up
New York, Published by the author, 1939.
136pp. Illus. by John Rupe.
An announcement on the title-page states that this book is published by a "Punch-Drunk Author", but there are but a few references to boxing.
The frontispiece carries a picture of Joe Madden in boxing kit, announced as "Clever New York Lightweight", with some drawings of him in training and in action in the ring. Most of the book relates to the author's experiences as a saloon-keeper, and of gambling on horses and at dice.

1290. MADDICK and POTTAGE
(Publishers)
The Shilling Illustrated Boxiana. How to Train and the Science of Boxing. Lives of the Champions &c. &c.
London. 1863.
Bound in light yellow boards, lettered in black.

This book is divided into sections, commencing with the Origin and Progress of Boxing in England, and reviewing a large number of prize-ring champions up to the International Fight (Sayers v. Heenan). There are articles on Training and Exercise, Time and Quantity of Eating, etc.
There are 6 full page plates of pugilists.

1291. MAETERLINCK, Maurice
Life and Flowers
English edition translated by Alexander Teixeira de Mattos.
London, George Allen, 1907.
311pp.
Bound in light green cloth lettered in gold, with black designs on front cover and spine.
Consists of 12 essays, the ninth of these is entitled "In Praise of the Fist" and it deals with boxing.

1292. MAGRIEL, Paul (Compiler)
Bibliography of Boxing
A Chronological Check-List of Books
published in English before 1900.
New York, The New York Library, 1948.
28pp. white paper covers.
120 boxing items are listed, with reproductions of title-pages of some of the rare books.

1293. MAGRIEL, Paul (Editor)
Memoirs of the Life of Daniel Mendoza
Edited with an Introduction by Paul Magriel.
Dedicated to Nat Fleischer.
London and Sydney, B.T. Batsford Ltd., 1951.
111pp. Illus.
Bound in red cloth with gilt lettering on the spine. The illustrations consist of 2 coloured plates and reproductions of boxing illustrations by Hogarth, Cruikshank and others. The 4th plate of this modern reproduction shows the title-page of the original edition.
In his introductory remarks on the dust-wrapper the editor points out that Mendoza was the first Jewish champion and the most scientific boxer of his time, his four fights with Humphreys making a milestone in the history of boxing, demonstrating the advantages of scientific defence over mere strength.
There are 8 chapters in the book, with an Appendix entitled "Observations in the Art of Pugilism".

1294. MAILER, Norman
The Fight
The true story of the greatest heavyweight championship of all time.
London, Hart-Davis McGibbon Ltd., 1976, (First British Edition). Issued in Panther paperback, 1977.
207pp.

continued

Mailer's version of the Ali v. Foreman fight in Zaire, 1974.

1295. MALLALIEU, J.P.W., M.P.
Sporting Days
London, Phoenix Sports Books, 1953.
190pp. Illus.
A reissue of a series of articles giving accounts of sporting events covered by the author for the *Spectator*. There is an article on boxing, entitled "Boxing at the Bar".

1296. MALONEY, Thomas
The Value of Boxing to the Police
Dublin, A. Thorn, 1929.
75pp. Paper covers.

1297. MANCOUR PUBLISHING CO.
The Parade of Champions
(Pictures of Champions from Figg to Braddock)
Size 18ins x 30ins. Price $1.
Milwaukee, Wisconsin, 1937.
The size of each picture is approximately 3½ x 2 ins. and they are all on one large sheet.

1298. MANDEVILLE PUBLICATIONS (Publishers)
Tom Merry's Annual
London, 1949.
Bound in cream cloth, lettered in red on front cover and spine.
The annual includes "The Manassa Mauler" and "The Wild Bull" (Jack Dempsey v. Luis Angel Firpo) by Edward Northcott.

1299. MANNIN, Ethel
All Experience
London, Jarrolds (Publishers) Ltd., 1932.
284pp.
Chapter XVIII, "A Prize Fight, Black versus White" describes the bout between Larry Gains and Don McCorkindale at the Albert Hall on January 28th 1932, which resulted in a draw.
Six further impressions of the book were issued in 1932.

1300. MARCH, R. and Co. (Publisher)
Champions of the English and American Prize Ring
London, no date.
Includes Portraits, Exploits, Descriptions of the Battles, amounts of Wagers, Backers, etc.
All about John C. Heenan, Tom Sayers, Yankee Sullivan and others.

1301. MARCH, Joseph Moncure
The Set-Up
A Narrative Poem (A Thrilling Fight Story in Verse)
New York, Covici, Friede Inc., 1928.
New York, *Wild Party* and *The Set-Up* by Joseph Moncure March, published by Blue Ribbon Books, 1932.
London, Martin Secker, 1929. (Edition limited to 2000 copies)
199pp.
The English Edition bound in red cloth, gilt titles on front cover and spine.
The poem is divided into 6 parts, incorporating 54 stanzas.

1302. MARCHMONT, Frederick (Compiler)
The Three Cruikshanks
A Bibliographical Catalogue, Describing more than 500 works.
London, W.T. Spencer, 1897.
128pp.
This book contains short particulars of a number of pugilistic items; including Harrison Ainsworth, Pierce Egan and other authors illustrated by the Cruikshanks.

1303. MARCIANO, Rocky
Rocky Marciano's Boy's Book of Boxing and Body Building
With a simple section on Judo and contributions by Charles Goldman and Al Bochman.
London, Souvenir Press, 1960.
189pp. Illus. with portraits and plates.

1304. MAREK, Max
Mass Boxing Simplified
San Francisco (California), Simpson Publishers, 1941.
Bound in cloth
145pp.
This book is divided into three parts:

Book 1 – Deals with Mass Instruction, group form, drills on blows, counterpunches etc.; road work, bag punching, feinting etc.

Book 2 – Covers Priceless Ring Lore, with a secret of Bone-hardening the hands; gym equipment etc.

Book 3 – A detached account and method, of promoting a boxing show, with tips – all for a smooth and entertaining show.

1305. MARJORIBANKS, Edward
The Life of Sir Edward Marshall Hall
With an Introduction by the Rt. Hon. Earl
of Birkenhead, M.P.
London, Victor Gollancz Ltd., 1929.
483pp.
Chapter VII, "Setback", contains an account of
the Liverpool Bank Forgery, otherwise known as
"The Goudie Case", with mention of Dick Burge,
the lightweight boxer, who was involved in the
case.

1306. MARKS, Henry Stacey, R.A.
Pen and Pencil Sketches. 2 Vols.
London, Chatto and Windus, 1894.
Vol.II includes Chapter XVII, "A Pugilistic
Painter". References to Jem Ward, Pugilist, Pub-
lican and Painter.

1307. MARRIOT, A.E.
Hand to Hand Fighting
New York, Macmillan and Co., 1918.

**1308. MARSH, Irving, and EHRE, Edward
(Editors)**
Best Sports Stories of 1944.
With Sixteen of the Year's Best Sports
Pictures
New York, E.P. Dutton and Co. Inc., 1945.
(4 printings up to January 1946)
Includes articles on Sam Langford, Lou Nova,
Dempsey v. Firpo, and on Stillman's Gymnasium.
The *Best Sports Stories* series was issued annually
for a number of years following the first public-
ation; each issue contained articles on boxing taken
from various papers and periodicals.
The featured writers included W.C. Heinz, John
Lardner, Jesse Abramson, James J. Cannon,
Harold Rosenthal, James P. Dawson, Bob
Considine, and others of similar calibre.

1309. MARSHALL, Howard (Editor)
Great Boxing Stories
London, George Routledge and Sons Ltd.,
1936.
244pp.
This anthology includes excerpts from *Lavengro,
Boxiana* etc. and also from the works of Fred
Dartnell, J.B. Priestley and other authors.

**1310. MARSHALL STILLMAN
ASSOCIATION (Publishers)**
Boxing and Self Defence Taught by the
Marshall Stillman Principle
New York, copyright, 1919.
92pp. 102 Illus.

Included in the course was a separate complimentary volume of Mike Donovan's famous book
Science of Boxing, specially bound for home
study; including the rules and articles on training,
generalship in the ring, and every good blow and
guard known to boxing.
Chapters IV and V of the main work are devoted
to Ju-Jitsu and Wrestling. Mike Donovan posed
for the pictures in Chapter I, entitled "Five Sub-
Conscious Lessons on Boxing". Donovan also
posed for the pictures shown in his own work.

1311. MARTIN, John (Compiler)
Radio Quiz
Over 1500 Questions and answers on your
favourite topics.
London, Danceland Publications Ltd., 1947.
Illus. paper covers. Price 2s-6d.
The contents of boxing interest comprise a section
entitled "Boxing", with 50 questions and answers
on the sport. There are also boxing questions in
the section entitled "Sporting Salad".

1312. MASEFIELD, John
The Everlasting Mercy
London, 1911.
New York, Bridgehead Books, 1954.
230pp.
Although this famous narrative poem commences
with a grudge fight on turf by moonlight, with the
internal evidence dating the contest as definitely
taking place in 1867, it is fought under Queensberry Rules, "round on round, three minutes
each", and "my seconds ... gloved me". A serious
fight would almost certainly have taken place
under London Prize-Ring Rules at that date, with
bare knuckles. Indeed, the narrator says: "They
drove (a dodge that never fails) / a pin beneath
my finger nails". How this could have been done
with the boxer wearing gloves Masefield does not
make clear. He obviously knew more about
poetry than he did about pugilism.

1313. MASON, Michael and ROSE, Charles
The Story of Boxing
(40 pictures of Boxing Stars, including all
World Heavyweight Champions from James
Jeffries to Joe Louis; with articles, etc.)
Windsor, Cedric Day, 1947.
27pp. Illustrated paper covers.
The text in this booklet consists of 16 sections,
each relating to a famous pugilist or to a particular
contest; this ranges from Daniel Mendoza through
the ages to Tunney, Loughran, Carnera, Baer,
Schmeling and Louis.
There is an additional section entitled "Famous
Fights", giving accounts of the outstanding prize-
fights during the past ninety years, from Sayers
v. Heenan to Len Harvey v. Jack Petersen; there
is also a list of championship fights from 1873.

1314. MASTERMAN, Harland
The Challenger's Come-Back.
A Boxing Novel.
London, Grant Hughes Ltd.,1947.
Paper covers. Boxing picture on front cover.

1315. MASTERMAN, J.C.
Fate Cannot Harm Me
London, Victor Gollancz Ltd., 1935.
Reissued by Penguin Books, 1940.
285pp.
Chapter XI contains a reference to boxing, where a lightweight champion takes on a booth boxer.

1316. MATSELL, George (Compiler)
Vocabulums; or The Rogue's Lexicon
Compiled from the Most Authentic Sources.
New York, George Matsell and Co. Proprietors of the National Police Gazette, 1859.
Includes in the Appendix: Technical Words and Phrases in General Use by Pugilists.

1317. MATTHISON, Arthur L.
Art, Paint and Vanity
London, Heath Cranton Ltd., 1934.
256pp. Illus.
This story of the Matthison family is mostly concerned with their lives and careers in the theatre; included in Chapter II is an account of the author's grandfather, a well-known pugilist who fought under the name of Arthur Matthewson.
The frontispiece, taken from a miniature, shows Arthur Matthewson in the year 1820.
See also *Less Paint, More Vanity*, by the same author.

1318. MATTHISON, A.L.
Less Paint, More Vanity
London, Heath Cranton Ltd., 1937.
223pp. Illus.
Contains a number of references to pugilism, including:
"Boxing contests, even one or two at "The Swan With Two Necks" when Alf Greenfield was Licensee."
See also *Art, Paint and Vanity* by the same author, 1934.

1319. MATTHISON, A.L.
Bullocks at Stamford Fair
With an Introduction by W. Macqueen Pope.
Birmingham, Cornish Brothers Ltd., 1951.
128pp. Illus.
Includes a section entitled "Bare Knuckles" which deals with the author's grandfather, Arthur Matthison (or Matthewson), known as the "Fighting Basketmaker" of Birmingham.

1320. MAXWELL, Alan
(Boxing Referee and ex-Lightweight Champion of New Zealand)
Ring Recollections
Wellington (New Zealand), *New Zealand Free Lance*

1320A. MAXWELL, Alan
Tom Heeney, His Meteoric Career
(From Plumber's assistant to Fistic Star)
Wellington (New Zealand), H. E. Geddes and Co. Ltd., 1928.
25pp. Illus. Pictorial wrappers.
The subject of this biography was Dominion Contender for the World's Heavyweight Championship.

1321. MAYES, Harold
Rocky Marciano
London, Panther Books, 1956.
(Panther Books No. 550)
153pp.

1322. MAYHEW, Augustus
Paved with Gold, or The Romance and Reality of the London Streets
London, Chapman and Hall, 1858.
London, Downey and Co., 1899.
Illustrated by H.K. Browne ("Phiz")
Includes the following chapter in Book the Second, "Childhood in the Streets".
Chapter XII. The Fight for the Championship.
(Ned Tongs and Jack Hammer)
This is, in fact, an account of the fight between Tom Sayers and Tom Perry, The Tipton Slasher, on June 16th, 1857.
Includes one plate, "The Prizefight interrupted by the Police".

1323. MAYHEW, Henry
London Labour
London, Charles Griffin and Co., 1861-1862.
(4 volumes)
Volume III (1861) includes mention of James Shaw, lightweight pugilist.

1324. McBRIDE, P., M.D., F.R.C.P.E., F.R.S.E.
The Philosophy of Sport
London, Heath Cranton ltd, 1902.
Includes boxing references in Chapters III and IV.

1325. McCALLUM, John D.
The World Heavyweight Boxing Champion-

continued

ship. A History.
Foreword by Dr. Charles P. Larson, Former
President W.B.A.
Radnor, (Pennsylvania), Chilton Book Co.,
1974.
278pp. plus Appendix. Illus.

1326. McCALLUM, John D.
The Encyclopedia of World Boxing
Champions
All the Champs from Heavyweight to Fly-
weight since 1882.
Radnor (Pennsylvania) Chilton Book Co.,
1975.
Bon Mills, (Ontario), Thomas Nelson and
Sons Ltd., 1975.
227pp. Illus. with over 170 photos. 4to.

1327. McCANN'S TOURS INC.
(Publishers)
The "Sportsmen's" Special
New York, 1910.
This was a 12-page pamphlet, being the pro-
gramme of a "Tour de Luxe" to the Pacific Coast
in connection with the Jeffries-Johnson contest
for the World Title, July, 1910.
The tour was a 20-day trip under the direction of
Tom O'Rourke, Managing Director of the National
Sporting Club of America, and Business Manager of
McCann's Tours Inc.
The Pamphlet contained a daily synopsis of the
tour, a letter from Tom O'Rourke, and other in-
formation.

1328. McCAUSLAND, Hugh
Old Sporting. Characters and Occasions
from Sporting and Road History.
London, The Batchworth Press Ltd., 1948.
172pp.
Includes in "Horse and Highway" sections en-
titled "Newmarket Matches" and "Lord
Lonsdale against Time".
The first of these sections refers to Captain
Barclay's training of Tom Cribb for the second
match with Molyneaux.

1329. McCONNELL, J. Knox
The Boxer and the Banker. A Biography of
Billy Conn.
New York, Vantage Press, 1984.
109pp.

1330. McCORMACK, Lily
I Hear You Calling Me.
The Story of John McCormack.
London, W.H.Allen and Co. Ltd., 1950.

232pp. Illus.
In this biography of her husband, Mrs McCormack
refers to a visit to Ireland by Gene Tunney in
1924; with a picture of McCormack and Tunney.

1331. McCORMICK, John B.
(Macon)
The Square Circle; or, Stories of the Prize-
Ring
Being Macon's Description of Many Pugil-
istic Battles, Fought with Bare Knuckles
or Boxing Gloves, with Numerous Anec-
dotes of Famous Fighters, to which are
added How to be Young at Fifty, a Treatise
on the Proper Method of Living; of Great
Value to All Men.
Copyrighted 1896 by J.B. McCormick.
New York, Continental Publishing Co.,
1897.
274pp. Illus.
Bound in red cloth. Gilt titles on cover and
spine.
A number of famous fighters are dealt with in the
text, including Dan Donnelly, Yankee Sullivan,
Tom Hyer, Bill Richmond, Tom Molyneux, John
Morrissey, Big Mike McCoole, John L. Sullivan,
Bob Fitzsimmons, Peter Jackson, George Dixon,
Peter Maher and many others.
There are 22 illustrations, many of these being
copies of old prints.

1332. McFADDEN, George (Elbows)
Blocking and Hitting
New York, Richard K. Fox Publishing Co.
1905.
Reissued in New York, 1909.
58pp. Illus. Wrappers.

1333. McGOVERN, Terry, and others
How to Box and Win – How to Build Muscle
– How to Breathe, Stand, Walk or Run –
How to Punch the Bag. A Book of Health
and Strength, By Terry McGovern, James
J. Corbett, J. Gardner-Smith, M.D., Gus E.
and Arthur R. Keeley.
Reprinted by permission of the New York
Evening World.
Chicago, Shrewesbury Publishing Co., 1920.
Copyright 1899 by the New York *Evening
World*.
Illus.
The book is divided into sections, as indicated,
each section by a different author.

1334. McGUIGAN, John
A Trainer's Memories
Sixty Years' Turf Reminiscences and Experiences at Home and Abroad.
Edited by J. Fairfax Blakeborough.
Introduction by Lord Hamilton of Dalziell, K.T.
London, Heath Cranton Ltd., 1946.
171pp.
The book contains many references to boxing, including the following:

Chapter VII —	Some Scottish Sportsmen. (Dick Burge and Bobby Dobbs boxing on Tyneside, etc.)
Chapter VIII —	Australian and South African Impressions. (Tommy McInnes of Scotland, Australia and New Zealand)
Chapter XIV —	Racing in South Africa. (Boxing in South Africa)

1335. McILVANNEY, Hugh
McIlvanney on Boxing
London, Stanley Paul and Co. Ltd., 1982.
190pp. Illus.
The author is a well-known sporting journalist.

1336. McINNES, Peter
Tackle Boxing This Way
London, Stanley Paul and Co. Ltd., 1960.
127pp. Illus.

1337. McINNES, Peter
Ten and Out!
(Being the Life Story of Benny Lynch)
Bournemouth, The Epsilon Press, 1961.
198pp. Illus.
This book concentrates more on Benny Lynch's brilliance as a boxer, rather than on the weaknesses that finally made it impossible for him to pursue his career in the ring.

1338. McINNES, Peter
Clouting for Cash
London, P.R.M. Publications Ltd., 1962.
219pp. Illus.
Each of the 21 chapters is devoted to a famous boxer or a notable contest; includes Boon v. Danahar, Joe Louis v. Billy Conn, Tony Zale v. Rocky Graziano, etc.

1339. McKENZIE, F.A.
The Mystery of the *Daily Mail*, 1896-1921.
London, Associated Press Ltd., 1921.
128pp. Illus.
Chapter III, "The Secret of Vereeniging, and other Great Adventures", includes: Jack London's Prize-Right Narratives, and tells how London was commissioned by the *Daily Mail* to report on the Jack Johnson v. Tommy Burns World Title fight at Sydney in 1908, and how he expedited the news of the result; his following description of the fight was described as one of the most vivid word-pictures of a great glove fight ever written.

1340. McKINNEY, Roland
Thomas Eakins
Photo Research and Bibliography by Aimee Crane.
New York, Crown Publishers (American Artists' Series), 1942.
112pp. Illus.
Refers to the artist's interest in prize-fighting and his pictures on the sport; four of these pictures are included in the illustrations to this book.

1341. McLAGLEN, Victor
Express to Hollywood
London, Jarrolds (Publishers) Ltd, 1934.
112pp. Illus.
Several chapters refer to the author's career as a boxer, eg: "My First Fight" — "My First Boxing Match" — "My Fight with Jack Johnson", etc.
The illustrations include "Victor McLaglen, Heavyweight", a picture of his arrival in Hollywood, where his boxing record was used for publicity purposes.

1342. M'CRACKEN, Mike
Blood on His Gloves (Fiction)
London, Hamilton and Co. (Stafford) Ltd., 1951.
128pp. Illustrated paper covers.
A story of the tough New York fight racket.

1343. M'CRACKEN, Mike
The Black Hammer (Fiction)
London, Hamilton and Co. (Stafford) Ltd., 1951.
128pp. Paper covers.
Described as "Another Tough Two-Fisted Yarn, Featuring that Rising Negro Battler, Liberty Jones".

1344. MEAD, Chris
Champion, Joe Louis — Black Hero in White America
New York, Charles Scribner's Sons, 1985.
330pp. including a 16-page bibliography. Illus.
Issued in U.K. by Robson Books, 1986.

1345. MEANEY, Joseph
Scribble Street
London, Sands and Co. (Publishers) Ltd.
144pp. Illus.
The reminiscences of a Fleet Street journalist, particularly devoted to murderers and their trials; it includes an account of the trial of Del Fontaine for murder. (Del Fontaine was a Canadian boxer, domiciled in London)

1346. MEDEWINE, Captain (Editor)
Recollections and Conversations of Bob Gregson
A work under the title was reviewed in *The Annals of Sporting and Fancy Gazette* Volume VI, No.36 (Dec.1, 1824) pages 334-336; The article opened: "This volume, which is forthcoming and from the proof-sheets of which we have been favoured with the following extracts . . ."
Later in this issue of *The Annals of Sporting* there is an announcement of the death of Bob Gregson; it is therefore possible that the *Recollections etc. of Bob Gregson* were never published.

1347. MELLIFONT PRESS LTD (Publishers)
Mellifont Sports Series
This series was published at 3d each, with coloured illustrated covers; it included a number of boxing titles, chiefly fiction; a list of these is given as follows:

1 — Elliott, William J. – *Great Stars of the Prize Ring*
2 — Ruthen, Jack – *The Champion of the World*
3 — Worthing, Temple – *The Boxer's Sweetheart*
4 — Gill, Patrick – *The Fighting Tramp*
5 — Pearce, Charles E. – *Corinthian Jack*
6 — Elliott, William J. and Wilson, Major Arnold M.C. – *Cameos from the Prize Ring*
15 — Dartnell, Fred – *Seconds Out!*
17 — Martin Peter – *The Midget Marvel*
18 — Wallace Francis – *Kid Galahad*
23 — Maydwell, W.D. – *The Russian Heavyweight*
25 — Gilmour, R. – *Death in the Ring*
32 — Gilmour, R. – *Dynamite Dave*
33 — Whitley, Reid – *Down for the Count*
36 — Rowe, John C. – *The Roped Square*
37 — Worth, Richard – *A Bantam Champion*
53 — Kenyon, James W. – *"Beau Nash" Heavyweight Champion*

1348. MELLIFONT PRESS LTD (Publishers)
The Mellifont Twopenny Series
This series includes a number of boxing items; they were all fiction and bound in coloured wrappers. Information on these is given as follows:

Rowe, John G. – *The Boxing Baronet, or Showman Boxer*
Rowe, John G. – *The Boxing Twins*
Rowe, John G. – *Sparring Partners*
Gilmour, R. – *Knuckle-Duster Jim*
Gilmour, R. – *Jim Lang's Secret Punch*
Gilmour, R. – *The Spartan Boxer*
Gilmour, R. – *Champion Paddy O'Kane*
Marsden, James – *Ned Cartwright, Middleweight Champion*
Gill, Patrick – *The Laughing Lightweight*
Elliott, William J. – *The K.O.*

1349. MELVILLE, Don
The Fighting Sportsman
The Adventures of a Sporting Baronet.
(Fiction Library No.47)
London, Fiction House Ltd., 1941.
Blue paper covers.

1350. MEMBER OF TATTERSALLS, A.
Tales of the Turf and the Ring
Drawings by H.M. Bateman.
London and Kingswood, The World's Work (1913) Ltd., 1936.
Dedicated with respect and admiration to the Right Honourable Lord Hamilton of Dalziell, K.T.
The section entitled "Tales of the Ring" includes the following chapters:

Chapter 1 — "The First Fight for the Pictures" (Jim Corbett and Peter Courtenay Sept. 7th, 1894)
Chapter 2 — "The Autography of Jem Mace"
Chapter 3 — "When the Fist Beat the Gun" (Nelson v. Gans at Goldfield, etc.)
Chapter 4 — "Carson City, March 17th, 1897" (Corbett v. Fitzsimmons)
Chapter 5 — "The Killing of Jimmy Elliott".

1351. MENDOZA, Daniel P.P. (Professional Pugilist)
The Art of Boxing, with a statement of the Transactions that have passed between Mr.

continued

Humphreys and Myself since our Battle at Odiham.

Printed and sold for Daniel Mendoza, 1789.

xi, 95pp. One plate showing a pugilist in Action.

1352. MENDOZA, Daniel

The Modern Art of Boxing. As Practised by Mendoza, Humphreys, Ryan, Ward, Watson, Johnson, etc, etc,

London, Printed for the author and sold at No.42 Little Britain, sold also by C. Stalker, Stationers Court and T. Axtell, Royal Exchange (1790). A New Edition.

There are 8 chapters and a frontis, which bears the caption "The First Position or setting-to of Humphreys and Mendoza at Stilton". The chapters are headed as follows:

1. Of the Requisites to form a Good Boxer
2. The Rules Necessary to be Observed
3. Of the Several Sorts of Blows, and Their Probable Effect
4. Of Closing and Throwing
5. Different Methods of Training
6. A Short Explanation of the Technical Terms Used Among Boxers.
7. Mendoza's Treatise, with the Six Lessons (Also including "Rules of Boxing")
8. A Circumstantial Account of the Battle between Humphreys and Mendoza at Stilton.

As this book is stated to be a "New Edition" it is possible that it was a later edition of *The Art of Boxing* by Daniel Mendoza (1789) q.v.

1353. MENDOZA, Daniel

Memoirs of the Life of Daniel Mendoza, etc. etc. A New Edition.

London, Printed for D. Mendoza by G. Hayden, Covent Garden, 1816.

A cardboard bound volume of 320pp. being the autobiography of D. Mendoza including his numerous contests, anecdotes of distinguished characters, observations of pugilism, Rules for Training, etc. There was a new edition of a book under this title, edited by Paul Magriel and published by B.T. Batsford in 1951 (q.v.)

1354. MENDOZA, Daniel

Cautions to the Amateurs of Pugilism
ca. 1823.

A review of this item, with extracts, is printed in *The Sportsman's Magazine or Chronicle of Sports and Pastimes* Vol. II (Feb.1824), in the section entitled "Review of New Sporting Works". The review consists of five pages.
Mention of the Mendoza items is also included in an article by Jon Bee in *The Fancy Gazette* for April (*Annals of Sporting*, Vol.III No.17), May, 1823.

1355. MENKE, Frank G.
(Compiler and Editor)

All Sports Record Book
New York City. All Sports Record Book Inc. 1930-1936.

This record book appeared annually from 1930 to 1936. Each issue included a section on boxing. These sections included Facts about Prize-Fighting, The Roll of Champions, Boxing Laws of America, British Bare-Knuckle Champions, details of champions through the various weights and other similar entries.

1356. MENKE, Frank G.

Encyclopedia of Sports
New York, Published by the author, 1939

1939= 319pp. 1944 = 628pp. 1953 = 1018pp.
Contains a section on boxing, which includes the following:

Early facts about Prize-Fighting and Boxing
National Association Members (1938)
Roll of Heavyweight Champions
Jack Dempsey's Ring earnings
Roll of Champions under various Rules

1357. MENKE, Frank G.

The New Encyclopedia of Sports
New York, A. S. Barnes and Co. 1947.

Dedicated "To John T. O'Neil, San Antonio, Texas, and Louis B. O'Neil, Missouri, Montana and Los Angeles; Sportsmen and Gentlemen.
Bound in red cloth, yellow lettering on front cover. 1007pp.
Contains a section on boxing, including:

Introduction – Mainly Historical
Broughton's and Marquess of Queensberry Rules
Roll of Champions
Data on Fistic Greats
Ring Names – Real Names
Ring Earnings – of various Champions
Lists of Famous boxing Promoters and Managers

There are also many other articles and statistics.

1358. M.E.P. BOOKSHOP (Publishers)

Boxing Self Taught
Wellington (New Zealand), 1947.

Twelve illustrated lessons based on the best advice of World's Champions; All the fundamentals in the Art of Self Defence.
Illustrated instructional. Price 2s 6d.

1359. MERRILL, Walter Anthony

"K.O.". A Novel.

Printed in U.S.A. by Keystone Publishing Co. Inc. 1933.

continued

First edition limited to 1000 copies.

Bound in light grey boards.
The book is dedicated by the author to James J. Jeffries.
The Foreword is by Dan Tobey, who states "in my opinion 'K.O.' is the most original story of the great profession of boxing that it has been my privilege to read".
(Dan Tobey was a famous boxing announcer, and a familiar figure to boxing fans)

1360. MEYERS, Harold (Editor)

The Big Fights
Eye-witness stories by Arthur Brisbane, Arthur "Bugs" Baer, James Cannon, Bob Considine, Bill Corum, Robert Edgren, Bob Fitzsimmons, Gene Fowler, Frank Graham, Hype Igoe, Dan Parker, Westbrook Pegler, Damon Runyon, etc.
With a thrilling album of the greatest fight action photos.
New York, Avon Publishing Co. Inc., 1950.
160pp. Stiff paper covers. Picture of Dempsey v. Gibbons on front cover.

1361. MEYNELL, Miss Viola (Editor)

A Memoir of Julian Grenfell
London, Burns and Oates, May, 1920.
37pp.
The boxing item from the above work was first published in *The Dublin Review* in January, 1917, and was issued as a reprint by Burns and Oates in April, 1917, and then reissued in Miss Meynell's book as above.
The extract consists of an account of a fight in which he was involved, by Julian Grenfell in a letter from South Africa when his regiment was stationed in that country.
Bohun Lynch, in the *Sporting and Dramatic News*, dated January 26th, 1926, quoted the extract as "The best account of a fight I ever read, for simplicity and directness".

1362. MICHELSON, Vic (Compiler)

The *Tribune* Boxing Annual, 1947.
Johannesburg, *The Weekly Tribune*
48pp. Illus.

1363. Miles, C. W. (Editor)

They're Off! A Journalistic Record of Sports By Leading Writers of the Press
Edited by C. W. Miles, with a Foreword by The Right Hon. The Earl of Derby, K.G.
London, Dennis Archer, 1934.
278pp. Illus.
Includes a section on boxing by James Butler.
There are mentions of boxing in the Epilogue by Percy Rudd.

The illustrations include one of Len Harvey.

1364. MILES, H.D. (H.D.M.)

A Handbook of Boxing and Training for Athletic Sports
London, W.M. Clark, 1838.

1365. MILES, Henry Downes

Pugilistica
Being One Hundred and Forty Four Years of the History of British Boxing — The Only Complete and Chronological History of the Ring, from Figg and Broughton, 1719-1740, to the Championship Battle of King and Heenan, in December, 1863.
There appears to have been at least five issues of this work, as follows:
1. One volume, issued in 1866, published for the proprietor, at the office of the *Sporting Life*, London, 1866. 499pp. Illus.

2. Twenty monthly parts, issued by Weldon & Co. London, 1880.

3. Three volumes, issued by Weldon and Co.,
London, 1880. Vol. 1 — 499pp., Vol II — 538pp., Vol. III — 528pp. Illus.

4. Three volumes, published by John Grant, Edinburgh, 1906. These are similar in text and plates to Item 3 above, except for slight variations, mentioned later. The pagination of these is the same as in the Weldon volumes.

5. An American edition, Miles, H D., *Pugilistica*, 20 parts, 1880.

Before giving information on the volumes, it should be mentioned that H.D. Miles was a versatile and prolific writer. His credentials are given on the title-page of *Pugilistica* as follows:
"Many years Ring Reporter to the *London Daily Press* and *Bell's Life in London*, Editor of the *Sportsman's Magazine*, Author of the *Book of Field Sports, English Country Life*, etc."
Among the other works from the pen of Mr. Miles were *The Life of Grimaldi* (1838), *Dick Turpin* (1845), *The Anglo-Indian Word Book* (1858), and *Miles' Modern Practical Farrier* (1863-1864).
Due to the scarcity of the single volume dated 1863, there is sometimes doubt expressed regarding its existence. An illustration of the title-page is shown in the present work, where it will be noted

continued

that it is designated Volume 1, thus indicating that there was at that time an intention to issue further volumes. For some reason the work was held over until its appearance in parts and in three volumes in 1880, with the history completed up to the year 1863.

The texts of the single 1866 volume and the first volume of the set issued in 1880 are the same; however, the 1880 issue carries a Preface not given in the earlier volume.

Regarding the 3-volume sets, these are occasionally found in the form of bound-up weekly parts. These sets are identifiable as they contain the bound-in green paper covers, each bearing a picture of a pugilist or a subject of pugilistic interest.

The sets issued by Weldon in 1880 and by Grant in 1906 are very similar in content; the bindings are different in that the 1906 edition is bound in a cloth of lighter brown than that of the earlier set, and that the books are of a slightly larger format. The gilt decorations on the covers are the same in both cases; these consist of a picture of Humphries and Mendoza on the front cover, and a portrait of Gentleman Jackson on the spine.

An inscription on the covers of the volumes state that they contain one hundred portraits and illustrations. This is not correct, as there are only sixty-one plates in the Weldon set and sixty-three in that issued by John Grant.

As may be anticipated in a work consisting of more than 1,500 pages, covering a period of 144 years of the history of boxing, these volumes give comprehensive coverage of the period under review – probably the most comprehensive of all the similar works.

1366. MILFORD, L. S.
Haileybury College – Past and Present
London, T. Fisher Unwin, 1909.

340pp. Bound in red cloth with gilt lettering on front cover and spine.
Chapter XIV, "The Gymnasium and School of Arms", includes some reference to boxing, and says (*inter alia*) "We were equally successful at Boxing".
The illustrations include one of a group outside the Old School of Arms, two of the group wearing boxing gloves.

1367. MILLARD, Joseph
The Wickedest Man
The Extraordinary Story of the "Gentleman from Hell"
London, Frederick Muller Ltd (A Gold Medal Original) (1960)

160pp. Paperback
The fictionalised biography of Ben Hogan, 19th century American prize-fighter.

1368. MILLER, Colonel Harvey L., U.S.M.C.
Would You Call This Murder?
Washington D.C., Published by the author, 1951.
21 chapters.

This book is a reply to the anti-boxing lobby; the author states his case in support of the sport.

1369. MILLER, John (Publisher)
The Literary Expose, and Fashionable Proteus
London, 1823.
Being a New Series continued from No.6 of *The Literary Humbug and Weekly Take In*
See under Chappell and Sons' *The Literary Humbug*

1370. MILLER, Margery
Joe Louis, American
New York, A.A. Wynn, 1945.
London, Panther Books, 1956.
(Paper Boards)
157pp. Illus.
A contemporary review describes this book as "vivid, authentic and portraying Louis, a fine American".
The English edition of this book is entitled *Brown Bomber – the Life Story of Joe Louis* (q.v.)

1371. MILLER, Margery
Brown Bomber – The Life Story of Joe Louis
London, Mark Goulden Ltd., 1946.
This is the English edition of Margery Miller's *Joe Louis – American.*
Coloured paper covers with a portrait of Joe Louis on the front cover.
The 28 chapters are similarly-titled to those in the American edition. There are 16 illustrations, differing slightly from those in the original edition.

1372. MILLHAUSER, Bertram, and BEULAH, Marie Dix
Hot Leather
(the Life of Jimmy Dolan)
Copyright 1938 by the Macauley Company.
New York, Bantam Books, 1948.
151pp. Paper covers.
Originally published as *The Life of Jimmy Dolan*

1373. MILLIER, W.H.
Francois Descamps
(*Boxing* Handbooks, Personalities of the Ring, No.1)
London, Fleetway Press (1930) Ltd., 1934.
32pp. Paper covers

1374. MILLS, Freddie
Twenty Years
An Autobiography
London, Nicholson and Watson Ltd., 1950.

continued

(There were a number of reprints of the book in the following years)

212pp. Illus.
Bound in black cloth, lettered in white on front cover and spine. Foreword by W. Barrington Dalby.
The book traces Freddie Mills' career from his early days in the fight game to the loss of his World Title to Joey Maxim and his retirement. The final chapter gives Freddie's Thoughts on the Fight Game.

1375. MILLS, Freddie
Freddie Mills' Boxing Annual for Boys
London, Andrew Dakers, ca.1950.

95pp. Card covers, Illus.
Includes articles by George Whiting, Charlie Rose, Harry Carpenter, etc.

1376. MILLS, Freddie
Battling for a Title
London, Stanley Paul and Co. Ltd., 1954.
186pp. Illus.

1377. MILLS, Freddie
Learn Boxing With Me
London, Nicholas Kaye Ltd., 1955.
143pp. Illus. with line drawings.

1378. MILLS, Freddie
Forward the Light Heavies
London, Stanley Paul and Co. Ltd., 1956.
222pp. Illus.

1379. MINGAUD, Edward
Life and Adventures of James Ward
Viewed as "The Champion" and as "The Artist".
Published by James Ward, 1882.
The date of this item has also been given as 1853.

1380. MINTER, Alan
Minter
An Autobiography
London, Queen Anne Press, 1980.
184pp. Illus.

1381. MIRROR OF LIFE (Publishers)
Life and Battles of J. J. Corbett
Illustrated by Portraits of the Principal Pugilists whom Corbett has beaten, and descriptions of the Battles.
London, 1904.

1382. MITCHELL, Charles
Art of Boxing
New York, Street and Smith, 1891.
82pp. Illus.
Also appeared as number 22 in Street's Manual Library, as the *Manual of Boxing*, 1893.

1383. MITCHELL, Charlie
Manual of Boxing
New York, Dick and Fitzgerald, 1893.
See also *Art of Boxing* by the same author, 1891.

1384. MITCHELL, Elmer D. (Editor)
Sports for Recreation and How to Play Them
By the Staff of the Intermural Sports Department, University of Michigan
New York, A. S. Barnes and Co. Inc., 1946.
This book covers a wide range of subject matter, including boxing. A section covers the place of boxing in the programme, boxing hints and a bibliography.
There are 12 instructional cuts in the text.

1385. MITCHELL, Ray
The Fighting Sands
Sydney, Horwitz Publications Inc. Pty. Ltd., 1965.
130pp. Paper covers. Illus.
This book traces the careers of the members of the Great Australian boxing family; Clem, Ritchie, Dave, George, Alfie and Russell Sands.

1386. MITCHELL, Ray
Ray Mitchell's Boxing Quiz
Sydney (N.S.W.), Horwitz Publications Inc. Pty. Ltd., 1966.
190pp. Paper covers. Illus.

1387. MITCHELL, Ray
Fight for Your Life
Death in the Ring. Ray Mitchell probes boxing's bloody past.
Sydney, Scripts Pty. Ltd., 1967.
First published in New Zealand, and simultaneously in Australia.
130pp. Paper covers, Illus.
The Dedication reads — "To all those boxers who died so unnecessarily, and to those who have helped boxing".

1388. M'LEAN, Thomas (Publisher)
The Sporting Repository
Originally printed in London by W. Lewis

continued

for Thomas M'Lean, 1822.

This publication first appeared monthly and ran to 6 issues from January to June, 1822; it covered a number of sports including Horse Racing, Hunting, Coursing, Shooting and Pugilism.

There were 19 coloured lithographic plates by H. Alken, and I. Barrenger; none of these were of boxing interest.

The work was reissued in 1904 in an edition limited to 500 copies. The publisher in this case was Kegan Paul, Trench, Trubner and Co. Ltd. The text of the 1904 edition is similar to that of the original, but some of the original plates were left out and substituted by others, one of the latter being a plate of Molineux (The Prize-Fighter) by Dighton.

The new issue was bound in green cloth with gilt titles on the spine and a design of a huntsman on the front cover.

Each of the 6 issues (Vol.I numbers I to VI), bound into one volume, include pugilistic items, such as results of matches, reports and parodies in verse.

1389. MOFFATT, Frederick C.

Linament (sic) and Leather
Sixty Years of the Fight Game in the North.
Morpeth, Published by the author. N/date, (ca. 1980)

50pp. Stiff paper covers. Illus.
In his little book, the author revives memories of Northern Boxers, their battles, and the fight venues. He recalls the days when almost every street in those cities and towns held its quota of brave, ringwise fighters.

The book is well illustrated; it includes the records of some of the boxers.

1390. MOIR, Gunner

(Heavyweight Champion of the British Army etc.)

The Complete Boxer
London, *Health and Strength* Library, 1908.
Second Edition 1909.

79pp.
Red paper covers with a picture of the author on the front. Also issued in blue cloth.
Many instructional illustrations.
There were further editions of this book, one issued by *Boxing* in 1919.

1391. MOISEWITCH, Maurice

The Hands of Woolf Sarasan
This boxing story appeared in *Penguin Parade No. 7*, 1940; published by Penguin Books, Harmondsworth, Middx.

1391A. MOLEN, Sam

The Mid-West's number One Sports Commentator

They Make Me Laugh

A Collection of Stories and Anecdotes About the Greats and Also-Rans of Sport.

Laugh at — Tony Galento, Frank Gotch, Benny Leonard, Jack Dempsey, Jim Thorpe and scores of others.

Philadelphia, Dorrance and Co., Publishers, 1947.

210pp.

1392. MONAGHAN, Paddy

Black Crusoe, White Friday
London, Satellite Books, 1979.

103pp. Illus.
The story of the No.1 Muhammad Ali fan in the U.K.

1393. MONTGOMERY, Robin Navarro

Cut'n Shoot Texas. The Roy Harris Story.
Austin (Texas), Easkin Press, 1984.

180pp. Illus.

1394. MOON, Buckley (Editor)

Champs and Bums
Extracts from Hemingway, Jack London, Budd Schulberg, etc.
New York, Lion Books, 1954.

Paper covers.

1395. MOONEY, Bernard F.

Boxing for Beginners
(M. & M. Publishing Company's Sports Series No.2)
Columbus (Ohio), M. and M. Publishing Co., 1936.

Price one dollar.

1396. MOORE, Archie

The Archie Moore Story
London, Nicholas Kaye, 1960.

240pp. plus Moore's record.
The autobiography was also issued in a Sportsmans Book Club edition.

1397. MOORE, Archie, and LEONARD, Pearl

Any Boy Can. The Archie Moore Story.
Eaglewood Cliffs (New Jersey), Prentice Hall Inc., 1971.

303pp. including Moore's record.

1398. MOORE, Thomas

Tom Cribb's Memorial to Congress
With a Preface, Notes and Appendix.
By One of the Fancy.
London, Printed for Longman, Hurst, Rees,

continued

Orme and Brown, 1819.

There were 2nd, 3rd and 4th editions published in the same year, the title-pages are the same except for the number of the edition shown thereon.

This item is a small book of verse; there were 2 issues of the 3rd edition, one with 4 pages of advertisement at the commencement of the book, which is undated; the other issue of the 3rd edition carries 12 pages of adverts, and is dated April, 1819.

The text of the book is contained in pages 1 to 30 (10 chapters) and there is a 57 page appendix.

An edition was reprinted in New York in 1899 for Kirk and Mercein, C. Willey and Co., W.B. Gilley and A.T. Goodrich and Co., William A. Mercein, Printer.

The book includes very full notes on all the items, explaining pugilistic terms, etc.

1399. MORAN, Vic
Joe Mandot, the Fighting Fool
A Complete Review of Mandot's Career.
Published in U.S.A.
159pp.

1400. MORELL, Parker
Diamond Jim
The Life and Times of James Buchanan Brady.
London, Hurst and Blackett, 1935.
286pp. Illus.
John L. Sullivan is mentioned several times in this work, in chapters IV, IX, XI and XXI.
The book also includes a full-page action picture of Sullivan.

1401. MORGAN, Dan
(with McCALLUM, John)
Dumb Dan
New York, Tedson Publishing Co., 1953.
Introduction by Frank Graham, Foreword by Dan Parker.
The biography of Dan Morgan, a gentleman with a prodigious memory for fight facts and anecdotes.

1402. MORGAN, Johnny
The Square Jungle
A Boxing Novel.
London, Secker and Warburg, 1965.
192pp.

1403. MORGAN, Tom
(Sports Editor of *The People*)
Wembley Presents -- Twenty Two Years of Sport
Wembley, Published by Wembley Stadium

Ltd., 1945.
79pp.
Illustrated paper covers. Fully illustrated.
The Text contains many boxing items, including the following:

Chapter IV —	Sports Centre of the British Empire (Boxing and Ice Hockey Stars — A Gallant Boxer) (Jack Petersen)
Chapter V —	Petersen the Money Spinner
Chapter VI —	The Ride to Nowhere (The Golden Gloves)
Chapter VII —	1937 — A Great Year (World Title Fight, Benny Lynch v. Small Montana)
Chapter IX —	War Comes to Wembley (Boxing for the Red Cross)

There are a number of illustrations of boxing matches staged in the Empire Pool.

1404. MORGAN W. A.
(Compiler and Editor)
The House on Sport
By Members of The London Stock Exchange
London, Gale and Polden Ltd., 1898 (Vol. I)
470pp.
This book includes a section entitled "Boxing — The Noble Art" by B. J. Angle.
There are 13 illustrations showing portraits of boxers.

1405. MORISON, Stanley
John Bell, 1745--1831. Bookseller, Printer, Publisher. Founder or Part-Proprietor of *The Morning Post* etc.
London, The First Edition Club, 1930.
165pp.
Illustrated by portraits of John Bell (from original prints), facsimiles of John Bell's publications etc.
Gives interesting facts and details about *The Weekly Despatch, Bell's Life in London*, and publications by Pierce Egan.
There was an edition of 100 special copies, bound and printed for members of The First Edition Club, by courtesy of Mr Stanley Morison.

1406 MORRISON, Alex
Body and Soul (The Book of the Film)
Metro-Goldwyn-Mayer Release, Produced by Enterprise Studios.
London World Film Publication Ltd. (In association with Hollywood Publications)
94pp. With additional matter, including description of the film and actors.
Stiff illustrated paper cover.
The star of the film was John Garfield.

continued

1407. MORRISON, Arthur
Tales of Mean Streets
London, Methuen and Co. Ltd., 1894.
301pp.
Bound in green cloth, gilt titles on front cover and spine.
This book includes a story on boxing entitled "Three Rounds".

1408. MORRISON, Ian
Guinness Boxing Records
Enfield, Guinness Superlatives, 1986.
168pp. Paper covers. Illus.

1409. MORRISON, Morie
Here's How in Sports
Garden City, New York, Doubleday and Co. Inc., 1948.
This book is by a veteran sports writer who offers an unusual method of instruction consisting of short captions illustrated by line drawings, includin tips on how to improve your boxing. There is also material on training methods and how to avoid injury.

1410. MORTON, H.V.
The Nights of London (A Book of Essays)
London, Methuen and Co., 1926.
194pp.
This includes an essay entitled "The Gladiators" on the subject of boxing.

1411. MOTT, Edward Spencer
(Nathaniel Gubbins)
A Mingled Yarn (Autobiography)
London, Edward Arnold, 1898.
In chapter XXVIII "More Turf Celebrities", the author asserts that J.C. Heenan was drugged in his fight with Tom King.

1412. MOTTRAM, R. H.
Old England
(Illustrated by English Paintings of the 18th and early 19th Century)
London, The Studio Limited, 1937.
New York, Studio Publications Inc., 1937.
Chapter XI, "Sports and Games" includes a section on boxing. The illustrations include No.45, The Boxing Match between Richard Humphries and Daniel Mendoza at Odiham, January 9th, 1788.

1413. MOULT, Thomas
Great Stories of Sport
London, Leonard Stein (with Victor Gollancz Ltd), 1931.
602pp. Bound in red cloth
Includes a section "Knuckles and Gloves" (pages 25 to 106), which gives extracts from the works of William Hazlitt, George Borrow, Pierce Egan, Jack London and A. Conan Doyle.

1414. MULDOWNEY, T. (Editor)
Seconds Out: Round 2
Dublin, Libra House, ca.1980.
60pp. Paperback, Illus.

1415. MUMFORD, Clive Tregarthen
Fighters of the Old Cosmo
A History of Plymouth Boxing from 1907 to 1924.
Plymouth, Published by the author, 1975.
189pp. Stiff paper covers. Illus.

1416. MURALT, Mr
(A Gentleman of Switzerland)
Letters Describing the Characters of the English and French Nations
London, Translated from the French, printed and sold by Thomas Edlin and N. Prevost, 1726.
Letter No.3 refers to the rules and practice of box - ing.

1417. MURRAY, Jim
The Sporting World of Jim Murray
Garden City, New York, Doubleday and Co. Inc., 1968.
236pp.
There is some boxing material in this selection from the author's newspaper articles; including a section entitled "Last of the Fancy", an obituary of A. J. Liebling.

1418. MURRAY, John
(Editor of *Boxing*)
Footwork and How to Cultivate It (*Boxing* Handbook No.11)
Illustrated with Special Photographs.
London, Ewart Seymour and Co. (publishers of *Boxing*), 1909.
4 chapters, 5 Illus.

1419. MURRAY, John
(Editor of *Boxing*)
How to Train for Boxing Contests
(*Boxing* Handbook No.5)
London, Ewart Seymour and Co. Ltd., 1913.
The text consists of 4 chapters on Training Theory, The Development of Muscles and Hints on Diet. The 6 illustrations include pictures of Fred Welsh, Tommy Burns, and Packy McFarland in training.

1420. MURRAY, John
(Editor of *Boxing*)

continued

P

How a Boxing Contest is Judged. With
National Sporting Club and other
Recognised Rules.
(*Boxing* Handbook No.2)
London, Ewart Seymour and Co., 1913.
Contains 8 chapters on various aspects of refereeing and judging.
4 Illus.

1421. MURRAY, John
(Editor of *Boxing*)
How to Become a Boxer
(*Boxing* Handbook No.7)
London, Ewart Seymour and Co., 1913.
Illus.

1422. MURRAY, John
(Editor of *Boxing*)
Ring Strategy and Tactics
London, Ewart Seymour and Co. Ltd., 1914
(*Boxing* Handbook No.8)

4 Instructional chapters. 9 Illustrations showing
action pictures of famous boxers, including Packy
McFarland, Freddy Welsh, Jim Driscoll, Tommy
Burns, Digger Stanley, Joe Bowker, etc.

1423. MURRAY, John
(Editor of *Boxing*)
Favourite Ring Tricks of Boxing
Champions
(Fred Welsh, Jim Driscoll and Bombardier
Wells)
London, Ewart Seymour and Co. Ltd., 1914
(*Boxing* Handbook No.3)
Issued in two sizes at 6d and 1/- respectively
54pp. 6 Illus.
Bound in card covers.

1424. MURRAY, John
(Editor of *Boxing*)
First Lessons in Boxing
(*Boxing* Handbook No.14)
London, Ewart Seymour and Co. 1914.

1425. MURRAY, John
(Editor of *Boxing*)
The American Style and How it is Learnt
(*Boxing* Handbook No.9)
London, Ewart Seymour and Co. Ltd, 1914
Six Instructional Chapters 16 Illus.

1426. MURRAY, John (Publisher)
Adventures in British Sport
by Various Authors
(Modern English Series)

London, 1926.
The chapter on boxing is entitled "In the Ring".
It consists of an extract from Sir Arthur Conan
Doyle's *Rodney Stone* entitled "The Smith's
Last Battle".

1427. MURRAY, John (Compiler)
Boxing News Annual, 1945
London, War Facts Press.

Bound in stiff paper covers.
This was the first of a series which was
published annually from the offices of *Boxing
News*.
It contained records of British amateur and professional boxers, together with World Title
holders and the British rankings.
After the first issue the title of the annual was
changed to *Boxing News Annual and Record
Book* (q.v.)
There was also a *Boxing News Amateur Boxing
Annual*, issued under the editorship of Gilbert
Odd for the years 1948, 1950 and 1951 (q.v.)

1428. MUSEUM OF THE CITY OF NEW YORK, THE (Publishers)
The Ring and The Book
A Survey of Boxing
New York, 1947.

32pp. Stiff paper covers.
This is the catalogue of an exhibition held in the
Museum from November 9th, 1947 to April 4th,
1948.
There is an introductory article entitled "Jimmy
Walker, Fight Fan", by Edward P. F. Eagan,
Chairman, New York State Athletic Commission.
The Foreword is by Paul Magriel.
The exhibition consisted of Prints, Paintings,
Lithographs, Photographs, Sculptures and
Ceramics. Many of these were lent by Paul Magriel
from his collection.

1429. MUSPRATT, Eric
Ambition
London, Gerald Duckworth, 1924.
328pp.
An Autobiographical Novel, with the author as
the hero (thinly disguised). The boxing reference
occurs in the account of the author sparring with
the Australian Heavyweight Champion.

1430. MUYBRIDGE, Edward
The Human Figure in Motion. An Electro-
Photographic Investigation of Consecutive
Phases of Muscular Actions.
London, Chapman and Hall Ltd, 1907.
Copyright 1901 by the author.

This book, commenced 1872 and completed in
1885, shows the first consecutive action pictures
of Athletes.
Includes on page 223 — Some Phases of a Boxing
Match. (Two lines, each showing three pictures)

1431. MYLER, Patrick
Regency Rogue
Dan Donnelly, His Life and Legends.
Dublin, O'Brien Press, 1976.
159pp.

1432. MYLER, Patrick
The Fighting Irish
Dingle (Ireland), Brandon, 1985.
250pp. Illus.
Includes a bibliography and an index.

TOM SAYERS,

SOMETIME CHAMPION OF ENGLAND,

HIS LIFE

AND PUGILISTIC CAREER.

CONTAINING

THE WHOLE OF HIS BATTLES, FROM CONTEMPORARY REPORTS;
PERSONAL ANECDOTES; AND THE LITERATURE OF
THE GREAT FIGHT AT FARNBOROUGH

FROM

The 'Times,' 'Punch,' 'All the Year Round,' the 'Saturday Review,' &c.

EDITED BY

THE AUTHOR OF "PUGILISTICA."

LONDON:
S. O. BEETON, 248, STRAND.
1866.

Title-Page *Tom Sayers, Champion of England* (Philopugilist) (Bib. Ref. 1553)

1433. NAGLER, Barney

James Norris and the Decline of Boxing
Indianapolis, The Bobbs Merrill Co. Inc.,
1964.

249pp.
Looks at the state of the boxing game against
the background of monopolistic promoters, fixed
fighters, and the infiltration of mobsters into the
sport.

1434. NAGLER, Barney

Brown Bomber, The Pilgrimage of Joe
Louis
New York, The World Publishing Co., 1972.
Published simultaneously in Canada by
Nelson, Foster and Scott Ltd.

235pp. Illus.

1435. NAIDOO, Bobby

20 Years, the Story of the World Boxing
Council
Weybridge (Surrey), Bobby Naidoo Assoc-
iates Ltd., 1983.

274pp. Illus.
This book, as its title suggests, covers the first
two decades of the existence of the WBC.

1436. NATIONAL UNION OF BOXERS, THE

The Boxer's Bulletin
(The Official Organ of the National Union of
Boxers)
President, Jimmy Wilde, Vice-President, Len
Harvey, Secretary Harry A. Fowler.

There were eight issues of this Bulletin; the first
seven in printed form, price 2d, and the last in
typescript, Price 1d.
Vol 1, No.1 appeared in July, 1936 and the final
issue was for May–June, 1937.

1437. NATTY, Bill

The Complete Second
London, Ewart Seymour and Co. Ltd.,
ca. 1900 (*Boxing* Handbook No.1). Seven
Chapters from 'The Elements of a Good
Second" to "After the Contest is Over".
Illus.
The Author acted as Principal Second in many
Championship contests of his period.

1438. NAUGHTON, W. W.

The Fight of the Century
An Album of the Contest at Carson, March,
1897.
(Fitzsimmons v. Corbett)
Published in America, 1897.

1439. NAUGHTON, W. W.

(America's Best Known Sports Authority)
Kings of the Queensberry Realm
Being an Account of every Heavyweight
Championship Contest Held in America
under Queensberry Rules. A Sketch of every
Contestant who has taken part therein and
an account of the Invasion of Australian
Boxers, Together with a Defence of Boxing,
a Comparison of Old Methods of Boxing and
Training with Those in Vogue Today, and a
Comparative Ring Record of Heavyweight
Pugilists.
Chicago, The Continental Publishing Co.,
1902.

315pp.
32 Illustrations. Bound in green cloth with inset
portrait of Jim Jeffries on the front cover.
This book is divided into parts, as follows:

Part I –   The Art of Self Defence

Part II –   The Invasion of America by Australian
             Pugilists

Part III –   Individual Sketches of World Champion
             ship Candidates

Part IV –   World Heavyweight Championship Con-
             tests under Queensberry Rules

1440. NAUGHTON, W. W.

Heavyweight Champions
San Francisco, California News Co., 1912.

208pp.
Gives a graphic description of every heavyweight
Championship contest from Sullivan and Corbett
to Jeffries and Johnson, together with a complete
record of every contestant. Extended fighting
life sketches of both Johnson and Jeffries – the
story of the making of the match and the original
articles of agreement.

1441. NEILL, Bobby
(In Collaboration with Bill Martin)

Instructions to Young Boxers
London, Museum Press, 1961.

128pp. Illus.

1442. NEILSON, Harry B.

Auld-Lang-Syne
Recollections and Rural Records of Old
Laughton, Birkenhead and Bidston, with
other Reminiscences.
Birkenhead, Willmer Brothers and Co. Ltd.,
1935.

296pp. Illus.
Contains a section entitled "Sports and Pastimes"
with a section on boxing.

1443. NELSON, Battling

Life, Battles and Career of Battling Nelson, Lightweight Champion of the World. By Himself.

Hegewisch (Illinois), Published by the author 1908.

264pp.

Bound in grey cloth, lettered in green, with cartoon illustrations on the front cover.

The illustrations include cartoons by 'Tad' (T.A. Dorgan) and by Robert Edgren.

The Introduction speaks of Nelson as the richest pugilist in the World, telling of his progress in the ring and the shrewd investment of his earnings.

The 25 chapters relate the story of the author's career, from his birth in Denmark on June 5th, 1882, to his victory over Joe Gans to become the undisputed Lightweight Champion of the World.

The book includes stories of Nelson's career by various contributers, including W. J. (Spike) Slattery, Jack London, R. H. Guelich, and others.

In addition to the 'Tad' and Edgren caroons there are a number of photographic illustrations; these include pictures of Eugene Corri and R. P. Watson, the English Referees.

1444. NEVILL, Ralph

Old Sporting Prints

(*Connoisseur* Extra Number)

London, *The Connoisseur Magazine*, 1908.

67 reproductions of prints; none on boxing.

The list entitled "A Few Exceptionally Attractive Prints" contains a section "Boxing"; this includes details of some 34 items.

There are also a few boxing items in the section "A Record of the Principal Sporting Prints Sold by Auction 1901–1908", by Mr. G. Menzies.

1445. NEVILL, Ralph

Sporting Days and Sporting Ways

London, Duckworth and Co., 1910.

313pp. Illus.

This book contains many references to pugilists and the prize-ring, particularly in Chapters V, VI and VII; the last two being wholly devoted to the subject.

The chapters include some legendary names from the bare-knuckle period, including Broughton, John Gully, Gentleman Jackson, Langan, Mendoza, Sayers v. Heenan, Shaw the Lifeguardsman and others.

The venues mentioned include the Fives Court and The Castle Tavern.

1446. NEVILL, Ralph

Old English Sporting Books

Edited by Geoffrey Holme.

London *The Studio* Ltd., 1924.

The contents of this book consist of a Prefatory Note, and Introduction, a Bibliography and 107 reproduced plates; 24 of the plates are coloured.

The bibliography contains a number of items of pugilistic interest, including the works of Pierce Egan, Henry Lemoine, Thomas Fewtrell and others. Information is also given on Sporting Periodicals such as *The Annals of Sporting, The Fancy, The Sporting Magazine*, etc.

5 of the plates (including 2 coloured) are of boxing interest.

1447. NEVILLE, Bob

Who's Who in Sports.

Interesting Facts About more than 600 celebrities.

New York, Modern Sports Publishing Co., 1931.

Magazine size, paper covers, Profusely illus.

The boxing section includes short biographies of Jack Dempsey, Max Schmeling and Gene Tunney.

1448. NEWBOLD, George (Publisher)

Life of Tom Sayers

(Retired Champion of England)

London, 1860.

Bound in reddish/brown cloth, gilt lettering on front cover.

This book gives a full account of all Sayers' battles, Verbatim from *The Times, Bell's Life in London*, and other journals; with letters from both Sayers and Heenan written to *The Times* after their historic contest.

There is also a key plate to Newbold's Giant Representation of the Sayers-Heenan contest. This Representation contained upwards of 250 portraits of pugilists, patrons and other connections of the ring, from specially taken photographs.

The text of this work is identical with that of *The History of the Great International Contest between Heenan and Sayers, Farnborough, on the 17th April 1860*. (George Newbold) (q.v.)

1449. NEWBOLD, George (Publisher)

History of the Great International Contest Between Heenan and Sayers, at Farnborough on 17th April, 1860

London, Printed by J. Miles, 1860.

Bound in light brown cloth.

This item gives the History of the Contest, including the Full Reports from *The Times*, Dickens' *All the Year Round, Punch*, etc., with biographies and histories of the combatants.

Among the illustrations is a folding plate showing Newbold's Representation of the contest, containing upwards of 250 portraits from photos specially taken for this work. There is also a Key to Newbold's representation, each portrait on the key being numbered for identification of the people on the main picture.

1450. NEWBURY, Harold
World Champions. A Pictorial Review.
London, The Howes Publishing Co., 1950.
Illustrated paper covers, Price 6d.
This book contains an article, with illustrations, covering all the current World Boxing Champions.

1451. NEWCOMBE, Jack
Floyd Patterson, An Original Life Story
U.S.A., Bartholomew House, 1961.
159pp

1452. NEWMAN, Gordon
The Streetfighter
London, W. H. Allen and Co. Ltd., 1975.
(A Star Book)
220pp. Paperback.
A Novel based on the screenplay by Walter Hall, Bryan Gendoff, and Bruce Henstell, made into a Columbia picture, starring Charles Bronson.

1453. NEWMARKET (Pseud.)
Chapters from Turf History
London, Published at the *National Review*, 1922.
159pp Illus. Including a portrait of John Gully.
Chapter IV is entitled "The Ring, The Turf and Parliament" (Mr. John Gully).

1454. NEWTON, Andrew, Junior
(England's Premier Boxing Instructor and Straight from the Shoulder Critic)
Guide For Beginners. Learn How to Box.
Training Methods, Guards, Blows, etc.
London, Published by the author, 1945.
52pp. Stiff paper covers, with picture on the front, "Professor Newton instructing Nipper (Pat) Daly".

1455. NEWTON, A. J.
Boxing (With a Section on the Singlestick)
London, C. Arthur Pearson, 1904 and 1907.
123pp. Illus.
The author was Amateur Lightweight Champion of England, 1888 and 1890.

1456. NEWTON, H. Chance ("Carados" of the
Referee)
Cues and Curtain Calls
The Theatrical Reminiscenes of the Author.
With an Introduction by Sir Johnston Forbes Robertson.
London, John Lane, The Bodley Head, 1927.
292pp. Illus.

Although this is mainly a theatrical item it also includes references to well known pugilists who performed in the theatre; notably Tom Sayers and Jem Mace.

1457. NEW YORK STATE LEGISLATURE
(Publishers)
Report of the Joint Legislative Committee on Professional Boxing
Albany, (N.Y.), 1963.
88pp.
Legislative Document, 1963. No.83

1458. NEW YORK *WORLD-TELEGRAM*, THE
(Publishers)
The World Almanack and Book of Facts
New York City, Published Annually, Commencing 1885.
This issue for 1944, the 59th year of publication includes:
Sporting Events of 1943 and Records; contains a section devoted to Boxing, this is divided into sub-sections as follows:

Boxing Champions by Classes
Ring Champions of the Past (with weights)
Joe Louis and His Record of 57 Ring Contests
History of the Heavyweight Championship Bouts
Largest Championship Battle Gate Receipts
Amateur Boxing in 1943
Golden Gloves Championships, 1943
Boxing Results in 1943.

1459. NICKALLS, G. O. (Editor)
With the Skin of Their Teeth
Memories of Great Sporting Finishes in Golf, Cricket, Rugby and Association Football, Lawn Tennis, Boxing, Athletics, Rowing, and Horse Racing.
Recalled by Bernard Darwin, Herbert Sutcliffe, G. H. Gadney, Bernard Joy, John Olliff, Harold Abrahams, G. O. Nickalls and Geoffrey Gilbey.
London, *Country Life* Ltd., 1951.
168pp. Illus.
The Boxing section includes the following fights, by Barrington Dalby:

Bombardier Wells v. Georges Carpentier (First fight at Ghent, 1/6/1913)
Against All the Odds (Jack Roberts v. Will Curley, at the N.S.C., 21/1/1901)
A Fight that Made History (Jack Meekins v. Arthur Evernden, at Camberwell Baths, 25/10/1909)
Almost Out – But Won (Joe Fox v. Eugene Criqui, at Holland Park Rink 29/5/1922)
A Great Heavyweight Fight (Larry Gains v. Don McCorkindale, at the Royal Albert Hall 3/3/1932)
The Killer Instinct (Jack Petersen v. Charlie Smith,
continued

at Cardiff, 28/3/1932)
The Mizler Classic (Harry Mizler v. Gustave Humery, at the Royal Albert Hall, 2/10/1935)
A Memorable Evening at the White City (Len Harvey v. Jock McAvoy 10/7/1939)

There are 6 illustrations showing some of these fights.

1460. NICHOLS, Beverley

Twenty Five. An Autobiography.
London, Jonathan Cape Ltd., 1926.
(Reprinted a number of times from 1926 to 1929)

The boxing interest is in Chapter XV: "Two Artists in a Different Sphere" – Interviews with Pachmann and Georges Carpentier.

1461. NICHOLS, Beverley

Oxford – London – Hollywood
An Omnibus, containing *Twenty Five, Are They the Same at Home* and *The Star Spangled Banner.*
London, Jonathan Cape, 1931.
Reprinted 1932, 1934, 1935 and 1938.

See separate entries under *Twenty Five* and *Are They the Same at Home.*

1462. NICHOLS, Beverley

Are They the Same at Home?
London, Jonathan Cape, September, 1937.
Reprinted three times in the same year.

349pp.
Also included in an omnibus volume: *Oxford – London – Hollywood*, in 1931. q.v.
Includes in Chapter LXI "Georges Carpentier, or why do they do it".

1463. NICHOLSON, Geoffrey

The Professionals
London, Andre Deutsch Ltd., 1964.

219pp. Illus. (2 associated with boxing)
A general sporting book by a journalist; the chapter on boxing is entitled "You're born with your fists closed".

1464. NICHOLSON, Renton

Boxing
With a Chronology of the Ring and a Memoir of Owen Swift.
London, Published at 163 Fleet Street, 1837.

1465. NICHOLSON, William

An Almanack of Twelve Sports
With Verses by Rudyard Kipling
London, William Heinemann, 1898.

First English Edition, including a calendar for the year and Nicholson's twelve coloured illustrations. A Library Edition was also issued, printed on Japanese vellum.
New York, R. H. Russell, 1898.
Small Folio, with pictorial cloth binding.

Another U.S. Edition was issued in 1899 with a calendar for 1900.
A Copyright Edition, verses only, was issued in U.S.A. by Bill Bradley at the Wayside Press, Springfield, Massachusetts, for William Heinemann, in 1897.

The boxing reference is in the calendar entry and the plate for November. This shows a boxing match between a white and a coloured boxer, with an appropriate verse.
All the verses and plates were included in Rudyard Kipling's *Verses*, Inclusive Edition, published by Hodder and Stoughton, London, 1919, in three volumes, the heading being "Verses and Games, an Almanack of Twelve Sports".

1466. NICKERSON, Kate

Ringside Jezebel
New York, Macfadden-Bartell Corporation, 1953.

160pp. Paperback (Fiction)

1467. NIMROD

(Charles James Apperley)
My Life and Times
Edited and with Additions by E. D. Cuming
London and Edinburgh, William Blackwood and Sons, 1927.
New York, Charles Scribner's Sons, 1927.

This book contains 28 chapters, the illustrations include 2 coloured plates of Nimrod. The chapters XX to XXVIII are headed "Additions".
There are some references to pugilism as follows:
Chapter XXIV – tells (*inter alia*) of Nimrod travelling the country as a reporter for the *Sporting Magazine* in which role he attended the fight between Spring and Neat at Andover. As well as reporting on the fight he expressed doubts on the expediency of prize-fighting, and also its influence on morals.

Chapter XXVI – Includes reference to Nimrod's presence at the prize-fight between Hannan and "A Provincial" which took place on the border of Leicestershire with Nottinghamshire.

1468. NISENSON, Samuel

Giant Book of Sports
Designed and Illustrated by Samual Nisenson
Text by Myron Openheiner, S. N. Nelson and Gene Schoor.

continued

Introduction by Mel Allen
Garden City, New York, Garden City Publishing Co., 1948.

187pp. Illus.
Includes sections on Baseball, Boxing and other sports.

1469. NISENSON, Sam
A Handy Illustrated Guide to Boxing
New York, Permabooks (Perma Sports) Ltd, 1949.

192pp. Coloured stiff paper covers, with picture of Joe Louis on front.
The illustrations include over 80 instructional pictures in the text. Other illustrations include Joe Louis, Henry Armstrong, Gene Tunney, Jack Sharkey, Ezzard Charles, Jake LaMotta and others. Included in the contents are a History of Boxing, Fundamentals of Boxing, and other instructional

chapters; there is also an article by Commissioner Eddie Eagan.

1470. NOEL, Baptist Wriothesley
The Fight Between Sayers and Heenan
A Letter to Noblemen and Gentlemen who attended the Fight.
London, James Nisbet and Co., 1860.
Printed by James Nisbet and Co. Edinburgh.

21pp. Price 1s.
The author was a Baptist Minister: his letter commences with a description of the fight from *The Times* and other newspapers, and continues with an attack on pugilism.

1471. NORTON, Pete
Boxing Builds Burns
Published in U.S.A, 1942.

1472. OAKELEY, Sir Atholl
Blue Blood on the Mat. The All-in Wrestling Story.
London, Stanley Paul and Co. Ltd., 1971.
163pp. Illus.
The story of a baronet who became a successful wrestler. The author, whose grandfather took a great interest in the Prize-Ring, discusses the relationship between wrestling and boxing, emanating from the time when wrestling holds and throws were permissible in the boxing ring.

1473. O'BRIEN, Brian F.
Kiwis with Gloves On
A History and Record Book of New Zealand Boxing.
Wellington, A. H. and W. Reed, 1960.
270pp. Illus.
Traces the history of the sport in New Zealand, from the early days when Jem Mace visited that country and opened a boxing school in Timaru, and the emergence of Bob Fitzsimmons as World Champion.

1474. O'BRIEN, Philadelphia Jack
(Former Light Heavyweight Champion of the World). In collaboration with S.E. Bilk, M.D. (Former World Athletic Trainer, University of Illinois)
Boxing
New York and London, Charles Scribner's Sons, 1928 and 1936.

1475. OBEYESEKERE, Danton Gammenu,
B.A. (Hons), M.A. (Trin.Coll.) Cantab.
(Cambridge University Half-Blue 1927-28-29 -30. Ceylon Amateur Welter-Weight Champion 1932-33-34-35-36)
The Scientific Art of Boxing
Colombo. *The Times* of Ceylon Co. Ltd., 1937.
Also published in London at the above Company's London Office.
Consists of 9 chapters and a 4 part Appendix, dealing with boxing in Ceylon, India and other lands; The Technique of Boxing, Training, etc.
The Appendix gives the Rules of the Amateur Boxing Association of Ceylon, and the International Amateur Boxing Federation. There is also a boxing bibliography.

1476. ODD, Gilbert, and WHITING, G. W.
(Compilers)
The Boxers Annual, 1944-45
London, The British and Colonial News Services, 1944.
64pp. Illus. Price 2s-6d.

Stiff paper covers with full-length portrait of Joe Louis on front cover.
Gilbert Odd compiled the information on professional boxing and G. W. Whiting that on amateur boxing.

1477. ODD, Gilbert E. (Editor)
Boxing News Annual and Record Book
London, War Facts Press, commencing 1946.
This was the first of the annuals to appear under the above title; the series has continued to appear each year to 1985, and it is established as a source of information for statisticians and record compilers.
Gilbert Odd continued as Editor of the *Annual* for a number of years; retirement and changes in the editorship of *Boxing News* has resulted in different names appearing on the title-page.
There were also changes in the publishing houses responsible for production of the book; it was issued under the imprints of such as Ring Publications, City Magazines, Williams Publishing, and Byblos Productions Ltd.

1478. ODD, Gilbert
Ring Battles of the Century
London, Ivor Nicholson and Watson, 1948.
243pp. Illus.
The author chooses 22 glove fights for his selection, commencing with the Carpentier v. Dempsey bout in 1921 and finishing in 1946 with Freddie Mills v. Gus Lesnevitch and Tony Zale v. Rocky Graziano.

1479. ODD, Gilbert (Editor of *Boxing News*) and KENRICK, Jim (Former Flyweight Champion of England, and Class 'A' Referee)
How to Box — All the Modern Moves
London, War Facts Press, 1950.
94pp. Stiff paper covers.
Contains a descriptive commentary and 48 diagrams.

1480. ODD, Gilbert
Was the Referee Right? Foreword by Freddie Mills.
London, Nicholson and Watson Ltd., 1952.
Each chapter looks at a boxing bout involving a controversial decision. Typical chapter headings are given as follows:

Chapter 1 — Did the Long Count Save Tunney's Title?

Chapter 3 — When Phil Scott Lost His Cahnce. (Jack Sharkey v. Phil Scott, 28th Feb. 1930)

Chapter 5 — Decision Rendered at Revolver Point (Mike McTigue v. Young Stribling,

continued

at Columbus (Georgia), 4th Oct. 1923, for the Lightheavyweight Championship of the World)

Chapter 13 — How Max Baer Beat Tom Heeney. (Madison Square Garden, 6th Jan. 1931)

1481. ODD, Gilbert
Debatable Decisions. Foreword by Freddie Mills.
London, Nicholson and Watson, 1953.
236pp. Illus.
Each of the chapters deals with a bout involving a controversial decision.

1482. ODD, Gilbert
Great Moments in Sport. Heavyweight Boxing.
London, Pelham Books, Ltd., 1973.
218pp. Illus.

1483. ODD, Gilbert
Boxing — The Great Champions
London, The Hamlyn Publishing Group Ltd., 1974.
171pp. 4to. Illus.
Gives potted biographies of 160 champions.

1484. ODD, Gilbert
Great Moments in Sport: Boxing: Cruisers to Mighty Atoms.
London, Pelham Books Ltd., 1974.
204pp. Illus.
A selection by Mr. Odd of what he regards as the most outstanding contests between boxers in all the weight divisions from light-heavyweight to flyweight.

1485. ODD, Gilbert
Ali,
The Fighting Prophet
London, Pelham Books Ltd., 1975.
(Sporting Prints Series)
96pp. Illus.

1486. ODD, Gilbert
The Fighting Blacksmith
The Story of Bob Fitzsimmons, Foreword by Len Harvey.
London, Pelham Books Ltd, 1976.
217pp. plus a bibliography and the record of Bob Fitzsimmons.

1487. ODD, Gilbert
Boxing, The Inside Story
London, Hamlyn Publishing Group Ltd., 1978.
128pp. Illus. (Some coloured)

1488. ODD, Gilbert
The Woman in the Corner
London, Pelham Books Ltd, 1978.
190pp. Illus.
Stories of the women behind the boxers.

1489. ODD, Gilbert
Len Harvey, Prince of Boxers
Foreword by Mrs Florence Harvey
London, Pelham Books Ltd., 1978.
251pp. Illus.
The Biography of a great champion.

1490. ODD, Gilbert
Encyclopedia of Boxing
London, Hamlyn Group, 1983.
Reprinted, 1984.
191pp. 4to. Illus.
Full of Facts and Figures; the book to settle all arguments on boxing.

1491. ODD, Gilbert
Kings of the Ring
100 Years of Heavyweight Boxing.
London, Newnes Books, 1985.
155pp. Stiff paper covers. 4to. Illus.

1492. ODETS, Clifford
Golden Boy. A Play in Three Acts.
London, Victor Gollancz Ltd., 1938.
125pp.
This is a presentation in book form of the boxing drama first presented in U.K. at the St. James' Theatre on June 21st, 1938.

1493. ODHAMS PRESS LTD (Publishers)
The Great Encyclopedia of Universal Knowledge
Includes short entries entitled 'Boxing' and 'Prize-Fight'; the former including a picture of a Roman Boxing Glove.
There are also short biographies of 9 boxers or pugilists, including James Belcher, J. J. Corbett, Tom Cribb, Jem Mace, Tom Sayers and others.

1494. ODHAMS PRESS LTD (Publishers)
England Today in Pictures
With an Introduction by A. G. Street

continued

London, 1947.

In the section entitled 'England at Play – Popular Sports' is included a picture of the ring at the Queensberry Club, with a note on the Queensberry name, as associated with boxing.

1495. O'FARRELL, Dick

How to Box

Larry Foley's Method, and the Story of His World Famous Pupil, Griffo.

Sydney, (Australia), Frank Johnson, 1944.

Bound in wrappers. Illus.
Contents Include:

Part 1 –   Reminiscences of Larry Foley

Part 2 –   How to Box – The Science as Taught by Larry Foley. (Including 38 instructional cuts in the text)

Part 3 –   Two Great Fights and a Fighter (Larry Foley v. Abe Hickman, Jem Mace v. Sam Hurst, 'Griffo' The World's Cleverest Boxer.

1496. O'HARA, B.

From Figg to Johnson

Complete History of the Heavyweight Championship, containing dates and accurate descriptions of every contest for the world's boxing title from the time of the first championship down to the present day.

Chicago, The Blossom Book Bourse, 1909.

1497. O'HARA, John

Pipe Night (Short Stories)

London, Faber and Faber, 1946.

Thirty-one stories, twenty of which first appeared in *The New Yorker*, and four in *Collier's Magazine.*
No.29 is entitled 'The Handler', a boxing story.

1498. O'HARA, Patrick

The Red Sailor

London, Neville Spearman, 1963.

220pp.

A strong autobiographical first novel, largely dealing with boxing in the Royal Navy during the Korean War period in the Far East. O'Hara may be counted among that small band of originally ill-educated fighters, like Jim Tully, who developed themselves into capable novelists and poets.

1499. O'HARA, Patrick

God Came on Friday

London, Neville Spearman, 1964.

219pp.

The second boxing novel by the the young author who went on to write exciting adventure tales in the tradition of Alastair MacLean.

1500. OKAPU, Joseph

Superfight II.

Muhammad Ali vs. Joe Frazier

New York, The Third Press, 1974.

126pp. Illus.

1501. O'KEEFE, Pat

(British Middleweight Champion)

The Whole Art of Boxing

London, Amalgamated Press Ltd., 1915.

This paper-covered booklet was issued as a supplement to the Christmas Number of *The Marvel* (a paper for boys), dated Dec. 18th, 1915. Printed in black on white paper, illustrated by cuts in the text.

The booklet consists of 22 instructional sections, announced on the title-page as 'A Complete Book of Instruction on the Art of Ringcraft'.

1502. OLD BUSHMAN, THE

(W. H. Wheelwright)

Sporting Sketches – Home and Abroad

London, Frederick Warne and Co., 1866.

There was another edition of this work issued by the same publisher in 1870 with original illustrations in colour by G. Bowers; none of these are of boxing interest.

The text of both issues is the same, it includes: Melbourne Heath Cambridgeshire Oct. 25th, 1842, Bungaree beat Sam Sutton, 72 rounds, 1 hour 11 minutes.

On the Encouragement of Manly and Athletic Exercises, Such as Sparring, and a Few Remarks in Defence of the Much-Abused Custom of British Boxing.

1503. OLD KNUCKLE FIGHTER, AN

Championship Glove Contests

Specially written for the *Licensed Victualler's Gazette*, London.

London, *The Licensed Victuallers' Gazette*, 1899 and 1900.

There were at least two issues of this item, one for 1898–1899 and the other for 1899–1900. Both were priced 6d and on the title-page in each case was inscribed 'The Chief Prize Fights of . . .', but the Main Title *Championship Glove Contests* appears on the cover.

1504. OLSEN, Jack

Cassius Clay

London, Pelham Books Ltd., 1967.

214pp. Illus.
The author wrote as Senior Editor of America's *Sports Illustrated.*

1505. OLVER, Ron, and RILEY, Tim

Boxing

continued

London, W. and G. Foyle Ltd., 1962.

92pp. Card covers. Illus.
This book of instruction, from the pens of two noted boxing journalists, is illustrated with line drawings and photographs of actual contests.

1506. OLVER, Ron

The Professionals
London, Glenport Press, 1983.

183pp. Paper covers. Illus.
A reprint in book form of Ron Olver's articles from *Boxing News*.

1507. "ONE OF THE FANCY"

The Ring v. The Knife
This item was published with No.16 of *Tom Spring's Life in London and Sporting Chronicle* (Sept. 27th, 1840)

An Advertisement, which appeared in the journal mentioned above, read as follows:
'Will be given full and complete instructions in the Manly Art of Self-Defence, with a beautiful print, illustrating the most approved method of setting-to, as practised by the most eminent pugilists of the present day. Also the new rules of Prize-Fighting and a History of the Prize-Ring, from the earliest period to the present time.'

1508. "ONE OF THE FANCY"
(Thomas Moore)

Tom Cribb's Memorial to Congress
See entry under Moore, Thomas

1509. "ONE OF THE OLD BRIGADE"
(Donald Shaw?)

London in the Sixties. With a Few Digressions.
London, Everett and Co., 1908.
A further edition was issued in 1909 and a new edition in 1910.

312pp. Illustrated by Henry Pollard.
There were a number of references to prize-fighting in this book, as follows:

Chapter III —	speaks of 'Young Broome, the pugilist, who was to pilot one to the big fight between Sayers and Heenan'.
Chapter IV —	refers to 'The Kangaroo' a negro pugilist of somewhat ill repute. Known as 'Nat Langham's Black'.
Chapter V —	refers to the Night Houses of the Haymarket area, where J. C. Heenan lodged.
Chapter XXI	mentions Young Reed's sparring rooms at the 'Rising Sun' in Whitehall

Chapter XXII	refers to Tom King sparring at Jimmy Shaw's.

The pseudonym 'One of the Old Brigade' is believed to be that adopted by Donald Shaw, who also wrote under the name of 'Captain Stewart'.

1510. ONE OF THE OLD SCHOOL
(W. West)

Tavern Anecdotes and Reminiscences of the Origins of Signs, Clubs, etc.
See entry under West, W.

1511. "ONE WHO THINKS FOR HIMSELF"

Metropolitan Grievances, or a Serio-Comic Glance At Minor Mischiefs in London and its Vicinity, Including a Few which extend to the Country. The whole critically and satirically exposed and interspersed with sly remedial hints, and anecdotes visable and appropriate.
London, Printed by Charles Squire, for Sherwood, Neely and Jones, 1812.

Bound in paper boards, with folding frontis: 'Grievances of London', signed G. Cruikshank. Includes: 'Grievance LVI', 'Pugilism', including 'Milling, or the Progress of Civilisation' (An attack on Pugilism).

1512. O'NEIL, Chief Instructor J., R.N.

The Art of Boxing
Aldershot and London, Gale and Polden Ltd
1919 and 1925.
Price 1s-6d.

1513. ONYEAMA, Dillibe, and WALTERS, John

"I'm the Greatest"
The Wit and Humour of Muhammad Ali.
London, Leslie Frewin, 1975.

93pp. Illus. with photographs and with cartoons by Roy Ullyett and Jon. 4to, bound in pictorial boards.
An oddity in boxing literature, with much 'wit and humour' which is surely ephemeral. Ali himself probably had the minimum to do with this volume.

1514. "OPERATOR, AN" (Jon Bee)

The Fancy: or The True Sportsman's Guide. Being Authentic Memoirs of the Lives, Actions, Prowess, and Battles of the Leading Pugilists, from the Days of Figg and Broughton, to the Championship of Ward.
This work was first issued in 55 parts, and in 2 volumes, (Volume I - 28 parts, 680pp; Vol

.continued

II - 27 parts, 743pp).

Publication was first started by John Bysh, of Paternoster Row, London, and was subsequently taken over by John McGowan later John McGowan and Son, of Great Windmill Street, London. The first number was issued on April 21st, 1821, and publication continued until 1826.

There is evidence to indicate that Jon Bee (John Badcock) was responsible for at least the first 16 numbers of the work. This evidence is derived from some of the other works produced by Jon Bee, notably his *Sportsman's Slang* (1825), and *The Annals of Sporting and Fancy Gazette*, 1822–1828. Bee was also described in the title-pages of several of his books as "The Editor of the Original *Fancy*".

The woodcut heading of the wrappers of the parts was designed by George Cruikshank. The volumes were illustrated throughout with 46 engraved portraits and 3 coloured plates.

1515. O'REILLY, John Boyle
Ethics of Boxing and Manly Sport
Boston (Mass), Ticknor and Co. 1888.
358pp. Illus.
This book is divided into four sections; the first of these is entitled "Ethics and Evolution of Boxing". There is one full-page illustration, "The Boxer", engraved by permission from the statue by John Donoghue; there are further illustrations in the text.

1516. O'REILLY, John Boyle
Athletics and Manly Sport
Boston (U.S.A.) Pilot Publishing Co., 1890.
Bound in Black cloth, gilt titles on spine, with gilt decorations on front cover.
This is a later edition of *Ethics of Boxing and Manly Sport* by the same author, published in 1888.
The contents and illustrations are very similar (q.v.).

1517. OSBERN, E. B.
Anthology of Sporting Verse
Selected with a Preface by E. B. Osbern,
(Literary Editor of the *Morning Post*)
London, W. Collins Sons and Co. Ltd., 1930.
288pp.
Includes "The Great Fight" (From *Everlasting Mercy*, by John Masefield, 1911).

1518. O'SULLIVAN, J.B.
Death Stalks the Stadium
A Steve Silk Story.
Dublin, The Pillar Publishing Co. Ltd., 1946.
Distributed in Great Britain by Fudge and Co. Ltd.
80pp. Stiff paper covers, with coloured picture of a boxing match on the front cover.

1519. OTTENHEIMER
The Art of Sparring and Boxing and Science of Self Defence.
An American Publication, 1945.

1520. OTTLEY, Roi
Inside Black America
London, Eyre and Spottiswoode Ltd, 1948.
280pp.
Chapter XIV includes "Joe Louis and His People".

1521. OTTLEY, Roi
Black Odyssey
The Story of the Negro in America.
London, John Murray, 1949.
340pp.
There is reference to coloured boxers in the text, including Tom Molineux, Peter Jackson, Joe Walcott, Joe Gans, Jack Johnson, and Joe Louis.

1522. OXBERRY, William
Pancratia, or A History of Pugilism
London, Published and sold by W. Oxberry, and also by Sherwood Neely and Jones, 1812.
A Second Edition was published by G. Chapple in London in 1815.
The frontis shows a portrait of Tom Cribb, in private dress.

Part I —	(Pages 1 to 18) deals with the boxing of the Classical ages; including The Amusements Depending upon Bodily Exercises and Personal Contests.
Part II —	(Pages 29 to 371) gives the History of Boxing in this country, from the time of Figg and Broughton to Cribb's second fight with Molineux, 1811.

An explanation of the derivation of the title of this book is given in *Sportsman's Slang etc* — Addenda of Obsolete and Far-Fetched Words and Phrases, by Jon Bee (1825).

"Pancratium — a place of boxing in Rome, their wrists circled with iron, their knuckles defended with bullocks' hide, they larruped away incontinently, and two or three score Romans were thus murdered annually. Hence derived we have 'Pancratia', which is the title of a 'History of Pugilism', partly done by Bill Oxberry in 1811, the first fifty pages by another hand".

In the Boxing Bibliography given in the Harold Furniss *Famous Fights* magazine (1901–1903), the publication date of *Pancratia* is given as 1811,
continued

and the publisher as George Smeeton. The authorship is here attributed to "J.B.", London; thus indicating that Jon Bee was involved in compilation of this book.

1523. OXBERRY, William

A History of Pugilism and Memoirs of persons who have distinguished themselves in that science.
London, 1814.

1524. OXFORD UNIVERSITY PRESS, HUMPHREY MILFORD (Publishers)

Early Victorian England, 1830–1865.
London, 1934. Two Volumes.

References to pugilism occur in Volume I, Chapter V: "Country Life and Sport" by Bernard Darwin, where reference is made to pugilists and pugilistic personalities of the period, such as Captain Barclay Tom Cribb, Tom Molineux, etc.

The section ends with the Sayers-Heenan contest in 1860, stating "The old prize-ring ended with Tom Sayers, and ended in a blaze of glory".

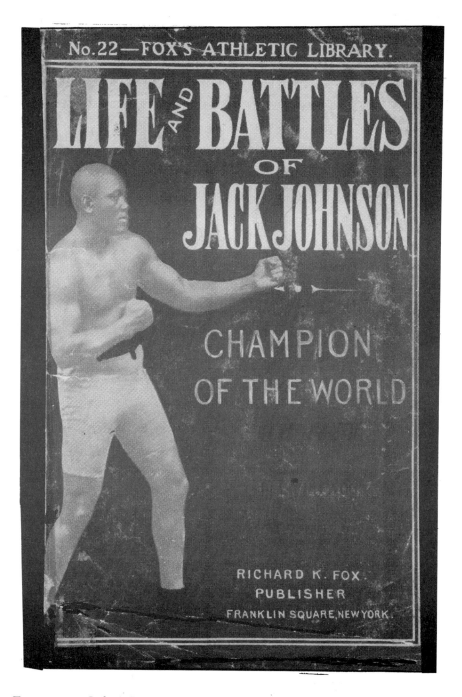

Front cover *Life & Battles of Jack Johnson* (Fox Pub.) (Bib. Ref. 744)

1525. PACHECO, Ferdie, M.D.
Fight Doctor
Introduction by Muhammad Ali.
New York, Simon and Schuster, 1977.
London, Stanley Paul and Co. 1978.
(Revised and enlarged edition).
262pp. (U.K. Edition) Illus.

1526. PAGE, L. C, and Co. (Publishers)
Famous American Athletes of Today
Boston (U.S.A.) 1928 to 1952. ca.
350pp. per issue.

There was a total of 12 series under this title, issued between the dates shown above. They appeared under the names of various editors and writers, including Charles H. Johnston, Leroy Atkinson, Austen Lake, Al Hirschberg, and Frank Waldman.

Some mention of boxing and boxers occurred in each of the series, referring to contests and boxers contemporary with the year of publication, with some reference to athletes, including boxers,, mentioned in previous volumes. The articles were often accompanied by photographs.
The following boxers were among those who were the subjects of articles:– Gene Tunney. Jack Sharkey, Ernie Schaaf, Max Baer, Young Stribling, James J. Braddock, Joe Louis. Billy Conn and Ray Robinson.

1527. PALMER, Joe
Recollections of a Boxing Referee
London, John Lane, The Bodley Head Ltd., 1927.
Introduction by Bohun Lynch.
235pp. Illus.
The author was a vastly-experienced boxing referee and in his book he tells of his early interest in boxing and of his experiences during his career as 'third man' in the ring for 3,000 or more bouts.
Joe Palmer was a relative of Pedlar Palmer and he officiated in contests involving champions at all weights, including Elky Clark, Frank Goddard, Jack Bloomfield, Tommy Burns, Tommy Milligan, Jim Higgins and many others.
Among the controversial decisions given by Mr. Palmer were those involving Ted Kid Lewis v. Georges Carpentier and Len Harvey v. Johnny Sullivan in 1926.
In the latter contest the verdict in favour of Sullivan resulted in the withdrawal of Joe Palmer's licence to referee.

1529. PARISH, Charlie (Editor)
Charlie Parish's Continental Boxing Guide, 1956.
Records of 250 Boxers from all parts of the Continent: National Title Holders; Managers' Directory; Boxing History.

London, Atlas Publishing Ltd.
99pp. Stiff paper covers.

1530. PARISH, Charlie, (Editor)
European Boxing Guide, 1958–1959
Records of all Leading European and Empire Boxers.
London, Atlas Publishing Ltd., 1958.
75pp. Stiff paper covers. Illus.

1531. PARKER, Eric
British Sport
(Britain in Picture Series No.1)
London, William Collins, 1941.
44pp Illus.
Includes twelve plates in colour and seventeen illustrations in black and white.
One coloured plate is entitled 'Boxing' after an engraving by Henry Alken.

1532. PARKER, Eric
Highways and Byways in Surrey
Illustrated by Hugh Thomson
London, Macmillan and Co. Ltd., 1908.
Reprinted 1909 and 1919.
452pp. Illus.
Chapter XIX – Chobham and Bisley, mentions Sayers v. Heenan.

1533. PARKER, Eric (Editor)
The Lonsdale Anthology of Sporting Prose and Verse.
Volume XII of the Lonsdale Library of Sports, Games, and Pastimes.
London, The Seeley Service Co. Ltd., 1931.
376pp. Illus.
This volume was issued with 3 varying types of binding. Full Leather, Quarter Leather, and Light Brown Buckram.
There was also a Special Edition, limited to 100 copies, bound in Full Persian Calf, and signed by Eric Parker; and a thin paper pocket edition.
The book includes a section on boxing, with the following items:

"A Bully Served Out", by William Hazlitt.

"The Fighting Tinman", from George Borrow's *Lavengro.*

"Ringcraft", by "Klaxon", from *Heather Mixture.*

"Three Schools", by Viscount Knebworth, from the Lonsdale Library *Boxing.*

"The Fight" from William Hazlitt's *Essays.*

The plates include 'The Interior of the Fives Court'.

1534. PARKYNS, Sir Thomas, of Bunny Park,
continued

Baronet

The Inn-Play; or Cornish Hugg Wrestler. Digested in a Method which teacheth to break off Holds, and Throw Most Falls Mathematically. Easy to understand by all Gentlemen etc and of great use to such who understand the Small sword in Fencing. And by all Tradesmen and Handicrafts that have competent Knowledge of the use of Stillyards, Bar, Grove-Iron or Lever.
1st Edition, 4to, 1713.
2nd Edition, 4to, 1714 (with woodcuts)
3rd Edition, corrected with large Additions, London.
Printed for Thomas Weekes and sold by Humphrey Wainwright, at Bunny in Nottinghamshire, 1727.
There was also a further issue of this book, published by J. Bailey, Chancery Lane, London, which contained one, or possibly two, folding plates by I. R. Cruikshank: this issue was included in the *Book of Sports*, or *Man of Spirits Companion*, published by J. Bailey in 1819.

Sir Thomas Parkyn's book contains references to pugilism, particularly in section (G), 'Boxing'.
Henry Lemoine, in his *Modern Manhood* (1788) gives at the end of his book an advert for *Inn Play* as follows:
"In a short time will be published in Octavo, price 2s-6d, Ornamented with the Head of the Author, and other Copper-Plate Prints, Sir Thomas Parkyn's *Inn-Play Wrestler and Cornish Hugg*. Originally printed in 1728".
Sir Thomas Parkyns died in 1741.

1535. PARRY, Judge Edward Abbot
Drama of the Law
London, T. Fisher Unwin, 1924.
Reissued in Benn's Essex Library Series (no.9) 1929.
319pp.
Refers in Chapter VIII to the Liverpool Bank Robbery, involving Dick Burge.

1536. PATRICK, Vic
(Australian Lightweight Champion)
Vic Patrick — The Champ
Daily Telegraph Sports Book No. 3.
Sydney, Printed by Compress Printing Ltd., 1946.
32pp. Stiff paper covers. Illus.

1537. PAUL, Louis
The Pumpkin Coach. A Boxing Novel.
London, William Heinemann, 1936.
360pp.

1538. PATTERSON, Floyd
(with Milton Gross)
Victory Over Myself
An Autobiography.
New York, B. Geis Association.
Distributed by Random House, 1962.
244pp. Illus.

London, Pelham Books Ltd., 1962
205pp. Illus.

1539. PATTERSON, Floyd
Inside Boxing
Published in Chicago, 1974.
78pp.
Mainly instructional. (A Step by Step Guide)

1540. PATTERSON, Ralph W.
The Square Ring
London, Arthur Barker and Co., 1954.
(Fiction)

1541. PEARCE, Charles E.
Corinthian Jack
A Novel of the Prize Ring.
London, Benman, 1927.
Also published in London by Stanley Paul & Co.
254pp.
See also Mellifont Press Ltd., Sports Series, No.5.

1542. PEARSON, Hesketh
Conan Doyle, His Life and Art
London, Methuen and Co. Ltd., 1943.
193pp. Illus.

This book contains a number of references to Conan Doyle's interest in boxing and the prize-ring, and to his books on the subject. These are particularly referred to in Chapters IX, XI and XII.

1543. PEARSON, John
The Profession of Violence
The Rise and Fall of the Kray Twins.
London, Granada Publishing Ltd., 1972.
London, Panther Books, 1973.
Includes information on the Kray twins' association with boxing and famous boxers.

1544. PEGG, Harry W., Sr. (Editor)
Boxiana Review
Philadelphia, Published Annually by the Editor.
This annual publication was first issued in 1965 as a large format magazine, printed on
continued

art paper.

Mr. Pegg was formerly President of the World Boxing Historians' Association. He was the driving force behind the accumulation of material for his magazine. In the first year he lost money on the publication; fortunately in the subsequent years a number of enthusiasts came to the rescue and assisted with cash and with distribution.

The contents consisted mainly of pictures of old-time fights and fighters, supported by articles; publication continued for at least 12 years.

1545. "PENDRAGON", (Henry Sampson)
(Editor of *The Referee* etc.)
Modern Boxing
(The Referee Series)
London, E. J. Francis and Co., 1879.

154pp. Stiff paper covers.

This item was announced to appear in 2 parts, but so far as can be ascertained, Part II was never issued.

Part I was entitled "The Decay and Downfall of the Prize Ring". 9 chapters, bound in yellow paper wrappers.

1546. PEP, Willie,
with SACCHI, Robert
Friday's Heroes. Willie Pep Remembers.
Special Materials — Co-ordinated by David Wilson.
Foreword by Joey Adams.
New York, Friday's Heroes, Inc., 1973.

195pp. incuding Willie Pep's boxing record, Illus.

1547. PEPE, Phil
Come Out Smokin'
Joe Frazier — The Champ Nobody Knew
New York, Coward, McCann and Geoghegan Inc., 1972.

224pp. Illus.
The remarkable story of Joe Frazier and his determined and courageous rise to the top.

1548. PERIODICAL PUBLICATIONS
(Publishers)
Championship Boxing Annual
(British Edition)
London, 1963.

1549. PERUGINI, Mark Edward
Victorian Days and Ways
London, Jarrolds (Publishers), 1932.
Price 18s.
Also published by Hutchinson and Co.
(Publishers) in their Booklovers Library at 2s.

288pp.
Illustrated by reproductions from *Punch* and from Contemporary Prints.
Includes Chapter XVI: "Sports and Pastimes" which deals with Racing, Boxing, Cricket, etc.

1550. PETERS, Harry T.
Currier and Ives
Printmakers to the American People
New York, Doubleday, Doran and Co. Inc., 1942.

41pp. plus 192 plates.
The illustrations include examples of prints issued by this famous American company, including those of Tom Sayers and John Morrisey and a plate showing the Great Fight for the Championship between Sayers and Heenan.

1551. PHILLIPS and PROBERT LTD
(Printers and Publishers)
Fox Hunting Reminiscences of Gin and Beer, and Two "Turpin" Romances of local
Interest
Worcester, 1930.

"Gin and Beer" was the pseudonym of Tom Andrews, of Harkaway, Whittington, Worcestershire.
The book includes a plate entitled "The Battle of Worcester", beneath which is written:
"The Great Contest between Spring and Langan on Worcester Racecourse, January 7th, 1824, for the Championship of England"
Note — The author's grandfather (The Reverend Tom Boulter, Vicar of Kempsey) and Mad Jack Mytton on the left of the ring. (From an old print)

1552. PHILLIPS, Thomas
Cheap Glory
A Boxing Novel
London, Geroge Harrap and Co. Ltd., 1939.
London, Pendulum Popular Sports Series, 1946 (Cheap Edition)

283pp.
The Author was a well-known sporting journalist.

1553. PHILOPUGILIS
(Henry Downes Miles)
Tom Sayers Champion of England:
A Fistic Biography
London, S.D. Beeton, ca. 1865.

188pp.
Green paper wrappers. Picture of Sayers (seated in fighting kit) on the front cover.
The contents consist of 4 chapters and an appendix these cover the birth and early life of Tom Sayers in Sussex, his migration to London, his early battles and his later career and his death.
The appendix contains prose and poetry originated
continued

by the Great Battle with J.C. Heenan and In Memoriam notices form the *Daily Telegraph* and the *Sporting Life*

1554. PICTUREGOER MAGAZINE,
Famous Film Supplement (Publishers)
The Crowd Roars
November, 1938.

The illustrated story of the film of this title, which featured Robert Taylor, Maureen O'Sullivan, Frank Morgan and Edward Arnold.

1555. PINK RECORD BOOK
Published in U.S.A., 1916.

1556. PLATT, Charles
Famous Fights and Fighters
London, Odhams Press Ltd., 1920.

188pp. Card covers.
The Introduction quotes Eugene Corri as saying "The next best thing to witnessing a great glove fight is to read a good account of one".
The chapters range from "The Historic Fight Between Mendoz and Gentleman Jackson" (1795), to "Our Modern Fighting Giants" (1920).
The dust cover carries an action portrait of Georges Carpentier.

1557. PLIMPTON, George
Shadow Box
London, Andre Deutsch Ltd., 1978.

343pp. Illus.
Boxing experiences and stories by the U.S. journalist, embracing many well-known boxers and devotees of the sport.
Portions of this book had previously appeared in different form in papers and magazines, such as *Harper's, Sports Illustrated*, etc.

1558. POLLINI, Francis
The Crown
London, Neville Spearman Ltd., 1967.
284pp.
A highly dramatic novel of the boxing world.

1559. POPHAM, H. E.
The Taverns in the Town
Introduction by Sir John Squire.
Illustrations by J. K. Popham, F.R.S.A.
London, Robert Hale Ltd., 1937.

220pp.
There are no illustrations of pugilistic interest, but the book includes many references to prizefighters and to taverns kept by them, including:

"The Union Arms" Panton Street (kept by Tom Cribb)

"The Queen's Head and French Horn", Little Britain, (once kept by Peter Crawley)
"The Coach and Horses", St. Martin's Lane, later known as "Ben Caunt's Head", after the famous pugilist.
"The Horns" Kennington, where Jack Martin, the pugilist, was landlord, and a number of other similar references.

1560. POPULAR PUBLICATIONS Inc.
(Publishers)
Sports Novels Magazine
Chicago, from April–May 1937.
This was a bi-monthly magazine, the first issue appeared for April–May 1937.

Volumes 1 to 4, to April–May 1939, contained a number of articles on boxing; the subjects of these were Mickey Walker, Tony Canzoneri, Jim Braddock and a number of mentions of Joe Louis.

1561. POPULAR PUBLICATIONS Inc.
(Publishers)
Sports Novels
Chicago (Published Monthly)
The following numbers contained items of boxing interest.
Volume 15, No.1 – March 1948 – " Sam Langford's Way" – by Edwin Laird Cady.

Volume 15, No.3 – May 1948 – "That Vertical Man" (The Brown Bomber, Joe Louis) by David Cooke.

1562. POWER, Bob
Fighters of the North
A Saga of the Early Battling Days on the Northern Fistic Front.
New Lambton (Australia), Published by the author, 1976.

162pp. Stiff paper covers. Picture of Frank Slavin on the front cover.
Tells of boxers and contests in the Hunter Valley of New South Wales, with records of local fights. The boxers include Frank Slavin, Paddy King, Bill Squires, Les Darcy, and others.

1563. "P.P" – Boston
Ring Record and Fistic Facts
Containing Reliable Records of Prominent English, Australian and American Pugilists.
Boston, 1896.
This item was also sold in England by *The Mirror of Life* Co., London.
Records of many contemporary boxers were given in the text.

1564. PRESTIDGE, Dennis

continued

Tom Cribb at Thistleton Gap
Wymondham, Melton Mowbray (Leicester-shire), Brewhouse Publication, 1971.

Limited Edition of 450 copies.
Bound in brown buckram, gilt decoration on the cover.
Illustrated by Rigby Graham (some coloured)
Tells the background story of the second Cribb v. Molineux fight, September 28th, 1813, with a detailed look at the location of the bout.

1565. PRESTON, Harry

Memories
With a Portrait by Richard Sickert, A.R.A., and other illustrations.
London, Constable and Co 1928.
There was also an edition of this work pub-lished in New York in 1928.

288pp. Illus.
Bound in red cloth with gilt lettering on the spine.
This item contains a quantity of boxing material, including stories of Bob Habbijam's, The Pelican Club, the National Sporting Club and also boxing personalities with whom the author was involved over a number of years, covering the last of the bare-knuckle and the first of the glove fighters.
The text includes stories of B. J. Angle, Abington Baird, Sam Langford, Joe Jeanette Jack Johnson, Dick Burge, Bobby Dobbs, J. L. Sullivan, Jim Driscoll, Charles Ledoux, Willie Ritchie, Billy Wells Joe Beckett, Tom Berry, Ted Moore, Jimmy Wilde, Jack Dempsey, Harry Mason and many others.

1566. PRESTON, Sir Harry

Leaves from My Unwritten Diary
London, Hutchinson and Co. (Publishers) Ltd., 1936.
Dedicated to "My Daughter Nancy and her generation, the younger generation".

Sir Harry died shortly after completion of this book.
The book contains a quantity of boxing material, as follows.
Chapter I - Includes the author's experiences as an amateur boxer.
Chapter II - A funny fight at Woodbury Hill Fair.
Chapter IV - Experiences at Bob Habbijam's, White's Rooms, The Pelican and the National Sporting Club.
Chapter VI - Sport Scene, mentions Joe Louis, Max Baer, Tommy Loughran and others.
Chapter VII - Mentions J. J. Corbett.
Chapter XI - Old Timers, deals with bare fist fighters, including Charlie Mitchell, Sullivan, Corbett, Fitzsimmons, Jackson, etc.
Chapter XII - A Terror for His Size, Jimmy Wilde and Teddy Baldock.
Chapter XIII - Big Men: Mickey Walker, Iron Hague and Sam Langford, Wells v. Carpentier, Beckett, Dempsey and Tunney.
Chapter XIX - The Helping Fist, Charity Boxing

Tournaments at Brighton.

1567. PRESTON, Thomas

The Yeomen of the Guard; Their History from 1485 to 1885. And a Concise Account of the Tower Warders.
London, Harrison and Sons, 1885.

198pp.
The section "George II, 1727 to 1760" includes a sub-section entitled "The Yeoman Boxer", which deals with John Broughton, the first Champion Boxer, who was for a long period one of the Ushers of the Yeoman of the Guard.

1568. PRICE, E.E.

Science of Self Defence
New York, Dick and Fitzgerald, 1867.

This item is described as follows:
"A Treatise on Sparring and Wrestling, Including Complete Instructions on Training and Physical Development"
Bound in coloured boards, green cloth hinge, picture of a sparring match on the front cover.
There are 24 instructional illustrations.

1569. PRIESTLEY, J. B.

Self Selected Essays
London, William Heinemann Ltd., 1932.

319pp.
This book includes a section entitled "The Ring (Blackfriars Road London)". This essay originally appeared in *The Saturday Review* Sept. 27th, 1929 and is also reproduced in Cox W.D. *Boxing in Art and Literature* (q.v.)

1570. PROCTOR, Richard Wright

Our Turf, Our Stage, and Our Ring
Manchester, Denham and Co., 1862.
London, Simpkin, Marshall and Co., 1862.
Illustrated by William Morton
100pp.
Part Fourth "Sporting Life in Manchester" includes references to boxers such as Isaac Perrins, Robert Gregson, Edward Painter, Spring and Langan etc.
One Illustration "The Turf, the Stage and the Ring" includes at the head a framed picture of two pugilists in action.

1571. PROFESSIONAL BOXER, A

Science of Self Defence, or The Art of Sparring and Boxing
Bound in wrappers.
(Reprint of a 1915 booklet)

1572. PUGILIST, A (Owen Swift)

The Modern English Boxer, or Scientific Art and Practise of Attack and Self Defence, etc.
continued

etc.

London, Printed by H. Smith, 27 Holywell Street, 1835.

The frontis is a folding plate entitled "Attitudes and Positions in the Art and Practise of English Boxing"; this shows 8 attitudes or positions. There are 35 pages of instructional text.

This pamphlet is probably an earlier edition of the work under the same name, published by E. Hewitt (1848), (q.v.). The text is the same, though set out in a different manner.

See also SWIFT, Owen.

1573. PUGILISTIC BENEVOLENT ASSOCI-ATION OF ENGLAND

The Lives and Battles of Tom Sayers and John C. Heenan. To which is added the New Rules of the Ring, as revised by the Pugilistic Benevolent Association of England.

New York, R.M. De Witt. Copyright, 1860.

84pp.

1574. PUGNUS

History of the Prize Ring

London, B. T. Gale, 1876 and 1877. In 2 parts.

This item consists of reprints, with all necessary additions, or a series on Great Battles which had appeared from time to time in *The Licensed Victuallers' Gazette*.

The parts are dealt with as follows:

Part I   Contents include – James Figg, the Founder of English Pugilism – Figg's fight with Ned Sutton and other bouts up to and including the bout between Tom Tyne and Elisha Crabbe.

Part II   Contains the History of the Prize Ring 1788–1795, from the bout between Jacob Doyle and William Dean to that between Hooper and William Wood.
This volume was bound in yellow paper covers with a portrait of Jackson on the front cover.

At the end of the second volume was an announcement that Part III would follow in due course: it is doubtful whether this additional volume was ever issued.

1575. PUPIL of BROUGHTON, A

Art of Defence, or a System of Attack and Defence, with a Description of the Stops, Parries and Blows of the Leading Professors of Smallsword, Backsword, Quarterstaff and Pugilism.

1780.

The above description is taken from the short boxing bibliography included in the magazine edited by Harold Furniss *Famous Fights Past and Present*, 1901–1904. The bibliography is given in No.63 of the series; this is contained in Volume II

of the bound annual volumes. (q.v.)

1576. PUNSHON, E. R.

Old Fighting Days

First Issued in New York in 1921.

London, John Bale and Sons and Danielson Ltd.

321pp.

Bound in red cloth, lettered in black.

This is a novel of the old prize-fighting days. 39 Chapters.

1577. PUPIL OF THE LATE TOM CRIBB, A (Editor)

The British Boxer, or Guide to Self Defence

London, R. Winn. ca.1850. Price 1d.

16pp.

There is a copy of this item shown as being published by W. Winn of 34 Holywell Street, London; it is the same in all respects to the item described above, except for the name and address of the publisher.

1578. PUPIL OF HUMPHREYS (sic) AND MENDOZA, A

The Art of Manual Defence, or System of Boxing. Perspicuously explained in a Series of Lessons and Illustrated by Plates.

London, Printed for G. Kearsley, 1784.

Second Edition, 1789.

Third Edition, 1799.

133pp. 12mo.

The text and plates in the second and third editions are similar and contain a descriptive account of the merits of modern boxers, including Big Ben, Johnson, Ryan, Ward, Mendoza, Crabbe, Oliver and others.

There is also a unique Table of Merit, listing seventeen fighers, with points awarded for various attributes i.e. Weight, Strength, Activity, Skill and Bottom.

1579. PUPIL OF MENDOZA AND HUMPHRIES, A

Boxing Made Easy, or The Complete Manual of Self Defence Clearly Explained and Illustrated in a Series of Easy Lessons, with Some Important Hints to Wrestlers.

By a Pupil of Mendoza and Humphries, both Celebrated Professors of the Science.

New York, Dick and Fitzgerald, (1865)

46pp. Brown paper covers.

Illustrated with ten woodcuts.

The work includes a Real Scale of Merit among the boxers. The scale lists 17 boxers, with marks given to under the headings – Weight, Strength, Activity, Skill and Bottom.

1580. PURCELL, Edmund D.
Forty Years at The Criminal Bar —
Experiences and Impressions
London, T. Fisher Unwin and Co., 1916.
352pp.
Includes in chapter IX "Glove Fighting and Prize-
Fighting".

JACK SLACK, of Bristol, the Conqueror of Broughton,
From a Bust sculptured by SIVIER.

PART VIII.　　　(To be Completed in 20 Parts.)　　ONE SHILLING.

PUGILISTICA.

ONE HUNDRED AND FORTY-FOUR YEARS OF

BRITISH BOXING.

WITH 100 AUTHENTIC PORTRAITS OF CELEBRITIES.

PETER CRAWLEY'S PORTRAIT.

LONDON :

WELDON & CO., 9, SOUTHAMPTON STREET, STRAND, W.C.

Handsome Cloth Covers for Binding Vol. I. now Ready, price 1s. post free.

Cover of Part VIII *Pugilistica*, as issued in parts (Bib. Ref. 1365)

1581. QUEEN, Ellery

The New Adventures of Ellery Queen
London, Victor Gollancz Ltd., March 1940.
Second Edition (First cheap edition) April,
1941.

307pp.
This item includes a "Group of Ellery Queen
Sports Mysteries", one of which is entitled "Pugil-
ism, Mind Over Matter".

1582. QUEEN, Ellery (Editor)

Sporting Detective Stories
London, Faber and Faber, 1946.

This book carries a section entitled "Outdoor
Sports" includes Prize Fighting: "His Brother's
Keeper" by Dashiell Hammett. (From *Collier's
Magazine*, February 17th, 1934)

1583. QUEENSBERRY

The Tenth Marquess Of

The Sporting Queensberrys
London, Hutchinson and Company (Publishers) Ltd., 1942.

273pp. Illus.
Bound in red cloth with gilt titles on spine.
There was also a Limited Edition of 250 copies,
numbered and signed.
This book includes "unrevealed episodes" in the
lives of the author's sporting forbears, together
with other reminiscences, consisting of old and
modern episodes.

1584. QUEENSBERRY, The Marquess of
(In collaboration with Percy Colson)

Oscar Wilde and the Black Douglas
London, Hutchinson and Co. (Publishers)Ltd
1949.

273pp.
Chapter I – "Introduction to The Clan Douglas",
gives information on William Douglas, Fourth
Duke of Queensberry (Old Q), and his kinsman,
Sir Charles Douglas, and their interest in and sup-
port of the prize-ring.

1585. QUENNELL, Marjorie and C.H.B.

Everyday Things in Homeric Greece
London, B. T. Batsford, 1929.

139pp.
The text includes a number of references to boxing, and one illustration is entitled thus.

1586. QUENNELL, Marjorie and C.H.B.

A History of Everyday Things in England
London, B. T. Batsford, 1933.
(Second edition, new and enlarged, 1938)

Chapter VIII – "Nineteenth Century Clothing",
includes an illustration in the text of two pugilists. There is no other mention of boxing in the
book.

APPENDIX.

SCALE OF RELATIVE MERIT

Among nearly One Hundred Boxers, made up to the Period of the latest Battle of each Man.

** The existing degree of every man's qualifications for fighting, as regards his weight, strength, activity, skill, or bottom, are each taken at 10 for the *highest ;* as these descend in excellence, the *number* is lower, so that if he had *no merit* at all, he would stand at 0. Again, if any man could be found, the total of whose *five points* of excellence, should reach 50 altogether, he might be considered the perfection of all pugilistic acquirement— or *ne plus ultra ;* with this exception, the totals (simply taken as such) are little *comparative,* unless the *weights* nearly agree; for, where this is greatly deficient, his strength must fall commensurately short, and then what signifies his *skill,* or his *activity,* unless to aid in running away with his *bottom ?*

THE MEN'S NAMES.	Wgt.	Str.	Act.	Skill.	Bott.	Total	THE MEN'S NAMES.	Wgt.	Str.	Act.	Skill.	Bott.	Total.
Aaron, Barney . . .	4	5	8	5	6	28	Dutch Sam	5	6	9	8	8	36
Abbott, Bill . . .	6	9	1	3	9	28	Eales, Bill	6	6	7	7	6	32
Acton, Dick . . .	9	8	4	4	6	31	Firby, (*i. e.* Fearby) Jack	9	9	6	6	4	34
Belasco, Aby . . .	5	5	7	7	5	29	Gamble, Andrew . .	10	10	4	1	2	27
Belcher, Jem . . .	8	9	10	10	10	47	Gibbletts, Charley .	5	7	8	8	7	35
Belcher, Tom . . .	5	6	10	9	9	39	Gregson, Bob . . .	10	10	2	2	8	32
Pitton, Isaac . . .	8	7	6	7	6	34	Gully, John . . .	8	8	9	9	10	44
Brown, Ned . . .	3	4	8	7	7	29	Hall, Tom (Isle of Wight)	6	6	7	6	5	30
Broughton, Jack . .	8	9	6	10	9	42	Hall, Bill (Birmingham)	5	5	5	4	3	22
Burn, Ben . . .	9	10	6	5	7	37	Hares, Dick . . .	4	5	5	6	8	28
Burn, Jem	6	6	6	7	8	33	Harmer, Harry . .	7	7	9	8	9	40
Cabbage, Jack . .	5	6	6	7	7	31	Head, Gorge . . .	5	6	9	10	7	37
Cannon, Tom . . .	7	7	8	7	8	37	Hickman, Tom . .	6	8	9	3	10	36
Carter, Jack . . .	8	8	9	5	5	35	Holt, Harry . . .	4	4	9	7	5	29
Cooper, George . .	7	6	6	8	8	35	Hudson, Josh (Hodgson)	9	8	7	6	9	39
Cooper Jack . . .	5	5	5	3	6	24	Hudson, Dav. . . .	5	5	10	4	7	31
Crawley, Peter . .	8	7	6	9	7	37	Humphries, Dick . .	5	5	8	9	8	35
Cribb, Tom	9	9	4	5	10	37	Inglis, Peace . . .	4	6	6	8	10	34
Curtis, Jack . . .	4	5	6	7	10	32	Jackson, John . .	8	8	7	10	7	40
Curtis, Dick . . .	4	4	6	8	9	31	Johnson, Tom . . .	8	9	9	10	10	46
Davis, Cy	5	5	8	7	6	31	Jones, Tom (Paddington)	5	6	9	9	8	37
Dogherty, Dan . .	5	6	7	7	6	31	Kendrick, John. . .	9	8	6	3	7	33
Donnelly, Dan . .	10	10	2	1	5	28	Langan, Jack . .	9	10	5	3	10	37

Comparable Table of Merit, from *Memoirs of Jack Scroggins* (Bib. Ref. 1033)

1587. RAINBOLT, Richard
Boxing's Heavyweight Champions
Minneapolis, Lerner Publications, 1974.
(Sporting Heroes series)
70pp.

1588. RAY, Oscar
Joe Louis the "Brown Bomber"
"How They Did It" Life Stories, 1st Series,
Volume 5.
London, The Pallas Publishing Co. Ltd.,
1938.
126pp. Illus.

1589. READ, Herbert
(Of the Victoria and Albert Museum)
Staffordshire Pottery Figures
London, Duckworth, 1929.
This includes, Plate 61 — Tom Cribb: White
Earthenware, painted in enamel colours.
About 1820. height 9 inches.

1590. READ, Jack
(Former Lightweight Champion of
Australia)
Griffo — His Life Story and Record
Sydney (Australia), Fine Art Publishers,
1926.
32pp. Coloured paper covers, picture of Griffo on
the front cover.
5 Illus.
This biography was issued in the year before
Griffo's death.

1591. READ, Jack (Editor and Compiler)
Australian Boxing Records – 1927
An Almanac of records made by Australian
Boxers, past and present, and a few world-
famous fighters who are known to ring
followers in this country.
Sydney N.S.W., Jack Read, c/o the *Sporting
Globe*.
Bound in red paper covers. Illus.

1592. READ, Jack (Editor and Compiler)
Australian Boxing Annual, 1928
An Almanack of records made by Australian
boxers, past and present, and a few items of
interest to ring followers.
Published by the author.
Blue paper covers, with a picture of Griffo on the
front cover.
Dedicated to W. F. (Bill) Corbett, the greatest box-
ing authority of his day.
Includes a review of champions the world over,
Australian boxing records and other features.
Illus.
Further issues of this Annual were published in
1930, 1934, 1935, 1938 and 1945; all compiled
and edited by Jack Read.

1593. READ, Jack (Compiler)
Mick Simmons' Australian Boxing Annual
Sydney (N.S.W.), Mick Simmons Ltd., 1938.
88pp. Illus.
Yellow paper covers; pictures of Australian boxers
on front cover.
The contents include articles by Australian and
American boxing writers and a number of boxers
records up to 1st January 1938, with 27 illust-
rations.

1594. READ, Jack
Read's Australian Boxing Records, 1947.
Sydney, Melbourne etc., Invincible Press,
1947.
80pp.
Includes records of sixty-three Australian boxers
and many illustrations.

1595. READE, Sir Charles
Readiana
London, Chatto and Windus, 1883.
329pp.
This item contains a chapter "The Coming Man",
with some references to boxing.

1596. READING, The Marquess of
Rufus Isaacs, First Marquess of Reading,
P.C., G.C.B., G.C.S.I., G.C.V.O., 1860–1914
By His Son.
London, Hutchinson and Co. (Publishers)Ltd
1942.
Chapter I includes details of the relationship of
Daniel Mendoza with the Isaacs family. (Mendoza
was the uncle of Lord Reading's grandmother.)
Mention is also made of the friendship between the
First Marquess and B. J. Angle the well-known
amateur boxer and boxing referee. The enthusiasm
of the Marquess for boxing led him to become a
pupil of Ned Donnelly at the boxing school behind
the Cafe Royal.
The illustrations include a cartoon of the Marquess
of Reading as a boxer; this was drawn by Sir F.
Carruthers Gould.

1597. REED, Gregory
This Business of Boxing and "Its Secrets"
Washington D.C., New National Publishing
Co., 1981.
280pp. Illus.

1598. REED, Milton

continued

The Fight on Wrecker's Rock
(The Pocket Series — Adventure Stories)
No.40.
London, Pocket Edition (1945)
Coloured paper covers. Pictures of a fight on the front cover.
There are 3 other boxing illustrations.

1599. REEVE, Henry (Editor)
The Greville Memoirs. A Journal of the Reigns of King George IV and King William IV.
By the late Charles C.F. Greville, Esq., Clerk to the Council of those Great Sovereigns.
London, Longmans Green and Co., 1874, 3 volumes.
(With 5 volumes following later to complete the set)
Volume II, Chapter XIX (Brighton, Dec. 17th 1832), contains references to John Gully, several of a very offensive character, but these were withdrawn in subsequent editions.
Editions were published in 1927 and 1929 by William Heinemann and Eveleigh Nash and Grayson respectively included the original passages, but with some omissions.

1600. REID, G. W.
Descriptive Catalogue of the Works of George Cruikshank
London, Bell and Daidy, 1871.
This work carries details of a number of boxing items which are included in other entries on the Cruikshank brothers contained in this bibliography

1601. REID, J. C.
Bucks and Bruisers — Pierce Egan and Regency England
London, Routledge and Kegan Paul, 1971.
220pp, plus Notes and Bibliography.
The story of the life and writings of the famous journalist, the first boxing historian.

1602. REYNOLDS, John Hamilton
The Fancy. A Selection from the Poetical Remains of the Later Peter Corcoran of Gray's Inn, with a Brief Memoir of His Life.
London, Printed for Taylor and Hessey, 1820.
London, Published by Elkin Matthews, 1905 (reissue)
This item contains a quantity of material about the old prize-ring and pugilists; the following poems are of particular interest:
"Lines to Philip Samson, The Brummagem Youth"

"Sonnett on The Nonpareil" (Jack Randall)
"Sonnett on Hearing St. Martin's Bells on my way home from the Fives Court"
The Introduction to the 1905 edition was written by John Masefield; this included references to the prize-ring.

1603. REYNOLDS, Quentin
Don't Think It Hasn't Been Fun
London, Cassell and Co. Ltd, 1941
282pp.
An account of the author's voyage to England from America in wartime, each day bringing back memories of past events. There are a number of references to American boxers and boxing, particularly in the section "Seventh Day Out" which includes mention of Mickey Walker, Harry Greb, Tony Canzonieri and others.

1604. RIBALOW, Harold
The Jew in American Sports
New York, The Bloch Publishing Co. "The Jewish Book Concern", 1948.
Bound in blue cloth, gilt lettering on cover and spine.
288pp. Illus.
Contains stories of 25 of the greatest Jewish stars in America, covering a wide range of sports endeavour.
The preface is by Barney Ross. Other boxers mentioned include Joe Choynski, Benny Leonard, Benny Bass, Jack "Kid" Berg and Al Singer.
There are 6 boxing illustrations.

1605. RIBALOW, Harold U. (Editor)
The World's Greatest Boxing Stories
New York, Twayne Publsishers Inc., 1952.
309pp.
Includes stories by Ernest Hemingway, Jack London, Damon Runyon, Dashiell Hammett and others.

1606. RIBALOW, Harold
Fighter From Whitechapel. The Story of Daniel Mendoza.
Illustrated by Simon Jeruchim.
New York, Farrar, Straus and Cudahy. Jewish Publication Society, 1962.
Published simultaneously in Canada by Ambassador Books Ltd., Toronto.
144pp.

1607. RICE, Elmer
Imperial City. A Novel.
London, Victor Gollancz, 1937.

continued

(First published in U.S.A.)
554pp.
Bound in black cloth.
Part of this novel deals with Clifford Austrian, World Lightweight Champion, a young man of extraordinary accomplishments.

1608. RICE, Grantland
Sportslights of 1923.
New York and London, G. P. Putnam Sons, 1924.

1609. RICE, Grantland, and
POWEL, Hartford (Editors)
The Omnibus of Sport
Illustrated by Lee Townsend
New York, Harper and Brothers, Publishers, 1932.
809pp.
This book contains a section entitled "Combat", with the following items of boxing interest:

'The Croxley Master', by A. Conan Doyle

'The Story of a Smile' (Johnson v. Jeffries), by Jack London

'Sullivan versus Corbett', from *The Roar of the Crowd* by J. J. Corbett

'A Piece of Steak', by Jack London

'Cobb Fights it Over' (Feature Story of the Carpentier v. Dempsey fight) by Irvin Cobb, of the *New York Times*

'The Chickasha Bone Crusher', by H. C. Witwer (from *The Bone Crushers*)

'Guilty', by Westbrook Pegler (Story of the Godfrey-Carnera fight in the *Chicago Tribune*)

'A Large Number of Persons', by Paul Gallico.

There is also a section entitled "The Ancient Pageant Passes"; this includes The Roman Ideal of a Boxing Match from Virgil's *Aeneid*, and the essay "The Fight" by William Hazlitt.

1610. RICE, Grantland
The Tumult and the Shouting
My Life and Sport
South Brunswick and New York, A. S. Barnes and Co. Inc. 1954.
Toronto, The Copp Clark Co., 1954.
356pp. Illus.
Among the boxing references are one chapter each devoted to Jack Dempsey and Gene Tunney.

1611. RICE, Harold
Within the Ropes (Champions in Action)

New York, Stephen-Paul Publishing, 1946.
Bound in Yellow cloth, lettering in black on cover and spine.
194pp.
This is a blow-by-blow account of heavyweight championship bouts from the 18th Century to the 20th.
The chapters progress through the stages of the championship from the English Prize-Ring Champions, the American Champions and other bouts, to the emergence of Max Baer, James Braddock and Joe Louis.
The final chapter gives the various sets of Ring Rules, Famous Referees and Announcers, and Training Methods.

1612. RICE, James
History of the British Turf, From the Earliest Times to the Present Day
London, Sampson, Low, Marston, Searle and Rivington. 1872. (2 Volumes)
In Volume I, Chapters VII and XII there are references to John Gully.

1613. RICHARDS, Grant
Author Hunting. By an Old Literary Sportsman.
Memories of Years spent mainly in publishing.
London, Hamish Hamilton, 1934.
295pp.
Chapter XIII – *Plays Pleasant and Unpleasant, Cashel Byron's Profession* and Georges Carpentier.
This chapter includes a letter from Bernard Shaw, extracts from articles by Shaw, and the author's own memories of boxing.
Mention is made of the Carpentier v. Beckett bout and Shaw's article on this in the *Nation*, with other boxing references.
See also "The Great Fight" by Bernard Shaw, 1921.

1614. RICHARDSON, A.E., F.S.A., F.R.I.B.A.
Georgian England
A Survey of Social Life, Trades, Industries and Art from 1700 to 1820.
London, B. T. Batsford Ltd, 1931.
202pp. Illus.
Chapter V, "Sport, Pastime and Recreation", contains a section entitled "Boxing". There is an illustration of the Cribb v. Molyneux fight, from a drawing by Rowlandson.

1615. RICHARDSON, The Reverend John, LLB
Recollections, Political, Literary, Dramatic and Miscellaneous of the Last Half Century.
London, Printed for the author, 1855. 2
continued

Volumes.

The work includes anecdotes of pugilists including George Alexander Lee (son of Harry Lee) and Deaf Burke.

1616. RICKARD, Mrs 'Tex', and OBOLER, Arch

Everything Happened to Him.
The Story of Tex Rickard.
New York, Frederick A. Stokes and Co., 1936.
London, Rich and Cowan Ltd., 1937.
311pp.
Illus. by a frontis. showing Tex Rickard.
Tex Rickard was a famous American boxing promoter; among the bouts he staged were those for the World Title between Johnson and Jeffries and Dempsey and Tunney.

1617. RING RECORD BOOK

See *Nat Fleischer's All Time Ring Record Book*, or the entry under *All Time Ring Record Book* for further information.

1618. RIPLEY, Robert R.

Believe It Or Not. (The Omnibus)
A Modern Book of Wonders, Miracles, Freaks, Monstrosities and Almost Impossibilities, Written, Illustrated and Proved by Robert R. Ripley.
London, Stanley Paul and Co. Ltd., ca.1930s
384pp. Illus.
The contents include notable statistics concerning boxing; such as:

'The Longest Fight'
'Commodus Fought and Won 1031 Battles'
'Jim Corbett Fought in the Prize-Ring for 18 Years'

There are three boxing illustrations.

1619. RITCHIE, J. Ewing

The Night Side of London
First and Second editions published by Tweedie in 1857 and 1858. Third edition (revised) published by Tinsley Brothers, London, 1861. New edition, revised and enlarged. 1869.
This includes a section 'The Sporting Public House' which contains mention of many of the old time pugilists and also Ben Caunt's house in St. Martin's Lane.
The 1869 edition contains a section entitled 'Public Houses' which is similar to the section 'The Sporting Public House' in the earlier edition, though somewhat extended.

1620. RIVERS, James

(Compiler and Editor)
The Sports Book
London, Macdonald and Co (Publishers) Ltd 1946.
This book was described as 'An Introduction to post-war sport'. The contents include 'Boxing' by Paul Irwin.
There are 4 boxing illustrations showing Bruce Woodcock, Vince Hawkins, Freddie Mills and Cyril Gallie.
There were further annual issues of this book as follows:

The Sports Book-2 "Britain's Prospects in the Olympic Games and in Sport Generally", 1948.
Compiled and edited by James Rivers.
There are 2 sections devoted to boxing:

Olympic Contests – Boxing, by George Whiting
General Sports – Boxing, by Lainson Wood.

The sections include 8 boxing illustrations.

The Sports Book-3 Compiled and edited by James Rivers.1949.
This edition includes 'Boxing' by Lainson Wood.
With 3 boxing illustrations.

1621. RIVERS, Joe

Ringside Reviews
(Records, Humour of the Ring, Sketch of the Life of Les Darcy,etc)
Brisbane (Australia), *Truth* and *Sportsman* Ltd., 1933.
Paper covers, coloured purple and white.
This book is divided into 2 parts:

Part I – Boxing
Part II – Wrestling

The boxing contents include:

A Brief History of Boxing
The Growth of the Game
Early Days of the Sport in Australia
Notable Fights
Famous Fights and other similar material

There are 25 boxing illustrations.

1622. ROBB, Frank Maldon, B.A., L.L.B. (Editor)

Poems of Adam Lindsay Gordon
London, Oxford University Press, 1912.
The volume includes the poet's poems with a boxing theme.

1623. ROBBINS, Harold

A Stone for Danny Fisher
London, Brown, Watson, 1958.
Issued as a Corgi paperback, 1962.
319pp.
A novel with boxing content.

1624. ROBERTS, Bechofer
("Ephesian")
Sir Travers Humphries
His Career and Cases
London, John Lane, The Bodley Head,
1936.
Chapter 3, 1910–1911, includes the case regarding in the proposed Jack Johnson v. Bombardier Wells boxing match.
The illustrations include one of Jack Johnson.

1625. ROBERTS, Kenneth
The Captain of the Push
London, Angus and Robertson, 1964.
137pp. Illus.
The story of Larry Foley, owner of the famous saloon and gymnasium in Sydney, used by many prominent fighters.

1626. ROBERTS, Randy
The Manassa Mauler
Baton Rouge, Louisiana State University
Press, 1979.
270pp. plus notes on the text and a bibliography giving Source Material. Illus.
A biography of Jack Dempsey.

1627. ROBERTS, Randy
Papa Jack
Jack Johnson and the Era of White Hopes.
New York, The Free Press, 1983.
London, Robson Books, 1983.
267pp. Illus.

1628. ROBINSON, John Robert
"Old Q". A memoir of William Douglas, Fourth Duke of Queensberry, K.T., One of "The Fathers of The Turf", with a full account of His Celebrated Matches and Wagers etc.
London, Sampson Low, Marston and Co.
Ltd., 1895.
Includes items of pugilistic interest as follows:
Chapter VII (*inter alia*). Anecdote of John Smith, alias "Buckhorse".
Chapter XXIV. Claims that the Fourth Duke did not support the noble, or ignoble, Art of Self Defence.
Note. Nothwithstanding the assertion given in Chapter XXIV, there is evidence that "Old Q" did take an interest in pugilism and was indeed a friend and patron of John Jackson. This is shown by Fred Henning in his *Fights For The Championship*, (Volume 1).

1629. ROBINSON, C.E.

Everyday Life in Ancient Greece
Oxford, The Clarendon Press, 1933.
Illus.
Chapter IX – Recreation 1. "Athletics", contains a reference to boxing.

1630. ROBINSON, Joe
Claret and Crossbuttock, or Rafferty's Prize-Fighters
London, George Allen and Unwin Ltd., 1976
150pp. Illus.
The Story of the Robinson family of North Country Prize-Fighters.

1631. ROBINSON, John Robert
The Last Earls of Barrymore
London, Sampson Low, Marston and Co.,
1894.
250pp. plus Appendix.
This book contains a number of references to pugilism and the prize-ring, particularly to Hooper "The Tinman" who was under the patronage of the Earl.
Among these references are the following:

Chapter V   – The Earl bestows his patronage on the prize-ring. (Humphries v. Mendoza at Odiham)
Chapter IX   – Hooper "The Tinman's" adventure at Vauxhall Gardens
Chapter X   – Some account of the meeting between Big Ben and Johnson, and the latter with Isaac Perrins
Chapter XII   – Hooper's encounter with a bargee
Chapter XIII   – Encounter between Hooper and Watson
Chapter XIV   – An encounter took place this year, 1790, between the Earl of Barrymore's Pet, Hooper, and "Tom Tight", alias Howard, a Reading bargee
Chapter XV   – Encounter between Big Ben and Hooper
Chapter XVIII   – Fight between Johnson and Big Ben
Chapter XXIII   – Hooper thrashes Mr Donadieu, also a draper
Chapter XXXIV – Anecdote of, and death of Hooper.

1632. ROBINSON, Sugar Ray, and ANDERSON, Dave
Sugar Ray
London, Putmam and Co. Ltd., 1970.
369pp. plus Ray Robinson's record, 1940 to 1965. Illus.

1633. ROBSON, Spike
How to Box Six Rounds.
A Manual of Instruction for the Young

continued

Boxer (*Boxing* Handbook No.4)
London, Ewart Seymour and Co. Ltd., 1913.
47pp.
In this instructional item the author discusses the contrasts between American and English training and boxing methods.
The 8 illustrations include some from Robson's contests in America.

1634. RODDA, John and
MAKINS, Clifford
The Sporting Year
A Selection of the Best Sports Writing 1977-1978
London, Collins and Co., 1978.
208pp.
Includes 3 boxing items:

"One Gamble Too Many" (Muhammad Ali)

"Last Fight", by Benny Green

"The Weight on a Boxer's Mind" (Death in the Ring) by Alan Hubbard.

1635. RODWELL, G. Herbert
Woman's Love.
A Romance of Smiles and Tears.
London, Willoughby and Co., 1846. Price — 10s6d.
Also published by Lea in 1853 at 2s.
Illustrated by Alfred Crowquill.
In Chapter XIV the story introduces a character named Mr Jobber Gristelung, "Formerly a distinguished ornament of the prize-ring" and gives a description of his methods of teaching a young boy the art of boxing.
One of Mr Gristelung's principal maxims was "if a man throws a pebble at you, always return him a paving stone".
Chapter XIV is illustrated by a plate entitled "A First Lesson in the Noble Art of Self Defence".

1636. ROE, F. Gordon
Sporting Prints of the 18th and Early 19th Centuries.
With an Introduction by C. Reginald Grundy.
(The *Connoiseur* Series of Books for Collectors)
London, The *Connoiseur* Ltd., 1927.
50pp of text, 48 plates in colour, 2 in monochrome
Although there are no boxing prints reproduced in the book, there is mention of boxing subjects in the text.
There is a comment on the picture by T. Blake, engraved by Turner, entitled "The Interior of the Fives Court" Randall and Turner Sparring". This reports a criticism in *The Annals of Sporting* dated April 1st, 1822; he criticises the picture on the grounds of anatomy, portraiture, etc., and states that some of the sporting celebrities named

in the key to the picture could not have been present. It quotes as an instance that Randall and Turner could not have sparred in the presence of Jem Belcher, as Belcher died before either of the sparrers took up the ring.

1637. ROGERS, Agnes and
ALLEN, Frederick Lewis
I Remember Distinctly
A Family Album of the American People, 1918–1941.
Assembled by Agnes Rogers, Assembler of the *American Procession* and *Metropolis*. With Running Commentary by Frederick Lewis Allen, author of *Only Yesterday* and *Since Yesterday*.
New York, Harper and Brothers, 1947.
London, Hamish Hamilton, 1948.
251pp.
This book is a panorama of American Life during the years of peace from 1918 to 1941.
The boxing interest is centred on the World Heavyweight Champions of that period, discussing the bouts involving Dempsey, Willard, Firpo, Tunney, Heeney, Max Baer, Carnera, Joe Louis and Braddock.

1638. ROMANO, John J.
Fifty Years at the Ringside
New York City, Everlast Publishing Co. Inc. 1932.

1639. ROMANO, John J. (Editor)
Post Boxing Record Book and Sports Annual
New York, *Post* Sports Records Corporation, 1934.
264pp (including adverts), Cartoons by Ted Carroll
New York, *Post* Sports Records Corporation, 1935.
288pp (including adverts), Cartoons by Ted Carroll
New York, John J. Romano, 1936.
160pp (including adverts), Cartoons by Ted Carroll

New York, John J. Romano, 1937.
174pp (inc. adverts), Cartoons by Phil Berube.

These Annuals contain the full records of all champions under the Marquess of Queensberry Rules, together with many articles, cartoons and photographs on boxing subjects.
All the annuals were issued with paper covers.

1640. ROMANO, John J., and
RICHARDS, Jimmy
How to Box and How to Train
New York City, *Post* Sports Records Corporation.

continued

Copyright 1934.
Reissued in illustrated wrappers, 1946.
94pp. Illus.

1641. ROMANO, John J.
(Boxing Coach to Yale University, and Sports
Columnist)
How to Box Correctly
New York, Benlee Sporting Goods Manufac -
turing Co., 1944.
Copyright by John J. Romano.
67pp. Bound in stiff paper wrappers, illustrated by
cuts in the text.

1642. ROPER, Edward
A Sportsman's Memories
Edited by Fred W. Wood
Liverpool, C. Tinling and Co. Ltd., 1921.
295pp. Illus.
This book is mainly dedicated to cricket, with
some racing reminiscences. The author also re-
lates anecdotes concerning Tom Sayers, J. C.
Heenan, Bendigo, Ben Caunt, and Peter Jackson.
There is a story of the author taking part in a
boxing contest at Carlisle.

1643. ROSE, Charlie
Errors That Lose Decisions, or Blunders of
Boxers
Illus. by Special Drawings.
London, Ewart Seymour and Co. Ltd. (Pub-
lishers of *Boxing*), 1914.
79pp. 14 Illus.
This book deals with such things as "Errors of
Style" and "The Open Glove".

1644. ROSE, Charlie
Boxing Taught Through the Slow Motion
Film. (Carpentier, Beckett, Drake, Wells,
Lewis, Berry, and their Methods)
London, Athletic Publications Ltd., 1924.
71pp.
Includes six chapters of text and many pictures of
the boxers mentioned in the sub-title.
A second edition was issued in 1943 by the same
publishers; this was similar in most respects to the
first edition except for the illustrated cover. That
on the later edition shows scenes from the bout
between Joe Louis and Charlie Retzlaff.

1645. ROSE, Charlie (Editor)
The Story of British Boxing.
(50 pictures of British Champions — Story
of the British Heavyweights — By Charlie
Rose — 9 Masters of the Ring — Record of
Lonsdale Belt Holders)

Windsor, Cedric Day, 1949.
Illustrated paper covers, front cover showing
Woodcock v. Mills and the Lonsdale Belt.
There are 5 sections in the text, as follows:

How British Titles Have Changed Hands
The Story of British Boxing, by The Editor
Famous British Title Holders
Top Men in British Boxing
British Heavyweight Champions, by Charlie
Rose

The illustrations show the boxers individually and
in some of their contests.

1646. ROSE, Charlie
Life's a Knock-Out
London, Hutchinson's Library of Sports and
Partimes, 1953.
208pp. Illus.
These are the personal reminiscences of "Britain's
oldest active boxing writer", who at 83, told the
story of watching a bare-knuckle contest 75 years
earlier, his part in the Australian gold rush at the
start of the century, his managing of three British
heavyweight champions, and his journalistic
activities.

1647. ROSE, Henry
Before I Forget
London, W. H. Allen and Co. 1942.
143pp.
A Cavalcade of Recollections, Pen-Pictures, Anec-
dotes and Personalities by one of Britain's Ace
Sportswriters.
Including many boxing references.

1648. ROSE, Lionel
Lionel Rose, Australian
The Life Story of a Champion.
As told to Rod Humphries.
Sydney, Angus and Robertson Ltd, 1969.
150pp. Illus.

1649. ROSENTHAL, Bert
Sugar Ray Leonard. The Baby Faced Boxer.
Chicago, Children's Press, 1982.
43pp. Illus.
This book is catalogued as Juvenile Literature.

1650. ROSS, Barney
(Former World Lightweight and Welter-
weight Champion)
Fundamentals of Boxing
Chicago, Ziff-Davis Publishing Co. (Little
Technical Library), 1942.
127pp. Small 8vo, 38 Illus.
The majority of the pictures were posed for by
continued
R

Barney Ross. The book is dedicated to the Youth of America.

1651. ROSS, Barney, and ABRAMSON, Martin
No Man Stands Alone
London, Stanley Paul and Co. Ltd., 1959.
231pp. Illus.
The prize-fighting career of Barney Ross, an American sports legend.

1652. ROUTLEDGE, George and Sons (Publishers)
Athletic Sports and Manly Exercises
Published 1864.
Illus.
Includes Cricket, Rowing, Sailing, Swimming, Skating, Boxing, Fencing, Broadsword Etc.
See also "Stonehenge", "Forrest" and Co., *The Handbook of Manly Exercises.*

1653. ROYAL ARMY AND NAVY BOXING ASSOCIATION (Publishers)
Boxing Rules and Guide to Refereeing and Judging etc.
No date.
47pp. Hard covers
Titles etc. on front cover.

1654. ROYAL PUBLISHING COMPANY (Publishers)
How to Box
The Science of Self Defence, or The Art of Sparring and Boxing — Taught Easily Without a Master.
Philadelphia (U.S.A.), 1910.
Light purple paper covers, with a picture of Griffo and a partner on the front cover.
Illus.
This instructional material is presented in 3 parts, dealing with methods of Defence, Attack and Training.

1655. RUBENS, Alfred
Anglo-Jewish Portraits
A Biographical Catalogue of Engraved Anglo-Jewish Portraits from the Earliest Times to the Accession of Queen Victoria
With a Foreword by J. M. Hake, C.B.E., Director of the National Portrait Gallery.
London, The Jewish Museum, 1935.
This item contains details of the portraits of many Anglo-Jewish pugilists and of their battles, including Abraham Belasco, Isaac Bittoon, Samuel Elias (Dutch Sam), Daniel Mendoza and others.
Illustrations include Isaac Bittoon, Dutch Sam, Mendoza, and Mendoza v. Humphries.

1656. RUNYON, Damon
More Than Somewhat
Stories selected by E. C. Bentley.
London, Constable and Co. Ltd., 1937.
311pp.
Includes stories of boxing interest.

1657. RUNYON, Damon
Short Takes
(With a Memoir of the author by Don Iddon)
London, Constable and Co. Ltd., 1948.
(1st English Edition)
435pp.
There are many boxing references in this book, both in Don Iddon's Memoirs and in the text.

1658. RUSSELL, Fred
I'll Try Anything Twice
A Collection of Sport Humour and Anecdotes
Nashville (U.S.A.) Editions for the Armed Services Inc., published by arrangement with The McQuiddy Press
276pp. Illus.
This item contains a number of boxing items, including "Heavyweight Champions", and "The Reign of Heavyweight Champions".

1659. RUSSELL, Lord John (First Earl Russell, 1792–1878) (Editor)
Memoirs, Journal and Correspondence of Thomas Moore
8 volumes 1853–1856, with 2 portraits.
Moore's interest in the prize-ring and pugilism is mentioned in these volumes, notably in volumes 2 and 5, as follows:
Volume 2 — contains an account of Moore's visit, with Gentleman Jackson and Scrope Davis, to the fight between Turner and Randall at Crawley Down on 4th Dec., 1818.
Volume 5 — gives an account on Moore's visit to Gentleman Jackson on Feb. 23rd, 1828, when Jackson showed two or three letters of Lord Byron, which Moore copied out.

1660. RUSSELL, The Reverend John
Memoirs of the Rev. John Russell and His Outdoor Life
First Edition 1878
New Edition 1883
London, Chatto and Windus, (with James G. Commin, Exeter), 1902.
(New edition, with illustrations, by N.H.J. Baird)
Chapter II tells of the Rev. Russell learning to spar
continued

at Oxford, Set-to's with others, and wrestling matches in Devon and Cornwall.

1661. RUSSELL, Leonard (Editor)

The Saturday Book.
1951 Edition.
This was announced as "The 11th Annual Appearance of this Renowned Repository of Curiosities and Looking Glass of the Past and Present".
The contents include "Sports for All Seasons" by Olive Cook and Edwin Smith where there is mention of pottery plaques commemorating the two fights between Tom Spring and Jack Langan. These plaques also show ballooning, with men and women in appropriate dress; the comparison between the two sports was used by Lord Palmerston in his heated defence of boxing following the Sayers v. Heenan contest.
Information is also given on other pottery figures which feature pugilists.

1662. RYLEY, Samuel William, 1759—1837

The Itinerant, or Memoirs of an Actor
This work was first published between 1808 and 1827, in 3 series with 3 volumes in each series. Another edition was published in 1880 from the *Chronicle* offices in Oldham.
Volume III contains an anecdote on Isaac Perrins, the well known pugilist, who fought the champion Tom Johnson. This anecdote is mentioned in Volume I of *Boxiana* under "Biography of Isaac Perrins" where it is stated that the anecdote is taken from the very popular and amusing work *The Itinerant*.

DEFENSIVE EXERCISES;

COMPRISING

WRESTLING,

AS IN CUMBERLAND, WESTMORELAND, CORNWALL, AND DEVONSHIRE;

BOXING,

BOTH IN THE USUAL MODE AND IN A SIMPLER ONE;

DEFENCE AGAINST BRUTE FORCE, BY VARIOUS MEANS;
FENCING AND BROAD SWORD, WITH SIMPLER
METHODS; THE GUN, AND ITS EXERCISE;
THE RIFLE, AND ITS EXERCISE;

&c. &c. &c.

WITH ONE HUNDRED ILLUSTRATIONS.

By DONALD WALKER.

LONDON:
THOMAS HURST, 5, ST. PAUL'S CHURCH-YARD;
MACHIN AND CO. DUBLIN;
SOLD ALSO, BY WILLIAM F. ORR, AND CO. PATERNOSTER ROW;
AND J. THOMAS, FINCH LANE, CORNHILL.

1840.

Title-Page *Defensive Exercises* (Walker) (Bib. Ref. 1904)

1663. SABINE, T.
Athletic Exercise, or The Science of Boxing
Displayed
London, 1788.
32pp.
Containing an account of the most celebrated
boxers of this country, from the time of Broughton to that of the present heroes, Johnson, Ryan,
Humphreys, and Mendoza the Jew. Including
their battles, manoeuvres, names, letters, challenges
and puffing advertisements, from the papers of
that time to the present day.

1664. SALDO, A. M. (A.M. Woollaston)
How to Excel at Games and Athletics
London, Published for Maxalding by Press
and General Publishing Services Ltd. 1937.
80pp.
Includes a section entitled *Boxing.*

1665. SAMPSON, Edmund
Tales of the Fancy
With Original Illustrations by Robert Prowse
Published at *Sporting Truth* Office, Covent
Garden, London, 1889.
160pp. Coloured paper covers. Price 1s.
The "Tales" include the following of pugilistic
interest:
A Night at Bill Richardson's. (With Some Recollec-
tions of Mine Host)

Maurice Brady's Fight (As told by A Pugilist)

An Episode at "Ould Nat's" St Martin's Lane (As
told by Himself)

Benjamin Bellacose Bunkum, and his black boxer
(As Told by Himself)

1666. SAMPSON, George
A Concise History of English Literature
Cambridge, The University Press, June, 1941
Reprinted November 1941, also 1942, 1943,
1944 and 1945.
Chapter XIV, "The Nineteenth Century", Part III
"Post Victorian Literature", Section VI "Character
and the Literature of Sport".
This section refers to Pierce Egan and his work.

1667. SAMUELS, Charles
The Magnificent Rube
The Life and Gaudy Times of Tex Rickard.
New York, The McGraw-Hill Book Co. Ltd.,
1957.
296pp. plus Bibliography. Illus.
A biography of the progenitor of the first million-
dollar gate in boxing.

1668. SANDFORD, Harry
Stand Up and Fight. The Fight Game and
the Men Who Make It.
New York, Exposition Press, 1962.
204pp.

1669. SARGENT, Harry R.
Thoughts Upon Sport
A Work Dealing Shortly with Each Branch
of Sport.
London, Simpkin, Marshall, Hamilton, Kent
and Co., 1895.
426pp.
The boxing references occur in the following chapters:

Chapter XVII – Manly Games and Exercises

Chapter XIX – The Prize-Ring and the Cockpit

Chapter XXII – Osbaldeston, Ross, Kennedy,
Budd and Barclay Allardyce

There is one boxing illustration.

1670. SAROYAN, William
The Human Comedy. A Novel.
London, Faber and Faber Ltd., 1943.
222pp.
Young Corbett of Fresno (Young Corbett III) is
frequently mentioned in this novel.

1671. SAYE, Charles
The Boxer
A Below-the-belt story of an international
sportsman.
London, New English Library, 1971.
110pp. Paperback.

1672. SAYERS, Henry
Fights Forgotten
A History of Some of the Chief English and
American Prize Fights Since the Year 1788.
London, T. Werner Laurie, 1909.
260pp. 10 Illus. Bound in red or blue cloth.
Consists of 24 chapters, each dealing with a famous
bout and including many heroes of the prize-ring,
such as John Jackson, Jem Belcher, Tom Cribb,
Tom Spring, Jem Ward, Tom Sayers, Jem Mace,
Jim Corbett, Bob Fitzsimmons and others.

1673. SAYERS, Tom
A Catalogue of the Trophies Won by, and
Presented to the Late Tom Sayers
London, 1865.

1674. SCANNELL, Vernon

continued

The Fight
London, Peter Nevill, 1953.
London, Corgi Books, 1958. (Paperback)
190pp.
A powerful novel of human emotions and the drama of the ring.

1675. SCANNELL, Vernon
The Big Time
London, Longmans, Green and Co. Ltd., 1965.
208pp.
A novel about professional boxing.

1676. SCANNELL, Vernon
Ring of Truth
London, Robson Books, 1983.
342pp.
A novel with the background of the harsh and demanding world of professional boxing.

1677. SCARROTT, John
50 Years of Boxing
Reprinted from the *South Wales Echo and Express*
Cardiff, Western Mail and Echo Ltd. No date
23pp. Stiff paper covers.
Includes reminiscences of Jim Driscoll, Freddie Welsh, Jimmy Wilde, Johnny Basham and other leading boxers.

1678. SCHIFFER, Paul
Never a Champion
Winnipeg (Canada), published by the author 1966.
175pp.
The author was a well-known Canadian welter and middleweight boxer in the 1930's, when he fought under the name of Paul Schaeffer.
Paul campaigned successfully in England, meeting a number of our leading boxers.
This book is a novel, based on his life and career.

1679. SCHOOR, Gene
Giant Book of Sports
Introduction by Mel Allen
An American Publication, 1948.
187pp. size 11ins x 8½ins
How the stars play the game; stories of the sports stars, including Dempsey, Tunney and many others

1680. SCHOOR, Gene
Sugar Ray Robinson
New York, Greenberg, Publisher, 1951.
Bound in grey-brown cloth; design of boxing gloves on front cover.

119pp. including Robinson's ring record.
31 illustrations.
Covers the great boxer's career, from Chapter 1 "In the Beginning", to Chapter 15 "His Greatest Win".
Also published in Canada by Ambassador Books Ltd. 1951.

1681. SCHOOR, Gene
The Jack Dempsey Story
London, Nicholas Kaye Ltd., 1956.
181pp. Illus.

1682. SCHOTT, Dr Carl P., and RILEY, Hugh R. Jr. (Editors)
The Official National Collegiate Athletic Association Boxing Guide.
Including the Official Rules, 1943.
New York, A. S. Barnes and Co. (The American Sporting Library), 1942.
Stiff paper covers, with boxing picture on the front cover.
The contents include: A Brief History of Collegiate Boxing by Hugh R. Riley Jr — The Role of Boxing in Military Training, by Commander Gene Tunney, and other articles by various contributors on the Medical aspects of Boxing and also on Refereeing and Judging.
The illustrations show pictures of some of the colleges and their boxers, some of whom are shown in action.
The Official National Collegiate Athletic Association Boxing Guide was issued annually until 1947 when the final issue appeared. Dr. Carl P. Schott was the sole editor for all except the first issue.

1683. SCHULBERG, Budd
The Harder They Fall
New York, Random House Ltd. 1947.
Toronto, Random House of Canada, 1947.
London, The Bodley Head, 1948.
343pp.
Some critics reviewed this novel as presenting professional prize-fighting as a thoroughly crooked and brutal business.
Gene Tunney is quoted as stating that he did not get the full significance of its gems of wit until the second reading.

1684. SCHULBERG, Budd
Some Faces in the Crowd
London, The Bodley head Ltd, 1954.
3rd Impression, 1975.
175pp.
A book of short stories, some with a boxing theme.

1685. SCHULBERG, Budd
Loser and Still Champion:

continued

Muhammad Ali
New York, Doubleday and Co. Ltd., 1972.
London, New English Library, 1972.
160pp. Illus.
This book is not so much a biography of Muhammud Ali as a celebration of his talents and abilities after he had been defeated for the first time in his professional career, by Joe Frazier.

1686. SCHULIAN, John
Writers' Fighters and Other Sweet
Scientists
Foreword by Studs Terkel.
Kansas City, Kansas, Andrews and McMeel,
1983.
252pp. Limp card covers.
Pen portraits of such boxers as Muhammad Ali, Sugar Ray Leonard, Roberto Duran, Jake La Motta, Archie Moore, Henry Armstrong, and others, by a man who was voted the number one sports columnist in the USA by his peers at the 1980 Associated Press Sports Editors' Convention.

1687. SCOTT, Fraser
Weigh In; The Selling of a Middleweight
New York, Thomas Y. Crowell Co., 1974.
Published simultaneously in Canada.
213pp. Illus.
The story of a speedy rise to fame of Fraser Scott, and of how the fight game lost its glamour for him.

1688. SCOTT, Neil
Joe Louis. A Picture Story of His Life.
New York, Greenberg, Publisher, 1947.
Foreword by Frank Sinatra.
122pp. mostly illustrations.
Issued in paper covers and also in a De-Luxe Edition, bound in cloth.

1689. SCOTT, Phil
(Ex-Heavyweight Champion of England),
with JAMES, Alexander R.
The Complete Boxer. A Textbook on Boxing.
London, Alston Rivers Ltd (1929)
80pp. Illus.
Illustrated with 7 photographic poses by Phil Scott and 8 woodcut pictures of boxing positions.
Paper covers, with a picture of Scott on the front.

1690. SEARLE, Mark (Compiler)
Turnpikes and Tollbars
Special Introduction by The Right Hon. The Earl of Birkenhead, P.C., G.C.S.I.
London, Hutchinson and Co. (Publishers) Ltd., 1930 (2 volumes)

12 coloured plates.
This edition is limited to 500 numbered copies.
Volume II contains a section entitled "Milling" which includes the following pugilistic references:

Turner and Scroggins (*Sporting Magazine*, Vol. 51, 1817)

Road to the Fight (*Real Life in London*, 1821)

Battle between Josh Hudson and Jem Ward for £200 (*Bell's Life in London* Nov. 16th, 1823)

On the Road to the Fight between Neal and Tom Gaynor for £200 (*Bell's Life in London*, March 20th, 1831).

This section also contains the following illustrations:

The Great Fight between Jem Mace and Tom King for 400 sovs. and the Championship of England at Thames Haven, Nov.26th, 1862. (*Illustrated Sporting News*, Dec. 13th, 1862).

Mill Fight (An aquatint in the compiler's possession)

The Man Wot Won a Fight (*Bell's Life in London*, Aug. 22nd, 1830)

The Man Wot Lost the Fight (*Bell's Life in London*, Sept. 19th, 1830).

1691. SEEBACK, Harry
(*Police Gazette* Champion, and holder of the Richard K. Fox Gold Medal, and Challenger of the World)
Scientific Bag Punching.
New York, Richard K. Fox Publishing Co., 1913.
80pp. Illus.
The chapters of instruction fully cover all punches, movements and variations in the use of the punchbag.
There are also hints on training for boxing.

1692. SELLAR, R.J.B.
Play!
The Best Sporting Stories.
London, John Hamilton Ltd.
191pp.
The section entitled "A little bit of everything" contains some boxing stories.

1693. SELLER, Nat
(Britain's Premier Boxing Trainer)
My Road to Boxing Stardom
Compiled and edited by Leslie Bell.
London, Linden Lewis Ltd.

continued

This book was advertised for publication on Dec. 10th, 1947, as "An Intimate instructive book in which this world famous trainer of champions reveals the secrets of successful ring preparation . . .".
Other contributors include Jack Solomons, Ted Broadribb, Freddie Mills and many other Sporting Personalities.

1694. SELLER, Nat
Improve Your Boxing.
With Instructional Photos Posed by Freddie Mills.
The Whole Collated and Edited by Leslie Bell
London, Findon Publications Ltd., 1948.
77pp. Illus.
Paper covers, picture of Nat Seller with Freddie Mills on front cover.
Foreword by Jack Solomons.
There are a number of illustrations, mostly of Freddie Mills.
The text consists of 10 instructional chapters; the final one is entitled "The Boxer in Private Life".

1695. SERLING, Rod
Requiem for A Heavyweight
Copyright in U.S.A., 1957.
London, Corgi Books, 1962.
128pp. Paperback.
Based on the television play of the same title.

1696. SERVICE, Robert W.
The Rough-Neck
London, T. Fisher Unwin, 1923.
448pp.
This novel, divided into Books I – V, and a total of 65 chapters, deals with the life of a pugilist; but only Book I really deals with the prize-ring.
Book I is entitled "The Bruiser".

1697. SHAFTESBURY PUBLISHING COMPANY (Publishers)
How to Box to Win – How to Build Muscle – How to Breathe, Stand Walk or Run – How to Punch the Bag.
A Book of Health and Strength.
Chicago, 1920.
The sections under the title-headings are contributed to Terry McGovern, James J. Corbett, J. Gardner-Smith, M.D., and Gus E. and Arthur R. Keeley.
Fully illustrated, reprinted by kind permission of the New York *Evening World*.
Copyright 1899 by the New York *Evening World* – 1900 by Rohde and Jenkins – 1920 by Shaftesbury Publishing Co.
The first two contributors were of course famous as World Champion boxers; J. Gardner-Smith, M.D. was a medical man and Gus E. and Arthur R.

Keeley were Champion Bag-Punchers of the World

1698. SHAPIRO, E.
Peddlers of Flesh
Hollywood (Calif.), Vantage Press Inc., 1959.
61pp.

1699. SHARKEY, Tom
United States Navy Drill. Known as Physical Training Without Arms.
Illustrated with Photographs Specially Posed for this Book by Sharkey and photographed by Norman of New York.
New York City, Richard K. Fox Publishing Co., 1912.
(Fox's Athletic Library No.11)
Red paper covers.
The contents include: Introduction, Hints on Training, Position for Exercises, Exercises Nos. 2 to 25.
There are 4 illustrations plus 25 photos showing the exercises.

1700. SHARPLES, William (Printer)
The Complete Art of Boxing, Teaching the Practical and Elementary Principles, Attitudes and Movements of the Science in the Present Day. Also the Art of Attack, as practised by the Most Celebrated Pugilists. With Broughton's Rules, as was Practised at his Amphitheatre in Tottenham Court Road.
Philadelphia, Sold Wholesale and Retail, No.118 North Fourth Street, William Sharples, Printer, 1829.
The paper wrapper continues the title: "To which is added, Biographical Sketches of the Most Celebrated Pugilists".
This book is based on *A Treatise on Boxing including a Complete Set of Lessons on the Art of Self Defence*, London, 1802, and Sir Thomas Parkyn's *Inn Play*.
The frontispiece is a folding plate on which are 9 small cuts, taken from the two books mentioned above.
This is one of the earliest books on boxing published in the U.S.A.

1701. SHAW, Bernard
Cashel Byron's Profession
London, The Modern Press, 1886.
164pp.
New York, Harper's 1886.
New York, Brentano, 1889.
This boxing novel first appeared as a serial in the magazine *Today*, commencing in 1885. Following
continued

the first edition in book form it was reissued many times by various London publishers.

The book was turned into a play under the title *The Admirable Bashville*, written by Shaw in Elizabethan verse, and first performed at the Imperial Theatre on June 3rd, 1903, with Ben Webster playing the title-role. C. Aubrey Smith was also in the cast.

The novel and the play were issued together in book form, together with an essay on "Modern Prizefighting", notably by Constable and Co. in 1905. This edition contained 349pp.

Cashel Byron, the hero of the novel and the play, absconded from school and went to Australia, where he made good as a fighter. He won his battles in the ring and also the heart and hand of an heiress.

1702. SHAW, Bernard
The Great Fight, 1921.

This 16-page pamphlet is described by the publisher Grant Richards in his book *Author Hunting*, Chapter XIII. "Plays Pleasant and Unpleasant". G. B. Shaw attended the contest between Carpentier and Beckett in December, 1919, and wrote an article in the *Nation* about the fight; this was later issued in New York under the title as given above as "By the author of *Cashel Byron's Profession*".

1703. SHAW, Edwin F.
(Late Instructor at Harvard University)
The Teacher of Sparring
(With illustrations photographed from life)
Boston, (U.S.A.), John P. Lovell's Sons, 1886.

63pp. Illus.
Bound in greenish-brown cloth, lettered in black, with sparring picture on front cover.
This item contains a number of sections covering positioning, defensive and attacking positions, a glossary of terms, etc.

1704. SHAW, Fred G., F.G.S.,Assoc. M. Inst. C.E., M.M.S.
The Science of Self Defence
London, Published by the Author, 1919.

179pp. Illus.
Bound in purple cloth, lettered in gold on front cover and on spine.
Design showing boxers in action on front cover.
15 Instructional chapters, with addendum and index.

1705. SHAW, Fred, F.Z.S.
Blackie's Boys Annual, 1922.
London and Glasgow, Blackie and Sons Ltd.
This annual contains an article by Mr. Shaw entitled "Boxing for Youths".

1706. SHAW, Irwin

Mixed Company
New York, Random House Inc., 1937.

480pp.
This selection contains items of boxing interest, including "Return to Kansas City".

1707. SHAW PUBLISHING COMPANY LTD (Publishers)
Vital Sayings of the Year, 1933
The Annual Record of the ideas and opinions expressed by leading thinkers on problems & topics of the year.
London, 1934.

The book includes four quotations on boxing.

1708. SHEED, Wilfred
Muhammad Ali
A Portrait in words and photographs
Lose Angeles (California), Alskog Inc., 1975.
London, Weidenfeld and Nicholson, 1975.

226pp. Profusely Illus. 4to.

1709. SHORE, Saxon, and GILROY, J.T.
Rough Island Story
News Reel (and Unreal) of the Depression, 1931–1935.
Commentary by Saxon Shore –
Pictures by J. T. Gilroy.
London, Methuen and Co., 1935.

110pp.
Includes references to Carnera boxing at the Albert Hall (with a picture). Also "Opening of the Baldwin-Churchill Battle for the All-India Belt", with a picture of the two gentlemen in boxing kit.

1710. "SHEFF" (Capt. C. V. Sheffield)
Boxing. All About It.
World, Empire, British, Olympic, A.B.A.
Birkenhead (Cheshire) The Liverpolitan Ltd, ca.1960.

94pp. Paper covers. Illus.
Contains sixty years of records, with other items of useful information on boxing.

1711. SHEPHERD, Jim
Australian Sporting Almanack
Dee Why West (N.S.W.), Paul Hamlyn Pty. Ltd., 1974.

295pp.
The Almanack includes a 33-page section on Australian boxing.

1712. SHEPHERD, T.B. (Compiler)
The Noble Art. An Anthology.

continued

With an Introduction by Colm Brogan
London, Hollis and Carter Ltd., 1950.

265pp. Illus.
Bound in red cloth.
The contents consist of 9 sections and 2 appendices. The parts are entitled as follows:
Boxiana – Train Up a Child in the Way He Should Go – The Glory That was Greece – The Craft of Boxing – The Augustan Age – The Corinthian Age – The Passing of Prize Fighting – The New Age etc.
These sections contain extracts from the works of William Hazlitt, George Borrow, John Masefield, Jack Dempsey, Charles Dickens, Robert Graves, Pierce Egan and many others.

1713. SHEPPEY, M.

The Bruiser
Contained in a pamphlet with the following title page:
A Hint on Duelling in a Letter to a Friend. The Second Edition, to which is added The Bruiser or an Inquiry into the Pretensions of Modern Manhood, In a Letter to a Young Gentleman.
Printed for Mr. Sheppey, under the Royal Exchange, Cornhill, 1752.

Price One Shilling.
44pp.

1714. SHERIDAN, Barnett

King Sol (A Novel)
London, Chatto and Windus, 1939.
Toronto, The Macmillan Company of Canada Ltd., 1939.

298pp.
Dedication "To the Memory of Riffka Shrensky".

1715. SHERIDAN, Jim

Leave the Fighting to McGuigan
The Official Biography of Barry McGuigan.
Harmondsworth (Middx.) Viking Division of Penguin Books Ltd., 1985.

216pp. Illus.

1716. SHERWOOD, NEELY and JONES (Afterwards Jones and Co) (Publishers)

The Annals of Sporting and Fancy Gazette
London, 1822–1826.

This magazine was described as "Entirely Appropriated to Sporting Subject and Fancy Pursuits. Containing every Thing worthy of Remark on (inter alia) Pugilism".
Was originally issued in monthly parts; there were thirteen half-yearly volumes and one part, (June, 1828) following which issue publication ceased.
It included 155 plates, of which 50 were coloured, by such artists as Samuel Alken, Herring, and the Cruikshank brothers. There were also many woodcuts in the text.
Each issue contained a section entitled "The Fancy Gazette", which was edited by Jon Bee (John Badcock), and almost entirely devoted to pugilism. Other sections of the magazine also included items of boxing interest.

1717. SHOAF, Pal

The World Is Mine. A Novel.
A Dramatic Love Story of the Prize Ring.
Hollywood and New York, Pal Shoaf Publishers, 1948.

272pp. plus biography of the author. Frontis.
This novel was highly acclaimed on its appearance, by personalities such as Frank Sinatra, Mickey Walker, Max Baer and by representatives of the press. The frontis. is a reproduction of a photograph of Greats and Near Greats of the Prize-Ring, taken at the Manhattan Gym in Sept. 1925. Among the fighters shown are Jack Dempsey, Mickey Walker, Tommy Loughran, Pete Herman and Bermondsey Billy Wells.

1718. SHORTER, Clement King

George Borrow and His Circle
London, Hodder and Stoughton, 1913.

450pp. Illus.
Contains many references to pugilism, including Chapter III "George Borrow and the Fancy".

1719. SHORTER, Clement K.

The Life of George Borrow
London, J. M. Dent and Sons Ltd., 1919.
New York, E. P. Dutton and Co., 1919.
This is a later and enlarged version of *George Borrow and His Circle.*
Includes Chapter XI, "Borrow and the Fancy".

1720. SHULMAN, Milton

How To be a Celebrity
London, Reinard and Evans, 1950.

215pp.
Caricature by "Vicky" of the *News Chronicle.*
Includes on pages 111 to 117 "Joe Louis", with a caricature of Louis. Joe Louis is also depicted on the front of the dust-wrapper.

1721. SICCHIO, Richard R.

Thirty Day Drill for Amateur Boxers
The Pocket Guide to Better Boxing.
Hurley (Wis.), Published by the Author, ca.1953.

1722. SICKLEMORE, Richard

continued

Pugilism, or an Address to Thomas Spring
Brighton, 1824.

1723. SILER, George
The Battle of the Century
Being a review of the World Championship
Battle between Robert Fitzsimmons and
James J. Corbett at Carson City, March 17th
1897.
Chicago, W. J. Jefferson Printing and Publish
ing Co., 1897.
51pp.
George Siler, who was the chief correspondent of
the Chicago *Tribune*, was the referee of the Fitzsimmons v. Corbett contest. His account of the
battle was reputed to be one of the best things of
its kind ever written. The account was printed in
book form as above, dealing with the two principals.
In his *Gentleman Jim* (1943), Nat Fleischer mentions *The Battle of the Century* as being a very
rare book; a copy being held in the fistic library
of *The Ring*.
See the entry *The Fight of the Century*, under
Naughton, W.W., and also the same title by George
Siler and Lou M. Houseman.

1724. SILER, George
Inside Facts of Pugilism
Chicago, Laird and Lee, 1907.
92pp. Bound in cloth. Illus.

**1725. SILER, George, and
HOUSEMAN, Lou M.**
The "Fight of the Century"
Chicago, W.J. Jefferson Printing and Pub-
lishing Co., 1897.
51pp.
This is a review of the World Championship con-
test between Bob Fitzsimmons and James J.
Corbett at Carson City, March 17th, 1897.

1726. SILKS, Donald K.
Your Book of Boxing
Written and illustrated by D. K. Silks
London, Faber and Faber, 1954.
48pp.

**1727. SILTZER, Captain Frank
(Late of H. M. Grenadier Guards)**
The Story of British Sporting Prints
First Published 1925.
New Edition (One Thousand Copies) Pub-
lished by Halton and Truscott Smith, Ltd.
London, 1929. (Revised and enlarged)
409pp. Illus.
Bound in green cloth with gold titles on front

cover and spine.
The New Edition was issued after the death of the
author; this was in response to many requests.
The book includes a section entitled "Prize-
Fighters and Prize Fights", including plates.
There is also mention of the long coloured prints
by Henry Alken "Going to a Fight" and "Return-
ing from a Fight".

1728. SIMPSON, S. L.
Notes on Boxing
Cambridge, 1933.
Cambridge Review "New Blue" series, No.9.

**1729. SINGER, Isadore
(Projector and Managing Editor)**
The Jewish Encyclopedia
A Descriptive Record of the History, Re-
ligion, Literature and Customs of the Jewish
People from the Earliest Times to the Pres-
ent Day.
New York and London, Funk and Wagnall's
Co., 1901 onwards. (12 volumes)
The volumes contain short biographies of a number
of Jewish pugilists.
The relevant volumes are:
Nos. II, III, IV, V and VIII, and the boxers men-
tioned include: Benjamin Bendoff (or Bendorff),
Abraham Belasco, William Benjamin, Joseph (Joe)
Bernstein, Isaac Bittoon, Joe Choynski, Samuel
Elias, Samuel Evans (Young Dutch Sam), and
Daniel Mendoza.

1730. SINGH, Benny
Champions Past and Present
(A Commentary on South African Boxing)
Durban, Central News Agency, 1949.
24pp. Illus.

**1731. SINGH, Benny
(The Father of African Boxing)**
My Champions Were Dark
Foreword by Jack Solomons
Durban (S.Africa), Pennants Publishing Co.
(Pty) Ltd., 1963.
199pp. Illus.
The author tells of his life in boxing, as a boxer,
trainer, manager and promoter.

1732. SKEHAN, Everett M.
Rocky Marciano
Biography of a First Son, written with the
family assistance of Louis, Peter and Mary
Ann Marciano.
Boston (USA), Houghton Mifflin Co., 1977.
London, Robson Books Ltd., 1977.
363pp. plus Appendix showing Marciano's record.
continued

Illus. from photographs.

1733. SKENE, Don
The Red Tiger. A Boxing Novel.
New York and London, D. Appleton-Century Co. Inc., 1934.
Bound in red cloth, yellow lettering on front and
on spine.
196pp. Foreword by Damon Runyon.
24illus.

1734. SLADEN, N.St.Barbe, F.R.S.L.
The Real Le Queux
The Official Biography of William Le Queux
London, Nicholson and Watson Ltd., 1938.
239pp. Illus.
Chapter 19 includes reference to Frank Slavin.

1735. SMEETON, George
Doings in London, or Day and Night Scenes
of the Frauds, Frolics, Manners and Deprad-
ations of the Metropolis
London, G. Smeeton, 1828.
Illus. by engravings by Bonner from engravings by
Mr. Robert Cruikshank.
On the subject of pugilism is included "The Doings
in the Tennis Court" with an illustration of the
same title depicting two boxers on a raised stage,
with spectators.
There were a number of editions of this work; the
tenth edition published in London by Orlando
Hodgson has no reference to George Smeeton,
although it is similar in text, etc. to the first
edition. A later edition in 1850 refers to the
illustrations being by Mr. G. Cruikshank.

1736. SMITH, Ed.W.
Knockouts I Have Seen
With decorations and drawings by Wallace
E. Smith.
Chicago, The Sutton-Spinner Publishing
Co (Copyright) 1922.
67pp.
Bound in stiff grey paper covers, lettered in yellow
and purple, with a picture of a knock-out on the
front cover.
The author was a well known sports writer and
boxing referee.
The book is dedicated to "The memory of the late
lamented George Siler, a writer on Fistiana and a
referee of utmost honesty".
The text refers to many knock-outs in boxing
bouts in U.S.A., including Joe Choynski v. Kid
Carter and knock-outs by Bob Fitzsimmons, Kid
McCoy and others.
In addition to the decorations there are 6 illustrations.

1737. SMITH, James and Horace

Rejected Addresses
London, Printed for John Miller, Covent
Garden, 1812.
This work ran through a number of editions
including a modern edition edited by
Andrew Boyle and published by Constable
and Co. 1929.
There is discussion in this book regarding the
authorship of *The Fancy*, q.v.

1738. SMITH, Lady Eleanor
The Spanish House. A Novel.
London, Hutchinson and Co. (Publishers)
Ltd. 1938.
415pp.
This book includes a description of life in a boxing
booth.

1739. SMITH, Lady Eleanor
Life's A Circus
(Reminiscences of Lady Eleanor Smith)
London, Longmans Green and Co., 1939.
294pp. Illus.
Includes in chapter 9 "Ballet and Boxing" and
other references to the sport.

1740. SMITH, Maurice (Editor)
The People Boxing Guide
London, Odhams Press Ltd, 1950.
96pp. Stiff paper covers, Illus.

1741. SMITH, Owen
Boxing without a Master; or The Scientific
Art and Practice of Attack and Self Defence
With several illustrations of current pugilistic
attitudes
Philadelphia. A. Winch, Publisher, ca. 1854.
This item is probably the same as that under the
same title by Owen Swift, with a mistake in the
name of the author; alternatively it may be a copy
of Swift's work.

1742. SMITH, Dr. William, etc. (Editors)
A Dictionary of Greek and Roman
Antiquities.
Third Edition Revised and Enlarged.
London, John Murray, 1914. Two Volumes.
Volume II includes a short illustrated article en-
titled "Pugilistica", which refers to several other
works on boxing in the context of the main title.

1743. SNELLING, O. F.
(see also FREDERICK, Oswald)
Rare Books and Rarer People

continued

Some Personal Reminiscences of "The Trade"
London, Werner Shaw Ltd, 1982.
256pp. Illus.
This book, by the well-known author and journalist on boxing is primarily concerned with the characters he met in the antiquarian book business, but Chapter III, "Old Jim", relates of how the subject lived in the same Lambeth Street which produced four champions, two of them being Jem Smith and Johnny Curley.

1744. SNELLING, O.F.
(see also FREDERICK, Oswald)
A Bedside Book of Boxing
London, Pelham Books Ltd., 1972.
196pp. Illus.
The author delves into the archives and into his own memory to provide a pot-pourri of immense interest to fight-fans.

1745. SNOWDEN, W. Crawford
London, 200 Years Ago.
With an Introduction by E.G.H. Taylor, D.Sc.,
F.R.G.S., F.R.Hist.Soc.
London, A *Daily Mail* Publication, 1948.
63pp.
Stiff pictorial paper covers. Comprising old maps, plans, pictures, and text.
Includes the following boxing references:
North of Oxford Street: refers to the tea gardens on the site of the Adam and Eve Public House, where John Broughton had his amphitheatre. Barbaric Sports and Fighting Women, describes Hockley in the Hole, near Camberwell Green, where there was a beer garden which was the scene of bear-baiting, bull-fighting and prize-fights in which the contestants were ocasionally women.

1746. "SOLAR PLEXUS"
(Will Lawless) (Editor)
Records of Australian Boxers
This book was advertised on the back of "Boxing Made Easy" by "Solar Plexus" 1919, as follows:

"Records of Australian Boxers/Edited by 'Solar Plexus'/Profusely Illustrated. Ready Shortly. Order Your Copy Early/Price: One Shilling:/Publishers: New Century Press Ltd./431 Kent Street, Sydney"

1747. "SOLAR PLEXUS" (Will Lawless)
The Darcy Story
A rare Australian publication, dealing with the legendary Les Darcy.

1748. SOLOMONS, Jack
Jack Solomons' 1948 Annual of the Ring.
Compiled by L.N. Bailey.

(Full Records of the Leading British and World Boxers)
London, Playfair Books Ltd., 1948.
Bound in stiff paper covers, picture of famous boxers on front cover, with Jack Solomons.
124pp.
The contributors include Peter Wilson, Joe Bromley, Euan Wellwood and others.

Complete lists are given of World, British, British Empire, European and other amateur and Professional Champions. There are 65 pages of boxers records (Indexed). The book is illustrated by a number of full page pictures and some smaller portraits of boxers among the records.
A similar annual was issued by Jack Solomons in the following years under the title of *Jack Solomons' International Boxing Annual* q.v.

1749. SOLOMONS, Jack
Jack Solomons' International Boxing Annual
This Annual was published by Playfair Books Ltd, London, in the years 1949, 1950, 1951 and 1952. Information is given on these issues as follows:

1949 Edition
184pp. bound in red and yellow stiff paper covers, lettered in red, white and black. Adverts on end papers and back cover.
The features include articles by Norman Bell, Joe Bromley, Freddie Mills, Bruce Woodcock, etc. There is also a summary of World Title Fights promoted by Jack Solomons and details of other promotions by him during the year 1948.
The illustrations are mostly full page except for the boxers' portraits shown among the boxers' records.

1950 Edition
112pp. Bound in yellow, black and red stiff paper covers, lettered in black, with a picture of Turpin v Sands on the front cover.
The features include articles by Norman Bell, Peter Wilson, Lee Savold, Merv Williams, Dr. Herbert Kramer and Robert King.
The ranking lists, championship fight results and similar returns are as given in the issues of the Annual for previous years.

1951 Edition
96pp. Bound in stiff paper covers, front cover coloured red, black and blue with picture of a boxing match. The articles in this issue are by Tom Phillips, Walter Bartleman, Freddie Mills and others. World Ratings are given for 1951 and Championship Fights for 1950; there are also statistics regarding A.B.A. Champions etc.
The book is profusely illustrated and gives the usual boxers' records (40 pages).

1952 Edition
Bound in stiff paper covers, front cover coloured yellow with pictures of Boxers, including Robinson

continued

v. Turpin.

The principal articles are by Jack Solomons and L.N. Bailey; there are the usual lists of champions and title fights as given in previous issues, together with the illustrations and 43 pages of boxers' records.

1750. SOLOMONS, Jack
Jack Solomons Tells All
London, Rich and Cowan, 1951.

196pp. Illus.
Bound in black cloth, gilt titles on spine, design of boxing gloves on front cover.
This is an autobiography telling of the author's early days and of his rise to become a leading figure in World boxing promotion.

1751. SOREL, Julia
Rocky. A Love Story about the World's Heavyweight Championship.
Based on the screenplay by Sylvester Stallone.
New York, Ballantine Books, 1976.
(Paperback)
118pp.

1752. SOUTAR, Andrew
Battling Barker. A Novel.
London, Hutchinson & Co. (Publishers) Ltd., 1923.
288pp.

1753. SOUTAR, Andrew
My Sporting Life
London, Hutchinson and Co. (Publishers) Ltd., 1934.

254pp. Illus. (6 of boxing interest)
There are 11 chapters devoted to boxing in this book of sporting reminiscences. Among those mentioned are Carpentier, Jim Driscoll, Sam Langford, Jimmy Wilde, and Jack Johnson. The final chapter is entitled "Boxers and Their Earnings".

1754. SOUTAR, Andrew
The Wolves and the Lamb.
(A Detective story featuring Phineas Spinnet)
London, Hutchinson & Co. (Publishers) Ltd., 1940.
223pp.

1755. SOVIET NEWS (Publishers)
Sport in the Soviet Union
London, 1946.

Printed on art paper, illustrated paper covers.

Includes a short section "Boxing's Rapid Development".
There are 3 boxing illustrations, including one showing a group of champions of the Soviet Union.

1756. SOWDEN, Samuel (Compiler)
The Law and Testimony in The Case of John C. Heenan versus Tom Sayers. Compiled from Public Journals by Samuel Sowden.
Columbus (Ohio), E. K. Lundy, 1860.
130pp.

1757. SOWDEN, S.
The Heenan and Sayers Fight
Columbus, O.E.K. Dundy, 1869.

1758. SPILLER, Andrew
Crooked Highway
A Crime Detection Story
London, Denis Archer, 1947.

318pp.
This detective novel contains many references to boxing, boxers and characters connected with the sport.
Chapter VII "Count Ten" contains a very good description of a boxing match.

1759. SPADE, Mark
Fun and Games
(How to Win at Almost Anything)
Illustrated by W. M. Hendry
London, Hamish Hamilton, Publishers, 1936.

155pp.
section VII refers to boxing.

1760. SPORT MAGAZINE The Editors of
Sport Annual, 1949.
New York, Macfadden Publications Inc.,1949
The Complete Record Book of 1948.

The chapter headings include:

Two Ring Titles go Overseas
Boxing's Heavyweight King
Death Hunts the Ring
Boxing War Gets Hot

The portraits in full colour include one of Joe Lous

1761. SPORTING CHRONICLE, The (Publishers)
The Sporting Chronicle Annual
Published in Manchester, commencing 1876, continuing for 53 issues.

Each issue contains a boxing section, and in some cases pictures of boxers.
The boxing content of each issue is very similar
continued

and was made up as follows:

> Lists of current champions
> Facts about boxers (Birthplace, Weight, etc.)
> Sporting Obituary for the previous year (inc. boxers)
> Principal boxing matches fought in the previous year
> The Amateur Championships (English and Scottish)

1762. SPORTING CLUB OF WALES
(Publishers)

Ringsport

The Official Journal of the Sporting Club of Wales Ltd., and the Good Sports

Caerphilly, 1964.

1763. SPORTING LIFE, The
(Publishers)

The Sporting Life Companion

(Containing Complete Turf and Miscellaneous Sports Records, Olympic Games Winners and a Variety of other Useful Information)

Published in London

This Annual was first issued in 1875 and continued to appear annually except for the war years.

Each issue contained a section entitled "The Ring".

1764. SPORTING LIFE, The (Publishers)

Sayers v. Heenan

A Pamphlet

London, 1909, Price 1d.

1765. SPORTING LIFE, The
(Publishers)

Olympic Boxing Competitions

London, 1909. Price 1s and 2s.

This report of the Olympic boxing competition, which took place at the Northampton Institute (London) in 1908, was a supplementary work to "The Olympic Games of London 1908"; it contained portraits of all the boxing winners.

1766. SPORTING LIFE, The
(Publishers)

Battling Balfour (The City Pet) v. Boss Asquith (The Temple Slasher)

Being a Reproduction in Book Form of the Letterpress and Illustrations published in *The Sporting Life* during the General Election. The contest is described as being for the Heavyweight Championship of Great Britain and the King's Purse, and the referee is Mr. John Bull (Appointed by *The Sporting Life*). A unique and Mirth-Provoking Pro-

duction, reprinted by Special Request. (Price 1d).

Issued by *The Sporting Life*, 1910.

1767. SPORTING LIFE, The
(Publishers)

Boxing Records, 1910.

144pp.

Contains records up to October, 1909.

This item is mentioned in *Boxing* magazine as follows:

"Records of all English fighters, complete ring careers of over a hundred of the best English mitt artists".

1768. SPORTING LIFE, The
(Publishers)

The *Sporting Life* International Inquiry Into the Necessity for a Board to Control International Boxing

Reprinted from *The Sporting Life* (London), of various dates from November 30, 1909 to April 19, 1910.

London, *The Sporting Life* 1910.

A pamphlet of 24 pages.

Among the contents of this pamphlet were opinions given by a number of well-known patrons of boxing (English and American), including the following:

J. H. Douglas, Eugene Corri, A. F. Bettinson, Sir Claude Champion De Crespigny, Bart., T. S. Andrews, Jack Gleason, J. J. Corbett, and a number of American newspapers.

There were also opinions expressed from France and Australia, including those of Hugh D. McIntosh.

1769. SPORTING LIFE, The (Publishers)

Sporting Life Boxing Records, 1923.

Containing Records of all World Champions and other Leading Professional Boxers.

Also records of Amateur (A.B.A.), Navy and Army, Oxford and Cambridge, Public Schools &c. &c.

London, 1923

166pp. Illus.

Yellow paper covers with picture of Bombardier Billy Wells on the front cover.

In addition to the boxers' records there are pictures of 18 contemporary boxers.

1770. SPORTS PICTURES (Publishers)

Sports Pictures Boxing Handbook

London, ca. 1920.

80pp. Paper covers.

This small handbook includes a list of holders of various championships, it also gives short biog-
continued

raphies of famous boxers, some contemporary and some from the early days.

1771. SPORTS PICTURES
(Publishers)
Sports Pictures Boxing Handbook
London, 1921.

Brown paper covers. Lettered in black.
The contents include:
Boxing Weights, List of Champions, Present Holders of Titles (Amateur and Professional) National Sporting Club and other Rules, Rules for Lonsdale Belt Contests; also Biographical Records of approximately 100 boxers.

1772. "SPORTSMAN, THE"
(Compiler and Editor)
British Sports and Sportsmen
London, British Sports and Sportsmen, 1908

This work comprises a series of some fifteen volumes, folio, illustrated with photogravure and coloured plates, portraits and woodcuts.
Two of the volumes are entitled "Past Sportsmen" containing biographies of some of the old personalities of the prize-ring.

1773. STAFFORD, Helen
A Leprechaun Abroad
Ilfracombe (Devon), Arthur H. Stockwell, 1968.

136pp. Illus.
A biography of Dr. John Ingham Stafford, alias Jackie Stafford, the Irish Amateur Flyweight Champion.

1774. STANLEY, Arthur Penrhyn, D.D.
(Dean of Westminster)
Historical Memorials of Westminster Abbey
London, John Murray, 1868.
Second revised edition, 1868.
A Supplement to these editions was issued in 1869.
3rd and 4th Editions (revised) appeared in —
1869 and 1876.
A 5th Edition with the author's final revision in 1882; with a popular edition in 1911.
The boxing reference is found in information given regarding the tomb of John Broughton, "Prince of Prizefighters".

1775. STANLEY, Louis T.
Sports Review
London, Macdonald and Co. (Publishers) Ltd., 1951.
Bound in blue cloth, yellow titles on the spine.
Every sport is dealt with, month by month, from September 1950 to August 1951, including a review of each month's boxing.
There are 4 boxing illustrations.

1776. STANLEY, Louis T.
The Sporting Collector
London, Pelham Books, 1984.

163pp. Illus.
This is a book on collecting sporting trophies and ephemera. Chapter 9 is entitled "The Lure of the Ring"; there are other references to boxing in the text.

1777. STAPLETON, Alan
London Alleys, Byways and Courts
Drawn and described by Alan Stapleton.
London, John Lane, The Bodley Head Ltd., 1924.
New York, Dodd Mead and Co. 1924.
(Reprinted 1925)

183pp
The boxing interest is in Chapter II; it refers to Hanway Street "running out of Oxford Street into Tottenham Court Road" and tells that John Broughton, the first of the champion pugilists and pupil of James Figg, had a booth or ground where Hanway Street now stands.
The illustrations include one of Hanway Street.

1778. STAUGHTON, George
The Roped Ring Racket
A Novel
London, Gramol Publications Ltd., 1938.
128pp.
Coloured paper cover with pictures of a fight on the front cover.

1779. STEELE, L.E., M.A.
(Trinity College, Dublin)   (Editor)
Essays of Richard Steele
Selected and Edited by L.E. Steele, M.A.
London, Macmillan and Co. Ltd., 1902.
(Re-issued in 1907, and 1914).

128pp. Coloured paper
In the section entitled "Various Essays" is included an essay "A Combat at Hockley-in-the-Hole". This deals with the quarter-staff, the forerunner of pugilism, and of which James Figg (the first boxing champion) was an expert.

1780. STEGMAN, H.H. (Owner & Editor)
Fight Parade
1948 Illustrated Year Book — Ring Ratings
San Francisco *Fight Parade* Magazine, 1948.
56pp. Stiff paper covers
This item is made up of articles and hundreds of pictures of famous boxers and their contests; there are 6 pages of ratings.

1781. STENNER, Tom
Sport for the Million
London, Stanley Paul and Co. Ltd., 1958.
192pp. Illus.
Includes many boxing references, and also pictures of Jack Doyle, Tony Galento, Larry Gains, and Carnera engaged in wrestling contests.

1782. STEPHEN, Sir Leslie, and LEE, Sir Sidney (Editors)
The Dictionary of National Biography
London, Smith Elder and Co., 1903.
63 Volumes
Three later volumes were published under the title of *The Twentieth Century Dictionary of National Biography*. Details are given as follows:

1910–1911, edited by Sir Sidney Lee
1912–1921, edited by H.W.C. Davis and
J.R.H. Weaver
1922–1930, edited by J.R.H. Weaver

There was an index and an Epitome to the main work published in 1903, and further Epitomes for the periods 1901–1911, 1912 –1921, 1922–1930.
The Epitome published in 1930 contains two sections, one to 1900 and the other from 1901 to 1930; these include biographies of a number of pugilists and others connected with the prize-ring; these are arranged in alphabetical order from Captain Barclay to Tom Spring.

1783. STERN, Bill (Famous Sports Announcer)
My Favourite Sport Stories
New York, Mac Davies Features, 1946.
New York, Pocket Books Inc., 1948.
The Pocket Book edition was re-issued at least 4 times.
126pp. Illus.
This item is divided into 8 sections, the section dealing solely with boxing is entitled "Say it with Cauliflowers".
There are also references to boxing in the sections entitled "The Lame, the Halt and the Blind" and "Out of the Land of Legend".

1784. STERN, Bill
Bill Stern's Favourite boxing Stories
New York, Pocket Books Inc., 1948.
244pp. Stiff paper covers.

1785. STILLMAN, Marshall
Mike Donovan, the Making of a Man
New York, Moffatt, Yard and Co., 1918.
291pp. 4 Illus

1786. STIX, Thomas L. (Editor)
Say It Ain't So, Joe
Published in the U.S.A. by Bony and Caer, ca. 1948.
This book was reviewed in *Sports Week* for March 1st, 1948, as follows:
"No book since Paul Gallico's *Farewell to Sport* so completely coincides with *Sports Week's* policy of spotlighting the insidious, sinister, cruel, false and greedy in sports as *So It Ain't So, Joe*, a compilation of 18 stories edited by Thomas L. Stix. Readers who disbelieve some of the revelations regarding the fouler elements of sport MUST read this book."
Among the authors whose stories are used in this book are Damon Runyon, Stanley Frank and Milton Gross.

1787. STODDART, Joseph
(Editor of *Athletic Journal*)
Men I Have Met (Sports and Pastimes)
Manchester, John Heywood, 1888–1889.
There were 2 and possibly 3 volumes of this item.
Volume 1 was published in 1888 and Vol. II in the following year.
The work consists of portraits and short biographies of prominent sportsmen and athletes.
Volume II includes Charles Henry Kain, a prominent Manchester boxer.

1788. STONE, Shephard, and BALDWIN, Hanson W. (Editors)
We Saw It Happen
by Thirteen Correspondents of the New York Times
London, George G. Harrap and Co., 1939.
Chapter VII, "Sports of the Times" includes a quantity of boxing material, particularly about Gene Tunney.

1789. "STONEHENGE", "FORREST" & Co.
The Handbook of Manly Exercises
Comprising Boxing, Walking, Running, Leaping, Vaulting etc. With Chapters on Training for Pedestrianism and Other Purposes.
London, George Routledge and Sons, 1864.
64pp. Bound in boards, the front board showing a picture of two boxers in action.
The boxing section of the book is illustrated by three cuts in the text.

1790. STRAUSS, Gustave Louis Maurice
Reminiscences of an Old Bohemian
London, Tinsley Brothers, 1882 (2 volumes)
London, Tinsley Brothers, 1883 (1 volume)
London, Tinsley Brothers, New Edition,1884

continued

S

(1 volume)
London, Downey, 1895 (1 volume)
This book, which is not divided into chapters or sections, includes reference to some of the old pugilists, including Tom Sayers (to whom the author was introduced), Perry (The Tipton Slasher) Evans (Young Dutch Sam), Deaf Burke, Ben Caunt, Owen Swift and others.

1791. STRONG, L.A.G.
Sea Wall
A Novel
London, Victor Gollancz Ltd. 1933.
360pp.
Chapter X is entitled "Mainly Pugilistic"; there are also other references to school boxing.

1792. STRONG, L.A.G.
"The Minstrel Boy"
A Portrait of Thomas Moore
London, Hodder and Stoughton Ltd., 1937.
317pp. Illus.
In this work the author refers to Moore's visit to Gentleman Jackson, the boxer, seeking material for his book "Tom Cribb's Memorial to Congress".

1793. STRONG, L.A.G.
Shake Hands and Come Out Fighting
London, Chapman and Hall Ltd., 1938.
274pp. Illus.
Bound in red cloth, gold titles on spine.
The text is divided into 6 sections, the 1st, 3rd and 5th sections are entitled "The Big Stuff" and deal with heavyweights from Corbett and Fitzsimmons to Dempsey and Tunney.
Sections 3 and 4 entitled "Interlude" include general chapters and section 6 "Odds and Ends" includes chapter headings "Things Remembered" and "An Afternoon's Entertainment"; the latter tells of a daytime boxing tournament at a small London Hall.
This item was issued later in the Sportsmans Book Club series.

1794. THE STUDIO LIMITED
(Publishers)
Famous Sporting Prints
VI – Boxing
London, 1930.
New York, William Edwin Rudge, 1930.
Contains eight coloured plates; these are copies of well-known engravings showing pugilists and scenes from famous contests, with an introduction by George Kendall.
The subjects include – Deaf Burke, Bold Bendigo, The Interior of the Fives Court, Spring and Langan etc.
The prints are contained in stiff paper covers, size 12½ins x 10ins with the heads of two pugilists

decorating the front cover.

1795. SUFFOLK and BERKSHIRE, The Earl of and AFLALO, F.G. (Editors)
The Encyclopedia of Sports and Games
(Two volumes 1897)
London, William Heinemann, 1911 (Revised edition)
Four Volumes
The New Edition contains a section entitled 'Boxing' contributed by B. J. Angle and G.W. Barroll. The section includes instruction in the Art of Boxing, a glossary of boxing terms and a bibliography.
There are three boxing illustrations showing bouts between Sayers and Heenan, Welsh and McFarland and Jimmy Britt v. Johnny Summers.

1796. SUGAR, Bert Randolph, and the Editors of Ring Magazine.
100 Years of Boxing
London, Produced exclusively for W. H. Smith, 1982.
256pp. Illus. 4to.

1797. SUGAR, Bert Randolph
(with John Grasso)
Five Hundred and Five Boxing Questions Your Friends Can't Answer
New York, Walker and Co., 1982.
144pp.

1798. SUGAR, Bert Randolph, and the Editor of The Ring Magazine
The Great Fights
A Pictorial History of Boxing's Greatest Bouts.
New York City, Gallery Books, ca. 1983.
255pp. 4to. Illus.
Takes the reader through a number of the greatest fights of all time in words and pictures.
The coverage extends from John L. Sullivan v. Jake Kilrain 1889 to Sugar Ray Leonard v. Thomas Hearns 1981.
There are a number of pages of boxers' records.

1799. SULLIVAN, Alex
(Editor and Publisher)
Complete Records of World heavyweight Boxing Champions
From John L. Sullivan to the Present Time. How the Title has been won and lost. All the Facts and Figures worth knowing – Also records of the Leading Contenders –
continued

Kayo percentages for all the Men who won the Crown.
New York, 1941.
Contains portraits of all the champions from Sullivan to Joe Louis and additional portraits of many heavyweight contenders.

1800. SULLIVAN, George
The Cassius Clay Story
New York, Fleet Press, 1964.
116pp. Illus.

1801. SULLIVAN, John E.
Life and Battles of James J. Corbett
New York, American Sports Publishing Co., 1892.
Spalding's Athletic Library, Vol.1. No.1.
58pp. Illus.

1802. SULLIVAN, John L.
Champion of the World
Life and Reminiscences of a Nineteenth Century Gladiator
With Reports of Physical Examinations and Measurements, Illustrated by Full-Page Half Tone Plates, and by Anthropometrical Chart by Dr Dudley A. Sargent.
Boston (Mass.), J. A. Hearn and Co., 1892.
London, George Routledge and Sons Ltd., 1892.
294pp. Illus.
Brown cloth, gilt titles on spine.
A Publisher's Note to this volume states as follows: "As several fragmentary sketches have been issued purporting to give the record of John L. Sullivan, but proving to be both incorrect and unfair, it is proper to inform the public that this work, prepared by himself, is the only complete and authentic account of his life"
This book was re-issued in London and U.S.A. in 1979, under the title *I Can Lick Any Sonofabitch in the House*. (q.v.)
This edition was edited by Gilbert Odd.

1803. SULLIVAN, John L.
I Can Lick Any Sonofabitch in the House!
Edited with an afterword by Gilbert Odd.
London, Proteus (Publishing) Ltd. N/Date.
First published in U.S.A. in 1892 under the title *Life and Reminiscences of a 19th Century Gladiator* (q.v.)
238pp. Illus.

1804. SULLIVAN, Stephen (Translator)
Select Fables from Gulistan, or The Bed of Roses
(Translated from the Original Persian of Sadi)
London, Printed in 1773 and 1774.
84pp. Thirty "Select Fables".
Select Fable XXV is about boxing.

1805. SUMMERSKILL, Dr. Edith, P.C., M.P.
The Ignoble Art
London, William Heinemann Ltd., 1956.
104pp. Illus.
Dr. Summerskill was an anti-boxing Member of Parliament; in her book she makes her case, chapter by chapter, for the abolition of the sport.

1806. SUNDAY PICTORIAL NEWSPAPERS (1920) LTD (Publishers)
Sports Parade
Drawn by Jon
Written by the *Sunday Pictorial* Team of Sports Writers (including George Casey, Stan Russell and Peter Wilson).
An oblong book, stiff paper covers, red in colour, lettered in white and black.
The fascinating story of 24 of the world's leading sportsmen; these include Peter Kane, Freddie Mills, Gwyn Williams and Rinty Monaghan.

1807. SUTHERLAND, Douglas (with Henry Gilfond)
The Yellow Earl
The Life of Hugh Lowther, 5th Early of Lonsdale, K.G., G.C.V.O. 1857–1944. With a Preface by the present Earl.
London, Cassell and Co. Ltd., 1965.
236pp. plus Family Tree and Appendices. Illus.
Includes material reflecting the Earl's life-long connection with boxing.

1808. SUTTON, Charles (Editor)
Don Iddon's America
With a Preface by Sir Alan Herbert.
Illustrated by "Trog"
London, The Falcon Press (London) Ltd., 1951
Part 2, Chapter IX – The Business of Sport, is largely devoted to boxing.
There is one boxing illustration.

1809. SWAFFER, Hannen
Hannen Swaffer's Who's Who
London, The Falcon Press (London) Ltd., 1951.
Foreword by Edgar Wallace.
255pp.
The following entries include material of boxing interest:
Gene Tunney – W. Maqueen Pope – Charles Chaplin – Tom Webster – Jim Driscoll – The
continued

Earl of Lonsdale.

1810. SWANN, Gerald G. (Publishers)

Dale Boxing Novels
London, ca. 1939–1940.

These novels were issued in paper wrappers; authors and titles as follows:

1. Graham, Harold – *From Gutter to Prize Ring*
2. Worth, Richard – *A Bantam Champion*
3. Monk, Richard – *Rogues in the Ring*
4. Woodruff, Peter – *The Battling Tramp*
5. Monk, R.C. – *Champion of Two Worlds*
6. Lloyd, Tom – *Knocked Out*
7. Worth Richard – *The Boxing Squire*
8. Worth, Richard – *The Young Corinthian*
   also, – *The Art of Seconding*
9. Batten, P.W. – *The Greenhorn Champion*
10. Whitley, Reid – *Down for the Count*
11. Whitley, Reid – *The Boxing Earl*
12. Whitley, Reid – *Silky Jim*

The novels numbered 5, 9, 10, 11 and 12 also include a feature "What do you Know About Boxing".

1811. SWANWICK, Raymond

Les Darcy
Australia's Golden Boy of Boxing.
Sydney, Ure Smith Pty, Ltd. 1965.
238pp. including Appendix listing Darcy's 50 fights. Illus.

1812. SWIFT, Frank

Football from the Goalmouth
Edited by Roy Peskett
London, Sporting Handbook Ltd, 1948.
177pp. Illus.
The author was a famous footballer, playing for Manchester City and England.
The boxing reference is included in Chapter XVII, which refers to Frank Swift's friendship with Joe Baksi when the latter was training at Brighton for his fight with Bruce Woodcock.
One illustration shows Frank Swift with Joe Baksi.

1813. SWIFT, Owen

The Handbook of Boxing
London, Renton Nicholson, 1840.
62pp. including Index. Bound in pink paper covers with a picture of two boxers shaking hands. The illustrations include a steel portrait of the author by Henning and a number of diagrams in the text.
The chapter headings include.
A Defence of Pugilism – Antiquity of Boxing – Modern History of Pugilism – The Art of Boxing – New Rules of Prize-Fighting – Chronology of Boxing, etc.

1815. SWIFT, Owen
(Professor of the Art)

The Modern English Boxer, or Scientific Art and Practice of Attack and Defence, etc. etc.
London, E. Hewitt, 1848 and 1863. Price 1d
Bound in paper wrappers.
The frontis is a folding plate entitled "Attitudes and Positions in the Art and Practice of English Boxing". This shows 8 attitudes or positions in 2 rows. The text is headed "The Art of Boxing" and consists of instructional matter, covering Preparation, Guard, Various Blows, and Falls.
See also "A Pugilist".

1816. SWIFT, Owen

Boxing Without a Master; or The Scientific Art and Practice of Self-Defence.
New York, O.A. Roorbach, ca. 1852.
This item was first published in 1848.
Note. It is possible that the English edition was that entitled *The Modern English Boxer, or The Scientific Practice of Attack and Defence and Self Defence* by Owen Swift, 1835 and 1848.
There were other American issues of this book, as follows:

New York, R. M. De Witt, ca. 1853
Boston, W. Berry and Co. ca. 1854
New York, Ackerman, 1856.

1817. SYDNEY, William Connor

England and The English in the Eighteenth Century.
Chapters on the Social History of the Time.
London, Ward and Downey, 1892.
Two Volumes.
Includes some small reference to prize-fighting during the period, mostly between women.

1818. SYDNEY, William Connor

The Early Days of the Nineteenth Century in England.1800–1820.
London, George Redway, October, 1898.
Includes some references to pugilism during the relevant period.

1819. "SYLVANUS" (Robert Cotton)

The By-Lanes and Downs of England, with Turf Scenes and Characters.
London, Richard Bentley, 1850.
348pp.
The book is dedicated to Joseph Whitaker, of Ramsdale House, Nottinghamshire.
Includes references to pugilists, in particular to John Gully.
The frontis shows Lord George Bentinck, from a sketch by Count D'Orsay.

**1820. TALON, Henri
(Professor of English Literature in the
University of Dijon) (Editor)**
Selections from the Journals and Papers of
John Byrom, Poet-Diarist and Shorthand
Writer.
Edited with notes and biographical sketches
of some of his notable contemporaries.
London, Rockliff Publishing Corporation
Ltd, 1950.

The boxing content is in the following
chapters:
Chapter II – 1723–1725 (inter alia) –
Figg's Amphitheatre.
Chapter VI – 1733–1735 – The Castle
Tavern, Holborn, designated as "the head-
quarters of the Prize-Ring", kept by Tom
Belcher and Tom Spring.

1821. TAYLOR, Foulproof
Prizefight Government
New York, Published by the author, 1946.

88pp. Illus.
(Issued in illustrated paper covers)
The author was the inventor of the foul-proof
cup, widely used by boxers for protection against
foul blows.
The book contains one hundred and fifty true
stories, fifty-one on boxing.

1822. TAYLOR, J. H.
Golf: My Life's Work
Introduction by Bernard Darwin
London, Jonathan Cape. May 1943, Second
Impression, June 1943.

236pp.
Chapter XIV, "A Boxing Interlude" mentions Kid
McCoy, J. J. Corbett, Jimmy Wilde, Bombardier
Billy Wells and Hugh D. McIntosh (The Australian
Promoter).

1823. TEARLE, Robert
Sports Quiz. Over 1000 questions and
answers
London, Danceland Publications Ltd, 1947.

This includes 47 questions on boxing (with
answers).

1824. TEMPLE-CLARK, Oldrid
Some Views on Boxing
Published for the author by Delderfield of
Exmouth, N/D.

85pp. Paper covers.
Reprint of a series of articles from a magazine.

**1825. TEMPLE-CLARKE, Captain A.O.,
R.A.S.C., (T.F.)**

Transport and Sport in the Great War Period
London, Quality Press, 1938.

Chapter XIX deals largely with boxing, being de-
voted mainly to Amateur and Army boxing; the
following boxers are mentioned:
Capt. H. Bruce Logan, Jack Greenstock, Alec
Lambert, A. Gutteridge, W. Baxter, Capt. M.
P. Leahy, Corporal Jack Meekins, Captain
E. V. Chandler, and others.
There are 3 boxing illustrations, including one of
the author.

1826. TENNYSON, Lionel Lord
Sticky Wickets
London, Christopher Johnson Publishers
Ltd, 1950.

173pp. Illus.
Chapter X, "Some Impressions of the Americans
at Home" includes some mention of boxing at
Madison Square Garden, New York.

1827. THACKERAY, William Makepeace
Several books by this author, or items edited
by him, include references to pugilism and
the prize-ring; among these are the following:

1. "The Combat of Sayerius and Heenanus,
   A Lay of Ancient London". This work is
   mentioned in Volume 1 of H. D. Miles'
   Pugilistica where it is included in the
   Bibliography of Boxing. There is also
   mention of the Thackeray piece in Vol-
   ume 3 of Miles' work. See also Cox, W.D.
   Boxing in Art and Literature.

2. *The Virginians*, 1st Edition, 2 volumes
   1858–1859, includes reference to James
   Figg, the first Champion of the Prize-
   Ring, 1719–1734.

3. *Thackeray in the United States, 1852–
   1853, 1855–1856. Including a variety of
   Thackerayana*, by James Grant Wilson,
   with six score illustrations and a Bibliography, by Frederick S.Dickson.

Published in 2 volumes by Smith Elder and
Co., London, 1904.
Volume I contains 2 plates of the Sayers-
Heenan contest, with comments on the
plates and on the fight.

1828. THOM, Walter
Pedestrianism.

continued

Or an account of the performance of cele-brated Pedestrians, with narrative of Captain Barclay's matches.

Aberdeen, Printed by D. Chalmers and Co. for A. Brown and F. Frost, 1813.

Also produced in London during the same year.

286pp. Frontis. showing Captain Barclay.
This book includes a number of references to pugilism; including the process observed by Tom Cribb for his battle with Molineux.

1829. THOMAS, Art
Boxing Is For Me
Minneapolis, Lerner, 1982.
(Sports for Me books)
47pp. Illus.

1830. THOMAS, Edward
George Borrow, The Man and His Books
London, Chapman and Hall Ltd., 1912.
333pp. Illus.
Includes several references to the prize-ring, including two plates. Tom Shelton–Jack Randall and Ned Turner–Tom Cribb.

1831. THOMAS, S. Evelyn
(Producer and Publisher)
The 1948 London Olympic Games.
(Programme-Olympic, Worlds' and British Records and Useful Visitors' Guide to London)
London, 1948, Price 2s 6d.
Paper covers. Illus.
The boxing contents include:
Governing Bodies – Provisional Timetable, and articles on some of the boxers.
There is a picture of Johnny Ryan, European Amateur Welterweight Champion.

1832. THOMAS, S. Evelyn
(The World's Humour Service)
(Publishers)
Laughs for All Sports
London, 1948.
Paper covers, Price 1s 6d.
Includes many boxing items and pictures.

1833. THOMPSON, James, F.R. Hist. Soc.
The History of Leicester
(Pocket Edition)
Leicester, F. Hewitt, Caxton House, Granby Street, 1876.
Chapter XII, "The Late Hanoverian Period, AD 1760–1837" includes references to prize-fighting,

especially "a pugilistic display between Lydall the celebrated Whitwick collier and Dore of Leicester, which was witnessed by 5000 people".
This work is based on two earlier works by the same author:
1. *The History of Leicester from the Times of the Romans to the end of the Seventeenth Century, 1849.*

2. *The History of Leicester in the Eighteenth Century, 1871.*

1834. THOMSON, D. C. and Co. Ltd.
(Publishers)
The *Topical Times* Sporting Annual
(Facts, Figures and Fixtures)
London and Dundee, 1935, 1936 and 1937-1938.
The annual appeared for at least the 2 years shown above.
Illustrated coloured covers.
There were a number of boxing items in the annuals, as follows:

1935) Action picture of Jock McAvoy on the front cover.
1936) A short biography and portrait of Benny Lynch.
Prominent Young Men of the Sporting Year an illustrated section which includes articles on Dave McCleave, Benny Caplan and George Daly.
1937) Action picture of Peter Kane on the front cover.
1938) A short biography of Peter Kane.
A boxing section containing statistics and tables of title-holders; also Interesting Fights, June, 1936 to April, 1937.

1835. THOMSON, Prudence Yolden
English Country Life (The Colour Art Books Edited by Charles Mitchell)
London, William Collins, 1942.
21pp. 11 plates.
Contains a brief reference to the prize-ring, and a picture of the fight between Broughton and Slack.

1836. THORBURN, Horace
How to Learn Boxing Without a Master
London, The General Publishing Co., 1889.

1837. "THORMANBY" (W.Wilmot Dixon)
Famous Racing Men
With Anecdotes and Portraits
London, James Hogg, 1882.
Paper covers.
Includes references to John Gully.
This item was also published with *Tales of the Turf and the Chase* in cloth binding.

1838. "THORMANBY" (W.Wilmot Dixon)
Kings of the Turf
(Memoirs and Anecdotes of Distinguished Owners, Backers, Trainers and Jockeys who have figured on the British Turf, with Memorable Achievements of Famous Horses)
London, Hutchinson and Co. 1897.
378pp. 32 portraits.
Contains a memoir and portrait of John Gully and also refers to other personalities of the prize-ring, including Tom Sayers and Jem Mace. This book ran to several editions.

1839. "THORMANBY" (W.Wilmot Dixon)
Boxers and Their Battles. Anecdotal Sketches and Personal Recollections of Famous Pugilists.
London, R. A. Everett and Co., 1900.
Reissued 1902.
340pp. Illus.
Bound in coloured boards with a picture of the Heenan-Sayers contest on the front cover.
The later issue was bound in paper covers.

1840. "THORMANBY" (W.Wilmot Dixon)
The Spice of Life. A Motley of Memories.
London, Everett and Co. Ltd., 1911.
275pp.
This book includes a few references to pugilism and the prize-ring.

1841. THORNTON, Alfred
Don Juan
London, Printed for Thomas Kelly. Two volumes 1821–1823. With coloured plates.
In volume II are descriptions of The Fives Court and a journey to Moulsey Hurst for the fight between Weaver and Pounder (Fictitious names) with Crib and Belcher as seconds to one of the boxers.
One of the plates in volume 2 shows "A Set-to at The Fives Court for the Benefit of One of the Fancy".
A further edition of this work was published in 1825–1826.

1842. *TIMES* PUBLISHING COMPANY, The
A Newspaper History, 1785–1935 (Reprinted from the 150th Annual Number of the Times, January 1st, 1935)
London, 1935.
Chapter XVII "Sunday Newspapers" contains reference to the start of the *Weekly Despatch*, Pierce Egan's *Life in London, Bell's Life in London* and also to Pierce Egan, George Kent, and others.

1843. TIMONY, Patrick (Pseud.)
The American Fistiana
Containing a History of Prize-Fighting in the United States, and a precise and full account of the great $ 10,000 match between Sullivan and Hyer.
New York, J. Johnson, 1849.
22pp. Paper covers.
There were further editions of this work, listed as 1867 and 1873.

1844. TOM SPRING'S LIFE IN LONDON
The Editor of
Whole Art of Boxing
London, W.M. Clark, 1841.
This item was advertised as follows in *Tom Spring's Life in London:*
"Clark's Sparring Handbooks, Price Sixpence Each, Price by Post 10d. The First Book of This Series is Now Ready, beautifully bound, with gilt edges, and forms the most complete instructor on THE WHOLE ART OF BOXING Ever Published. By the Editor of *Tom Spring's Life in London.*
"By a perusal of this little manual, the aspirant may learn the whole art of Self Defence, and become thoroughly acquainted with this truly national and manly science. Every stop, guard and manoeuvre will be found treated of, and practically illustrated, under the separate heads . . . "

1845. TONKIN, James E.
The English, Australian and American Sporting Calendar 1884
Sydney (Australia), W. M. Maclardy 1884–1885.
Contains entries entitled "Fistiana" and "The Ring"; including Longest Fights, Shortest Fights, Colonial Fistiana, etc.

1846. TOOLEY, R.V.
Some English Books with Coloured Plates. Their Points, Collations and Values.
London, Ingpen and Grant, 1935.
288pp.
This work includes information on many items of pugilistic interest, including works by Henry Alken, Pierce Egan, etc.

1847. TOOLEY, R. V.
English Books with Coloured Plates. 1790 to 1860.
A Bibliographical Account of the Most Important Books Illustrated by English Artists in Colour Acquatint and Colour Lithography.
London, B. T. Batsford Ltd., 1954.
continued

This is a reissue of the same author's *Some English Books With Coloured Plates*, 1935, (q.v.) with additional material to cover the extended period given in the sub-title.

The first book included 300 titles covering 400 volumes, while the later issue contains 517 titles covering 700 volumes, listing several thousand engravings.

1848. TOPHAM, Captain

Hints and Observations on the Art of Self Defence

This item was published as a series of articles ca. 1783 to 1799. Mention of the series occurred in *The Annals of Sporting and Fancy Gazette*, Vol. II No.17 (May 1st, 1883), claiming that the ground work for the articles was the work of Captain Godfrey, issued in 1747 as a *Treatise on the Useful Art of Self Defence*.

1849. TOPOLSKI, Feliks

The London Spectacle, 1935. Seen by Feliks Topolski. With notes and introduction by D. B. Wyndham Lewis.
London, John Lane the Bodley Head, 1935.
Includes "Boxing Club, Interval for Refrehsment".

1850. TORRES, José

Sting Like a Bee. The Muhammad Ali Story.
New York, Abelard Schumann, 1971.
Preface by Norman Mailer, Epilogue by Budd Schulberg.

223pp. Illus. with sketches by Le Roy Neiman.
This remarkable work, with books like those of Gene Tunney and Harry Legge's *Penny a Punch*, is one of the few ever actually written without extensive editorial aid, by a former professional boxer. José Torres was light-heavyweight champion of the world and later became a columnist on the New York *Post* and featured contributor to many journals.

1851. TOSSWILL, Major Leonard

Boxing Up-To-Date
(Spalding's Athletic Library, Group XIV, No.6)
New York, American Sports Publishers.
London, British Sports Publishing Co. Ltd., 1906 and 1923.
112pp. Illus.

1852. TOSSWILL, Leonard R.

Famous Fights
Foreword by Eugene Corri.
London, C. Arthur Pearson Ltd., 1915.
140pp. 8 Illus. Paper covers.

Ten chapters, covering bouts from Jem Belcher v. Tom Cribb to Carpentier v. Gunboat Smith.

1853. TOUSEY, F.

How to Box. The Manly Art of Self Defence made Simple and Easy, arranged by a professional boxer.
New York, Copyright, 1862.
Reissued 1902.
60pp. Illus.

1854. TOWEEL, Willie, and McINNES, Peter

Somebody Ring the Bell
London, Stanley Paul, 1961.
202pp. Illus.
The story of the Toweel family of boxers.

1855. TOWN CRITIC and CENSOR GENERAL, Mr.

The Connoissuer. No. 1, Jan. 31st, 1754 to No. 140, Sept. 30th, 1756.
Edited by George Colman, Bonnell Thornton and others.

This item was subsequently published in four volumes. A second edition, also in four volumes was published by A. Baldwin in Paternoster Row, London; the first two volumes in 1755 and the other two in 1757. There were further editions, including one in four volumes, published in Oxford in 1774.

The issue of this journal dated 22nd August,1754 contained an article on boxing, including reference to the fight between Slack and Perrin and to Jack Broughton.

1856. TOY, Eddie

The Technic on How to Become Scientific in the Manly Art of Self-Defence
An American Publication.
Copyright 1923 by Eddie Toy, 250 West 42nd Street, New York City.

122pp. Illus. Bound in red cloth, lettered in black.
Eddie Toy, with 25 years experience as a Professional Boxer and Instructor, boxed Abe Attell, Eddie Santry, Jack McClelland, Brooklyn Tommy Sullivan. Taught Boxing for ten years in two of New York's large gymnasiums.
Includes over fifty photographs demonstrating various slips, blocks, ducks, punches, and footwork, covering a complete course of instruction in boxing.

1857. TREHARNE, E. R.

Conditioning for Fighting

continued

Caerphilly (Glamorgan), Treharne Boxing
Publications, 1946.

A four-page leaflet.

1858. TREAHARNE, E. R.

Famous Heavyweight Fights
Caerphilly (Glamorgan), E. R. Treharne,
Treharne School of Physical Culture, 1948.

40pp. Illus. paper covers.
14 chapters, ranging from Willard v. Dempsey to
Woodcock v. Baksi.

1859. TREHARNE, E. R.

Among the Heavyweights
Caerphilly (Glamorgan), Treharne (Boxing)
Publications Ltd, 1949.

28pp. Illus. Paper covers.

1860. TREHARNE, E. R.

The Fighting Guardsman, Jack Gardner
Cardiff, Adventure Enterprises, 1951.

31pp. Illus.
Traces Gardner's career from his professional
debut to his European title victory.

1861. TREHARNE, E. R.

British heavyweight Champions
London, F.C. Avis, 1959.

144pp. Illus.
Introduction by Joe Erskine
Deals with 17 champions, from Bombardier
Billy Wells to Henry Cooper.

1862. TREMBATH, Hedley

The Fighting Cartoonist Detective
London, Gerald G. Swann, 1946.

96pp. Coloured paper covers.
The theme of this novel is gangsterism and
boxing.

1863. TREMBATH, Hedley (Editor)

British Sport. With a Foreword by Sir
Arthur Elvin, M.B.E.
London, Skelton Robinson – British Year-
books, 1947.

246pp. including biographical index. Illus.
A mention of boxing is given in the editor's intro-
duction; there is also an article by Ronnie James:
"The Future of British Boxing".
The reference section includes a directory of Box-
ing Promoters and Managers and short biographical
notes on about 150 Boxers.
There are two illustrations, both featuring Bruce

Woodcock.

1864. TREVELYAN, George Macauley, O.M.

British History in the Nineteenth Century
and After (1782–1919)
London, Longmans Green and Co. 1922
(1st Edition).
Twelve new impressions of this work appeared between 1922 and 1936.
The Second Edition entitled *British History
in the Nineteenth Century and After (1782–
1919)* appeared in 1937, with new impressions in 1941 and 1943.

Chapter X of the second edition includes a section
dealing with boxing and "The Ring, 1822–1829".

1865. TREVELYAN, G.M., O.M.

English Social History. A Survey of Six
Centuries, Chaucer to Queen Victoria.
First published in U.S.A. and Canada –
Copyright 1942 by Longmans Green and
Co. Inc.
First edition in Great Britain printed by
Novographic Process, 1944.
The work was first published in America
because of the wartime paper shortage in
Great Britain, it was not possible to pub-
lish in U.K. until 1944.

Chapter XVI, "Cobbett's England", contains a
section on the Prize-Ring.

1866. TROTTER, J.C.

Boxing
Dedicated to B. J. Angle
London, George Routledge and Sons Ltd.,
1896.
("The Oval" Series)
Re-issued: 1899, 1913 and 1914 (with
minor variations)

128pp. Illus.

1867. TROUP, Major W.

Sporting Memories
My Life as Gloucestershire County Crick-
eter, Rugby and Hockey Player, and Member of Indian Police Service.
London, Hutchinson and Co., 1924.

312pp. Illus.
There is a small reference to boxing in Chapter I
of this book.

1868. TRUSTEES of the NATIONAL PORTRAIT GALLERY (Publishers)

continued

297

Catalogue of the National Portrait Gallery, 1932
Oxford, Printed for the Trustees at the University Press
The Catalogue includes particulars of the following pugilistic items:
54. John Gully, 1783–1863, in a group of the House of Commons.
246. Tom Sayers, 1826–1865. A 12-inch high terracotta statuette, full-length, standing in fighting attitude.

1869. TULLY, Jim
Emmett Lawler. A Semi-Autobiographical Novel.
New York, Harcourt Brace and Co. Inc., 1922.
London and New York, Andrew Melrose Ltd 1922.
315pp.
Includes a considerable quantity of boxing material in chapters entitled "A Hobo Fight", "Battling Galore", etc.

1870. TULLY, Jim
Jarnegan. A Novel.
New York, A. and C. Boni, 1926. Price $2
New York, Sun Dial Library, 1929, Price $1
London, Brentano's Ltd, 1928, Price 7s.6d.
London, Brentano's Ltd, 1929, Price 3s.6d.
255pp.
This item is described as "An episodic novel of the lusty life of a man who is jailed for killing his opponent in a fist-fight"
There is mention of Stanley Ketchel in the book.

1871. TULLY, Jim
The Bruiser. A Boxing Novel.
New York, Grossett and Dunlap, 1936.
London, Michael Joseph Ltd., 1937 (First English Edition)
U.S. Edition – 248pp.
English Edition – 288pp.
Dedicated to "My Fellow Road Kid, Jack Dempsey"
Each edition has an illustrated dust-wrapper showing boxers.

1872. TULLY, Jim
A Dozen and One
Introduction by Damon Runyon
Hollywood, U.S.A. Murray and McGee Inc. 1943.
Dedicated to Arnold Gingrich and Damon Runyon.
242pp.

Boxing references include Jack Dempsey and Henry Armstrong.

1873. TULLY, John
Muhammad Ali. King of the Ring.
London and Glasgow, William Collins Sons and Co. Ltd., 1978.
(Collins English Library, Level 2)
48pp. Paper covers. Illus.
This is one of the series of graded readers for students of English as a second or as a foreign language.

1874. TUNNEY, Gene
Boxing and Training
New York, A. G. Spalding Bros. 1928.
20pp.

1875. TUNNEY, Gene
(James Joseph Tunney)
A Man Must Fight
Boston and New York, Houghton Mifflin Co., 1932.
London, Jonathan Cape Ltd., 1933.
254pp. Illus.

This book appeared as a serial in *Collier's National Weekly* (U.S.A.) and in *Cassell's Magazine* (London), before publication in bound form. It was also published in French and German.
There are 8 illustrations in the American edition, and 4 in the one issued in London.
There was also a paper covered edition, this was produced for the Armed Services by Guild Books of London, in 1944.
This book is one of the very few works attributed to a champion boxer which was written unaided, without the assistance of a "ghost writer".

1876. TUNNEY, Gene
Arms for Living
New York, Wilfred Funk Inc., 1941.
279pp. Illus.
This is virtually an autobiography of Gene Tunney, expressing his views on boxing and on life in general.
The illustrations are included in a short section on physical fitness at the end of the book.

1877. TURBEVILLE, A.S.
(Professor of Modern History in the University of Leeds)
(Editor)
Johnson's England
Account of the Life and Manners of His Age.

continued

Oxford, The Clarendon Press, 1933 (2 volumes)

Volume I includes, Chapter XIII "Sports and Games" by E.D. Cuming, with a sub-section entitled "Pugilism".

There is an illustration in the same volume Broughton v. Slack, April 10th 1750, from Pierce Egan's *Boxiana*.

1878. TURNER, E.C. (Ted)

The Life Story of Bobby Blay

Sydney, The Market Printers Ltd, 1933. Set up and printed under the personal supervision of Jack Johnson, Editor of the Australian *Ring* Magazine.

56pp. Illus. Price 1s.

Includes portraits of many Australian boxing celebrities, including Fred Henneberry, Ambrose Palmer, Tod Morgan, etc.

1879. TURNER, E. S.

Boys Will Be Boys

The story of Sweeney Todd, Deadwood Dick, Sexton Blake, Billy Bunter, *et al.*

Introduction by Capt. C.B. Fry.

London, Michael Joseph Ltd, 1947.

269pp.

Includes Chapter XVI, "Vive Le Sport", in which mention is made of boxing stories.

1880. TURNER, Herbert Kyle (Compiler)

The World's All Sports Who's Who for 1950.

Hove (Sussex), Wex Press, 1950.

Bound in light blue cloth, gilt titles on cover and spine.

Foreword by H.R.H. The Duke of Edinburgh.

This book opens with a number of articles; the following are of boxing interest:

World Sportsmen I Have Met, by Trevor Wignall (including boxing)

American Sport. by W. Buchanan-Taylor (including boxing)

Boxing is My Sport, by Peter Wilson

The Who's Who is set in alphabetical order; some of the short biographies include caricatures of the subject by Mickey Durling.

There are 42 entries on boxers and boxing personalities.

1881. TURNER, Tommy

Famous Fights in the Prize Ring

Sydney (Australia), Published by the Author, 1946.

64pp. Stiff paper covers.

The author was an Ex-Instructor to the Police Force and other similar organisations on Ju-Jitsu and Unarmed Combat.

Parts of the work refer to various aspects of boxing, with chapters on J. J. Braddock, J. L. Sullivan, Larry Foley, Les Darcy, etc.

1882, TURPIN, Guy

Forgotten Men of the Prize Ring

Texas, Naylor Co. 1963.

76pp. Illus. Card Covers.

1883. TWENTIETH CENTURY SPORTING CLUB (The),
Publishers

Madison Square Garden, New York City

General Editor, Harry Markson

The Club (under whose auspices boxing was held at Madison Square Garden) published a magazine and programme which contained an inset of the contestants at any of their boxing shows, otherwise the magazine varied only from time to time.

As an example particulars are given of a 1947 issue of the magazine:

Boxing—1947—Magazine and Programme

Volume XXI, No.2, Price 25 cents per copy.

The articles include:

"Jacobs Wins Biggest Fight" by Lester Bromberg

"Joe Louis — Then and Now" by Lewis Burton

"The Fight of the Year — Any Year" (Zale v. Graziano), by Ed Van Every

"Where are the Service Boxers" by Jim Jennings

and other similar articles.

There are 16 portrait illustrations.

THE

AUTOBIOGRAPHY

OF

JOSEPH F. HESS,

THE

CONVERTED PRIZE-FIGHTER.

A BOOK OF THRILLING EXPERIENCES AND TIMELY
WARNINGS TO YOUNG MEN.

Dedicated to the causes of Total Abstinence and Religion.

SECOND EDITION.

ROCHESTER, N. Y.
1888.

Title-Page *Autobiography of Joseph F. Hess* (Bib. Ref. 976)

1884. UDEN, Grant
Strange Reading
London, George Newnes Ltd, 1936.
Includes a section in chapter XX entitled "Strange Fights· and Wagers". This mentions a number of boxing matches and prize-fights, with extracts from the *Sporting Magazine* and other papers.

1885. UNITED STATES COMMISSION ON TRAINING CAMP ACTIVITIES
(Publishers)
Rules for Boxing
Washington, Government Printing Office, 1918.
16pp. including diagrams

1886. UNMACK, William (Publisher)
Unmack's Annual
(Sports Almanack and Record Book)
San Francisco, 1916.
111pp. Paper covers.
A small booklet containing records of all sports, including boxers of the period.

TOM CRIB'S MEMORIAL

TO

CONGRESS.

WITH

𝔄 𝔓𝔯𝔢𝔣𝔞𝔠𝔢,

NOTES, AND APPENDIX.

BY ONE OF THE FANCY.

Αλλ' ᴄᴋ' οιει ΠΥΚΤΙΚΗΣ ΠΛΕΟΝ ΜΕΤΕΧΕΙΝ της πλκσικς επι-
στημη τε και εμπειρια Η ΠΟΛΕΜΙΚΗΣ; Εγω, εφη.—PLATO *de Rep.*
Lib. 4.

" If any man doubt the significancy of the language, we refer
him to the third volume of Reports, set forth by the learned in the
Laws of *Canting*, and published in this tongue."—BEN JONSON.

LONDON:

PRINTED FOR LONGMAN, HURST, REES, ORME,
AND BROWN, PATERNOSTER-ROW.

1819.

Title-Page *Tom Cribb's Memorial to Congress* (Moore) (Bib. Ref. 1398)

1887. VAN COURT, Carroll
The Van Court Scientific Boxing Course
Los Angeles, Published by the author, 1937.
41pp. Illus.

1888. VAN COURT, De Witt
The Makers of Champions in California
An American Publication, 1926.
This is a rare item with probably only a few
copies being printed. It deals with the start of
many Californian fighters; champions and near-
champions.

1889. VAN den BERGH, Tony
The Jack Johnson Story
London, Hamilton and Co (Stafford) Ltd.
1956 (Panther Paperback)
144pp. Paper covers. Illus.

1890. VAN EVERY, Edward
Gene Tunney, The Fighting Marine. And the
Great Dempsey-Tunney Fight.
Told by his old friend Ed Van Every.
New York, Dell Publishing Co. 1927.
64pp.
Coloured paper covers. Illus. Price 25 cents.
The front and back covers are identical, each show-
ing a head and shoulders portrait of Tunney.
The book is presented in 6 parts with a following
section in which the author analyses the first
Tunney v. Dempsey contest for the Champion-
ship of the World. Information is given in the
text as follows:

Part I   The Boy
Part II   The Man
Part III   The Fighting Marine
Part IV   The Pugilist
Part V   The Challenger
Part VI   The Champion

Second Section:
After the Battle. Van Every's Vivid Interviews
with Winner and Loser.
  1. The Talk with Tunney
  2. The Talk with Dempsey

The final part of this section is entitled "Picking
the Winner and How an Expert Does It".
Van Every's remarkable analysis of the situation
before the battle. "The Winner Picked! Here is the
Climax of Van Every's Shrewd Veteran Analysis
and Judgement: Tunney will gain the Decision."

1891. VAN EVERY, Edward
Muldoon, The Solid Man of Sport
The Amazing Story as related for the first
time by him to his friend, Edward Van Every
Foreword by Jack Dempsey.
New York, Frederick A. Stokes Co. 1929.
364pp.

With 18 illustrations from photos.
30 chapters of this book begin with the boyhood
of Muldoon and continue with his life as a wrestler,
boxer, actor and trainer. There are also chapters
on the great figures of boxing, such as Sullivan,
Corbett, Fitzsimmons, Jeffries, Johnson, Willard,
Dempsey, Tunney and Tex Rickard.

1892. VAN EVERY, Edward
Sins of New York (As "Exposed" by the
Police Gazette)
New York, Frederick Stokes and Co., 1930.
299pp.
The text is presented in 2 parts:
Part 1 – The Original *Police Gazette* 1845
Part 2 – The Richard K. Fox *Gazette* 1876.

The whole text is full of references to prize-
fighters and the old boxers.
The chief references to pugilism are given as
follows:
Part 1
  The Publican, The Pewterer and the Pugilist.
  (An Oustanding Case of Mistaken Identity)

  When Men were Manhandlers. (About John
  Morrisey and Murder, and Bill Poole and
  Politics)

Part 2
  Up Hill's and Down the Road to McGlory's.

  Mr. Sullivan and Mr. Fox. (How the Sport of
  Boxing Came to be Big Business)

There are 120 reproductions of the original woodcuts from the *Police Gazette* of 1845 to 1876;
a number of these are connected with boxing.

1893. VAN EVERY, Edward
Joe Louis, Man and Super Fighter
New York, Frederick A. Stokes Co. 1936.
183pp.
Bound in brown cloth, full length action portrait
of Louis on the dustwrapper.
Dedicated to John Roxborough and Julian Black
who helped to make the Ideal into a Reality. Alec
W. W. Edgar and Michael S. Jacobs, who had a
part in the making of Joe Louis and of this book.
12 chapters. Frontis showing an action picture of
Joe Louis.

1894. VAN LOAN C.
Inside the Ropes. A Novel.
Illus. by Arthur Hutchins
Boston (Mass) Small, Maynard & Co. 1913.
411pp.

1895. VAN LOAN, Charles E.
Taking the Count
New York, George H. Doran Co. 1919.
continued

Foreword by Irvin S. Cobb
354pp.
This book is made up of 11 short stories with a boxing theme.

1896. VASEY, William
Remarks on the Influence of Pugilism on Morals
Newcastle, Members of the Newcastle Debating Society, 1824.
This publication consists of the substance of a talk given at The Newcastle Debating Society on 4th November, 1824.

1897. VESEY-FITZGERALD, Brian (With Other Writers)
The Lonsdale Book of Sporting Records
Volume XXV of the Lonsdale Library of Sports, Games and Pastimes.
London, The Seeley Service Co. Ltd., 1937.
Brian Vesey-Fitzgerald contributes to this volume on boxing.
The items of boxing interest are as follows:

Controlling Bodies; Amateur Boxing; Professional Boxing.

Regarding professional boxing there is a table of the earliest champions at each weight; showing champions of the World and of Great Britain.

The two boxing illustrations show two outstanding events in the past year's boxing, Benny Lynch v. Small Montana and Walter Neusel v. Jack Petersen.

1898. VESEY-FITZGERALD, Brian, F.L.S., F.R.E.S., N.B.O.U. (Editor of *The Field*)
Gipsies in Britain. An Introduction to their History
London, Chapman and Hall, 1944.
204pp.
In Chapter X the author refers to the natural usefulness of gipsies with their fists and names those of the Gipsy Race who became Champions under Prize Ring Rules; Romany descent is also claimed for later Champions with the gloves, such as Digger Stanley, Gipsy Daniels and Jim Driscoll.

TOM SAYERS
(Champion of England)

1899. WACE, Alfred, I.C.S.

The Story of Wadhurst, As told in a lecture given in Wadhurst School by Mrs Rhys Davies, D.Litt., E.A., in 1894
With the notes on which it was based, edited amplified and brought up-to-date.
Tunbridge Wells, Courier Printing and Publishing Co.Ltd. (1923)
The boxing interest is contained in references to the fight between Tom King and J.C.Heenan, December 8th, 1863.

1900. WAGNER, Leopold

A New Book About London
London, George Allen and Unwin, 1921.
233pp.
Includes boxing references as follows:

Chapter III — Round the Town, Evans' Supper Rooms in Covent Garden, afterwards the National Sporting Club.
"The Union Arms" in Panton Street, Haymarket (Landlord Tom Cribb)

Chapter V — Tavern Curiosities; "The Two Brewers" in Church Street, Greenwich, where there is a portrait of Jem Mace, done in oils, with his own fighting gloves suspended above.

Chapter VII — Historic Landmarks: "The Ring" in Blackfriars Road, once the Surrey Chapel and subsequently used as a warehouse and showrooms before being adapted as a boxing arena.

1901. WAGNER, Leopold

London Inns and Taverns
London, George Allen and Unwin, 1924.
252pp.
This book includes a number of references to pugilists and to places of boxing interest, including the following:—

Chapter I — The Union Arms, Panton Street, (Tom Cribb's Parlour)

Chapter VIII — The Ring, Blackfriars Road, previously the Surrey Chapel

Chapter XII — Around Clerkenwell. Hockley-in-the Hole, scene of prize fights and bear-baiting; Sporting Taverns, including the Horse and Groom, kept by Tom Spring

Chapter XIII — Due West of the City; Ye Olde Blue Anchor and Ye Olde Napier

Chapter XV — The National Sporting Club, etc.

Chapver XVI — Bygone London Night Haunts

See also *More London Inns and Taverns* by the same author.

1902. WAGNER, Leopold

More London Inns and Taverns
London,George Allen and Unwin, Ltd., 1925.
256pp.
As in the case of its predecessor *London Inns and Taverns*, by the same author, this book carries a number of references to boxers and places of boxing interest; including the following:

Introduction — A notorious prize-ring on the site of the Bricklayers' Arms Goods Station in the Old Kent Road, opposite "The Swan"

Chapter III — Leicester Square and Soho, a sparring saloon owned by "Gentleman George"

"The Round Table" in St. Martin's Court, where Heenan stayed when he came to fight Sayers

The erstwhile "Pelican Club" on the site of the great Telephone Exchange of today

"The Street of Adventure", Panton Street, and Tom Cribb's Parlour

Chapter X — North London Pleasure Gardens, including the "Adam and Eve Tavern", The Long Room used as a boxing academy

Chapter XV — The Kentish Quarter, with memories of Jem Mace and Tom Cribb

1903. WALKER, Donald

British Manly Exercises
London, T. Hurst, 1834 (2 editions), 1835, 1837 etc.
Bound in dark green cloth, gilt titles on the spine.
The first edition of this book carried no reference to boxing, the second and later editions included sections on boxing and wrestling. The 8th edition appeared in 1847 and was edited by "Craven".
The following information is given on the 3rd edition:— The Title-Page reads: "British Manly Exercises, Containing Rowing and Sailing, Riding and Driving, &c, &c." by Donald Walker. With Fifty Engravings, London, T. Hurst, 85 St. Pauls Church Yard.

The boxing contents are as follows:

Utility of Boxing
Physical Qualities of Boxers
Art Essential in Boxing
Position of the Body
Mode of Striking
Most Effective Blows
Guarding
Closing
Bottom
Rules in Boxing (Taken from those drawn by Broughton)

There are 4 illustrations showing boxing positions,
continued
T

blows and guards, and also a section on training.
An American edition of this work was published
by Thomas Wardle in Philadelphia in 1836.

1904. WALKER, Donald
Defensive Exercises
London, Thomas Hurst, 1840.

193pp. Bound in dark green cloth, gilt titles and
design on the front cover.
The Title-Page reads:

Defensive Exercises, Comprising Wrestling, as in
Cumberland, Westmorland, Cornwall and Devon-
shire; Boxing, in the Usual Mode and in a Simpler
One; Defence against Brute Force, by Various
Means; Fencing and Broad Sword, With Simpler
Methods; The Gun and its Exercise; &c, &c, &c.
With One Hundred Illustrations, by Donald Walker.
London; Thomas Hurst, 6 St. Paul's Church Yard.

The contents include:

Wrestling
Boxing (As in *British Manly Exercises* q.v.)
Simpler Method of Boxing

The illustrations include the four plates as in
British Manly Exercises, and seven cuts in the
text illustrating "The Simpler Method of Boxing".

1905. WALKER; John, and
MacGILL, James
(National Gallery of Art, Washington D.C.)
Great American Paintings, from Swibert
to Bellows, 1729–1924.
London, New York and Toronto, Oxford
University Press, 1943.
Copyright 1943 by Oxford University Press,
New York, Inc.
Second printing with corrections, 1944.
Printed in U.S.A.

This work contains considerable material about
Bellows and Eakins, who were responsible for
pictures of interest to followers of boxing.
The plates include "Between the Rounds" by
Thomas Eakins and "Stag at Sharkey's" by George
Wesley Bellows.

1906. WALKER, Johnny
The Life and Adventures of the Renowned
Johnny Walker
Winchester, Printed for the Author and
Proprietor by Hugh Barclay, 1857.

Bound in green-brown paper covers, printing on
the front cover similar to that on the title-page.
The title-page reads:
"The Life and Adventures of the Renowned
Johnny Walker in the Old World and the New,
Containing Facts About His Professional Career
Now Made Public: Including a Succinct Narrative

of His Performances in the P.R. To Which is Added
An Original Guide to the Theory and Practice of
Self Defence. Founded on the Experience of the
Author".
The first two chapters give an account of Walker's
birth and early encounters and a further account
of his career and his retirement. Then follows a
section of instruction on the Theory and Practice
of British Boxing.
An announcement at the foot of the last page
states "Boxing taught by Mr. J. Walker at Gentlemen's own residences. Gentlemen may always hear
of J.W. by addressing through *Bell's Life*.

1907. WALKER, Mickey, "The Toy Bulldog"
The Will To Conquer
A Great Champion Speaks from His Heart!
Hollywood (California), House-Warven,
Publishers, 1953.
112pp.

1908. WALKER, Mickey (with Joe Richler)
The Toy Bulldog and His Times
New York, Random House Inc., 1961.
305pp. Illus.
Described on the dust-wrapper as "The ram-
bunctious Life Story of one of the most colorful
personalities of the Golden Twenties".

1909. WALKER, Robert
Muhammad Ali. His Fights in the Ring.
Speldhurst (Kent), Midas Books, 1978.
152pp.

1910. WALKER, "Whimsical"
From Sawdust to Windsor Castle
London, Stanley Paul and Co., 1922.

The author was a celebrated clown who performed
at Drury Lane and elsewhere.
Chapter XIII includes (*inter alia*) the following
sections:
"A bogus boxing match" – "Dispersed by hose-
pipe" – "Jem Mace and Joe Goss" – "I second
Mace and get the worst of it".

1911. WALLACE, Francis
Kid Galahad. A Boxing Novel.
Boston (U.S.A.), Little Brown and Co. Ltd.,
1936.
Toronto, McClelland and Stuart Ltd., 1937.
New York, Grossett and Dunlap Inc., 1937.
London, Robert Hale, 1937, Price 7s.6d.
London, Robert Hale, 1939, Price 3s.6d.
286pp.
A paper-covered edition was issued in London in
1950 by Pocket Books Ltd.

1912. WALLACE, William
"Quitter" Grant
Lloyd's Sports Library No.1
London, United Press Ltd.
48pp. Coloured paper covers.

1913. WALLENDER, A.W.
Physical Training Manual
New York, Siebel Publishing Corporation,
1924. Price $2.

1914. WALPOLE, Horace
(4th Earl of Oxford)
Anecdotes of Painting
First Edition published in London in 5 volumes 1762–1771 (4to), followed by six further editions up to 1849.
A reprint of the 1788 edition appeared in 1872, published in London by Alex Murray and Son.
The pugilistic reference is given under the heading "Statutaries"; the sculpture mentioned being the "Hercules" executed by J. Michael Rysbrach 1693–1770. The statue was compiled from various parts and limbs of seven or eight of the strongest and bestmade men in London, chiefly the bruisers and boxers from the leading boxing amphitheatres. The arms were Broughton's, the breast Stevenson's (the coachman). The statue, and Walpole's book, are mentioned in the preface to Henry Lemoine's *Modern Manhood*, 1788.

1915. WALSH, John J.
(in association with Otis J. Dymwick)
Boxing Simplified
New York, Prentice-Hall, 1957.
110pp. Illus.
(Prentice-Hall books on Health and Sports)

1916. WALSH, Maurice
The Key Above the Door
London (?), 1923.
264pp.
Although this is not a boxing novel its central character, Tiger Enright, is a pugilist.

1917. WALTER, Gerald
(Boxing Report of the *News Chronicle*)
White Ties and Fisticuffs
The Story of Patsy Hagate, the Famous Boxing Announcer.
London, Hutchinson's Library of Sports and Pastimes, 1951.
162pp. Illus.

This book tells the story of Patsy Hagate's career as a Master of Ceremonies at boxing, and to a lesser extent, wrestling matches; commencing with his humble beginnings in the Notting Hill area. Mr. Hagate officiated for a number of years at the Blackfriars 'Ring'.
The illustrations include Jack Doyle, Len Harvey, Freddie Mills, Danny O'Sullivan and Bruce Woodcock.

1918. WALTERS, The Rev. Dan
(Principal Christ Church School Madras)
Boxing for Character. (A Manual for Schools and Clubs). Foreword by the Lord Bishop of Madras.
Madras, 'The Field Madras', 1937.
Illustrated by fifteen plates.
A note at the end of this book states 'Most of the instructions contained in this little book originally appeared in a series of articles in the *Madras Mail*, with whose permission they now appear, (having been revised in book form)'.

1919. WARD'S READABLE BOOK DEPOT
(Publishers)
The Batchelors Guide to Life in London, with its Saloons, Clubs, Exhibitions, Debating Societies, and all Gaieties that possess 'A Local Habitation and a Name'. Useful Sporting Information, Boxiana, Gymnastics, etc.. Enriched with Characteristic Coloured Illustrations.
London, 1830.
The section "Boxiana &c" comprises a list of public houses kept by well-known pugilists, it has a cut of a pugilist above the section.

1920. WARNER, P.F. (Editor)
The Boys' Own Book of Outdoor Games and Pastimes
London, *The Boys Own Paper* Office for the R.T.S. (Lutterworth Press), 1913.
Includes a section " Boxing and its Values" by J.W.H.T. Douglas; with a photogravure plate of Mr. Douglas.

1921. WARREN, John, and
WHITTAKER, G. and W.H.
(Publishers)
Takings, or The Life of a Collegian
Illustrated by 26 Etchings from Designs by R. Dagley.
London, 1821.

continued

This book is divided into 6 cantos; 7 of the verses in Canto I relate to pugilism.
One of the plates is entitled "Taking Courage" and shows two pugilists on a stage, one of them supported by the back of a supporter or second.

1922. WATSON, Alfred E.T. (Editor)

Fencing, Boxing, Wrestling
The Badminton Library of Sports and Pastimes
London, Longmans, Green and Co., 1889.
Boston, (U.S.A.), Little Brown and Co., 1889.
293pp. including Appendix. Illus.
The standard 8vo edition was issued in blue and gold half-calf bindings, and also in brown pictorial cloth.
A large Paper Edition, limited to 250 copies was issued by Longmans, Green and Co in 1889; this was also bound in blue and gold half-calf.
A second edition of the standard edition was published in 1890; further editions followed in later years.
The three chapter section on "Boxing and Sparring" was edited by E.B. Michell and comprised 67 pages with 16 illustrations.
The 3 chapters are entitled:— "The History of Boxing", "The Old School" and "The Art of Boxing".

1923. WATSON, Alfred E.T.

The Young Sportsman
London, Lawrence and Bullen Ltd, 1900.
663pp.
The Preface says (inter alia) — "By far the greater part of it is reprinted from the Encyclopedia of Sport.
The contributors to the Boxing section are B.J. Angle and G.W. Barroll. This section is mainly instructional and includes at the end a Glossary of Boxing Terms.
There are 7 instructional illustrations on boxing.

1924. WATSON, Eric R., L.L.B.

Barrister-at-Law of the Inner Temple
Trial of Thurtell and Hunt
Edinburgh and London, William Hodge and Co., 1920.
(Notable British Trials Series)
217pp.
The Introduction contains many references to Thurtell's interest in the prize-ring, and says (inter alia):
"By degrees he wormed himself into some intimacy with the champions of the ring, and for several years acted intermittently as a trainer and backer of pugilists".

1925. WATSON, E.H. Lacon

Notes and Memories of a Sports Reporter

London, Herbert Joseph, 1931.
287pp.
This book includes a number of references to boxing, particularly in chapter IV "A Few Words on Champions" in which mention is made of many old-time pugilists.

1926. WATSON, J.

(Printer and Publisher)
The Life and History of Tom Sayers, The Renowned Champion of England
London, 1860.
294pp. Bound in light brown boards, 15 Illus.
The description of this item is continued on the title-page as follows.
In which is fully detailed his Birth and Parentage from Original and Authentic Sources, together with full particulars of All His Battles in the Ring, with Aby Crouch, Dan Collins, Jack Grant, Jack Martin, etc., Down to his Great Fight with Jack Heenan.
Giving a Detailed Description of all the Battles, with accompanying Extracts from the Public Journals of the Day, respecting the Most Important Events that ever occurred in the Prize-Ring.
To which are added, New Rules for the Ring, Form of Articles for a Prize Battle, Duties of Seconds and Bottle Holders, Duties of Umpires and Referees, Hints on Sparring, Counter Hitting, In-Fighting, Suit in Chancery, The Cross Buttock, &c, &c. Indispensable Attributes and requirements for a Successful Pugilist. Science, Right Training, Exercise &c, Forming a Complete Manual of Boxing.
With Portraits of Tom Sayers, and Numerous Cuts of his Various Contests &c.

1927. WATSON, R.P.

Memoirs of Robert Patrick Watson
Journalists Experiences of Mixed Society.
London, Smith, Ainslie and Co., 1899.
513pp.
Dedicated (by Permission) to The Earl of Lonsdale
This book contains 75 chapters and includes a great deal of material on the last days of the prize-ring and the early days of glove fights. Examples of some chapter headings are given as follows:
Chapter I   — Tom Sayers' Funeral, Medical Science, and Interesting Frauds

Chapter VI   — Red Lion Square, Dr. Gilmour and the Pugilistic Bookseller

Chapter VIII — Prize-Ring Fatality, Flight from London as a Priest, Old Clay Hall, Queensberry Rules, and Mr. Henry Sampson

Chapter X   — Remarkable Episodes in the Career of "Hanky-Panky", Jem Goode, Allen Hawkins, Dowsett etc.

continued

Chapter XI – Friction between Police and Boxers; re Chesterfield Goode, Dick Roberts and Jim Kenrick, Harrison and Greenfield Sensation etc.

Chapter XII – The Prize-Fight, Boylan v. Keogh, Peter Maher's Rise and Progress, Boxing across the Irish Channel

Chapter XIII – Charley Mitchell, John L. Sullivan, Billy Madden's Championship, and the Fight at Apremont

Chapter XIV – Pugilism Proper, Smith v. Davis, Knifton v. Smith and Greenfield v. Smith, etc.

Chapter XV – The Pelican Club, International Prize-Fights, Kilrain v. Smith and Slavin v. Smith etc.

Chapter XVII – Remembrances of Charley Mitchell v. Mace, Toff Wall v. Goode, Dixon v. Wallace, Burge v. Carney and Burge with Connelly.

Chapter XIX – The National Sporting Club, Corfield v. Moore; Professional Referees, etc.

Chapter XLII – Sir Henry Hawkins and Prize-fighting.

1928. WATSON, Rowland
A Scrapbook of Inns
Being a miscellany of curious and instructive items from magazines, news-sheets, journals, diaries and letters and other sources concerning the old inns of England.
London, T. Werner Laurie Ltd, 1949.
218pp. Illus. Bound in green cloth, gilt titles on the spine.
This book includes pugilistic items as follows: Panton Street, "The Union Arms" – Tottenham Court Road "The Adam and Eve" (including a picture of this Inn).

1929. WATT, Jim
Watt's My Name
An Autobiography
London, Stanley Paul and Co. Ltd., 1981.
175pp, Illus.

1930. WAUGH, Bobby
My Life in the Prize-Ring
Fort Worth Texas, Printed privately by the author, 1926 and 1927.
76pp. Illus.

1931. WAXMAN, Maurice, and VACKNER, Charles (Editors)
Bang Boxing Record Book
New York, Maurice Waxman, 1938.
As well as boxing records this item contains many articles on boxing.
The book is similar to the 1938 issue of the *Everlast Boxing Record Book*.

1932. WEBSTER, Tom
Tom Webster's Sporting Cartoons
London, Associated Newspapers Ltd, 1920 onwards.
This famous cartoonist was born on July 17th, 1890, and joined the *Daily Mail* in 1919; among the cartoons he contributed to that paper there were many of boxing interest.
From 1920 to 1939 the *Daily Mail* published volumes of Webster's cartoons taken from that paper and from the other Associated Newspapers publications the *Evening News* and the *Weekly Despatch*.
Each volume of cartoons contained drawings of boxers and boxing matches executed in Tom Webster's inimitable style.
(See also Associated Newspapers Ltd., Item No. 80)

1933. WEHMAN, Henry J.
Book on the Art of Boxing and Self Defence
New York, Published by Wehman,
ca. 1910.

1934. WEINER, Ed
The Damon Runyon Story
New York, Longmans, Green and Co., 1948.
258pp.
Includes many references to Boxing, among these are the following: –

Chapter 5 – "By-Line", Damon Runyon (Jack Johnson and his fight with Jess Willard)

Chapter 8 – "Cider in His Ear" (One of Damon's most expensive luxuries was the sport of boxing).

1935. WELLING, R.A.J.
George Borrow, the Man and his Work
London, Cassell and Co. Ltd., 1908.
Contains many references to Borrow's interest in pugilism and his ability in the Art.

1937. WELLS, Bombardier Billy (Heavyweight Champion of England and Holder of the Lord Lonsdale Belt)

continued

Modern Boxing. A Practical Guide to Present Day Methods.
London, Ewart Seymour and Co. Ltd., (Publishers of *Boxing*).
This item was issued in 2 different types of binding:

1. Souvenir or Autograph Edition, printed on art paper, bound in red cloth with gold lettering. Price 5s.

2. The cheap edition, price 1s, was bound in paper boards with a picture of Wells on the front cover.

The book ran through at least 8 editions, the 8th edition being published by Athletic Publications.

78pp. Illus.
There are 8 instructional chapters with many illustrations; there are 2 extra illustrations in the Autograph edition.

1938. WELLS, Bombardier Billy

The Science and Art of Boxing
This is an illustrated booklet published in connection with a postal boxing course, and including Moving Pictures. The cinematograph effect was obtained by flicking the pages of small books of pictures of Billy Wells boxing with a sparring partner.
The course was distributed by Bombardier Billy Wells Ltd, 281 Regent Street, London.
The books of photographic pictures were produced by Industrial & Educational Film Co. Ltd., Compton House, 1 & 3 Old Compton Street, Charing Cross Road, London W1.

Among the contributors to the booklet associated with the course were Lord Lonsdale, Major Arnold Silson, Eugene Corri, Georges Carpentier, Jimmy Wilde, A.F. Bettinson, Jack Smith, etc.

1939. WELLS, Billy

How a Boxer Should Train
London, Athletic Appliance Co. 1914.
8pp.

1940. WELLS, Bombardier Billy

Physical Energy
Showing how Physical and Mental Energy may be developed by means of the Practice of Boxing.
London, T. Werner Laurie, 1923.
153pp. Illus.

1941. WELLS, Ernest ("Swears")

Chestnuts
London, Sands and Co., 1909.
256pp.
There are two chapters on prize-fighting in this book, and the author acknowledges his indebtedness for these to Mr. Davis Christie Murray, Mr. R.P. Watson and Mr. Byron Webber.

1942. WELLS, Matt, and DRACKETT, Phil

Come Out Fighting
With an Introduction by James Butler, and a Foreword by Ralph Ward.
London, Paul King, 1946.
40pp. Stiff paper covers. Illus.

1943. WENTWORTH-DAY, J.

Best Sporting Stories
London, Faber and Faber Ltd., 1942.
448pp.
The stories are all fiction and include two on boxing, "The Croxley Master" by Conan Doyle and "Pride of the Ring" by Andrew Soutar.
See also DAY, J. Wentworth.

1944. WEST, Rebecca

The Modern "Rakes Progress"
Paintings by David Low
London, Hutchinson and Co. (Publishers) 1934.
128pp.
A section of this book includes "The Rake Backs a Possible World Champion".
The illustration of the same title shows a fight in progress, with many famous personalities by the ringside, including Lord Lonsdale, The Duke of Windsor, Harry Preston, and many others. One of the boxers is Primo Carnera. (This item first appeared in *Nash's Pall Mall Magazine*).

1945. WEST, W. (One of the Old School)

Tavern Anecdotes, and Reminiscences of the Origin of Signs, Clubs, Coffee Houses, Streets, City Companies, Wards etc.
Intended as a Lounge-Book for Londoners and Their Country Cousins.
London, Printed for William Cole, 10 Newgate Street, 1825.
Price 5s. (Also listed as published by Maunder, London, 1825).
There are pugilistic references in the text as
continued

follows:
Origin of Signs
The Hole in the Wall (In Chancery Lane), kept by Jack Randall
The Castle Tavern, Holborn (A General House of resort for gentlemen of "The Fancy".
The Marquis of Granby. (Telling of the bout between the Marquis and Frank Hayman, the painter.
The Daffy Club (A Short History of the Club).

There are also some verses-Impromptu-On Seeing Cribb's new House, The Union Arms, Panton Street.

1946. WESTERBY, Robert
Only Pain is Real.
A Boxing Novel.
London, Arthur Barker Ltd, 1937.
First Cheap edition, 1938.
307pp.
The front of the coloured dust-wrapper shows a boxing scene.

1947. WESTERBY, Robert
Wide Boys Never Work
A Novel.
London, Arthur Barker Ltd., 1937.
300pp.
This novel contains an account of a boxing match.

1948. WESTERMAN, O.S.
Counter Back on a Counter
(Boxing without a teacher, or an aid to teachers; the Mysterious, uncanny skill possessed by some champions easily explained).
Ann Arbor, Michigan, U.S.A., O.S. Westerman, 1916.

1949. WESTMACOTT, Charles Molloy
The English Spy. An Original Work, Characteristic, Satirical and Humorous.
Comprising Scenes and Sketches in Every Rank of Society, being Portraits of the Illustrious, Eminent, Eccentric and Notorious. Drawn from life by Bernard Blackmantle. The illustrations by Robert Cruikshank.
London, Sherwood Jones and Co., 1825–1826. Two Volumes.
This work was first issued in 24 monthly parts in paper wrappers. There is a slight difference in the two volumes in that the publishers name in Volume II is given as Sherwood, Gilbert and Piper. The illus-

trations in the volumes total 71 coloured acquatints plus 74 woodcuts in the text. and one full page woodcut.

There is some reference to pugilism and the prize-ring, particularly in Volume I, under 'Metropolitan Sketches'. Here a number of pages are devoted to the Daffy Club, which met at the Castle Tavern in Holborn, kept by Thomas Belcher.
A plate devoted to the Club is included in Volume I.

1950. WESTON, Stanley
The Heavyweight Champions
New York, Ace Publishing, 1970.
This book is quoted by Randy Roberts as providing Source Material for his work *The Manassa Mauler* (q.v.)

1951. WHARTON, Wilfred G.
Boxing as a Career
Harrow (Middx), Riviere Sporting Publications, 1949.
25pp. Coloured paper covers.

1952. WHARTON, Wilfred G.
The Wharton Rapid Course in Scientific Boxing
London
London, Lionel Stebbing, 1962.
26pp.

1953. WHEATLEY, Henry B., F.S.A.
Hogarth's London. Pictures of the Manners of the Eighteenth Century.
London, Constable and Co., 1909.
467pp.

Chapter IV	– "Low Life" includes the following sections: 'Art of Self Defence', 'Figg', 'Taylor and Broughton'
Chapter XIII	– "The Suburbs", has the following sections: 'The March to Finchley', 'Tottenham Court', 'Southwark Fair', etc. etc. and contains reference to Broughton.

The illustrations include 'The March to Finchley' and 'Southwark Fair'.

1954. WHEBLE, J., and PITTMAN, I. (Publishers)
The Sporting Magazine
or Monthly Calendar of the Transactions of the Turf, the Chase, and every Other Diversion interesting to the Man of Pleasure and Enterprise.
London, 1792 to 1870.
This monthly magazine commenced public-

continued

ation in October 1792 and continued until December 1870. It made up 151 half-yearly volumes; details of these are given as follows:

Volumes 1 to 50, 1792 to 1817.

New Series, Vols 51 to 100, 1817 to 1842. (A Second Series commenced with Vol. 76)

Third Series, Vols 101 to 157, 1843 to 1870.

From July 1846 *The Sporting Magazine* was identical in content to *The New Sporting Magazine, The Sporting Review* and *The Sportsman.*

Details of the various publishers are given as follows.

From 1792 (Vol 1) to 1818 (Vol 50) the publisher was J. Wheble, 18 Warwick Square, Warwick Lane, London.

From 1818 (Vol 1, New Series) to 1821 (Vol 7, New Series) it was jointly produced at the same address by J. Wheble and I. Pittman.

From 1821 (Vol 8, New Series) to 1827 (Vol 20, New Series) the publisher was I. Pittman at the same address.

From 1828 (Vol 21, New Series) to 1846 it was produced by M.A. Pittman (widow of I. Pittman).

From 1846 to 1851 the publisher was J. Rogerson, 24 Norfolk Street, Strand, London, and from 1851 to 1852 Rogerson and Company at the same address.

For the final period, 1852 to 1870 the publishers were Rogerson and Tuxford st 246 Strand, London.

From the first issue in 1792 until about 1835 the magazine included reports of all the important prize-fights, in addition to many articles on prize-fighting and pugilism in general.

After 1835 there were few if any reports of boxing matches and hardly any reference to pugilism, and from 1846 onward the pugilistic items almost disappeared.

An interesting contributor to *The Sporting Magazine* was "Nimrod" (Charles James Apperly) who reported on the fight between Tom Spring and Bill Neat on May 29th 1823.

The pugilistic references in the different series of the magazine are too numerous to be given in detail; they consisted of many first-hand reports, the first of these being the Ward v. Mendoza fight at Bexley Common (November 12th 1794).

Other pugilistic items consisted of the obituaries of famous fighters, poems on pugilism, Histories of Boxing, Court cases connected with boxing (including trials resulting from the deaths of participants in contests), biographies of pugilists and other similar material.

1955. WHEELER, C.A. (Editor)

Sportascrapiana

Cricket and Shooting, Pedestrianism, Equestrian, Rifle and Pistol Doings, Lion and Deer Stalking, By Celebrated Sportsmen: With Hitherto Unpublished Anecdotes of the Nineteenth Century.

London, Simpkin, Marshall and Co., 1867. A Second Edition was issued in 1868.

301pp. (Second edition)

Bound in red cloth with gold lettering and designs on front cover and spine.

The second edition was bound in illustrated coloured boards.

This book is mainly about Squire Osbaldeston, Captain Horatio Ross, and Edward Hayward Budd. The pugilistic references are included in Chapters I, IX, XI and XIII with Material relating to Mr. Jackson, the Pugilist, Sparring before the Governor of Rome, Captain Barclay, Jack Randall, Cribb and Belcher, Gully and Gregson and others.

The text of the 2 editions is largely the same except for the heading of the final chapter, i.e. First edition 'Cricket', Second edition 'A Medley'.

1956. WHEELER, Harold Hon., D.Litt., F.R. Historical Soc., (Editor)

How Much Do You Know?

(A Book of Fascinating Questions and Answers on Every Subject)

London, Odhams Press Ltd., 1941.

Includes a section 'The World of Sport' with a few questions and answers on pugilism.

1957. WHISTLER, Rex and Laurence

Oho

London, John Lane The Bodley Head Ltd., 1946.

The illustrations by Rex Whistler consist of a series of 'Reversible Faces' each described in verse by Laurence Whistler.

One of the faces, in one position, depicts a boxer, to which is appended an appropriate verse.

1958. WHITCHER, Alec E.

Sportsman's Club

Brighton, Printed by the Southern Publishing Co. Ltd., 1948.

(All profits from the sale of this book will be devoted to the funds of the Brighton and Hove Football Club)

229pp.

The contents include:

Boxing Champions I Have Known (Bombardier Wells, Phil Scott, Tommy Farr, Harry Mason, Georges Carpentier).

Brighton's Boxing Tournament (Dec. 3rd, 1921)

The Boxing Booth.

1959. WHITE, Leslie Turner
Lord Fancy
A Novel of the Prize Ring.
London, Frederick Muller, 1961.
272pp.

1960. WHITEHEAD, Paul
(Poet Laureate)
The Gymnasiad, or Boxing Match. A Poem.
London, Printed for M. Cooper, 1744.
33pp. Paper covers.
Various boxing authorities, such as Frank Bradley,
H.D. Miles and Henry Lemoine, have given different publication dates for this work. Some of these
give the date as 1860, the year in which a volume
of Whitehead's Collected works was issued under
the title of *Satires*.

1961. WHITEHEAD, Will
Tripe and Onions
A small porition of the recollections, of, and
as served up by Will Whitehead.
Rushden (Northants), Northamptonshire
Printing and Publishing Co., Ltd., ca.1950.
64pp. Stiff paper covers. Illus.
These memoirs include several short chapters with
boxing content. There is mention of Jem Mace
and Bob Fitzsimmons, who were known to the
author. There are also stories of boxing and boxers
in Northants, including Jack Harrison of Rushden.

1962. WHITELAW, David
A Bonfire of Leaves
London, Geoffrey Bles, 1937.
276pp. Illus.
Contains a number of references to boxing, partic-
ularly in London, including Wonderland, etc.

1963. WHITING, George
(Award winning columnist of the
Evening Standard)
Billy Walker
Published in London, No date.
24pp. Including covers.
A magazine-type publication, with action-packed
photos.

1964. WHITING, George
Great Fights of the Sixties
London, Leslie Frewin Publishers Ltd., 1967.
276pp. Illus.
Ringside reports of 52 great contests.

1965. WHITTEN, Wilfred (John O' London)

and WHITTAKER, Frank (Editor of
John O' London's Weekly)
Good and Bad English. A Guide to Speaking
and Writing.
London, George Newnes Ltd., 1939.
Reprinted 1941.
Second Edtion 1944.
Includes a section "Prize Ring English: The Child
of Calamity".

1966. WHYTE-MELVILLE, G.J.
Digby Grand. An Autobiography.
London, John W. Parker and Son, 1835.
Two Volumes.
Includes some reference to pugilists and the prize-
ring in Volume I, Chapter IV and Volume II,
Chapter I.

1967. WIGHT, J.
(Bow Street Representative to the *Morning*
Herald)
Mornings at Bow Street
A Selection of the Most Humorous and
Entertaining Reports which have appeared
in the *Morning Herald*.
With 21 illustrative drawings by George
Cruikshank.
London, Printed for Chas. Baldwyn, New-
gate Street, 1824.
There were further editions of this work in
1824, 1825 and 1838. (The 1825 edition
included an extra plate by George Cruik-
shank). There was also a 'yellow back'
edition issued in 1875 by George Routledge
and Sons, London and New York.
The items of boxing interest, 2 woodcuts:
Tom Cribb and the the coppersmith – Tom Cribb
bringing William Bull, one of the coppersmiths,
before the magistrate.
Tom Cribb and the coppersmith: A wild elephant
chasing a man; this is a Figuration of Tom Cribb
running after William Bull, the coppersmith.
There is also an article, "One of the Fancy",
mentioning Burns' house in Windmill Street and
Spring's in Holborn.

1968. WIGNALL, Trevor
Jimmy Lambert. A Boxing Novel.
London, Mills and Boon Ltd, 1921, Price
3s6d.
Cheap edition issued in 1923, Price 3s6d.
282pp.

1969. WIGNALL, Trevor
Thus Gods are Made

continued

London, Hutchinson and Co (Publishers) Ltd., 1923.

286pp.

This boxing novel is bound in blue cloth, black titles on cover and spine.

Many years after having written this book the author observed how strangely the career of Young Stribling had followed the plot of his fictitious story, that of a young man almost literally bred for the highest boxing honours, only to fail at the last rung of the ladder.

1970. WIGNALL, Trevor

The Story of Boxing

London, Hutchinson and Co., 1923.

Dedication "To My Friend Harry J. Preston, who represents All That is Best in Boxing".

319pp. Illus.

This book consists of 17 chapters, with headings as follows:

Chapter I	The Earliest Fighters
Chapter II	Broughton, Slack and the First Frenchman
Chapter III	Mendoza, The Jew
Chapter IV	Jackson, 'The First of the Gentlemen'; The Belchers; and Pearce, 'The Game Chicken'
Chapter V	John Gully M.P.; 'Sir' Dan Donnelly; And Tom Cribb, The First Fighter to be Properly Trained
Chapter VI	Tom Spring; and Others Less Well Known
Chapter VII	Bendigo; Pugilist, Harlequin, Revivalist
Chapter VIII	Big Little Men
Chapter IX	The Great Champion (Tom Sayers)
Chapter X	The Most Memorable Fight (Sayers v. Heenan)
Chapter XI	James Mace, The Last of the Great Knuckle Fighters
Chapter XII	The Ring in America
Chapter XIII	The Inventors of the Modern Style of Fighting
Chapter XIV	Coloured Fighters
Chapter XV	Boxing in France
Chapter XVI	Men of Mark; and Clubs and Resorts
Chapter XVII	Some Impressions

Rules of Boxing, Broughton's Rules, 1743 — London Prize-Ring Rules. Marquess of Queensberry Rules — National Sporting Club Rules, 1923.

There are 32 illustrations, including 2 Original Cartoons by Charles Graves; the pictures include many of the old pugilists, together with boxers of the 1920's including Bombardier Wells, Jack Dempsey, Georges Carpentier, Jimmy Wilde, Joe Beckett and Jack Bloomfield.

1971. WIGNALL, Trevor C.

Comfort O'Connor

London, Hutchinson and Co. (1924).

286pp.

The subject of this novel is an actress; the story also involves a journalist and an American heavyweight boxer named Jeff Madden, a secondary character who supplies the pugilistic interest.

1972. WIGNALL, Trevor

The Sweet Science

London, Chapman and Hall Ltd., 1926. (There was also an edition published in America in the same year)

232pp. Illus.

Bound in red cloth, gilt titles on the spine.

This book gives wide coverage on boxing and boxers, from earliest days of Tom Figg to the date of publication and the advent of the 'Big Purse'. The final chapter, entitled 'Multum In Parvo' chronicles some facts on boxing, such as the identity of the original 'Nonpareil' (Jack Randall) and many other interesting pieces of information.

1973. WIGNALL, Trevor

Prides of the Fancy

London, Eveleigh Nash and Grayson, 1928.

Dedication "To My Brother Edwin".

256pp. Frontis. showing Gene Tunney.

Twelve Chapters dealing with all the various Boxing weights, and with the second Dempsey v. Tunney contest.

1974. WIGNALL, Trevor

The Ring

London, The Readers Library, 1928.

127pp.

Issued in paper covers. 6 Illus.

The contents comprise:

Introductory Note, by Carl Brisson
Editor's Note
The Text

This story started life as a film and was then turned into a novel by Trevor Wignall.

The film starred Carl Brisson. In his Introductory Note the star describes his part as "particularly interesting". The 'heavy' was played by Ian Hunter. Gordon Harker also played a part in the film, the fight scene was enacted at the Blackfriars 'Ring' and was refereed by Eugene Corri.

The Editor's Note gives a short biography of Trevor C. Wignall, a famous sporting journalist who specialised in boxing and wrote a number of books on the subject.

1975. WIGNALL, Trevor

I Knew Them All

London, Hutchinson and Co (Publishers) Ltd., 1938.

348pp.

This item gives many personal and intimate

continued

stories of sportsmen and boxers.

A number of sections are devoted to boxing and boxers, including: The Old Mauler (Jack Dempsey) One by Himself (Gene Tunney), The Mightiest Atom (Jimmy Wilde), and others.

1976. WIGNALL, Trevor

Sea Green. A Boxing Novel.
London, Hutchinson and Co., 1939.
Dedicated "To Frank, My Brother".

256pp.
The main character in this story is Green (known as 'The Incorruptible'), a famous sporting journalist.

1977. WIGNALL, Trevor
(Famous Sporting Journalist)

Never a Dull Moment
London, Hutchinson and Co (Publishers) Ltd
1940.

295pp.
This book is described on the dust-wrapper as "A foreceful, racy autobiography". There are 43 chapters, which include many references to boxing, boxers and personalities connected with the sport.

1978. WIGNALL, Trevor

Ringside
London, Hutchinson and Co (Publishers) Ltd
1941.

218pp.
This is described on the dust-wrapper as "A Fascinating Book about Boxers and Boxing".
The Dedication reads "To Jack Harding for reviving the National Sporting Club, and to Sydney Hulls, a good promoter".
In this Introduction Trevor Wignall describes this as "a book I said I would never write". He then describes how he was persuaded to give talks to R.A.F. personnel who were recovering from war wounds. The talks were so successful, that he was persuaded to turn them into a book.

1979. WIGNALL, Trevor

One Man's Road
London, Hutchinson and Co (Publishers) Ltd
1945.

192pp.
A description of the contents of this novel is given on the back of the dust-wrapper as follows:
This is a story, by a famous journalist of boxing affairs, to recommend to every boxing enthusiast for its entrancing history of boxing during the last hundred years, and to every fiction-reader in search of an intriguing and extremely well-written novel.

1980. WIGNALL, Trevor (Editor)

Sporting Record Boxing Annual, 1949
London, Country and Sporting Publications Ltd.

96pp.
Paper covers, with action picture of Freddie Mills on front cover.
Includes records and statistics relating to Boxing to December 31st 1948, with pictures of champions.
The text consists of articles by Trevor Wignall, Hugh Edwards, Nat Fleischer, C.B. Thomas, etc., together with boxers' records, lists of champions, and records of Olympic boxing.
The illustrations are on art paper and are at the centre of the book.

1981. WIGNALL, Trevor

Almost Yesterday
London, Hutchinson and Co., 1949.

218pp. Illus.
Contains a large quantity of boxing material; also includes other sports.

1982, WILD, Roland and
CURTIS-BENNETT, Derek

"Curtis", The Life Story of Sir Henry Curtis-Bennett, Q.C.
London, Cassell and Co. Ltd., 1937.
With 23 Photogravure Illus.
Foreword by St John Hutchinson, K.C.

311pp. Illus.
Chapter III contains the story of the Police Court case regarding the proposed promotion by James White of a fight between Jack Johnson and Bombardier Wells.

1983. WILDE, Jimmy

How I Won One Hundred Fights
(Boxing Handbook)
London, Ewart Seymour and Co., 1913.

1984. WILDE, Jimmy

Hitting and Stopping
(With Special Illustrations)
London, Ewart Seymour and Co. (Publishers of *Boxing*), 1914.
Boxing Handbook No.11.

75pp. Illus.
There were a number of editions of this book.
The text and illustrations are instructional.

1985. WILDE, Jimmy

The Art of Boxing

continued

Preface by Ted Lewis (Manager)
London, Webster's Publications, Ltd., 1923.
London, Foulsham and Co. Ltd., 1927.
Re-issued several times subsequently.
80pp. Illus.
(The pagination varies with the different editions)

1986. WILDE, Jimmy
Fighting Was My Business
(Autobiography)
Foreword by Lord Lonsdale
London, Michael Joseph Ltd., 1938.
284pp. Illus.
In his reminiscences the author chronicles his experiences in 20 chapters, from "Two Bob a day" in the coal mines to his winning of the World title and after.
There is an action picture of Jimmy Wilde on the front of the dust-wrapper and 17 illustrations in the book.

1987. WILKINSON, C.H.
Diversions. An Anthology selected by C.H. Wilkinson.
London, Oxford University Press, 1940.
(2nd and 3rd Impressions 1941 and 1942)
336pp.
Includes "The Fight" by William Hazlitt and "The Nonpareil", J.H. Reynolds *The Fancy*, 1820.

1988. WILKINSON, Dyke
A Wasted Life
London, Grant Richards, 1902.
392pp.
This book of reminiscences contains a number of references to the prize-ring and pugilists, particularly some associated with Birmingham, including the following:

Chapter XI –	Reminiscences of Birmingham. (A famous Inn – Notable Brums – A Case of Sudden Death – The Ruling Passion – A Short Boxing Bout – "Nibbler" Birch)
Chapter XII –	Reminiscences of Birmingham. (Palmer the Poisoner and Bob Brettle)
Chapter XXXII	Cases of Mistaken Identity. (Sir John Astley's Claim – Lord Marcus Beresford – A Fistic Preacher (Morris Roberts) – Taking a Liberty.

Some of the chapters which make up this volume had previously appeared in *The Licensed Victuallers' Gazette* under the pen name of "The Old Guv'nor".

1989. WILKINSON, Dyke

By-Gone Birmingham Part 1.
A Series of articles as they appeared in the *Birmingham Daily Mail*.
Birmingham, Moddy Brothers, 1923.
Part 2 of the series was not issued.
Contains a section entitled "Old Time Pugilists".

1990. WILKINSON, George Hatton
(M.A., Trinity College, Cambridge)
The Old Inmates of Harperly Park
Cambridge and London, Macmillan and Co., 1859.
Illustrated in 5 Paragraphs from the Odyssey of Homer.
The section "Irus", and the notes thereto refer to the old prize-ring.
Apparently the author was a pupil of Daniel Mendoza, the famous pugilist. There is a portrait of the author's old friend, Newbey Lawson, who was a patron of the prize-ring and also a pupil of Mendoza.

1991. WILLIAMS, Harry Llewellyn
The Art of Boxing, Swimming and Gymnastics made easy, giving complete and specific instructions for acquiring the Art of Self-Defence
New York, Published for the Trade, ca.1883.
99pp. Illus.

1992.WILLIAMS, Joe
(Nationally Known Sports Columnist)
T.V. Boxing Book
With a Foreword by Bob Hope
New York, D.Van Nostrand Co. Inc., 1954.
183pp., Illus.

1993. WILLIAMS, Montague, Q.C.
Leaves of a Life
London, Macmillan and Co. Ltd., 1890 (2 volumes).
2 new editions were issued in 1890 by the same publisher, and another in 1899 in Macmillans "Two Shilling Library".
Chapter XVIII deals with the author's defence of William Shaw and others who were charged with the manslaughter of Edward Wilmot, who died following his participation in a boxing match held in Great Windmill Street, Haymarket; the defendants were found 'Not Guilty'.
At the opening of the chapter, Montague Williams states: "I was always a favourite with the professors of the noble art of self-defence, and I do not think that, at any rate during the last fifteen or sixteen years of my professional career, there was a case in London associated with the ring in which I did not appear as defending counsel".

1994. WILLIAMS, Robert V.
Shake This Town
London, Rupert Hart-Davis, 1961.
373pp.
A novel featuring an ex-boxer who is forced back into the profession.

1995. WILLIAMSON, Dr. G.C.
Memoirs in Miniature — A Volume of Reminiscences
London, Grayson and Grayson, 1933.
272pp.
Chapter 18 "Sixty Years Ago" includes a memory of the Old National Sporting Club in King Street, Covent Garden, with its historical and literary associations.

1996. WILLIAMSON, J.N., and WILLIAMS, H.B.
The Illustrious Clients Case Book
Published in U.S.A., 1947.
67pp. Bound in stiff paper covers.
The Illustrious Clients is a society formed for the study of the Illustrious Sherlock Holmes.
The book includes a section "Sherlock Holmes on Boxing".

1997. WILLICK, A.F.M.
The Domestic Encyclopedia, or a Dictionary of Facts and Useful Knowledge.
London, Printed for Murray and Highley; Verner and Hood; D.Kearsley; H.D. Symonds; Thomas Hunt and the Author. 1802. Four Volumes.
The first volume contains a section on boxing.

1998. WILMOT, Sir John Eardley
Reminiscences of The Late Thomas Asheton Smith, Esq., or The Pursuits of an English Country Gentleman.
With 10 portraits by Cooper and others.
London, George Routledge, 1860.
London, John Murray, 1860.
London, Geroge Routledge, 1862.
London, Routledge, Warne and Routledge, 1862 (New and Revised Edition)
There were also 5th and 6th editions issued in 1893 and 1902.
212pp.
Chapter I of this book includes:
His Fight with John Musters.
Subsequent pugilistic encounters.

1999. WILSON, Major Arnold
Kings for a Day

This book was announced for publication ca. 1937 by Hutchinson and Company but was withdrawn.

2000. WILSON, B.R.
Muhammad Ali
Illus. by Floyd Sewell
New York, G.P. Putnam's Sons, 1974.
62pp.

2001. WILSON, Sir Daniel, L.L.D., F.R.S.E.
Left Handed News
Macmillan and Co. Ltd., 1891.
This book contains references to boxing; it was first published under the title of *The Right Hand; Left Handedness,* 1891. (q.v.)

2002. WILSON, Sir Daniel, L.L.D., F.R.S.E.
The Right-Hand; Left Handedness
London, Macmillan and Co. Ltd., 1891.
(Macmillans Nature Series)
215pp.
This work contains reference to boxing.

2003. WILSON, F.B.
Sporting Pie
With a Preface by A.J. Webbe
London, Chapman and Hall Ltd., 1922.
The boxing references are in Chapter III, including Corbbtt v. Fitzsimmons, Corbett v. Jeffries, Joe Choynski, Jack Johnson, Joe Walcott, Tom O' Rourke and others.

2004. WILSON, Ishmael, and Sons (Printers and Publishers)
This was an old-established firm in Nottingham who published a number of pamphlets dealing with the lives and records of the old prize-fighters. The pamphlets usually included cuts of the pugilists on the front covers; some were issued with different coloured covers.
Herewith is a list of some of the pamphlets issued by Wilson and Son:

1. Life, Battles, Conversion and Death of Bold Bendigo, 1901.
2. Life, Battles, Conversion and Death of Bold Bendigo, 1927. (Issued with both blue and yellow covers)

continued

3. Bendy's Sermon (Sir Arthur Conan Doyle), 1929 (Issued with both blue and yellow covers)
4. Portraits and Battles of Bendigo; also career, Portrait and Death of George Fryer, 1930.
5. Careers and Battles of Chick Soles and Bendigo.
6. Bendigo's Last Battle (Local Notes), 1930.
7. Ben Caunt's Tombstone (Local Notes), 1932.
8. Career and Battles of Patsy Clay (Born 1820, weight 8st 7lbs)
9. Sketch of George Fryer.
10 Life, Battles and Portrait of Jem Mace, 1891. (Issued with both green and orange covers)
11 Career, Battles and Death of Sam Merriman, 1891. (Nottingham; born 1808, died 1847. Weight 9st. 5lbs)
12 Famous Boxers of Petticoat Lane
13 Life, Battles and Death of Tom Sayers, 1892. (Issued with both green and pink covers)
14 Bob Smith (A Modern Boxer), Portrait etc.
15 Career and Battles of Sam Turner (Nottingham)

2005. WILSON, John
(Christopher North)
Christopher and His Sporting Jacket
New York, McClure Phillips and Co., 1901.
This Edition limited to 2500 copies, for distribution in England and America.

Includes boxing references in the Introduction and an account of a village fight on pp51 to 90.
There is a coloured plate of the fight among the illustrations.

2006. WILSON, Peter
Ringside Seat
London, Rich and Cowan, 1949.

174pp Illus.
Bound in black cloth, gold lettering.
Dedication "To the spivs, eels, drones and butterflies of fistiana without whose constant, although unconscious, co-operation this book could not have been written".
The book consists of 22 chapters, divided into 2 parts:

　　Part I – We Shoulda Stood in Bed
　　Part II – Eight Greats

There are 15 illustrations.

2007. WILSON, Peter
How To Watch Boxing
London, Sporting Handbooks Ltd,, 1952.
135pp.
Gives hints on assessing a fight, with a chapter on the history and origins of boxing, with sets of rules.

2008. WILSON, Peter
More Ringside Seats
London, Stanley Paul and Co. Ltd., 1959.

224pp. Illus.
A sequel to the same author's *Ringside Seat*, published in 1949 (q.v.)
This book was also issued in the Sportsman's Book Club series.

2009. WILSON, Peter
Old Holborn Book of Boxing
London, Gallaher Ltd., 1969.
160pp. Stiff paper covers. Illus.
Contains a number of articles and features on fights and fighters, a boxing and a photo quiz. 14 of the contributions are by Peter Wilson.

2010. WILSON, Peter
King Henry
The Fighting Life of Henry Cooper.
Reported from the ringside by Peter Wilson.
London, *Daily Mirror* Books, 1971.
80pp. Many illus. Stiff paper covers. 4to.

2011. WILSON, Peter
The Man They Couldn't Gag
London, Stanley Paul and Co. Ltd., 1977.
372pp. Illus.
More reminiscences from this articulate and outspoken sportswriter.

2012. WILSON, Peter
Boxing's Greatest Prize
London, Stanley Paul and Co. Ltd, 1980
240pp. Illus.

London, Arrow Books Ltd, 1982 (Paperback)

270pp. Illus.
The famous sporting journalist recreates the twelve greatest heavyweight championship bouts he witnessed in his career in Fleet Street.

2013. WILTON, Hal.
Rockfist in the Kingdom of the Khan
Billericay (Essex), Stuart Pepper and Son, N/d.
147pp.
The hero of these stories is Rockfist Rogan, some of whose activities were located in the boxing ring.
These stories first appeared in *The Champion* magazine.

2014. WILTON, Hal.
The Boxing G-Man
London, *Champion* Library No.245, 1940.
64pp.

2015. WINCH, A. (Publisher)

Life and Battles of Yankee Sullivan
Embracing Full and Accurate accounts of
His Fights
Philadelphia, 1854.

Brown paper covers.
96pp.
This book describes Yankee Sullivan's fights
with Hammer Lane, Tom Secor, Harry Bell, Bob
Caunt, Tom Hyer and John Morrissey, together
with his training for some of these fights and
with anecdotes concerning his opponents.

2016. WINN, George
(Editor and Publisher)

Boxing News Record
New York, *The Boxing News* Inc., 1937
New York, George Winn, 1938 and 1939.

1937 Edition = 224pp.
1938 and 1939 Edition = 320pp. each.
Each edition includes boxers' records, articles on
boxing and wrestling, and is illustrated with
portraits, pictures and cartoons.
The first two issues refer to the *Boxing News
Magazine* (U.S.), but the third issue contains no
reference to the magazine.

2017. WINTER, David

Low Design
London, Michael Joseph Ltd, 1937.

Chapter XIV gives an account of a championship
fight at the Albert Hall.

2018. WISCONSIN STATE ATHLETIC
COMMISSION (Publishers)

Law, Rules and Regulations for the government of Boxing in the State of Wisconsin
Madison (Wisconsin), 1919, 1924 and
1926.

2019. WITWER, H.C.

Kid Scanlan
Boston (U.S.A.), Small Maynard and Co. 1920
394pp.
The author, in the role of the boxer's manager,
tells of Kid Scanlan's entry into films after winning
the world welterweight title.

2020. WITWER, H.C.

The Leather Pushers, A Novel.
New York, G.F. Putnam's Sons, 1921.
New York, Grosset and Dunlap, N/d.
341pp. Bound in light brown cloth.

2021. WITWER, H.C.

Fighting Blood, A Boxing Novel.
New York, G.P. Puntnam's Sons, 1923.
London, G.P. Putnam's Sons, 1923.
Another edition was published in New York
by Grosset and Dunlap (No date)
377pp

2022. WITWER, H.C.

Fighting Back. A Sequel to *The Leather
Pushers*.
(Illustrated with scenes from the photo-
play in the Universal Jewel Series)
New York, Grosset and Dunlap, 1924.
339pp.

2023. WITWER, H.C.

Love and Learn: The Story of a Telephone
Girl who had Loved not Too Well, but
Wisely.
New York, G.P. Putnam's Sons, 1924.
New York, A.L. Burt Co., 1925.

2024. WITWER, H.C.

Bill Grimm's Progress. A Boxing Novel.
New York, G.P. Putnam's Sons, 1926.
London, G.P. Putnam's Sons, 1926.
Re-issued in New York, 1927.
336pp.

2025. WITWER, H.C.

Roughly Speaking
New York, G.P. Putnam's Sons, 1926.
(English Edition) G.P. Putnam's Sons,
1926.
New York, Grosset and Dunlap, 1927.
335pp.
This item is described thus:

The adventures of Gladys, the telephone girl,
Hazel, the film flapper and their heavy friends
–Gladys describes her beloved's pugilistic
progress.

2026. WITWER, H.C.

The Classics in Slang
New York and London, G.P. Putnam's Sons,
1927.
New York, Grosset and Dunlap, 1928.
331pp.
The stories are narrated by a character named

continued

"One Punch" McTague. He relates the plots of Shakespeare, Dickens, and other great writers, with references to his own profession of boxing.

2027. WITWER, H.C.
Yes Man's Land
New York, G.P. Putnam's Sons, 1929.
312pp.
The story of a boxing champion who gets to Hollywood to make films, and his various adventures there.
H.C. Witwer also wrote numerous light novels with a baseball or sporting theme. Most have some small allusion to the ring.

2028. WODEHOUSE, P.G.
The Pothunters. A School story.
London, A. and C. Black, 1902.
272pp.
Ten full-page illustrations by Noel Pocock.
Chapter 1 "Patient Perseverance Produces Pugilistic Prodigies", relates to Public School boxing at Aldershot.

2029. WODEHOUSE, P.G.
The Gold Bat. A School Story.
London, A. and C. Black, 1904.
277pp.
8-full-page illustrations by T.M.R. Whitwell.
Includes 2 chapters devoted to boxing:
    Chapter XXII – A Dress Rehearsal
    Chapter XIII – What Renford Saw
There is one boxing illustration.

2030. WODEHOUSE, P.G.
The White Feather, A School Story.
London, Adam and Charles Black, 1907.
284pp. 12 full-page illustrations by W. Townsend.
The school story if concerned largely with boxing.

2031. WODEHOUSE, P.G.
Psmith, Journalist
London, A. and C. Black, 1915.
247pp.
Containing twelve full-page illustrations from drawings by T.M.R. Whitwell.
There is a quantity of boxing material in this novel, which features a character named Kid Brady, the coming Lightweight Champion of the World.
The scene is laid in New York.

2032. WOLFE, Thomas
Look Homeward, Angel
New York, Charles Scribner's Sons, 1929.
London, William Heinemann Ltd., 1930.
613pp.
There is slight reference to boxing when the central

character's father reminisces about the night of the Corbett v. Sullivan fight, when an attempt was made to rob him.

2033. WOLFE, Thomas
Of Time and the River. A Legend of a Man's Hunger in His Youth. A Semi-Autobiographical Novel.
New York, Charles Scribner's Sons, 1935.
92pp.
There is mention of Dempsey and Carpentier in this book.

2034. WOLFE, Thomas
The Web and the Rock
New York City, Harper Brothers, 1939.
695pp.
The chapter entitled "Gotterdammerung" includes a very good description of the Dempsey-Firpo fight and the training period, all interwoven into the autobiographical fiction of the novel.

2035. WOLSTENHOLME, Kenneth
Sports Special
London, Stanley Paul and Co. Ltd., 1956.
160pp. Illus.
This book by the famous sportswriter and commentator, includes some references to boxing.

2036. WOOD, Don (Editor)
Great Moments in Boxing
London, Queen Anne Press, 1973.
Revised Edition, 1975.
(Park Drive Leisure Library)
144pp. Stiff paper covers. Illus.
Covers famous contests from Corbett v. Fitzsimmons (1897) to George Foreman v. Muhammad Ali (1974)

2037. WOOD, Ira L., Jr.
Boxing for Skill and Health, or How to Box
New York City, Physical Culture Publishing Co. 1901.
(Copyright 1901 by Bernarr Macfadden)
80 pages including 30 instructional plates.

2038. WOOD, William R., BACON, Francis L., and CAMERON, David
Just for Sport. Stories and Articles about Sports and Those Who Engage in Them.
Philadelphia, 1943.
423pp.

2039. WOODCOCK, Bruce

Two Fists and a Fortune (Autobiography)
London, Hutchinson's Library of Sports and
Pastimes, 1951.

192pp. Illus.
Bound in black cloth, gilt lettering on the spine.

2040. WOODGATE, Walter B., M.A., Barrister-at Law

Reminiscences of an Old Sportsman
London, Eveleigh Nash, 1909.

499pp.
This book contains mention of a number of the old
pugilists, including:
Part I, Chapter IV – School Days, recalls the
staging of prize-fights in Worcestershire, how
the author witnessed a fight at Rubery Hill,
when he shook the hand of Bob Brettle who
was in attendance. There is also a claim that
Worcestershire possessed the spirit of the prize-
ring better and later than the majority of
counties.
Part I, Chapter VIII – Oxford (continued). Gives
an account of the visit to Abingdon of a travelling amphitheatre with Tom Sayers giving daily
exhibitions; the author accepted an invitation
to spar with Sayers and tells of his experiences.

2041. WOODWARD, Stanley

Sports Page. The Story behind Newspaper
Sports Writing
New York, Simon and Schuster, 1949.
This book includes some boxing material.

2042. *WORLD SPORTS* (Publishers)

British Olympic Association-Official Report
of the London Olympic Games, 1948.

Includes reports in detail of bouts at the boxing
venues, Earls Court Empress Hall and Empire Pool,
Wembley.
One picture shows George Hunter (S.Africa)
beating Donald Scott (G.B.).

2043. WORTH, Richard

The Amateur Boxer
London, The Modern Publishing Co. ca.1939.
23 chapters
This work of fiction carries on the dust-wrapper a
picture of a boxer being declared the winner of a
bout.

2044. WREN, Percival Christopher

Soldiers of Misfortune
The Story of Otho Belleme
London, John Murray, 1929.

432pp. Bound in red cloth, gilt titles on cover and
spine,
This novel tells of the story of a young man who

wins the heavyweight championship of England
and Europe.

2045. WRIGHT, J. Murray

Boxing at a Glance (With Birds-Eye Illustrations)
London, The Bazaar Exchange and Mart,
1909.

26pp. Includes thirty-five illustrations, drawn as
though from above the boxers.
An American edition of this item was published in
New York in 1909.

2046. WRIGHT, Richard

Black Boy. A Record of Childhood and
Youth.
First Published in U.S.A. in 1937.
London, Victor Gollancz Ltd., 1945.

194pp.
This novel contains an account of a fight between
two black boys.

2047. WRIGHT, William (Publisher)

Memoirs of Tom Sayers
London, 1858, Price 1s.

Bound in Red Cloth.
Dedicated "To his Most Esteemed Friend and Early
Patron, Jack Atchelor, This Memoir is Inscribed by
His Most Grateful Servant Tom Sayers Champion
of England January 5th, 1858".
The text includes:
History of the Championship of England and
Memoirs of Tom Sayers. It then proceeds to give
accounts of battles between Tom and a number of
opponents between 1849 and 1857; these include
Aby Crouch, Dan Collins, Jack Grant, Jack Martin,
Nat Langham, George Sims, Harry Poulson, Aaron
Jones, The Tipton Slasher etc.

2048. WYLIE, Andrew

Ali, Fighter, Prophet, Poet
New York, Freeway Press, ca.1974.

2049. WYMER, Norman

Sport in England
A History of Two Thousand Years of Games
and Pastimes
London, George G. Harrap and Co. Ltd.,
1949.

271pp.
This includes the following references to boxing:
Chapter I – An Ancient Tradition
Chapter II – Sport in the Middle Ages
Chapter VII – The Golden Age (Boxing in
Georgian Times)
Chapter XI – The Dawn of a New Era (Boxing in
Victorian Times)

continued

U

There are 2 boxing illustrations.

2050. WYNDHAM, Horace

This Was the News. An Anthology of Victorian Affairs (What They Said and Why They Said It)

London, Quality Press Ltd, Publishers, 1948.

167pp.

Includes in Chapter X – Tom Sayers and The "Benecia Boy".

The illustrations include a portrait of Heenan.

2051. WYNDHAM, The Hon, Mrs Hugh, (Editor)

Correspondence of Sarah Spencer, Lady Lyttleton, 1787–1870.

London, John Murray, 1912.

424pp.

Illus.

Chapter I, 1804–1808, contains two letters to the Hon. Robert Spencer, dated May 8th and 11th 1808, which refer to the fight between John Gully and Bob Gregson on May 10th of that year.

The editor of this book was great-grand-daughter of the writer of the letter.

2052. WYNNE, Hugh

Leather Socking Tales

Philadelphia (U.S.A.), Majestic Press, 1947.

80pp.

Bound in green stiff paper cover.

Design of boxing gloves on the front cover.

The majority of the stories in this book are of boxing interest, they were selected from a series published in the *Philadelphia Observer* and include such items as "Philadelphia's No.1 Fight Fan", "The Man Who Saw 25000 Fights", "The Four Square Ringster", etc.

2053. WYNNE-JONES, G.V.

Sports Commentary

London, Hutchinson and Co. (Publishers) Ltd, 1951.

(Hutchinson's Library of Sports and Pastimes)

191pp.

Includes in Chapter II – "Boxing Commentaries"

There are 3 boxing illustrations.

2054. YATES, Arthur

(In collaboration with Bruce Blunt)

Arthur Yates, Trainer and Gentleman Rider.

An Autobiograpjy.

London, Grant Richards, 1924.

278pp.

This book includes references to the Yates' family interest in pugilism.

Chapter IV is entitled "Boxers and the Turf" and mentions Dick Cain, Tom King (who became a successful bookmaker), and the Sayers v. Heenan contest.

Mention also occurs of "The Squire" (Abington Baird)

2055. YOUNG, A. S.

The Negro in Sports

Chicago, Johnson Publishing, 1963.

301pp. Illus.

This title is given by Randy Roberts in giving source material for his book *The Manassa Mauler* (q.v.)

2056. YOUNG, A. S.

Sonny Liston

The Champ Nobody Wanted

Chicago, Johnson Publishing Co., 1963.

224pp.

2057. YOUNG, M.

The Complete Instructor, in Boxing, Swimming, Gymnastics, Pedestrianism, Horse Racing and other Sports.

Printed in U.S.A., 1881.

94pp. Paper wrappers. Illus.

Includes two sections on boxing; the first including 3 instructional cuts and the second giving short biographies of Champions of the American Prize Ring, with portraits of Joe Goss, Ned O'Baldwin, Yankee Sullivan and Tom Sayers.

2058. "YOUNG ENGLAND"

The Yorkshire Fancy-Ana for 1845.

Leeds, Printed by Milner, Stephenson and Co. Kirkgate. For the Editor.

Bound in dark blue cloth; gilt designs and lettering on both covers and spine.

The title-page of this item reads as follows:

The Yorkshire Fancy-Ana for 1845. Comprising A Faithful Record of The Ring and The Turf: With Chronological Tables (Alphabetically Arranged), of All The Fights of The Prize Ring &c. &c. &c. During The Last 144 Years; A List of the Champions of England from 1719 to 1844. Also The History of British Boxing. Rules of The Ring (Ancient and Modern) Form of Articles, Duties of Seconds, Bittle-Holders, Umpires and Referees, Intstructions to Amateurs (Illustrated With Engravings), on Setting-To, Hitting, Stopping, Cross-Buttock and Prevention Thereof, The Chancery Suit, The Prevention Thereof &c. &c.

Then follows a similar lay-out describing the Horse-Racing contents of the book.

Pages 38 to 52 contain "Hints on Sparring" by

continued

Mr. Dowling, Editor of *Bell's Life*. This section is illustrated by woodcuts showing the positions as described in the text.

The Chronology of the Ring extends from 1785 to 1845.

The boxing contents of this item appear to be taken largely from Dowling's *Fistiana* (q.v.)

2059. ZINBERG, I.

Walk Hard —Talk Loud. A Boxing Novel.
Indianapolis and New York City, The Bobbs Merrill Co. 1940.

354pp.

Bound in light blue cloth, yellow lettering on front cover and spine.

17 untitled chapters.

This book is described on the dust-wrapper as follows:

"The boxing racket is hard and loud, and rich men's sons are not found in it because 'hunger is the fighter's best second'. Andy Whitman fell into it because he was a fighter at heart and because he was a Negro and hoped that boxing would make him enough money to free himself from everything he suffered for the color of his skin. *Walk Hard — Talk Loud* is a story of fights and fighters, and it is as brash as the white spotlight over the ring and as direct as a straight left to the jaw."

"TUG" WILSON.

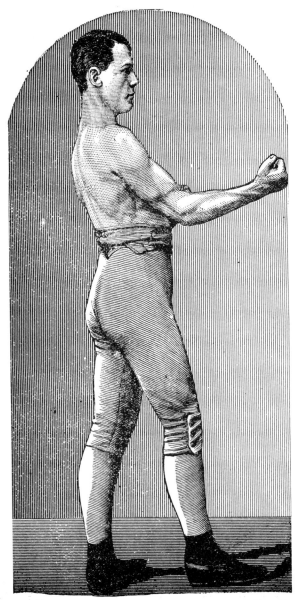

PROF. JOHN DONALDSON.   19

ADDENDA
and
INDEX

JACK DEMPSEY.

THE HISTORY & BIBLIOGRAPHY OF BOXING BOOKS

ADDENDA TO BIBLIOGRAPHICAL SECTION

2060. ADELER, Edwin, and WEST, Con.
Remember Fred Karno?
The Life of a Great Showman
London, John Long Ltd., 1939.
This volume includes two incidents relating to boxing. How Fred Karno put on an act to deputise for Jem Mace, who was taken ill when topping a variety bill with his exhibition of boxing. The second relates to a sketch staged with scenery representing the N.S.C.; Johnny Summers and Young Joseph, both professional boxers, were engaged to appear in this.

2061. AUTHORS Various
Adventures in British Sport
London, John Murray, 1926. (Modern English Series)
177pp. Illus.
This miscellany of sporting stories includes one boxing item – "The Smith's Last Battle" from "Rodney Stone" by Conan Doyle

2062. ARNOLD, Peter
All-Time Greats of Boxing
Leicester, Magna Books, 1987.
127pp. Illus. 4to.

2063. BRUCCOLI, Matthew J. and LAYMAN, Richard (eds.)
Some Champions; Sketches and Fiction by Ring Lardner
This volume contains "The Battle of the Century", a fictionised account of the 1921 contest between Dempsey and Carpentier. Jim Dugan (Dempsey), Big Wheeler (Willard), Goulet (Carpentier) and LeChance (Descamps), are easily recognisable.

2064. BRUNO, Frank
Rigor Mortis
London, Robert Hale Ltd., 1966.
188pp.
A boxing novel set in Australia, the homeland of the author; that he bears the same name as the British Heavyweight, who fought for the World Title, appears to be pure coincidence.

2065. BUCHANAN, Ken with DUNCAN, Nigel
My Life and Hard Times
Edinburgh, Mainstream Publishing Co. Ltd., 1986.
160pp. Illus.
An Autobiography; issued in hardback and in paperback editions.

2066. BUTLER, Frank
The Good, The Bad and the Ugly. The Story of Boxing.
London, Stanley Paul, 1986.
216pp. Illus.

2067. CHAMPIONS OF ENGLAND, The
The British Boxer, or The Art of Self Defence
London, H.May, 1865, Price: one penny.
Bound in yellow wrappers, with the title-page on the front cover; the contents are described as follows:–
Containing Valuable Information on Training for the Ring, Exercise, Diet & c. With the Most Complete Instructions in the Art of Boxing. Illustrated with Nine First-Rate Engravings. The New Rules of the Ring, and Hints to Pedestrians; with Champions of England from 1719 to 1863.

2068. CHESNEY, Kellow
The Victorian Underworld
London, Maurice Temple Smith Ltd., 1970.
384pp. plus a bibliography and index. Illus.
Chapter 9, entitled "The Sporting Underworld", includes a quantity of pugilistic material. There are two boxing illustrations; one showing the Sayers v Heenan contest, and the other a series of pictures of Tom Sayers in action.

2069. COTTRELL, John
Muhammad Ali, Who Once Was Cassius Clay
New York, Funk and Wagnall, 1967.
363pp.
This book was also issued under the title "The Story of Muhammad Ali/Cassius Clay" (q.v.)

2070. D'AMATO, Cus
Making Neighbourhood Heroes. An Oral History.
New York, Community Workshop of St. Marks Church in the Bowery, 1982.
28pp.

2071. DAVIE, Maurice R.
Negroes in American Society
New York, Whittlesey House, 1949.
542pp.
Contains mention of negro boxers, including Joe Louis.

2072. EDWARDS, Audrey, and
WOHL, Gary
Muhammad Ali, The People's Champ
Toronto and Boston, Little Brown and Co., 1977.
181pp. Illus.

2073. FITCH, Jerry
Cleveland's Greatest Fighters of All Time
Privately published in U.S.A., 1980.
Pages un-numbered, paperback.

2074. FRASER, Raymond
The Fighting Fisherman
The Life of Yvon Durelle
New York, Doubleday and Co. Inc., 1981.
Toronto, Doubleday Canada Ltd.,
282pp. including Durelle's record. Illus.
The book follows the subject's career from obscurity in a remote fishing village to the top of the boxing world, and the Canadian and British Empire titles.

2075. GORN, Elliott J.
The Manly Art. Bare Knuckle Fighting in America.
Ithaca, Cornell University Press, 1986.
316pp. Including a bibliography and index. Illus.

2076. GRAHAM, J.W.
Eight, Nine, Out. Fifty Years a Boxing Doctor.
Manchester, Protel Ltd., N.d.
133pp. Illus. Paperback.

2077. GUTTERIDGE, Reg and
GILLER, Norman
For Whom the Bell Tolls
London, W.H. Allen and Co., plc, 1987.
224pp.
A biography of Mike Tyson.

2078. HARDING, John with
BERG, Jack "Kid"
Jack "Kid" Berg
London, Robson Books, 1987.
224pp.
A biography of the celebrated "Whitechapel Whirlwind".

2079. HAYES, Teddy
With Gloves Off
Houston (Texas), Lancha Books, 1977.
184pp. Illus.

2080. HOFF, Syd
Gentleman Jim and the Great John L.
Tadworth, The World's Work, 1979.
48pp. Illus.

2081. HUGMAN, Barry
Frank Warren's International Boxing Year 1988, compiled by Barry J. Hugman
London, McDonald, 1987.
192pp. Illus. (some col.)

2082. JOHNSON, D.
Barefist Fighters of the 18th and 19th Century, 1704–1861
Foreword by Henry Cooper
Lewes (Sussex), The Book Guild Ltd., 1987.
165pp. Illus.

2083. LIPSYTE, Robert
Free to be Muhammad Ali
London, Bantam Paperback, 1979.
117pp.

2084. LOUIS, Joe
The Joe Louis Story. Written with the editorial aid of Chester L. Washington and Haskell Cohen.
New York, Grossett and Dunlap, 1953.
167pp. Illus.

2085. LOY, John W. Jr and
KENYON, Gerald S.
Sport, Culture and Society
A Reader on the Sociology of Sport
Pub. in the U.S.A. by The MacMillan Company, 1969.
464pp. including a supplement containing further reading on the subject.
The section entitled "Sport in Small Groups" includes a sub-section entitled "The Occupational Culture of the Boxer".

2086. LUCAS, Bob
Black Gladiator. A Biography of Jack Johnson.
New York City, Dell Publishing, 1970.
189pp. Paperback.

2087. MAILER, Norman
King of the Hill.
On the Fight of the Century.
New York, New American Library, 1971.
93pp. Illus.

2088. McCORMICK, John
The Square Circle
New York, Continental Publishing Co., 1897.
274pp. Illus.
See item No.1331 in Main Bibliography.

2089. MORRISON, Ian
Boxing. The Records.
Enfield, Guinness Books, 1986.
160pp. Illus.

2090. MULDOWNEY, T. (Editor)
Seconds Out; Round 2
Dublin, Libra House, 1980.
60pp. Illus.

2091. MYLER, Patrick
The Fighting Irish
Dingle, Ireland, Brandon, 1985.
250pp. Illus.
Includes a bibliography and an index.

2092. NISENSON, Sam
Handy Illustrated Guide to Boxing
New York, Permabooks, 1949.
192pp. Illus.
Parts of this book appeared previously in the same
author's "Great Book of Sports".

2093. OATES, Joyce Carol
On Boxing
With Photographs by John Ranard
London, Bloomsbury, 1987.
128pp.

2094. O'CONNOR, Ulick
Sport Is My Lifeline
London, Pelham Books, 1984.
135pp. Illus.
A series of essays from "The Sunday Times", in-
cluding seven short pieces of boxing.

2095. OLSEN, Jack
Black is Best. The Riddle of Cassius Clay.
New York, Putnam, 1967.
255pp. Illus.

2096. "AN OPERATOR" (Jon Bee)
Selections from The Fancy
Barre (Massachusetts), Imprint Society, 1972
136pp. Illus.
A limited edition of 1950 copies.

2097. PAYNE, Leslie
The Brotherhood
London, Michael Joseph Ltd., 1973.
167pp. Illus.
The Story of the Kray twins, includes some reference to their boxing careers and to their friendship
with well-known boxers.

2098. PAZDUR, Ed.
Television Boxing Guide
Chicago, Windsor Press, 1954.
160pp. Illus.

2099. PICK, J.B.
The Spectator's Handbook. An Aid to
Appreciation of Athletics, Boxing, etc.,
etc.
London, Phoenix Sports Books, 1956.
144pp. Illus.
The boxing section is covered in pages 45 to 65; it
includes articles on The Marking System, Class
and Type of Boxer, with other aspects of the
sport.
There is one boxing illustration.

2100. PROSPERO, Angelo Jr.
Great Fights and Fighters
Published privately in U.S.A., ca. 1970's.
33pp. Illus. Paperback.

2101. SEVERS, Malcolm
The Frank Bruno Scrapbook
London, McDonald, 1986.
126pp. Illus.

2102. SLATER, J. Herbert
Illustrated Sporting Books
A Descriptive Survey of a Collection of
continued

English Illustrated Works of a Sporting and Racy Character. With an Appendix of Prints Relating to Sports of the Field
London, L.Upcott Gill, 1899. ("The Bazaar Exchange and Mart")

The main portion of this book "Illustrated Sporting Books" contains details of boxing items.
The "Appendix of Sporting Prints" contains a section "Boxing", and another section "Portraits of Sporting Celebrities" which contain many boxing subjects.

2103. SLATER, J. Herbert
Round and About the Book Stalls. A Guide for the Book Hunter.
London, J. Upcott Gill, 1891.

119pp.
Chapter IV "Rough Diamonds" refers to the interest in all works of a sporting nature, among these being books on boxing.

2104. S.M. (Septimus Miles)
A Lecture on Pugilism
Delivered at the Society for Mutual Improvement, established by Jeremy Bentham Esq., at No.52 Great Marlborough Street, Oxford Street, April 14th, 1820.
Published by White in 1820.

This defence of pugilism was included in "Boxiana" Volume III.

2105. SMEETON, George (Publisher)
The British Dance of Death
Exemplified by a series of Engravings from drawings by Van Assen
London, 1823.

Paper covers, 18 coloured plates.
This item consists of a series of Explanatory and Moral Essays.
Among the plates is one entitled "Death and the Pugilists" showing two boxers in action, with a skeleton of Death in the background. This is followed by a four page essay with the same title as that on the plate.

2106. SMEETON, George (Pubblisher)
Observations on the Practice of Self Defence
London, 1814.

Contains Explanatory Remarks on the requirements which form the English Boxer, so that the novitate may become complete master of the Art of Milling, with opinions of Captain Godfrey and Fewtrell.
Includes a folding plate frontis, entitled "The Manner of Setting To of the Leading Professors", showing Johnson, Perrins, Humphries, Mendoza, Cribb and Molyneux.

2107. SMITH, H. Allen
The Life and Legend of Gene Fowler
New York, William Morrow and Co. Inc., 1977.

320pp. Illus.
The subject of this biography was an eminent American newspaperman, in addition to being a successful author of books. He was a great friend of Jack Dempsey, who is frequently mentioned in the book.

2108. SMITH, Robert W.
Western Boxing and World Wrestling
Story and Practice by John F. Gilbey
Berkeley, California, North Atlantic Books, ca 1986.

149pp. Illus. Including Bibliographical References.

2109. SUGAR, Bert Randolph
The 100 Greatest Fights of All Time
New York, Bonanza Books, Distributed by Crown Publ. 1984.

224pp. Illus.

2110. THOMAS, Champ;
Sean O'Grady, Living Legend
Denver (Colorado), Celebrity Book Co. 1981.

69pp. Illus. Paperback.

2111. TOPEROFF, Sam
Sugar Ray Leonard and Other Noble Warriors
New York, McGraw Hill, ca. 1979.

212pp.

2112. VAN DEUSON, John G.
Brown Bomber
The Story of Joe Louis
Philadelphia, Durrance and Co., 1940.

163pp. Illus.

2113. VITALE, Rugio
Joe Louis
Biography of a Champion
Los Angeles, Holloway House Publishing Co, 1979.

163pp. Illus.

INDEX OF ABBREVIATED TITLES

The books relating to boxing have been listed heretofore alphabetically under the names of the authors, editors, or compilers — except in those cases where no information of the person or persons responsible for the particular work has been traced, when the names of the publishers or printers have been appended.

Thus, while it is simple for a collector to refer to a specific book if he is aware of who wrote or compiled it, it is not always so easy when the title might be known but its author is not. For this reason the following index of titles has been compiled as an aid to cross-reference.

The full titles have been abbreviated as much as possible for the sake of compactness, dispensing with the preliminary definite and indefinite articles, and deleting lengthy sub-titles. The names of the authors or those who were responsible for the works appear in brackets afterwards. The numerals which follow signify the *item number* in the bibliography and not that of the page on which it appears.

The abbreviations which appear within brackets signify as follows:

book.	=	bookseller
comp.	=	compiler
ed.	=	editor or editors
engr.	=	engraver
print.	=	printer
pseud.	=	pseudonym
pub.	=	publisher or publishers
trans.	=	translator

E

Eagle Book of Records (Hulton Press, pub.) 1028
Earls Court (Langdon) 1175
Earl's Handbook of Boxing (Earl) 571
Early American Sport (Henderson, comp.) 963
Early Days of the Nineteenth Century (Sydney) 1818
Early Life of William Windham (Ketton-Cremer) 1146
Early Victorian England (O.U.P., pub.) 1524
Edwardian Story (Desmond) 506
Ego 1 (Agate) 9
Ego 3 (Agate) 10
Ego 5 (Agate) 12
Ego 6 (Agate) 13
Ego 8 (Agate) 14
Ego 9 (Agate) 15
Eighteenth Century (Andrews) 55
Eighteenth Century London Life (Bayne-Powell) 129
Elliott's Guide to the Art of Boxing (Coeburn) 379
Emblematical Synopsis of Life in London(Cruikshank) 444
Emmett Lawler (Tully) 1869
Empire of Deceit (Allinson & Henderson) 39
England in the Eighteenth Century (Sydney) 1817
England Today in Pictures (Odhams, pub.) 1494
English, Australian and American Sporting Calendar, 1884 (Tomkin) 1845
English Books with Coloured Plates (Tooley), 1847
English Country Life (Thomson) 1835
English Inn Signs (Larwood & Hotten) 1189
English Nightlife (Burke) 275
English People (Brogan) 246
English Saga (Bryant) 258
English Social History (Trevelyan) 1865
English Sports and Pastimes (Hole) 1001
English Spy (Westmacott) 1949
Encyclopedia Britannica (Ency. Brit. Co., pub.) 611
Encyclopedia of Boxing (Golesworthy) 821
Encyclopedia of Boxing (Odd) 1490
Encyclopedia of Rural Sports (Blaine) 181
Encyclopedia of Sports (Amalgamated Press, pub.) 42
Encyclopedia of Sports (Menke) 1356
Encyclopedia of Sports and Games (Suffolk & Aflalo, eds.) 1795
Encyclopedia of World Boxing Champions (McCallum) 1326
Entertainer (Kent) 1138
Epics of the Fancy (Farnol) 653
Ernest Hemingway. A Life Story (Baker) 101A
Errors That Lose Decisions (Rose) 1643
Esquire's First Sports Reader (Graffis, ed.) 831
Esquire's Second Sports Reader (Gingrich, ed.) 791
Essays (Henley) 966
Essays of Richard Steele (Steele, ed.) 1779
Essays of Today and Yesterday (Agate) 16
Ethics of Boxing (O'Reilly) 1515
European Boxing Guide (Parish, ed.) 1530
"Everybody Boo – " (Deyong) 509
Every Boy's Book of Sport (Clerke & Cockeran, pub.) 367
Every-day Book (Home) 1009
Everyday Cameos (Finn) 665
Everyday Life in Ancient Greece (Robinson) 1629
Everyday Things in Homeric Greece (Quennell) 1585
Every Gentleman's Manual (Egan) 597
Every Idle Dream (Darwin) 466
Every Night Book (Clarke) 361
Everything Happened to Him (Rickard & Oboler) 1616

Everlast Boxing Records, 1922–1938 (Everlast, pub.) 617–634
Everlasting Mercy (Masefield) 1312
Evil Firm (MacConnell) 1276
Exhortation on Christian Love (Eddowes, print.)572
Express to Hollywood (McLaglen) 1341

F

Fair Play (Kircher) 1153
Falcon on St. Paul's (Day) 478
Famous American Athletes of Today (Page, pub.) 1526
Famous Boxers of Petticoat Lane (Wilson, pub.) 2004
Famous Fighters (Allied Newspapers, pub.) 38
Famous Fights (Tosswill) 1852
Famous Fights and Fighters (Bettinson & Bennison) 165
Famous Fights and Fighters (Platt) 1556
Famous Fights at the Stadium (Jeffries) 1090
Famous Fights in the Prize-Ring (Fox, pub.) 735
Famous Fights in the Prize Ring (Turner) 1881
Famous Fights – Past and Present (Furniss, ed.) 759
Famous Heavyweight Fights (Treharne) 1858
Famous Last Rounds (Dalby) 455
Famous Racing Men ("Thormanby") 1837
Famous Sporting Prints *(Studio*, pub.) 1794
Fancy ("Operator") 1514
Fancy (Reynolds) 1602
Fancy Ana ("Jon Bee") 1113
Fancy Chronology ("Jon Bee ") 1111
Fancy List ("Jon Bee") 1114
Fancy Togs Man (Egan) 592
Farewell to Sport (Gallico) 770
Fashion Then and Now (Lennox) 1219
Fat City (Gardner) 773
Fate Cannot Harm Me (Masterman) 1315
Favourite Ring Tricks (Murray) 1423
Fellow Countrymen (Farrell) 656
Fencing and Fighting ("EBT") 571A
Fencing, Boxing, Wrestling (Watson, ed.) 1922
Fifty Famous Fights in Fact and Fiction (Birkenhead, ed.) 171
Fifty Leaders of British Sport (Elliott) 605
Fifty Two Years of Sport (Bland, ed.) 183
Fifty Wonderful Portraits (Cooper & Page, eng.) 406
Fifty Years a Fighter (Mace) 1283
·50 Years at Ringside (Fleischer) 718
·Fifty Years at the Ringside (Romano) 1638
Fifty Years in the Ring (Corri) 419
50 Years of Boxing (Scarrott) 1677
Fifty Years of my Life (Astley) 81
Fifty Years of Song (Dawson) 477
Fifty Years of Sport at Oxford and Cambridge (Croome) 441
Fifty Years of Sport (Bland, ed.) 182
Fight (Hazlitt) 927
·Fight (Mailer) 1294
Fight (Scannell) 1674
Fight Between Sayers and Heenan (Noel) 1470
Fight Doctor (Pacheco) 1525
Fighter Blake (Frudd) 754
Fighter from Whitechapel (Ribalow) 1606
Fighter in the Naptha Ring (Goldberg) 806
Fighters (Greyvenstein) 860
Fighters of the Old Cosmo (Mumford) 1415
Fighters of the North (Power) 1562

V

ADDITION TO INDEX
ALPHABETICALLY BY TITLE
The numbers carry on from the last in the original Index (2059)